ISLAMIC URBAN STUDIES

ISLAMIC URBAN STUDIES

Historical Review and Perspectives

Edited by
Masashi HANEDA and Toru MIURA

Routledge
Taylor & Francis Group
LONDON AND NEW YORK

First published in 1994 by
Kegan Paul International

This edition first published in 2010 by
Routledge
2 Park Square, Milton Park, Abingdon, Oxfordshire OX14 4RN

Simultaneously published in the USA and Canada
by Routledge
711 Third Avenue, New York, NY 10017

First issued in paperback 2014

Routledge is an imprint of the Taylor & Francis Group, an informa business

British Library Cataloguing in Publication Data
A catalogue record for this book is available from the British Library

ISBN 13: 978-0-7103-0492-6 (hbk)
ISBN 13: 978-0-415-76010-2 (pbk)

Publisher's Note
The publisher has gone to great lengths to ensure the quality of this reprint but points out that some imperfections in the original copies may be apparent. The publisher has made every effort to contact original copyright holders and would welcome correspondence from those they have been unable to trace.

CONTENTS

LIST OF COLLABORATORS

Masashi HANEDA	Associate Professor of Institute of Oriental Culture, University of Tokyo History of the Islamic Iran
Kayoko HAYASHI	Assistant Professor of Department of Middle Eastern Studies, Tokyo University of Foreign Studies Ottoman History
Masatoshi KISAICHI	Associate Professor of Institute of Asian Cultures, Sophia University Medieval History of the Maghrib and the Islamic Spain
Hisao KOMATSU	Associate Professor of Department of Middle Eastern Studies, Tokyo University of Foreign Studies Modern History of Central Asia
Toru MIURA	Associate Professor of Faculty of Letters and Education, Ochanomizu University Medieval History of Egypt and Syria

PREFACE

This study traces the history of urban studies concerning the Islamic world, in terms of theme, motif and methodology. Its purpose is to reveal the concerns of scholars in the field over the past century or so and to isolate topics for future research.

The term "Islamic cities" has been a favoured form of reference for the cities of the Islamic world, centring on the Middle East. As this indicates, scholarship has tended to link the cities of the Islamic world with Islam as a religion and a culture in an attempt to understand them as a whole in a unified and uniform way. However, there have been insufficient studies which examine and compare the cities in their diversity of climate, landscape, population and historical background. A frequent argument has been to say that the particular phenomena of an area are themselves the characteristics of the "Islamic city." As a result, as studies divided into particular areas such as Turkey, Iran and the Arab lands have progressed, there has been growing difficulty in undertaking research which sufficiently integrates the results obtained in the individual fields. Likewise there has been very little interest in thinking about cities by synthesizing the results of the various disciplines, whether they be in the field of the humanities, like history, geography or art and architectural history, in the social sciences, like sociology, law or economics. This volume will attempt to make up for such deficiencies.

This study may be said to have two characteristics. First, it coordinates, without distinction of academic field, the main research that has been done since the 19th century in regard to the cities of five regions that came under the sway of Islam comparatively early: the Maghrib (the Western Arab lands), Mashriq (the Eastern Arab lands), Turkey, Iran and Central Asia. Second, through comparing the history of scholarship regarding the cities of those five regions, it throws light on the issues that have exercised academic concern in urban studies of the Islamic world as a whole to the present and tries to suggest new perspectives for future research.

Such a survey of the history of the scholarship covering the vast area of the Middle East and Central Asia has not been undertaken previously, even in the West with its long tradition of urban studies. This in itself speaks of the difficulty of the project. We have nevertheless taken up the challenge because we are convinced that if no such attempt is made at consolidating and examining the scholarship, it will be impossible to understand truly the cities of the Islamic world. Further, the issues studied here are closely connected with debates now occurring within the fields of Japanese, Chinese and European urban studies, and we believe that they have wide application to urban studies and the study of history in general.

It has not been our intention however to provide either comprehensive bibliographies or a systematized history of scholarship and academic theories. Rather than merely criticizing what has been done in the past, we have placed weight on clarifying currents of research and exploring topics that look to the future, and aimed, not at a uniform review, but at a study of selected, epochal work, in order to bring into relief study motifs and questions of method and approach.

The book examines studies (books, articles, maps, bibliographies) of cities which existed in the Middle East and Central Asia in the period from the rise of Islam to the beginning of the 20th century. In principle, historical materials themselves have not been included. The majority of works surveyed are historical and geographical studies written by Western scholars, since from the 19th century they have taken a lead in these areas, but we have tried to relativize them by paying attention also to fields such as architecture, sociology and anthropology and by considering the contributions of local scholars. We have limited our study temporally, since after the beginning of the 20th century industrialization and urbanization progressed at great rapidity, and different approaches are needed to examine cities after this time. More than 1500 studies, in various Middle Eastern and European languages and in Japanese are mentioned, and details of works cited will be found in the bibliographies at the end of each chapter. Indexes of the names of authors, cities and terms are also provided.

This book was first published in Japanese in July 1991 by the University of Tokyo Press, as one of the outcomes of the project entitled "Urbanism in Islam: A Comparative Study" (Professor Yuzo Itagaki, chair) funded by the Japanese Ministry of Education, Science and Culture. This project, centred on the Institute of Oriental Culture at the University of Tokyo, which ran for three years from April, 1988, was divided into 24 study groups involving approximately 120 scholars from the humanities, the social sciences and the natural sciences. More than two hundred seminars, as well as two large scale international conferences in 1989 and 1990, were held in that time and several hundred reports were made. It was an epoch-making achievement for Islamic Studies in Japan, and contributed to the creation of networks among scholars both at home and abroad. This book was planned as part of the project by the five authors at the suggestion of the late Professor Johei Shimada. In the process of collecting material and writing the various chapters, we have received the support and encouragement of great many colleagues and have also discussed each other's drafts at length. Therefore the introductory and concluding chapters should not be thought of as the work of one person, but the result of the combined efforts of many, though the ultimate responsibility lies with the five authors.

The English translation is based on the original Japanese version, though the authors have taken the opportunity to revise and enlarge the text. While the Japanese version considers work published through 1990, the English edition furthers the discussion by taking later publications also into consideration. The translation was undertaken by Gaynor Sekimori (Introduction, Maghrib, Mashriq, Conclusion) and Misako Nagasawa (Turkey, Iran, Central Asia); Mrs. Sekimori also revised the whole. The authors remained in touch with the translators through to the final draft and so retain the ultimate responsibility for the contents. This book should be considered the Enlarged and Revised English Edition, rather than a simple translation of the original. We realize all the same that in the short span of five years we have not been able to make an adequate study of the subject and are conscious that we have been guilty of many omissions and errors. We await the critical response of our readership.

This translation has been made possible by a Grant-in-Aid for Scientific Research (Publication of Scientific Research Results) from the Ministry of Education, Science and Culture and by a grant from the Mitsubishi Foundation. Each of the authors has also been enabled through the auspices of the Ministry to visit the locality of his or her field of interest and gather the necessary material and information. We thank the people concerned for the trouble they have taken to assist us in our research. We would also like to take this opportunity to express our gratitude to Professor Yuzo Itagaki and to Professor Akira Goto for the encouragement they have given us in regard to both the Japanese and the English version.

Masashi Haneda
Kayoko Hayashi
Masatoshi Kisaichi
Hisao Komatsu
Toru Miura

NOTES

1. Transcription: Arabic and Persian terms and references have been transcribed as follows.

   Arabic ', b, t, th, j, ḥ, kh, d, dh, r, z, s, sh, ṣ, ḍ, ṭ, ẓ, ', gh, f, q, k, l, m, n, h, w, y

   Persian ', b, p, t, ṯ, ǧ, č, ḥ, ẖ, d, ḏ, r, z, ž, s, š, ṣ, ḍ, ṭ, ẓ, ', ġ, f, q, k, g, l, m, n, h, v, y

   Transcription for Russian, Tajik and Uzbek follows a modification of the system and tables published in Edward Allworth, *Nationalities of the Soviet East* (Columbia University Press, 1971). Turkish terms have been cited according to modern Turkish orthography.

2. Well-known place names, the names of historical personages and terms common throughout Islamic history have been transliterated in terms of English and diacritical marks have been omitted.

3. Names of authors: in the text, names are given generally as initial plus surname, or common name.

4. Names of publications: in the text, Arabic, Persian, Turkish, Russian and Japanese titles have been translated into English. The original language is indicated by a capitalized initial (see below). Works in other European languages are referred to in an abbreviated version of the original. Full titles and details of publication are given in the bibliographies following each chapter.

   A: Arabic P: Persian T: Turkish

   R: Russian J: Japanese

5. Periodicals and serials are abbreviated according to the usage in the *Encyclopaedia of Islam* and *Index Islamicus*.

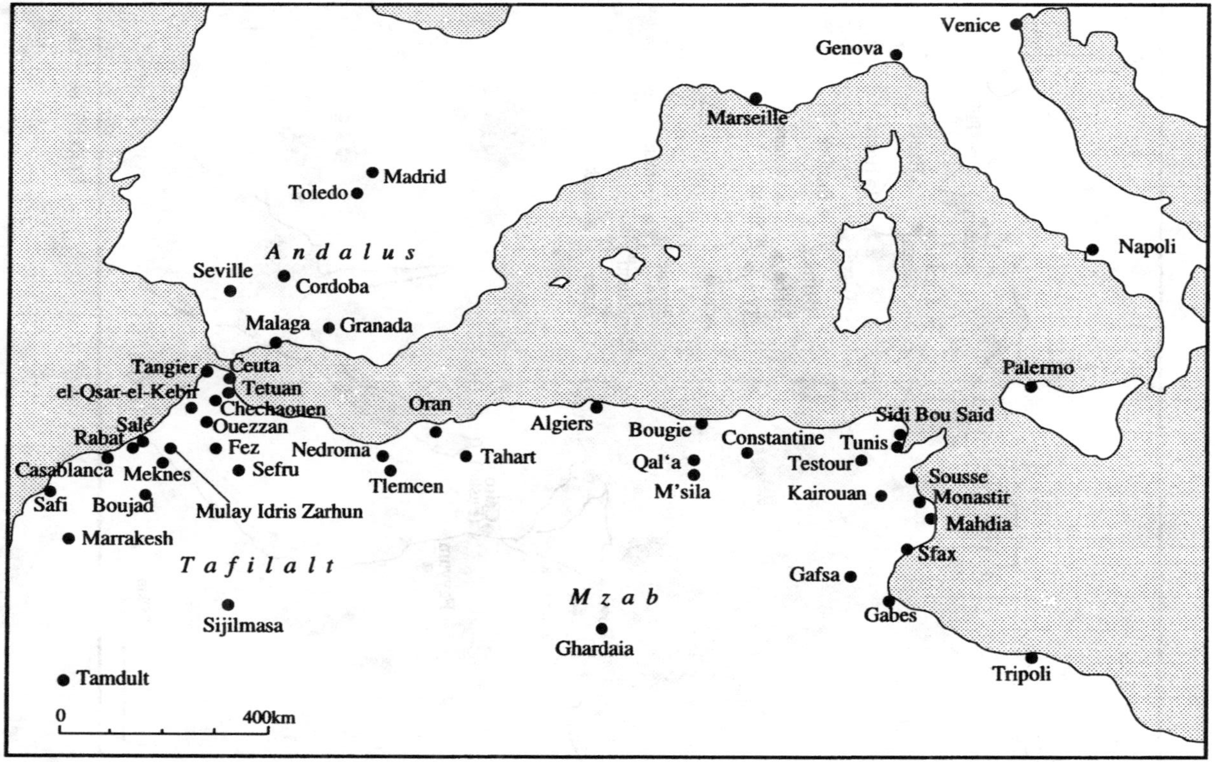

THE MAGHRIB & ANDALUS

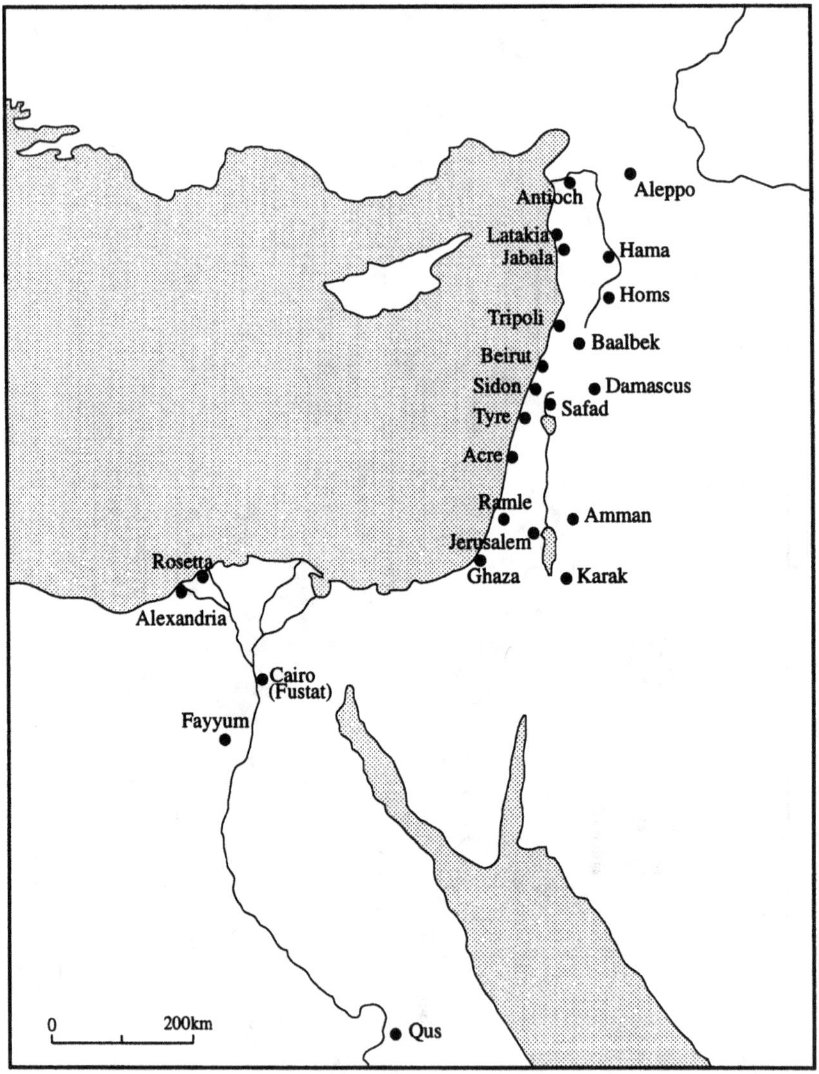
Aleppo
Antioch
Latakia
Jabala
Hama
Homs
Tripoli
Baalbek
Beirut
Sidon
Damascus
Safad
Tyre
Acre
Ramle
Amman
Jerusalem
Ghaza
Karak
Rosetta
Alexandria
Cairo
(Fustat)
Fayyum
Qus
0
200km

EGYPT & SYRIA

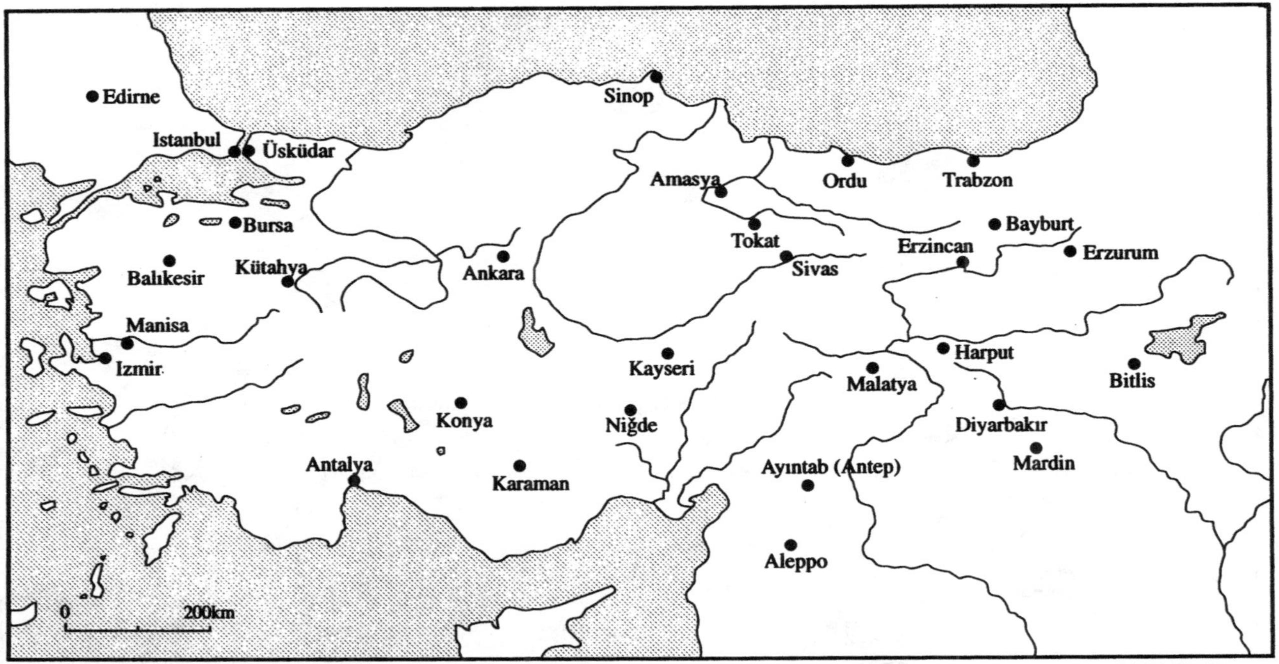
Edirne
Istanbul
Üsküdar
Sinop
Amasya
Ordu
Trabzon
Bursa
Bayburt
Tokat
Erzincan
Erzurum
Balıkesir
Kütahya
Ankara
Sivas
Manisa
Izmir
Kayseri
Harput
Malatya
Bitlis
Konya
Niğde
Diyarbakır
Mardin
Antalya
Karaman
Ayıntab (Antep)
Aleppo
0
200km
TURKEY

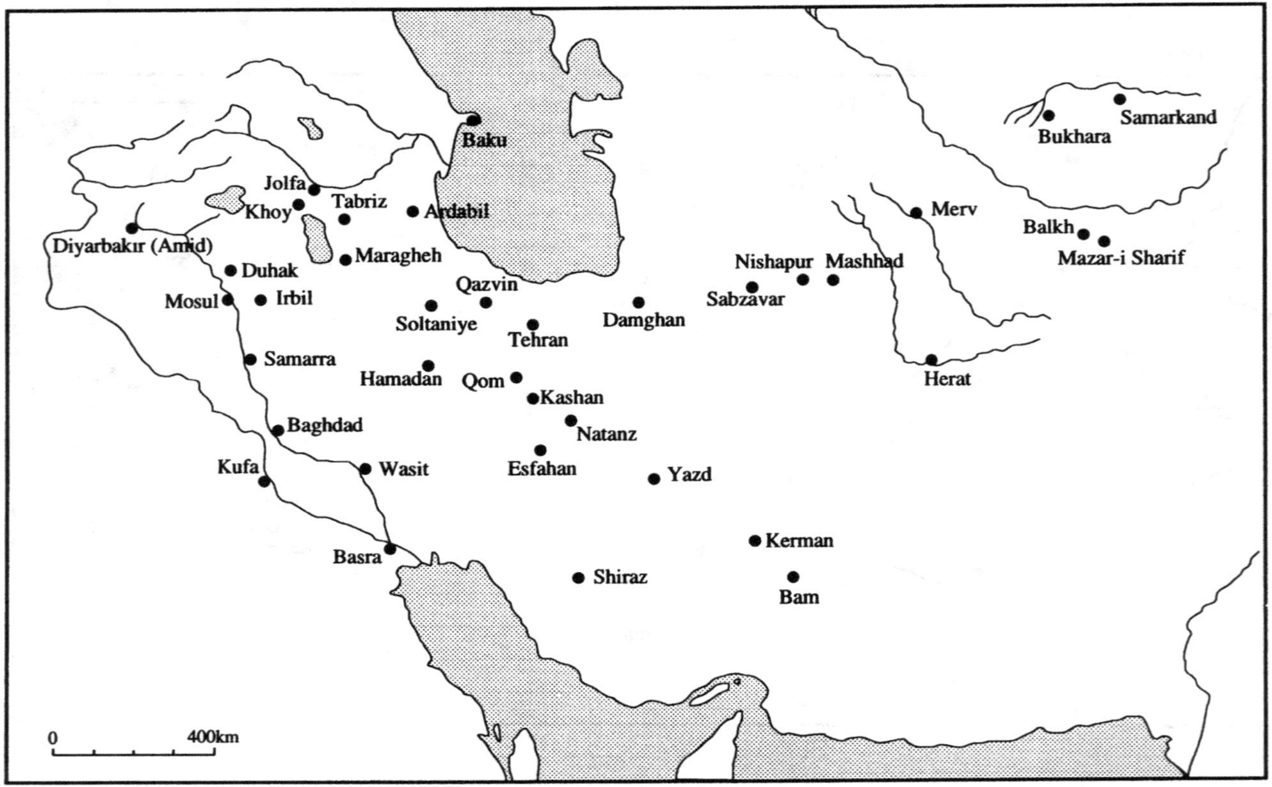
Samarkand
Bukhara
Baku
Jolfa
Khoy
Tabriz
Ardabil
Merv
Balkh
Mazar-i Sharif
Diyarbakır (Amid)
Maragheh
Duhak
Nishapur
Mashhad
Qazvin
Mosul
Irbil
Sabzavar
Soltaniye
Damghan
Tehran
Samarra
Hamadan
Qom
Herat
Kashan
Baghdad
Natanz
Kufa
Wasit
Esfahan
Yazd
Kerman
Basra
Shiraz
Bam
0
400km

IRAQ & IRAN

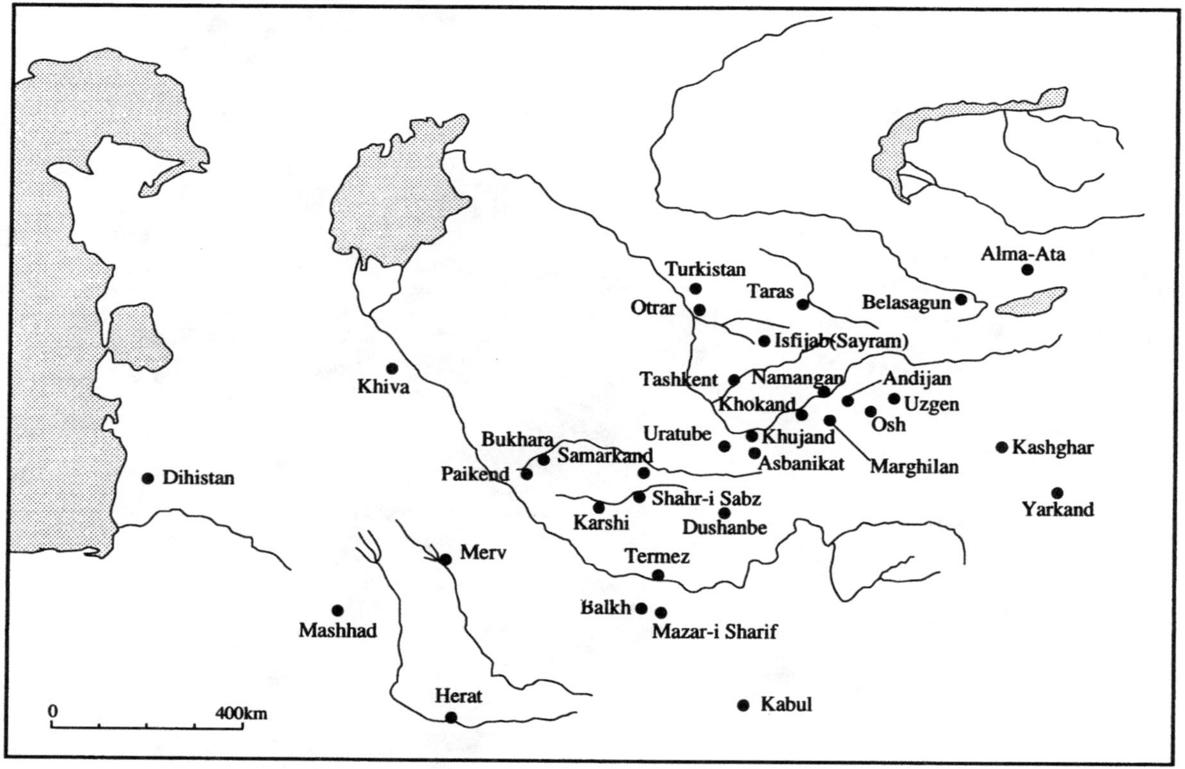

CENTRAL ASIA

INTRODUCTION
An Interpretation of the Concept of the "Islamic City"

Masashi Haneda

I

Compared with Islamic countries in the Indian subcontinent, South East Asia and West Africa, the Islamic lands which extend from the countries of former Soviet Central Asia in the east to the Maghrib in the west came comparatively early under the sway of Islam and in an historical sense have come to form the core of the Islamic world. The central purpose of this volume is to bring together research concerning the cities of this area, divided broadly into five regions according to differences in race and culture, to elucidate what has been studied, when and where. By having each chapter focus on a particular region, it is hoped that the distinctive features of the history of urban studies in each region will be highlighted, as will be the issues peculiar to the various cities.

The second purpose in bringing together the five regional studies into one volume is to enable scholars to gain a better understanding of issues common to Islamic urban studies as a whole by presenting them with a wider view. The reader will no doubt make various connections based on his or her own interests or concerns. The five writers met a number of times to discuss together issues concerning the history of Islamic urban studies as a whole and prospects in the directions of future research. They also benefited from the opinions of various scholars about individual chapters. The Introduction and Conclusion have therefore been written to include the various thoughts that have been raised. In the Introduction we will concentrate on the past history of urban studies and on the main lines of research at present, and explore the central issues involved. Our key theme will be the "Islamic city," a topic which has long occupied an important place in the field.

II

It is appropriate, when looking at the currents of research down to the present, to divide the five areas discussed above into two broad groups: first, the Eastern and Western Arab lands and Central Asia, and second, Turkey and Iran. Whereas the former area was colonized by the European powers in the late 19th and early 20th centuries, the latter was never colonized in the strict sense of the word. Of course, even Iran and Turkey could not escape European economic and political influence, but the fact they never actually became colonies was one of the chief reasons they can be separated from the first group.

After France's colonization of the Maghrib in the 19th century, and its taking of Syria as a Mandate after the First World War, exceedingly systematized field surveys were carried out in conjunction with the needs of colonial administration. The surveys extended to the whole of the particular regional society, and those dealing with the cities, with their concentrations of population, were both large-scale and thorough. As a result, detailed city maps (for example, the *Plan cadastral* of Damascus) and sketches of buildings were made, and the political, economic and religious systems were "discovered" and described. Such systematic large-scale surveys had been a specialty of French Oriental studies ever since the compilation of the *Description de l'Égypte* at the time of Napoleon's expedition to Egypt. As will be described below, there were considerable problems with such surveys and research, stemming from the notions Europeans had about the region and the premises on which they based their analysis of local society, and this coloured to some extent the voluminous writings of the Marcais brothers about the Maghrib, the Fez research of R. Le Tourneau, and the series of studies on Aleppo and Damascus made by J. Sauvaget.

Urban surveys in the lands of former Soviet Central Asia, which became Russian territory in the late 19th century, though not undertaken as systematic research, were energetically carried out by colonial officials and military administrators. Several of them attracted the interest of French authorities concerned with colonial administration in the Maghrib and they appear even to have been translated for French reference. But Russian research in Central Asian cities was, comparatively speaking, not as established as that done in the Maghrib and Syria. It was not in a strong position in the years before and after the 1917 Revolution. However, during the Soviet era, Soviet scholars promoted the study of the cities of the region using the conceptual framework of "feudal cities" and "medieval cities." Their work will be discussed by Komatsu in the chapter on Central Asia.

In Iran and Turkey, on the other hand, countries that were never completely colonized, the situation was quite different. Though both countries, which somehow or other preserved their independence throughout the age of Imperialism, attracted fact-finding expeditions from a number of European countries, what was surveyed was significantly limited in comparison to what had been done in those countries which had been colonized. Though Iranian art and architectural history, for example, were described in the great work of A. U. Pope, very little was done in terms of city maps. There was little attention given to urban administrative or religious organizations; the interest of Europeans was fixed rather on ancient Persian civilizations and ruins such as Persepolis rather than on cities of the Islamic period. It was the same in Turkey. Expeditions from various countries in Europe devoted their efforts to excavating pre-Hellenic and Hellenic sites on the Mediterranean coast and in Anatolia and only conducted very inadequate examinations of cities at that time and their society. Reasons for this include the absence of any of the concerns of direct rule (colonial authorities did not exist), an interest in and nostalgia towards the ancient Orient and the Hellenistic world as the well-spring of European civilization——there was a certain amount of Orientalist character in this——, and limitations on the activities of foreign expeditions in sovereign states. As a result research by European scholars involving Iranian and Turkish cities was, with the exception of specialized fields like art history, scanty compared with what had been done in the Arab lands. Thus the degree to which a particular area was studied by Europeans is closely related to whether it had been colonized or not.

III

The concept of the "Islamic city" came into being as a topic of discussion among European scholars who were involved in the study of the Arab regions during the period of colonial rule. It is of great interest that no such general debate existed in Iran and Turkey, where studies by Europeans were scanty.

The development of the debate about the concept of the "Islamic city" has been covered concisely in Japanese by Miura,[1] and Kisaichi also introduces the topic in detail in his chapter on the Maghrib in this volume. Therefore, rather than studying the ideas and arguments of the various scholars in depth here, I will focus on the problems inherent in the concept itself. In doing so, it is convenient to divide the history of the debate into two periods: one, up till the 1960s when the question was discussed principally among historians, and two, after the 1970s, when scholars from other fields joined their voices to the argument.

The origins of the concept of the "Islamic city" lie in Maghribi urban studies. French scholars such as the Marcais brothers, L. Massignon and R. Brunschvig described the characteristics of Maghribi cities from a variety of angles such as the urban landscape, facilities and law, on the basis of the knowledge gained from surveys of Maghribi cities under colonial rule. Despite the fact that they were at that time concerned only with Maghribi cities, they tended to include in the titles of their papers words such as "Islamic city," "Muslim city" and "Muslim law." Leaving aside the question of whether they used such expressions consciously or not, they were, under the influence of concepts—of Max Weber and others—of the medieval European city, popular at the time, attempting to describe the cities of the Islamic world as contrasting to those of Europe. This was the starting point of the concept of the "Islamic city."

As Kisaichi shows in his chapter on the Maghrib, we can also understand the various concepts of the "Islamic city," conceived in terms of a biased view of history regarding Maghribi society current since the 19th century, to have been a way for French scholars of the time to understand the place of their own society, civilized Europe. In order to represent Maghribi society, with its value system different to that of France or Europe, they employed terms that denoted a duality, like "Islamic society" or "Islamic city." It is easy to perceive a typical Orientalist attitude in their failure to recognize the variegated nature of Muslim society and their attempt to explain everything in terms of a dichotomy between an advanced Europe and a stagnant Islamic world. In the same way the cities of prerevolutionary Central Asia were generally designated after the rise of the Soviet Union "feudal" or "medieval," and studied in terms of their place in the socialist system.

IV

It was G. von Grunebaum who brought together the studies of French Orientalists and gave the model of the "Islamic city" a general shape. His "Die islamische Stadt," "The Structure of the Muslim Town,"[2] published in 1955, despite the fact that it mainly looked to the studies of the Maghribi city to that time, and only partially treated Syria (Sauvaget's studies),[3] succeeded, in hand with the thesis of H. A. R. Gibb and H. Bowen that Islamic culture was first and foremost an urban culture,[4] in disseminating the concept of an "Islamic city" to the world at large. As a result the concept gained credibility in the academic world. As both Kisaichi and Miura show (pp. 34-5, 88-9), von Grunebaum employed Weberian typology without alteration, generalizing about the cities of the Islamic world in terms of a dichotomy by asking where and how the "Islamic city" differed from the image of the European city as described by Weber. In this he was part of the same stream as the French Orientalists.

Cl. Cahen and E. Ashtor revised von Grunebaum's model as a result of their detailed studies of autonomy and guilds in 10th to 12th century Syrian and Iraqi cities based on historical sources. (Their arguments are outlined on pp. 112-3) Their work is of great value as empirical historical research, and they brought something new to methodology. We may question, however, how much meaning there was in a partial revision and criticism of the Orientalist type image of the "Islamic city," constructed on the base of the image of the "stagnant pre-modern Islamic society," in another words, of general characteristics of Maghribi cities of no particular period, by means of studies limited to a certain time and place (the 10th to 12th centuries, and the Eastern Arab lands, not the Maghrib).[5] What needed to be addressed was rather the concept of the "Islamic city" in terms of a framework, and a recognition of a simple dichotomy between the "Islamic city" and European cities. Nevertheless, a large number of scholars besides Cahen and Ashtor involved themselves in the discussion of the "Islamic city." For them the concept itself was sufficiently valid as a framework for discussion, whether or not the "Islamic city" actually existed or not. I will return to this point below.

The above criticism can also be applied to the research of I. M. Lapidus, considered an epoch-making achievement in the tradition of debate about the "Islamic city." His method of analysis, an attempt to describe urban society dynamically, focused on a system based on the indivisibility of city and village and the various social networks among people. Although his works are not urban studies in the narrow sense of the word,[6] being rather a detailed historical study of Mamluk society, they are persuasive and arresting. It must be pointed out, however, that though he criticized those scholars who until then had been using the same analytical methodology as Weberian discussion of the European city and who considered the city in a static way, focusing upon urban systems and landscapes, he still did not question the efficiency of the concept itself. Lapidus himself in the preface to the second edition of his first published work, *Muslim Cities in the Later Middle Ages* (1984), recalls the time the work was first published (1967) and writes, "The crucial issue then seemed to be the differences among European and Muslim societies,"[7] which suggests that his own concern, whatever the methodology used, was whether or not it was possible satisfactorily to identify and describe the differences between European society and cities and Muslim society and cities. To do so he devised a new way of studying the "Islamic city." In this sense, he had not broken away from the traditional Orientalist dual-contrastive pattern of Europe versus Islam.

All the same, Lapidus has never used the expression "Islamic city." He invariably describes Islamic society and cities prudently in the plural as "Muslim cities" or "Islamic societies." Neither does he necessarily try to make his own model of Islamic society and cities apply without restriction to any place or period. Excluding his most recent major work, *A History of Islamic Societies*(1988), he limits his area of study more or less to the area from Egypt to Central Asia. His model of Islamic societies, because it is so flexible, responds to changes in social groupings and can therefore be altered to become a specialized model for each period or region. Thus his research itself, when it moves away from Orientalist type comparisons with European societies to an analysis of an Islamic society in its own terms, is valid in methodology, the value of which will be shown as individual studies appear which employ it.

V

Until the 1960s, the concept of the "Islamic city" was discussed almost exclusively among historians. After 1970, the discussion became much more diversified with the contributions of geographers, sociologists, social anthropologists, architects, etc. as well, although a certain deadlock seems to have transpired. Whereas until the 1960s the discussion of the "Islamic city" tried to set forth a general model of the physical and social features of the cities of the Islamic world, from the 1970s the center of the argument shifted to the question of the extent of the influence of Islam as a religion on urban structures and society in the Islamic world. The arguments of E. Wirth and B. S. Hakim on this point are all the more interesting for the contrasting conclusions they offer. Wirth made a study of the common geographical characteristics of cities in Western Asia and North Africa and concluded that there were problems about calling them "Islamic," since none of those characteristics could be directly related to Islam as a religion.[8] Hakim, on the other hand, said that cities in the Arab lands at least could be called "Arab-Islamic," since Islamic law functioned as the guideline for urban construction and life.[9] The arguments of both scholars are persuasive in that they are well-grounded and logical in comparison to the confused discussion of the former period. One says that the "Islamic city" does not exist, and the other uses the term "Arab-Islamic city," limited in application to the Arab lands. This shows that the further the dispute is pursued, the more cautious one has to become of broaching the concept of the "Islamic city". The social anthropologists K. Brown and D. Eickelman have also developed their own arguments about the "Islamic city" based on field research in Morocco,[10] but again the debate remains limited to the Maghrib.

J. Abu-Lughod's article published in 1987 deserves attention in that it consolidates the arguments about the "Islamic city," based on a fine understanding of the subject, and offers new proposals. She first examines and criticizes the tradition of Orientalism in the concept of the "Islamic city" and warns of the dangers inherent in making generalizations from single case studies,[11] and then speaks of the importance of resolving the fundamental question, why Islamic cities are expected to be similar, and in what ways. She goes on to describe from her own experience differences between Muslim and Hindu urban quarters in India, then, in order to explain the "Islamic city" she sums up into three points the role played by Islamic legal provisions in the shaping of cities. In itself it is a persuasive study, but as Eickelman pointed out, it is easy to find examples among cities in the Islamic world which do not fit Abu-Lughod's definition.[12] The first half of the article is a clearly written criticism of the tradition that led to the growth of the concept of the "Islamic city," but it is undeniable that a number of ambiguities remain in the second half, the author's own suggestions. Why persist on using the concept when it needs to be supported by such forced argument? As would be expected, Abu-Lughod retreated a little in her report to the international conference in Tokyo in 1989, saying that when comparing cities of different cultural spheres, the role of Islam as a religion should not be overrated.[13]

There has been virtually no European or American scholar who has expressed doubts about the validity of the concept of the "Islamic city" itself. Abu-Lughod, who attempted to present a new view of it while criticizing the old Orientalist concept, is a case in point. Scholars from the Arab region too have not been able to ignore the debate entirely, even when they have not participated in it directly. In one sense, it is possible to say that the great majority of research to the present has served to give substance to the concept from a variety of angles. All the same, the question remains why people have not had doubts about the concept itself and its validity. Decades have already been spent pursuing this elusive quarry, and the debate continues with no sign of resolution. We cannot help feeling, when looking at the examples of Wirth, Hakim and Abu-Lughod, that the argument has reached an impasse and the quarry has flown.

VI

The history of urban studies treated in this volume reveals the extremely interesting fact that local scholars (that is, those who are native to the Muslim regions in question) themselves have remained on the whole indifferent to the debate about the "Islamic city." Of course some scholars in Arab lands have expressed an interest in the concept and have spoken about it, chiefly in terms of specific cities in Arab regions such as the Maghrib and Syria. All the same it is interesting to note that a good many of the Arab scholars who have contributed to the debate have, like Hakim, been educated abroad in Europe or the United States. The lack of interest in the topic by Turkish and Iranian scholars will become obvious from what is written in the appropriate chapters. Until very recently the cities of these areas were not made the subject of study in the discussion of the "Islamic city." How should this lack of interest by local scholars be interpreted?

One possible interpretation lies in differences in the meaning of knowledge (*connaissance*) and the academic tradition between Europe and the Islamic Middle East. The European method of learning, to study and comprehend an object through the analytical method of comparison, contrasts with the tradition of the Islamic Middle East where the object of knowledge itself is examined directly and described from as many angles as possible in order to grasp it in its entirety. Typical of such an approach are 'Alī Mubārak's *Enlarged and Newly-edited Topography of Egypt* and Ṣāliḥ Aḥmad al-'Alī's *The Topography of Basra in the Early Islamic Period.*[14] Even the recently published *Social History of Tehran in the 13th Century A. H.* by Ǧ. Šahrī attempts to understand the object Tehran by means of a comprehensive description of 13th century Tehran society from a number of angles.[15] It contains no sign of any form of comparative analysis such as examining how the characteristics of Tehran society differ from those of contemporary society in Istanbul or London. The only object of interest is Tehran itself. There will be other examples in the various chapters below of such works, which have been criticized by those trained in European and American methods of learning as being deficient in analysis and argument. However, it must be remembered that they belong to the academic tradition of the Islamic Middle East. People often comment that Arab, Turkish and Iranian scholars seem little interested in other regions, but this is to judge from a stance that European academic methods are absolute. We must understand that the Islamic Middle Eastern academic tradition remains different to that of Europe.

What must not be forgotten when considering the concept of the "Islamic city" is that it derives from a model for comparison according to the European academic tradition. This has been consistent from the time of the Orientalists in the first half of this century until almost the present. In most cases the model for comparison has been the European city and its society. Even Eickelman, who attempted to make comparisons with a number of different societies, was not able to break completely free from Europe-Islam dualism.[16] Why is it always necessary to make comparisons with Europe when considering

Islamic society? This approach clearly shows the limitations in the concept of the "Islamic city," for it is above all the way European and North American scholars seek to comprehend a foreign culture. The indifference of local scholars to the question is certainly not unconnected with this point. It may be fair to say that even the question itself, whether the "Islamic city" exists or not, or of what exactly is the true "Islamic city," is a product of the European way of understanding the Islamic world.[17]

Today, the way by which Western scholars sought in the past to understand the East has been labelled as "Orientalism" and criticized.[18] The concept of the "Islamic city," which developed from an Orientalist base, has not a great deal of possibility. No longer should we need adhere to the framework of that well-worn theory. It is time urban studies in the Islamic world were given a new framework and methodological direction. A new outlook might emerge even if comparative methodology was retained, if detailed comparisons were made among cities not only of the Arab lands but also of Iran and Turkey and other areas of the "peripheral regions" such as the Indian subcontinent, Indonesia and West Africa, and these were further compared with different cultural areas such as China and Japan. The academic tradition of the Islamic Middle East should also be considered. I would be delighted should this volume provide the starting point for such a new outlook in urban studies.

Notes

1. T. Miura, "The Nature of the 'Islamic City'" (in Japanese), *Chichukaigaku Kenkyu* 13 (1990).
2. G. von Grunebaum, "Die islamische Stadt," *Saeculum* 6 (1955); id., "The Structure of the Muslim Town," *Memoir* (The American Anthropological Association) 81: *Islam: Essays in the Nature and Growth of a Cultural Tradition* (1955).
3. J. L. Abu-Lughod, "The Islamic City: Historic Myth, Islamic Essence, and Contemporary Relevance," *IJMES* 19 (1987), p. 158.
4. H. A. R. Gibb and H. Bowen, *Islamic Society and the West*, vol. 1 (London, 1950), p. 276.
5. Cahen held that there are no basic differences between cities of the Byzantine period and of the Islamic period before the 11th century, and that Islam as a religion did not exert all that much influence on urban life. He felt it was not appropriate to use the term "Islamic city." In this sense he did not necessarily confine himself to partial revision but anticipated the arguments of the post-1970s period. However it is inescapable that by dealing with the question and offering criticism, he stood in the

same Orientalist camp. Cl. Cahen, "Mouvements populaires et autonomisme urbain dans l'Asie musulmane du moyen age, I," *Arabica* 5/3 (1958), pp. 225-9.

6. D. F. Eickelman, "Is There an Islamic City? The Making of a Quarter in a Moroccan Town," *IJMES* 5 (1974), p. 277. id., "The Comparative Study of 'Islamic' Cities" (paper presented at the 2nd International Conference on Urbanism in Islam, Tokyo, 27-29 November 1990), p. 9.
7. I. M. Lapidus, *Muslim Cities in the later Middle Ages,* student edition (Cambridge, 1984), p. viii.
8. E. Wirth, "Villes islamiques, villes arabes, villes orientales? Une problématique face au changement," in *La ville arabe dans l'Islam,* eds. A. Bouhdiba and D. Chevallier (Tunis and Paris, 1982). Concerning H. Djaït's criticism to Wirth's article, see Kisaichi's comments of this volume (pp.43-4).
9. B. S. Hakim, *Arabic-Islamic Cities: Building and Planning Principles* (London, 1986).
10. K. L. Brown, *People of Salé: Tradition and Change in a Moroccan City 1830-1930* (New York, 1976). Eickelman, "Is There an Islamic City?"
11. Abu-Lughod, "The Islamic City," pp. 155-60.
12. Eickelman, "The Comparative Study of 'Islamic' Cities," p. 10.
13. Abu-Lughod, "What is Islamic about a City? Some Comparative Reflections," in *Urbanism in Islam: The Proceedings of the International Conference on Urbanism in Islam,* vol. 1 (Tokyo, 1989). See particularly pp. 204-5.
14. 'Alī Mubārak, *Enlarged and Newly-edited Topography of Egypt* (in Arabic), 20 vols. (Bulaq, 1304-5/1886-8). Ṣāliḥ Aḥmad al-'Alī, *The Social and Economic Systems of Basra in the First Century of the Hijra* (in Arabic) (Bayrut, 1953).
15. Ğ. Šahrī, *Social History of Tehran in the 13th Century A. H.*(in Persian), 6 vols. (Tehran, 1367-8/1988-9).
16. For such a comparison, see Eickelman, "Is There an Islamic City?" pp. 277-88.
17. It is possible to foresee a concept of an "Islamic city" from the point of view of Islam, in terms of Islam not simply as a religion but as the norm influencing all of social life, making cities where Muslims live "Islamic." The traditional concept of the "Islamic city," looking almost totally at premodern times, recognized that religion had a great influence on society, in the same way Christianity had on Europe, and so this outlook is not confined just to the Islamic world.
18. Concerning Orientalism, see E. W. Said, *Orientalism* (New York, 1978). For Orientalism and the problem of comparative studies, see Y. Itagaki, "Area Studies and Orientalism" (in Japanese), in *Comparative Studies in Social and Political Change in the Asia-Africa Region and Islam* (Tokyo, 1988) for a concise synopsis of the problem.

THE MAGHRIB

Masatoshi Kisaichi

Introduction

This chapter deals with the cities of the Maghrib from the 7th to the end of the 19th century. On occasion I may go beyond these temporal limits when discussing a particular problem. I had originally intended to treat the cities of Andalus as well, but reluctantly will have to remain content with mentioning them only episodically.

When studying the cities of the Islamic world, or more broadly, the Islamic culture of the region, it is important to recognize that certain historical factors exist which make the Maghrib different from other Islamic lands. First, the influence of "Orientalism" has been long and profound in the Maghrib and Andalus. Ever since Andalus came under Islamic rule in the 8th century, the region constantly provided a window through which Europeans viewed Islamic civilization, and it would be quite correct to say that European knowledge and study of Islam began with the creation of the province of Andalus. The Maghrib too, like Andalus, was affected by the fortunes of history, with Italy and France close neighbours across the Mediterranean Sea. Second, the countries of the Maghrib were long under French colonial rule. This is important in that the concept of the "Islamic city" derived from urban studies conducted in the Maghrib by French scholars, initially as a facet of French colonial policy. The ideas formulated by them subtly influenced urban studies in other Islamic lands.

These two points mean that while urban studies of the Maghrib are a part of Arab urban studies in general, because they gave birth to the general concept of an "Islamic city," they have both strongly local colorations and a close connection with urban studies over the entire Islamic region. Taking this into consideration, I will survey urban studies centering on French scholars from the latter half of the 19th century until 1970 as they were connected with political events, such as colonial rule, moves towards independence, and changes in the international environment since independence. Following this survey, I will first examine trends in research undertaken between 1970 and 1990 in terms of the concept of the "Islamic city" and its attendant problems and mention changes in research methodology. Naturally the majority of examples given will concern the Maghrib, but depending on the nature of the question, I will also include cities of Mashriq and other Islamic regions. Next I will indicate characteristics and problem areas in urban studies according to important themes. I hope that this overview of the history of urban studies will give scholars a vantage point for new research.

I. Historical Overview

1. 1830-1880

There is some uncertainty about from when the history of Maghribi urban studies should be considered to begin. If we include descriptions of cities such as the *Topographia e historia general de Argel* (1612), a topography and history of the town of Algiers by the Spanish Benedictine monk Haëdo, based on his four years of captivity there, and *An Account of the Empire of Morocco* (1809), a travel record by the English consul in Mogador, J. Grey-Jackson, the beginnings become somewhat obscure in terms of objective exposition. Since though it was after the French occupation of Algiers in 1830 that descriptions became more consciously objective and academic, both numerically and quantitatively, we will begin our discussion at that date.

There were among the 37,000 strong occupying army of Algiers a group of scholars who had been added to it following the previous example of Napoleon in Egypt. They began their actual work in 1837, when the French Ministry of the Army set up a commission for the scientific investigation of Algeria (Commission chargée de l'Exploration Scientifique de l'Algérie). Two years later, in 1839, Bory de Saint-Vincent, a naturalist and member of the Academy of Science, arrived in Algeria at the head of a scientific commission of twenty-five men, including fourteen soldiers. The commission's results were published in a massive report of thirty-nine volumes between the years 1844 and 1867 (*Exploration scientifique de l'Algérie*), astonishing for its multi-disciplined approach, covering geography, history, medicine, earth science, zoology, botany, archaeology and the arts. Some reports, such as C. Carette's *Recherches sur la géographie et le commerce de l'Algérie méridionale* (1844) and E. Pellissier's *Mémoires historiques ou géographiques sur l'Algérie* (1844), mention topics concerning the towns, but overall, interest was with tribal society, and moreover the reports were obviously intended as general sketches to aid eventual full-scale colonial rule. This is not unconnected with the fact that many of the members of the expedition were soldiers, civil servants and interpreters rather than independent scholars. By the 1850s, scholars who had mastered Arabic and Berber had appeared on the scene, energetically translating and editing historical material. Among the works published were M. G. De Slane's translation and edition of the geographies of al-Bakrī and Ibn Ḥawqal, R. Dozy's edition of the historical writings of Ibn 'Idhārī and 'Abd al-Wāḥid al-Marrākushī, and M. J. De Goeje's edition and partial translation of the geographies of al-Idrīsī and al-Ya'qūbī. Even though such studies were not undertaken at the direct request of the French colonial administration, as may be surmised by the fact that both Dozy and De Goeje were Dutch, research by scholars fluent in Arabic and Berber and with a deep interest in the local society was of a practical character beneficial to the colonial government.

Translation and editorial work on medieval Arabic historical material promoted in a very short time an understanding among Europeans of Islam and Maghribi society, and reports about cities like Marrakesh, Fez, Tlemcen and Kairouan brought about a heightening interest in urban studies. The first such studies undertaken include the pioneering work concerning topography and architecture of J. J. L. Bargès, *Tlemcen, ancienne capitale du royaume de ce nom* (1859), A. Devoulx, "Notes historiques sur les mosquées" (1860-2), id. "Les édifices religieux de l'ancien Alger" (1862-70), id. "Alger: Étude archéologique et topographique" (1875-8), and A. Berbrugger, "Les anciens établissements de Constantine" (1868). Devoulx's study (1862-70), for example, is a detailed report on the religious architecture existing in Algiers in 1830; in it are recorded not only a total of 176 buildings, including 13 congregational mosques, 109 mosques for daily prayer, 32 marabouts and 12 *zāwiyas*, and descriptions of their physical characteristics, but also translations of inscriptions and commentaries. Berbrugger (1868) throws light on the incomes and expenditures of large mosques by means of waqf documents. The priority of geography and architecture in the discipline of urban studies remains true for the later colonies of Tunisia and Morocco, perhaps since one of the tasks of the colonial administration was the practical work of making maps and surveying buildings.

It is interesting therefore that studies on guild organizations and the Sufi orders began early side by side with topographical and architectural research. Ch. L. Féraud's "Les corporations de métiers à Constantine" (1872) is a brief work which details how commerce and industry in Constantine before the French occupation (1837) were supervised by various *amīns* (headmen), listing the names of forty-one guilds. *Les Khouan* (1859) by Ch. Brosselard, deputy governor of Tlemcen, discusses the organization, hierarchies and initiation rituals of seven powerful Sufi orders active in the cities and villages.

Those who undertook research from the time of the occupation to around 1880 were in the main soldiers, colonial officials and interpreters, who made the most of their ability to study local society directly. Brosselard's examination of the history of prominent ulama families in Tlemcen in his study of inscriptions, "Les inscriptions arabes de Tlemcen" (1864), E. Mercier's comprehensive histories of Constantine, *Constantine avant la conquête francaise* (1878) and *Constantine et histoire de Constantine* (1903), and Féraud's *Histoire des villes de la province de Constantine: Bougie* (1869) are all products of their authors' local experience. However, in the works of Carette (1844) and E. Mercier, Algerian history is seen as a contrast between the high civilization of the Roman period and its destruction by the Arab nomads, a view that became established as the ideology legitimating the French conquest and control as the restoration of civilization. It was only natural that such an outlook on history encouraged scholars to be interested in the Roman period. As a result, studies of the Islamic period were outside the mainstream, and research into the urban society of Islamic times lagged behind that of tribal society and rural villages in the same period.

2. 1880-1904

As the apparatus of French colonial control was consolidated with the transfer of control to a civil administration in 1871 and the enactment of the Warnier law in 1873, conditions were steadily changing. Already in Algeria scholarly societies, such as Société Archéologique de Constantine (1852), Société Historique Algérienne (1856) and Société Géographique et Archéologique d'Oran (1878) had been set up. La Société Historique Algérienne published the *Revue Africaine,* which contributed greatly to research into Algerian and Maghribi history, geography, archaeology and tribal society. The University of Algiers was founded around the same time (1874), and by the 1880s, scholars active in the societies or at the university had earned the name of the Algerian School and were promoters of Maghribi studies.

The Algerian School at first followed the established methodology and view of history, that historical research of the Roman period was cut off and separate from that of the Islamic period. Studies of the Roman period were appraised affirmatively as justifying the rationality of French colonial control as the herald of Western civilization, and many such works appeared, for instance E. Cat's *Essai sur la province romaine de Mauritanie césarienne* (1891) and successive studies. The majority of these were based on historical sources or fieldwork, but they were similar in that they looked at the Maghrib only as a Roman province, not in terms of the native Berber culture and society. At the same time many studies of the history of the Islamic period were also produced. E. Mercier, *Histoire de l'Afrique septentrionale* (1888-90) is noteworthy as the first general history of the Maghrib as a whole, an enormous work filling three volumes and 1500 pages. However, the work saw history in terms of conflicts with incoming peoples and tribal hostility, and was biased in that Mercier did not recognize any order or historical coherence in Maghribi society. His interpretation was elaborated by G. Marçais in *Les Arabes en Berbérie* (1913), and brought to completion by E. F. Gautier, a professor of geography and history at the University of Algiers, in *Le passé de l'Afrique du Nord* (1927). G. Marçais, *Berbérie musulmane* (1946) is evidence that this view continued unchanged even into the middle of the 20th century. This bias was considered established theory in a large number of studies of tribal society, such as A. Hanoteau and A. Letourneux, *La Kabylie et les coutumes kabyles* (1893), and became the established, if stagnant, explanation of Maghribi and Islamic society. Needless to say, this distortion in methodology and historical understanding was to have a considerable influence on the formation of the concept of the so-called "Islamic city."

With the French conquest of the cities and their surroundings virtually complete by the beginning of the 1880s, a certain over-familiarity with local culture, and with the beginning of concerted efforts to extend control over tribal society and the rural villages, urban studies lost momentum to some extent. All the same a number of new trends can be identified. For example, Aumerat, "La propriété urbaine à Alger" (1897-8) investigates the possession of landed property during the Ottoman period, according to whether it was owned by the *beys* (Turkish governors), the *Bayt al-Māl* (the state treasury), individuals, or in common. E. Masqueray, *La formation des cités* (1886) is a comparative study of three Berber regional societies, Kabylie, Aurès and Mzab. In that he avoids judgments based on racial inferiority or superiority and looks at differences in the character of settlements as being based on differences in occupation, such as farming or herding, he represents a new attitude towards research. As French colonial power spread to neighbouring countries (Tunisia became a protectorate in 1883), the field of urban studies expanded from Algeria to Tunisia and Morocco. This was also a new trend. Ch. Lallemand, *Tunis et ses environs* (1890) is a detailed study of the distribution and activities of commercial and craft guilds in Tunis, which shows that respectable crafts occupied the town's centre, that in their relationship with the city administration, each guild was under the control of an *amīn* (headman), and that though the *amīn* had the authority to resolve business disputes, all occupations were subordinate to the *shaykh al-madīna* (the town head). This study is worthy of attention since it sets out the important issues about the guild in the city of Islamic region, later a popular subject for research. Moroccan cities were covered in the form of a topography by T. de Cuevas in "El Ksar-el-Acabir" (1897). Among geographers in Algiers there were a number who also had an interest in historical geography. For example, A. Coudray, "Relations commerciales de Tlemcen avec le Sahara et le Soudan" (1892) uses historical materials to trace changes in trade routes and goods across the Sahara and argues that Tlemcen was a base for this trade. Though somewhat later, a further new area of study emerged during the period under discussion, the study of waqf, pious endowments. This development was linked with French colonial land policy, which had seen a land law similar to that of Algeria enacted in 1885 after Tunisia was made a protectorate. E. Mercier, *Le Habous ou Ouakf* (1896), J. Terrasse, *Essai sur les biens habous en Algérie et en Tunisie* (1899) and J. Abribat, *Essai sur les contrats de quasi-aliénation* (1902) are examples of such studies. Mercier's was a Hanafi law treatise; the conscious study of waqf in terms of urban studies was yet to begin.

3. 1904-1920

1904 was an epoch-making year for Maghribi urban studies, and indeed for the Islamic lands in general, being the year France organized the Mission Scientifique to undertake a general survey of the cities and tribes of Morocco. Its headquarters were situated in Tangier, and a good many of the cities studied were in the northern part of Morocco. The result was a concentrated study by historians, sociologists, linguists and others, which covered the administrative structure and the political, religious and economic organization of a number of cities including Tangier, el-Qsar-el-Kebir, Tetuan, Rabat, Casablanca and Fez. The leading members of the Mission, like G. Salmon, E. Michaux-Bellaire, E. Doutté, M. A. Joly and L. Mercier, were not exempt from a sense of the strategic in their work for they agreed with the intent of colonial policy, but they were scientifically trained Orientalists whose historical descriptions of the cities, based on old documents, were of a considerable level of scholarship. The Mission is important in that it heralded the beginning of urban studies. Its reports were published in stages in the *Archives marocaines* (1904-36) and the *Revue du monde musulman* (1906-26); they were collected and published by Michaux-Bellaire and others in eleven volumes (*Villes et tribus du Maroc*) between 1915 and 1932.

In terms of the Maghrib, 1904 was also the year that urban studies moved its centre of gravity from Algeria to Morocco. The reason that urban studies developed in earnest in Morocco was that France, contemplating the colonization of the whole Maghrib following the annexation of Morocco (made a protectorate in 1912), used cities as their points of control; also, Morocco was chosen as the testing ground for a modern urban policy and town planning. J. Abu-Lughod, *Rabat: Urban Apartheid in Morocco* (1980) is an incisive analysis of the contradictions in French urban policy at the time.

G. Salmon, "Les Chorfa idrissides de Fès" (1904) and "Les Chorfa Filāla et Djilāla de Fès" (1905) are historically documented studies tracing the *sharīf* families of Fez. Salmon's research also included "Confréries et zaouia de Tanger" (1904-5), discussing the activities of the 'Īsāwā and Tijaniya and other Sufi orders in Tangier, "Le culte de Moulay Idriss" (1905), an analysis of the process how Mulay Idris, a saint of Fez, grew into the most important saint of the town, and "Notes sur Salé" (1905), an annotated translation of historical material concerning the saints and buildings of Salé. His contribution to urban studies has been his investigations of the connection between cities and the cults of saints using historical materials. L. Mercier, "Les mosquées et la vie religieuse à Rabat" (1906), though basically a report of a survey of Rabat, is of particular interest for the wealth of detail it includes about religious life in urban society. There were at the time in Rabat six congregational mosques, where a Friday sermon was given, thirty-three so-called congregational mosques, which had no Friday sermon, twenty-six ordinary mosques, and thirteen *zāwiyas*. In addition he describes *mūsims* (saints' festivals) run by ten Sufi confraternities, and the membership and activities of a number of "sociétés" (*rbāyi'*) with religious functions or the organizational characteristics of the cofraternities, such as seven groups of musicians and five groups of militia which protected the town from outside threat.

Fez was the main city of Morocco, not only in cultural, but in economic terms also, and so more than any other city it received the attention of investigators and scholars. *Une ville de l'Islam: Fès* (1905) by the French consul H. Gaillard is a penetrating study based on original historical sources, though it was surpassed in many areas by R. Le Tourneau (1949). Michaux-Bellaire and Salmon, "Description de la ville de Fès" (1907) and L. Martin, "Description de la ville de Fès" (1909) are both survey reports of the quarter (*ḥoma*). Michaux-Bellaire's survey was carried out in the quarter of Zoqaq al-Rommān with Salmon's collaboration; it concludes that the distinctive features of the town were its numerous blind alleys and the unplanned nature of its urban architecture. Martin's work was also a detailed report of a survey he made of the buildings and streets of the Ḥoma al-Keddan. A. Pèretie, "Les Médrasas de Fès" (1912) is a detailed monograph which examines the history, function, management, architectural construction, educational methods, etc. of nine madrasas in Fez.

During this period the traditions of late 19th century urban studies were still being continued. For example, research on inscriptions in the towns began by Brosselard was continued by the brothers W. Marçais and G. Marçais, *Les monuments arabes de Tlemcen* (1903), W. Marçais, *Musée de Tlemcen* (1906) and A. Bel, "Inscriptions arabes de Fès" (1917) and the geographical and archaeological tradition by Ch. Monchicourt, "La région de Tunis" (1904) and E. T. Hamy, "Cités et nécropoles berbères de l'Enfida" (1904). Bel's research in particular is a detailed analysis of inscriptions (95 from mosques, madrasas and tombs) dating from the Marinid period in Fez; it also includes waqf accounts. E. Doutté, a former soldier, compiled a monograph, *Marrakech* (1905), a religious study of the veneration of saints from Casablanca to Marrakesh based on his own investigation.

Completely new trends are also apparent. Al-Moutabassir, "Les Habous de Tanger" (1907) discusses waqf in terms of the city (also apparent in the above-mentioned study of Bel), and J. Abribat, "Notes sur la hisba" (1911) deals with urban law and morals in the process of discussing the functions of the muhtasib. It should be noted that studies of *ḥisba* occupy an important position in urban studies of the Maghrib and Andalus. Ch. Monchicourt, "La fête de l'Achoura" (1910) examines the observance of *'āshūrā'* in Tunisians cities; at its base he discerns two elements, one, an agricultural ritual involving sacrifices and the other the tradition of the Prophet Muhammad, and relates that the former (the non-Islamic element) was the more vigorous. Because also many Jews lived in Maghribi cities and played a supplementary role in colonial administration, studies of Jewish communities throve in this period, influenced by the anti-Semitism of late 19th century Europe. Examples of such include D. Cades, *Essai sur l'histoire des Israélites de Tunisie* (1889) and J. Chalom, *Les Israélites de la Tunisie* (1906). M. A. Joly, "Le siège de Tétouan" (1905) discusses the critical incident of 1903-1904 when Tetuan was besieged and looted by nomads, clarifying in the process relationships between the town and the nomads and the fact that the Jews incurred the greatest harm during that troubled time. The period 1904-1920 was then a time when urban studies, like research into rural villages and the tribes, were becoming independent and research topics diversifying.

4. 1920-1956 (1962)

From around 1920 a number of important changes can be discerned in Maghribi urban studies. These new trends maintained their impetus until the end of French colonial rule (Morocco and Tunisia achieved independence in 1956, Algeria in 1962). The first point to be noted is the maturity of the research organizations and apparatus in the three countries of the Maghrib. We have already noted the development of academic societies in Algeria. In Tunisia, Institut des Hautes Etudes was established in 1894, and published the *Revue tunisienne* (1894-1942, continued from 1953 as *Les Cahiers de Tunisie*). An institute of the same name was founded in Rabat in 1920, and it published *Hespéris* (1921-59, known as *Hespéris-Tamuda* from 1960). Members of the latter institute included E. Pauty, H. Terrasse, L. Brunot and G. S. Colin, who published work in urban studies concerning history, geography, the arts, archaeology and handicrafts. Institut d'Etudes Orientales was newly set up in Algiers in 1934, and the urban theories of Pauty and E. Lévi-Provençal were published in its journal *Annales* (1934-61). The same year Fédération des Sociétés Savantes de l'Afrique du Nord was also established in Algiers. G. Marçais, "L'urbanisme musulman" (1940) was actually the proceedings of the fifth conference of the federation, held in Tunis. The fact that the concept of the "Islamic city" could be discussed at such a conference as a commonly recognized issue by French historians of the Maghrib points to the influence of the post-19th century colonialist view of history, which incorporated this concept. This growth shows how new organizations were brought into being to support colonial policy and to strengthen the colonial system and also, especially after the 1930s, to cope with the nationalist movement.

A second extremely important point, which will be examined later in the discussion about the development of Islamic urban studies, is that it was from this period that the concept of the "Islamic city" began to be discussed, primarily among scholars of Maghribi cities. Two factors favoured this development. One was the trend among European historians to admire the medieval Commune, deriving from a tradition of German romanticism, and to pursue a comparative methodology and a historical universalism, as best represented by Max Weber. Weber's *Wirtschaft und Gesellschaft* (1922) and Henri Pirenne's *Les villes du moyen âge* (1927) exerted a great influence on contemporary European historians. Second, there was already a formidable store of research about Maghribi cities, which provided ample material for historians wishing to make comparative studies with European cities and to form theoretical conceptualizations about the "Islamic city." One conclusion thus reached was that Islamic society was stagnant.

Here I will outline the main theories of the concept of the "Islamic city," before elaborating on them in a later section, which can be broadly divided into (a) the argument between L. Massignon and G. von Grunebaum regarding commune-like functions and (b) the universalism of the three characteristics described by W. Marçais, that Islam is an urban religion, that the elements of the Islamic city are the congregational mosque, the suq and the public bath, and that cities were founded in relation to the expansion of Islam and the establishment of dynasties.

It is true that there is considerable historical and epistemological distortion in these theories, but the research into urban structures and functions required to elucidate them is itself of great interest in many ways. Massignon compared Islamic urban guilds (professional corporations) and European guilds in lectures he gave in 1920 to the Collège de France; these were published as "Les corps de métiers et la cité islamique" (1920) and "Enquête sur les corporations d'artisans" (1924). He recognized the autonomous character of Islamic urban guilds in the medieval period (9th-12th centuries). Though there are many problems with this view, his contributions to learning cannot be ignored. In the former essay he emphasizes that the suq is an essential of the "Muslim city" and that the guild constitutes the basic structure of the city. Here we see clearly his interest in the essential qualities of the "Muslim city"; his pioneering role in the urban theory elaborated by W. Marçais and others needs to be appreciated. The latter essay, a field report concerning guilds in Moroccan cities is of great value. In it, Massignon gives the names of 164 guilds in Fez, 115 in Marrakesh, 89 in Rabat, 93 in Salé, and 106 in Meknes, as well as an analysis of their distribution in the quarters, their techniques, the organization of their members, initiation and their relations with the Sufi orders. He emphasizes the social integrative functions of the guilds from below, centring on the *amīn* (the guild headman), but also discusses how they operated following the regulations of the muhtasib, the agent of the ruling power (in the control of guilds). E. Buthaud, "Le gardiennage des souks" (1942, an examination of the authority of the *shaykh al-madīna* in terms of the issue of theft in the suqs and the employment of guards to prevent it, is influenced by Massignon's ideas.

W. Marçais's thesis is contained in his "L'islamisme et la vie urbaine" (1928), where his main point is the linking of Islam with the city. His ideas were elaborated by his brother, the architect and geographer G. Marçais, who brought together an abundance of materials in "L'urbanisme musulman" (1940) and "La conception des villes dans l'islam" (1945), and further systematized by von Grunebaum in "The Structure of the Muslim Town" (1955). The understanding of history which underlies this systematization is that Islam (civilization) is the ideology of the townspeople and that this ideology was confronted by the nomads. Such a schema of historical development, contrasting nomads as the destroyers of civilization with urban dwellers as its upholders, was held in common among scholars of the Maghrib at the time, including E. Mercier (1878), Gautier (1927), G. Marçais (1913) (1946) and W. Marçais, "Comment l'Afrique du Nord a été arabisée" (1938-56). L. Gardet, "Humanisme musulman" (1944) and *La cité musulmane* (1954) too emphasize that Islam is the religion of the city and that the essential quality of the structure of the "Islamic city" is the suq, where the various guilds are centred. Such is the view of history evident behind the concept of the "Islamic city" and we must bear it in mind when tracing the results of the research done during this period.

The first result was the sociological surveys concerning commerce, crafts and the organization of the guilds that were undertaken in the main by members of the Institut des Hautes Etudes in Rabat. L. Brunot, "Vocabulaire de la tannerie" (1923) is a collection of terminology related to the tanning industry in Rabat, and G. S. Colin, "Noms d'artisans et de commerçants" (1931) and P. Ricard, "Les métiers manuels à Fès" (1924) are field reports listing the names of 192 types of merchants and artisans in Marrakesh and 126 occupation names in Fez respectively. Brunot also wrote "La cordonnerie" (1946), a field report about the shoe-makers' guild of Rabat. Systematic investigations were also undertaken by scholars from the university. R. Guyot, Le Tourneau and L. Paye surveyed guilds in Fez: for example, potters in "L'industrie de la poterie à Fes" (1934), tanners in "La corporation des tanneurs" (1935) [see Le Tourneau for details], bookbinders in "Les relieurs de Fès" (1935), and shoemakers in "Les cordonniers de Fès" (1936). In content they are detailed monographs dealing with, in the case of the field report on the tanners' guild for example, history, the present circumstances, the work process, the leather market, and the guild organization. The above mentioned "Enquête sur les corporations" (1924) and "Complément" (1927) of Massignon are masterpieces of such practical research. E. Lecuyer, "Les métiers constantinois" (1950) studies the organization of some twenty guilds in Constantine (Algeria) before the French Occupation. P. Marty, "Corporations et syndicats" (1935) is a contemporary report on the silk goods guild of Tunis. J. Quemeneur, "Contribution" (1942) studies the history, work process, materials, apprenticeship system and social life of the *belghajia* (slipper makers) guild of Tunis. Le Tourneau, "L'activité économique de Sefrou" (1938) is a field report about economic activity centring on the suqs of Sefru (Morocco). G. Lucas, *Fès dans le Maroc moderne* (1937) analyzes contemporary urban society in Fez from the standpoint of population, transport and communications, and commercial and industrial activities.

Specific research was also beginning to be done more extensively in the field of urban social life. I. S. Allouche, "Un plan des canalisations de Fès" (1934) clarifies an aspect of urban life through the question of water, being a translation and commentary of a document written in 1715. It discusses the canal network in Fez at the time, the problems of distributing water to the quarters, plans for new canals, and the functions and organization of the guild (*qawādisīya*) carrying out maintenance and repairs on the canals. A further study about water in the cities is J. M. Solignac, "Travaux hydrauliques Ḥafṣides de Tunis" (1936), which shows by a study of historical sources and archaeological investigation changes in the construction of facilities for the water supply to Tunis between the 13th and 15th centuries. While the successive Sultans restored the aqueduct built at the time of Hadrian, they also encouraged the excavation of *foggara* (underground channels) and the construction of diversion channels, indicating the importance of water for urban life and city dwellers. J. Berque, "Ville et université" (1949) does not look at social life directly, but by tracing the development of the Qarawiyyin Mosque in Fez, it touches on the strength of social integration in the city, centring on the ulama. Though its area of interest is different, the aforementioned G. Marçais (1940), which deals with the idea of the "Islamic city," also throws light on an aspect of urban society. When a city was built, he said, the necessary geographical conditions were security and water. Water in particular was important, and its acquisition was a determining factor in a city's construction. The problem of water was not just a matter of supply; drainage was also vital to the maintenance of urban life. In a city (to take Old Cairo for example), the establishment of a system to separate lavatory and ordinary household drainage, the existence of guilds of effluent collectors, and the importance of the role of the muhtasib as the supervisor of urban sanitation, all attest to a powerful concern with drainage. id., "Considerations sur les villes musulmanes" (1954) discusses the problem in terms of the role of the muhtasib. R. Brunschvig, "Urbanisme médiéval" (1947) specifically points out that Islamic law was concerned with various facets of urban life, such as roads, walls, drainage and relations between neighbours. id., *La Berbérie orientale sous les Ḥafṣides* (1940-7) discusses in detail urban life in Tunis, Kairouan and other cities under the Ḥafṣid dynasty. L. Torrès Balbas, "Les villes musulmanes d'Espagne" (1942) emphasizes that urban structure was formed to maintain the quiet, safe and private life of the family.

Very important for an understanding of urban social life are the manuals of *ḥisba* (market inspection and the censorship of public morals), and many historical sources and studies exist particularly for the Maghrib and Andalus. E. Lévi-Provençal, "Un document sur la vie urbaine" (1934) is a detailed analysis of information concerning city administration and merchants and artisans in early 12th century Seville, appended to a commentary of a manual of *ḥisba* by Ibn 'Abdūn. M. Talbi, "Quelques données sur la vie sociale" (1954) is a study of a manual of *ḥisba* by the 15th century Tlemcen scholar, Muḥammad al-'Uqbānī. M. Gaudefroy-Demonbynes, "Sur quelques ouvrages du ḥisba" (1938) divides manuals of *ḥisba* into four types according to content: theoretical works (al-Māwardī and others), collections of *fatwā* (*niṣāb*), practical examples from Andalus (Saqatī and others) and practical examples from Mashriq (Ibn al-Ukhuwwa). Though somewhat removed from urban social life, Ch. Monchicourt, *Kairouan et les Chabbia* (1939), which deals with the history of the family of Sufi notables, the Shābbīs, who governed Kairouan in the middle of the 16th century, is extremely interesting in terms of the connections between the city and a family of notables. Monchicourt also wrote a series of studies on the history and life of Kairouan, "Études kairouanaises" (1931-6). H. R. Idris, "Contribution à l'histoire de l'Ifrikiya" (1936) uses the late 10th century *Riyāḍ al-Nufūs* (biographies of jurists of Kairouan) to paint a clear picture of urban religious life at the time. It is apparent that in the 10th century jurists actually participated in rites for rain and healing, indicating the types of connections that existed between them and the people. A comprehensive study of the physical form, functions and social life of the cities, one that retains its value today, is Le Tourneau, *Fès avant le protectorat* (1949). The value of this study is that it combines a wealth of historical documentation with actual surveys, going beyond merely describing the physical form of Fez to give a detailed analysis of the urban life in terms of government, economy, culture, society and religion. According to D. E. Eickelman, *The Middle East* (1981) he was nevertheless unable to break away from a static view of history.

Examples of studies using chronicles and geographies are E. Lévi-Provençal, "La fondation de Fès" (1938), an examination of the circumstances surrounding the establishment of Fez; id., *Las ciudades y las instituciones urbanas* (1950), an outline of the facilities and institutions of medieval Andalus and the Maghrib, using historical materials; R. Blachère, "Fès" (1934), a compilation of descriptions concerning Fez from over ten geographies (from Ibn Khurdādhbih to al-'Umarī); and H. Terrasse, "Note sur les ruines de Sijilmassa" (1936), an attempt to throw light on the ruins of Sijilmasa through historical sources. However these works seem to lack a certain vividness in comparison with the practical studies being done in the same period in conjunction with field work. The study of waqf also continued to be a very important part of colonial policy. Noteworthy is the appearance of M. Mercier, *Étude sur le 'waqf' abadhite* (1927), an analysis based on historical documents concerning waqf set up by the Ibadites of Mzab (in the Ghardaia district of Algeria) in both theory and practice. id., *La civilisation urbaine au Mzab* (1922) is a doctoral thesis discussing the physical form, structure, social life and history of Ghardaia, the city of the Ibadites.

On the other hand descriptive general histories in the traditional mould continued to be produced energetically. Examples include Ch. Dessort, *Histoire de la ville Tunis* (1924), A. Pellegrin, *Histoire illustrée de la ville de Tunis* (1955), J. Caillé, *La ville de Rabat* (1929), and A. R'honi, *Historia de Tetuán* (1953). Dessort's study is an outline by a self-confessed enlightened man of the history of Tunis since Carthaginian times using photographs and illustrations. R'honi's history of Tetuan, a Spanish translation from the original

Arabic, deals with history, geography, monuments and the records of notables, and reflects the purposes of Spanish cultural policy in the northern part of Morocco, which Spain then controlled from its base in Tetuan. All of these works share a common view in that they purport to be overviews of the city's history from earliest times to the present in terms of natural features and cultural and social characteristics, but they are no more than stereotyped historical outlines, closed to the idea of social change.

Geography and archaeology gradually gave rise to a great deal of research. R. Lespès, *Alger* (1925) deals with pre-1830 Algiers, the statistics of demographic change between 1830 and 1921, and the history of developments between 1830 and 1925. Similar in kind are *Alger* (1930) and *Oran* (1938), both by the same author. Studies of the cities of Tunisia include J. Despois, "Kairouan" (1930) and id., *La Tunisie orientale: Sahel et basse steppe* (1955). G. Marçais also wrote *Tunis et Kairouan* (1937) and *Tlemcen* (1950), the latter a general history of Tlemcen from earliest times. In the former, Marçais expounds his view of history, that historical development is a product of destruction by nomads, asserting that Kairouan and Tunis are linked by history, in that the invasion and destruction of Kairouan by Arab nomads, the Hilal, led to the growth of Tunis as a city. A. Lézine, *Mahdiya* (1956) is an archaeological study. According to X. Yacono, "Peut-on évaluer la population de l'Algérie en 1830?" (1954), the majority of scholars of Algeria made estimates of Algeria's population during the period of French occupation. Examples are P. Boyer, "L'évolution démographique" (1954) and Yacono himself. Yacono's research makes an extremely precise examination of the subject using a great many estimates. A. Nouschi, "Constantine à la veille de la conquête française" (1955) investigates society in Constantine between the 1830s and the early 1840s and give an excellent synopsis based on population, commerce, craft and manufacturing activities, the constitution of the inhabitants, and the numbers of mosques (35), madrasas (7) and Koranic schools (90). J. Célérier, "Les conditions géographiques du développement de Fès" (1934), which seeks the reasons for the development of Fez in geographical (as opposed to topographical) terms, gives three conditions for that development: regional (climate, land forms, geology), that specific to Fez (its position on a river) and general (its strategic position in terms of communications).

The outstanding achievement of the period in terms of architecture and the arts is G. Marçais, *Manuel d'art musulman* (1926). This large work in two volumes and covering close to a thousand pages is a comprehensive guide to virtually all Islamic buildings in the Maghrib, Andalus and Sicily up to the 19th century and is the greatest work of Marçais, then a professor at the University of Algiers. A distinctive part of his work is his analysis of building plans and designs. The book is also rich in photographs and illustrations. This work of Marçais, and the aforementioned work of Le Tourneau on Fez (1949), together rank in the highest class even today. G. Marçais, *L'architecture musulmane d'Occident* (1954) is virtually a supplement to the previous work. In "Les portes de l'arsenal de Salé" (1922) and "Trois bains mérinides" (1950), H. Terrasse examines plans of Marinid city gates and public baths and their inscriptions. B. Maslow and H. Terrasse, "Une maison mérinide" (1936) states that plans of dwellings in 14th century Marinid Fez are the essence of the Islamic-Spanish style. P. H. Koehler, "La Kasba saadienne de Marrakech" (1940) examines the plan of the kasbah of Marrakesh as it then existed in comparison with a map of the kasbah included in a 1585 Portuguese manuscript. A. Lézine, "Deux ribats du sahel tunisein" (1956) is an architectural study of the physical form of the *ribāṭ* in Sousse and Monastir.

An important topic regarding the origins of cities was raised during the period. In a conference at the Institut d'Etudes Orientales in Rabat in 1947, E. Pauty, acknowledging the work of G. Marçais, H. Terrasse, Pirenne, J. Sauvaget and others in this field, discussed the difference between the "spontaneous" city and the "created" city in "Villes spontanées et villes créées en Islam" (1951). This concept was closely connected with that of the "Islamic city," and had already been discussed by G. Marçais in "La conception" (1945). It had also been mentioned in P. Lavedan, *Géographie des villes* (1936). Pauty systematized the concept in the course of a comparison with medieval European cities. His points are as follows: (1) Cities of the Islamic regions, and particularly those of the Maghrib, are overridingly created cities. (2) These created cities were virtually always built for the rulers by the rulers. (3) The definition of the medieval city in Europe does not fit the city of Islamic land, since citizens, juridical personalities and the community did not exist in a European sense in the city of Islamic land. (4) When, particularly in Ottoman times, city people first began building mosques, madrasas and *qaysarīyas* for themselves, the muhtasib came to play an important role regarding building plans. (5) Good examples of created cities are Fez, Kairouan, Granada, Marrakesh, Tunis and Meknes. In the course of his conclusions, Pauty criticized the inflexible urban planning of the state leadership. He had in fact twenty-five years previously published "Rapport sur la défense des villes" (1922) clearly indicating the need for the protection of historical monuments in Fez, Marrakesh, Rabat and other towns in Morocco and stating the validity of a colonial urban policy which separated the new towns from the medinas. He also averred that the Arabs lacked both the will and the ability to preserve cultural remains. Few of the historians of the period were able to escape such racial bias completely. Worthy of note however is Ch. A. Julien, *Histoire de l'Afrique du Nord* (1931), an attempt to write a new history of the Maghrib based on textual criticism, not bound by prevailing opinion. According to M. Djender (1968), though, Julien can be criticized in that he too saw the history of the Maghrib as the history of conflicts between the nomads and the settled communities. P. De Cenival produced two extremely interesting papers about Christians in Maghribi society: "L'église chrétienne de Marrakech" (1927), showing the existence of a Christian church in Marrakech in the 13th century, and "Le prétendu évêché de la kal'a des Beni Ḥammād" (1932), which state there was a church in the early 12th century Qal'a (Algeria), the Banu Ḥammad capital, and perhaps even a bishop, and contend that Christianity remained firmly fixed even after the Arab conquest. Would it be possible perhaps to see such an emphasis on Christian culture, which after all was of small importance in the wider Islamic culture, to be in a way an example of historical bias?

Studies continued in this period also about the cities and their saint cults. Le Torneau (1949) is of course such an example; individual papers on the subject include H. De Castries, "Les sept patrons de Marrakech" (1924) about the origins of the seven patron saints of Marrakesh and the order of pilgrimages (*ziyāra*) to their tombs, P. Durand, "Boujad, ville sainte" (1931), a physical description and history of Boujad, the religious centre of the Sharqāwa order, P. Marty, "La zaouia de Sidi Ben Achir" (1933), dealing with a Sufi who moved to the Maghrib from Andalus in the 14th century and whose tomb became the most famous of saints' monuments in Salé, W. Fogg, "Wazzan" (1934), a discussion of the role of the *sharīf* in the holy city of Ouezzan before the Protectorate, and A. Pellegrin, "Sidi Bou Said" (1955), a history of Sidi Bou Said.

Research concerning Jews includes M. Eisenbeth, "Les juifs" (1952), a study of the Jewish population of Algeria and Tunisia under Ottoman rule, the autonomy of Jewish communities, and their relations with political authority, based on a large number of documents; H. Cornet, "Les juifs de Gafsa" (1955), a field report on the population, family and social life of Jews in Gafsa (Tunisia) in the first half of the 20th century; and V. Danon, "Les niveaux de vie dans la Hara de Tunis" (1955), a field report concerning the Jewish quarter of Tunis (based on a study of 100 families selected from the 2,500 families and 10,000 people who then resided in the quarter, focusing on family composition, age, occupation, income, etc.). The issue of the establishment of the state of Israel was probably connected with such research. Ch. E. Dufourcq, "La question de Ceuta" (1955) discusses the role of Ceuta in 13th century Mediterranean trade. A similar study is A. Sayous, *Le commerce des européens à Tunis* (1929). It should also be added that studies of the urban proletariat began around this time, as a result of growing urban industrialization, an example being R. Montagne, "Naissance du prolétariat marocain" (1951). Though M. A. al-Kānūnī, "Āsfī and the Surroundings" (A., n. d.) was published during the 1980s, this history of Safi (Āsfī) was actually written considerably earlier, probably before 1940. With its descriptions of the city walls, mosques and other buildings, important families, notables and rulers, it is a pioneer of the urban histories that were written by local historians after Independence.

Thanks to the firm research base which had been established, the period gave rise to a large number of works, based on both surveys and on documentary analysis, and many of the monographs published remain of great value today. However the accumulated research also caused a distorted concept of the city to emerge, an issue which had to be addressed in the next period. In this sense the research undertaken in the period prior to independence provides a comprehensive survey of urban studies under colonial rule.

5. 1956 (1962) -1970

Changes in the region in the later 1950s (Moroccan and Tunisian independence in 1956, and the fierce conflict in Algeria between 1954 and 1962) were reflected also in urban studies. First, with independence, the fulcrum of research shifted from the colonial facilities to faculties or institutes within universities. The lead was taken in France by the University of Paris, the University of Aix-Marseilles, the University of Tours, the CNRS (Centre national de la recherche scientifique) and others, and in the Maghrib by the University of Tunis, Muhammad V University and the University of Algiers. Second, this shift meant that local scholars began to be involved in urban studies, though not in earnest until after 1970. Third, Mashriq moved to centre stage in discussions about the "Islamic city" and English and American scholars came to play a prominent role. For example, in 1965 leading scholars such as Cl. Cahen, S. Stern, A. H. Hourani and I. M. Lapidus discussed the "Islamic city" at Oxford University (*The Islamic City,* eds. A. H. Hourani and S. M. Stern, 1970) and in 1966 Lapidus, S. D. Goitein, Ch. Issawi, J. Abu-Lughod and others held a symposium at the University of California on Middle Eastern cities (*Middle Eastern Cities,* ed. I. M. Lapidus, 1969). In terms of the overall issue it is apparent that at the level of studies on individual cities, urban studies in the Maghrib were relatively behind those of Mashriq. Fourth from this period, urban studies were promoted particularly as part of area studies. As a result of the Heyter Report of the 1960s, area studies were promoted in earnest in Great Britain, and soon Harvard University and other American universities followed suit, establishing institutes of Middle Eastern Studies. Urban expansion as a result of industrialization, the growth of slums, and the appearance of a class of urban poor attracted interest in the city, and a large number of urban studies were produced, in connection with area studies.

Le Tourneau, who had earlier produced the excellent study of Fez, generalized about the characteristics of Maghribi cities in *Les villes musulmanes* (1957). Here he consolidated and reasserted the traditional view of the "Islamic city" whose elements are the mosque, the central market and the citadel of the rulers. The city is surrounded by a wall and is separated from and stands in contrast to the rural village. The quarters have no autonomous functions. There is no overall city plan, and therefore the city comprises winding roads and blind alleys. The Muslim city consists of various religions and races. The cities of the Maghrib lack the intellectual vigour of medieval European cities. Le Tourneau also published a work on Marinid Fez, *Fez* (1961), which is practically identical with his earlier *Fès* (1949). G. Deverdun, formerly head of the Institut des Hautes Etudes in Rabat, published a history of Marrakesh, *Marrakech des origines à 1912* (1959-66) focusing on political history, for which he utilized a large amount of historical sources and research reports. L. Golvin, *Aspects de l'artisanat* (1957), which, while following Massignon, "Enquête" (1924), discusses connections between artisans and the Sufi orders and the patron saints of guilds. P. Boyer, *La vie quotidienne à Alger* (1963) throws light on daily life in the urban setting of Algiers under Ottoman rule, based on European historical sources and research. An Orientalist flavour is discernible but the work is of great interest for its detailed descriptions of food, clothing, women's cosmetics, etc. If the above studies are considered a continuation of the research that was conducted in colonial times, A. Adam, *Casablanca: Essai sur la transformation de la société marocaine* (1968) is an excellent study emerging from the new research order, liberated from the colonial past, in France. It analyzes the development and transformation of Casablanca as a city from various angles, such as architecture, religion and family life.

Studies by Maghribi scholars include M. Dā'ūd, *A History of Tetuan* (A., 1959-62), a voluminous history of Tetuan, M. Naciri (Professor of Geography at Muhammad V University in Rabat), "Salé: Étude de géographie urbaine" (1963), and A. Ben Talha, *Moulay-Idriss du Zerhoun* (1965), a sociological analysis of the holy city of Mulay Idris Zarhun. Dā'ūd's study is a valuable description of the history of his birthplace from its beginnings until the Spanish-Moroccan War of 1860 and it paints a detailed picture, through the use of historical materials, of the rulers, the qadis, the notaries, the Sufis and urban life. Unfortunately Ben Talha's work lacks sharp analysis, since research by local scholars was then only beginning and research experience was still minimal. Muḥammad al-Marzūqī, *Gabes: A Paradise of the World* (A., 1962) is a descriptive study of the history of Gabes and N. Ziadeh, *Arab Cities* (A., 1965) also contains descriptions of Maghribi cities.

The concept of the "Islamic city," constructed by French scholars in the course of their studies on Maghribi cities, was during this period submitted to severe criticism and revision by English and American researchers of the cities of Mashriq. Compared with French scholars, they perhaps had a certain freedom of viewpoint since they were not tied to the same extent to Islamic society. Related topics such as the criticism by Stern and Cahen of Massignon's guild theory will be dealt with in the chapter on Mashriq. J. Berque, "Médinas, villeneuves et bidonvilles" (1958) represents a new approach to the subject by a scholar of Maghribi cities. Berque bases his work on the presupposition that there is a clear differentiation between city and rural village. He says that this differentiation can be made according to function rather than form, such as the three elements of congregational mosque, public bath and suq, as defined by W. Marçais. He holds that whereas the city is a place of "exchange and testimony" (*un lieu d'échange et de témoignage*) where Islamic law functions, the village (*bādiya*) is place where custom rather than law prevails and so stresses the importance of the functioning of Islamic law in the cities. R. Brunschvig, "Justice religieuse" (1965), though not directly related to the concept of the "Islamic city," deals with the legal and court systems of Tunis during the Ottoman period. Many scholars at the time under discussion were interested in studying the *ḥisba,* spurred by Lévi-Provençal's edition of three *ḥisba* manuals (Ibn 'Abdūn, Ibn 'Abd al-Ra'ūf, al-Jarsīfī), *Documents arabes inédits* (1955). G. M. Wickens, "al-Jarsīfī" (1956-7) is a commentary and English translation of the *ḥisba* manual of al-Jarsīfī in Lévi-Provençal's work. J. D. Latham, "Observations and the Text and Translation" (1960) points out errors in Wickens's translation and makes a detailed examination of the text. R. Arié, "Traduction annotée et commentée" (1960) is a commentary on and French translation of 'Abd al-Ra'ūf's *ḥisba* manual, and G. E. García, "Unas ordenanzaz del zoco" (1957) is a commentary on and Spanish translation of the suq manual of the 9th century Kairouan jurist Yaḥyā b. 'Umar. P. Chalmeta, "La ḥisba en Ifriqiya et al-Andalus" (1970), read at an international conference held in 1969 on the historical and cultural relationships between Tunisia and Spain, is a comparative study of *ḥisba* sources recorded by eight people, from Yaḥyā b. 'Umar (9th century) to al-'Uqbānī (15th century). Chalmeta shows that the sources changed in character as Islamic law and the legal system became consolidated. At first, with the beginnings of Islamic law in the 9th century, provisions related to the government administration of the suq. Provisions (*ḥisba*) became more minute and related to the juristic control of the suq. Eventually, *ḥisba* came to apply to life as a whole. Behind the popularity of such research is the realization that *ḥisba* manuals are important documents for analyzing urban society. This is shown by Chalmeta's later major consolidation of his work, *El señor del zoco* (1973), a study of urban life and economy through *ḥisba* manuals.

A number of studies deal with cities which prospered as a result of their trade with the Mediterranean or the Sahara. B. J. Vallvé, "Descripción de Ceuta" (1962) is a Spanish translation of the portion of al-Anṣārī's *Ikhtiṣār,* a 15th century Arabic source, concerning Ceuta, a city on the Mediterranean in the northern part of Morocco; Latham, "Reconstruction and Expansion of Tetuan" (1965) deals with the growth of Tetuan as a result of immigration from Andalus; and Ch. E. Dufourcq, *L'Espagne catalane et le Maghrib* (1966) throws light on the activities of Catalonian merchants in the Maghrib. Dufourcq's richly original study analyzes through an analysis of many historical documents the activities of Catalonian merchants riding the wave of the Reconquest. Works dealing with the Saharan trade include T. Lewicki, "L'état nord-africain de Tāhert" (1962), a work by a Polish scholar referring to the close trading relations between Rustamid Tahart (Algeria) and Ghāna and Gao in the western Sahara; J.-M. Lessard, "Sijilmassa" (1969), a compilation of descriptions of Sijilmasa found in al-Bakrī's geography; and B. Rosenberger, "Tamdult" (1970), a documentary and archaeological study of the rise, economic life and collapse of Tamdult, a city situated south of the Anti-Atlas mountains in Morocco, near the present Akka, which prospered until the 14th and 15th centuries through gold mines and the caravan trade.

In addition, J. Hopkins, "Sousse et la Tunisie orientale médiévales" (1960) is a study by a scholar of London University of the cities of Ifriqiya between the middle of the 9th and the middle of the 11th centuries based on the geographies of Ibn Khuradādhbih, al-Bakrī, al-Ya'qūbī, Ibn Ḥawqal and al-Muqaddasī, which concludes that the cities had a long tradition of urban prosperity which predated Islam. A. Lézine, "Sur la population des villes africaines" (1969) calculates that a city's population would be four times the number of people attending the Friday mosque (limited to adult males), on the basis of the mosque's seating capacity, estimating that one person requires 0.6 x 1.35 m of space to worship.

Studies of Jews include D. Corcos, "The Jews of Morocco" (1964), a discussion of the conditions of the Jews in Marinid Fez, and P. Sebag, "Les juifs de Tunisie" (1959), a translation of the travel record of the Roumanian Jew, Benjamin II, in which are detailed descriptions of the manners and customs of Tunisian Jews in the middle of the 19th century. Sebag has also produced a series of studies concerning Tunis, including *L'évolution d'un guetto nord-africain* (1960), a survey of the Jewish quarter of Tunis, "La peste dans la Régence de Tunis" (1965), an account of plague epidemics in Tunis in the 17th and 18th centuries, and "Le bidonville de Borgel" (1958), a sociological study of the slum of Borgel formed through the rapid population increase of Tunis. H. Z. Hirschberg, *A History of the Jews in North Africa* (in Hebrew, 1965) is probably the first extensive study of the Jewish Mediterranean community, using Hebraic and Arabic sources, and it provides a basis for S. D. Goitein's comprehensive study, *A Mediterranean Society* (1967-88). These studies are not intended as an urban study in themselves, but they contain many useful pieces of information regarding the study of the social and economic activities of Maghribi cities. I would further add that there are several urban studies in Hebrew that should be consulted: for example, Hirschberg, "The Salars and Negidim of Kairouan" (in Hebrew, 1958-9).

A point to note about the research of this period is the work of Marxist historians. At a seminar in 1968 about feudalism, J. Poncet, A. Prennant, R. Gallissot and others reported on the relationship between the cities and rural villages of the Maghrib in pre-colonial times. They were strongly influenced by the thesis of Ibn Khaldūn that while the cities and villages mutually depended on one another, the city dwellers not only dominated and exploited those who lived in the villages but were the major landowners there as well. Their reports were published by the Centre d'Etudes et de Recherches Marxistes under the title of *Sur le féodalisme* (1971). The Algerian historian M. Djender suggests in his *Introduction à l'histoire de l'Algérie* (1968) that pre-19th century society should be seen as a confrontation between city and village. Though such studies were significant when Marxism was influential in historical studies, now their appeal is greatly reduced because of their lack of analysis of contemporary sources and their ideological component.

It is clear from the above survey that the changes in the style of urban studies mentioned at the beginning of this section have been reflected in the great strides forward made in the examination of the concept of the "Islamic city" centred on Mashriq rather than in specific research. In this sense the period under discussion should be thought of as transitional, at least with regard to urban studies of the Maghrib.

II. Recent Trends

Here we will examine urban studies in the Maghrib from 1970 to 1990, paying particular attention to the nature of the influence exerted by methods and issues in urban studies since 1830 and the direction the most recent studies are taking.

Very simply, post 1970 research can be characterized as a continuation and development of lines of research begun in the 1960s, though there are a number of points concerning results and organizations which should be noted.

First, it was during the 1970s that actual results began to issue from the various departments of area studies set up in Great Britain and the United States. Maghribi urban studies therefore emerged from the domination of French scholars. For example, the American scholar K. L. Brown published two excellent monographs in 1971 and 1976 based on field work undertaken in Salé (Morocco) in 1965-7, and R. I. Lawless and G. H. Blake published *Tlemcen: Continuity and Change in an Algerian Islamic Town* in 1976, the results of an urban survey of Tlemcen undertaken in 1971 and 1974 with a grant from the Centre for Middle East and Islamic Studies of the University of Durham. Such work is being continued through to the present by Eickelman, C. Geertz, L. Rosen, Abu-Lughod and J. S. Woodford. In addition, it should be noted with regard to this first point that local scholars have begun to organize conferences on urban studies. For example, La Faculté des Lettres et des Sciences Humaines d'Ibn Msik (ed.), *al-Madīna fī ta'rīkh al-maghrib al-'arabī (La cité dans l'histoire du Maghreb)* (A., 1990) is the proceedings of a colloquium held at the Faculty of Letters and Human Sciences of the University of Ibn Msik (Casablanca) in 1988. Second, the contributions of cultural anthropologists and sociologists have been notable. Most of the scholars mentioned above have done their work in urban studies employing the disciplines of cultural anthropology and sociology, but in that their interests are grounded in an historical perspective they have brought a new and effective viewpoint to premodern urban studies and the concept of the "Islamic city." This is particularly striking in the research of Brown, Eickelman and Abu-Lughod. Third, the structure of research and research organizations has become internationalized, in two aspects. One concerns organs and the reporting media. For example, *The Maghreb Review* (bi-monthly since 1976) carries reports concerning the politics, economy, history, religion, architecture, etc. of the Maghrib and is published in London (England, not France!). *Revue d'Histoire Maghrébine,* focusing on Ottoman period Maghribi history, has been published since 1974 in Tunis (since 1985 in Zaghouan, a suburb of Tunis) and is an important outlet for the work of Tunisian scholars in the field. Stimulated by a growing interest in Maghribi studies, it should also be added that A. I. M. S. (The American Institute for Maghreb Studies) and C. E. MA. T. (Center for Maghrib Studies in Tunis) were established in 1984 and in 1985 respectively, and that both made an academic agreement to promote research among Tunisian and American scholars and students. The second aspect of internationalization is the international conferences being held to discuss comprehensively urban problems in Middle Eastern Islamic society, with the rapid rise of urbanization in the Third World. There is also growing recognition of the need for multi-disciplined research and of the increased costs such research entails.

The first full-scale international conference on Islamic cities was held at Oxford University in 1965, attended by the scholars like Cahen, Stern and Hourani who discussed the traditional concept of the "Islamic city," centring on the idea of the guild. A conference at the University of California in 1966 on the theme of the Middle Eastern city incorporated subjects ranging from the cities of the ancient Orient to cities in the Islamic period and the urban problems of modern Middle Eastern cities, but discussion centred on relations between the traditional cities and villages and the transformation of the internal structure of urban society. A conference at Cambridge University in 1976, sponsored by UNESCO, discussed issues relating to the preservation of traditional cities, such as the character of the cities, their physical forms and structure, changes which have affected them, and their preservation. In contrast to such international conferences, a conference at Carthage, outside Tunis, in 1979 was devoted to modern Arab urban problems, though in fact these problems were elucidated in historical terms through a multi-disciplined approach. Conferences following the same approach have since been held in 1984, at Birkbeck College in London, in 1986, in Tunis, and in 1989, in Tokyo. (See the bibliography at the end of this chapter for details of the proceedings of those conferences.)

1. The Concept of the "Islamic City"

As I have mentioned already a number of times, the issue of the "Islamic city" is central to any discussion of Maghribi urban studies. The importance of the question is reflected by the fact that since the 1970s American sociologists and cultural anthropologists have begun to revise the concept of the "Islamic city" through studies of individual Maghribi cities.

The concept of the "Islamic city" was consolidated and debated from the 1920s and to understand the essence of the issue it is necessary to identify the sources of the theory. Between the 19th and early 20th centuries studies and surveys of the Maghrib in France reached massive proportions. The view of history they propounded, though, was that the region's period of greatest cultural fluorescence was during the Roman empire, and that the Islamic period was characterized by continuous confrontations between the nomads (the destroyers of civilization) and the city dwellers (the upholders of civilization), which prevented any development. This theory was compounded of two elements, the separation and conflict between the urban (dweller) and the non-urban (dweller), and the stagnation of Islamic society. It is particularly clear in the work of G. Marçais (1913, 1946), one of the pioneers of the theory of the "Islamic city."

W. Marçais (1928) offered an interpretation of the concept which can be summarized as follows: Islam is essentially an urban religion conforming to urban life, and it disdains and is distrustful of nomadic life. This outlook is evident in the dislike and hostility that the Prophet Muhammad expressed towards the nomads. Islam being an urban religion, its growth occurred necessarily in conjunction with the building of cities. The elements of the city are the congregational mosque, the suq (permanent market) and the public bath. In terms of the confrontation between urban and non-urban, this construction equates Islam with civilization (the city), and ignores Islam as it was accepted by the nomads and the rural population. Furthermore, it follows that urban society is regulated by Islam as a religion. This view was linked to the one-sided, distorted understanding of Islamic civilization that had prevailed since the 19th century.

A second important theme is the debate concerning commune-type autonomous functions, which began with the assertion by Massignon (1920, 1924) that the guilds provided virtually the same functions in the Muslim city that the European commune possessed. Behind his argument was the concept of the medieval European commune, as analyzed by Pirenne and Weber. The result of the debate was the eventual denial that Muslim city had any commune-type functions at all and this added fuel to the idea that Islamic society was stagnant. Even Le Tourneau, in his outstanding monograph (1949), asserted that a city of Fez had remained unchanged in the several centuries since the Middle Ages. It is hard therefore to escape the conclusion that the source of the concept of the "Islamic city" lies in the epistemological methodology regarding Maghribi society devised by scholars under French colonial rule. How deep the roots of the problem are can also be surmised. A. H. Iḥsāyan, "The Moroccan City in French Studies" (A., 1990) is an example of a local scholar criticizing such distorted points of view by French scholars.

Let us now examine how the debate developed. The concept of the "Islamic city" quickly became an important theme with the elucidation by W. Marçais of the three characteristics of a Muslim city (that Islam is an urban religion, that the elements of the Muslim city are the congregational mosque, the suq and the public bath, and that the building of cities was closely related to the expansion of Islam and the founding of dynasties) and by Massignon of urban autonomous functions. G. Marçais (1940, 1945) and E. Pauty (1951) continued the emphasis that Islam was an urban religion, divided cities into spontaneous and created, and asserted that most Muslim cities were created by dynasties and rulers (and therefore never developed autonomy). von Grunebaum, "The Structure of the Muslim Town" (1955) and id., "The Muslim Town and the Hellenistic Town" (1955) further systematized and consolidated these arguments. He paid particular attention to the physical form of cities, and on the premise that there is a distinction between the city and the rural village said that the elements identified by W. Marçais were inherent to the city. Other elements noted by numerous observers, such as the narrow, winding, maze-like streets, the many blind alleys, and the inner courtyard of buildings were, he said, derived from the unplanned nature and the chaos of the cities. Another of his points concerned autonomous functions; he denied that the Muslim town had autonomy in the sense of the European commune. However he agreed with Massignon, saying that the heads of quarters and the heads of guilds were intermediaries between townspeople and the state, and in that sense they fulfilled a definite autonomous function. In particular the quarters, being enclosed spaces composed of a racially homogenous group, were important as unifying residents of the quarter as a community. They did not however achieve overall integration and the city remained therefore a collection of separate quarters. Three important points to note are that von Grunebaum recognized a limited autonomy, though different to that of the commune, that he understood the importance of the quarter as an integrating structure for urban dwellers, and that he described the Muslim town as a mosaic society. E. Ashtor and Cl. Cahen later took up the theme of autonomy, Lapidus and Eickelman further elaborated the theory of the quarter, and the idea of the mosaic society was linked to H. A. R. Gibb and H. Bowen, *Islamic Society* (1950-7), published around the same time, to become the dominant image of the "Islamic city." The view of Gibb and Bowen was similar to that of von in that they recognized a clear separation between city and rural village, denied that the city was an organic whole, and saw Islamic society as being segmented by guild, tribe and sect and their constant mutual disputes (that is, the mosaic society). Ashtor and Cahen carefully analyzed Islamic historical materials to develop a new theory of the autonomous city through the particular elements extracted from those sources. In "L'administration urbaine" (1956) and "Républiques urbaines" (1975), Ashtor asserts that 11th and 12th century Damascus did have a system of urban autonomy, centring on the *ra'īs* (city headman). Cahen, "Mouvements populaires" (1958-9) analyzes Syrian and Iraqi cities in the 10th-12th centuries and concludes that urban autonomy was maintained by orginization of the urban outlaws called *aḥdāth* in Syria and *'ayyārūn* in Iraq.

During the 1960s the concept of the "Islamic city" constructed by French scholars through their studies of Maghribi cities was vehemently attacked by British and American scholars studying the cities of Mashriq. At the international conference in 1965, Stern gave a paper entitled "The Constitution of the Islamic City" (1970). The core of his argument was a criticism of Massignon's guild theory, for he denied the existence of guilds in Islamic cities. Also, in stressing that it was meaningless to make comparisons with the commune cities and that autonomous organizations were extremely immature in Islamic cities, he criticized von Grunebaum, Ashtor and Cahen as well. In "Muslim Cities and Islamic Societies" (1969), a paper presented to the international conference of 1966, and *Muslim Cities in the Later Middle Ages* (1967), Lapidus, who criticized past views and presented a new methodology, examined Mamluk period Syrian cities and, in that he asserted that there was no essential difference between cities and rural villages and that there could not have been any autonomous city centring on gangs (*zu'ar*) who lacked political ability, he denied the tenability of the city as a morphological study or as a model of an autonomous urban commune. Moreover, he talked of organic networks among people encompassing both urban centres and rural villages. Though of course cities were ruled by the amirs and the governors, at the level of ethnic groups, religious sects, law schools, Sufi orders, etc. there existed definite communities among the townspeople, and the quarters constituted their base. Thus Lapidus by denying the validity of the dichotomy between the urban and rural and looking rather at an order based on the various social relationships between people (stratified but mutually intersecting) escaped from the static constructionist and functionalist theories. However, in that he attached special importance to the consciousness of solidarity among the various social groups centring on the quarter, and considered that they combined or struggled to gain urban power, he can be criticized as doing no more than refashioning the theory of the mosaic society, as was pointed out in B. S. Turner, *Marx and the End of Orientalism* (1978).

In the 1970s the discussion of the "Islamic city" was resumed around the cities of the Maghrib. The lead in such studies was indisputably taken by American sociologists, cultural anthropologists and scholars interested in the area study. The pioneer in such work was K. L. Brown, who conducted a field study of Salé between 1965 and 1967. He was motivated in his study by the arguments of Stern and Hourani and by Lapidus's urban theory, and extended their discussion, which had previously been centred on Mashriq, to the cities of the Maghrib. In 1971 he published "An Urban View of Moroccan History," in which he maintained that while Salé in many ways exhibited the characteristics of the traditional Muslim city (the Friday mosque, public baths, the marketplace, administration), it differed from the model in that the inhabitants of Salé had a sense of citizenship and autonomous organizations (though not in a legal sense) and had hardly any sense of factionalism, in terms of religion, race or language. His views were expressed even more clearly and specifically in *People of Salé* (1976). He differed from Lapidus's opinion that "Muslim cities are never regarded as communities but as collections of isolated internal groups unable to cooperate in any endeavour of the whole," that it was social relationships that made order and community possible, saying that the people of Salé had "a highly developed sense of solidarity and municipal pride," and that they participated in local government willingly, without coercion. They did so because they possessed a civic consciousness through the fact they had been born in Salé, had lived there over an extensive period and had family ties there, through social networks, and through the unitary ties of religion, language and quarter. The autonomy and identity of the city and urban dwellers are discussed in N. Cigar, "Société et vie politique à Fès" (1978-9) and "Conflict and Community in an Urban Milieu" (1978). Cigar analyzes the power structure of Fez between 1660 and 1830, citing the *shurafā'* (the sharifs), the *bildīyīn* (rich Jews who had converted to Islam), the masses and the *zāwiyas* (centres associated with saints' cults) as the structural elements in the urban population, and pointing out the fact that the cities developed autonomy as political power weakened during the period, and that its base was the unity of identity of the urban populace. Brown and Cigar agree in that they see the base of autonomy in the ties fostered by a mutual culture and belief and in the consciousness of the townspeople as belonging to a particular city.

In "The City-State in Medieval Ifriqiya" (1986), Michael Brett, the English historian of medieval Maghrib, deals with the concept of the "Islamic city" as it was established by a comparison with, for example, Pirenne's description of the cities of medieval Western Europe, in terms of the issues of autonomy and self-government. He summarizes the views of the main scholars in the field since von Grunebaum and extends to the cities of Ifriqiya the unresolved question implicit in Ashtor (1975) of why municipal self-government arose in 11th century Syrian cities centring on the *ra'īs* (head of the municipality) and why it ultimately failed. Since, as Brett points out, few individual studies of cities exist for the time under question, he examines the issue through documentary analysis, focusing on the history of the Ifriqiyan city of Tripoli from about 1000 to about 1400. He describes how in Tripoli there did not exist any powerful government authority and the city was ruled by merchants and a council of notables (*shūrā*). By the 14th century however a city-state had been founded by a powerful *ra'īs*, and eventually the position of *ra'īs* came to be contested between two powerful clans. Just as it seemed a kingdom might be formed by the winning faction, Tripoli was subjugated in 1402 by the Hafsids of Tunis. Brett suggests the collapse of self-government was connected with the preeminent interest of the townspeople in economic profit, that they did not see any essential need for self-government. Therefore it was natural that they would choose a powerful government rather than a small and weak local dynasty once a dynasty had appeared that destroyed any urban autonomy. Brett understands that the political autonomy of Tripoli developed in connection with the commercial elite, and agrees with Ashtor (1975) and P. von Sievers, "Military, Merchants and Nomads" (1979) that "the origin of urban autonomy in medieval Islam lay in the development of an urban society and a commercial economy out of the Arab conquests and the Arab empire." He concludes that self-government in the Islamic city established after the 10th century is unrelated to pre-Islamic systems such as the Byzantine system, that city states were supported by commercial elites and urban autonomy was principally motivated by commercial interests, and that the whole constitutional, republican model of medieval Western European cities should be abandoned in regard to Arab cities. He sees the "Islamic city" as neither lacking in organization nor defence in relation to the central power above or the warrior tribes outside, while he agrees with Brunschvig (1947) that because Islamic law, which gives priority to private over public interest, lacks the concept of legal persons other than human beings, it was difficult for autonomy like that in the European Commune to develop in Muslim cities. Brett therefore maintains that autonomy is a significant subject in the study of the Islamic city, and that Lapidus's portrait (1967, 1970) of the Syrian city with its lack of organization among artisans, merchants and the ulama may not provide a general model for the Muslim city. He also suggests that the Islamic city conforms to the standard of Islamic monarchy, not to that of the European republic, and that the autonomy of the Islamic city is variable. J. D. Latham (see below) shows that Ceuta too exhibited similarities to Tripoli in terms of self-government, and it may in fact be possible to show that the Tripoli pattern was a characteristic of the prosperous commercial cities of the Mediterranean coast as a whole (including those of Lebanon and Syria), which were considerably distant from central authority (See also Raymond, 1986). Ceuta as an autonomous city and its rule by the Azafids is discussed in Latham, "The Strategic Position" (1971), "The Rise of the 'Azafids" (1972) and "The Later 'Azafids" (1973). On the other hand, H. Ferhat, "Le role de la minorité andalouse" (1991) observed the functions of Andalusians in Ceuta of the first half of the 13th century and stated that Ceuta in this period enjoyed independence under the Andalusian immigrants who were a minority group of townspeople and that the rise of 'Azafids who represented the native Ceuta people, if their origin being Andalusian but "nationalized", meant a reaction of the anti-Andalusians in Ceuta society.

Stambouli and Zghal, "La vie urbaine dans le Maghreb précolonial" (1974) analyzes Maghribi cities through a general concept comprising three elements (the central authority, urban dwellers, and the Bedouin), and discusses the mutually dependent relationships of those elements in three dimensions, political, economic and religious. The authors state that urban administration in Ottoman times was subject to external authority, as symbolized by the kasbah, but that in economic and religious matters a partially autonomous life existed for the townspeople. M. Kisaichi, "The Character of the Islamic City and the Stages of its Urban History" (J., 1989) shares a similar concept, broadened both spatially and temporally. Such studies show an interest in comparing cities in the Islamic lands with those of different civilizations and regions, such as Europe and China.

The American cultural anthropologist Dale Eickelman added his voice to the debate about the "Islamic city" with his field study of a quarter (*darb*) in the small Moroccan city of Boujad ("Is there an Islamic City?," 1974). He is interested in comparisons with cities of other cultural zones and therefore finds the three urban elements (because found in rural villages as well) of W. Marçais and Massignon's thesis of the guilds (as rejected absolutely by Stern) inadequate in terms both of a conceptual standard and an ideal model. While acknowledging the usefulness of Lapidus's "system of relations as a whole" as an analytical concept, he rejects it since it compares social structures rather than cities. Rather Eickelman applies Weber's concept of social relations within cities in order to elucidate by means of an analysis of the quarter (*darb*) as the basis of social relations whether or not it is possible to distinguish between city and village or to determine characteristics and concepts through a comparison with European cities. In his view, social relations are formed through a mutual sense of closeness (*qrāba*); they comprise family relationships, patron-client relationships, and relationships among neighbours, which are further deepened by the festivals of daily life, marriage, birth, funerals, and participating in events such as the recitation of the *Koran*. Social unity through this sense of *qrāba* is, he says, if extended in terms of physical space, the quarter, which is not static but which expands or contracts according to conditions. Eickelman does not give precise answers to the questions he has raised, but his conclusion seems to be that it is not possible to make a distinction between the city and the rural village. However, since the concept of *qrāba* applies also to the village and the family (at times, strikingly so), the question remains whether it is valid to discuss the differences between the city and the village, and particular urban characteristics, using *qrāba* as an analytical concept. Despite this, Eickelman in his article has given us a new way of understanding the quarter.

Previous research on the quarter had focused on several methods of understanding its nature: the investigations of E. Michaux-Bellaire (1907) and L. Martin (1909) saw it more or less as a fixed physical space and as a unit of urban social life, while scholars like Le Tourneau (1949), von Grunebaum (1955) and Gibb and Bowen (1950-7) regarded it as the basic unit of urban life, characterized by racial and religious homogeneity, and as a mosaic society within an enclosed space. Lapidus (1967, 1969), while continuing to regard the quarter as the basic unit of the urban dweller, at the same time suggested the importance of those connections between people which transcend the framework of the quarter. By contrast, Eickelman denies the theory of the quarter which presupposes an enclosed space and puts forward the very useful idea that the real quarter consists of personal and mental relationships, not physical space. It will be up to future historical research to show to what extent this can be backed by historical documentation. A similar point is made in T. Miura, "The Quarter and Popular Movements" (J., 1989), which, in a discussion about Mamluk Damascus, suggests that the quarter can be considered in two ways, singly as a small-scale unit of urban social life, and compoundly as a large-scale political and economic unit.

The connection between Islam and the city is the pivotal issue in the concept of the "Islamic city." Since 1970 this question has been approached from a number of different angles. At the international conference in Carthage in 1979, the German geographer Eugen Wirth read a paper entitled "Villes islamiques, villes arabes, villes orientales?" (1982) in which he states that it is undeniable that there are numerous features in common among cities in North Africa and Western Asia. If they are all to be called "Islamic cities" then, he says, we must explain whether these common features occur as a result of the influence of Islam, and how much so. Being a geographer, he does not look at the distinctive features of the city from a religious viewpoint, but only in terms of actual remains and archaeological evidence. He then categorizes five distinctive features of cities in the Islamic period: (1) cities founded in the Islamic period were systematic and planned; their labyrinthine and unsystematic nature increased in later centuries (2) blind alleys which riddled the space between the main access routes were consciously planned, not a result of haphazard development (3) houses with an inner courtyard (4) independent quarters (5) suqs. Wirth shows that characteristics 1 to 4 existed in the Orient before Islam and that it was the suq as the commercial centre which existed neither in the ancient Orient nor in medieval Europe. Of the five characteristics, the suq has the weakest connection with Islam as a religion. As a result Wirth suggests it would be more accurate to call these cities "Oriental" rather than "Islamic." He rejects the designation of "Arab city" since the above five characteristics can also be found in Iranian and Turkish cities and that further detailed comparative study would be necessary before its use could be advocated. Wirth's thesis met with severe criticism from H. Djaït, whose work will be examined below.

K. Chater, who in "La ville tunisienne au XIXe siècle" (1978) pays special attention to the suq from the point of view of differences between the city and the rural village, notes that while both cities and villages have congregational mosques and public baths, villages contain only one suq, which contains a mixture of trades, while cities have numbers of suqs, differentiated according to trade. Chater also touches on the unity of the city as a whole and claims that the city maintained economically independent wealth (taxes on the grain and vegetable markets, seized property, *ḥabs* etc.) to support urban facilities like mosques and city walls, jurists and teachers. While the city had no political authority, the quarters, segregated according to ethnic group, functioned as administrative units under the sheikh, had a sense of solidarity (*'aṣabīya*) stronger than that of the city as a whole. L. Gardet, *La cité musulmane* (1954) also focuses on the suq, asserting that urban life, in terms of refined Islamic learning and the arts, derived from the suq, with its economic power and its ability to attract crowds, and he links this with the idea that Islam is the religion of the great merchants. H. al-Junḥānī, "Tahart: A Capital of the Rustamid Dynasty" (A., 1975) is also based on the precondition that Islamic society is an urban society, and utilizes Gardet (1954) and others to discuss the political, economic and intellectual life of Tahart from its foundation.

J. L. Abu-Lughod, "The Islamic City" (1987) is an attempt to redefine the "Islamic city" in the knowledge that the concept contains considerable prejudice and bias. Abu-Lughod takes a broad look at Islamic urban studies since the time of W. Marçais and points out that the theory of the Islamic city was built on a small sample from a specific region (chiefly the cities of the Maghrib) and that the city should be depicted as a process of urban formation, not according to an *a priori* model. She then states that of the important elements in the creation of the Islamic city—terrain and climate, a technology of production, distribution and transportation, a system of social organization, and a legal/political system—the determining element is the Islamic legal/political system, which includes (1) spatial segregation by juridical distinction, (2) gender segregation by architecture and space, and (3) spatial segregation between public and private (the residential area as private space and the commercial area as public space). An Islamic city is one where all of these latter three elements function effectively. This article strongly suggests the influence of Islam, but in a paper given at an international conference in Tokyo, "What is Islamic about a City?" (1989), she asks "How is it that we have a large body of literature about an intellectual construction of reality called the "Islamic city," while we have few or no articles, books, and conferences about the Christian City, the Buddhist City, the Hindu City, or the Pagan City?" She says that it is a mistake to put too much value on the role of Islam as a religion when making comparisons with cities of other cultural spheres, that it is natural that diverse urban characteristics grew up within the same Islamic region, due to differences in geography, history and institutions, and that Islam is only one element that gave rise to such differences.

Abu-Lughod recognizes the significance of the connection between Islam and the city, and having denied the concept of the "Islamic city" as it was constructed historically, she advocates a redefined concept. K. L. Brown, "The Uses of a Concept: 'The Muslim City'" (1986) on the other hand criticizes the work of Cigar (1978; 1978-9), Eickelman (1981) and Abu-Lughod (1980) for being too neglectful of Islam's importance.

This argument extends also to the connections between the Islamic legal system and urban architecture and between the Islamic legal system and social life. According to R. Brunschvig, "Urbanisme médiéval" (1947), the first scholar to focus on the application of Islamic law not only to roads and houses but also to city life was O. Spies, in "Islamisches Nachbarrecht" (1927). He however had only a narrow conception of the law as that which was expressly provided, and looked at it from the viewpoint of the Shafi'i law school alone. Brunschvig criticizes Spies, and uses the legal texts of Ibn al-Imām (d. 996 in Kairouan) and Ibn al-Rāmī (a skilled stonemason who lived during the Hafsid dynasty and died in 1334) to analyze how the law was applied in cases relating to roads, walls, rebuilding and problems relating to water, neighbourly relations, and the location of businesses like tanneries, forges, stables, etc., the origination and abolition of easement, and the legal procedures. From this he educed certain characteristics: that provisions are given only in outline (for example they recommend damages be avoided but do no clarify the concept of "damages"), that there is a tendency to go with the circumstances (to minimize the amount of damages and to tolerate that amount), to favour private over public rights, and to preserve the freedom of the family and the individual over government compulsion. B. S. Hakim continued Brunschvig's line of thinking and proved through an examination of a great many historical sources, including Ibn al-Rāmī's treatise, combined with a survey of the modern Islamic city of Tunis, that Islamic law acted as a guideline for urban construction and life (*Arabic-Islamic Cities,* 1986), systematically discussing elements such as blind alleys, the windowless courtyard construction of houses, and the labyrinthine network of streets. S. Mouline, "La ville et la maison arabo-musulmanes" (1983) maintains that the fact the Arab-Islamic cities which grew up in various regions possess a common style and organization of space is due to the influence of an Islamic ethic and ideal, and that a certain principle and order underlie the construction plan of the city. It is important to note that studies like these which look to the importance of Islamic law tend to be linked with a new type of urban stereotype, a different kind of historical "Islamic city" concept. In this sense, Hakim, "The Role of the Urf" (1989) is important as a study (rather than an analysis) focusing on the connections between the *'urf* (regional customary law) and urban construction and life.

Recurring themes regarding the "Islamic city" since the publication of "L'islamisme et la vie urbaine" by W. Marçais in 1928 have been whether or not a sharp dividing line can be drawn between town and countryside, whether there are certain essential characteristics of the "Islamic city," and how the "Islamic city" should be defined. B. Johansen, "The All-Embracing Town and its Mosques" (1981) has reexamined those questions through an analysis of the Hanafite legal texts. Johansen states that in the early Islamic period, Friday mosques represented a difference between town and countryside, since they were constructed exclusively in towns. Later, once Friday mosques began to appear in the countryside as well, whether or not there was a Friday mosque was no longer a distinguishing characteristic between the two. What came to characterize the city was the existence of a number of Friday mosques and an elaborate hierarchy of places of worship. More important elements, though, in distinguishing town and village were the *finā' al-miṣr*, the open space serving the interests of all town residents, and a number of *ṭawābi'*, places and settlements dependent on the town locate between the town and the village. These separated the town from the village not only in space but also in the consciousness of the urban residents, who recognized those spaces as places of common use, to serve such community interests as public prayer, cemeteries and military parades. Johansen therefore concludes that there was a consistent difference between town and countryside. Since his information is drawn in the main from lawyers' opinions, Johansen's conclusion tends to represent the ideal characteristics; nevertheless the study merits attention as a criticism of the recent dominant view (as represented by Lapidus) which emphasizes the relationships between town and village, saying that there is no substantial difference between the two, either in topography or function.

A study which discusses the problem of planning and order in the "Islamic city" not in terms of Islamic law is Hichem Djaït, *al-Kūfa: Naissance de la ville islamique* (1986). Djaït, of University of Tunis, in a chapter called "L'orientalisme et la ville islamique," asks what is an Islamic city and severely criticized Wirth who studied the connections between Islam and the city from a geographical viewpoint, and saw a problem in the designation "Islamic city" because of the weakness of the relationship between the two. Wirth's theory, Djaït said, was weakened by misconceptions such as his attempt to understand Islam purely as a religion and his conviction that such an Islam should have given the city an original character and therefore should have appeared in some concrete form; he was therefore guilty of the same prejudices as Orientalists from the time of G. Marçais who criticized Islamic civilization by saying the "Islamic city" lacked originality and could not perceive any development of unity or order in the city as a whole because of the mosaic fragmentation of the quarters. However, Djaït says that Wirth rejected the designation of "Oriental city" (*ville orientale*), which is a mistake, since Wirth in fact defended that usage, rejecting rather the designation of "Islamic city" (*ville islamique*). Following his criticism, Djaït suggests that the Islamic city as seen in classical form in the garrison towns was originally planned and ordered, since for political rationality such towns were divided into quarters, residential areas for each Arab tribe. The city and the nomads had a close relationship and it is a mistake to think of them as being in confrontation to each other. We should consider the Islamic city in terms of historical and cultural continuities, rather than in terms of opposing elements like Islam and Greece/Rome or Islam and the ancient Orient. Djaït's work is valuable for its analysis of construction plans for cities in the early Islamic period through the use of historical sources. Nevertheless the urban planning and order that he advocates are described only in terms of examples from the early Arab period. Though he subtitles his work "Naissance de la ville islamique," we must ask when and how the Islamic city of his definition emerged and whether other non-Arab cities within the Islamic cultural sphere like those of Iran and Turkey have the same character and construction. Unfortunately Djaït does not provide clear answers to these questions.

Discussion about the character and concept of the "Islamic city" is thus moving in a new direction. Some studies are attempting to throw light on urban autonomy through an analysis of historical materials, like those of Brown, Cigar and Brett, who do not completely disallow its existence. Eickelman's understanding of the quarter breaks through earlier interpretations of it as static space, as in the mosaic theory, and hints how historical sources should be read. The next question is how this idea will be used by historians. The relationship between Islam and the city has hitherto been approached from two mutually contradictory directions. An example of the first is Wirth, and his view that Islam and the city are separated, and of Djaït, with similar views. If Djaït stresses cultural continuity and change and maintains that the Islamic city emerged in its individual character and form (not clearly specified) as the civilization of Islam (not Islam in the narrow sense of religion) gradually permeated it, then his stance comes close to that of Abu-Lughod and Hakim and B. Johansen, who represent the second direction, that of scholars who are trying to reconstruct the concept of the "Islamic city" by focusing on the influence of Islamic law.

The great interest shown in the topic by sociologists and cultural anthropologists arises from the fact that many of them did field work in the Islamic lands and then used their results to construct theories. Their participation in the discussion may be attributed to the fact that they experienced for themselves the undeniable points of commonality that join the cities of the Islamic societies, and the correlation between Islam and the city. Since the idea of the "Islamic city" as an historical concept cannot be brought as is into the discussion, historians must reexamine the question through historical sources.

The above-mentioned studies are conscious to a certain extent of the traditional concept of the "Islamic city," and new patterns of urban research are discernible in their criticism of the problems inherent in the concept, even if those new patterns do not take up the question explicitly. As mentioned below, M. Ben Achour: *Catégories* (1989), M. Mazzīn (1986) and A. A. Sebti (1984) are brilliant studies by local scholars which may open up a new field beyond the concept of the "Islamic city." We will next look at the research of the past twenty years organized into a number of important themes.

2. Waqf Endowment

Waqf research started in conjunction with the needs of colonial land policy rather than from an awareness of the potential importance of waqf in urban studies. This is exemplified for instance in E. Mercier (1896), J. Terrasse (1899) and J. Abribat (1902). With the beginning of urban studies *per se*, there grew more interest in the functioning of the waqf in urban society, as in al-Moutabassir (1907), A. Bel (1917) and Y. de La Motte (1949). For example, al-Moutabassir examined waqf (*ḥabs*) in Tangier and argues that waqf in Morocco was based on Maliki legal theory and was of two types, the public and the private (mainly family endowments). Private endowments were the most numerous and were administered by a *nāẓir* under the supervision of the qadi. He points out two interesting facts. First, sources of waqf revenue could become dangerous to the authorities, since ulama in cities like Fez, Marrakesh, Rabat and Tangier used waqf revenues to purchase weaponry to use against rulers who did not follow the direction they wanted. Second, these revenues could be leased (*tanfidh*) as a usufruct. Many urban waqf were personal property and so shops could be leased to specified individuals through leasing procedures (the procedures being under the authority of the ruler) and the lessor could then sublet the property without permission at a higher rent even to Jews or Christians. Waqf had therefore become capital to invigorate the urban economy. Sociological research has been undertaken concerning this point. In *Meaning and Order in Moroccan Society* (1979), C. Geertz analyzes in a more theoretical way waqf in the Moroccan city of Sefru to show that waqf endowments were important elements in giving vigour to the suq economy in the cities (and in the rural villages also).

Studies of the waqf in Maghribi cities have been slow to use historical documentary material, but recently this deficiency is being remedied and papers utilizing such material are appearing in succession. Abdeljelil Temimi, head of the Centre d'Etudes et de Recherches Ottomanes, Morisques, de Documentation et l'Information in Zaghouan, Tunisia, in "On the Documents of the Great Mosque in Algiers" (A., 1980), has published in microfilm with revisions the contents of Ottoman period waqf documents in the Algerian National Archives. A. Kacem, "The Ḥabs and the Inzāl of the Early Ottoman Period in Tunisia" (A., 1985) studies the question of leasing the sources of waqf revenue in Ottoman period Tunis. J. Luccioni, *Les fondations pieuses (Habous) au Maroc* (n. d.) examines the development of the waqf system in Morocco from its beginnings until 1956 and gives a detailed analysis of subjects such as waqf application, functioning, administration, collapse, and reconstitution under the Protectorate. (Considering the author's scholarly activity, this research was probably done before 1970.)

A *fatwā* (*nawāzil*) document contains much information about waqfs. M. Lahmar, "Les hubus dans la société" (1990) asserts that the 15th century *fatwā* document *al-Mi'yār* of al-Wansharīsī is an important source and studies the problems of water supply, residence, commerce and the leasing and renting of farmland through an analysis of the chapter on waqf in this document. *Fatwā* documents are a treasure-house of information, containing materials lacking in the chronicles. M. Mazzīn, *Fez and its Rural Surroundings* (A., 1986) and Ben Achour (1989) are also examples of the possibilities for historical study in the discovery and analysis of waqf documents. Such work is very important in that it provides a concrete analysis of urban social life and organization, areas that have hitherto be inadequately researched. Potential research based on newly discovered documents offers bright prospects for urban studies.

3. Guilds

Urban commerce and the craft industry, especially the latter, were early identified as distinctive elements in Islamic urban society. Pioneering studies like Ch. L. Féraud (1872), Ch. Lallemand (1890) and A. Atger (1909) promoted research into the guild through sociological investigations. As mentioned above, Lallemand's work suggested important points at issue in later guild theory, but in terms of the depth of discussion, L. Massignon (1920, 1924) is very important. We have seen how Massignon maintained that as a result of their guilds, the "Muslim city" possessed functions virtually the same as the European commune, but here I would like to take up the point that he saw the commune as originating under the influence of Islam. Massignon (1920) says that the 9th century Qarmatians (thought to be the kernel from which developed the Fatimid state) formed from guild organization and that the prototype of the European commune developed from outlying Christian areas like Galicia, Lombardia and the Balkans, situated on trade routes and bordering Islamic lands (and to which Qarmatian activities extended), and conjectures that the European commune thus developed under Islamic influence. Sociological type investigations were to continue energetically, related to government policy; examples include L. Brunot (1923, 1946), P. Ricard (1924), G. S. Colin (1931), R. Guyot (1934), P. Marty (1935), J. Quemeneur (1942), and E. Lecuyer (1950). Of a somewhat different type are E. Buthaud, "Le gardiennage des souks" (1942) and L. Golvin, *Aspects de l'artisanat* (1957). Buthaud argues that when the guilds employed guards to prevent theft in the suqs, they could select the people to be employed, but rights of appointment and dismissal rested with the *shaykh al-madīna,* who also decided upon questions like sharing expenses relating to the guards' wages, the length of time they should be on duty, and the opening and closing times of the suq, meaning that he also exercised some of the authority of the muhtasib. Golvin shows that 95% of artisans in Morocco were affiliated with a Sufi order, and that also the majority of guilds had a particular patron saint regardless of that order. Research into guilds declined rapidly after the traditional organization broke up because most information came from surveys rather than documentary material, which is sparse.

Noteworthy in this respect is a study by H. Touati, a professor at the University of Oran entitled "Les corporations de métiers à Alger à l'époque ottomane" (1988), an analysis of guilds in Algeria during the Ottoman period through unpublished historical documents. Criticizing Massignon (1924), Lecuyer (1950), Golvin (1957) and other researchers who laid excessive emphasis on the control function of the guild from the authority and fixed negative image of the guild in Algeria by denying the guild the function of settling disputes between artisans, by negating its function of mutual aid and companionship, and by disregarding the existence of guild documents, Touati says that by using documents in the National Library of Algiers he has been able to show that fifty-seven guilds existing in the 17th century were supervised by a head *amīn,* who controlled the guilds as a whole, and by *amīns* responsible for each guild, that the guilds were under the power of the *bey* not directly, but through two *shaykh al-balad,* that some guilds, like those of Fez, had a single patron saint for each guild, and others, like those of Algiers (and Tunisia also), had different patron saints according to the ethnic groups within each guild, that unlike the saints of Mashriq, who were linked with lineages going back to Muhammad, Ali and Salmān al-Fārīsī, those of the Maghrib were independent figures possessing supernatural powers (*baraka*), for whom such lineages were unnecessary, and that through participation in religious and trade rituals by members, and the existence of a consciousness of social unity among members, the guild functioned firmly as the organization of the urban populace. id., "Note sur l'organisation des corporations de métier" (1986) is of much the same tenor. Though not dealing with the guild directly, T. Chenntouf, "L'évolution du travail en Algérie" (1981) states that the formation of wage labour in Algeria from the 19th century progressed first within agriculture but eventually spread to urban centres where it dismembered the craft industry. However, as Touati's research shows, the contributions historiography can make in this area will depend largely on what new documents turn up.

4. Ḥisba

We have seen already that the study of *ḥisba* has been an important pillar in research into Maghribi and Andalusian history. The study of the functions of the muhtasib by J. Abribat (1911) is of deep interest in that it explained the various regulations of legal ethics in urban life. Later studies, such as E. Lévi-Provençal (1934, 1955), M. Gaudefroy-Demonbynes (1938), M. Talbi (1954), G. M. Wickens (1956-7), G. E. García (1957), J. D. Latham (1960), R. Arié (1960) and P. Chalmeta (1970) are either research into particular *ḥisba* sources or introductions to the historical material. For example, Lévi-Provençal (1934), introducing the *ḥisba* manual of Ibn 'Abdūn, describes in great detail one segment of urban life in his discussion of the authority held by various administrative posts in 12th century Seville, such as the *ra'īs,* the *ṣāḥib al-madīna,* the *qubbād,* the *ḥākim,* the muhtasib, and the *amīn* (especially the very important supervisor of river traffic, vital to the economy of Seville), and of the various craft industries and commerce in terms of their products, sales and placement of shops, etc. Chalmeta (1970) introduces a manual of suq regulations of 9th century Kairouan, the *Kitāb aḥkām al-sūq,* compiled by Yaḥyā b. 'Umar, which contains a precise description of both administrative participation in the suq and the business of the various trades.

An epoch-making study of *ḥisba* is Chalmeta, *El señor del zoco* (1973), which uses a number of *ḥisba* manuals, chronicles and geographies to analyze in depth the form the suq took in Andalusian cities, its physical characteristics and its operation and management, the organization of merchants and craft workers, and the economic life of the urban populace. While *ḥisba* manuals themselves are considered to belong to the wider genre of legal texts, because they are manuals for the muhtasib in his supervision of urban society and give specific regulations governing the life of the urban population, they are a fair reflection of the realities of urban life. Islamic sources are very scanty regarding urban economic life in the medieval period, and so the value of *ḥisba* manuals used in conjunction with chronicles and such like cannot be underestimated. Latham's research ("Ibn 'Abd al-Ra'ūf," 1971, a discussion of marriage regulations and procedures, "Towards the Interpretation of al-Saqaṭī's Observations," 1978, dealing with varieties of flour used for bread, "The Interpretation of a Passage on Scales," 1978, concerning how scales are made, and "Some Observations on the Bread Trade," 1984, discussing the sale of bread in Malaga around 1200) uses *ḥisba* manuals to describe urban social life from various angles. P. Cuperly, "Un document ancien sur l'urbanisme au Mzab" (1981) is an edition and French translation of the third part of the text of the *Kitāb al-uṣūl,* by the Ibadite scholar Abū al-'Abbās (d. 1049), which describes rights and responsibilities in domestic construction in the Mzab according to the regulations of the Ibadites. The unpublished first and second parts cover regulations dealing with roads and commerce. Such studies employing *ḥisba* manuals should stimulate a greater knowledge of the actualities of the urban economy and of urban life, about which there is a great deal more to be known.

5. Ulama

It is a little difficult to define exactly when research into the ulama began, since the ulama, being the intellectuals of Islamic society and in many cases purveyors of the law, are mentioned to some extent in most studies. In terms of Maghribi urban studies alone, research into the ulama up to the 1960s understood them to be a single-layered and fixed group, whose members were jurists and an intellectual elite with common interests. Specialist studies which analyze them as having mutual antagonisms and consisting of varying social classes and functions began to appear in the 1970s. This change in perception reflects the way historical sources are being used, and sociological and statistical theories (and in certain cases the resources of the computer) can now be applied to some ulama research in analyzing the different types of biographical dictionaries which contain records of an enormous number of ulama.

In this sense A. H. Green and D. Urvoy have been outstanding in the field. Green, "The Tunisian Ulama and the Establishment of the French Protectorate" (1974) and id., *The Tunisian Ulama, 1873-1915* (1978) examine the various reactions of the ulama to Tunisian modernization and the ulama. Green employs biographical dictionaries and other documents to identify professors of the Zaytūna Madrasa, qadis in the sharia-courts, imams in mosques, to trace family genealogies and describe briefly the lives of powerful ulama, and to analyze, in terms of the human element, how the various ulama reacted to the secularization and Westernization that accompanied the process of modernization in Tunisia. He draws a vivid picture of the sufferings, the conflicts and the concord of a wide range of ulama, from those who supported armed resistance to those who positively promoted change during the period from the 19th century until the present. Urvoy looks at the medieval ulama in "La structuration du monde des Ulémas à Bougie" (1976) and *Le monde des Ulémas andalous* (1978). The former uses the biography of al-Ghubrīnī (d. 1304) to discuss the ulama of Bougie (Algeria) in terms of their field of learning, their movement and their motivations, and how they formed links with leading ulama. The latter study looks at the same questions in relation to the cities of Andalus in the 11th-13th centuries in a detailed analysis using a large number of biographical dictionaries and chronicles. A sociological quantitative analysis in terms of period of time is also employed (for example, a statistical representation of the number of ulama in each academic field over twenty year periods).

Recently several excellent studies on the topic have been produced by local scholars, particularly those from Tunisia. Mohamed Ben Achour, "Islam et contrôle social à Tunis" (1982) analyzes Tunisian society in the 18th and 19th centuries in terms of social control and discusses the central function of the ulama in this, dividing this function broadly into two parts: (1) the coexistence of the Hanafis and the Malikis, and the coexistence of formal Islam and Sufi Islam, and (2) the control of the people and the supervision of arbitrariness on the part of the Turkish power. Ben Achour's interest is in the analysis of the social structure through the notables represented by the ulama. This interest is apparent in an important recent work, *Catégories de la société tunisoise* (1989), which examines urban elite families in Tunis in the late 19th century. He states that just as Tunis functioned both as a capital city and as a city of the townspeople (*madīna*), the dominant elites, centring on twenty families, can be grouped into two categories, the political elite serving the state (Mamluk and Hanafite *a'yān,* officers of the *makhzan*) and the religious elite of the city's society (rich merchants, the Zaytūna professors, marabouts, etc.). Ben Achour sees these groupings as not only being between families but between members of the same family, and says that notable families lost their social influence when traditional systems such as the waqf, the positions of *shaykh al-madīna* and *amīn,* and the education in the madrasa ceased functioning effectively when society underwent a total change in the late 19th century. This study, an analytical approach based on the use of public and private archives, is a masterpiece by a local scholar which throws light on areas such as household economy and endogamy that have remained obscure. Perhaps his observation that families of the urban elite were generally monogamous does not seem of any particular account, but it is important for an unbiased understanding of Islamic society. It is to be hoped that more studies will be able to penetrate inherent changes in society in the medieval and modern periods so that the view that Islamic society was stagnant may be rectified. Unfortunately, Ben Achour has not sufficiently addressed this point. His views are a development of his doctoral thesis, *Les Ulama à Tunis aux XVIIIe et XIXe siècles* (1977). Ben Achour: *Catégories* (1989) discusses the role of families of notables in urban society; the question of their participation in urban administration is studied in a very interesting work by 'Ali Chebbi, "New Sources for the Study of the History of the Shābbīya" (A., 1979), which shows that when in the mid-16th century the Hafsids became powerless before the encroachments of the Ottoman armies and the Christians, the Shābbī family of Kairouan gained the confidence of Muslims through Sufi ideas and built a Sufi state in that city in the years 1537 to 1557. A. Chebbi, *Aḥmad b. Makhlūf al-Shābbī* (A., 1979) is a religio-historical study of Aḥmad, the founder of the Shābbī Sufi order in Kairouan.

As far as the state was concerned, the ulama were the pivot of urban rule. For example, M. Shatzmiller, "Les premiers Mérinides et le milieu religieux de Fès" (1976) examines the question in detail and says that the people of Fez, heirs of a long history of urban culture, did not have amicable relations with the Marinids, an outsider group of nomad origin held in contempt by the townspeople. Therefore the Marinids had to employ the policy of attaching religious leaders (imams, jurists, *khaṭībs*) from Fez to the court in order to control the city. F. R. Mediano, "Los ulemas de Fez y la conquista de la ciudad por los Sa'dies" (1992) stated that after the conquest of Fez by the Sa'dids, new leading ulama had come to the fore in place of the great ulama who were oppressed by the Sa'dids because of their desapproval of the Jazuli Sufi order which the Sa'dids supported, and lost their influence. The building of madrasas by the state was part of the same policy. Sa'd Ghrad, in the introduction to his edition (A., 1976) of *The Origins of Debates* of al-Sakūnī (d. 1317), discusses the history of the Sakūnī family from the time they were in Andalus to the beginning of the 15th century, including their move to Tunis in the middle of the 13th century. M. Kisaichi, "Three Distinguished Ulama Families of Tlemcen" (J., 1983) studies the history of the Maqqarī, the Marzūq and the 'Uqbānī families, affluent families who combined control of the positions of qadi and *khaṭīb* in Tlemcen with commercial activities. Kisaichi also discussed ulama contributions to social unity and stability through the various connections linking the ruling power and the people in "Medieval Islamic Society of the Maghrib and the Social Role of the Ulama," (J., 1982) using like Urvoy (1976) biographical dictionaries. In addition, M. García-Arenal, "The Revolution of Fās in 869/1465" (1978) examines the role of the *sharīf* as a mediator between the people and the rulers in Fez urban society in terms of the uprising of 1465; J. Berque, "Cadis de Kairouan" (1973) studies the role of the qadi in Kairouan based on a manuscript of al-Jawdī concerning the position of judge; and N. Sghaïr, "En marge d'une lecture du chroniqueur Mahmud" (1986) clarifies the important role borne by the ulama of Sfax in the vigorous intellectual traffic between Egypt and Tunisia in the 18th and 19th centuries. Abdel Moula, *L'université zaytounienne* (1971) is a study of the Zaytūna Madrasa, the most prestigious educational and research facility for ulama in Tunisia, from its foundation to the 1950s, focusing on the characteristics and social functions of its system of education and research. It is clear from the above that the ulama were particularly active in the cities (only a few lived in rural villages) and any study of them as a large group is virtually limited to the city. When the number of reports concerning the ulama are considered, as well as the breadth of their social functions, it is readily apparent that studies of the ulama are an important means of understanding the distinctive features of the city in Islamic society.

6. The Jews

The question of ethnic groups in Maghribi cities is not all that meaningful outside the Jews, and so research in this field is confined almost exclusively to them. Relevant works already cited include D. Cades (1889), J. Chalom (1906), M. Eisenbeth (1952), H. Cornet (1955), V. Danon (1955), P. Sebag (1959), D. Corcos (1964) and H. Z. Hirschberg (1965, 1974). It is clear though that these represent only a tiny proportion of the studies that have been made when it is considered that R. Attal, *Les juifs d'Afrique du Nord: Bibliographie* (1973) lists a total of 5,640 such works. This number is far too great for adequate treatment here, but I would like to make specific mention of a number of recent studies which look at Jews in urban society.

J. S. Gerber, *Jewish Society in Fez* (1972) studies the Jewish community (*mellah*) in Fez up to 1700 in detail using relevant historical materials to describe its autonomous organization and religious system, and the mercantile and craft activities of the Jews. This is a valuable study of the Jewish community in the Maghrib. Gerber points out that the arrival of the Sephardim (Jews from the Iberian peninsula) was a turning point for the Jews of Fez in two regards. First, because the native Jewish community had been severely shaken prior to the arrival of the Sephardim by the pogrom of 1465, the latter came to hold a predominant position in the Fez Jewish community. Second, the newcomers introduced social, communal and economic conflicts into the Jewish community. Gerber understands that particularism was expressed institutionally between the Toshavim (native settlers) and the Megorashim (those expelled from the Iberian peninsula) and the two groups had their own institutions for worship, litigation, education, animal slaughter and matters concerning death. The study is indeed fruitful for deepening urban understanding. G. Ayache, "La minorité juive dans le Maroc précolonial" (1987) examines the social position, standing and social life of Jews in Morocco before French colonial rule; after having shown that the Jews lived in a condition of intimate coexistence with the Muslims, it goes on to describe how the seed of discord was planted in both communities through European colonization and the implantation of the mistaken idea that the two races had always been in conflict, making peaceful coexistence increasingly difficult. As this reveals, modern studies of Jews, even if primarily historical, have a certain political edge. M. Kenbib, "Les relations entre musulmans et juifs au Maroc" (1985) and id. "Les juifs de Tétouan" (1986) are historical studies of relations betwen Jews and Muslims with the interest firmly directed towards the breakdown of coexistence and its origins. L. Rosen, in a sociological study, "Muslim and Jewish Relations in a Moroccan City" (1972) attempts to describe the relations between Jews and Muslims in what is probably Sefru from the perspective of an outsider, but even here a concern about the modern Israel-Arab question can be perceived.

7. Saints' Cults

The veneration of saints in the cities is not an issue particular to the Maghrib, but it can be considered one distinctive topic within Maghribi urban studies. G. Salmon recognized comparatively early on that the saints' cults had a role within urban society and he deals with the topic in a number of reports between 1904 and 1905. For example, "Notes sur Salé" (1905) an annotated translation of a manuscript in the possession of the jurist Aḥmad, names marabouts buried within and without the city walls, mosques, quarters, and public baths, etc. and describes pilgrimages to the marabouts in Salé. H. De Castries (1924) is a study of the seven saints of Marrakesh but it does not specifically mention the significance of the cult to urban society. P. Marty (1933) deals with Sidi ben Achir, a saint renowned for powers of healing. Marty shows that his *zāwiya* also functioned as a hospital and sanitarium and was visited annually by several thousands of pilgrims who made donations to it and also throws light on its budgeting and the management of its waqf endowments. The resulting strong links between the saint and the townspeople may be readily surmised. The topic of the relation between guilds and saints is touched upon not only in L. Golvin (1957) in the section on guilds in this chapter, but also in most of the studies concerning cities and saints' cults. A. Ben Talha (1965), a study of Mulay Idris Zarhun, the most historical of Morocco's holy cities, discusses the origins of the city, the present state of the quarters, the economic life of the people, family life and festivals. Ben

Talha concludes that Mulay Idris preserves the functions of a traditional city more than Fez and Meknes, and gives as evidence the facts that Koran recitation could (then) be heard in the streets and that a daughter of a *sharīf* family could not marry a son of a non-*sharīf* family. Further examples of pre-1970 studies include Ch. Brosselard (1859), P. Durand (1931), W. Fogg (1934), and Le Tourneau (1949).

Noteworthy amongst modern research is W. Hoenerbach and J. Kolenda, "Šefšāwen (Xauen)" (1973-5), a detailed examination of the history and geography of Chechaouen in northern Morocco which discusses among other things the city's saints, mosques, *sharīf* families (many of them descended from Idrīs), the nature of saints' cults, pilgrimage to the tombs of the city's seven saints and the patron saints of the craft guilds. M. al-Ḥabīb "The Zawiya and its Influences on Kairouan Society" (A., 1975) uses the biographical dictionary *Ma'ālim al-Īmān* of Ibn Nājī (d. 1435) to analyze the functions of saints and *zāwiya*s in urban society in 13th and 14th century Kairouan. The study shows that many of the saints cooperated with the ruling power and effectively made use of their influence among the townspeople to quell insurrections or prevent outside attack and that they played an important role in pacifying surrounding Arab nomads and spreading Islam among them. As a result their *zāwiya*s were thronged with followers, and there is one case where an extra mural quarter (*rabaḍ*) formed around a *zāwiya*. Some of the *zāwiya*s had characteristics of a sanctuary. If it is thus possible to understand so clearly relations between the *zāwiya*s and the townspeople through biographical literature about saints, a new vista may perhaps be opened for urban studies by supporting them through the use of chronicles and other such records.

There is a certain amount of material concerning the urban saints' cult in Marinid Fez. H. L. Beck, "L'image d'Idrīs II" (1989) is a superb example of such research. It uses a wide variety of sources, including manuscripts, lithographs and printed books to analyze the process by which the tomb of Idris II (1437/8) was discovered as it is related to changes in the way the government and the people of Fez imaged Idris II. Beck says that when the tomb was discovered, Idris II was not yet regarded as an object of veneration in the saints' cult, and it was only after his tomb was discovered that it became a pilgrimage site as a saint's mausoleum. After the Marinid Sultan enlisted the Idris family to govern Fez society, the Idris *shurafā'* increased their prestige, so that the image of its ancestor Idris II also changed. The *shurafā'* who wielded power in Fez society were not a solid block but a number of different family lineages who struggled among themselves for power; the influential *'Imrān* family (a branch of the Idris family who occupied the former dwelling of Idris II), asserted their own orthodoxy and heightened their prestige by claiming through the fact they had discovered the tomb (the body showed no signs of decomposition!) in the Shurafa mosque opposite their house that they were true descendants of Idris II. Saints cults have been generally associated with the villages and the countryside, but this research is important in that it shows that the saints' cult in urban society can be clarified through historical sources. M. Shatzmiller, "L'historiographie mérinide" (1982) also notes that the histories of Fez began to be compiled from around the 14th century and that its historiography represents the ideological struggle of people of Fez against the Marinid rulers, to which can be ascribed the rise of Idris prestige and Sharifism and also the resurgence of the saints' cult of Idris II. Shatzmiller calls the cult a resurgence because he believes that Idris II was revered as a saint during the Almohad dynasty; Beck denies this as being contrary to fact.

The contributions made by sociologists and cultural anthropologists in this filed cannot be ignored. Representative examples include D. F. Eickelman (1974), which discusses the meaning and social and political functions of the *zāwiyas* of the Sharqāwa brotherhood in Boujad, id. *The Middle East* (1981) and A. Būkārī, *The Zāwiya of the Sharqāwīya* (A., 1985) and Geertz, *Meaning and Order in Moroccan Society* (1979), which takes the example of Sefru to analyze that the *zāwiyas* functioned as the pivot for the daily rituals of the townspeople (worship, communal meals, weddings and funerals, etc.), and the saints' festivals, through their close connections with the guilds (*ḥinṭa*) and their waqf endowments were an element in the economy of the city and the rural village. The interests of sociologists and cultural anthropologists are not confined to the topic of saints' cults but extend over a wide range of subjects but here is not the place to treat them exhaustively. I will therefore confine my attention to three such scholars. G. Grandguillaume, "Une médina" (1971) and *Nédroma* (1976) discuss changes in the medina (the old city) around the framework of city-village relations using the western Algerian town of Nedroma as an example. M. Miyaji, "Formation of the National Society" (J., 1980) uses Granguillaume's studies to extend the relations between rulers and ruled in Nedroma and its environs into an international system. K. Takagi, "Tunisia: Spatial Symbols in Sidi Bou Said" (J., 1990) is a report on the significance of the placement of religious facilities (mosques, saints' tombs), wells, coffee shops and the doors of houses. Though the examples cited are not numerous, they serve to indicate ways historians might use the fieldwork of sociologists and cultural anthropologists in conjunction with documentary analysis for the study of the city and its saints' cults.

8. Social History

Here I do not define social history in precise terms, and so exclude what would normally be considered to be a concern here like Urvoy's studies of the ulama (1976, 1978) and deal with research into daily life and illness, topics that have tended to be ignored in the past. Survey reports by sociologists such as L. Mercier (1906), which dealt in part with Muslim daily life appeared early on, but research based on historical documents has not appeared in any substantial form since P. Boyer (1963). A study that could be included is L. Golvin, "Alger à la période ottomane" (1986), which examines features of and changes in urban life according to the concept of the rhythms of life. Golvin says that traditional urban life (culture) in Algiers was maintained by the luxurious modes of living of a wealthy urban class comprising the Turkish ruling class and affluent Arab and Jewish merchants (for example they used Dutch ceramics and Venetian glass, and left the medina to spend summer in their villas), but between the 19th and 20th centuries, when a widening gap was evident between rich and poor, wealthier Arabs (Moors) began renting their homes in the medina to Kabyle people and going to live in the suburbs, which led to the dilapidation of the city.

Surveys and studies concerning diseases began with the colonial period. For example, A. Berbrugger, who was a member of the French scientific mission to Algeria from 1839, compiled a report entitled *Histoire sur la peste en Algérie* (1847). P. Sebag (1965), which discusses plague epidemics in 17th and 18th century Tunis, is the first example of an historiographical study of disease. Probably the pioneer of a thorough study of disease with careful attention to its historical significance is B. Rosenberger and H. Triki, "Famines et épidémies au Maroc" (1973-4). The authors, acknowledging the fact that little study has been done on the connections between population decrease and economic and social change or political movements, studied famines and plagues in 16th and 17th century Morocco through historical sources. Records (ones relating to Fez being the most numerous) show outbreaks of plague occurring about forty times between 1493 and 1680, with five of those major epidemics. Tables indicate whether famine occurred at the time of the epidemic and how many people died (the extent being indicated as a large number, a fairly large number, or a small number based on the sources). This research has been continued in M. A. El-Bezzaz, "La peste de 1798-1800 au Maroc" (1985), an examination of the plague of 1798-1800, the most serious of the three large plagues which broke out in Morocco in the 18th century in terms of its traces, its spread, estimates of the number of dead (123,500 for the cities of Fez, Marrakesh, Safi and Assaouira alone), and its social and political effects. F. El-Ghoul, "Histoire d'une rumeur"

(1988) deals with the rumour that spread throughout France in 1792 that plague had broken out in Tunis. He explains that the spread of the rumour and its origins lay in the fear that both people and state had of the plague at that time. Another study of plague in Tunis is N. E. Gallagher, "Colonial Enthusiasts and Plague in Tunis" (1984). Connected also with epidemics is M. Jole, "L'hygiène publique et l'espace urbain" (1983), a study of urban public health policy during the French colonial period. Jole states that the main concern of public health between the late 19th and early 20th centuries was that epidemics be prevented from infecting the French, and that there was no idea of an urban public health programme which included Moroccans also.

Fatwā documents are very useful for the study of social history. Halima Ferhat, "Famille et société à Sabta" (1992) is a good case study that examines the situation of the family and women of 12th century Ceuta by analyzing the *fatwā* document *Madhāhib al-Ḥukkām* of Qadi 'Iyyāḍ. Ferhat shows that many women were referred to in this document and that most families were monogamous, with polygamy being exceptional and the nuclear family usual, the average number of children not exceeding three. Women could specify in their marriage contract that they had the right to continue their work and visit the family of their parents, and they could also dispose of property and buy and free slaves. Ferhat implies that the social status of women in medieval times was not as low as is supposed. Also of note here is that the abovementioned Ben Achour (1989) points out that monogamy was dominant among notable families in Tunis in the late 19th century. V. Lagardère, "Droits des eaux et des installations hydrauliques" (1988-9), a description of water rights and irrigation technology in the Maghrib and Andalus in the 11th and 12th centuries through an analysis of the *fatwā* document *Mi'yar* of al-Wansharīsī, indicates that information concerning social history is available in waqf documents. The same can be said about Lahmar (1990). Such studies of social history attract attention as a new form of urban studies, but so far very little has been done and it is not possible to describe their characteristics or areas of concern.

9. Urban Architecture and Planning

Architectural studies of the cities have been a thriving area of interest, in combination with surveys, since the French conquered North Africa. Studies include J. J. L. Bargès (1859), A. Devoulx (1860-2, 1862-70, 1875-8) and A. Berbrugger (1868), but the best of any before 1970 is G. Marçais (1926). Studies of urban planning virtually were one with E. Michaux-Bellaire and G. Salmon (1907) in saying that the cities were characterized by their unplanned nature. Recent research has suggested new points of view and methodologies, and have given rise to a number of important results.

B. S. Hakim (see p. 42) explains that urban architecture and composition is systematic according to the principles of Islamic law. The planning and design of structures are dealt with in J. Revault's excellent architectural studies of Tunis and Fez, *Palais et demeures de Tunis* (1968-71) and *Palais et demeures de Fès* (1985). In contrast to the importance G. Marçais (1926) puts on religious buildings, Revault looks at domestic structures classified into four types and states the unity and common principles exist in their structures, by analyzing the planning and design based both on documents and surveys. C. Cambazard-Amahan, *Le décor sur bois dans l'architecture de Fès* (1989) analyzes the designs of wooden structures in Fez of the Almoravid, Almohad and Marinid periods and A. Gaudio, *Fès* (1982) discusses the heritage and value of traditional Islamic culture through the buildings, arts and ornamentation in Fez. A. H. al-Tāzī, "City Planning through Arabic and Non-Arabic Sources" (A., 1990) states that astrologers participated in the planning of urban buildings, and gives as an example that when building New Fez the Marinids listened to the opinions of astrologers before constructing mosques, palaces and dwellings. M. Ḥannānī, "Reasons and Myths Related to the Foundation of the Islamic Cities in the Maghrib" (A., 1990) introduces a new theme, that the various legends relating to the land affected the foundation of the cities. Revault, *Le fondouk des Français* (1984) examines the *funduq* as an historical and cultural legacy.

A detailed examination of the history of Tunis from its foundation to the present from an architectural point of view is J. S. Woodford, *The City of Tunis* (1990). Other works include H. Bressolette and J. Delarozière, "El Mosara" (1978-9), a study of the location of the now lost park of Marinid Fez, using documentary sources and aerial photographs, L. Golvin, "Mahdia" (1979), which cites the necessity of reexamining the structure and locations of the walls, gates and palaces of Fatimid Mahdia using documentary sources, A. Lézine, *Deux villes d'Ifriqiya* (1971), which sees the existence of the principle of privacy from the structure of buildings in Sousse and Tunis (but it does not touch on the legal side), and J. H. Benslimane, "Salé" (1979), a study of the structure of traditional dwellings in Salé. Lézine has also published "Sur deux châteaux musulmans" (1971), an archaeological study of palaces. F. Cresti, "Apports et influences européens dans le domaine de la structure et de la construction des villes du Maghreb" (1991) indicates European influences on the Mahgribi urban construction.

Many architectural studies show an interest in the preservation of the cultural heritage. A. Daoulati, *Tunis sous les Ḥafṣides* (1976) looks at urban expansion in Hafsid Tunis primarily in terms of building activity, and S. M.

Zbiss, *La médina de Tunis* (1981) examines the history of religious buildings in Tunis, including fourteen large mosques, fifteen madrasas, ten *zāwiyas* and six tombs (*türbe*).

It was early pointed out that there was a fixed pattern of utilization of urban space according to occupation (for example, Ch. Lallemand, 1890). Hakim (1986) shows that this pattern was systematized throughout the entire city according to the principles of Islamic law. F. Stambouli and A. Zghal, "Urban Life in Precolonial North Africa" (1976) theorizes the question in terms of a pattern of space ordering. Eickelman (1981) divides that pattern into four elements: (1) the relation of towns to the state, (2) the market (suq) or economic complex, (3) the relation of religious institutions to the town, and (4) the organization of residential and domestic space. The rulers build a citadel in the centre of the city or in a place nearby, and their living become separated from urban life. There is a tendency for commercial and industrial activity to become separated from the residential area, and for the various occupations to be located in a hierarchical fashion. The large mosque was both the symbolic and physical centre of the city. The quarters were constructed according to the concept of closeness (*qrāba*). Geertz (1979) discusses the second point fully. Eickelman (1981) and J. Abu-Lughod (1975, 1980) look at another aspect of land use, the colonial city. The separation of the new town, where the Europeans lived, and the old city (medina) of the Arab population is a reflection of the values of the ruling Europeans as well as a separation according to social class. They criticize French efforts to maintain the medinas of Fez and Meknes as a cultural isolation policy based on a biased concept. These arguments are difficult to apply as such to historical research but they are certainly capable of broadening the way scholars look at cities and read historical sources. T. Bachrouch, "Le Sahel: Essai de définition d'un espace citadin" (1986) attempts to define urban space and says that the common elements of the Ifriqi coastal cities of Sousse, Mahdia and Monastir are that the inhabitants own their homes, olive groves and graveyards individually. Despite the wealth of detail, it is difficult to gauge what the writer is trying to say.

10. Population, Trade, and Urban-rural Relations

It has been only relatively recently that questions concerning the markers that are at the base of urban development have been raised. We have seen in section I that the history of studies of urban population and transportation dates from the 19th century, with many of them being analyses of trade activities themselves undertaken often in response to the needs of colonial policy.

A. Raymond, the French scholar of the Ottoman period, criticized the commonly held idea that Arab cities declined overall in the 16th to 19th centuries in "La conquête ottomane et le développement des grandes villes arabes" (1979), claiming that at the very least there was development in the 16th and 17th centuries. Though he did not completely discount the reliability of chronicles, consular reports and travel records in establishing population figures, and used to some extent the size and distribution of mosques in determining them, his most important material was the public bath. (See also id. *Les grandes villes arabes à l'epoque ottomane,* 1985.) In "Le déplacement des tanneries" (1978) he looked at the movement of tanneries away from the city centres in Aleppo, Cairo and Tunis in the Ottoman period and said this was proof of urban expansion. F. Cresti, "Quelques observations et hypothèses sur la population et la structure sociale d'Alger" (1986) supports Raymond's hypothesis and infers from a large number of travel records by Europeans and the number of public baths and great mosques the population of Algiers from the 16th to the 19th centuries, and the population of slaves, Jews and *kulughlis*, the offspring of Turks and Arabs (Berbers).

R. I. Lawless, "Tlemcen, Capital City of the 'Abd al-Wadids" (1974) disagrees with Le Tourneau's claim that a general characteristic of Maghribi cities was their dealings with neighbouring rural villages, and that trade over a distance was of secondary importance. In Tlemcen of the 'Abd al-Wadid period (13th-16th centuries), he claims, trade with sub-Saharan Africa and Europe thrived and Tlemcen's prosperity was based on its international, long-distance trade. However he does point out that this was an exception among Maghribi cities. The relationship between the city and its hinterland has been discussed in D. Largash, "The City and its Outskirts: Monastir in the 19th Century" (A., 1988), which says that Monastir in Tunisia did not develop as a great city, though it possessed all the conditions to do so, because it did not control its surroundings either economically or politically. A. Kraiem, "La résistance de Gabès" (1988) is an interesting discussion taking the Tunisian city of Gabes as an example. This city held out the longest and the most furiously against the French for three reasons: the city was formed out of two settlements with an uninhabited space between them, the inhabitants, who were engaged in agriculture, had a deep attachment to their land, and there were strong links between the townspeople and the semi-nomadic people living in the vicinity. A. Qaddūr, "The Influence of the Big Cities on the Urban Network" (A., 1990) examines the influence of the great cities on urban civilization in Almohad Maghrib. He points out the following: (1) the most important element in determining a city's scale and its political, economic and social power was its population, (2) the basis of urban development was closely related to the agriculture and commerce of the surroundings, and it was because of this that the cities were open to the villages and named their gates for local tribes, (3) the cities were a meeting place for diverse ethnic groups, and the entry of new groups changed the composition and character of the city, and (4) as the large cities gradually grew in population, they dominated the fate of smaller cities absorbed in their network and in many cases caused their decline. In December 1984, scholars from Morocco, Algeria and Tunisia discussed from an historical perspective relations between Maghribi cities and villages from the 16th century to the present at a conference held at Muhammad V University in Rabat. Its proceedings were published by the University as *L'évolution des rapports villes-campagnes au Maghreb* (1988). One of the scholars present, Muḥammad Mazzīn, published a detailed analysis of the relations between Fez and the surrounding rural villages in the 16th and 17th centuries in "Fez and its rural surroundings" (A., 1986). This is a noteworthy study. Mazzīn attempts to disinter an obscure society and so has consulted many unpublished documents and manuscripts. He presents concrete and clear facts concerning the economic and social life of Fez. He implies that urban studies should not be done in total isolation from the rural surroundings, making frequent mention of the relationship between Fez and its surroundings in terms of population movements by the ulama and tribal people, and the interdependence of rural and urban society in commerce and agriculture.

Mazzīn's study indicates a new direction in studies by local scholars, one that is neither too theoretical nor too descriptive and which makes full use of the accessibility of sources. Similarly, A. Sebti, *Aristocratie citadine, pouvoir et discours savant* (unpublished thesis, 1984) is an excellent study of Fez society between the 15th and 19th centuries. Mazzīn and Sebti represent differences in terms of analytical approach, but both deserve high praise for their originality.

Trading activities of the city are discussed in B. Doumerc, "La ville et la mer" (1986), which employs Venetian commercial documents to show the great economic and cultural benefits 15th century Tunis received as a port-of-call for galleys plying between Venice and Alexandria; N. Pacha, *Le commerce au Maghreb du XIe au XIVe siècles* (1976), a study of the flourishing north-south trade in the western Mediterranean in the 11th to 14th centuries intended as a reexamination of Pirenne's thesis; M. Ḥ. al-Sharīf, "Imports and Importers in Tunis in the 18th Century" (A., 1986), a documentary examination of imports into Tunis in the years 1763-4; P. Sebag, *Tunis au XVIIe siècle* (1989), an analysis of the flourishing of Tunis society in the 17th century, when the Barbary pirates were at their peak, the physical structures of the city, its commercial and industrial activity, and its diverse ethnic composition; and M. al-'Ināwī, "The Coastal Cities of Medieval Maghrib until the End of the 4th Century A. H." (A., 1990), which states that north-south trade across the Mediterranean between the coastal cities of the Maghrib and Ifriqiya and Andalus and Christian Europe flourished generally, and that Rustamid Tahart also prospered due to the visits of Andalusian merchants, but that its economic base was not replaced by the sub-Saharan trade.

11. General Histories, Histories of Relations with Other Countries

A large amount of work has been done in these fields and since their content often relates to other fields I will cite here only those works I have not mentioned before.

The origins of the tradition of writing histories (especially political) of a particular city by Arab scholars can be found in the Arab chronicles. The style of research also reflects the long lineage of Islamic studies from the earliest period and the importance given to the citing of copious references rather than theorization. Examples of this are A. A. al-Sawīsī, *A History of Rabat* (A., 1979), M. Ibn Tāwīt, *A History of Ceuta* (A., 1982) and M. A. al-Ṭammār, *Tlemcen in History* (A., 1984). *A History of Rabat,* for instance, uses various historical sources to describe the history of Rabat from its founding until modern times, the origins of buildings and the various government offices. M. A. W. Khallāf, *Islamic Cordoba in the 11th Century* (A., 1984) describes the politics, economy and culture of 11th century Cordoba using a large number of Arabic sources. Sulaymān 'Abd al-Ghannī, "Social Life in Marrakesh in the Almoravid and Almohad Periods" (A., 1986) attempts to deal with urban social life as a whole by dividing the urban population into various groups according to political class and religious or ethnic differences, while M. al-'Arūsī, *Legend of Kairouan* (A., 1981) looks at the contributions made by medieval Kairouan to Maghribi-Islamic culture. A. A. al-Filālī, "On the Arabic and Islamic Conquest of Constantine" (A., 1986) examines the process of the conquest, A. Bouali, *Les deux grands sièges de Tlemcen* (1984) examines the sieges of Tlemcen by the Marinids, and L. Mezzine, *Le Tafilalt* (1987) uses four historical sources to describe the history of the Tafilalt region in the 17th and 18th centuries. Studies by non-Arab scholars include H. Bressolette and J. Delarozière, "Fès-Jadid" (1982-3) a general survey of the history of Fās al-Jadīda (the New Fez built by the Marinids), and P. Massiera, "M'sila du Xe au XVe siècle" (1974), a study of the history of M'sila, built by the Fatimids in central Algeria, from its foundation until its collapse. M. Benchekroun, *La vie intellectuelle marocaine* (1974) discusses urban intellectual life and cultural activity in the Marinid and Wattasid periods, and D. R. Lourido, "Documentos ineditos sobre el nacimiento de Dār al-Bayḍā" (1974) studies the foundation of Casablanca.

Studies which are not just general histories but look to the academic tradition of Europe and America, being more analytical than descriptive, have begun to appear. Examples include Tawfiq al-Ṭayyibī, "Study on the History of the Islamic City of Ceuta" (A., 1989) and A. I. Khalīfa, "The Maghribi History of the City of Ceuta" (A., 1988).

The history of the foreign relations and foreign contacts of the cities is studied in R. Mantran, "L'évolution des relations entre la Tunisie et l'Empire ottoman" (1959), a comparatively early work dealing with foreign contacts in a defined area. It examines particularly in terms of the movement of people through pilgrimage or commercial relations between Ottoman period Egypt and Tunisia, and reveals the existence of a Tunisian community in Cairo. More recent research includes G. Ayache, "Beliounech et le destin de Ceuta" (1972), a discussion of Spanish-Moroccan relations centred on Ceuta, J. D. Latham, "Contribution à l'étude des immigrations andalouses" (1973), an analysis of the historical significance of immigrants from Andalus to Tunisia, id. "Towns and Cities of Barbary" (1972), a study of the influence of Andalusian immigrants on the culture, especially building techniques, of Maghribi cities, J. B. Weiner, "Anglo-Moroccan Relations in the First Decade of the Occupation of Tangier" (1978-9), an examination of Anglo-Moroccan relations during the English occupation of Tangier (1662-72), and D. Meunier, "Le consulat anglais à Tétouan" (1980), which deals with Anglo-Moroccan foreign relations based on the Tetuan consulate.

Why do general urban histories and histories of particular periods tend to lack appeal? It is not that the wealth of quotations from historical sources and the compilation of facts are without interest, but many such works are just dull. Collections of individual papers do not constitute a general history and periodization and historical description based on a critical view of history are topics that should be treated in Islamic historical studies in the future. On the other hand, histories of foreign and cultural contacts may be significant for dissecting the static framework of the cities. In particular links between cities and the outside world constitute an important topic for clarifying the actuality of "openness," what has been called a characteristic feature of the cities of the Islamic region.

12. Urban Power Structure and Politics

Recent urban sociology has begun looking at social class in premodern Islamic cities. F. Stambouli, "Système social et stratification urbaine au Maghreb" (1977) divides Maghribi urban society into three social classes, the *makhzan* (rulers), the *baladī* (the urban bourgeoisie-affluent townspeople, the ulama, etc.) and the urban people, and sees them as having come into being under imperialist and colonial rule. M. Ben Achour, *Catégories de la société tunisoise* (1989) discusses social class using 19th century Tunis as an example, and id. "Cadre urbain, habitat et structures sociales à Tunis" (1986) analyzes the social structure of 19th century Tunis in terms of the hierarchy of the quarters, structures, the living environment, the economic system of the suq, etc. For outsiders, especially nomadic tribes who had no tradition of city culture, ruling the cities was difficult. A. W. al-Dubīshī, "The Relation of the Marinid Sultanate to Fez Society" (A., 1990) examines how the uncouth Marinids of outsider and tribal background were able to rule Fez, with its long tradition of urban culture. The Marinids adopted a policy of supporting the Malikis in terms of ideology and thereby won the understanding of the townspeople. However, the people they employed as jurists (*fuqahā'*) to promote their ideology were not from Fez but from the Zanāta tribes and particularly men who had moved to Morocco from Andalus.

N. S. Hopkins, "Testour au XIXe siècle" (1980) deals with urban rule. It analyses the society of 19th century Testour, a small city in northern Tunisia and discusses the downfall of the oligarchy centring on a traditional family of Andalusian origins as a result of the rise of new power holders after the French land reforms of 1904-10 and the conflict between the two. As the examples of Tripoli and Ceuta above-mentioned suggest (pp. 37-8), small regional cities, in contrast to the large central ones, were ruled by local urban power holders, and it appears to be necessary to divide between large central cities and small regional cities when discussing the relationship between cities and the ruling power. This question is discussed with a considerable difference in point of view by A. Raymond in "Les caractéristiques d'une ville arabe <moyenne> au XVIIIe siècle: Le cas Constantine" (1986). He says that in small to middle size cities like Constantine, where the Turkish occupying force was on a small scale, city government was in many cases in the hands of local power holders. In the case of Constantine, the pro-Turkish Bin al-Fujjun family combined Turkish power and amicable relations to control urban administration. In large cities, families of local notables did not play a significant role in urban administration, and in this sense there is a large difference between the large cities and the medium to small ones. Another example of a medium to small city is Mosul in Iraq. Ben Achour, "Autorités urbaines de l'economie et du commerce de Tunis" (1988-9) is a detailed study which shows that in 19th century Tunis, the *shaykh al-madīna* and the *amīn*s of the guilds increased their economic and political functions during the period of European commercial pressure and the French protectorate.

Ali Oumlil, "Ibn Khaldoun et la société urbaine" (1982) and K. Nakamura, "Ibn Khaldūn's Image of City" (1989) examine the meaning and image of the city for Muslims through an analysis of the preface (the *Muqaddima*) to

Ibn Khaldūn's *Kitāb al-'Ibar*. A. Abdesselem, "La sémantique sociale de la ville d'après les auteurs tunisiens" (1982) uses chronicles and travel records of the 18th and 19th centuries to analyze terms concerning the city (like *ḥaḍāra, baladī, madīna, rabaḍ*, etc.) expressed in them, thereby clarifying among other points the meaning of physical structures and their location in the urban setting and the self-consciousness of the urban dweller. A. R. al-Talīlī, "Description of the Maghribi Cities in *Sūra al-Arḍ*" (A., 1986) gives an outline in terms of climate, people, economy, etc. of the cities of the Maghrib as they are described in Ibn Ḥawqal's geography. M. Barrucand, *Urbanisme princier en Islam* (1985) is an interesting study of the similarities and differences in terms of form and function between the "royal cities," built by the order of princes with structures centring on the needs of the prince and his court, and the "bourgeois cities." Barrucand analyses the significance of points of commonality and difference in the extent, placement and functions of bazars (in royal cities bazars and artisans' areas were small, and the palace occupied the central space), mosques, walls and storehouses. She gives as examples of royal cities Meknes (her main object of study), Sa'did Marrakesh, Istanbul, Safavid Esfahan and Mughul Fathpūr Sīkrī.

To generalize on the power structure and politics of the city, the viewpoints of comparative as well as individual studies are necessary. In this we have much to learn from the work of Raymond and Barrucand. These topics also have a connection with the concept of the "Islamic city" (see pp. 34-44).

Conclusion

Such is the vast quantity of studies done on the topic of the city it is inevitable that I have almost certainly omitted much of value in attempting to consolidate the research undertaken since the 19th century. While on the subject of the history of resarch, I would like to add that though it is easy to criticize as prejudiced or biased those urban studies begun as part of French colonial policy, the results of that scholarship should not be discarded for that reason alone. The accumulated results have an important meaning even today. In this sense, a part of the series, *Villes et tribus du Maroc,* edited by Michaux-Bellaire at the beginning of the 20th century, has been translated into Arabic with supplementary notes: *The City of Azammūr and its Vicinity* (A., 1989) translated by M. al-Shiyāẓimī and H. al-Subā'ī.

When setting out to write this chapter, I perused quite a number of urban studies written by Arab scholars of the countries of the Maghrib and had several discussions with local scholars when attempting to analyze the work that has been done. Though as individual studies they were of a satisfactorily high level, I was not able to get a clear vision of the direction they are taking as a whole. As in previous years, descriptive studies are numerous, but such perhaps are a feature of Maghribi Arab urban studies (or historical research). Further examination remains to be done on this topic.

Many modern urban studies, while not yet challenging the theories of the Chicago School or the thesis of Lapidus, are denying there is any clear distinction between the city and rural village and are concerned rather in studying the relations between them and the region incorporating both. All the same I feel it is necessary to discover on what basis the terms "city" and "village" are used. The people of 19th century Tunis derided the inhabitants of regional cities and rural villages as "Āfaqīya" (people of the horizon), and it is easy to see in their attitude a pride in their polished urban culture. Until very recently in Japan the expression "Going to the city" was quite common; the idea of "city" had very clear cultural connotations. I received two very different impressions of the concept of "city" from a small survey I did in the cities of the Maghrib and of the Uigur region in China. The city of Uigur does not have clear boundaries between it and the vast farmlands surrounding it, and it might be more accurate to call it an enormous rural village. This is an apt reminder that in discussing the city it is necessary to continually return to the question, "What is a city?" The work of sociologists and cultural anthropologists mentioned in this chapter have a high utilization value, though care must be taken in how they are used, for I feel that the value of joint studies is in those areas of urban studies capable of a multi-disciplined approach. Such studies make sense when used to compare cities of different regions. The distinctive features of the cities in the Islamic lands will gain in precision through comparisons with cities in Europe, China and Japan.

I have not covered the available literature in anything like a comprehensive way in this chapter. In addition, I was not able to see for myself several of the works dating from the 19th and early 20th centuries. I used a number of bibliographic studies, and owe a particularly great debt to P. Shinar, *Islam maghrébin contemporain: Bibliographie annotée* (1983). I also used M. Jole, "Les villes et la politique de recherche française au Maroc" (1983) and Cl. Liauzu, "Orientations et redéfinitions des recherches françaises sur les villes du monde arabe" (1986) to gain an overview of the history of French urban studies, and referred to M. Djender, *Introduction à l'histoire de l'Algérie* (1968) and Kazuo Miyaji (J., 1971) amongst others for the relationship between colonial rule and Maghribi research.

BIBLIOGRAPHY

Abdel Moula Mahmoud. *L'université zaytounienne et la société tunisienne*. Tunis, 1971.

Abdesselem Ahmed. "La sémantique sociale de la ville d'après les auteurs tunisiens du XVIIIe et XIXe siècles." In *La ville arabe dans l'Islam*, eds. A. Bouhdiba & D. Chevallier. Tunis & Paris, 1982.

Abribat, J. *Essai sur les contrats de quasi-aliénation et de location perpétuelle auxquels l'institution des Habous a donné naissance*. Alger, 1902.

———. "Notes sur la hisba (police)." *Revue tunisienne* 85 (1911).

Abu-Lughod, J. L. "Moroccan Cities: Apartheid and the Serendipity of Conservation." In *African Themes: North Western University Studies in Honor of Gwendolen Carter*, ed. I. Abu-Lughod. Evanston, 1975.

———. *Rabat: Urban Apartheid in Morocco*. Princeton, 1980.

———. "The Islamic City: Historic Myth, Islamic Essence, and Contemporary Relevance." *IJMES* 19 (1987).

———. "What is Islamic about a City? Some Comparative Reflections." In*Urbanism in Islam: The Proceedings of the International Conference on Urbanism in Islam*. Vol. 1. Tokyo, 1989.

Adam, A. *Casablanca: Essai sur la transformation de la société marocaine au contact de l'Occident*. Paris, 1968.

Allouche, I. S. "Un plan des canalisations de Fès au temps de Mawlāy Ismā'īl d'après un texte inédit, avec une étude succincte sur la corporation des <ḳwādsīya>." *Hespéris* 18 (1934).

Arié, R. "Traduction annotée et commentée des traités de ḥisba d'Ibn 'Abd al-Ra'ūf et de 'Umar al-Garsīfī." *Hespéris-Tamuda* 1 (1960).

al-'Arūsī, Muḥammad. *Sīra al-Qayrawān: Risālatuhā al-dīnīya wa al-thaqāfīya fī al-Maghrib al-islāmī (Legend of Kairouan: Its Religious and Cultural Message in the Islamic Maghrib)*. Libya & Tunis, 1981.

Ashtor, E. "L'administration urbaine en Syrie médiévale." *Revista degli studi orientali* 31 (1956). Reprinted in *The Medieval Near East: Social and Economic History*. London, 1978.

———. "Républiques urbaines dans le Proche-Orient à l'époque des Croisades." *Cahiers de civilisation médiévale* 18 (1975).

Atger, A. *Les corporations artisanales en Tunisie*. Paris & Roussea, 1909.

Attal, R. *Les juifs d'Afrique du Nord: Bibliographie*. Jerusalem, 1973.

Aumerat. "La propriété urbaine à Alger." *R. A.* 41 (1897); 42 (1898).

Ayache, G. "Beliounech et le destin de Ceuta entre le Maroc et l'Espagne." *Hespéris-Tamuda* 13 (1972).

———. "La minorité juive dans le Maroc précolonial." *Hespéris-Tamuda* 25 (1987).

Bachrouch, T. "Le Sahel: Essai de définition d'un espace citadin"*C. T.* 34/137-138 (1986).

Bargès, J. J. L. (Abbé). *Tlemcen, ancienne capitale du royaume de ce nom: Souvenirs d'un voyage*. Paris, 1859.

Barrucand, M. *Urbanisme princier en Islam: Meknès, et les villes royales islamiques post-médiévales*. Paris, 1985.

Beck, H. L. *L'image d'Idrīs II: Ses descendants de Fās et la politique Sharīfienne des sultans marīnides (656-869/1258-1465)*. Leiden, 1989.

Bel, A. "Inscriptions arabes de Fès." *JA*, 11th ser., 9 (1917); 10 (1917); 12 (1918); 13 (1919).

Ben Achour, Mohamed El Aziz. *Les Ulama à Tunis aux XVIIIe et XIXe siècles*. Paris, 1977.

———. "Islam et contrôle social à Tunis aux XVIIIe et XIXe siècles." In *La ville arabe dans l'Islam*, eds. A. Bouhdiba & D. Chevallier. Tunis & Paris, 1982.

———. "Cadre urbain, habitat et structures sociales à Tunis dans la deuxième moitié du XIXe siècle." *C. T.* 34/137-138 (1986).

———. "Autorités urbaines de l'économie et du commerce de Tunis au XIXe siècle. *IBLA* (Tunis) 162 (1988); 163 (1989).

———. *Catégories de la société tunisoise dans la deuxième moitié du XIXe siècle*. Tunis, 1989.

Ben Talha, Abdelouahed. *Moulay-Idriss du Zerhoun*. Rabat, 1965.

Benchekroun, Mohamed. *La vie intellectuelle marocaine sous les Mérinides et les Waṭṭāsides*. Rabat, 1974.

Benslimane, Joudia Hassar. "Salé, étude architecturale de trois maisons traditionnelles." *Études et travaux d'archéologie* (Rabat) 7 (1979).

Berbrugger, A. *Histoire sur la peste en Algérie*. Vol. 2. of *Sciences médicales, Explorations scientifiques de l'Algérie*. Paris, 1847.

———. "Les anciens établissements de Constantine." *R. A.* 12 (1868).

Berque, J. "Ville et université: Aperçu sur l'histoire de l'école de Fez."*Revue historique de droit français et étranger* 27 (1949).

———. "Médinas, villeneuves et bidonvilles." *C. T.* 6/21-22 (1958).

———. "Cadis de Kairouan d'après un manuscrit tunisien." *R. O. M. M.* 13-14 (1973).

Bezzaz, Mohammed Amine El-. "La peste de 1798-1800 au Maroc." *Hespéris-Tamuda* 23 (1985).

Blachère, R. "Fès chez les géograghes arabes du moyen âge." *Hespéris* 18 (1934).

Bouali, Sid-Ahmed. *Les deux grands sièges de Tlemcen*. Alger, 1984.

Boyer, P. "L'évolution démographique des populations musulmanes du département d'Alger (1830/66-1948)." *R. A.* 98 (1954).

———. *La vie quotidienne à Alger à la veille de l'intervention française*. Paris, 1963.

Bressolette, H. & J. Delarozière. "El Mosara, jardin royal des Mérinides." *Hespéris-Tamuda* 18 (1978-9).

———. "Fès-Jadid de sa fondation en 1276 au milieu du XXe siècle." *Hespéris-Tamuda* 20 (1982); 21 (1983).

Brett, M. "The City-State in Medieval Ifriqiyā: The Case of Tripoli." *C. T.* 34/137-138 (1986).

Brosselard, Ch. *Les Khouan: De la constitution des ordres religieux musulmans*. Alger & Paris, 1859.

———. "Les inscriptions arabes de Tlemcen." *R. A.* 30 (1864).

Brown, K. L. "An Urban View of Moroccan History: Salé 1000-1800." *Hespéris-Tamuda* 12 (1971).

———. *People of Salé: Tradition and Change in a Moroccan City 1830-1930*. Manchester, 1976.

———. "The Uses of a Concept: 'The Muslim City'." In *Middle Eastern Cities in Comparative Perspective*, eds. K. Brown, M. Jolé, P. Sluglett & S. Zubaida. London, 1986.

Brunot, L. "Vocabulaire de la tannerie indigène à Rabat." *Hespéris* 3 (1923).

———. "La cordonnerie indigène à Rabat." *Hespéris* 33 (1946).

Brunschvig, R. *La Berbérie orientale sous les Ḥafṣides des origines à la fin du XVe siècle*. 2 vols. Paris, 1940-7.

———. "Urbanisme médiéval et droit musulman." *REI* 15 (1947).

———. "Justice religieuse et justice laïque dans la Tunisie des deys et des beys jusqu'au milieu du XIXe siècle." *SI* 23 (1965).

Būkārī, Aḥmed. *al-Zāwiya al-Sharqāwīyā al-Zāwiya Abī al-Ja'd, dawruhā al-ijtima'īyu wa al-siyāsīyu (The Zāwiya of the Sharqāwīyā The Zāwiya of Boujad, its Social and Political Role)*. Casablanca, 1985.

Buthaud, E. "Le gardiennage des souks de Tunis." *IBLA* (Tunis) 5 (1942).

Cades, D. *Essai sur l'histoire des Israélites de Tunisie*. Tunis, 1889.

Cahen, Cl. "Mouvements populaires et autonomisme urbaine dans l'Asie musulmane au moyen âge." *Arabica* 5/3 (1958); 6/1 (1959); 6/3 (1959).

Caillé, J. *La ville de Rabat jusqu'au protectorat français*. 2 vols. Paris, 1929.

Cambazard-Amahan, C. *Le décor sur bois dans l'architecture de Fès*. Paris, 1989.

Carette. C. *Recherches sur la géographie et le commerce de l'Algérie méridionale*. Vol. 2 of *Sciences historiques et géographiques, Explorations scientifiques de l'Algérie*. Paris, 1844.

Cat, E. *Essai sur la province romaine de Mauritanie césarinne*. Paris, 1891.

Célérier, J. "Les conditions géographiques du développement de Fès." *Hespéris* 19/1-2 (1934).

Centre d'Etudes et de Recherches Marxistes. *Sur le féodalisme*. Paris, 1971.

Chalmeta, P. "La ḥisba en Ifriqiya et al-Andalus: Étude comparative." *C. T.* 18/69-70 (1970).

———. *El señor del zoco en España*. Madrid, 1973.

Chalom, J. *Les Israélites de la Tunisie*. Paris, 1906.

Chater, Khélifa. "La ville tunisienne au XIXe siècle: Théorie et réalités." *C. T.* 26/103-104 (1978).

Chebbi,'Ali. "Maṣādir jadīda li-dirāsa ta'rīkh al-Shābbīya (New Sources for the Study of History of the Shābbīya)." *Rev. hist. maghreb* 13-14 (1979).

———. *Aḥmad b. Makhlūf al-Shābbī*. Tunis, 1979.

Chenntouf, Tayeb. "L'évolution du travail en Algérie au XIXe siècle: La formation du salariat." *R. O. M. M.* 31 (1981).

Cigar, N. "Conflict and Community in an Urban Milieu Fez under the Alawis (ca. 1666-1830)." *Maghreb Review* 10 (1978).

———. "Société et vie politique à Fès sous les premiers 'Alawite (ca. 1660-1830)." *Hespéris-Tamuda* 18 (1978-9).

Colin, G. S. "Noms d'artisans et de commerçants à Marrakech." *Hespéris* 12/2 (1931).

Corcos, D. "The Jews of Morocco under the Mérinides." *Jewish Quarterly Review* 54-55 (1964).

Cornet, H. "Les juifs de Gafsa." *C. T.* 3/10 (1955).

Coudray, A. "Relations commerciales de Tlemcen avec le Sahara et le Soudan." *Bulletin de la société de géographie d'Alger et de l'Afrique du Nord* 63/573 (1892).

Cresti, F. "Quelques observations et hypothèses sur la population et la structure sociale d'Alger à la période turque (XVIe-XVIIIe siècles)." *C. T.* 34/137-138 (1986).

———. "Apports et influences européens dans le domaine de la structure et de la construction des villes du Maghreb entre les XVIe et XIXe siècles." *C. T.* 44/157-58 (1991).

Cuevas, T. de. "El Ksar-el-Acabir." *Boletín de la sociedad geográfica de Madrid* 39 (1897).

Cuperly, P. "Un document ancien sur l'urbanisme au Mzab." *IBLA* (Tunis) 148 (1981).

Danon, V. "Les niveaux de vie dans la Hara de Tunis." *C. T.* 3/10 (1955).

Daoulati, Abdelaziz. *Tunis sous les Ḥafṣides: Evolution urbaine et activité architecturale*. Tunis, 1976.

Dā'ūd, Muḥammad al-Tiṭwānī. *Ta'rīkh Tiṭwān (A History of Tetuan)*. 8 vols. Tétouan, 1959-62.

De Castries, L'-Colonel H. "Les sept patrons de Marrakech." *Hespéris* 4 (1924).

De Cenival, P. "L'église chrétienne de Marrakech au XIIIe siècle." *Hespéris* 7 (1927).

———. "Le prétendu évêché de la ḳal'a des Beni Ḥammād." *Hespéris* 15/1 (1932).

Despois, J. "Kairouan: Origine et évolution d'une ancienne capitale musulmane." *Annales de géographie* 39 (1930).

———. *La Tunisie orientale: Sahel et basse steppe*. Paris, 1955.

Dessort, Ch. *Histoire de la ville Tunis*. Alger, 1924.

Deverdun, G. *Marrakech des origines à 1912*. 2 vols. Rabat, 1959-66.

Devoulx, A. "Notes historiques sur les mosquées et autres édifices religieux d'Alger." *R. A.* 4 (1860); 5 (1861); 6 (1862).

———. "Les édifices religieux de l'ancien Alger." *R. A.* 6 (1862); 7 (1863); 8 (1864); 9 (1865); 10 (1866); 11 (1867); 12 (1868); 13 (1869); 14(1870).

———. "Alger: Étude archéologique et topographique." *R. A.* 19 (1875); 20 (1876); 21 (1877); 22 (1878).

Djaït, H. *al-Kūfā: Naissance de la ville islamique.* Paris, 1986.

Djender, M. *Introduction à l'histoire de l'Algérie.* Alger, 1968.

Doumerc, B. "La ville et la mer: Tunis au XVe siècle." *C. T.* 34/137-138 (1986).

Doutté, E. *Marrakech.* Paris, 1905.

al-Dubīshī, 'Abd al-wahhāb. "'Alāqa al-salṭana al-marīnīya bi al-mujtama' al-fāsī (The Relation of the Marinid Sultanate to Fez Society)." In *The Proceedings of the Colloquium of 1988: al-Madīna fī ta'rīkh al-maghrib al-'arabī.* Casablanca, 1990.

Dufourcq, Ch, E. "La question de Ceuta au XIIIe siècle." *Hespéris* 42 (1955).

———. *L'Espagne catalane et le Maghrib aux XIIIe et XIVe siècles.* Paris, 1966.

Durand, P. "Boujad, ville sainte: Les marabout Cherkaoua." *Renseignements coloniaux de l'Afrique française* 41/2 (1931).

Eickelman, D. F. "Is there an Islamic City? The Making of a Quarter in a Moroccan Town." *IJMES* 5 (1974).

———. *The Middle East: An Anthropological Approach.* 2nd edition. New Jersey, 1989. Originally published in 1981. Translated into Japanese as *Chuto: Jinruigakuteki kosatsu* by Kazuo Otsuka. Tokyo, 1988.

Eisenbeth, M. "Les juifs en Algérie et en Tunisie à l'époque turque (1516-1830)." *R. A.* 96 (1952).

Exploration scientifique de l'Algérie pendant 1840, 1841, 1842. 39 vols. Paris, 1844-67.

La Faculté des Lettres et des Sciences Humaines. *The proceedings of the Colloquium of 1988: al-Madīna fī ta'rīkh al-maghrib al-'arabī (La Cité dans l'Histoire du Maghreb).* Casablanca, 1990.

Féraud, Ch. L. *Histoire des villes de la province de Constantine: Bougie.* Constantine, 1869.

———. "Les corporations de métiers à Constantine." *R. A.* 16 (1872).

Ferhat, Halima. "Le role de la minorité andalouse dans l'intervention Hafside à Sabta", *C. T.* 43/155-156 (1991).

———. "Famille et société à Sabta d'après l'ouvrage du cadi 'Iyyāḍ Madhāhib al-Ḥukkām (XIIème)." *Hésperis-Tamuda* 30/2 (1992).

al-Filālī, 'Abd al-'Azīz. "Ḥawl al-fatḥ al-'arabī al-islāmī li-madīna Qusanṭīna (On the Arabic and Islamic Conquest of Constantine)." *C. T.* 34/137-138 (1986).

Fogg, W. "Wazzan: A Holy City of Morocco." *Aberystwyth Studies* 13 (1934).

Gaillard, H. *Une ville de l'Islam: Fès.* Paris, 1905.

Gallagher, N. E. "Colonial Enthusiasts and Plague in Tunis 1818-1819." *Rev. hist. maghreb* 33-34 (1984).

García, G. E. "Unas 'ordenanzaz del zoco' del siglo IX: Traducción del más antiguo antecedente de los tratados andaluces de Ḥisba, por un autor andaluz." *al-Andalus* 22 (1957).

García-Arenal, M. "The Revolution of Fās in 869/1465 and the Death of Sultan 'Abd al-Ḥaqq al-Marīnī." *BSOAS* 41/1 (1978).
Gardet, L. "Humanisme musulman d'hier et d'aujourd'hui: Éléments culturels de base." *IBLA* (Tunis) 7 (1944).
———. *La cité musulmane: Vie sociale et politique*. Paris, 1954.
Gaudefroy-Demonbynes, M. "Sur quelques ouvrages du ḥisba." *JA* 230 (1938).
Gaudio, A. *Fès: Joyau de la civilisation islamique*. Paris, 1982.
Gautier, E. F. *Le passé de l'Afrique du Nord: Les siècles obscurs du Maghreb*. Paris, 1927.
Geertz, C., H. Geertz & L. Rosen. *Meaning and Order in Moroccan Society: Three Essays in Cultural Analysis*. Cambridge, 1979.
Gerber, J. S. *Jewish Society in Fez: Studies in Communal and Economic Life*. Ph. D. dissertation, Columbia University, 1972. Published in Leiden, 1980.
El-Ghoul, Fayçal. "Histoire d'une rumeur: La peste de Tunis de 1792." *C. T.* 36/143-144 (1988).
Gibb, H. A. R. & H. Bowen. *Islamic Society and the West*. 2 vols. London, 1950-7.
Goitein, S. D. *A Mediterranean Society*. 5 vols. Berkeley, 1967-88.
Golvin, L. *Aspects de l'artisanat en Afrique du Nord*. Paris, 1957.
———. "Mahdia à la période fatimide." *R. O. M. M.* 27 (1979).
———. "Alger à la période ottomane (rythme de vie)." *C. T.* 34/137-138 (1986).
Grandguillaume, G. "Une médina de l'ouest algérien: Nédroma." *R. O. M. M.* 10 (1971).
———. *Nédroma. L'évolution d'une médina*. Leiden, 1976.
Green, A. H. "The Tunisian Ulama and the Establishment of the French Protectorate, 1881-1892." *Rev. hist. maghreb* 1 (1974).
———. *The Tunisian Ulama, 1873-1915: Social Structure and Response to Ideological Currents*. Leiden, 1978.
Grey-Jackson, J. *An Account of the Empire of Morocco and the Districts of Sus and Tafilelt*. London, 1809.
Grunebaum, G. von. "The Muslim Town and the Hellenistic Town." *Scientia (Rivista di scienza)* 90 (1955).
———. "The Structure of the Muslim Town." *Memoir* (The American Anthropological Association) 81: *Islam: Essays in the Nature and Growth of a Cultural Tradition* (1955). Reprinted in London, 1961.
Guyot, R., R. Le Tourneau & L. Paye. "L'industrie de la poterie à Fès." *Bulletin économique marocaine* 2/10 (1934).
———. "Les relieurs de Fès." *Bulletin économique marocaine* 3/12 (1935).
———. "Les cordonniers de Fès." *Hespéris* 23 (1936).
al-Ḥabīb, Muḥammad. "al-Zāwiya wa āthāruhā fī al-mujtama' al-qayrawānī bidāya min muntaṣf al-qarn al-sābi' ilā nihāya al-qarn al-thāmin al-hijrī (The Zāwiya and its Influences on the Kairouan Society from the First Half of the 7th Century to the End of the 8th Century)." *Revue tunisienne de sciences sociales* 40-43 (1975).

Haëdo, D. *Topographia e historia general de Argel*. Valladlid, 1612.

Hakim, Besim Selim. *Arabic-Islamic Cities: Building and Planning Principles*. London, 1986. Translated into Japanese as *Isuramu toshi: Arabu no machizukuri no genri* by Tsugitaka Sato et al. Tokyo, 1990.

———. "The Role of the Urf." In *Urbanism in Islam: The Proceedings of the International Conference on Urbanism in Islam*. Vol. 2. Tokyo, 1989.

Hamy, E. T. "Cités et nécropoles berbères de l'Enfida, Tunisie Moyenne: Étude ethnographique et archéologique." In *Bulletin de géographie historique et descriptive*, Paris, 1904.

Ḥannānī, Muḥammad. "al-Asbāb wa al-asāṭīr al-murtabīṭa bi-ta'sīs al-mudun al-islāmīya bi al-maghrib (Reasons and Myths Related to the Foundation of the Islamic Cities in the Maghrib)." In *The Proceedings of the Colloquium of 1988: al-Madīna fī ta'rīkh al-maghrib al-'arabī*. Casablanca, 1990.

Hanoteau, A. & A. Letourneux. *La Kabylie et les coutumes kabyles*. 3 vols. Paris, 1893.

Hirschberg, H. Z. "The Salars and Negidim of Kairouan" (in Hebrew). *Zion* 23-24 (1958-9).

———. *A History of the Jews in North Africa*. 2 vols. Leiden, 1974. Originally published in Jerusalem, 1965 in Hebrew.

Hoenerbach, W. & J. Kolenda. "Šefšāwen (Xauen): Geschichte und Topographie einer Marokkanischen Stadt." *Welt des Islam* 14 (1973); 16 (1975).

Hopkins, J. "Sousse et la Tunisie orientale médiévales, vue par les géographes arabes." *C. T.* 8/31 (1960).

Hopkins, N. S. "Testour au XIXe siècle." *Rev. hist. maghreb* 17-18 (1980).

Hourani, A. H. & S. M. Stern, eds. *The Islamic City*. Oxford, 1970.

Ibn Tāwīt, Muḥammad. *Ta'rīkh Sabta (A History of Ceuta)*. Casablanca, 1982.

Idris, H. R. "Contribution à l'histoire de l'Ifriḳiya: Tableau de la vie matérielle et religieuse à Kairouan sous les Aglabites et les Fatimites d'après le Riyāḍ en Nufūs d'Abū Bakr el Mālikī." *REI* 10/1 (1936).

Iḥsāyan, 'Abd al-Ḥamīd. "al-Madīna al-maghribīya min khilāl al-tārikh al-faransī (The Moroccan City in French Studies)." In *The Proceedings of the Colloquium of 1988: al-Madīna fī ta'rīkh al-maghrib al-'arabī*. Casablanca, 1990.

al-'Ināwī, Muḥammad. "al-Mudun al-saḥilīya fī minṭaqa al-maghrib al-'arabī al-wasṭī ilā ḥudīd al-qarn al-rābi' al-hijrī (The Coastal Cities of Medieval Maghrib until the End of the 4th Century A. H.)." In *The Proceedings of the Colloquium of 1988: al-Madīna fī ta'rīkh al-maghrib al-'arabī*. Casablanca, 1990.

Johansen, B. "The All-Embracing Town and its Mosques: al-Miṣr al-Ǧāmi'." *R. O. M. M.* 32 (1981). Translated into Arabic as "al-Miṣr al-jāmi' wa masājiduhu al-jāmi'a." *al-Ijtihād* 7 (1990).

Jole, M. "L'hygiène publique et l'espace urbain: Exemple, Rabat." *Bulletin économique et social du Maroc* 147-148 (1983).

———. "Les villes et la politique de recherche française au Maroc." *Bulletin économique et social du Maroc* 147-148 (1983).

Joly, M. A. "Le siège de Tétouan par les tribus des Djebala, 1903-1904." *Arch. Mar.* 3 (1905).

Julien, Ch. A. *Histoire de l'Afrique du Nord: Tunisie-Algérie-Maroc*. Paris, 1931.

al-Junḥānī, al-Ḥabīb. "Tāhart: 'Āṣima al-dawla al-Rustamīya (Tahart: A Capital of the Rustamid Dynasty)." *Revue tunisienne de sciences sociales* 40-43 (1975).

Kacem, Ahmed. "Aḥbās al-'uthmānīya al-awā'il bi-Tūnis wa jam'īya al-awqāf al-inzāl (The Ḥabs and the Inzāl of the Early Ottoman Period in Tunisia)." *Rev. hist. maghreb* 37-38 (1985).

al-Kānūnī, Muḥammad b. Aḥmad al-'Abdī. *Āsfī wa mā ilayhi (Āsfī and the Surroundings)*. N. p., n. d.

Kenbib, Mohammed. "Les relations entre musulmans et juifs au Maroc, 1859-1945: Essai bibliographie." *Hespéris-Tamuda* 23 (1985).

———. "Les juifs de Tétouan entre la chronique et l'histoire." *Hespéris-Tamuda* 24 (1986).

Khalīfa, Aḥmad Idrīs. *al-Ta'rīkh al-maghribī li-madīna Sabta (The Maghribi History of the City of Ceuta)*. Rabat, 1988.

Khallāf, Muḥammad 'Abd al-Wahhāb. *Qurṭuba al-islāmīya fī qarn al-ḥādī 'ashara al-mīlādī al-khāmis al-hijri (Islamic Cordoba in the 11th Century A. D./5th Century A. H.)*. Tunis, 1984.

Kisaichi, Masatoshi. "Maguribu no chusei Isuramushakai to urama no shakaiteki yakuwari (Medieval Islamic Society of the Maghrib and the Social Roles of the Ulama: Based on the Biography of al-Ghubrīnī)."*Chuo Daigaku Ajiashi Kenkyu* 6 (1982).

———. "Toremusen ni okeru mittsu no meimon urama-ke (Three Distinguished Ulama Families in Tlemcen: Banū Maqqarī, Banū Marzūq and Banū 'Uqbānī)." In *Nairikuajia, Nishiajia no shakai to bunka*, ed. Masao Mori. Tokyo, 1983.

———. "Isuramutoshi no seikaku to toshishi no shodankai: Fesu no rekishi kara mita shiron (The Character of the Islamic City and the Stages of its Urban History: A Rough Sketch Based on the History of Fez)." *Isuramu no Toshisei Kenkyu Hokoku, Kenkyu Hokokuhen* (Institute of Oriental Culture, Univesity of Tokyo) 43 (1989).

Koehler, P. H. "La Kasba saadienne de Marrakech d'après un plan manuscrit de 1585." *Hespéris* 27 (1940).

Kraiem, Abdelmajid. "La résistance de Gabès à l'occupation française en 1881." *C. T.* 36/143-144 (1988).

La Motte, Y. de. *Aspects de la question des terres Habous dans le contrôle civile de Béjà*. Paris, 1949.

Lagardère, V. "Droits des eaux et des installations hydrauliques au Maghreb et en Andalus au XIème et XIIème siècles dans le Mi'yār d'al-Wanšarīsī." *C. T.* 37-38/145-148 (1988-9).

Lahmar, Mouldi. "Les hubus dans la société et le Šar' d'après le Mi'yār d'Wanšaīsī." *C. T.* 41-42/151-154 (1990).

Lallemand, Ch. *Tunis et ses environs*. Paris, 1890.

Lapidus, I. M. *Muslim Cities in the Later Middle Ages*. Cambridge, 1967.

———. "Muslim Cities and Islamic Societies." In *Middle Eastern Cites,* ed. I. M. Lapidus. Berkley, 1969.

———. "Muslim Urban Society in Mamlūk Syria." In *The Islamic City,* eds. A. H. Hourani & S. M. Stern. Oxford, 1970.

———, ed. *Middle Eastern Cities*. Berkeley, 1969.

Largash, D. "al-Madīna wa faḍā'uhā al-khārijīyū al-Munastīr fī al-qarn al-tāsi' 'ashara (The City and its Outskirts: Monastir in the 19th Century)." In *Mélanges Professeur Robert Mantran*. Zaghouan, 1988.

Latham, J. D. "Observations and the Text and Translation of al-Jarsīfī's Treatise on Ḥisba." *Journal of Semitic Studies* 5 (1960). Collected in London, 1986.

———. "Reconstruction and Expansion of Tetuan: The Period of Andalusian Immigration." In *Arabic and Islamic Studies in Honor of Hamilton A. R. Gibb,* ed. G. Makdisi. Leiden, 1965. Collected in London, 1986.

———. "Ibn 'Abd al-Ra'ūf on the Law of Marriage: A Matter of Interpretation." *The Islamic Quarterly*. 15. (1971). Collected in London, 1986.

———. "The Strategic Position and Defence of Ceuta in the Later Muslim Period." *The Islamic Quarterly*. 15. (1971). Collected in London, 1986.

———. "Towns and Cities of Barbary: The Andalusian Influence." *The Islamic Quarterly*. 16. (1972). Collected in London, 1986.

———. "The Rise of the 'Azafids of Ceuta." *Israel Oriental Studies* 2: *Memoriam Samuel Mikós Stern* (1972). Collected in London, 1986.

———. "Contribution à l'étude des immigrations andalouses et leur place dans l'histoire de la Tunisie." In *Recueil d'études sur les Moriscos andalous en Tunisie,* eds. M. de Epalza & R. Petit. Madrid & Tunis, 1973. Collected in London, 1986.

———. "The Later 'Azafids." *R. O. M. M.* 15-16 (1973). Collected in London, 1986.

———. "Towards the Interpretation of al-Saqaṭī's Observations on Grain and Flour-milling." *Journal of Semitic Studies* 23 (1978). Collected in London, 1986.

———. "The Interpretation of a Passage on Scales (Mawāzin) in an Andalusian Ḥisba manual." *Journal of Semitic Studies* 23 (1978). Collected in London, 1986.

———. "Some Observations on the Bread Trade in Muslim Málaga (ca. A. D. 1200)." *Journal of Semitic Studies* 29 (1984). Collected in London, 1986.

———. *From Muslim Spain to Barbary*. London, 1986.

Lavedan, P. *Géographie des villes*. Paris, 1936.

Lawless, R. I. "Tlemcen, Capital City of the 'Abd al-Wādids: A Study of the Functions of a Medieval Islamic City." *The Islamic Quarterly* 18/1-2 (1974).

Lawless, R. I. & G. H. Blake. *Tlemcen: Continuity and Change in Algerian Islamic Town*. Durham, 1976.

Le Tourneau, R. "L'activité économique de Sefrou." *Hespéris* 25 (1938).

———. *Fès avant le protectorat*. Casablanca, 1949.

———. *Les villes musulmanes de l'Afrique du Nord*. Alger, 1957.

———. *Fez in the Age of the Marinides*. Norman, 1961.
Le Tourneau, R. & L. Paye. "La corporation des tanneurs et l'industrie de la tannerie à Fès." *Hespéris* 21 (1935).
Lecuyer, E. "Les métiers constantinois à l'époque des Beys." *IBLA* (Tunis) 13 (1950).
Lespès, R. *Alger: Esquisse de géographie urbaine*. Alger, 1925.
———. *Alger: Etude de géographie et d'histoire urbaine*. Paris, 1930.
———. *Oran: Etude de géographie et d'histoire urbaine*. Alger & Paris, 1938.
Lessard, J-M. "Sijilmassa: La ville et ses relations commerciales au XIe siècle d'après El Bekri." *Hespéris-Tamuda* 10/1-2 (1969).
Lévi-Provençal, E. "Un document sur la vie urbaine et les corps de métiers à Seville au début du XIIe siècle: Le traité d'Ibn 'Abdūn." *JA* 224/2 (1934).
———. "La fondation de Fès." *AIEO* 4 (1938). Reprinted in *Islam d'Occident*. Paris, 1948.
———. *Las ciudades y las instituciones urbanas del Occcidente musulman en la Edad Media*. Tetouán, 1950.
———. *Documents arabes inédits sur la vie sociale et économique en Occident musulman au moyen âge*. Le Caire, 1955.
Lewicki, T. "L'état nord-africain de Tāhert et ses relations avec le Soudan occidental à la fin du VIIIe et au IXe siècles." *Cahiers d'études africaines* 8 (1962).
Lézine, A. *Mahdiya, recherches d'archéologie islamique*. Paris, 1956.
———. "Deux ribats du sahel tunisien." *C. T.* 15 (1956).
———. "Sur la population des villes africaines." *Antiquités africaines* 3 (1969).
———. *Deux villes d'Ifriqiyā: Sousse, Tunis*. Paris, 1971.
———. "Sur deux châteaux musulmans d'Ifriqiya, Raqqāda-Ajdabīya." *REI* 39/1 (1971).
Liauzu, Cl. "Orientations et redéfinitions des recherches françaises sur les villes du monde arabe." *C. T.* 34/137-138 (1986).
Lourido, Diaz R. "Documentos ineditos sobre el nacimiento de Dār al-Bayḍā' (Casablanca) en el siglo XVIII." *Hespéris-Tamuda* 15 (1974).
Lucas, G. *Fès dans le Maroc moderne*. Paris, 1937.
Luccioni, J. *Les fondations pieuses <Habous> au Maroc depuis les origines jusqu'à 1956*. Rabat, n. d.
Mantran, R. "L'évolution des relations entre la Tunisie et l'Empire ottoman du XVIe au XIXe siècle." *C. T.* 7/26-27 (1959).
Marçais, G. *Les Arabes en Berbérie du XIe au XIVe siècle*. Paris & Constantine, 1913.
———. *Manuel d'art musulman: L'architecture, Tunisie, Algérie, Maroc, Espagne, Sicile*. 2 vols. Paris, 1926.
———. *Tunis et Kairouan*. Paris, 1937.
———. "L'urbanisme musulman." In *5e Congrès de la Fédération des Sociétés Savants de l'Afrique du Nord*. Alger, 1940. Reprinted in *Mélanges d'histoire et d'archéologie de l'Occident musulman*. Vol. 1. Algér, 1957.
———. "La conception des villes dans l'islam." *Revue d'Alger* 2 (1945).

———. *Berbérie musulmane et l'Orient au moyen âge*. Paris, 1946.
———. *Tlemcen*. Paris, 1950.
———. *L'architecture musulmane d'Occident: Tunisie, Algérie, Maroc, Espagne, Sicilie*. Paris, 1954.
———. "Considérations sur les villes musulmanes et notamment sur le rôle du mohtasib." *La ville: Recueil de la société Jean Bodin* 6 (1954).
Marçais, W. *Musée de Tlemcen*. Paris, 1906.
———. "L'islamisme et la vie urbaine." In *L'académie des inscriptions et belles-lettres, Comptes rendus*. Paris, 1928.
———. "Comment l'Afrique du Nord a été arabisée." *AIEO* 4 (1938); 14 (1956).
Marçais, W. & G. Marçais. *Les monuments arabes de Tlemcen*. Paris, 1903.
Martin, L. "Description de la ville de Fès, quartier du Keddan." *RMM* 9 (1909).
Marty, P. "La zaouia de Sidi Ben Achir à Salé." *REI* 7 (1933).
———. "Corporations et syndicats de Tunisie: La corporation tunisienne des soyeux." *Extrait de REI* année 1934 (1935).
al-Marzūqī, Muḥammad. *Qābis: Janna al-Dunyā (Gabes: A Paradise of the World)*. Cairo & Baghdad, 1962.
Maslow, B. & H. Terrasse. "Une maison mérinide de Fès." *R. A.* 79 (1936).
Masqueray, E. *La formation des cités chez les populations sédentaires de l'Algérie: Kabyles du Djurdjura, Chaouia de l'Aouras, Beni Mezab*. Paris, 1886. Reprinted in Aix-en-Provence, 1983.
Massiera, P. "M'sila du Xe au XVe siècle." *C. T.* 22/85-86 (1974).
Massignon, L. "Les corps de métiers et la cité islamique." *Revue internationale de sociologie* 28 (1920).
———. "Enquête sur les corporations d'artisans et de commerçants au Maroc." *RMM* 58 (1924).
———. "Complément à l'enquête de 1923-1924 sur les corporations musulmanes." *REI* 1/2 (1927).
Mazzīn, Muḥammad. *Fās wa bādīyatuhā: Musāhamatu fī ta'rīkh al-Maghrib al-Sa'dī, 1549-1637 (Fez and its Rural Surroundings: Contributions to the History of the Sa'dids, 1549-1637)*. 2 vols. Rabat, 1986.
Mediano, F. R. "Los ulemas de Fez y la conquista de la ciudad por los Sa'dies." *Hesperis-Tamuda* 30 (1992).
Mercier, E. *Constantine avant la conquête française*. Constantine, 1878.
———. *Histoire de l'Afrique septentrionale depuis les temps les plus reculés jusqu'à la conquête française (1830)*. 3 vols. Paris, 1888-90.
———. *Le Habous ou Ouakf, ses règles et sa jurisprudence*. Alger, 1896.
———. *Constantine et histoire de Constantine*. Constantine, 1903.
Mercier, L. "Les mosquées et la vie religieuse à Rabat." *Arch. Mar.* 8 (1906).
Mercier, M. *La civilisation urbaine au Mzab: Étude de sociologie africaine*. Alger, 1922.
———. *Étude sur le 'waqf' abadhite et ses applications au Mzab*. Alger, 1927.

Meunier, D. "Le consulat anglais à Tétouan sous Anthony Hatfeild (1717-1728)." *Rev. hist. maghreb* 19-20 (1980).

Mezzine, Larbi. *Le Tafilalt: Contribution à l'histoire du Maroc aux XVIIe et XVIIIe siècles.* Rabat, 1987.

Michaux-Bellaire, E. & C. Justinard, eds. *Villes et tribus du Maroc.*
Vol. 1-2: *Casablanca et Chaâouïa.* Paris, 1915.
Vol. 3-6: *Rabat et sa région.* Paris, 1918-20.
Vol. 7: *Tanger et sa zone.* Paris, 1921.
Vol. 8: *Les Aït Ba Amran.* Paris, 1930.
Vol. 9: *Districts et tribus de la haute vallée du Drá.* Paris, 1931.
Vol. 10-11: *Région des Doukkala.* Paris, 1932.

Michaux-Bellaire, E. & G. Salmon. "Description de la ville de Fès." *Arch. Mar.* 11 (1907).

Miura, Toru. "Gaiku to minshuhanran: 15-16 seiki no Damasukusu (The Quarter and Popular Movements: Damascus in the 15th and 16th Centuries)." In *Sekaishi eno toi.* Vol. 4: *Shakaiteki ketsugo.* Tokyo, 1989.

Miyaji, Kazuo. "Furansu Kita-afurika (Recent Trends of African Studies Abroad: North African Studies in France)." *Afurika Kenkyu* (Tokyo) 11 (1971).

Miyaji, Mieko. "Kokuminshakai no keisei to toshi-sonraku kankei no henyo (Formation of the National Society and the Transformation of the Urban-Rural Relations: A Case of Nédroma in the Western Algeria)." In *Afurika shakai no keisei to tenkai,* ed. Morimichi Tomikawa. ILCAA, Tokyo University of Foreign Studies, 1980.

Monchicourt, Ch. "La région de Tunis." *Annales de géographie* 23 (1904). Reprinted in *C. T.* 22/87-88 (1974).

———. "La fête de l'Achoura." *Revue tunisienne* 17 (1910).

———. "Études kairouanaises." *Revue tunisienne* (nouvelle série) 7-8 (1931); 9 (1932); 13-14 (1933); 17 (1934); 26 (1936).

———. *Kairouan et les Chabbia.* Tunis, 1939.

Montagne, R., ed. "Naissance du prolétariat marocain." *Cahiers de l'Afrique et l'Asie* 3 (1951).

Mouline, Saïd. "La ville et la maison arabo-musulmanes." *Bulletin économique et social du Maroc* 147-148 (1983).

al-Moutabassir. "Les Habous de Tanger." *RMM* 1 (1907).

Naciri, M. "Salé: Étude de géographie urbaine." *Revue de géographie du Maroc* 3-4 (1963).

Nakamura, Kojiro. "Ibn Khaldūn's Image of City." In *Urbanism in Islam: The Proceedings of the International Conference on Urbanism in Islam.* Vol. 2. Tokyo, 1989.

Nouschi, A. "Constantine à la veille de la conquête française." *C. T.* 3 (1955).

Oumlil, Ali. "Ibn Khaldoun et la société urbaine." In *La ville arabe dans l'Islam,* eds. A. Bouhdiba & D. Chevallier. Tunis & Paris, 1982.

Pacha, Najet. *Le commerce au Maghreb du XIe au XIVe siècles.* Tunis, 1976.

Pauty, E. "Rapport sur la défense des villes et la restauration des monuments historiques." *Hespéris* 2 (1922).

———. "Villes spontanées et villes créées en Islam." *AIEO* 9 (1951).

Pellegrin, A. *Histoire illustrée de la ville de Tunis et de sa banlieue*. Tunis, 1955.

———. "Sidi Bou Said: Le site et son histoire." *Bulletin économique et social de la Tunisie* 107 (1955).

Pellissier, E. *Mémoires historiques ou géographiques sur l'Algérie*. Vol. 6 of *Sciences historiques et géographiques, Explorations scientifiques de l'Algérie*. Paris, 1844.

Pèretie, A. "Les Médrasas de Fès." *Arch. Mar.* 18 (1912).

Pirenne, H. *Les villes du moyen âge*. Bruxelles, 1927.

Qaddūr, Aḥmad. "Ta'thīr al-Mudun al-Kabīra 'alā al-Shabka al-ḥaḍarī fī al-'ahd al-muwaḥḥidīn (The Influence of the Big Cities on the Urban Network under the Almohad Period)." In *The Proceedings of the Colloquium of 1988: al-Madīna fī ta'rīkh al-maghrib al-'arabī*. Casablanca, 1990.

Quemeneur, J. "Contribution à l'étude des corporations tunisiennes: Les Belghajia de Tunis." *IBLA* (Tunis) 5 (1942).

Raymond, A. "Le déplacement des tanneries à Alep, au Caire et à Tunis, l'époque ottomane: Un <Indicateur> de croissance urbaine." *Rev. hist. maghreb* 7-8 (1978).

———. "La conquête ottomane et le développement des grandes villes arabes: Le cas du Caire, de Damas et d'Alep." *R. O. M. M.* 27 (1979).

———. *Les grandes villes arabes à l'époque ottomane*. Paris, 1985.

———. "Les caractéristiques d'une ville arabe <moyenne> au XVIIIe siècle: Le cas Constantine." *C. T.* 34/137-138 (1986).

Revault, J. *Palais et demeures de Tunis (XVIe et XVIIe siècles)*. Paris, 1968.

———. *Palais et demeures de Tunis (XVIIIe et XIXe siècles)*. Paris, 1971.

———. *Le fondouk des Français et les consuls de France à Tunis (1660-1860)*. Paris, 1984.

Revault, J., L. Golvin & A. Amahan. *Palais et demeures de Fès. 1. Époques mérinide et saadienne (XIVe-XVIIe siècles)*. Paris, 1985.

R'honi, Aḥmad Sidi. *Historia de Tetuán*. Tetuán, 1953.

Ricard, P. "Les métiers manuels à Fès." *Hespéris* 4 (1924).

Rosen, L. "Muslim and Jewish Relations in a Moroccan City." *IJMES* 3 (1972).

Rosenberger, B. "Tamdult, cité minière et caravanière présaharienne (IXe-XIV^{e}s)." *Hespéris-Tamuda* 11 (1970).

Rosenberger, B. & H. Triki. "Famines et épidémies au Maroc aux XVIe et XVIIe siècles." *Hespéris-Tamuda* 14-15 (1973-4).

Sa'd Ghrad. *'Uyūn al-Munāzalāt (the Origins of Debates)*. Tunis, 1976.

Salmon, G. "Les Chorfa idrissides de Fès d'après Ibn at-Tayyib al-Qadiry." *Arch. Mar.* 1 (1904).

———. "Confréries et zaouia de Tanger." *Arch. Mar.* 2 (1904-5).

———. "Les Chorfa Filāla et Djilāla de Fès d'après Ibn at-Tayyib al-Qadiry." *Arch. Mar.* 3 (1905).

———. "Notes sur Salé." *Arch. Mar.* 3 (1905).

———. "Le culte de Moulay Idriss et la Mosquée des Chorfa." *Arch. Mar.* 3 (1905).

al-Sawīsī, 'Abd Allāh. *Ta'rīkh Ribāṭ al-Fatḥ (A History of Rabat).* Rabat, 1979.

Sayous, A. *Le commerce des Européens à Tunis depuis le XII*e *jusqu'à la fin du XVI*e *siècle.* Paris, 1929.

Sebag, P. "Le bidonville de Borgel." *C. T.* 6/23-24 (1958).

———. "Les juifs de Tunisie au XIXe siècle d'après J. J. Benjamin II." *C. T.* 28 (1959).

———. *L'évolution d'un guetto nord-africaine: La Hara de Tunis.* Paris, 1960.

———. "La peste dans la Régence de Tunis aux XVIIe et XVIIIe siècles." *IBLA* (Tunis) 109 (1965).

———. *Tunis au XVII*e *siècle: Une cité barbaresque au temps de la course.* Paris, 1989.

Sebti, Abdelahad. *Aristocratie citadine, pouvoir et discours savant au Maroc précolonial.* Thesis of History and Civilizations, University of Paris VII, 1984.

Sghaïr, Noureddine. "En marge d'une lecture du chroniqueur Mahmud ben Said Magdish: Les relations culturelles Mashreq-Maghreb et les 'Ulama de Sfax." *Rev. hist. maghreb* 43-44 (1986).

al-Shābbī, 'Alī. see Chebbi, 'Ali

al-Sharīf, Muḥammad al-Ḥādī. "al-Wāridāt wa al-mustawridūn bi-Tūnis fī al-qarn al-thāmin 'ashar (Imports and Importers in Tunis in the 18th Century)." *C. T.* 34/137-138 (1986).

Shatzmiller, M. "Les premiers Mérinides et le milieu religieux de Fès: L'introduction des Médersas." *SI* 43 (1976).

———. *L'historiographie mérinide: Ibn Khaldūn et ses contemporains.* Leiden, 1982.

Shinar, P. *Islam maghrébin contemporain: Bibliographie annotée.* Paris, 1983.

al-Shiyāẓimī, Muḥammad & al-Ḥājjī al-Subā'ī, trans. *Madīna Azammūr wa ḍawāḥīhā (The City of Azammūr and its Vicinity).* Salé, 1989. The Arabic translation of the second part of *Villes et tribus du Maroc,* vol. 11 written by E. Michaux-Bellaire and C. Justinard.

Sievers, P. von. "Military, Merchants and Nomads: The Social Evolution of the Syrian Cities and Countryside during the Classical Period, 780-969/164-358." *Der Islam* 56/2 (1979).

Solignac, J. M. "Travaux hydrauliques Ḥafṣides de Tunis." *R. A.* 79 (1936).

Spies, O. "Islamiches Nachbarrecht nach schafiitischer Lehre." *Zeitschrift für vergleichende Rechtswissenschaft* 42 (1927).

Stambouli, F. "Système social et stratification urbaine au Maghreb." *Revue tunisienne de sciences sociales* 50-51 (1977).

Stambouli, F. & A. Zghal. "La vie urbaine dans le Maghreb précolonial." *Revue tunisienne de sciences sociales* 36-39 (1974).

———. "Urban Life in Precolonial North Africa." *The British Journal of Sociology* 27/1 (1976).

Stern, S. M. "The Constitution of the Islamic City." In *The Islamic City*, eds. A. H. Hourani & S. M. Stern. Oxford, 1970.

Sulaymān, 'Abd al-Ghannī. "al-Ḥayāt al-ijtimā'īya fī madīna Marrākush fī 'aṣr al-Murābiṭīn wa al-Muwaḥḥidīn (Social life in Marrakesh in the Almoravid and Almohad Periods)." *C. T.* 34/137-138 (1986).

Takagi, Keiko. "Chunijia Sidi Bu Saido no machi no kukanhyosho (Tunisia: Spatial Symbols in Sidi Bou Said)." *Isuramu no Toshisei Kenkyu Hokoku, Kenkyu Hokokuhen* (Institute of Oriental Culture, Univesity of Tokyo) 72 (1990).

Talbi, M. "Quelques données sur la vie sociale en Occident musulman d'après un Traité de Ḥisba du XVe siècle." *Arabica* 1 (1954).

al-Talīlī, 'Abd al-Raḥmān. "Waṣf al-mudun al-maghribīya fī Kitāb Ṣūra al-Arḍ (Description of the Maghribi Cities in Ṣūra al-Arḍ of Ibn Ḥawqal)." *C. T.* 34/137-138 (1986).

al-Ṭammār, Muḥammad b. 'Amr. *Tilimsān 'abra al-'uṣūr: Dawruhā fī siyāsa wa ḥaḍāra al-Jazā'ir (Tlemcen in History: Its Political Role and the Civilization of Algeria).* Alger, 1984.

Tawfīq al-Ṭayyibī, Amīn. *Dirāsāt fī ta'rīkh madīna Sabta al-islāmiya (Study on the History of the Islamic City of Ceuta).* Tripoli, 1989.

al-Tāzī, 'Abd al-Hādī. "Taṣmīm al-Madina min khilāl al-maṣādir al-'arabīyat wa al-ajnabīyat (City Planning through Arabic and Non-Arabic Sources)." In *The Proceedings of the Colloquium of 1988: al-Madīna fī ta'rīkh al-maghrib al-'arabī*. Casablanca, 1990.

Temimi, Abdeljelil. "Min ajli kitāba ta'rīkh al-Jāmi' al-A'ẓam bi-madīna al-Jaẓā'ir (On the Documents of the Great Mosque in Algiers)." *Rev. hist. maghreb* 19-20 (1980).

Terrasse, H. "Les portes de l'arsenal de Salé." *Hespéris* 2 (1922).

———. "Note sur les ruines de Sijilmassa." *R. A.* 79 (1936).

———. "Trois bains mérinides." In *Mélanges W. Marçais*. Paris, 1950.

Terrasse, J. *Essai sur les biens habous en Algérie et en Tunisie*. Lyon, 1899.

Torrès Balbas, L. "Les villes musulmanes d'Espagne et leur urbanisation." *AIEO* 6 (1942).

Touati, Houari. "Note sur l'organisation des corporations de métier à Alger au XVIIIe siècle." *C. T.* 34/137-138 (1986).

———. "Les corporations de métiers à Alger à l'époque ottomane." In *Mélanges Professeur Robert Mantran*. Zaghouan, 1988.

Turner, B. S. *Marx and the End of Orientalism*. London, 1978.

Université Muḥammad V, ed. *L'évolution des rapports villes-campagnes au Maghreb*. Rabat, 1988.

Urvoy, D. "La structuration du monde des Ulémas à Bougie au VIIe/XIIIe siècle." *SI* 43 (1976).

———. *Le monde des Ulémas andalous du V/XIe au VII/XIIIe siècle*. Genève, 1978.

Vallvé, B. J. "Descripción de Ceuta musulmana en el siglo XV." *al-Andalus* 27 (1962).

Weber, M. *Wirtschaft und Gesellschaft*. Tübingen, 1922.

Weiner, J. B. "Anglo-Moroccan Relations in the First Decade of the Occupation of Tangier (1662-1672)." *Hespéris-Tamuda* 18 (1978-9).

Wickens, G. M. "al-Jarsīfī on the Ḥisba." *The Islamic Quarterly* 3/3-4 (1956-7).

Wirth, E. "Villes islamiques, villes arabes, villes orientales?: Une problématique face au changement." In *La ville arabe dans l'Islam,* eds. A. Bouhdiba & D. Chevallier. Tunis & Paris, 1982.

Woodford, J. S. *The City of Tunis*. Cambridgeshire, 1990.

Yacono, X. "Peut-on évaluer la population de l'Algérie en 1830?" *R. A.* 98 (1954).

Zbiss, Slimane-Mostafa. *La médina de Tunis*. Tunis, 1981.

Ziadeh, N. *Mudun 'arabīya (Arab Cities)*. Beirut, 1965.

MASHRIQ

Toru Miura

Introduction

This chapter examines the cities of Mashriq, the central Islamic lands extending from Egypt in the west to the borders of Turkey and Iran in the east. Within Islamic urban studies, these cities, as represented by Mecca, Baghdad, Cairo and Damascus, are considered the prototypes of the "Islamic city" for two reasons. The first is historical, in that the Islamization which proceeded alongside Arabization developed from a city base: Islam had come into being among the mercantile cities of the Arabian Peninsula, and the Arab-Islamic armies, conquering Iraq, Syria and Egypt, set up garrison towns (*amṣār*), such as Basra, Kufa and Fustat, from which Islamization subsequently advanced. Umayyad Damascus, 'Abbasid Baghdad, and Fatimid and Mamluk Cairo were political and cultural centres for the whole Islamic world and the gathering places for a wide variety of people artisans and merchants, the ulama and pilgrims on their way to Mecca.

Secondly, these cities have been the subject of considerable historical documentation and research. The ulama, whose stage was the city, produced historical materials such as chronicles, topographies and geographies, biographical dictionaries and travel records, as well as legal texts and literary works, and in them were concerned not only with political events but also with the occupations of the inhabitants of the city, the architectural fabric, and the wider range of urban life. As a result, the Arab world is fortunate in possessing a variety of historical narrative material, unlike Iran and Turkey, whose authentic records are largely confined to those of the governing power, in a way comparable to the situation in China. In addition, travel records written by the enormous numbers of European merchants and pilgrims who visited the region contain descriptions of distinctive scenes and customs, while from the late 19th century Europeans living in the Arab lands they had colonized conducted surveys of historical sites in the cities and produced detailed maps and statistical data. Urban studies were in fact launched by

Europeans using such historical materials, and they gave rise to an image of the "Islamic city" which possessed a landscape and a culture different to those of European cities. As M. Kisaichi points out in the chapter on the Maghrib, the model of the "Islamic city" was formed by 19th century French studies, in the main, of the Maghrib and reworked into a more elaborate framework as a result of 20th century urban studies of Mashriq, centring on Syria. The result was a general acceptance of the concept that the Arab city and the Islamic city were identical. Though criticism of this view was advanced as a result of urban studies on Mashriq, particularly Syria, after the Second World War, there still remains a tendency to regard the Islamic city and the Arab city as being the same; for example, the 1976 symposium, "The Islamic City," discussed the traditional structure and the modernization of Islamic cities from a historical point of view, but the cities discussed were only those of the Arab world, including the Maghrib (*The Islamic City,* ed. R. B. Serjeant, 1980).

Studies of the cities of Mashriq have a long history, and since the Second World War there has been greatly increased activity in the field by scholars from the various Arab countries of the region, with histories of regional cities and towns being published in large numbers. Since it is beyond the bounds of possibility for the efforts of a single person to produce a bibliographical study that covers all of the documentation available, it is my hope in this chapter to throw light upon the trends and topics of urban studies through an examination of books and articles according to theme and approach. The bibliographies of the books mentioned in this chapter can be employed for further reading in the field.

Part One gives an historical outline of trends in urban studies from the 19th century until the present, with the intention of illuminating the process by which the general picture of the "Islamic city" was formed out of individual studies of Arab cities, and of clarifying the various questions raised by that process. Part Two introduces basic research that has been undertaken on the topography, politics, society and economy of the main cities of Iraq, Syria and Egypt respectively, and examines how the themes of topography, the ulama, the waqf, merchants and artisans, and the quarter have been dealt with in the various regions and how they differ. By so doing I hope to point out differences in the historical characteristics of the cities and in research viewpoints according to place and time even within the Arab heartland, and thereby to suggest how to comprehend the Arab city in a way that incorporates compound views. That I have not dealt with the cities of the Arabian Peninsula is due to my own limitations, and I await the day when this deficiency can be amended. I conclude by consolidating the various issues in research region by region and suggesting issues for further study.

I. Historical Outline

1. Physical Structures and Topography

European interest in the cities of Mashriq stemmed from the reports of travellers to holy and commercial sites in Syria and Egypt and their comments on the prosperity of the cities in Islamic lands and on their distinctive buildings and scenes. P. H. Dopp, *Le Caire* (1950) introduces such travel records from the time of the Mamluk dynasty; more recently, twenty-seven such works have been edited and published in the series *Collection des Voyageurs Occidentaux en Égypte* by the Institut Français d'Archéologie Orientale du Caire. What drew the interest of the enormous numbers of pre-twentieth century travellers from Europe and what appears over and over again in their travel records were the massive citadels (*qal'a*), religious facilities such as mosques and madrasas, the narrow zigzagging streets and the houses with few outer openings. Well-known works by long-term residents which give an outline of the geography and history of the cities include A. Russell, *The Natural History of Aleppo* (1794), A. von Kremer, *Mittelsyrien und Damascus* (1853), id., *Topographie von Damascus* (1854), E. W. Lane, *Cairo: Fifty Years Ago* (1896), S. Lane-Poole, *Cairo* (1892) and *The Story of Cairo* (1902), and D. Margoliouth, *Cairo, Jerusalem and Damascus* (1907). In addition, E. W. Lane, *An Account of the Manners and Customs of the Modern Egyptians* (1836), a best-seller during the Victorian era, is an important record of the life of the common people in Cairo. A large number of these books contain illustrations of buildings and famous places in the city, which allow glimpses of the life of the people at the time.

Experts in art and architecture conducted surveys of buildings like citadels and mosques, the results of which were published with drawings and plans. The pioneer of such works was P. Coste, *Architecture arabe ou monuments du Caire* (1837-9). Two comprehensive studies by K. A. C. Creswell of architecture in Iraq, Syria and Egypt from the Arab Conquest to the Mamluk dynasty are *Early Muslim Architecture* (1932-40) and *The Muslim Architecture of Egypt* (1952-9). They are useful aids to research, with bibliographies appended to each chapter organized according to city and structure, listing chronologically historical sources by Arabs and travel records and surveys by Europeans. E. Herzfeld and F. Sarre, *Archäologische Reise im Euphrat und Tigris Gebiet* (1911-20) deals with Iraq, and E. Herzfeld, "Damascus: Studies in Architecture," (1942-48) with Syria. K. A. C. Creswell, *A Bibliography of the Architecture, Arts and Crafts of Islam* (1961, 1973, 1985) gathers together materials on art and architectural history.

Urban topography can also be studied through chronicles, geographies and topographies written in Arabic. During the 'Abbasid Caliphate (9th-10th centuries) large numbers of geographies were written, which recorded brief information about the geography, history, industries, etc. of the cities. After the 10th century topographies and histories concerning particular cities began to be produced, typical of which were *Ta'rīkh Baghdād* (Chronicle of Baghdad) by al-Khaṭīb al-Baghdādī (d. 1071), *Ta'rīkh Madīna Dimashq* (Chronicle of Damascus) by Ibn 'Asākir (d. 1176) and *al-Khiṭaṭ* (Topography of Egypt) by al-Maqrīzī (d. 1442). This literary tradition has continued into this century and comprises an important source for information regarding urban history. Historical reconstructions of urban topography using these sources and the verification of monuments recorded in them on maps produced as a result of field research reached a peak in the period 1920-1930. The pioneer of such studies was G. Le Strange, *Baghdad during the Abbasid Caliphate* (1900). Similar studies for other sites include K. Wulzinger and C. Watzinger, *Damaskus* (1921-4), and two works by J. Sauvaget, *Alep* (1941) and "Esquisse d'une histoire de la ville de Damas," (1934), which deal with the urban development of Aleppo and Damascus respectively from Hellenic and Roman times until the Ottoman Empire. M. Clerget, *Le Caire* (1934) gives vital statistical information about the population in the form of maps and diagrams, using the aforementioned historical sources, the *Description de l'Égypte* produced by the Napoleonic expedition of 1798, and statistical data compiled at the beginning of the 20th century.

These works suggest a characteristic feature of prewar urban studies, the large number of elaborate surveys and studies that were made of buildings and the overall physical structure. Such surveys could no longer be carried out easily in the postwar period, after Arab states gained independence from European colonial rule and as antagonism grew during the decade 1950-1960. This meant that during this period the maps, drawings and inscriptions that had been collected and produced previously were quoted widely and diffused somewhat uncritically. Field research by Western scholars began again in the 1980s in cooperation with local authorities, with more weight being given to studies of suqs, domestic housing and the residential quarters than to monuments such as religious structures. Noteworthy are the attempts to reproduce the urban structure by means of historical materials and field research, such as the French study of Cairo, B. Maury et al. (ed.), *Palais et maisons* (1982-3), and the German studies, H. Gaube and E. Wirth, *Aleppo* (1984) and D. Sack, *Damaskus* (1989). In addition, M. Scharabi, *Der Bazar* (1985) is a survey by a town planner of markets and caravansaries in the main cities of the Middle East, from Andalus to Turkey and Iran. The study is richly supplemented with drawings and photographs, and there are bibliographies appended for each city. Université de Provence, *L'habitat traditionnel dans les pays musulmans* (1988-91) is a comprehensive study by a group of historians and architects concerning houses and housing in the Mediterranean world.

2. Political and Social Structures

If studies of buildings and overall physical structure may be termed research into the hardware of cities, those of the political and social structures such as the works of L. Massignon concerning the guild and of J. Sauvaget concerning the quarter are investigations into their software. In "Les corps de métiers et la cité islamique" (1920), Massignon states that the essence of an Islamic city is the market and the systematic organization of the various types of occupations associated with it, rather than the city walls and public law that characterized the Graeco-Roman city. He maintains that the origins of the autonomous corporations (guilds) are to be traced to the Qarmatians, who rallied merchants and artisans to their movement in the 9th and 10th centuries. His opinion was based initially on his own observations in Baghdad and Fez, but he later backed his views with a survey of artisan and merchant guilds in Morocco and Syria ("Enquête sur les corporations," 1924; "La structure du travail à Damas," 1953) and pointed out connections between the spiritual base of the guild and that of the Qarmatians and the *futuwwa* ("La 'futuwwa'," 1952). The distinctive feature of Massignon's theory is that he takes into consideration his own field surveys together with specialist research in the history of thought, so that there is a problem in establishing a positive historical base for his theories; nevertheless, his line of research was continued in B. Lewis, "The Islamic Guilds" (1937), which asserts that guilds with a religious character had proliferated in the Islamic world by the 15th century. The Massignon-Lewis theory of the "Islamic guild" was followed by H. A. R. Gibb and H. Bowen, *Islamic Society* (1950-7) and L. Gardet, *La cité musulmane* (1954), and in the 1950s, it was considered that autonomous corporations of merchants and artisans probably existed in the Islamic cities as well. T. Yukawa, "An Historical Outline of Studies concerning the Medieval Islamic Guild" (J., 1974) is a concise review of these studies.

While Sauvaget, in the course of studies on Aleppo and Damascus, showed on the one hand that the residential quarters performed the role of self-governing communities, he was of the opinion that they were "mosaic societies" without any sense of integration with the city as a whole ("Esquisse d'une histoire," 1934; *Alep,* 1941). The arguments of both Massignon and Sauvaget are based on the model of the commune, the self-governing municipality of medieval Europe, and they looked to the guilds and the residential quarters as being responsible for self-government in the "Islamic city". Since though on the whole they depended more on the field surveys they conducted themselves than on historical documents their work is defective as historical research. E. Ashtor, in "L'administration urbaine" (1956) and "L'urbanisme syrien" (1958), was the pioneer in systematic research using historical documents. He showed that in the cities of Syria between the 10th and 12th centuries the qadi (judge), the muhtasib (official overseeing artisans and markets) and the *ra'īs* (headman) performed an autonomous role by protecting the interests of the townspeople and the city as a whole with the help of the *aḥdāth* (urban militia). However, he was unable to go conceptually beyond the framework of the European commune, in that he saw the failure of a merchant or artisan class to develop as frustrating city self-government.

Studies in legal history, such as O. Spies, "Islamisches Nachbarrecht" (1927) and R. Brunschvig, "Urbanisme médiéval et droit musulman" (1947), showed that minute regulations concerning rights of streets, houses and walls developed in Islamic law (sharia), and that Islamic law also performed a role in providing for individual privacy in the crowded cities, in particular regarding the protection of women, and for public welfare. Such studies explain the background which gave rise to the zigzagging alleys and the closed-off houses that comprise the characteristic landscape of cities in Islamic lands, and at the same time suggest the existence of Islamic law as a special type of software.

G. von Grunebaum, "The Structure of the Muslim Town" (1955), skillfully combining the two streams of European research, physical and institutional, was instrumental in formalizing the concept of the "Islamic city," with its own landscape and values different from those of Western Europe. von Grunebaum's study revealed his opinion that unlike Greek and medieval Western European cities, which were integrated politically by the self-government of the citizens themselves, Islamic cities allowed the free entry and exit of people of different occupations and social classes, and a specified form of citizenship did not emerge; the townspeople lived in guilds and quarters differentiated according to religion, race and occupation, with no system in place for political integration, but with integration coming rather by religious ideology alone. Islam is the "religion of the townspeople," and only in towns which possessed a congregational Friday mosque (*jāmi'*) could the religious duties of a Muslim and Islamic social ideas be completely fulfilled. von Grunebaum's thesis was not so much his own creation as derived from the idea of the "Islamic city" as held by traditional Orientalists. The tenor of the arguments of both W. Marçais and Gibb had been that Islam was the religion and culture of the city, and A. Mez, *Die Renaissance des Islams* (1922) had placed strong emphasis on the role played by cities having a congregational mosque. Sauvaget had spoken of a mosaic society where the quarters and guilds were communes but the city as a whole lacked unity. von Grunebaum's argument brought together previous work in urban studies and he succeeded in building a model of the "Islamic city" through the integrating concept of an Islamic city which was not the Western European concept of the self-governing city but that of "Islam as a city culture," and visualized it in terms of the congregational mosque. (For the genealogy of this kind of idea of the "Islamic city," see J. Abu-Lughod, "The Islamic City" (1987), and T. Miura, "Some Remarks on Urbanism in Islam" (J., 1990). It is apparent that studies of urban political and social structure conducted up to the 1950s discussed Islamic cities in terms of their similarities and differences to the European commune cities. These studies assess the degree of self-government the Islamic cities had on the one hand, and emphasize their Islamic features on the other. Since both images were projected by the Western European commune model, either positively or negatively, there has been a growing criticism of the model itself since the 1960s.

Cl. Cahen, "Mouvements populaires et autonomisme urbain" (1958-9) led such criticism. In this work, Cahen voices his objection to arguments which stress the uniqueness of cities under Arab-Islamic domination and which contrast the autonomy of citizens in the cities of ancient and medieval Western Europe and the absence thereof in cities in Islamic lands and suggests there is a need to conduct comparative studies among the Western European, Byzantine and Islamic worlds, with no temporal or spatial demarcation between the Islamic world and the others. He investigated the autonomous role played by the *'ayyār* and *aḥdāth* gangs in their protection of the quarters and the city and the spiritual tradition of the *futuwwa* which underlay it and, in particular, by identifying the *futuwwa* as the encompassing spirit, he brought a new line of development to the methodology employed so far, which had discussed only comparatively whether or not self-government occurred. In "Zur Geschichte der städtischen Gesellschaft" (1958), he argues that Islamic cities maintained a social continuity from Late Antiquity until the 11th century and that cities with Islamic characteristics appeared only after the 12th century.

I. M. Lapidus also challenged von Grunebaum's theory of the Islamic city in *Muslim Cities in the Later Middle Ages* (1967) and "Muslim Cities and Islamic Societies" (1969) and has offered a new model for research. He criticizes such dichotomies as the European and the Asian, the communal and the noncommunal, and the urban and the rural as having given rise to an artificially created image of the "Islamic city" with a landscape and values system different to those of the rural village. In addition, he points out that in a structural analysis of Islamic society, with its high fluidity and non-differentiation in social terms, it is essential to elucidate the functions and mutual interaction of social organizations and networks (family, ethnicity, neighbourhood, law schools, Sufi orders, patron-client relationships, etc.) and that it is possible to transcend dichotomies such as those mentioned above through the study of the city as a "process" rather than through its physical form. He thus criticizes the methodology used by followers of Max Weber, who recognized city government, and especially self-government, only in terms of formal institutions and an urban-rural dichotomy. Lapidus took the position that basically both urban centres and rural villages achieve local integration through mutual and habitual traffic, and that they do not have a different structure at all, in physical, social, economic or cultural respects. By analyzing urban structure as a microcosm of society, it is possible, he says, to analyze social structure, to ascertain its historical development, and to make structural comparisons. In this he shares common ground with Weberian typology. Later "networks" became Lapidus's keyword, and he worked towards constructing a methodological model encompassing the historical development of Islamic societies and the total structure (for further details, see pp. 116-8).

Around the same time (1965) a symposium was held at Oxford University entitled "The Islamic City." There, Cahen delivered a severe criticism of Massignon's guild theory ("Y a-t-il eu des corporations professionnelles?," 1970), and S. M. Stern criticized the sterility of the statement that Islam is an "urban civilization," suggesting that specific questions need to be asked in order to examine the characteristics that constitute the city. Also, rejecting Massignon's theory of the medieval guild as a product of fantasy, Stern recommended a positive consideration of the elements of the absence of corporate municipal institutions, popular disorders, the notables, the quarters, and the militias as contributing to the loose structure of the Islamic city, rather than merely as the germ of self-government or its lack ("The Constitution of the Islamic City," 1970). The significance of Lapidus's and Stern's arguments is in their acknowledgment that it is not possible to analyze the pluralistic and fluid Islamic city in terms of formal systems and structures like citizenship and self-governing communities. Their method of analysis, an examination of networks, suits the social realities of the "informal and unstructured" (Lapidus). To summarize, while von Grunebaum was aware of the looseness of structure of Islamic cities, in that all could enter and leave freely, he was unable to discover a framework to evaluate it positively; Lapidus on the other hand has provided a new perspective by demolishing the model of the commune in urban theory.

As a result of Lapidus's epoch-making definition, since the latter half of the 1960s various internal and external networks have been discussed in detail, and research into the political and social structures of individual cities or regions is thriving. A typical example is Abdul-Karim Rafeq, *The Province of Damascus* (1966), which describes the political and social structures of the Ottoman province of Damascus through the multifaceted activities of the military, the ulama, merchants and the residential quarters. Since the 1970s he has been using sharia-court registers to examine the actual state of the economic and social relations between the city and the countryside. A. Raymond, also using sharia-court registers and similar materials, started out by describing changes in the political order through an examination of the situation of artisans and merchants in Ottoman Cairo in *Artisans et commerçants* (1973); he published many subsequent pioneering studies on the composition of the inhabitants, the institution of waqf, the quarters, and popular movements in Ottoman Cairo, Damascus and Aleppo and presented his general criteria of Arab cities in *Grandes villes arabes* (1985). S. D. Goitein, *A Mediterranean Society* (1967-88), using the wealth of documents and historical material found in the Jewish synagogue of Fustat, attempts a reconstruction of the occupations and classes, the family, and the daily life of the time, giving specific data and examples. J. Abu-Lughod, *Cairo* (1971) seeks to abstract the social characteristics marking the thousand-year-old city of Cairo, combining her own sociological survey with the historical research of Clerget and others. The study is extremely interesting for its sociologist's approach to urban history as a response to an historian's social research.

The 1980s have seen a large amount of detailed analytical study of political and economic conditions in cities at particular periods, employing waqf documents, sharia-court registers of the Mamluk and Ottoman periods, records of Ottoman Imperial Council (*mühimme defteri*)and the Ottoman land survey register (*tapu defteri*). One type of such study (such as works on Cairo by N. Hanna, D. Behrens-Abouseif, L. Fernandes, etc., and J.-P. Pascual's study of Damascus) uses waqf documents to make topographical reconstructions of particular localities and concrete investigations of the structure and function of religious institutions and waqf properties in the cities and of the role of governors, merchants and the ulama in urban development. A second type (studies on Damascus by M. A. Bakhit and K. K. Barbir) uses Ottoman government documents such as land survey registers and imperial commands to examine the city administration and its relationship to the central government. A third type (studies of Damascus and Aleppo by A. K. Rafeq and A. Abdel Nour, and studies of Jerusalem by H. Lutfi and A. Cohen) uses sharia-court registers to describe the social and economic conditions of townspeople in terms of private houses and commercial facilities. Because these studies all use primary materials they are able to paint a vivid picture of the multiple relationships and historical change in specific societies, and so provide concrete counter-evidence against the stereotyped view of the "Islamic city."

Since the 1970s, rapid urbanization and intensified urban-based social movements in the Middle East have called attention to the importance of urban research in political science and sociology. K. Brown et al. (eds.), *État, ville et mouvements sociaux au Maghreb et au Moyen-Orient* (1989) is the report of a symposium held by scholars in such fields as sociology, anthropology and history. E. Burke, "Towards a History of Urban Collective Action" (1989) shows that the Islamic state, whether described in terms of Marxism or Weberism, was recognized as the government of rulers and the bureaucracy and that society was not considered as a political process, and he discusses the characteristics and political meaning of collective action in cities from 1750 to 1980 from the viewpoint of the moral role of Islam. S. Zubaida, "Class and Community in Urban Politics" (1989) and Ch. Pickvance, "Social Movements in the City or Urban Movements" (1989) reexamine the validity of concepts such as class, community and city in Middle Eastern urban studies. Cl. Liauzu, one of the editors of the report, in an article "Sociétés urbaines et mouvements sociaux" (1986) introduces English documents concerning urban society and organizes them accurately by topic and outlook in terms of urban studies.

Today, scholars are taking as their subjects social networks such as the ulama, merchants, artisans, Sufi orders, the quarters, the family, outlaws, and patron-client relationships to shed positive light on cities and local societies at particular periods. At the same time though, it has become increasingly difficult to deal with questions which transcend a region or view a problem over a longer period of time. Can Lapidus's network theory, which took the first steps in this research and which provided the theoretical base for it, now be of use as a common framework for the studies of individual cities which have begun to fragment? As D. F. Eickelman, "Is There an Islamic City?" (1974) has already pointed out, Lapidus's theory is not one of the Islamic city but of Islamic society, and its direction is towards dissolving the individual meaning of the city as a framework for analysis and comparison. Regarding this, B. Johansen, "The All-Embracing Town and its Mosques" (1981) takes account of criticism of the theory of the Islamic city as held in the past and shows that Islamic legal texts accorded a position to cities different to that of rural villages, both socially, economically and politically. Of great significance is how Muslims themselves seek to understand the changing set of conditions of the city, using legal texts, rather than defending the Orientalist theory of the Islamic city. Further, as Komatsu has pointed out, the Soviet social and economic historian O. G. Bol'shakov stresses the significance of discussing the city as the concentration of surplus production and a center for redistribution, and in "The Medieval City of the Near East" (R., 1984), while he evaluates Cahen's socio-economic historical research highly, he exhibits a critical view of Lapidus and his lack of recognition of any difference between city and rural village (see pp. 290-3). When paying attention to socio-economic functions there is the need for further examination of the role the city plays within the region and the state.

3. Research in Arab Countries

Urban studies in Arab countries, like those in the West, began with research into the structure of, and changes in, religious and political monuments. For Cairo there is the "Map of Islamic Historical Monuments in Cairo" (A., 1948-51) compiled by the Egyptian Department of Survey (Maṣlaḥa al-Misāḥa), based on a survey in 1947 and for Damascus archaeological and historical investigations have been directed by La Direction Générale des Antiquités et des Musées (al-Mudīrīya al-'Āmma) as well as the historical research into historical remains by the scholars Muḥammad Aḥmad Dahmān and Ṣalāḥ al-Dīn al-Munajjid. In Iraq topographical studies of cities such as Baghdad, Basra, Kufa, Samarra, and Mosul were carried out by scholars centring on Ṣāliḥ Aḥmad al-'Alī of the Iraq Academy (al-Majma' al-'Ilmī al-'Irāqī). For Syria, there is a wealth of studies being published, using chronicles and topographies, concerning the history of regional cities such as Hama, Homs, Karak, Jerusalem and Ghaza.

These studies are on the whole concerned with an examination of historical sources and though they provide proofs concerning historical materials, some lack the analysis and conclusion valued by Western scholars; nevertheless, they do include valuable points of view that are missing from Western research. An excellent study is Ṣāliḥ's *The Social and Economic Systems of Basra in the First Century of the Hijra* (A., 1953). This work analyzes as far as feasible the actual state of urban administration in Basra in the 8th and 9th centuries, taking into account wages and prices, and food, clothing and lodging, using primarily historical sources, but also legal texts and literary works. Western research, even today, remains ensconced within the limits of historical narrative writings in the narrowest sense; Ṣāliḥ's work suggests that legal texts and literary works are of use in studies of social history. The same tendency can also be seen in B. M. Fahad, *The Common People of Baghdad in the 5th Century of the Hijra* (A., 1967). There are in addition a fairly large number of detailed and concrete studies being done by local scholars concerning artisans and their crafts, markets, houses, town planning, and genealogies of local notables.

A second type of research is the social and economic, employing sharia-court registers and waqf documents. A. K. Rafeq's study using a series of sharia-court registers reveals through inheritance and trade the state of society and economic activities of urban dwellers in Syria from the 16th to the 19th centuries. M. M. Amīn, *Waqf and Social Life in Egypt* (A., 1980) describes how the waqf system supported the economy, society and culture in Mamluk Cairo. The work of these scholars has a great depth of erudition, and is marked by an extensive use of historical documents.

A third type of study is the published memoirs and collections of photographs concerning the everyday life of ordinary people in the 19th and 20th centuries. They provide a means of knowing how the Arabs themselves saw their lives. A fourth type represents the growing interest in Arab countries in urban studies and the beginnings of a discussion on the "Islamic city." Symposia have been held in Cairo in 1969 to commemorate the 1000th anniversary of the founding of the city (*Colloque international*, 1972; *Abḥāth al-nadwa al-duwalīya*, 1970-1); in Syria, on the subject of Damascus; in Iraq, "The City and City Life" (ed. Ṣāliḥ A. A., 1988); and in Saudi Arabia in 1980, *The Arab City* (eds. I. Serageldin and S. El-Sadek, 1982) and in 1981, *Islamic Architecture and Urbanism* (ed. A. Germen, 1983) and in 1987, *The Middle East City* (ed. A. Y. Saqqaf, 1987). Among the work being done, B. S. Hakim, *Arabic-Islamic Cities* (1986) and M. A. S. 'Uthmān, *The Islamic City* (A., 1988) have taken up the subject of Islamic law as the criterion determining both the external and internal structures of city life, and have attracted attention by presenting the concept of the "Islamic city" from a Muslim Arab point of view as a city governed and managed by Islamic law. H. Djaït, *al-Kūfa* (1986) and N. AlSayyad, *Cities and Caliphs* (1991) reject the static Orientalist approach to the "Islamic city" and discuss the Islamic and Arab elements in city construction in the early Islamic period using historical sources. Their analyses cannot be said to be persuasive enough but they do represent a reaction to Lapidus's view of an unstructured urban society.

4. Japanese Research

So far we have been examining the directions urban research has taken, in terms of themes and methods of approach, primarily through Western studies from the 19th century to today. In broad terms, the Second World War marked the boundary between the study of external components and that of the internal structure, and the time around 1960 delineated research into the official institutions, such as the guild and the qadi, from that into the social groups making up the city and the operations of their networks. Even in physical studies interest has in recent years grown away from public facilities such as the mosque and the citadel toward private spaces, such as markets, houses and the quarter, in response to the growth of importance as research topics of artisans, merchants and the quarters in response to the network theory. In addition, research is being done to reconstruct the plans of houses and quarters by means of waqf documents and sharia-court registers. Means are thus being developed in various places to make a concrete clarification of the internal structure of the city in terms of both physical structures and internal components, rather that relying, as in the past, on an urban theory that touches only externals and on an abstract theory of civilizations.

Islamic urban studies in Japan, on the other hand, could not be said to have been popular before the beginning of the "Urbanism in Islam" project in 1988. Arab-Islamic historical research in Japan has centred on state systems, topics such as the taxation system, the land system and the military system, with little concern for the city as a subject for specific study. Given such conditions, in 1970, when Western academics were criticizing previously held ideas about the "Islamic city" and when there was a great turn in the direction that research was taking, interest was spurred by a study meeting, called "Islam and the City," held at ILCAA (the Institute for the Study of Languages and Cultures of Asia and Africa, Tokyo University of Foreign Studies), which produced an introduction to the debate between 1950 and 1960 about the "Islamic city', in Sh. Maejima, "Islam and the City" (J., 1971). T. Sato "The Characteristics of the Muslim City" (J., 1982) introduced the directions of research in Arab lands together with a summary of the condition of Islamic urban studies in the West; and Y. Itagaki, in works such as "Arab Political Culture and Nation Building" (J., 1978), pointed out the "urban character" of the Middle Eastern region and Islam from the latter half of the 1970s.

During the 1980s original research concerning urban society based on historical sources included T. Sato "'Ayyārūn in Baghdad" (J., 1983) and A. Goto, "The Free City of Mecca" (J., 1983) and "The People of the Free City of Mecca" (J., 1984). Goto sees Meccan society at the time of the rise of Islam as a free city where "no official system of headmen, councils and public institutions existed," and his theory of the free city is in antithesis to and criticism of the interpretation of M. M. Watt and others who regarded Mecca as a tribal society. Goto stresses that what is called the clan or the tribe were flexible units which realigned themselves according to circumstances and that the basis of society was contracts among independent individuals. Here he takes the same position as he did in "The Social Structure of Arab Society in the Early Islamic Period" (J., 1970, 1977) where he discussed the houses "of free entry" which welcomed as *ḥalīf* (confederates) not only blood kinsmen but also those who were unrelated. In "The People of the Free City of Mecca" he links society as the matrix for such individuals with the Mecca's characteristic as a mercantile city. He amplifies this point in the series of papers which include "Mecca and Medina in the 7th Century" (J., 1989) and "On Urbanism in Islam" (J., 1988), developing the ideas of the free Islamic city and the free society of the Middle East, and stressing the urban character of the whole Middle East and the growth of mercantile cities based on the great agricultural productive power of the region from ancient times, contrasting them with the "closed" European concepts of citizens and the city based on citizenship, and criticizing the European-centred urban studies carried out in the past and their historical distortions. His opinions are brought together in *Mecca and Islamic Urban Society*, (J., 1991). Goto's theory of the free city is refreshing in that it gives an unexpected twist to the concept of "freedom" as held in European urban theory. With this as a start, the journal *Sobun* (1988) published a series discussing the "free city of Islam." Goto shares common ground with Lapidus in that he does not make any distinction between the urban and the rural, and abstracts "an absence of institutionalization" in political and social structures from the actuality of the city, but differs from him in that whereas Goto sets up free individuals as the basis for his theory, Lapidus develops the network theory with his attention focused on the mutual relations and functions among social groups. Goto, both in terms of theory and social model, measures generalization and abstraction based on the free individual; in the future though it will be necessary for him to discuss how the social order was maintained among free individuals and over regional differences and temporal changes.

II. Studies According to Region and City

In section II, we will examine the history of studies of a number of cities in the regions of Iraq, Syria and Egypt, in that order. My intention in using such a structure is to elucidate the topic by taking up the particular characteristics of research into the cities that we are interested in, looking at differences in the types of historical documentation available and in the ways the subject has been examined, according to both city and period.

1. Iraq

Studies of the cities of Iraq allow us to know their plans from the earliest period of Islam, since Basra and Kufa were set up after the Arab-Islamic conquest and Baghdad was established with the founding of the 'Abbasid Caliphate.

Basra and Kufa

Basra, in southern Iraq, and Kufa, in central Iraq, are the oldest Islamic garrison cities (*amṣār*), set up in 638-639 as centres of government and military administration by the conquering army. L. Massignon, who visited Kufa and other Iraqi cities in 1908, wrote "Mission en Mésopotamie" (1912) and produced a pioneering work about the plan of the garrison town in "Explication du Plan de Kufa" (1935). Using the historical records of al-Balādhurī (d. 892), al-Ya'qūbī (d. 897) and others, he showed that seven quarters for each of the tribal units in the army were established around a central area consisting of the palace, the congregational Friday mosque and the plaza. K. al-Janābī, in *An Outline of the Planning of the City of Kufa* (1967), presents a rectangular city plan using historical records together with excavation reports of the governor's residence (*dār al-imāra)* and other places, and makes a detailed investigation of the governor's residence, the mosques, the streets, the houses, and the market. H. Djaït, *al-Kūfa* (1986), as Kisaichi points out (pp. 43-4), uses historical documents to compare the city plan of Kufa with other cities, such as Babylon, Mecca, Basra and Baghdad, and noteworthy is his investigation from a critical stance regarding the theory of the "Islamic city." He shows that the plan of Kufa is characterized by a planned duality of a central public space with the palace and the mosque, and a surrounding residential area (*khiṭaṭ*). Compared with Basra, which was constructed at the same time, it shows an intention towards urban life in the planned positioning of the residential area. In this it is an Islamic urban model, approximating the later cities of Wāsiṭ and Baghdad, and he stresses that here is a hallmark of Arab civilization.

In "Explication du plan de Basra" (1954), Massignon suggests that Basra consisted of central facilities like the palace and the congregational Friday mosque in conjunction with five quarters, for each of the tribes. Massignon's study only describes the outline of the city plan using geographies; Ṣāliḥ A. A., *The Social and Economic Systems of Basra in the First Century of the Hijra* (A., 1953) reconstructs the social life of the city through chronicles, legal texts and literary works, and he includes as much information as possible about the composition of the inhabitants, the administration, the work of merchants and artisans, as well as information about wages, prices and the essentials of food, clothing and accommodation. While he has skillfully collected and arranged separate reports, it is regrettable that he has not made a systematic analysis of them. He includes tables showing the organization of the inhabitants, taking the clans and tribes as units, and reveals that the quarters (*khiṭṭa*) were allocated according to tribe and clan and that they were used as administrative units, for example in the payment of allowances or blood money. Ṣāliḥ also wrote *Topography of Basra in the Early Islamic Period* (A., 1986), a compendium of the various topographies and their reports about the quarters, mosques, the palace, and canals. A. J. Naji and Y. N. Ali, "The Suqs of Basrah" (1981) examines the formation and the positioning of markets in Basra in the 7th and 8th centuries. F. M. Donner, "Tribal Settlement in Basra" (1984) uses biographical dictionaries to examine the composition of the inhabitants of Basra, focusing on ulama families who had moved to the city in the first century of the Hijra. This represents a forward step in this type of research, previous works having tended to use the descriptions in the chronicles indiscriminately. Ch. Pellat, *Le milieu baṣrien et la formation de Ǧāḥiẓ* (1953) discusses the cultural features of Basra, where the great Arab writer al-Jāḥiẓ had been born and brought up in the 9th century. Pellat writes that in ninth century Basra, with its diversity of population, the tribalism of the early period had melted into a cosmopolitan Muslim culture, with the different cultures of the Arabs, Persians, Indians, and Greeks mixed together, and that the literary form of al-Jāḥiẓ developed among the diverse types of people to be found in a port town. Though Pellat describes the features of Basra as a cultural background to the writings of al-Jāḥiẓ, such urban studies by literary scholars are so rare in the West as to make the work unique.

Wāsiṭ

Wāsiṭ was a base the Umayyad Caliphs placed in the province of Iraq halfway between Basra and Kufa to avert attempts at opposition in those cities. A. Q. S. al-Ma'āḍīdī, *Wāsiṭ in the Umayyad Era* (A., 1976) investigates the construction of the city, the migration of settlers, the financial and administrative systems, and the process of economic prosperity. In 1983, he published a sequel called *Wāsiṭ in the 'Abbasid Era* (in Arabic).

Baghdad

Baghdad, established by the order of al-Manṣūr, the second 'Abbasid Caliph, in 766, early drew the attention of scholars because of its distinctive plan, encircled by triple round walls. Topographical studies subsequently mounted. In 1900, G. Le Strange wrote *Baghdad during the Abbasid Caliphate*, combining the rich supply of topographical reports such as that of al-Khaṭīb al-Baghdādī (d. 1071; *Ta'rīkh Baghdād*) with maps made during the 19th century by Felix Jones and others, through which he was able to describe how the city grew and expanded around the Round City of al-Manṣūr's time with the construction of quarters such as al-Karkh and new palaces such as al-Ruṣāfa. In the eight maps of different areas he indicates important facilities such as palaces, mosques, madrasas and canals, and these maps have been used extensively by scholars. It appears that Le Strange identified the positions of buildings based on the placements of more than 500 edifices that had been listed by F. Jones in "Memoirs on Baghdad" (1857). E. Herzfeld, in *Archäologische Reise im Euphrat und Tigris Gebiet*, vol. 2 (1920), investigated surviving constructions such as the Mustanṣirīya Madrasa and reconstructed the triple walls of the Round City in plane and elevation. The four volume work includes studies of cities like Seleucia, Ctesiphon, Samarra, Mosul, and Raqqa and contains maps of the cities and numerous illustrations. Creswell, in *Early Muslim Architecture*, vol. 2 (1940) made a technical study of brick mounds and other remains and looked for the origins of the circular plan in the circular plans of Assyrian camps and of cities such as Ebra and Hatra. The 'Abbasid city was north-west of the modern Baghdad, and with the exception of the 'Abbasid palace, dating from the 12th century, and the Mustanṣirīya Madrasa, few buildings of the time remain. Therefore even now we are greatly dependent in the topographical study of Baghdad on the maps F. Jones made.

Further investigations were added to the above studies after the Second World War. J. Lassner, *The Topography of Baghdad in the Early Middle Ages* (1970), is an English translation of the first volume of al-Khaṭīb al-Baghdādī's *Ta'rīkh Baghdād*, the topographical introduction, together with descriptions from other historical documents. He makes a comparative study, including detailed notes, based on historical textual criticism, regarding the credibility of the descriptions and historical changes. He adds his own study at the end, in which he deals with the character of the Round City as the court of the 'Abbasid Caliphs, and addresses the questions of the increase in numbers of congregational Friday mosques with the growth of the city and of the formation of the markets. The importance of Lassner's annotated translation can be inferred from the fact that Ṣāliḥ translated it into Arabic in 1983. In "Massignon and Baghdad" (1966), reprinted in the above volume, Lassner shows, quoting R. M. Adams, *Land behind Baghdad* (1965) and having quantitatively considered the expansion of the villages surrounding Baghdad from the Seleucid period to the time of early Islam, that the prominent growth of Baghdad, with an area of 7000 hectares and a population of at least 300,000, was due to administrative factors related to Baghdad as the capital of the Caliphate and that in the city area multinucleurization proceeded outwards to the suburbs centring on marketplaces and mosques. Thus he criticizes Massignon's view of the city with a centre and organized occupational groups arranged around it. While Lassner explains the circular plan in terms of economic rationalism and security, Ch. I. Beckwith, "The Plan of the City of Peace" (1984) points out that Khālid, the designer of the plan, was of the family of ministers, the Barmaks, who were of Central Asian-Iranian origin, that the "round cities" of Iraq are not perfectly circular and their origins may be traced to Dārābgird and Ghūr in Iran, and that the construction of the circular fortification closely resembles the Buddhist temples of Balkh, a region associated with the Barmaks. This argument pierces a blind spot among Arab researchers, and it holds great interest in terms also of the cultural relations between Iraq and Iran. G. Makdisi, in "The Topography of Eleventh Century Baghdad" (1959) translates the description of Ibn 'Aqīl (d. 1119) into English and investigates topographical changes (such as the construction of the city wall on the east bank) under the Seljuks after the 11th century.

In 1971, the Iraqi Department of Archaeology and the Iraqi-Italian Institute of Archaeology of Baghdad began a joint investigation of Baghdad, conducting a grid survey of monuments in the Karkh and Ruṣāfa quarters. This study too was based on the list of buildings F. Jones had compiled; data concerning position, plan and date of construction were checked using historical sources, including waqf documents (the majority of which remains in Istanbul, having been removed there in 1840 by the Ottoman government), and field research. The results were published in V. Strika and J. Khalīl, "Preliminary Report" (1973-4) and id., "The Islamic Architecture of Baghdād" (1987). In his introduction to the latter work, Strika traces the history of research into the topography of Baghdad, and this is of use as bibliographical data.

Topographical studies by Arab scholars include M. Jawād and A. Sūsa, *Topographical Guide to Baghdad* (A., 1958), which gives an historical survey from the construction of Baghdad until 1918, but which includes little that is new since it only introduces the main madrasas and *ribāṭs* (Sufi convents). Sūsa, *A Collection of Maps of Baghdad* (A., 1952) consists of sixteen historical maps from the 'Abbasid, Buwayhid and Seljuk periods until the present century. The maps of the 'Abbasid, Buwayhid and Seljuk periods show the main buildings and the names of streets and quarters, and are useful when reading historical documents, but no indication is given regarding the authority on which the identification has been made. Jones's map showing the street network and the quarters has been reproduced, and on the modern map are given the names of the quarters, their size and statistics about the residents. The collection is an important resource for the study of Baghdad topography. An example of serious research is Ṣāliḥ, *Baghdad, the City of Peace: Buildings and the Residential System at the Beginning of the 'Abbasid Caliphate* (A., 1985). Only the first part concerning the west bank has so far been published; the first volume deals with the formation of the Round City and the second volume with suburbs such as the Karkh quarter. It is interesting that he deals with residential space such as houses, quarters, markets and streets (sg. *sikka*, *darb*) rather than public facilities such as the palaces and the congregational mosques, painstakingly gleaning information from chronicles and biographical dictionaries as well as topographies. The many street names that refer to individuals is indicative that the Caliph al-Manṣūr, the founder of Baghdad, allocated the streets *(sikka)* between the inner and outer walls of the castle to the military commanders, and distributed lots in the suburbs to his retainers. Ṣāliḥ's work concentrates on gathering reports from historical documents, but from this it is possible that he will go on to discuss the process of formation of quarters and shops.

Ṣāliḥ dealt with city administration in *Administrative Institutions and Public Facilities in Baghdad* (A., 1988), which supplements the previous work, using a wide range of historical material to discuss the institutions of city administration such as the *wālī* (governor), the *shurṭa* (police force) and the qadi, as well as their locations in the early part of the 'Abbasid Caliphate. Massignon, "Cadis et naqibs baghdadiens" (1948-52) lists those who filled the office of qadi or *naqīb* during the 'Abbasid Caliphate. For markets and the organizations of merchants and artisans there are two works, S. I. S. al-Shaykhlī, *Craft-Guilds in the 'Abbasid Period* (A., 1976) and H. A. M. al-Kubaysī, *The Markets of Baghdad until the Beginning of the Buwayhi Age* (A., 1979). The former suggests that the planning of Baghdad and other Islamic cities shows that areas were allocated according to occupational grouping, and that guilds formed in connection with popular movements such as the Qarmatians to represent the interests of merchants and artisans. al-Shaykhlī uses unpublished manuscripts such as the *Kitāb al-futuwwa* to investigate the conditions of artisan life, such as wages and dress, as well as morals and guild rituals. Finally he turns his attention to market inspection and the censorship of public morals (*ḥisba*) and studies the relationship between the state and the guilds. The latter work, dealing with the location of the suqs and urban development, activities of merchants and money changers, prices, and economic change, discusses the functioning of commerce in the 'Abbasid state. G. Makdisi, "Muslim Institutions of Learning" (1961) examines the constitution and educational content of the madrasas under Seljuk rule and was one of the first studies to consider the cooperation between the ulama and the military rulers. J. Chabbi, "La fonction du ribat à Bagdad" (1974) is an examination of the construction and functioning of the *ribāṭ* in Baghdad between the 11th and 13th centuries and points out that *ribāṭ* construction began under influence from Khurasan, that until the first half of the 12th century they were used not only by Sufis but as centres of political propaganda, and that their construction was stimulated by the traditionalist climate in the latter part of the 12th century, and that the Caliph al-Nāṣir tended to give them over to the sole use of mystics.

Between the latter half of the 9th century and the 12th century there was a surge in popular movements in Baghdad, beginning with the *'ayyār* gangs. The pioneer in these studies was Cahen, "Mouvements populaires" (1958-9). More detailed treatment of the subject is given in Fahad, *The Common People of Baghdad in the 5th Century of the Hijra* (A., 1967) and S. Sabari, *Mouvements populaires à Baghdad* (1981). By "common people" (*'āmma),* Fahad means everyone from artisans and merchants to farmers, soldiers, thieves and *'ayyārūn*. In the first half of the work he describes elements of daily life, such as what people ate and wore and where they lived, and their religious ceremonies, and in the latter half he discusses social relationships among the people, such as relations between men and women and relations between the people and the headmen (sheikhs) of the quarters; he concludes with the subject of revolts by the *'ayyār* gangs and the people. He divides popular revolts into two types, attacks by the *'ayyār* gangs on officials or the wealthy, and uprisings by the whole people against foreign dynasties (the Buwayhids, the Seljuks). He emphasizes the *futuwwa* spirit of the *'ayyār* gangs which meant they preyed on the rich, not the poor. As the foreign regimes became more and more corrupt, leaving the caliphs in a weak position before the corruption, there were formed movements like the second type, growing out of cooperation between the *'ayyār* gangs and the people. Sabari, on the other hand, divides popular movements in Baghdad at the same time into three: popular (*'āmma*), the *'ayyār* gangs, and the Hanbalis. Popular movements were no more than a reaction to military government. Movements by *'ayyār* gangs were planned to resolve directly social dissatisfaction under a military government by actions such as looting, and they were linked to the manifestation of the *futuwwa* spirit of correcting inequalities. This *futuwwa* spirit was a rediscovery of the cooperative spirit which had existed before urbanization and which had been lost amidst the egotism of merchant society, so it was by no means a new concept. The Hanbalis, on the other hand, criticized the present in terms of the traditions of the past, and in the sense that they defended the rights of the Caliph as the focus of government, there was the possibility that they might collaborate with the other two groups, but in conclusion Sabari sees them as doing no more than restoring the social morals of the past.

T. Sato "'Ayyārūn in Baghdad" (J., 1983) traces the *'ayyār* gangs back to the Buwayhid dynasty (mid 11th century); he sees them, because of their *futuwwa* spirit, as being quite distinct from ordinary bands of robbers, though they did set fire to places and loot, and for this reason they had the support of the people, because they maintained order within quarters, and sponsored events such as religious festivals. M. A. 'Abd al-Mawlā, *The 'Ayyārūn and the Shuṭṭār of Baghdad* (A., 1990) examines their spirit, their organization, and their relations with the authorities and suggests that they were in a weak position regarding social revolution, since they had no programme to put in place of the existing authority, which they opposed, and were not of a social position to win support. The above four studies cover virtually all movements by *'ayyārūn, shuṭṭār* and *fityān* that appear in historical records, and also examine through literary works how the people thought of the *'ayyārūn*. What now needs to be done is to use these studies as a base to reconstruct the total picture of the social and political structure of the city, including the reaction of the ulama and the authorities. In this sense, R. P. Mottahedeh, *Loyalty and Leadership* (1980) brings a fresh point of view in his analysis, in terms of the loyalty and leadership of the title, of the actual relations between rulers and people during the Buwayhid dynasty.

Works dealing with the life of the people of Baghdad during the 'Abbasid period include M. M. Ahsan, *Social Life under the Abbasids* (1979) and S. H. al-'Ubaydī, *Arab-Islamic Clothing during the 'Abbasid Period* (A., 1980). M. R. 'Abd al-Ḥusayn, *Public Policy in Baghdad* (A., 1987) examines government and popular concern regarding the public nature of grants, hospitality, waqf, price controls, public facilities, etc. between the 11th and the middle of the 13th centuries. Makdisi, "Autograph Diary of an Eleventh-Century Historian of Baghdād" (1956-7) is a revision and English translation of the diary of 1068-9 of Ibn al-Bannā (d. 1079), a Hanbali ulama. K. Shimizu, "The World of an Urban Dweller" (J., 1989-90) reorders the same source in terms of topic and seeks to understand through it the connections between the sultan, the caliph and the ulama in the everyday life in the city.

It is apparent that studies of Baghdad are centred on the time before the Mongol invasion of the city in 1258, in broad terms, the 'Abbasid period. In 1962 the journal *Arabica* issued a special edition entitled *Baġdad* to celebrate the 1200th anniversary of the city. Contributions were made by prominent scholars of Arab history such as D. Sourdel, M. Canard and Cl. Cahen, by J. Aubin, a scholar of Iranian history ("Tamerlan à Bagdad"), by the scholar of Turkish history, R. Mantran ("Bagdad à l'époque ottomane"), and the issue also contained articles concerned with the problem of non-Muslims: M. Allard, "Les chrétiens à Bagdad" and G. Vajda, "Le milieu juif à Bagdad."

There is at present a large number of memoirs being published concerning life in Baghdad in the 20th century. R. al-Jumaylī (ed.), *The People of Baghdad: Sketches of the Life of the People of Baghdad in Past Times* (A., 1982) describes customs from the time of the founding of the city until 1934. Other such works include A. J. al-Ḥajīh, *The Appearance of Baghdad: Society and Customs in Baghdad This Century* (A., 1981), A. al-Mumayyiz, *Baghdad as I Saw it* (A., 1985), and B. A. H. Ḥamūdī, *Customs of the People of Iraq* (A., 1986). Studies based on an examination of the modern city of Baghdad include H. Kh. al-Genabi (al-Janabī), *Der Suq (Bazar) von Baghdad* (1976), S. al-Azzawi, "Oriental Houses in Baghdad" (1985) and J. Warren and I. Fethi, *Traditional Houses in Baghdad* (1982).

Samarra

The eighth 'Abbasid Caliph, al-Mu'taṣim (r. 833-42) ordered the erection of a new capital, Samarra, 140 km north of Baghdad. An excavation of the site was carried out in 1910-1914 by a German team directed by E. Herzfeld and the remains of the 'Abbasid period such as the Great Mosque, the palace, and the enclosure walls were uncovered. Because virtually nothing remains of early 'Abbasid Baghdad structures, Samarra is of great interest to architectural and art historians. The results of the excavations are contained in Herzfeld, *Archäologische Reise*, vol. 1 (1911) and id. *Geschichte der Stadt Samarra* (1948), and in K. A. C. Creswell, *Early Muslim Architecture*, vol. 2 (1940). J. M. Rogers, "Sāmarrā: A Study in Medieval Town- Planning" (1970) uses these sources to investigate the town plan from the point of view of both motifs and architectural techniques. A. Northedge, "Creswell, Herzfeld, and Samarra" (1991) examines the work of Creswell and Herzfeld providing the results of recent researches by both European and Iraqi scholars. Y. Sh. I. al-Sāmarrā'ī, *History of Samarra* (A., 1968-73) is a history of Samarra from its foundation in the 9th century to the present, and A. A. al-Bāqī, *Samarra* (A., 1989) is a scrupulous study of the relations among the amirs, men of religion and others around the Caliph, focusing on the 'Abbasid period.

Mosul and Other Cities in the Jazira Region

Mosul is on the opposite bank of the Tigris from Nineveh, the Assyrian capital, and is different from the cities treated above in that its history goes back beyond the beginning of the Christian era and it was built before the coming of Islam. The director of the city museum, S. al-Dewuchi (al-Dīwuhjī), has been conducting research into the city's history since the 1950s. *Mosul in the Time of the Atabegs* (A., 1958) discusses agriculture, commerce, industry, culture and social life in Mosul in the 12th and 13th centuries when it was the capital of the Atabegs (Zangids) and had the Jazira and Syria under its control. "The Madrasas of Mosul" (A., 1957) and *The Friday Mosques of Mosul* (A., 1963) deal with the religious monuments. Secular architecture, such as bridges, the citadel and government offices, is treated in *A Study of the Historical Sites of Mosul* (A., 1982), a work which includes old photographs. *Biographies of the Artisans of Mosul* (A., 1970) is a collection of short biographies from historical documents about artisans in Mosul (including weavers, architects and metal workers) from medieval times. We see in his work the interest of the local historian towards social life. His *History of Mosul,* published in 1982, is the recapitulation of thirty years of work. The first volume deals with the history of Mosul from pre-Islamic times to the collapse of the Zangid dynasty (first half of 13th century). After relating the political history, it describes briefly the topographies dealing with history, position and structure of the main buildings, literary figures and culture, handicrafts, agriculture and commerce, the army, social life and the Sufi orders. We await publication of the second volume, which has apparently been completed in manuscript. Other studies that have been published are A. M. A. al-Sulaymān, *Mosul in the Time of the Orthodox Caliphs and the Umayyads* (A., 1985), which deals with the history and topography up to the Umayyad period, and I. A. S. Ra'ūf, *Mosul in the Ottoman Period* (A., 1975), a description of the family of regional powerholders, the Jalīlīs, using Ottoman government documents and chronicles written in Arabic and Ottoman Turkish. P. Kemp, "Mosuli Sketches of Ottoman History" (1981) and "Power and Knowledge in Jalili Mosul" (1983) use local historical materials from the Ottoman period to reconstruct the political and cultural situation in Mosul. In his "History and Historiography in Jalili Mosul" (1983) he leads us from the repetitive descriptive style of the historical works to the historical consciousness of the present.

Compared with Baghdad, much of the old city of Mosul remains intact, and a number of investigations of the city are being carried out. H. Kh. al-Janābī, *Inner Structure of the Old City of Mosul* (A., 1982) is a field survey of the old city by a geographer; detailed maps of the quarters (*maḥallas*) and the suqs are appended; in particular each building in the suq is identified by occupation, the like of which has not been achieved for other cities. al-Janābī has applied the same methodology in surveys of Irbil and Duhāk, and has published *Urban Geography of the City of Duhāk* (A., 1985) and *Urban Geography of the City of Irbil* (A., 1987). The Department of Construction of Mosul has conducted a survey of existing buildings, the results of which appear in the report Y. Dhannūb et. al. (eds.), *The Buildings of Mosul* (A., 1982). Volume 1 is concerned with domestic buildings, Volume 2 with public buildings (suqs, caravansaries), and Volume 3 with religious buildings. There are plans in plane and elevation for each building. It is difficult to trace the historical development of the urban structure of cities like Basra, Kufa and Baghdad through modern investigations, since the cities of today are recent phenomena built some distance from the site of the early Islamic cities which were subsequently destroyed. Mosul, though, can be investigated topographically by means of both field surveys and historical records, as is the case in Syria and Iran.

Studies like those of Mosul centring on architectural history are I. al-Sulaymān et al. *Arab-Islamic Architecture in Iraq* (A., 1982), dealing with palace and religious architecture, and F. Muṣṭafā, *Arab Dwellings in Iraq during the Islamic Period* (A., 1983), dealing with domestic architecture. Discussing the city from the broader perspective of the Arab and the Islamic city is Kh. al-Ash'ab, *The Arab City* (A., 1982), which covers from a geographer's point of view the range from the traditional Arab city to the modern city. M. A. al-Mawswī, *Historical Factors in the Formation and Development of the Arab-Islamic City* (A., 1982) is a discussion of the military, political, religious, geographical, cultural, social and economic factors leading to the formation of cities, considering also the examples of pre-Islamic Iraqi cities. Ṣāliḥ (ed.), *The City and City Life* (A., 1988) is a three volume collection of the work of Iraqi scholars. Volume 1 deals with the pre-Islamic period, Volume 2 with pre-modern times, and Volume 3 with the modern age. Contributions concerning the Iraqi city have been made by many of the scholars whose individual works we have been considering, such as Ṣāliḥ, al-Ma'āḍīdī, al-Kubaysī and Ra'ūf. The introduction stresses the importance of the city in Islamic culture, but does not take up the arguments that have been concerning Western scholars regarding the "Islamic city."

Perhaps because Iraq has had a tradition of urban culture since ancient times, urban studies have been popular in that country since the 1950s, with their mouthpiece being the journal *Sumer*. This journal was first published in 1945; scholars from the West, from Arab lands and from Japan have reported their archaeological findings and their historical-geographical research in it. We may describe the characteristics of Iraqi urban studies as being twofold. Firstly, because there are so many created cities, a popular line of research is the study of the earliest city plan by means of geographies. Interest has been manifested not only in public buildings but also in the streets, the quarters and domestic buildings. Secondly, fragmentary historical documents are being collected to investigate urban administration and the economy, popular movements, and social life. I would hope in the future that the topographical studies will be compared with and studied in conjunction with the traditions of the ancient pre-Islamic cities, and that the topographical studies will be combined with the research that has been conducted into the society and people in order to look at urban structures as a whole. I feel there is still a considerable gap in research for the period after the 'Abbasid Caliphate, and would like to see work being undertaken in particular on the 13th-18th centuries in order to examine the connections with the modern city.

2. Syria

This section considers Syria to be the region comprising the modern Syria, Lebanon, Jordan, Palestine and Israel, the territory historically known as Syria (*Bilād al-Shām*) until the modern borders were decided under the British and French mandates after the First World War.

Damascus

Damascus began as a village settled by ancient Aramaeans; its basic plan of a network of streets in a grid pattern surrounded by a rectangular wall was devised under Roman rule. The pioneering topographical study, A. von Kremer, "Topographie von Damascus" (1854) is of great value in that it refers to structures such as the walls, the citadel and the Umayyad Mosque as well as to the mid-19th century structure of the quarters and domestic architecture. The first study based on a full-scale investigation was K. Wulzinger and C. Watzinger, *Damaskus* (1921-4). The first volume deals with the ancient city, and the second with the Islamic period. Volume 2 gives an outline of the architectural history of Damascus, and then goes on to mention the Arabic historical sources and the travel records and research into art and architectural history of Western scholars, to present maps, based on field research conducted in 1917, of the streets and the waterways showing the position of the most important buildings, and to describe the names, origins, plan, inscriptions and decoration of the buildings and remains existing in the old city within the walls and in the main suburban quarters such as al-'Uqayba and al-Ṣāliḥiya. The methodical presentation, with each section divided into a grid pattern, makes reference easy.

During the 1930s, J. Sauvaget published a number of studies of the ruins and monuments from ancient times, including "La citadelle de Damas" (1930), *Les monuments historiques de Damas* (1932) and *Monuments ayyoubides de Damas* (1930), dealing in the main with religious buildings like churches, mosques and madrasas, and "Un bain damasquin du XIIIe siècle" (1930), concerning the public bath (*ḥammām*). In 1934, in "Esquisse d'une histoire de la ville de Damas," he outlined the evolution of the city and social changes from ancient times, particularly the Greek and Roman periods, until the 20th century. In "Le plan antique de Damas" (1949) he made a concentrated study of the ancient city plan. Sauvaget's studies on Damascus were never organized into a single volume, such as his *Alep* (1941); nevertheless they have exerted a great influence as classical research based on field-work and the use of historical texts. A motif of Sauvaget's work is his comparisons between the classical period and the Islamic period. He considers that externally the basic plan of the Roman city, its gates, its rectangular wall, and its temple, was maintained into the Islamic period, and that internally, the network of streets on the grid plan transformed into a mass of zigzagging streets leading to blind alleys, that the life of the residents of the city was organized on the bases of small communities such as the quarter, facing the alleys, or the guild, and that the city was a mosaic society with no overall integration. "Esquisse" also contains maps showing the main facilities and the road network in the Roman period, and in the 13th, 16th, 19th and 20th centuries, and these have been widely quoted by both Western and Arab scholars, despite the fact that he does not cite his authorities for demarking the roads and residential quarters in each period. It is possible that he based his calculations on some kind of survey that was made when the French, during their mandate in the 1930s, produced a *Plan cadastral* of the city, a 1/500 land register made by triangular surveying which included every building, from religious facilities to ordinary homes. The *Plan* had been drawn up to survey real estate, and it therefore records in minute fashion the streets and each house in them according to owner, and even their walls, their courtyards, the fountains therein, outside staircases, and projections over the street. There is no other example of such a detailed city map for anywhere else in the Islamic Middle East, and it is a valuable source not only for the topography of Damascus but also for investigating the structure of Arab-Islamic cities.

There are a relatively large number of textual sources and studies based on them for the religious buildings of Damascus, such as mosques, madrasas, and convents (*zāwiya, khānqāh, ribāṭ*). The first volume of the *Ta'rīkh Madīna Dimashq* of Ibn 'Asākir (d. 1176) is an historical topography, and it was incorporated in the historical geography written by Ibn Shaddād (d. 1285). Ibn al-Mibrad (d. 1503), al-Nu'aymī (d. 1521) and Badrān (d. 1927) also drew on the work for detailed information about religious buildings, such as their position, their origin, their successive imams and professors, their facilities, and the details of their endowments (waqf). An abridgment of al-Nu'aymī's *al-Dāris fī ta'rīkh al-madāris* by 'Abd al-Basīṭ called *Mukhtaṣar tanbīh* was translated as "Description de Damas" (1894-6) by H. Sauvaire. Both Wulzinger and Sauvaget used this as a basic source for their surveys. M. A. Ṭalas published a survey in 1943 of 307 mosques, with location and commentary, in conjunction with his edition of Ibn al-Mibrad's topography. Other works by Arab scholars include S. D. al-Munajjid, *Topography of Damascus* (A., 1949) and A. H. al-'Ulabī, *Topographie historique de la ville de Damas* (A., 1989), which deal with public baths, caravansaries and suqs as well as religious facilities. M. Ecochard and Cl. Le Coeur, *Les bains de Damas* (1942-3) is a detailed study of the *ḥammām* together with water courses. M. Kayyāl, *The Public Baths of Damascus* (A., 1966) is a study of baths based on textual sources. Works on art and architectural history include K. A. C. Creswell, *Early Muslim Architecture*, vol. 1 (1932) and E. Herzfeld, "Damascus: Studies in Architecture" (1942-8). Through such works the sites of several hundred religious buildings have been confirmed, and since they are waqf institutions their position has remained basically unchanged since their foundation, enabling them to be used as virtual coordinate axes for inferring the position of other facilities, such as suqs and quarters, from the descriptions in historical materials. The foundations of research into Damascus were built by French scholars before the Second World War, and much of their work on topography and their introductions and editions of historical materials appeared in the *Bulletin d'Études Orientales* and *Syria*, journals of the Institut Français d'Études Arabes de Damas.

After the Second World War, there was a pause in topographical research, but during the 1980s the Deutsches Archäologisches Institut has reinstated field surveys, the results of which are gradually being published in the *Damaszener Mitteilungen* (1983-) and reports have appeared on excavations at regional sites and on studies of *khāns*, domestic housing and the quarters in Damascus. One such is D. Sack, "Damaskus: die Stadt intra muros" (1985), which lists the origins and present circumstances of domestic as well as religious architecture in the old city, and shows the structure of the old city and historical changes through nine maps. In 1989 she published *Damaskus*, in which, based on the above report, she identifies the streets and quarters, the network of water courses, and the markets as being the basic elements in the construction of the city, and makes a penetrating analysis of these points in terms both of case studies and comprehensive research. The work also includes maps showing the distribution of the main facilities according to period, that is, under the Zangids, the Ayyubids, the Mamluks, and the Ottomans down to the present, and thematic maps giving the distribution of mosques, streets, the market and shops. It is possible to conclude from these that religious institutions were concentrated in the north-west section, which contained the Umayyad Mosque and the citadel. M. Meinecke, "Der Survey des Damaszener Altstadtviertels aṣ-Ṣāliḥīya" (1983) is the report of a study of the Ṣāliḥīya quarter in the northern part of Damascus, a comprehensive list and map of the historical buildings in the quarter, based on Dahmān's *Historical Map of al-Ṣāliḥīya* (A., 1947), the *Plan cadastral*, and his own investigation.

The centre of Syrian research is La Direction Générale des Antiquités et des Musées (al-Mudirīya al-'Āmma) which edits the journal *Les Annales Archéologiques Arabes Syriennes*, which featured a special issue on Damascus in 1985. Besides conducting joint investigations with foreign research bodies, it has published studies such as *A General Survey of Historical Monuments in Damascus* (A., 1983), based on its own survey, and A. Q. al-Riḥāwī (ed.), *A Map of Mamluk Damascus* (A., 1971). The Syrian Department of Construction (Niqāba al-Muhandisīn) has also supervised its own studies of Damascus from the point of view of town planning and sponsored a symposium, *Old Damascus* (A., 1982). The city authorities too are concerned with the preservation of the old city from an administrative angle and have compiled a collection of building laws according to occupational categories and edifices. It would be worth examining these laws to find out what place Islamic building regulations, as advocated by Hakim (*Arabic-Islamic Cities: Building and Planning Principles,* 1986) and others, have in the modern city.

Noteworthy geographical studies include R. Tresse, "L'irrigation dans la Ghouta" (1929) and R. Thoumin, "Notes sur l'aménagement et la distribution des eaux" (1934), both concerning the irrigation and water system of the Ghūṭa, the surrounding oasis of Damascus. Both are studies of the system of underground watercourses developed in Damascus, employing actual surveys, legal documents and ordinances. They show that water was diverted by a siphon system to facilities and homes in the quarters, and the waste sent back by the same method to irrigate the fields. Water rights were determined by the width of the intake and water supervisors were in charge of maintenance and inspection. The underground channels are thought to date from the Roman period, and it is possible to confirm from geographies that the distribution system was in place already by the 14th century. It is not clear, however, how the system of construction, maintenance and supervision was organized historically. The question of the construction and maintenance of roads and watercourses is very important when considering the public nature of the city. Thoumin also published "Damas: Notes sur la répartition" (1937), concerning how people lived segregated according to religion, and "Deux quartiers de Damas" (1931), his fieldwork in Christian quarters such as Bāb al-Muṣallā. After the Second World War scholars favoured analyses from a macro viewpoint rather than individual field studies. E. Wirth, in "Damaskus—Aleppo—Beirut" (1966) compared the three cities in terms of geographical conditions. Compared with Damascus, a city in a sandy oasis, Aleppo is surrounded by broad steppe country. The former is characterized as a political and cultural centre, the latter as an international trading city. The differences between them are reflected in the characteristics of their inhabitants, and Wirth analyzes the people of Aleppo as being more progressive, open and rational. He says that Beirut, a seaport that developed much later, greatly utilized the Christian merchants in its rapid expansion in the 19th century as a modern European-style trading city. K. Dettmann, in *Damaskus* (1967) and other publications, has studied the composition of urban dwellers, the development of urbanism, and urban problems. M. Naito,

"Change in Spatial Segregation by Race or Religion in Damascus" (J., 1985) discusses the process of residence differentiation with the movement of immigrants into suburban quarters such as al-Ṣāliḥīya and al-Mizza. T. H. Greenshields, "'Quarters' and Ethnicity"(1980) surveys the processes of the formation of ethnic clusters in the Middle Eastern cities such as Damascus, Aleppo, Jerusalem, Salé, and Tunis in relation to population movement like migration.

Historical focusing on the period from the Arab conquest up to the 10th century and the Ummayad and 'Abbasid domination have treated Damascus as part of Syrian history rather than as a particular city. Th. Bianquis, *Damas et la Syrie* (1986-9) deals with the political history of the Fatimid domination of Syria, and M. D. Yusuf, *Economic Survey of Syria* (1985) treats geography, production, and transport in Syrian cities in the 10th-11th centuries, based on descriptions in the geographies. Because Sryian scholars such as Ibn al-Athīr, Ibn al-Qalānisī and Ibn al-'Adīm arose after the 11th century and produced local histories, studies on the social structure of the city using these textual sources are proceeding apace.

The starting point for postwar studies of social structure was the model provided by Sauvaget's "Esquisse." He regarded the quarter (*ḥāra*) as being the city in miniature, a place where people of the same race or tribe, religion and birthplace gathered, separated from the outside by the gate built at the entrance to the narrow streets, provided with communal facilities such as a mosque, a public bath, a market, a well, and a bakery, and its safety guaranteed by a system of self-defence, comprising the headman (sheikh), night-watchmen and the militia (*aḥdāth*). While the quarter was self-governing regarding its internal functions, it was closed to the outside, and the city as a whole was no more than a mosaic formed of such quarters, its integration being achieved through the city walls, standing from ancient times, the Umayyad Mosque (the former temple) and the central market. Islamic civilization guaranteed the formation of the such small communities as the quarters, but in that the city as a whole had no communal nature, it was dependent upon the traditions that had existed since ancient times. His schema, which treats the Hellenistic-Roman period and the Islamic period contrastively, follows the tradition of Islamic urban studies in the Maghrib.

N. Elisséeff, "Damas à la lumière des théories de Jean Sauvaget" (1970) is a critical examination of the problems raised by Sauvaget's thesis. According to Elisséeff, Sauvaget's method focuses on the physical structure and topography of the citadel, the temple/mosque, the markets, the streets and the quarters, and he argues in terms of the similarities and differences in political and social structures between the Hellenistic-Roman period, which he takes as his ideal, and the Islamic period, and a reconsideration in historical terms shows that there are many elements which cannot be reconciled to the Islamic. For example, the change from grid to zigzag in the street network had already begun from the 2nd century, and in that the muhtasib and the jurists thought it necessary to regulate projections over the streets it is apparent that the growth in the tendency towards zigzagging streets owed a great deal to the weakness of regulated rights, and the marked increase in population and commercial activity. The formation of the quarters, religiously, economically and as autonomous bodies, is not a phenomenon particular to the Islamic city but one whose antecedents are to be found in the existence of tutelary deities for each residential district during Roman times and in the *paroisse* of the Byzantine period. During the Islamic period, suqs were not limited to the main markets in front of the ancient temple and on the east-west concourse; small suqs were dotted around the city and the suburbs selling the goods needed for daily use, so that Massignon's formula of occupational groups distributed around the great mosque does not apply to Damascus. Overall, Elisséeff emphasizes the social and economic factors rather than attributing change in the Islamic period as being equivalent to the presence of Islamic factors. Sauvaget's research was not a study of society based on textual sources but was based rather on a model of a social structure made from the physical structure of the quarters and the city. Elisséeff appealed that an examination should be made of Sauvaget's points one by one by recourse to historical sources. R. S. Humphreys, "Urban Topography and Urban Society" (1991) makes a similar and more theoretical criticism of Sauvaget's research methodology.

We will examine studies of the structure of urban society in terms of three periods, the Zangid dynasty and before (to the first half of the 12th century), the Ayyubid and Mamluk dynasties (latter half of the 12th century-15th century) and the Ottoman dynasty (from the 16th century). Syria in the 10th-12th centuries was where three forces met and clashed: the Fatimids, the Seljuks and the Crusaders. Attention has been given to movements towards self defence and self government within the city in face of these external powers. Ashtor, "L'administration urbaine en Syrie médiévale" (1956) discusses urban autonomy in Syria in the 10th and 11th centuries, comparing it with the basic concept of the medieval city in Western Europe, civil autonomy versus feudal lords. On one hand, he stressed the function of the muhtasib and that of the headmen (*ra'īs*), who controlled the militias known as *aḥdāth* and played a communal role in protecting the city and maintaining its security. This function he located in the continuing Hellenistic-Roman tradition of autonomy. However, since there was no artisan or merchant class to be the repository of the civil spirit or to bear the responsibility of self-government, urban autonomy was unavoidably frustrated by the appearance on the scene of powerful figures like Nur al-Din and Saladin. Ashtor, "L'urbanisme syrien à la basse-époque" (1958) continues the discussion into the Zangid and Ayyubid dynasties. In "Républiques urbaines" (1975), Ashtor deals with autonomous movements in the regional cities of Syria and the Jazira in the 10th and 11th centuries, and points out by comparison with Iraq, where such movements did not rise, the influence exerted by economic development and contacts with Europe in the case of the former. Cl. Cahen, "Mouvements populaires" (1958-9) discusses the activities and character of urban militias (*aḥdāth*) and headmen (*ra'īs*) in Damascus and Aleppo in the 10th-12th centuries, comparing them to the *'ayyārūn* and *fityān* of Iraq and Iran. In contrast to the strongly manifested voluntary and popular character of the latter, symbolized in the *futuwwa* (chivalrous) spirit, the *aḥdāth* were organizationally connected with the upper classes and so had a strong official colouration, though functionally they played a popular role as leaders of insurrections. The differences are seen as stemming from the Sasanian, Iranian tradition that prevailed in Iran and Iraq, and the Byzantine tradition of Syria. By linking the *aḥdāth* and the *ra'īs* with the Byzantine tradition, Cahen agrees with Ashtor, who compared them with the city heads of Hellenistic and Byzantine times, the *nictéparque*, the *vicomagistri* and the *préteur*. In "Tribes, Cities and Social Organization" (1975), Cahen, to verify his thesis, examined the Iranian tradition in the *futuwwa* spirit. A. Havemann, *Ri'āsa und Qaḍā'* (1975) takes up squarely the problem of the relationship between the *aḥdāth* and the *ra'īs* and their role in urban autonomy. He examines in detail period by period movements in 10th-12th century Damascus, Aleppo, Tyre, Tripoli, Baalbek, Amid (Diyarbakır) and Mosul. He concludes: (1) the *aḥdāth* and *ra'īs* received the support of the various classes of townspeople against the authority of outside rulers and assumed autonomous power as the city, (2) there were two types of *ra'īs*, that of the *aḥdāth* and that of the town, and they were appointed in turn from particular families; some also held public positions such as that of vizier or were involved in fiscal administration, diplomacy or tax collection, based on *ḥimāya*, and (3) autonomous urban power was built up under the qadis in the Mediterranean coastal cities such as Tripoli. From the middle of the 12th century, when the Zangids took control of Aleppo and Damascus, the authority commanded by the *ra'īs* and backed up by the power of groups such as the *aḥdāth*, gave way to public officials such as *shiḥna* (head of police) and muhtasib, upon which autonomous power belonging to the people of the city independent of the central authority faded away. G. Hoffmann, *Kommune oder Staatsbürokratie?* (1975) takes up the same question from another point of view. In "Fāṭimid Policy towards Damascus" (1981-2) and "The Fāṭimids and the Aḥdāth of Damascus" (1982), Y. Lev examines the connection between the Fatimids and the Damascene *aḥdāth* and shows that the frequent changes of governor under the Fatimids allowed the *aḥdāth* to expand, so that in 1024 the Fatimid troops garrisoned in Damascus fought together against an encirclement by Bedouin in an alliance with the *aḥdāth* brokered by the *ashrāf*.

The problem here is the nature of the internal factors which enabled the *aḥdāth* and the *ra'īs* to assume the authority to represent the city, and why this turned out to be only a temporary phenomenon. P. von Sievers, "Military, Merchants and Nomads" (1979) considers the background to the rise of the *aḥdāth* as an element of urban autonomy in terms of the changes of Syrian society as a whole in the 8th-10th centuries. Around the middle of the 9th century, Syrian society saw the collapse of the system whereby a privileged Arab military controlled both cities and rural villages, and a growing gap between town and country and between urban classes, based on occupation. It was from such conditions that the trend to urban autonomy grew. It was here in the 8th century that the word *aḥdāth* came to be used in the same sense of maintaining order as the *shurṭa* (police force); in the 9th century it indicated the lower urban classes, and then finally in the latter part of the 10th century its usage was changed to mean militia. Sievers sees in this an expression of a move towards autonomy from below. At the same time, though, there was growing stratification and confrontation between the upper classes (*ashrāf*, sheikh, merchants) and the lower classes (*aḥdāth*, etc.) and because this was not controlled, self-government was nipped in the bud by the outside authorities, in contrast to the Italian cities which moved towards the formation of communes. B. Shoshan, "The Politics of Notables" (1986) does not allow there to have any formation of an autonomous community in 9th-11th century Damascus, though there was political ascendancy of the notable class, such as the *ashrāf* and of those not of that class, like the *aḥdāth*. After the 11th century the notables were appointed as bureaucrats and incorporated into the state as officials entrusted with religious duties. In that the Middle Eastern bourgeoisie, with its economic power, did not move towards acquiring political and military rights or generate any political idea to support the independent town, it differed greatly from the bourgeoisie of the European cities. In response, Havemann wrote "The Vizier and the Ra'īs" (1989) in which he points out that in contrast to the *ra'īs* of Aleppo, who were appointed by the rulers and who achieved control over the city, the *ra'īs* of Damascus had financial administrative abilities and commanded the city economy through the collection of taxes. He contends that Syrian urban society in the 11th and 12th centuries had arrived at the formation of a body politic which protected individual interests against the central power. Havemann delineates what the *ra'īs* and the *aḥdāth* actually were, through historical documents like chronicles and shows that in the Fatimid period they were an autonomous influence against external authority. However the question of the internal factors according to which the *aḥdāth* and their leaders (*ra'īs*), called rogues by ulama chroniclers, secured the authority to represent the city still remain unidentified.

Elisséeff, *Nūr al-Dīn* (1967) is an important work dealing with the government, economy and society of Syria during the Nur al-Din period. One chapter covers elements of urban administrative organization, such as the muhtasib, the *ra'īs,* the *shiḥna* and the *shurṭa,* the organization of the city people, the markets and the quarters, and suburban expansion, but the contents owe much to the studies of Sauvaget, Ashtor and Cahen, amongst others, and offers very little that is original. "Corporations de Damas sous Nūr al-Dīn" (1956) by the same author identifies the location of sixty-nine suqs according to the 11th century topography of Ibn 'Asākir and concludes that there is no evidence of distribution according to occupation as held by Massignon and others. The Zangid period was a time when there began a sharp increase in the number of facilities, such as madrasas and congregational mosques, built in the cities of Syria through waqf endowments; the subject of Nur al-Din waqf monuments is taken up in Elisséeff, "Les monuments de Nūr al-Dīn" (1949-51) and T. Yukawa, "The Development of the Madrasa in Syria in the 6th/12th Century" (J., 1980).

Between the 12th and 15th centuries, Syria was under the control of the Cairo-based Ayyubids and Mamluks; during the Ayyubid period, the ruling family built principalities centred on Aleppo, Damascus and other cities, and they were organized into six provinces under the Mamluks. R. S. Humphreys, *From Saladin to the Mongols* (1977) deals with the political changes between the confederated state of the Ayyubid dynasty and the centralization of power under the Mamluks. Humphreys focuses on Ayyubid political organization, and analyzes the political relationship between the urban population and the local ruler. Humphreys, "Politics and Architectural Patronage" (1989) examines architectural activity in Ayyubid Damascus. He shows, through a quantitative analysis, that (1) a distinctively large number of structures were built during the Ayyubid period, compared with the Seljuk and Zangid periods, (2) the buildings were founded in the main by the ruling family, the ulama and members of the military class, and (3) the military, the ulama and the bureaucracy tended to be newcomers to Damascus rather than being born there. The growth in the number of architectural undertakings in Ayyubid Damascus was due not only to the patronage of the Ayyubids themselves; the invitation of military personnel and ulama to Damascus also played a role. N. Ziadeh, *Urban Life in Syria* (1953) discusses from a number of angles economic prosperity, the provision of social facilities, the workings of urban administration, the intellectual life of the ulama etc. in the cities of 13th and

14th century Syria after the threat of the Crusaders had receded. Throughout the book are statistical evaluations of population, the economy and social institutions (like madrasas), enabling us to gain an insight into the overview of the cities. The author considers that what supported the prosperity of the cities was the result of Mamluk policy to strengthen the state organization through the Sunnis, in order to oppose the threat of the Crusaders and the Mongols. As a result, state control of education and culture increased. In his *Damascus under the Mamlūks* (1964), Ziadeh uses travel records and other sources to describe in vivid terms the social life of Damascus at this time. Dahmān, "Damascus in the Mamluk Period" (A., 1964) gives an overview of the political structures and the rule of the governors in the province of Damascus under the Mamluks. He adds many episodes as a local historian resident in Damascus, but unfortunately does not cite his sources.

Lapidus, *Muslim Cities in the Later Middle Ages* (1967) investigates and analyzes more than 200 textual sources dealing with urban politics and social structure in Mamluk Syria and proposes a new model for Islamic urban society. The question he asks is why the Mamluks, formerly military slaves of a different race and religion, had been able to govern cities occupied principally by Arab Muslims for over 250 years. It was not simply a matter of the military and political superiority of the Mamluks; rather they linked the farmers and nomads to the cities through their active social and economic actions, and formed a variety of networks between them and the two main classes in urban society, the notables (great merchants and ulama) and the common people. First, he identifies the economic ties the Mamluks made with the people through merchant activity and building work (waqf endowments). Second, he looks at the diverse roles of the ulama. On the one hand they had a place in administration as qadis and financial officers and forged their position as an elite by means of remunerations and waqf foundation, while on the other they had a leadership role among the common people as teachers and scholars. Third, he found links between the Mamluk rulers and the city lumpenproletariat, like the gangs and the beggar bands, and studied their role in popular uprisings. The ulama class, exercising its leadership role in both the city and the quarter, had in itself no military power to oppose the Mamluks; those who were armed, like the gangs, perpetrated crimes like pillaging and assassination among the propertied classes, and as a result the two never merged into a single class and power. In rearranging the above relationships, the Mamluks, both in relation to the people and the ulama built up a network of individual and specific patronage, by means of which they separated the two to ensure that they themselves and nobody else were in a position to integrate all of urban society. What supported the rule of these outsiders was their command of networks, consisting mainly of such patronage, and he calls this type of society, focused as it was on the Mamluks, the "Mamluk regime."

The significance of Lapidus's work was that he was able to present political and social structures of the Mamluk period in a very clear model by analyzing the individual networks. Though both Sauvaget and Ashtor had already dealt with similar problems, they had not been able to see the city as any more than an imperfect autonomy or a mosaic. Lapidus on the other hand was able through his network method to grasp the distinctive characteristics of a flexibly structured society, and at the same time to discern the conditions making for the existence of the Mamluk regime. He has argued for the effectiveness of his method and model, extending his subject to the whole of the Middle East/Islamic region from the Mesopotamian period of 3000 B. C. to the present.

First, in "Muslim Cities and Islamic Societies" (1969), "The Evolution of Muslim Urban Society" (1973) and *Muslim Cities* (student edition, 1984) he argues that Islamic urban society was formed during the Seljuk period of the 11th and 12th centuries from three types of organization, and this system lasted until the Ottoman period. The three type of organization are (1) parochial groups (*'aṣabīya* ties), such as of families and lineages, quarters or outlaws, (2) religious associations (law schools, Sufi orders, sects, etc.), and (3) imperial regimes (slave soldiers, nomadic soldiers, the *iqṭā'* system). These are indeed the principal networks he had observed when analyzing Mamluk urban society. This work, which showed that his "Mamluk regime" could be generalized as a model common to Islamic urban society and to Islamic society as a whole, contain the core of his network theory, in his approach that the state was a network like any social group. Second, this pluralistic network society was formed at the beginning of the 9th century out of the growing duality of the Caliphate, the separation of the state and religion. Since the formation of the modern states since the 19th century too there has been on the one hand a centralizing of authority and the removal of intermediate groups, and on the other vigorous activity by religious movements concerned with the identity of the individual and by benefit associations; this Lapidus sees as the continuation of the pluralistic connections between state and religion ("The Separation of State and Religion in the Development of Early Islamic Society," 1975; "Islam and Modernity," 1987; "Muslim Cities as Plural Societies," 1989). He finds the distinguishing feature of Islamic society not to be the unity of state and religion, but the "ambiguous" nature of the interface between them as separated institutions, and understands Islam to be not something which has provided the inner workings of society a special prescription, transcending place and time, but rather an external receptacle which sanctions the state and the various groups which claimed legitimacy in the name of Islam, which, in a word, guarantees the pluralistic networks.

In a comparative study of Chinese and Islamic societies, Lapidus furthers his investigation of the social type of Islamic society, and uses the word "network" on three levels. First, it is used as an analytical tool, stressing mutual relationships and functions among groups rather than their particular structure or organization. Second, it is employed as a metaphor for "informal and unstructured interconnections." Third, it expresses those Islamic cultural characteristics in history and society seen as a constant formative process. Here, what he calls "network" is not an analytical method applicable to the mesh of combinations and connections seen in all societies, or to any society; rather, he uses it as an analytical tool connected intrinsically with the Islamic cultural style and social reality, making it thus possible to educe the characteristic Islamic cultural "unstructuredness." ("Hierarchies and Networks," 1975). T. Miura, "Some Remarks on Urbanism in Islam" (J., 1990) and "The Network Theory Reconsidered" (J., 1991) look at the development of Lapidus's theory expanding from urban society to Islamic society as a whole and examine its significance and problem areas.

J. E. Gilbert, in *The Ulama of Medieval Damascus* (1977) and "Institutionalization of Muslim Scholarship and Professionalization" (1980) presents a statistical analysis of the biographies of more than one thousand ulama active in Damascus from the time of the Seljuks to that of the Ayyubids (1076-1260). During this time, with the consolidation of religious and educational facilities like madrasas, there was growing institutionalization of learning and education and professionalization of the ulama. After the time of Nur al-Din those in power encouraged as a matter of policy the building of waqf-endowed institutions such as madrasas and tightened their control on the ulama by means of their powers of appointment and dismissal in regard to the teaching and judicial professions. As a result there grew up noted families among the ulama, which exercised a powerful influence over ulama society as a whole, and among which positions such as that of qadi were hereditary. The use of concepts such as "institutionalization" and "professionalization" is highly significant in pointing out changes in the social role and position of the ulama. H. Shumaysānī, *Madrasas in Damascus in the Ayyubid Period* (A., 1983) arranges the madrasas of Ayyubid Damascus according to the different schools (*madhāhib*) of law. L. Pouzet, "Maghrébins" (1975) examines the biographies and activities of ulama from the Maghrib in 13th century Damascus, and their affiliations with schools of law. In *Damas au VIIe/ XIIIe siècle* (1988), Pouzet sees the 13th century as a time of change in the social position of the ulama and makes a broad study of the ulama in Damascus during that century, incorporating the views of the Sunni four schools of law and their relationship with the Sufis, the Shiites and the

Christians. H. al-'Ulabī, *Damascus at the Turn from the Mamluk Period to Ottoman Rule* (A., 1982) is a study employing a large number of unpublished manuscripts from the national libraries of Cairo and Damascus. It contains detailed and unique accounts of the military, the taxation system, law courts, the people and social change in the late Mamluk period, after 1500. He divides the social classes into Mamluks, ulama, the common people and *zu'r* (outlaws); he defines the *zu'r* as those who were loyal neither to the rulers or the common people and were considered troublesome by both. Worthy of note is that he deals with tax collectors and the sheikh and *'arīf* of the quarters (*ḥāra*) on the same plane as the *zu'r,* since according to Lapidus, the sheikh and *'arīf* of the quarters were employed by the notables (ulama) of the quarter and played the part of middle-men between the rulers and the people. al-'Ulabī on the other hand sees them as the actual rulers of the quarters who had dealings with those in power for their own benefit, though he cites no documents to substantiate his claim.

T. Miura, "The Urbanization of the Suburbs of Damascus" (J., 1987) deals with the development of the Ṣāliḥīya quarter, formed in the northern suburbs of Damascus in the 12th century, and examines in detail the role of the Mamluks and the ulama, and their interaction in the process of urban development. The activities of ulama of the Hanbali law school who had moved to Damascus following the capture of Palestine by the Crusaders exerted a wide-ranging influence, far beyond law school and social class, and they stimulated the founding of madrasas and other religious institutions, and the formation of the quarter of which those madrasas were the core. Further, Miura discusses the relationship between law schools and the quarter by means of an analysis of madrasas and teachers, and shows that the Hanafis were predominant even in the "Hanbali city" of the Ṣāliḥīya, overturning previous ideas. Miura, "The Ṣāliḥīya Quarter in the Mamlūk Period" (J., 1989), a continuation of the previous article, is a detailed examination of both the physical form and the internal structure of the quarter. By comparing the historical maps of Dahmān and Meinecke with the topographical sources, he indicates that while in the Mamluk times the Ṣāliḥīya quarter was made up of thirty to forty smaller quarters (*ḥāra*) which centred on religious institutions, with each *ḥāra* being physically a separate unit independent of the others, the Ṣāliḥīya quarter as a whole was a complex structure regarded as a unit in terms of politics, administration and economics. Miura also deals with the internal structure by examining the ulama who occupied positions in the madrasas. After the latter half of the 14th century there was a growing tendency for ulama to hold and inherit such positions and for those offices to be very lucrative. As a result, waqf institutions collapsed through embezzlement, and the ulama lost their influence among the local people, while outlaw groups called *zu'r* held the key to the defence of the quarter and its resistance to oppression. These two articles are combined and expanded in "The Ṣāliḥīya Quarter in the Suburbs of Damascus" (1994). Miura, "The Quarter and Popular Movements" (J., 1989) uses 19th and 20th century memoirs and other sources to throw light on the twofold structure of (1) the small quarters centring on the alleys as the communities of the daily life of their inhabitants, and (2) the large quarter as a unit for government and administration. There he proposes that a characteristic feature of the Arab-Islamic city is the role played by outlaw groups and their leaders in controlling internal and external matters. The above series of papers clarifies the structure of the quarter, about the realities of which little is known although it is the basic unit of urban society. Miura's proposal that outlaw groups held leadership roles in the quarter in place of the ulama from the end of the Mamluk period throws doubt on the idea of the ulama as the leaders of the quarters and the common people, an idea that has become firmly established since the work of Lapidus. "The Structure of the Quarter and the Role of the Outlaws" (1989) makes a critical evaluation of the history of such research.

Miura, "Urban Society at the End of the Mamlūk Era" (J., 1989) discusses political and social change, particularly in Damascus, in the last fifty years of the Mamluk period. During that time, the Mamluks and the ulama polarized and powerful amirs and higher officials maintained their own mercenaries and officials in their domains, and formed factions (*jamā'a*) through which they performed their own administration and exploited the inhabitants of the quarters directly. The *zu'r* on the other hand built up their own territories where the arm of the authorities could not reach, making the quarters their stronghold, and were the faction closest to the common people, left with nowhere to go. Thus urban society at the end of the period was composed of warring factions of powerful amirs, higher officials and *zu'r,* and Lapidus's classification of Mamluk, ulama and common people was dissolving, in terms both of social strata and political power, as individuals began to join together on the basis of the faction. Miura criticizes Lapidus's contention that the Mamluk regime continued into the Ottoman period and he sees changes in urban society coming about as a result of ambiguous groups such as the *jamā'a* and the *zu'r* becoming the nuclei of administrative and social integration.

Research into Ottoman period Damascus was triggered by A. K. Rafeq, *The Province of Damascus* (1966). During the 1980s a number of works dealing with particular aspects of society and economics were published, works which had utilized documentary sources such as the waqf documents and sharia-court registers in the collections of the Zahiriya Library (al-Maktaba al-Ẓāhirīya) and the Center of Historical Documents in Damascus (Markaz al-Wathā'iq al-Ta'rīkhīya bi-Dimashq) and the land survey register (*tapu defteri*) and records of Ottoman Imperial Council (*mühimme defteri*) in Istanbul. J.-P. Pascual, *Damas à la fin du XVIe siècle* (1983) uses waqf documents to look in detail at the process by which urban expansion was continued in a centralized fashion through waqf endowments by Ottoman governors like Sinān Bāšā and Murād Bāšā at the beginning of the period. This is an important work for its detailed exposition, using the land survey register, of the quarters and their population at the time of the Ottoman conquest, and its examination of waqf documents to discuss the relationship between religious institutions and agricultural land and commercial facilities endowed as a source of revenue. M. A. Bakhit, *The Ottoman Province of Damascus* (1982) deals with the roles of the governor and the military, the ulama and the financial commissioners (*defterdar*) in the provincial administration of Damascus under Ottoman rule in the 16th century, and with the growing independence of locally prominent families and of tribal groups. The military class was concerned not only with military affairs and administration but also had the power to enter economic activities as landlords, bankers and merchants. Powers of appointment to public office, such as that of qadi or *muftī*, were assumed by the Ottoman government and so the ulama were brought into the system. By using the land survey register and the sharia-court registers, Bakhit's work incidentally throws light also on the yet scarcely elucidated fiscal situation of the city in the Mamluk period. For example, he shows that everything from everyday dealings in fruit and vegetables to taverns and gambling places was taxed. L. al-Ṣabbāgh, *Syrian-Arab Society in the Early Ottoman Period* (A., 1973) understands, on the other hand, that Ottoman rule could not touch the base of Syrian society, founded as it was on various separate factions (*jamā'a*). A.-R. Abu-Husayn, *Provincial Leadership in Syria* (1985) focuses on the rise of local power in the regions of Tripoli, Baalbek and Biqa' in the period 1575-1650.

The above four works deal with the actualities of Ottoman rule in Syria in the early period. We will now look at research concerning changes in local administration from the 18th century, after the relaxing of the so-called *timar* system. In *The Province of Damascus,* Rafeq established a framework for the study of Syrian society under the Ottomans, discussing in a multifaceted way government and society during the time that four members of the 'Aẓm family were provincial governors of Damascus, over a period of thirty-nine years and three generations, tracing the movements of the military, the ulama, merchants and artisans, mercenary soldiers, farmers and nomads. Since 1973 he has been making extensive use of sharia-court registers to show that the widespread development of buying and renting of land in rural villages encouraged the accumulation of profit from real estate among powerful people in the cities and the amassing of wealth, which stimulated the rise of local power. K. K. Barbir, *Ottoman Rule in Damascus* (1980) looks at the province of Damascus in the same period. Barbir uses documents of the Ottoman government to contend that this period should not be considered a time when regional power was being held just by local families such as the 'Aẓm, for Ottoman control was made effective by means of national events such as the hajj (pilgrimage). L. S. Schilcher, *Families in Politics* (1985) on the other hand says that the rule of the 'Aẓm family, based not so much on local power as on the *kapu kulu* (slave) regiments despatched by the central government and on traders, was centrally-oriented, and was the forerunner of the centralized bureaucratic system which developed with modernizing reforms in the Ottoman Empire in the latter half of the 19th century. The determining event in this period of change was the massacres of Christians in Damascus in 1860. The Ottoman government used this as a pretext to deal with local notable and ulama, and local power, on the rise since the 18th century, was incorporated in the centralized system of the empire. Ph. S. Khoury, *Urban Notables and Arab Nationalism* (1983) and *Syria and the French Mandate* (1987) is a study of Arab nationalism and politics under the Mandate, centring on the activities of the notables. Khoury understands that the ulama, the local military and secular dignitaries (merchants, tax farmers), who until around the middle of the 19th century had had different bases and who had been in opposition to one another, came to constitute a single class of notables based on land ownership and official appointments following the promulgation in 1858 of the Ottoman Land Code, which allowed the private ownership of land, and the 1860 riots. R. Roded, "Ottoman Service as a Vehicle for the Rise of New Upstarts among the Urban Elite Families of Syria"(1983) studies the birth places and appointments and positions held by 236 elite families in the years between 1876 and 1918 and shows that Ottoman executive officials appeared as the new elite. Specialized discussions on the causes and historical significance of the 1860 riots include K. S. Salibi, "The 1860 Upheaval in Damascus" (1968) and Rafeq, "New Light on the 1860 Riots" (1988).

The above studies are concerned with provincial government and regional society rather than with urban research *per se*. They are characterized by their studies of the relationship between the Ottoman government and regional society, and by the vivid descriptions, utilizing documentary sources, of the actuality of the various social networks, such as the Damascene military, the ulama, merchants and artisans, and the inhabitants of the quarters. In their examination of the military class, they show that the yerlīya, slave soldiers resident in Damascus, were linked with merchants and artisans in particular quarters, such as Maydān and Qubaybāt, and repeatedly opposed and fought the troops (*kapu kulu* slave regiments) under the direct command of the

Sultanate. Also joining in the conflict as private soldiers of the governor and others were military groups such as the Maghāriba, the Dalātīya, the Tüfenqji and the Lawand, as well as outlaw groups such as the *zorab*. The power of the central government was at its greatest when it came to appointments of the ulama to public offices such as qadi or *muftī*, and, since connections with, and bribery of, government officials were essential, there was a strong tendency to centralization among the ulama. As a result, according to J. Voll, "Old 'Ulama' Families and Ottoman Influence" (1975), there was a mounting swing of powerful ulama in the 17th and 18th centuries towards the Hanafi, the law school officially supported by the Ottoman government which commanded the position of chief qadi. A striking change from the Mamluk period was the increased influence of the *ashrāf* and the Sufis. The number of *ashrāf*, direct descendants of Muhammad, grew rapidly from 500 in the 18th century to 2000 in the 19th century and the *ashrāf* forged links with the Sufi orders and the guilds, becoming a power in the process. The *aghas*, commanders of army corps, with the ulama, formed powerful families, assuming, the position of *muftī* and head (*naqīb*) of the *ashrāf*, and factions centring on those families became a political power. Schilcher's research deals with the political and social changes of the 18th and 19th centuries in terms of the three important estates, the military, the ulama and the *ashrāf*, and the activities of the influential families. A. H. Hourani, "Ottoman Reform and the Politics of Notables" (1968) was a pioneering work in methods of analyzing Syrian society by looking at trends among the notables as a class and among notable families. His views have taken root in regards to modern history, and have been widely employed not only in the Syrian situation but regarding Iraqi society as well, as for example by H. Batatu, "The Old Social Classes" (1978). B. Shoshan, "The Politics of Notables" (1986) sees politics by give and take among the notables as being a distinctive feature of urban society in the medieval Islamic world as well, and advocates using it as the analytical framework. He discusses the work of Lapidus, R. W. Bulliet, Ashtor and Havemann from this point of view. However, differences have arisen depending on what the political, economic and social bases of the notables are and in determining class and power accordingly. R. Roded, "The Syrian Urban Notables" (1986) and Khoury, "The Urban Notables Paradigm Revisited" (1990) are pertinent studies of the efficacy of the urban notables paradigm and problems concerning it.

A. Abdel Nour, *Introduction à l'histoire urbaine* (1982) examines Syrian cities and their external networks in the 16th to 18th centuries with comparisons from the period before Ottoman rule, focusing on such points as the quarters, the composition of their inhabitants, administration and the supply of commodities. The work deals not only with Damascus and Aleppo, but other regional cities as well, and it provides an outline of cities in that period. Abdel Nour shows originality in his study of the structure of housing in the period, based on his investigation of sharia-court registers of buying and selling. Most were one-storey stone dwellings with rooms placed around a central courtyard. Only 1/5 had a separate kitchen and so the courtyard was also used for cooking. Y. J. Nu'aysa, *Urban Society in Damascus* (A., 1986) is a study, using Syrian sharia-court registers, of the social structure of Damascus in the period 1772-1840, up to the time Ibrahim Pasha was governor of Syria. Throughout the 18th century, the general populace proceeded to live segregated according to criteria such as race, religion, birthplace and occupation. The family, the quarter, the guild (*ṭā'ifa*), and groups such as the Sufi orders tended to have an increasingly important meaning as units of social life. In that situation, the yerlīya and the headmen (sheikh) of the quarters and the guilds acted as mediators with the rulers, maintaining the public interests (*maṣlaḥa*) of society. This work, in accordance with its title, takes up the subject of urban society directly; it uses sharia-court registers to ascertain the position of suqs and the role of guilds, and deals also with the family, clothing, worship, entertainment and other aspects of daily life, as well as the underside of urban life, such as bribery, prostitution, drinking, and illegalities in commercial transactions. However its discussion of social structure seems to have little originality. Rafeq also produced many pioneering studies about the actual state of society and the economy, using sharia-court registers, for example, "The Law-court Registers" (1976); "Syrian Craft Corporations in the Ottoman Period" (A., 1981), discussing the formation and internal organization of craft corporations (guilds); and "The Social and Economic Structure of Bāb-al-Muṣallā" (1988), an analysis of the social and economic conditions of people living in the Damascus suburb of Bāb al-Muṣallā. The former two throw light on the 163 craft corporations which existed in Syria during the 17th-19th centuries, on the functioning of tax collection and administrative control, and on the threefold structure of master, artisan, and apprentice. The latter study pioneers a new research methodology which uses sharia-court registers to investigate occupations, social class and family structure of the inhabitants of Bāb al-Muṣallā. "Public Morality" (1990) studies morality, using examples of complaints brought to the courts regarding instances of immoral conduct (drinking, prostitution, peeking at women, bad language, etc.) in the quarters of 18th century Damascus. Rafeq provides concrete data to show that more than 60% of incidents occurred in suburban quarters and that more than 60% of the accused were women. In conclusion, he sees the growing deterioration of public morality as being caused by the corruption of rulers and leading figures. J. -P. Pascual, "Meubles et objets domestiques quotidiens" (1990) offers a new insight into research using sharia-court registers which lay stress on immovable property in its analysis of household effects from court inventories. Khoury, "Syrian Urban Politics in Transition" (1984) is a study of the political role of the quarters during the French Mandate. Khoury gives data on the structure of the quarters and their population at the beginning of the 20th century and shows that the patron-client relationships among the leaders of the National Movement who moved from the Old City to the new suburban city, the *qabaḍāy,* outlaw bands in the quarters of the Old City, and the residents themselves comprised a network that supported the revolt of 1925 and that such networks were eventually changed through a modern elite organization that had no identity within the quarters. Particularly interesting is his direct survey of the *qabaḍāy,* elucidating their relations with the inhabitants and their self-consciousness. H. Gerber, "The Population of Syria and Palestine" (1979) is a study of population undertaken to examine 19th century economic conditions. He points out that previous research using travel records of Europeans was exaggerated in relation to large cities like Damascus and Aleppo and attempts to make estimates through conditions during plague epidemics. D. Chevallier, *Villes et travail en Syrie* (1982) is a collection of Chevallier's pioneering works on those Syrian cities which had close economic ties with Europe in the 19th and 20th centuries.

A feature of studies of Syria in the 19th and 20th centuries has been the enormous interest in families, quarters and craft corporations, and the lives of those people. Memoirs from the latter half of the 19th century have been the basis of the information reported in those studies. I. Qudsī, "Notice sur les corporations de Damas" (1885) presents information about the internal organization of guilds, discussing the role of their heads (sheikh) and their initiation ceremonies. *Dictionary of the Artisans of Damascus* (A., 1960) is an alphabetical listing of more than 300 occupations collected by a father and son, M. S. al-Qāsimī (d. 1900) and J. D. al-Qāsimī (d. 1914). A. H. al-'Allāf, *Damascus at the Beginning of the 20th Century* (A., 1976) is a memoir by the author, who was born in the Ṣāliḥīya quarter, which describes, mixing episodes and songs, children's education and festivals and the relationship between the outlaw bands and the quarter, etc. Q. al-Shihābī, *Damascus History and Pictures* (A., 1986) and *The Old Souks of Damascus and their Historical Monuments* (A., 1990) contain a large number of maps and photographs from the beginning of the 20th century. Q. H. Najāt, *Story of Damascus* (A., 1988) describes the life of the city during the century 1884-1983, and M. Kayyāl, *Tales of the People of Damascus* (A., 1987) is a collection of tales passed down by the people, organized by quarter. Some of the records of Europeans are of great importance too; J. Lecerf and R. Tresse, "Les 'arāḍa de Damas" (1937-8) describes the parades associated with festivals, etc. and A. Keusséoglou, *Le vieux Damas* (1988) records the street hawkers of the 1930s.

Aleppo

Aleppo has been known by that name since around 2000 B. C. It contains a large number of ruins and buildings dating back to ancient times, and the enormous citadel dominating the eastern part of the Old City and the covered Grand Bazar are the pride of the local people. There are a large number of topographies and chronicles by Arab historians such as Ibn al-'Aẓīmī (d. 12th century), Ibn al-'Adīm (d. 1262), Ibn Shaddād, and Ibn al-Shiḥna (d. 1485). Studies in considerable numbers were made of monuments under the French Mandate following World War I, and published for example in M. Soberheim, "Die arabischen Inschriften von Aleppo" (1926) and E. Herzfeld, "Inscriptions et monuments d'Alep" (1954-6). S. Mazloum, "L'ancienne canalisation" (1936?) surveys canals bringing water from the springs to the city and introduces court documents related to water disputes under Ottoman rule. It was Sauvaget who established the framework for research and who collected the documentary sources together. After publishing works such as "L'enceinte primitive" (1929) which discusses changes in the city wall and "Inventaires des monuments musulmans" (1931), a study of the development of religious and social facilities during the Islamic period, he brought his research together in *Alep* (1941). Here Sauvaget uses such sources as Arabic historical sources, travel records by Europeans, cartographic resources such as the *Plan cadastral,* field surveys of monuments, and inscriptions. He works from the topographical environment to give an overview of the political situation and urban development in each epoch from ancient times to the 20th century. During Hellenistic and Roman times, Aleppo was "a trading city" and "a Mediterranean city" standing on the crossroads of east-west trade, and it was then that the basic structures of the city, such as its walls, its citadel, its temples and its canals, were built. During the Islamic period, though the city to an certain extent continued to follow the ancient physical structure, particularity took precedence over generality, and anarchy over law, in terms of social structure, with the increasing fragmentation of the city into quarters, etc., and its unity as a city was lost. To back his thesis, he presents plans of the city in the Hellenistic period, in the Roman period, and in the 11th, 13th, 16th and 19th centuries. These show the important buildings of each period, and overall result in exhibiting a continuity in central functions such as the walls, the citadel, the market, and the temple (Friday mosque) at the same time as the urban area expanded and developed. A feature of Sauvaget's research is that he incorporates studies of physical form into historical research, and speaks boldly about the social structure of the city based on its physical features. Researchers have quoted widely from the city plans mentioned above, and from his map of the Grand Bazar and the quarters based on the *Plan cadastral*.

Topographical studies undertaken after World War II include M. A. Ṭalas, *Islamic Historical Monuments in Aleppo* (A., 1956), a description of the history and location of important buildings in Aleppo on the model of Sauvaget's work, and even surpassing Sauvaget methodologically, is H. Gaube and E. Wirth, *Aleppo* (1984), a geographer's view based on textual sources and close observation. Gaube and Wirth carried out comprehensive surveys of the monuments and ensembles of the old city of Aleppo in 1975 and 1979. They collated the surveys with the topographies of Ibn al-Shiḥna, al-Ghazzī (d. 1923) and others to trace the historical development of religious monuments, commercial facilities, quarters, streets and canals and assembled the information obtained in precise coloured maps. They also examined commercial and craft functions of Aleppo in the 19th and 20th centuries and showed how the city maintained its function as a centre for east-west trade even after the inflow of European goods. In contrast to Sauvaget's studies of physical structures, which tended to generalize in terms of partial illustrations and no citation of sources, Gaube and Wirth conducted exhaustive investigations, whether for religious monuments or street networks, and their results are shown in the maps and diagrams. Whereas, too, Sauvaget took as his motif the comparison between the Graeco-Roman and Islamic periods, Gaube and Wirth focus on the 19th century and seek to show both what is continuous with the premodern urban structure and what has changed through modern urbanization. For example, they use al-Ghazzī's topography, *Nahr al-Dhahab*, to assemble in tabular form facts about the number of inhabitants and houses, the composition of the inhabitants, and the area, etc. of ninety-nine quarters around 1900. As well, they use statistical data as a means to investigate the quarter in premodern and modern times, by showing differences in the composition of the inhabitants of each quarter, the population density, the housing density, and numbers of people per household. As a general study using both historical records and field observation, the work should become the basis for further research on Aleppo, but regrettably the map on which it bases its surveys and its own cartographic work is a 1/11,000 map published in 1951; it was only possible to use the *Plan cadastral* (1/500; 1/200 for the Grand Bazar) employed by Sauvaget after 1980, when the work was in the final stages of editing. If the *Plan cadastral* could have been used, it would conceivably have been possible to investigate structure and changes in domestic dwellings as well.

M. Hreitani and J.-Cl. David, "Souks traditionnels" (1984) makes a detailed investigation of the Grand Bazar in terms of its facilities, its occupations, and the constitutions of waqfs, etc. in 1930 and 1980, based on textual sources and field observation and examines its role in the Aleppo economy. Its analysis of the situation in 1930 is important, based as it is on registers and maps of cadastral surveys conducted during the French Mandate. M. Kh. D. al-Asadī, *Comparative Encyclopaedia of Aleppo* (A., 1986-8); *Quarters and Markets of Aleppo* (A., 1990) are the revised and published papers of al-Asadī, who died in 1971. The former is a seven volume encyclopedia of Aleppo which reveals the deep erudition of the author in the fields of history, the topographies, literature and the arts.

Works concerning the problems of modern urbanization include several studies by J.-Cl. David, "Alep" (1975); "L'urbanisation en Syrie" (1978); and "Les quartiers anciens" (1979). David investigates changes in dwellings, streets, public facilities, urban centres, etc. using statistical data and a wealth of examples taken from field research. In "L'espace des chrétiens" (1990) he examines, for the period 1750-1950, the dwellings and the social and economic conditions of Christians living in the northern part of Aleppo. Their growing activity since the end of the 19th century is noteworthy. A. Terasaka and M. Naito (eds.), *Geographical Views: Syria* (1990) is a report of a field survey of Aleppo, and the suburban quarter of Bāb al-Ḥadīd in particular; an appendix contains reproductions of eight city plans dating from the 19th century to the 1980s. M. Scharabi, "Bemerkungen zur Bauform des Sūqs" (1980) studies the Grand Bazar in terms of architectural history. There are also a number of enterprising investigations into traditional industries and artisans, such as J. Cornand, "L'artisanat du textile" (1986), dealing with weavers, and Th. Grandin, "La savonnerie traditionnelle" (1986), discussing the soap-making industry.

All of the authors of epoch-making historical studies, such as Ashtor, Cahen, Lapidus, Havemann and Abdel Nour, have treated Damascus and Aleppo together. To avoid repetition, I will discuss here only historical research that concerns Aleppo alone. Detailed studies of Aleppo politics and society under the Mirdasids and the Seljuks include S. Zakkar, *The Emirate of Aleppo 1004-1094* (1971) and M. Ḍāmin, *The Emirate of Aleppo under the Seljuks* (A., 1990). D. Sourdel has reconstructed the topography of the Ayyubid city by means of the 13th century topography of Ibn Shaddād in "Esquisse topographique" (1952) and deals with professors in the Aleppo madrasas in the 12th and 13th centuries in "Les professeurs de madrasa" (1949-51). K. Ota, "The Military Organization of the Mirdasid Dynasty" (J., 1986) discusses, in terms of military organization how the Mirdasids established themselves as the regional power by mustering Arab tribal force and the urban dwellers to escape foreign domination. She examines the military connection between city dwellers, beginning with the *aḥdāth,* and the Mirdasids. J. Taniguchi, "The Qal'a and Madīna of Aleppo in the 11th Century" (J., 1990) states that the great citadel (*qal'a*) in the old city was set up as the base of ruling power in the 11th century and that is meaningful in that it opposed the growing activity of the *aḥdāth* in the city (*madīna*). His conclusion, drawn from his close investigation of the term *aḥdāth,* raises the important question that the *aḥdāth* was an independent group including the slave soldiers (*ghulām*), demarcated from both the rulers and the townspeople in general. K. Ota, "The History of Bānaqūsa in Aleppo" (J., 1990) traces the history of the formation of the Bānaqūsa quarter in the north-east suburbs of the city, demonstrates its growth during the Mamluk dynasty as a centre of trade and commerce and the increase in activity of autonomous movements among the residents, and discusses how the geographical situation of its being in the suburbs outside the city walls contributed all the more to its economic development and its political unity. J. B. Evrard, *Zur Geschichte Aleppos und Nordsyriens* (1974) discusses the political and military roles of the provincial governor in northern Syria at the end of the Mamluk dynasty when the Ottoman and Mamluk rulers confronted each other.

As with Damascus, studies of Ottoman Aleppo using documentary sources are thriving. M. A. Bakhit, "Aleppo and the Ottoman Military" (1978-9) uses such sources to describe the confused conditions up until the time Aleppo seceded from the province of Damascus. A. Raymond, "The Population of Aleppo" (1984) is a study of the structure of the quarters in terms of inhabitants and numbers of households, etc., employing three types of document, Ottoman land survey registers, the travel record of the Frenchman D'Arvieux and al-Ghazzī's topography. It presents basic data concerning the population of the city. id. "Les grands waqfs" (1979) discusses the connection between the building of waqf foundations and urban growth in the 16th and 17th centuries. Regarding Ipšīr Pāšā's waqf-complex (mosques, *khāns, qaysarīya*s, cafés and shops) in the Judayda quarter that Raymond discussed here, J.-Cl. David, *Le waqf d'Ipšīr Pāšā* (1982) is a detailed study of their construction and functions based on field research and waqf documents. A. Abdel Nour, "Types architecturaux" (1979) and "Habitat et structures sociales" (1982) analyze the physical form of dwellings and residential space in 17th and 18th century Aleppo, using sharia-court registers. J. Tate, *Une waqfiyya du XVIIIe siècle* (1990) examines the types and distribution of 102 buildings donated as waqf endowments by a trader in the 18th century, based on waqf documents and field research, presenting material through which can be ascertained the assets of the trader, his purpose in making the endowment, and his connections with the quarter.

J. H. L. Bodman, *Political Factions in Aleppo 1760-1826* (1963) is a pioneering study in the field of political history. It explains Aleppo politics in the 18th and 19th centuries, a period of frequently occurring urban riots, through the relationship among three groupings, the Ottoman government, the *yeniçeri,* and the *ashrāf,* and holds that from the 1830s, the *yeniçeri* and the *ashrāf* with their growing closeness to the residents lost strength in the face of reform policies of the Ottoman government and economic decline. Whereas Bodman had used chronicles and European reports as his historical material, J.-P. Thieck, "Décentralisation ottomane et affirmation urbaine" (1985) employs Ottoman decrees and sharia-court registers to show how the *yeniçeri* and the *ashrāf* established an economic and social base spanning both rural villages and urban centres as Ottoman centralized power weakened in the 18th century, and he considers that because of conflicts between the factions in the city and confrontations between the city dwellers, urban integration did not take form. H. Kuroki, "The Social Structure of the City of Aleppo" (J., 1987) shows Aleppo in the premodern period, before the Egyptian occupation of 1832 to have been an international commercial city, where various religious groups, including Christians and Jews, linguistic groups, occupational groups and social groups, based on the quarters, etc., coexisted in a complex and multiple manner. In "Social Relations in an Urban Disturbance: Aleppo 1819-20" (J., 1988) and "Social Relations in an Urban Disturbance: Aleppo, 1850" (J., 1989), Kuroki analyses two disturbances that involved the whole city which took place at years sandwiching the Egyptian occupation in order to trace changes in social relations. Whereas during the former disturbance, a consciousness of being a townsman (*ahl al-balad*) transcended religious sect and was held in common by all inhabitants, during the latter that consciousness weakened, with attacks on Christians and the appearance of fissures between the religious sects. Kuroki points out the change that occurred between the two disturbances, the collapse of an urban social norm of peaceful coexistence and tolerance among the various religious groups and the loss of identity of the townsman, and seeks the origin of the change in the modernizing policies of the Egyptian Occupation Army and the Ottoman Empire in the 1840s. In contrast to the views of scholars such as M. Ma'oz ("Syrian Urban Politics," 1966), who see Aleppo society as a mosaic with its large numbers of residents who belonged to the different Christian sects or who were Jews, Kuroki stresses the complex society where various sects and various groupings coexisted. In this sense he shows a critical attitude towards the concept of the "Islamic city." Nevertheless in the above articles he only analyzes social relations during times of disturbance, and further study should be undertaken concerning the relationships of coexistence in social life during times of peace, and the norms supporting those relationships.

B. Masters, *The Origins of Western Economic Dominance* (1988) is a contribution to this theme from a social and economic historian. Masters regards the period 1600-1750 as the time when the Islamic economy lost to European mercantilism and were incorporated into "the modern world-system" (I. Wallerstein). Using Ottoman government documents as well as sharia-court registers he makes a detailed examination of changes in the caravan trade centring on silk and the Aleppo commercial system and confirms three main points. First, any Muslim with capital engaged in commerce, and individual organizations and interest groups of merchants did not appear. On the other hand, minority groups like Christians strengthened their solidarity as merchants. Second, wealth was amassed chiefly as money, which was invested in loans to the farmers rather than maintained as capital accumulation such as trading or industrial capital. Third, Islamic market ethics (justice) functioned through the sharia-courts. These characteristics were reflected also in Ottoman government political and economic policies. The Islamic economy, which as a whole tends to be open, stands in contrast to European mercantilism which sought profits for the individual nation in combination with the national authority. Because of this open character, European merchants were permitted to enter the markets of the Islamic world, and in the lattter half of the 18th century, the Islamic economy was incorporated into "the modern world-system". Masters's work is an advance on previous studies in that it leads to an analysis of the economic system from historical documents, and in addition it criticizes both modernists and Marxists in viewing the source of the Islamic world's being absorbed into "the modern world-system" as being the openness inherent in the Islamic economy. In "The 1850 Events in Aleppo" (1990), Masters analyzes the origins of the anti-Christian attacks in Aleppo in 1850 in terms of the previous analysis of the economic process. This incident, where Muslims in the Eastern quarters attacked Christians in the Judayda quarter, reveals the limits of consensus politics and the balance between the various religious sects and groupings of Aleppo. Masters sees its origin not as a conspiracy by members of the long-established notables class, or at their instigation, nor in the general economic confrontation that occurred as a result of the absorption of the Islamic economy into the European, but in the way the interests of both sides were strikingly revealed in the Judayda and Eastern quarters and in the action of the Christians of Judayda to seek European protection and sever themselves from the framework of consensus politics.

Marcus, whose results have been published since 1983, like Masters uses sharia-court registers to draw a picture of Aleppo society in the 18th century; his work has the character of the Annales School of social history. "Men, Women and Property" (1983) is an examination of real estate transactions in the 1750s. He considers such transactions to be related to prestige rather than investment; they were not made on the free market but among people of certain propertied classes (and frequently involved women and business that transcended religious sect). The economics and society that Marcus portrays here is does not depend on market mechanisms but upon reciprocity, dependence and power. "Privacy in Eighteenth-Century Aleppo" (1986) examines how privacy worked in an Islamic society through a discussion of disputes recorded in sharia-court registers. While the norms of male and female separation characteristic of the Muslim are realized here, they are easily broken among the poorer classes who do not have the material base to make them work. Thus Marcus continues to criticize the method of explaining what actually happened in a deductive manner from such Islamic norms. At the same time, he does not try to understand behaviour through economic or social constructs, but states the necessity of attaching importance to culture and norms as elements generating behaviour and change. In *The Middle East on the Eve of Modernity* (1989) he describes Middle Eastern premodern urban society based on Aleppo society in the 18th century. He examines space and people, and material and spiritual life, and discusses them in terms of the individual, the group and the community. He attaches particular importance to the role of the group (such as the family, the quarter and the guild), which stands between the individual and the society. His "group" incorporates people of different social and economic circumstances and even has a hierarchical structure. Society as a whole also has class characteristics and conflict within it, and at the same time the function to resolve them. This understanding of groups and society is demarcated from the theory of the mosaic society, essentially comprising a classless society and an overarching government. While Masters emphasizes the contrasts and shifts between premodern and modern society, Marcus rather concentrates on the structures which stabilized premodern society. "Privacy" (see above) and in "Poverty and Poor Relief" (1990) both exhibit his great interest in the distinctive features of Middle Eastern, Islamic society itself, in comparison with Islamic and European societies.

Jerusalem

The holy city of Judaism, Christianity and Islam, filled with religious sites and monuments, Jerusalem is a lodestone for travelers, pilgrims, archaeologists and historians.

Topographical studies include the prewar H. Vincent and F. M. Abel, *Jérusalem* (1926) and architectural surveys by the British School of Archaeology in Jerusalem (1977), as well as Hopkins, *Jerusalem: A Study in Urban Geography* (1970). In addition, M. van Berchem, *Matériaux pour un corpus inscriptionum arabicarum: Jérusalem* (1920-7) is a collection of inscriptions then remaining on Jerusalem buildings, and it has become an important source of data. Waqf institutions are studied in Tibawi, *The Islamic Pious Foundations* (1978) and in A. J. H. 'Abd al-Mahdī, *Madrasas of Jerusalem in the Ayyubid and the Mamluk Periods* (A., 1981). M. H. Burgoyne conducted a survey with the cooperation of the Waqf Council of Jerusalem (Dā'ira al-Awqāf al-Islāmīya bil-Quds), focusing in particular upon the flurry of building activity that took place in the Mamluk period after Jerusalem was retrieved from the Crusaders in 1244. He has published his findings in "Some Mameluke Doorways" (1971), an analysis of the grandeur of construction of the doorways of madrasas and other buildings, and "Ṭarīq Bāb al-Ḥadīd" (1973), in which he traced the course of buildings in an alley leading to Ḥaram Sharīf. In *Mamluk Jerusalem* (1986) he examines sixty-four buildings of the Mamluk period in terms of their position, history and construction, etc. in a profusely illustrated text. He shows that religious facilities were constructed adjacent to the holy area (Ḥaram Sharīf). From the Muslim side, the Department of Islamic Archaeology in the Islamic Waqf Department was set up in 1977; it has published an Arabic edition of the survey reports of the aforementioned British School of Archaeology in Jerusalem (1977) and is working to record and preserve Islamic institutions.

Among historical studies are S. D. Goitein, "The Sanctity of Jerusalem and Palestine in Early Islam" (1966) and E. Sivan, "Le caractère sacré de Jérusalem" (1967), both of which discuss Jersualem's holy character. id., "The Beginnings of the Fada'il al-Quds Literature" (1971) and I. Hasson, "Muslim Literature in Praise of Jerusalem" (1981) trace the development of Faḍā'il literature, which sang of Jerusalem's beauties. Goitein, "Jerusalem in the Arab Period" (1982) is an outline of Jerusalem under Islamic domination prior to the Crusades which pays attention to relations towards Christians and Jews. M. Gil, "Dhimmī Donations and Foundations" (1984) examines in detail how the religious facilities of Jews and Christians were maintained. During the Mamluk period Jerusalem was administratively only a regional capital in the Province of Damascus, but J. Drory, "Jerusalem during the Mamluk Period" (1981) shows how its distinctive role as a holy place continued. Historical studies by Arabs include A. B. al-'Ārif, *History of Jerusalem* (A., 1950), I. Rishād, *Medieval Jerusalem* (A., 1976), Y. D. Ghawānama, *History of Jerusalem District in the Mamluk Period* (A., 1982) and Shafīq J. A. M., *History of Jerusalem: Relations between Muslims and Christians until the Crusade* (A., 1984). M. M. al-Dabbāgh, *Our Homeland Palestine* (A., repr. 1991) is a dictionary of place names in eleven volumes covering the history and geography of the Palestine region. F. E. Peters, *Jerusalem and Mecca* (1986) is a unique study based on historical materials examining the nature of the holiness of Jerusalem and Mecca and the influence of that holiness on their history.

A new turn in historical research into Jerusalem was made with the discovery of the Ḥaram Documents, dating from the Mamluk period, and with the employment of Ottoman government land survey registers and sharia-court registers. The Ḥaram Documents were discovered in 1976 in the Islamic Museum in the holy area of Jerusalem called Ḥaram Sharīf. They consist of documents of every kind, including royal decrees, court records and waqf documents. D. P. Little, "Ḥaram Documents related to the Jews" (1985) examines those documents concerning the Jews and reveals that Jews lived with Muslims in the same quarters and conducted business together. H. Lutfi, *al-Quds al-Mamlûkiyya* (1985) is an analysis of Jerusalem society during the Mamluk period, using mainly 423 estate inventories of the dead from the end of the 14th century, which comprise almost half of the Ḥaram Documents. These estate inventories record precise details of the dead: their occupations, their origins and places of abode, their spouses, and their property, as well as their heirs. Totaling and organizing the data, Lutfi gives a detailed outline of areas rarely covered in historical narrative material, like the connections between religious facilities and their waqf properties, industry, movements of population, the form of dwellings, and the workings of local administration. Her findings cast a light on unexpected elements of urban life. For example, financial resources for the religious facilities of Jerusalem were largely derived from the harvest from the surrounding rural areas and from rents on houses. The majority of houses in any quarter were rented, and in many cases these rents provided waqf income. In addition, the ratio of men to women amongst the dead was about 4:6, and there were large numbers of unmarried women from other lands living in Jerusalem.

Studies employing Ottoman period historical documents include W. D. Hütteroth and K. Abdulfattah, *Historical Geography of Palestine, Transjordan and Southern Syria* (1977) and Hütteroth, *Palästina und Transjordanien* (1978). These make a statistical analysis of 16th century land survey registers and provide a commentary on the taxation system, organizing data concerning taxation areas, amounts of tax revenue, and lists of items collected in Palestine and Jordan by means of graphs and maps. They therefore allow a commanding view over a broad area (province) including villages and towns as well as large urban centres. A. Cohen, continuing the work of Lewis, has used the same documents to make a wide study of the administration of the towns of Palestine in *Population and Revenue in the Towns of Palestine* (1978). E. Toledano, "The Sanjaq of Jerusalem" (1984) and G. Makovsky, "Sixteenth-Century Agricultural Production" (1984) use 16th century land survey registers (*tapu defteri*) and in particular the detailed registers called *mufaṣṣal* to make a careful investigation into the location and population of villages and the types and amounts of harvests in the *sanjaq* of Jerusalem. A. Singer, "The Countryside of Ramle" (1990) outlines the population and tax items of *nāhiya* of Ramle in the 16th century. Bakhit, "The Christian Population of the Province of Damascus" (1982) uses 16th century land survey registers to examine the composition of the population by religious sect in the Province of Damascus (including Jerusalem, Ghaza, Safad and Nabulus). Such studies of regional towns and villages using land survey registers are expected to increase in the future. Cohen's vigorous research is also continuing; he has used sharia-court registers remaining in East Jerusalem to describe Jewish society in 16th century Jerusalem in *Jewish Life under Islam* (1984) and social and economic life in *Economic Life in Ottoman Jerusalem*(1989). 'Aṭā Allāh, *Documents relating to Guilds in Jerusalem* (A., 1991) arranges sharia-court documents relating to guilds according to occupation. D. S. Powders, "Revenues of Public Waqfs" (1984) uses 16th century Jerusalem waqf survey registers to examine the income and expenditure of fifty-eight waqf endowments; it shows that a good proportion of the financial sources for the waqf came from agricultural land. G. Baer, "The Dismemberment of Awqāf" (1979) studies the dismemberment of waqf properties, which appears frequently in sharia-court registers in the early 19th century. He reveals that important waqf were eroded by powerful families of notables, managers (*mutawallī*) and qadis.

Political history of the Ottoman period is studied in M. Rosen, "The Naqīb al-Ashrāf Rebellion" (1984). Rosen uses diaries of Jewish Rabbis to cover the rebellion which broke out in Jerusalem between 1702 and 1705, and shows that as in contemporary Damascus the qadis and the *naqīb al-ashrāf,* etc. were at the head of local power. H. Gerber, *Ottoman Rule in Jerusalem* (1985) discusses Jerusalem in the late 19th century. Y. Ben-Arieh, "Urban Development in the Holy Land" (1983) discusses the form and composition of population of towns in 19th century Palestine according to European sources. id., *Jerusalem in the 19th Century* (1984) takes up Jerusalem in the same period. A. Schölch, "The Demographic Development of Palestine" (1985) examines population movements in Palestinian towns in the latter half of the 19th century, revealing that period to have been a time of economic and social change.

From the 19th century Jerusalem became the focus of international diplomacy, with the Eastern Question and the issue of the holy land. Today, following the annexation of Jerusalem in 1967 by Israel and the subsequent reconstruction, the city of Jerusalem is again a focus of interest with questions arising concerning the position it should hold. Works related to this subject are too numerous to enumerate here. Since the second half of the 1970s, Yuzo Itagaki has been emphasizing the historic and symbolic character of

Jerusalem as a city of peace and suggesting ways to understand the structure of the Eastern and Palestine questions by means of an examination of the history of Jerusalem. Part of his study has been republished in *Listening to the Voice of the Stones* (J., 1992).

The Mediterranean Coast

Numerous studies exist concerning cities other than Damascus, Aleppo and Jerusalem, and share common ground in terms of the sources used and methods employed to those cities already touched upon. In the main though they have not been as well documented in terms of independent histories or topographies, and the majority of studies are descriptive rather than analytical, necessarily consisting of reports on related people and events culled from general chronicles and biographies, either chronologically or for a particular period. For the period covering the 19th and 20th centuries studies use the travel records and maps of Europeans, or the consular reports and trade reports of the period. Since the 1980s, Ottoman land survey registers, sharia-court registers and waqf documents have been used to study the composition of the inhabitants, administration, and economy, but at the present stage, most of them are only introductory to the historical source material. Because such historical documents are in themselves static information, to analyze economic changes it will be necessary to use statistical methodology, and to relate the documents to political changes they should be used in conjunction with imperial decrees, consular reports, etc.

The cities of the Mediterranean coast functioned as windows for the European world, and at times as outposts. A. El'ad, "The Coastal Cities of Palestine" (1982) is a study of their role up till the 10th century. The cities of the northern Syrian coast have been studied by Sauvaget, "Le plan de Laodicée-sur-Mer" (1934), an examination of the plan of the city of Latakia through field research, and by J. Weulersse, "Antioche" (1934), an analysis of the suqs and the composition of the quarters, based on ethnic and religious differences, of Antioch (Antakya). The rule of the qadis was established in Latakia during the Crusades, to which one chapter has been devoted in Havemann, *Ri'āsa und Qaḍā'* (1975). T. Sato has collected historical materials on Jabala, a town south of Latakia, and given an overview of its geography and history with an appendix of Arabic documents concerning the town in *The Syrian Coastal Town of Jabala* (1988). id., "The Revolt of al-Nuṣayrīs at Jabala, 1318" (J., 1989) discusses the background to the revolt of the Nusayrīs at Jabala in 1318; he ascertains that the policies of the Sultan al-Nasir to promote persecution of the Nusayrīs with the land surveys underlay the revolt. id. "Qāḍīs in the Syrian Coastal Towns" (J., 1991) deals with the role of the qadis in Tripoli and Jabala, who managed these municipalities with their economic and military power not only during the time when they were independent, but also under Byzantine and Crusader rule.

Studies of Beirut include S. Chehabe Ed-Dine, *Géographie humaine de Beyrouth* (1960), H. Ruppert, *Beirut* (1969) and M. Sh. 'Iṣām, *History of Beirut* (A., 1987), a comprehensive history from ancient times. L. Fawaz, *Merchants and Migrants* (1983) is a pioneering achievement analyzing modern Beirut society. 19th century Beirut grew rapidly in population from 60,000 to 120,000 people, transforming into a commercial city. With urbanization came religious conflict. A new stimulus to urban studies has been the focus on and analysis of the origins of those changes, in particular the role played by the region of Mount Lebanon behind the city and its relation with migration. Epoch-making research has been undertaken using the documents preserved in the Lebanon Archives, and Egyptian, English and French diplomatic and commercial documents. This research shows that until the first half of the 19th century Beirut was a tolerant society where people of different religions and sects lived peacefully together. With an increase of migrants from the mountain regions, particularly Christians, the religious composition of the town changed; furthermore, with the economic predominance of Christian merchants with ties with Europe, sectarian confrontations, by religion and race, became marked. Thus came into being the problem that remains with Lebanon to the present. id., "The City and the Mountain" (1984) examines the reasons why the attacks on Christians in 1860 in the Mount Lebanon area spread to Damascus but not to Beirut. D. Chevallier, "Signes de Beyrouth" (1972) describes the economy and facilities of Beirut in 1834, immediately before it underwent its rapid expansion as a port city. H. Ḥallāq has published two works, *A Social, Economic and Political History of Beirut* (A., 1987) and *Waqf Foundations in Beirut* (A., 1988), an introduction to and revision of sharia-court registers and waqf documents from Beirut. He has also written *Ottoman Beirut* (A., 1987). M. Johnson, *Class and Client in Beirut* (1986) examines post-1840 politics and society in Beirut and Lebanon through patron-client relationships, and has attracted notice for its use of sociological and anthropological methodology. id., "Political Bosses and their Gangs" (1977) examines, through fieldwork, the political and social relationship between the *za'īm* (bosses) and the *qabaḍāy* (gangs) in the Muslim quarters of Beirut.

Tripoli is taken up in Ṣamīḥ W. Z., *A History of Tripoli* (A., 1969), a general history from ancient times to the present, in U. A. S. Tadmurī, *History of Tripoli* (1978), a detailed history from the Arab occupation to the Crusades, and in N. S. H. Nahdī, *A History of Tripoli in the 17th Century* (A., 1986), a study of politics, society and the economy of Tripoli during the Ottoman period, based on sharia-court registers. H. Salam-Liebich, *The*

Architecture of the Mamluk City of Tripoli (1983) surveys the religious and economic facilities of Tripoli constructed in the Mamluk period and includes a large number of plans and illustrations. A. A. Sālim, *Sidon in the Islamic Period* (A., 1986) is a general history of Sidon (Ṣaydā) from Phoenician times until the time of Fakhr al-Din. M. A. Bakhit, "Sidon in Mamluk and Early Ottoman Times" (1981) is in the main a study of the composition of the population and tax items using 16th century land survey registers. A. Cohen, *Palestine in the 18th Century* (1973) examines the regimes of Zahir al-'Umar and Jezzar, based in Sidon in the 18th century using Ottoman historical records and European historical materials, and should be compared with the 'Aẓm regime of Damascus at the same period. Ghassān M. S., *Sidon 1818-60* (A., 1988) uses sharia-court registers to describe the architecture, administration, social life, food, clothing and housing, and economy of Sidon between 1818 and 1860. Th. Philipp, "The Rise and Fall of Acre" (1990) is a study of economic fluctuations, centring on the cotton trade in Acre between 1700 and 1850. Dealing with Tyre (Ṣūr) is M H. Chéhab, *Tyr* (1975, 1979), a study of the city's politics and society during the time of the Crusader states, using both European and Arabic historical materials.

T. Th. al-Ṭarāwina, *The Province of Safad in the Mamluk Period* (A., 1982) brings together trends in local provinces, based on sources such as chronicles and geographies. H. Rhode, "The Geography of the Sixteenth-Century Sancak of Ṣafad" (1985) studies administrative regions in 16th century Safad using land survey registers and Bakhit, "Ṣafad" (1990) investigates the condition of waqf endowments in mid-16th century Safad using waqf registers. With Powders's research on Jerusalem, further analysis is expected in the future, the waqf registers being eloquent records of social and economic conditions.

Ghaza is treated in M. A. Kh. 'Aṭā Allāh, *Ghaza Province in the Mamluk Period* (A., 1986) and S. M. 'Arafāt, *Ghaza* (A., 1987), a general history from the Neolithic period until the First World War to which is appended Ottoman period documents, city maps, and a large number of photographs. Rafeq, "Ghaza" (A., 1985) examines society and the economy in the mid-19th century using sharia-court registers. M. M. Sadek, *Die Mamlukische Architektur der Stadt Gaza* (1991) is a detailed study of building activity in Ghaza in the Mamluk period based on field research and historical records.

The Inland Region

Studies of inland cities include M. I. A. al-Khūrī, *History of Homs* (A., 1983-4), a two volume history from ancient times to the present, A. Mūsā and M. Ḥurba, *Hama District* (A., 1985), an outline of the geography, history, peoples, economy and culture, and A. Gh. Sabbānū, *Ayyubid Kingdom of Hama* (A., 1984), the fate of the Hama Principality under the Ayyubid regime. al-Bakhīṭ, *Karak in the Mamluk Period* (A., 1976) is a compendium of the economy, administration and culture of the author's birthplace. These are not urban studies in the narrow definition, but show how keen an interest there is in local history in Syria and Jordan.

The University of Jordan (al-Jāmi'a al-Urdunīya) is conducting surveys of Amman, regional villages and hamlets, whose results are being published in a number of detailed, illustrated reports including *Dwellings in Amman* (A., 1987), *Sūf: A Study of the Structure of a Town* (A., 1989) and *'Irāq al-Amīr: A Study of the Structure of a Jordanian Village* (A., 1988). Since 1974 the university has sponsored an international symposium on Syrian history (International Conference on the History of Bilād al-Shām) and published voluminous conference reports.

3. Egypt

Fustat and Cairo

Cairo has a history of more than a thousand years, and with a population of over ten million it is one of the world's leading cities. When the Arab armies conquered Egypt in 642, they built a garrison town (*miṣr*) called Fustat on the eastern bank of the Nile. A new capital, al-Qāhira, was established north-east of Fustat by the Fatimids in 969, and under the Ayyubids and Mamluks it became the centre of government and the economy. During the Ottoman period, the city began to develop in the direction of the western suburbs, near the banks of the Nile, and under the French and British occupation, the government centre was moved here and a new, modern city was formed between the Old City and the Nile. Syrian cities like Damascus and Aleppo consist of an old city within the city walls, which contains the citadel and the Friday mosque, and new suburbs which developed in concentric circles outside the walls. Cairo on the other hand is distinctive in that it developed and grew over a period of time as its core moved from Fustat to al-Qāhira to the western suburbs, and no encircling walls were ever built.

The numerous studies on the topography of Cairo all tend to employ al-Maqrīzī's (d. 1442) *al-Khiṭaṭ*, 'Alī Mubārak's (d. 1893) *al-Khiṭaṭ al-jadīda (Enlarged and Newly-edited Topography of Egypt)* and the maps in *Description de l'Égypte*, compiled by scholars accompanying Napoleon's occupation of Egypt in 1798. Egypt has a long tradition of surveying and cartography since the end of the 19th century and Egyptian Survey Authority (al-Hay'a al-Miṣrīya al-'Āmma lil-Misāḥa) has published various types of city maps on a scale of 1/500, 1/1000, 1/5000, etc. for the purpose of administration. *Map of Islamic Historical Monuments in Cairo* (A., 1948-51) was made by the Egyptian Department of Survey (Maṣlaḥa al-Misāḥa) and distinguishes by colour historical sites from the Fatimid period to the Second World War. An index of place names allows ready reference. S. W. Johnson (ed.), *The Monuments of Islamic Cairo* (1979) shows the sites of historical remains and the dates of their construction. Individual buildings are treated comprehensively in Creswell, *The Muslim Architecture of Egypt* (1952-9), L. Hautecoeur and G. Wiet, *Les mosquées du Caire* (1932), A. R. Zakī, *History and Historical Monuments of Cairo* (A., 1966), Su'ād M. M., *Egyptian Mosques* (A., 1971-3), and D. Behrens-Abouseif, *The Minarets of Cairo* (1985). The Deutsches Archäologisches Institut in Kairo is carrying out a detailed survey of buildings and publishing its successive reports in its organ, *Mitteilungen der Deutschen Archäologischen Instituts, Abteilung Kairo*. Studies dealing with the mosques, madrasas and *khānqāhs* (Sufi convents) built by the Mamluk sultans Barquq and Faraj include S. L. Mostafa, *Kloster und Mausoleum des Farağ* (1968), *Moschee des Farağ* (1972) and *Madrasa, Ḫānqāh und Mausoleum des Barqūq* (1982), detailed examinations of religious buildings with great mausolea attached, a popular architectural form in the Mamluk period. Behrens-Abouseif, *Islamic Architecture in Cairo* (1989) is an outline of historical changes in style and decoration, with comments on the history of important buildings and their stylistic characteristics for each period. More than just an introduction to buildings, it is an analysis worthy to be considered an architectural history. A. Raymond and G. Wiet, *Les Marchés du Caire* (1979) translates the section on suqs in al-Maqrīzī's topography into French, makes detailed annotations based on the *Description de l'Égypt* and other works, and in appendices brings together maps and lists of commercial facilities like suqs and caravansaries in Mamluk Cairo. Taken as a whole, it gives an overall view of commercial functions in Cairo. M. Scharabi, "Drei traditionelle Handelsanlagen" (1978) is a survey of the caravansaries in modern Cairo, compared with those of other cities. The quarter of al-Qarāfa in the southern suburbs of Cairo has been the site, since the Fatimid period, of the tombs of the 'Alids and the saints, and it is a venue of popular pilgrimage. It is also known as "the city of the dead," and has been studied by Massignon in "La Cité des morts" (1958), by Y. Rāġib in "Les sanctuaires" (1977), "Deux monuments fatimides" (1978) and "Les mausolées fatimides" (1981), and by C. Williams, "The Cult of 'Alid Saints" (1983-5). J.-Cl. Garcin, "Toponymie et topographie urbaines médiévales" (1984) discusses the period from the founding of Fustat to Ottoman Cairo, examining historical changes in the meanings of terms referring to the quarter, such as *khiṭṭa, khuṭṭ, ḥāra,* and *maḥalla*. For example, *khiṭṭa* was a legal unit at the time of the founding of Fustat, *ḥāra* was a military quarter at the time of the founding of Cairo, and *khuṭṭ* indicates a division formed centring on mansions. Their meanings changed with urban expansion and it is difficult to confirm the meaning over a broad period of time; therefore Garcin stresses that it is impossible to regard the *ḥāra,* for instance, as a basic and continuous unit in the construction of the city. In his opinion urban topography should be examined in terms of the social and political development of the city; this view appears clearly in his "Le Caire et l'évolution urbaine dans des pays musulmans" (1991). There he compares Cairo's evolution with that of Syrian and Maghribi cities, and, avoiding any use of the word "Islamic," presents three stages in the urban evolution of those cities: the tribal city (ville gentilice) of the 7th-11th centuries, the city of chivalry of the 10th-14th centuries, and the traditional Muslim city of the 15th-18th centuries.

One feature of studies on Cairo space is the large number of works dealing with the history of domestic architecture. Architectural historians like J. Revault, B. Maury and M. Zakariya published *Palais et maisons du Caire* (1975-83), based on field research, and this was followed by a joint study by historians such as Garcin and Raymond, published as Maury et al. (eds.), *Palais et maisons du Caire* (1982-3). The study looks at dwelling space, both palaces and houses, surveys their structure, and analyzes them, Volume 1 dealing with the Mamluk period, and Volume 2 with the Ottoman period. Included in the work is Garcin, "Habitat médiéval et histoire urbaine" (1982), an outline of the development of the courtyard house from the Arab conquest until the Ottoman period. A. Lézine, "Les salles nobles" (1972) and H. Fathy, "The Qā'a of the Cairene Arab House" (1972) are studies of the development and function of the *qā'a* (hall), a feature of domestic architecture in Cairo. Revault, "Espace comparé des habitations citadines" (1979) compares dwellings in Cairo and Tunis dating from the 16th to 18th centuries. Lézine and 'Abdul-Tawwab, "Introduction à l'étude des maisons anciennes" (1972) widens the area of study to Rosetta. The above works in the main confine themselves to the construction of existing Ottoman period upper class dwellings. However, M. Zakariya, "Le rab' de Tabbāna" (1980) investigates the mass rented dwellings called *rab'*, and N. Hanna, "Bayt al-Isṭambullī" (1980) examines the construction of middle class houses. A symposium was held at the Université de Provence in 1984 dealing with the construction and functions of domestic architecture of the Mediterranean region compared with that of Syria and the Maghrib. Its proceedings were published as *L'habitat traditionnel dans les pays musulmans* (1988-91). Archaeological excavations in Fustat have revealed ruins of dwellings dating from the 11th to the 13th centuries, and studies have been made on the structure of dwellings and the question of rights using records of transactions among the Geniza Documents, discovered at Fustat after 1890. Lézine, "Persistence de traditions pré-islamiques" (1972) points out similarities in the courtyard house with those in Samarra and other place in Iraq, but stresses that the seven-storied houses reported by Nāṣir Khusraw (d. 1061) in his travel record have continuities with the traditions of ancient Egypt. S. D. Goitein, "A Mansion in Fustat" (1977) and "Urban Housing in Fatimid and Ayyubid Times" (1978) study the structure of houses in the Fatimid and Ayyubid periods, prices and rents based on the Geniza Documents. Goitein supports the existence of courtyard houses and multi-storied rented housing from historical sources. H. I. Sayed, "The Development of the Cairene Qā'a" (1987) touches on these studies and uses waqf documents and the Geniza Documents to discuss changes in domestic styles between the 12th and 15th centuries, focusing on the inner courtyard and the hall. Scharabi, *Kairo* (1989) traces the development of European-style urban architecture from the second half of the 19th century using a wealth of illustration.

A large number of studies have been published in the postwar period which utilize the rich trove of historical sources concerning Cairo, Arabic chronologies and topographies as well as travel records of Europeans. Works such as E. W. Lane, *Cairo* (1896), S. Lane-Poole, *Cairo* (1892) and *The Story of Cairo* (1902), and D. Margoliouth, *Cairo, Jerusalem and Damascus* (1907) are classics which outline Cairo's historical development. 'Alī Mubārak, *al-Khiṭaṭ al-jadīda* (1886-9) is a great twenty volume work concerning the topography of Cairo, Alexandria and Egypt as a whole, using Arabic historical sources, statistical materials by both Europeans and the Egyptian government, waqf documents, and various European records, such as the *Description de l'Égypt*. The author, who worked for the Ministry of Waqf and the Ministry of the Railways as a technical expert and bureaucrat brought his experience to bear in the compilation of this work, and its value as a historical source is very great. Modern specialists in urban studies cannot neglect to study its composition and ideas. M. Clerget, *Le Caire* (1934) is a general study of the geography, history and society of Cairo, utilizing research by Europeans since the latter half of the 19th century. A feature of this work is that it utilizes data from the statistical surveys of the quarters and their inhabitants that fill the *Description de l'Égypte* and the statistical material compiled by the government at the beginning of the 20th century to make a close examination of the geographical environment, urban utilities (such as water and transport), industry, and the lives of the people. At the end of the book data based on statistics between 1907 and 1927 concerning the administrative districts (the twelve *qism*s and their subdivisions, *ṣiyākh*s), the population and number of households of each quarter (*qism, ṣiyākh*), and the distribution of employment according to occupation are tabulated and interpreted in maps, giving a commanding view of the population and employment distribution of Cairo. Sauvaget's studies of Damascus and Aleppo, also produced during the 1930s, moved from physical structures to social composition; Clerget's study of Cairo on the other hand heralds a statistical approach to urban social development and composition.

Continuing Clerget's methods in the postwar period in its sociological study of urban forms is J. L. Abu-Lughod, *Cairo* (1971). Abu-Lughod, as she states in the preface, is concerned with seeking "the orderly patterns and temporal sequences" from the past to the present and "viewing history not from the heights but from the narrow streets of Cairo." She has built on the work of past researchers such as Lane-Poole, Creswell and Clerget with a social survey under the auspices of the American University in Cairo in 1960 and fieldwork with the support of her husband, an Arab in order to draw a matrix for a Muslim city before industrialization. She concludes that medieval Cairo divisions according to religion and origin are mostly on the basis of social class, occupation and place of abode. A feature of the city is the land use mixture with its unclear differentiation of usage and between the public and the private, as exemplified by the congested quarters and narrow streets. Such social organization and physical construction were continued down to almost the present. From a sociological survey concerning lifestyle, such as family composition and living environment, dividing modern Cairo into thirteen sections, she maintains that the distinctive features of and differences between each area reflect premodern social structure. This work traces Cairo's thousand-year historical development through physical form and social organization, presenting a coherent explanation of both premodern and modern structures. If the research of Lapidus is considered a sociological study by an historian, that of Abu-Lughod is an historical study by a sociologist. However, the view that the organizational principle of race and occupation is connected with the physical form of the quarter invokes the theories of Sauvaget, Massignon, Gibb and others, concerning cities other than Cairo, and with the exposure of this theory to increasing criticism it is all the more necessary to examine it based on historical materials pertaining to Cairo. S. J. Staffa, *Conquest and Fusion* (1977) is also a survey of the historical structure of Cairo society by a sociologist using historical research. Such studies by sociologists generalizing about historical structures by tracing them back from the present are a feature of Cairo urban studies.

At the centre of archaeological and historical research in the postwar period is the Institut Français d'Archéologie Orientale du Caire. Its organs, the *Bulletin* and the *Mémoires,* have published a great many research reports since before the World War II. Since 1954 the Institut has also published

Annales Islamologiques, which carries much of the latest in research concerning Cairo and Egypt. In 1969 when Cairo was celebrating the 1000th anniversary of its foundation, an international symposium was sponsored by the Egyptian government, the proceedings of which were published in French as *Colloque international sur l'histoire du Caire* (1972) and in Arabic as *Abḥāth al-nadwa* (1970-1). Perhaps because the sessions were not organized according to theme, the overall impression is vague, but it includes the presentations of foremost scholars in the field, both Western and Arab. In 1964 Zakī compiled *Bibliography related to the History of Cairo* comprising material both in Arabic and European languages, allowing scholars to refer to historical sources and research literature.

We will now examine historical research period by period. Works about Fustat, using documentary records and historical sources, include A. R. Guest, "The Foundation of Fustat and the Khittahs of that Town" (1907), a study of constitution of the *khiṭṭa,* the unit allotted to the tribes at the foundation, and P. Casanova, "Essai de reconstitution topographique" (1919). Guest and Richmond, "Miṣr in the Fifteenth Century" (1903) examines the changes around 1400 when Fustat was heading towards decline. Goitein, *A Mediterranean Society* (1967-88) uses the Geniza Documents found in a synagogue in Fustat to describe the Mediterranean world in the 10th to 12th centuries. The Geniza Documents, written in Arabic using the Hebrew script, are contracts, letters, and other writings, which show the close relations that existed at the time between the Jews of Fustat and Jewish communities around the Mediterranean. Goitein already used the Geniza Documents in his *Studies in Islamic History* (1968) to illustrate the citizens' ideas about man and society, and the lives of merchants and artisans. In the five volume *A Mediterranean Society* he analyzes more than 10,000 documents showing concretely contemporary society and its economy (industry, rents, labour, etc.), the family, and daily life to describe the free trade society between the Jews and the Muslims who operated in the Mediterranean region. In "Cairo" (1969) Goitein investigates, using the Geniza Documents, the possession of houses in Fustat and how people lived. He finds existing side by side both a clannish principle, whereby people of the same clan live together, and a free mercantile principle, whereby people of different religions live together, and regards such free connections as an attractive feature of the trading city of Fustat. In that he considers the city to be a place of freedom in contrast to the rural town, Goitein stands in contrast to Lapidus, who denies any difference between the city and the rural town.

A second feature of studies about Fustat is that excavations have revealed brick houses built on a grid of narrow streets. Due to the fact that the major part of the city was destroyed by a fire in 1168, and then was left largely deserted after the centre moved to Cairo in the Mamluk period, dwellings remain under the ground. Excavations were first conducted by the Egyptian 'Ali Baghat in 1912, and have been continuing since 1963 and 1978 by the American Research Center in Egypt and the Middle Eastern Culture Center of Japan (initially by Waseda University, Tokyo) respectively. The American excavation has been summarized in G. T. Scanlon, "Fusṭāṭ: Archaeological Reconsideration" (1972) and "Fustat Expedition" (1981). Scanlon, "Housing and Sanitation" (1970) examines how a public sense operated in Islamic cities by tracing housing and sanitation in Fustat. The Japanese excavations through to the 7th season have been reported in K. Sakurai and M. Kawatoko, "Excavations in al-Fustat" (1979-87). Walls, cement foundations, pits and *dakka* (concrete floors) have been unearthed, and it has been possible to reconstruct part of a quarter of between five and ten houses and a road. A surprising find has been the provisions for sewerage and drainage. Further analysis is attempted on the vast amounts of pottery, lamps and glass weights found to learn about the life and culture and the flow of merchandise. These excavation reports are enlarged and collected with many figures and maps in K. Sakurai and M. Kawatoko (eds.), *An Islamic City of Egypt, al-Fustat* (J., 1992). W. B. Kubiak, *al-Fustat* (1987) is the most recent study about Fustat. It uses both historical sources and archaeology to examine closely the process of the formation of the earliest city. *An Islamic City of Egypt, al-Fustat* (J., 1980) reports on the proceedings of a symposium held by the Middle Eastern Culture Center of Japan. In it, H. Yajima, "al-Fustat in the History of East-West Contacts" (J., 1980) is an excellent exposition that the reason for Fustat's growth as the entrepot in the east-west trade evolved out of the differences in the ecosystems of the Indian Ocean and Mediterranean world and the time lag in the voyages of the dhows which utilized the seasonal winds joining the two. Yajima gives an overview of the process of change in Fustat, sustained by the east-west trade, between its foundation and its decline in the Mamluk period. P. Sanders, "From Court Ceremony to Urban Language" (1989) focuses on how the ceremonials of festivals (*'īd*) lost their 'Isma'ili elements and took form as popular celebrations as Fatimid Cairo became urbanized, joining the more open city of Fustat with its population of Sunnis, Christians and Jews.

Ayyubid and Mamluk politics, administration and economy as a whole are treated in S. A. F. 'Āshūr, *The Mamluk period in Egypt and Syria* (A., 1965) and many other later works, but there are comparatively few studies specifically relating to Cairo, and so 'Āshūr's work with its independent section on city life draws attention. The aforementioned Lapidus, *Muslim Cities* (1967) makes a good deal of mention about the construction of waqf foundations in Cairo, the quarters, *zu'r* and so on. id., "Ayyubid Religious

Policy" (1972) points out that the Ayyubid rulers attempted to control the schools of law through the founding of madrasas in Cairo and their appointments of qadis. G. Leiser, "The Madrasa and Islamization" (1985) sees the reason for the building of more than forty madrasas in Cairo during the Ayyubid period as not so much an anti-Shiite policy but as a means of diffusing the Islamic law schools and training ulama bureaucrats to stand against the Christians, who held a deeply-rooted position in the bureaucracy. N. D. MacKenzie, *Ayyubid Cairo* (1992) studies military affairs, the economy, religion and the distribution of social facilities in the Ayyubid period. D. Ayalon, "The Muslim City and the Mamluk Military Aristocracy" (1968) stresses the isolation of the Mamluk slave soldiers from the people of the cities, noting the differences between Egypt and Syria, with its tradition of a free soldiery and militias. His thesis is of interest as contrasting with that of Lapidus stressing the pluralistic networks between the Mamluks and the townspeople. R. S. Humphreys, "The Expressive Intent" (1972) studies the architectural ideas in the erection of Mamluk period madrasas, etc. and says that the majestic appearance of the facades, domes and minarets symbolizes the power of the Mamluks in both the religious and social terms indispensable to the existing regional society. Humphreys attempts an architectural and artistic approach from the field of history. Behrens-Abouseif, "The Citadel of Cairo" (1988) examines the form and function of the citadel, which acted as a complex of palace, mosque and plaza.

Popper's annotated edition, *Systematic Notes* (1955-7) of Ibn Taghrī Birdī's chronicle, *al-Nujūm al-Zāhira*, presents basic information about Mamluk period Cairo place names, administrative structures, prices and wages, as well as plans of Cairo and the citadel. C. F. Petry, *The Civilian Elite of Cairo* (1981) collects data from two biographical dictionaries on ulama who lived or worked in Cairo in the 15th century and uses the computer to analyze patterns of birthplace, residence and occupation. J. H. Escovitz, *The Office of Qâḍî al-Quḍât* (1984) examines the careers and activities of the chief qadis of the four law schools in the Mamluk period. Promotion to chief qadi depended on gaining the position of *nā'ib* (judicial deputy) and marital and other connections with those in power rather than on scholarship or experience as a professor in the madrasa. Those who were able to do so would be promoted regardless of family or birth, and because those who became qadis then tried to seek personal profit through bribery, etc., they were unable to stand as upholders of Islamic law against the Mamluks. A. A. S. Nāṣif, *The Police in Islamic Egypt* (A., 1987) is a detailed study of the careers and duties of the *shurṭa* (police force) until the end of the Mamluk period. A. 'Abd al-Rāziq, "La ḥisba et le muḥtasib" (1977) and "Les muḥtasibs de Fosṭāṭ" (1978) examine the careers of the muhtasibs of Cairo and Fustat who with the *shurṭa* had the responsibility of maintaining public order. T. Kikuchi, "Muḥtasib in Cairo during the Mamluk Dynasty" (J., 1983) is a similar study, which concludes that before the 15th century ulama of ability were appointed muhtasib and acted as intermediaries between the people and the sultan's authority, but that later the position was used to amass personal funds and persons without scholarship like merchants and eventually the military gained the appointment for their own profit, which encouraged political corruption and decline. It is valuable for its use of chronicles and other historical documents to describe the actual figure of the muhtasib, but since this phenomenon alone does not explain political and bureaucratic corruption of the upper classes, further study is necessary to clarify the relations between the muhtasib and the common people. B. Shoshan, "Grain Riots" (1980) studies the relations between ruler, administrator and people from the viewpoint of "moral economy." It is an analysis of the food riots of Cairo between 1350 and 1517, and concludes that they were not spontaneous and purposeless riots but demands to the muhtasib and Sultan to take responsibility for price control and the provision of food; they were therefore motivated by a "moral" consciousness demanding a responsible policy. id., "Fāṭimid Grain Policy" (1981) sees the same mechanism in the Fatimid period food crisis. F. Hasebe, "Food Riots in Cairo around the Turn of the 15th Century" (J., 1988) finds, from a close study of the mechanism of food price rises, an artificial element in the food crisis, and concludes that the food riots were an expression of dissatisfaction with public order. id., "Food Disturbances in a City of the Islamic World" (J., 1990) examines the culture of the people and rulers that underlay the food riots. Popular protest and demands for a policy were backed with a strong belief in an absolute and eternal God. The government, whether it answered those demands or backed away from them, had to respond in terms of the Islamic idea. Hasebe holds that in Cairo, the *ḥāra* did not have much meaning in terms of the organization of social movements, like it did in Damascus, and rather than uselessly hypothesizing a closed society like the quarter as a crucial factor of analysis, he proposes as a basis of urban studies assuming open and fluid human relationships mediated by God. H. N. al-Ḥajjī, *Condition of the People under Mamluk Rule* (A., 1984) examines the reaction of the ulama and the people to growing bribery, confiscations (*muṣādara*) and injustice (*ẓulm*) under Mamluk rule. 'Āshūr, "Women of Cairo in the Mamluk Period" (A., 1971) examines items in historical records related to the social activities and lives of women in the city.

Egyptian waqf documents and sharia-court registers remain spanning the period from the Mamluk to the Ottoman dynasties. Studies utilizing waqf documents include the pioneering works of 'Abd al-Laṭīf Ibrāhīm dating from the 1950s. Bibliographical introductions are D. Crecelius, "The

Organization of Waqf Documents" (1971), which introduces where Cairo waqf documents are stored and how they are organized and M. M. Amīn, *Catalogue des documents* (1981), a list of waqf documents of the Mamluk period and before kept in the Egyptian National Library (Dār al-Wathā'iq al-Qawmīya) and in the Ministry of Waqf (Wizāra al-Awqāf bil-Qāhira), etc., with one portion edited and introduced. The waqf documents record donated waqf properties, and the officials of the institutions and their wages, etc. and they can be used to learn internal management and functions. Amīn used the documents in his *Waqf and Social Life in Egypt* (A., 1980) a general study of the social, economic and cultural meaning of waqf. In contrast to Amīn's comprehensive and exhaustive research, L. Fernandes and Behrens-Abouseif have studied the subject more in terms of theme and period. T. Kikuchi has long been interested in the studies of Egyptian waqf, and introduces trends in the field in "Some Remarks upon Recent Studies on Waqf" (J., 1988). Fernandes, *The Evolution of a Sufi Institution* (1988) focuses on the rapid increase of Sufi convents, especially the erection of *khānqāh,* during the Mamluk period, especially after the 14th century. From an analysis of waqf documents she shows that the *khānqāh,* unlike the *zāwiya* of specific sheikhs (spiritual instructors) and Sufi orders, were facilities which guaranteed in a broad sense the lives and training of Sufis and these were managed based on the regulations of the waqf documents. *Khānqāh*s were built in preference to madrasas, and Sufis made stronger ties with the Sultans than did the ulama. A three-storied residence typified the *khānqāh* construction, and Fernandes considers that this move to multi-storied buildings was in response to urbanization. She points out the changes that occurred between the latter part of the Mamluk period and the early part of the Ottoman period, and suggests that the merits of the *khānqāh* declined with the weakening of the economic power of their patrons, the sultans, and it was the Sufis from more humble origins and their *zāwiya* that attracted the people, in place of the corrupt and degenerate ulama ("Three Ṣūfī Foundations," 1981; "Some Aspects of the Zāwiya," 1983; "Two Variations," 1985). Behrens-Abouseif sees a weakening of differentiation, literally and actually, in the mosque, madrasa and *khānqāh* by the latter part of the Mamluk period, and all had become arenas for an open Sufism which no longer sought the secluded life ("Change in Function and Form," 1985). She has also studied the architectural features of the *zāwiya* and suggests that the building of the dome, in place of the *īwān* and *qā'a,* is more in keeping with the religious training of the Sufis, such as the *dhikr,* spiritual exercises ("An Unlisted Monument," 1982; "Four Domes," 1981). Fernandes, "The Foundation of Baybars al-Jashankir" (1987) and Behrens-Abouseif, "The Takiyyat Ibrahim al-Kulshani" (1988) are studies of Sufi conventual facilities in the early 14th century and the beginning of the Ottoman period respectively, employing waqf documents and field research. Fernandes, "Mamluk Politics and Education" (1987) studies madrasa management in the latter half of the 14th century, and shows that the Mamluks had begun to shift the balance of their support from the Shafi'is to the Hanafis.

The research of Fernandes and Behrens-Abouseif has opened ways of understanding the construction and functions of individual buildings through the use of waqf documents. Behrens-Abouseif, *Azbakiyya and its Environs* (1985) traces, using waqf documents how Ezbekiya, in the western suburbs during the Mamluk period, became a central suburb between the beginning of the Ottoman period and the rule of Muhammed 'Ali, and examines the factors in its growth. Behrens-Abouseif is interested in the expansion of the city to the suburbs, and deals with the growth to the north and east in "A Circassian Mamluk Suburb" (1978) and "The North-Eastern Extension" (1981). In "Locations of Non-Muslim Quarters" (1986) she studies non-Muslim residential quarters between the 11th and 18th centuries, and does not detect any clear residential segregation according to religion.

Similarly, N. Hanna traces the development of the Būlāq quarter in the suburbs of Cairo on the bank of the Nile from the Mamluk to the Ottoman periods in *An Urban History of Būlāq* (1983). Using waqf documents and *Description de l'Égypte,* she verifies the sites of forty-five trading buildings (*wakāla,* in text *wikāla*) and religious foundations and examines the planning of the Būlāq section. She shows that there was a commercial zone of a network of roads radiating to four docks and trading buildings occupying positions on a straight street parallel to the river bank. By contrast there were quarters of the dwellings of artisans and working people in the lanes behind the commercial zone. Such main roads and connected back lanes is a feature common with Cairo as well, but Būlāq is distinctive in that it was a wholesale zone centring on the port, which developed large-scale commercial facilities but none of the many mausolea to be seen in Cairo itself. id., *Construction Work* (1984) analyzes the building process of Ottoman period waqf institutions and gives concrete examples to discuss building materials, workers, planning and the problems of maintenance. As the research of Behrens-Abouseif and Hanna shows, a distinctive feature of the waqf study of Cairo has been their use as historical documents in investigating architecture and urban plans. Waqf documents and other historical documents were similarly used in the studies of dwellings cited above (Zakariya, "Le rab'" etc.). The demarcation between architectural historians confining themselves to field surveys and historians using only documentary sources no longer has any meaning. Hanna's most recent work, *Habiter au Caire* (1991) uses sharia-court registers to make a general examination of the construction, costs and distribution of ordinary Cairo housing in the 17th and 18th centuries, and moves towards an analysis of social structure.

T. Walz, "Wakālat al-Ğallāba" (1977) uses waqf documents and sharia-court registers to investigate the form of the trading buildings (*wakāla*) that conducted the slave trade with the Sudan, which developed at the end of the Mamluk period, their officials, and their management methods and reveals a system of acquisition of actual proprietary rights according to ninety-nine year loans and of the allotment of earnings according to guild organization. It is to be hoped more studies will in the future make similar use of historical documents to investigate the internal structures of commercial facilities. A. M. El-Masry, *Die Bauten von Ḫādim Sulaimān Pascha* (1991) examines documents of waqf founded by the 16th governor of Egypt, including mosques, madrasas, *zāwiya* and commercial facilities. Crecelius has translated waqf documents relating to the foundation of a mosque-madrasa complex in central Cairo by Muhammad Bey, a powerful Mamluk general in the latter part of the 19th century ("The Waqfīyah of Muḥammad Bey," 1978-9), and in "The Waqf of Muhammad Bey" (1991) he investigates the details of waqf income and expenditure through sharia-court registers and other documents. He reveals that when the waqf was first established, there were included a large amount of other waqfs and private property acquired by exchange and sale, as well as newly donated waqf properties. After Muhammad Bey's death, the wealth from the waqf was usurped by other Mamluks, and the income of the foundation substantially decreased. Crecelius understands that such transfer of waqf wealth was widespread, and was a link in the privatization of state land and tax collection rights in the course of the Ottoman period.

A. Raymond has been publishing pioneering studies concerning Ottoman period society since the 1960s, and is a leading scholar in the field. *Artisans et commerçants au Caire* (1973) uses narrative sources, sharia-court registers and waqf documents to examine prices, the organization and management of artisans and merchants, and their connections with the government and the military in 18th century Cairo. Here Raymond clarified the economic and political meaning of the city in an area where studies of rural villages had taken the lead. He has collected information concerning the social and economic conditions of artisans and merchants from voluminous and comprehensive historical sources and organized his findings in numerous diagrams, graphs and maps. In the latter half of the 17th century, the garrison regiments (*ojak* / *ocak*) protected the traders and built a base in the city through their acquisition of tax collection rights from the inhabitants. By the late 18th century, when the *ocak* were exhausted by the power of the governor (*pacha*) and internal conflicts, the Mamluk soldiers and particularly their generals, the *beys*, were dependent on tax farm (*iltizam*) in the rural villages and grasped for power, fighting amongst themselves and increasing their exploitation of the city people. With the French occupation of 1798, the people of the quarters rose up and for a while a collaboration of ulama, traders and small scale merchants and artisans established political power. This he sees as the result of deepening and spreading social contradictions in the 18th century. "The Sources of Urban Wealth" (1977) is a concise summing up of the economic situation of artisans and merchants from sharia-court registers. Raymond has covered the political process of the people in "Quartiers et mouvements populaires" (1968) and "La géographie des ḥāra" (1980). Here he examines the main quarters and popular movements in the 18th century, showing that the quarters on the outskirts, like Ḥusaynīya, had vigorous movements and an important role was played by organizations of guilds and Sufi orders and members of outlaw bands known contemptuously as *shuṭṭār, zu'r* and *ghawghā'*. In "Problèmes urbains" (1972) he studies how Cairo administration was carried out in the 17th and 18th centuries and shows that the Ottoman government had only minimal interest in city administration and urban planning, with the guilds and the quarters acting as intermediaries between the government and the people and maintaining on the whole natural equilibrium. id., "Une 'révolution' au Caire" (1965) deals with the characteristics of the insurrection of 1711.

Raymond, as he showed in *Artisans et commerçants,* on the one hand draws basic social and economic data from a comprehensive study of historical documents, and on the other merges this data with political events to examine historical change. "Essai de géographie des quartiers" (1963) is a detailed investigation of the residential quarters of the military elite in the 18th century, and since the 1970s Raymond continued his studies on Cairo with "La population du Caire" (1975) and "Cairo's Area and Population" (1984), an examination of residential area and demographic change in Cairo from the 15th to the 18th century, "Les grandes épidémies" (1972), concerning population movements and the plagues epidemics of the 17th and 18th centuries, and "Les bains publics" (1969), "Les fontaines publiques" (1979) and "Les grands waqfs" (1979), studies using waqf documents of the role of waqf foundations like water fountains (*sabīl)* and public baths (*ḥammām*). "Les quartiers de résidence des commerçants et artisans maghrébins" (1983) looks at the occupations and places of residence of people from the Maghrib in 17th and 18th century Cairo, and "L'activité architecturale" (1991) analyzes architectural activity in Ottoman Cairo according to types of buildings, their geographical distribution and founders. "Signes urbains" (1974) and "La conquête ottomane et le développement" (1979) look at the cities under Ottoman rule like 16th and 17th century Aleppo and Damascus, confirming their growth both economically and population-wise and stressing that their decline came with the growth of European power after the end of the 18th century. Raymond also expresses his deep interest in the common features of Arab cities in the Ottoman Empire in *The Great Arab Cities* (1984) and *Grandes villes arabes* (1985). The former work consolidates the tendencies of the most recent works in urban studies, like Hanna and Lézine, criticizing the views of scholars like Clerget who consider that the cities deteriorated or became chaotic under Ottoman rule and showing that public spaces like the suqs as well as private residential space grew in an orderly way. Regarding residential space, he criticizes the opinions which emphasize a particular Islamic urban principle in residential space simply characterized by the inner courtyard and the coexistence of rich and poor, using the clear example that with suburban expansion there grew up quarters with a particular class identity and an increase in domestic architecture without the inner courtyard. Raymond emphasizes the Mediterranean tradition and the economic development of Arab regions under Ottoman rule and raises questions about the tendency to make an a priori assumption about an "Islamic" organization of space or social structure. *Grandes villes arabes* is comprehensive compilation of twenty years of research, dealing with the various problems of urban studies like the composition of the inhabitants, organization of space, urban facilities, and the economy. He presents a basic outline of Arab cities, remaining aware of differences between them. "Urban Networks" (1989) shows that diverse social networks (professional, residential, and socio-religious) gave coherence to the native society and played a role in organizing the popular movements in Cairo and Aleppo from the end of the 18th century to the beginning of the 19th century.

Other scholars present different points of view to Raymond in regard to the military and the ulama in 18th century Cairo. A. L. al-Sayyid-Marsot, "The Political and Economic Functions of the 'Ulamā'" (1973) uses sharia-court registers to examine the economic base of the ulama and shows that from the 18th century powerful ulama, bolstered by their religious prestige, built fortunes as tax farmers (*multazim*) and waqf controllers (*nāẓir*) and drew close to the ruling classes; lower ranking ulama on the other hand took part in popular uprisings, indicating a class division within the ulama. "Religion or Opposition?" (1984) investigates the role of the ulama as mediators and leaders from the 19th century to the present. Baer, in "Popular Revolt in Ottoman Cairo" (1977) studies the participants and leaders in popular revolts at the end of the 18th century and at the beginning of the 19th century, and points out that it was not the lower class ulama participating in the uprisings who became their leaders but the wealthy and powerful ulama who established patron-client relationships with a particular group of the population. He thus calls into question the view of the ulama class as mediators between the rulers and the ruled. "Patrons and Clients" (1980) discusses the process of the formation of patron-client relationships between powerful ulama and the people. M. Winter, "The Ashrāf and Niqābat al-Ashrāf" (1985) examines the formation of the *ashrāf* class in Egypt. G. Piterberg, "The Formation of an Ottoman Egyptian Elite" (1990) deals with the formation of the garrison regiments (*ocak*) and the Mamluk *beys* as a single class of "Egyptian military" and suggests that inasmuch as powerful ruling families were then formed through the acquisition of tax farm rights and the control of dependants they should be compared with the phenomenon of the *a'yān* (notables) of Anatolia.

Studies concerning Egyptian society from the 19th century until recent times focus on topics of political and economic history like modernization, industrialization and nationalist movements. Those dealing exclusively with the city itself are very few. Baer, for instance, looks at both the city and the rural village in the period from the Ottoman period until the First World War and makes suggestions concerning the nature of Egyptian society. In *Studies in the Social History of Modern Egypt* (1969), discussing modern Egyptian society, he states that compared with Iraq and Syria, strongly centralized Egypt had little tradition of urban autonomy, and even during the process of modernization the upper class urban dwellers were separated from the great mass of Egyptian people. Though guilds and village communities broke up as modernization progressed, an urban bourgeoisie whose principal interests were concentrated in the towns and urban municipalities did not arise.

In "Village and City" (1981) he compares Egyptian and Syrian cities from the Ottoman period to the beginning of the 20th century and criticizes the thesis of Lapidus that places emphasis on the similarity, contact and integration of urban centres and rural villages based on the example of Mamluk period Syrian cities. He first points out differences between Egyptian cities and villages in terms of physical form, economy and culture (education, dress, etc.), saying that the social and economic ties and integrating connections between them were weak, and that such integration and contact, both politically and economically, only came about with the rise of a centralized nation after the 19th century. In Syria, by contrast, there were relatively close connections between city and village in the case of Damascus and Aleppo, but in the mountains of Lebanon there were deeply-rooted distinguished families who depended on the rural village, and Baer emphasizes the need therefore for further discussion of the problem considering differences in geography and period. In *Egyptian Guilds in Modern Times* (1964) he deals with changes in the social and economic roles of the guild, and in "Guilds in Middle Eastern History" (1970), comparing the historical situation of guilds in Egypt, Syria and Turkey, he points out that in comparison to Egypt, where in the 17th and 18th centuries guilds became more obvious and played an important role in the mechanism of tax collection, in Syria they had no administrative function since tax collection was done on the basis of the quarter. (Rafeq and Nu'aysa have disproved this, however.) In summary, not only did the city in Egypt have no meaning in terms of autonomy either socially or politically, but in modern times when a strong national authority was established this became the basis of power, and this fact may account for the loss of meaning of the city as an individual object of study.

H. Kato, using 19th century taxation revenue documents shows that in contrast to the city, which whether large or small displayed a uniform character, rural villages were of great diversity, both socially and economically, in each region. He criticizes previous research stressing the uniformity of the rural village and at the same time warns of the danger of attaching too much importance to urban studies. All the same he asserts the need to continue Egyptian social research examining both city and village from a multifaceted viewpoint (Kato, "Urban and Rural Societies," 1989). Perhaps the paucity of studies of individual modern cities may stem from modern urban uniformity.

There exist a number of specialized theses concerning post-19th century urbanization and urban problems accompanying modernization and industrialization. R. Ilbert, "Note sur l'Égypte" (1981) and P. Marthelot, "Le Caire" (1969) deal with the expansion of residential districts and changes in the transport network that have come about as a result of urbanization. Gh. Alleaume, "Hygiène publique" (1984) and "Politiques urbaines" (1985) are studies of government policy regarding public hygiene and the building industry. J. Berque and M. al-Shakaa, "La Gamāliya" (1974) describes the people and life of the quarter of Gamālīya in 19th century Cairo. Y. Itagaki, "On Muslim Brethren" (J., 1971) proposes that the Muslim Brethren movement of 1930-40 should be understood to reflect the contradictions of the modern Egyptian city, being stamped with urban characteristics in both its organization and its methods of action. If political history could be reexamined from this viewpoint, it might encourage urban studies to rise above static research which dissects only the inert physical and political forms of the city.

Another point to be noted is the existence of modern urban studies by social anthropologists. S. el-Messiri, *Ibn al-Balad* (1978) is a unique example of fieldwork relating to the identity of the urban dweller. *Ibn al-balad* (son of the city) is what native Egyptians originally called themselves in contrast to the Turco-Circassian rulers of Egypt, and it has become joined with the consciousness of the traditional *futuwwa* and its chivalrous spirit. With the Europeanization of the Egyptians during the 20th century, the consciousness of *ibn al-balad* is in danger of disappearing. id., "The Changing Role of the Futuwwa" (1977) discusses the 20th century *futuwwa* (chivalrous gangs), swaying between *ibn al-balad* and *baltagi* (outlaws). T. Hayashi, "Urbanization and Human Types" (J., 1972) is a similar analysis of changes in the *ibn al-balad* consciousness in the context of changes in its basis reflected in the quarter and in city-village relationships, that is, in urbanization. N. al-Messiri Nadim has conducted a sociological survey of social relationships in the quarter; in "The Concept of the Ḥāra" (1979) she reports on the dwellings, occupations and consciousness of people living in one quarter (*ḥāra*) of the old city, and in "Changing Lifestyle" (1989) she sums up the distinctive features of the traditional lifestyle of the *ḥāra* and ways in which it has changed. U. Wikan, *Life among the Poor* (1980) is based on the field-notes of a female anthropologist who lived in a working class area of Cairo and studied the human relationships and behavior of the people there, of families and women in particular. S. el-Messiri, "Self-images of Traditional Urban Women" (1978) describes the consciousness of *banat al-balad* (daughter of the city) among the women in the working class quarters of Cairo.

Cairo, as Egypt's capital, has drawn the attention also of a large number of travellers. R. Blachère, "L'agglomération du Caire" (1969) studies the descriptions of the city by medieval Arab travellers such as al-Muqaddasī, while J. Berque, "Les capitales de l'Islam méditerranéen"(1969) examines the image of Cairo held by Ibn Khaldūn and others. B. Blanc et al., "A propos de la carte" (1981) is a translation and study of the Venetian Matheo Pagano's account of the map of Cairo (published 1549), and V. Meinecke-Berg, "Eine Stadtansicht des mamlukischen Kairo" (1976) examines Cairo using maps made by Europeans in the same period. Ch. Vial, "Le Caire des romanciers égyptiens" (1969) deals with the image of Cairo in the works of 20th century novelists such as Najīb Maḥfūẓ. G. Wiet, "Fêtes et jeux au Caire" (1969) uses historical sources to extract information concerning the festivals and enjoyments of the people of Cairo; such studies of urban life will probably become more and more necessary. W. Miki, "Wholesale Druggists in Cairo" (J., 1984) describes the urbanism and internationalism of wholesale druggists (*'aṭṭār*) standing at the point of intersection between people, merchandise and information. In his opinion this represents the urban character previously held by the ulama as mediators of information.

Other Cities

Though Cairo and the Nile occupy a markedly large proportion of Egyptian society, economy and politics, distinctive studies of regional cities have also been made. E. Combe and G. P. al-Shayyāl have produced work on Alexandria, and A. 'Abd al-Rāziq, "Les gouverneurs d'Alexandrie" (1982) introduces those works while examining the careers of 103 governors of the city during the Mamluk period. M. Müller-Wiener, *Eine Stadtgeschichte Alexandrias*

(1992) is a long-awaited comprehensive study on the history of Ayyubid and Mamluk Alexandria. Baer, "The Beginnings of Municipal Government" (1968) discusses municipal government in Alexandria, established there for the first time in Egypt in 1864. M. J. Reimer, "Social and Spatial Change in Alexandria" (1988) analyzes social changes in Alexandria, the bridgehead for European colonization in the 19th century, and the anti-European riots of 1882. D. Panzac, "Alexandrie" (1978) is a demographic analysis of the rapid urbanization of the 19th century. *Alexandrie entre deux mondes* (1987) is a special issue of *ROMM* which contains eighteen multifarious articles concerning Alexandria from ancient times to the present. T. Sato, "A View of Islamic Social History" (J., 1977) studies the society of the Fayyūm area, 100 kilometres south of Cairo, based on the 13th century "History of Fayyūm" and describes the organic relationship of the central town and around one hundred villages situated around it. T. Walz, "Asyūṭ" (1978) sketches how the boom in the Sudan trade in the mid-19th century rocked society in Asyūṭ, a city in Upper Egypt. Garcin, *Qūṣ* (1974) is a detailed study of aspects of and important factors in the medieval development of Qūṣ, a central city in Upper Egypt. T. Yukawa, "The Ulama Community in Medieval Upper Egypt" (J., 1979) examines the ulama networks centring on Qūṣ.

CONCLUSION: PROBLEMS AND PERSPECTIVES

Having examined the history of research in terms of Iraq, Syria and Egypt there is striking evidence of particular concerns and methodologies regarding the different periods and cities under consideration rather than any indication of mutual exchanges in methodology or an awareness of common problems. First, morphological and topographical studies in Iraq are dominated by an interest in reproducing, through historical sources, the plans of the early garrison cities (*miṣr*) and of planned cities like 'Abbasid Baghdad and Samarra; in Syria by research into the quarters and suqs combining fieldwork and documentary sources; and in Egypt by using similar methods to discover the form and function of individual dwellings and religious facilities. Despite such differences there is ample scope for using the results attained to discuss similarities and differences of some forms that have been seen as characteristics of the "Arab-Islamic city," such as the courtyard house and the structure of the quarter, taking note of differences according to time and place. As research in Syria and Egypt shows, there has been rapid growth in studies of the form and function of urban facilities using waqf documents and sharia-court registers, and problems common with Ottoman cities in Turkey have been identified. In this sense, what V. Strika has pointed out concerning the existence of waqf documents related to Ottoman Iraq is important, and there is a possibility that like in Syria and Egypt, sharia-court registers remain in Iraq.

Second, research on Syria has produced pioneering studies about social structure. The impetus has been the model of Sauvaget, which in the early 20th century discussed society from the physical forms. Sauvaget early showed an interest in social structure and produced studies on it. This model was drawn in terms of dichotomies, like the Roman period as opposed to the Islamic period, and cities as opposed to villages and nomads, and sees Islamic society as a mosaic, without any centre. His research methodology and design was indebted to those systematically developed in the Maghrib by French scholars, as M. Kisaichi has shown in the chapter on the Maghrib. That this model has retained for such a long time its dominance and influence is due to the fact that it was a paradigm that urban studies in the Maghrib and Syria found easy to understand, since these areas had a strong tradition of cities in the Graeco-Roman pattern. The artificiality of the model was criticized by Lapidus in his network theory, and since the latter part of the 1960s a large number of analyses of politics and society have been published which give their attention to social networks. However in Iraqi studies there has been no discussion of the network theory as a methodology or model, and in Egyptian studies there have not been many works looking at the city or the quarter as independent social units. Studies of the ulama and the bureaucracy, and of individual buildings and institutions, are flourishing, but they are not focusing on the problem of the city itself but rather on questions concerned with a particular state or period. This actually provides a good contrast to Syria, flooded with concerns about the city itself. Despite the fact that the two regions were under the same rule for a long period of time their geographical, social and political differences cannot be ignored.

Third, Egypt is fortunate to have a wealth of statistical information dating from the 19th century, and a feature of Egyptian studies has been sociological analyses and anthropological surveys employing that data. If similar work could be done for Syria and Iraq, it would provide basic data for mutual comparisons. Differences in the research situation according to region are probably attributable to differences in the types of historical document mostly used and in research method. If research methods were shared it would be possible to make mutual comparisons among Iraq, Syria and Egypt despite their different geographical environments and cultural traditions in the Arab sphere.

The image of the "Islamic city" so far has been directly derived from individual urban studies in Arab lands, such as those of the cities of Baghdad, Damascus and Cairo, without close examination from a comparative viewpoint. As more concrete and positive studies are being done, it is becoming clearer that the concept is an abstract and ideological one. On the other hand, urban studies as a whole may be in the process of becoming dissolved in a mass of individual studies limited to a particular time or city or topic, losing sight of common paradigms and research methods. Scholars who consider all three regions in their research may be said to include only the historians Cahen, Lapidus and Raymond and the geographer Wirth; leading local Arab scholars like Ṣāliḥ, Rafeq and Amīn do not seem inclined to go beyond their own fields. However there are a large number of topics shared by the individual fields, such as the ulama, the madrasa, the qadi and the muhtasib, Sufis and the Sufi orders, the waqf, the quarter, the outlaws and gangs, notables and distinguished families, and merchants and guilds. It is to be hoped there will be more studies of these topics in terms of a common framework, by means of concrete investigations into similarities and differences in how they operated in different places and at different times. It would also be meaningful to do transtemporal studies of a single topic.

I have been constrained in many instances from dealing with problems common to all three regions because of the way I have organized my material, treating research trends city by city. For example, referring to the ulama, H. J. Cohen, "The Economic Background" (1970) shows from an analysis of ulama occupations through to the 11th century by *nisba* (affiliation) that many of them earned their livings as artisans and merchants. N. J. Coulson, "Doctrine and Practice" (1956) reveals that ulama in the early period had the idea that public appointments such as qadi should be avoided. This contrasts greatly to Escovitz's study of ulama in Mamluk Cairo who sought offices such as that of chief qadi and the change should be considered in terms of the institutionalization of scholarship and the professionalization of the ulama with the spread of the madrasa after the 11th century, as pointed out by Gilbert. In this sense, G. Makdisi, *The Rise of Colleges* (1981), which traces the development of the madrasa and the scholarship and life of the ulama, is an important study. J. Berkey, *The Transmission of Knowledge in Medieval Cairo* (1992) deals with the Islamic educational system more broadly, including Mamluks, women and the common people as well as the ulama, and examines individual relationships more closely. There are many studies dealing with inter-city commerce and trade relations, such as Ashtor, *Studies on the Levantine Trade* (1978) and *East-West Trade* (1986) and Labib, *Handelsgeschichte Ägyptens* (1965), but space limitations prevent me from dealing with them specifically here. Ashtor, *Histoire des prix et des salaires* (1969), a detailed study of medieval prices and wages, is a basic work on social and economic history and contains invaluable data for considering the life of urban dwellers.

BIBLIOGRAPHY

'Abd al-Ḥusayn, Mahdī al-Raḥīm. *al-Khidmāt al-'āmma fī Baghdād: 400-656 A. H./1009-1258 A. D. (Public Policy in Baghdad).* Baghdād, 1987.

'Abd al-Mahdī, 'Abd al-Jalīl Ḥasan. *al-Madāris fī Bayt al-Maqdis fī 'aṣrayn al-Ayyūbī wal-Mamlūkī: Dawrhā fī al-ḥaraka al-fikrīya (Madrasas of Jerusalem in the Ayyubid and the Mamluk Periods).* 2 vols. 'Ammān, 1981.

'Abd al-Mawlā, Muḥammad Aḥmad. *al-'Ayyārūn wal-shuṭṭār al-Baghādida fī al-ta'rīkh al-'abbāsī (The 'Ayyārūn and the Shuṭṭār of Baghdad in the 'Abbasid Period).* 2nd ed. Iskandarīya, 1990.

'Abd al-Rāziq, Aḥmad. "La ḥisba et le muḥtasib en Égypt au temps des mamlūks." *Annales Islamologiques* 13 (1977).

———. "Les muḥtasibs de Fosṭāṭ au temps des mamlūks." *Annales Islamologiques* 14 (1978).

———. "Les gouverneurs d'Alexandrie au temps des mamlūks." *Annales Islamologiques* 18 (1982).

Abdel Nour, A. "Types architecturaux et vocabulaire de habitat en Syrie au XVIe et XVIIe siècle." In *L'espace social de la ville arabe,* ed. D. Chevallier. Paris, 1979.

———. "Habitat et structures sociales à Alep aux XVIIe et XVIIIe siècles d'après des sources arabes inédites." In *La ville arabe dans l'Islam,* eds. A. Bouhdiva & D. Chevallier. Tunis, 1982.

———. *Introduction à l'histoire urbaine de la Syrie ottomane (XVIe-XVIIIe siècle).* Beyrouth, 1982.

Abu-Husayn, Abudul-Rahim. *Provincial Leadership in Syria 1575-1650.* Beirut, 1985.

Abu-Lughod, J. L. *Cairo: 1001 Years of the City Victorious.* Princeton, 1971.

———. "The Islamic City: Historic Myth, Islamic Essence, and Contemporary Relevance." *IJMES* 19 (1987).

Adams, R. M. *Land behind Baghdad: A Historical Settlement on the Diyala Plains.* Chicago & London, 1965.

Ahsan, M. M. *Social Life under the Abbasids: 170-289 A. H./786-902 A. D.* London & N. Y., 1979.

'Alī Mubārak. *al-Khiṭaṭ al-tawfīqīya al-jadīda li-Miṣr al-Qāhira wa mudunhā wa bilādhā al-qadīma wal-shahīra (Enlarged and Newly-edited Topography of Egypt).* 20 vols. Būlāq, 1304-5/1886-8.

al-'Allāf, Aḥmad Ḥilmī. *Dimashq fī maṭla' al-qarn al-'ishrīn (Damascus at the Beginning of the 20th Century).* Dimashq, 1976.

Alexandrie entre deux mondes. Revue de l'Occident Musulman et de la Méditerranée 46, Aix-en-Provence, 1987.

Alleaume, Gh. "Hygiène publique et travaux publics: Les ingénieurs et l'assainissement du Caire (1882-1907)." *Annales Islamologiques* 20 (1984).

———. "Politiques urbaines et contrôle de l'entreprise: Une loi inédite de 'Alī Mubārak sur les corporations du bâtiment." *Annales Islamologiques* 21 (1985).

AlSayyad, Nezar. *Cities and Caliphs: On the Genesis of Arab Muslim Urbanism*. Westport, 1991.

Amīn, Muḥammad Muḥammad. *al-Awqāf wal-ḥayāt al-ijtimā'īya fī Miṣr 648-923 A. H./1250-1517 A. D. (Waqf and Social Life in Egypt)*. al-Qāhira, 1980.

———, ed. *Catalogue des documents d'archives du Caire de 239/853 à 922/1516*. Le Caire, 1981.

Anonymous. *Baġdād*. Leiden, 1962.

'Arafāt, Salīm al-Mubayyid. *Ghaza wa qiṭā'hā (Ghaza)*. al-Qāhira, 1987.

al-'Ārif, 'Ārif Bāshā. *Ta'rīkh al-Quds (History of Jerusalem)*. al-Qāhira, 1950.

al-Asadī, Muḥammad Khayr al-Dīn. *Mawsū'āt Ḥalab bil-muqārana (Comparative Encyclopaedia of Aleppo)*. Indexed by Muḥammad Kamāl. 7 vols. Ḥalab, 1986-8.

———. *Aḥyā' Ḥalab wal-aswāqhā (Quarters and Markets of Aleppo)*. Edited by 'Abd al-Fattāḥ Riwās Qal'at Jī. Dimashq, 1990.

al-Ash'ab, Khālid. *al-Madīna al-'arabīya (The Arab City)*. Baghdād, 1982.

Ashtor, E. "L'administration urbaine en Syrie médiévale." *RSO* 31 (1956).

———. "L'urbanisme syrien à la basse-époque." *RSO* 33 (1958).

———. *Histoire des prix et des salaires dans l'Orient médiéval*. Paris, 1969.

———. "Républiques urbaines dans le Proche-Orient à l'époque des Croisades?" *Cahiers de civilization médiévale* 18 (1975).

———. *Studies on the Levantine Trade in the Middle Ages*. London, 1978.

———. *East-West Trade in the Medieval Mediterranean*. London, 1986.

'Āshūr, Sa'īd 'Abd al-Fattāḥ. *al-'Aṣr al-mamlūkī fī Miṣr wal-Shām (The Mamluk Period in Egypt and Syria)*. al-Qāhira, 1965.

———. "Nisā' al-Qāhira fī 'aṣr al-mamālīk (Women of Cairo in the Mamluk Period)." In *Abḥāth al-nadwa al-duwalīya li-ta'rīkh al-Qāhira*. Vol. 3. al-Qāhira, 1971.

'Aṭā Allāh, Maḥmūd 'Alī. *Wathā'iq al-ṭawā'if al-ḥirfīya fī al-Quds fī al-qarn al-sābi' 'ashara al-mīlādī (Documents relating to Guilds in Jerusalem in the Nineteenth Century)*. Vol. 1. Nābulus, 1991.

———. *Niyāba Ghaza fī al-'ahd al-mamlūkī (Ghaza Province in the Mamluk Period)*. Bayrūt, 1986.

Ayalon, D. "The Muslim City and the Mamluk Military Aristocracy." In *Proceedings of the Israel Academy of Sciences and Humanities*. Vol. 2. 1968. Reprinted in *Studies on the Mamlūk of Egypt (1250-1517)*. London, 1977.

al-Azzawi, Subhi. "Oriental Houses in Baghdad: Concepts, Types and Categories." *Ur* 1 (1985); 2 (1985); 3 (1985).

Baer, G. *Egyptian Guilds in Modern Times*. Jerusalem, 1964.

———. "The Beginnings of Municipal Government." *Middle Eastern Studies* 4/2 (1968).

———. "Social Change in Egypt, 1800-1914." In *Political and Social Change in Modern Egypt*, ed. P. M. Holt. London, 1968.

———. *Studies in the Social History of Modern Egypt*. Chicago, 1969.

———. "Guilds in Middle Eastern History." In *Studies in the Economic History of the Middle East*, ed. M. A. Cook. London, 1970.

———. "Popular Revolt in Ottoman Cairo." *Der Islam* 54/2 (1977).

———. "The Dismemberment of Awqāf in Early 19th Century Jerusalem." *Asian and African Studies* 13 (1979).

———. "Patrons and Clients in Ottoman Cairo." In *Memorial Ömer Lûtfi Barkan*. Paris, 1980.

———. "Village and City in Egypt and Syria: 1500-1914." In *The Islamic Middle East, 700-1900: Studies in Economic and Social History*, ed. A. L. Udovitch. Princeton, 1981. Reprinted in *Fellah and Townsman in the Middle East*. London, 1982.

al-Bakhīṭ (Bakhit), Muḥammad 'Adnān. *Mamlaka al-Karak fī al-'ahd al-mamlūkī (Karak in the Mamluk Period)*. N. p., 1976.

———. "Aleppo and the Ottoman Military in the 16th Century: Two Case Studies." *Al-Abḥāth* 27 (1978-9).

———. *The Ottoman Province of Damascus in the Sixteenth Century*. Beirut, 1982.

———. "The Christian Population of the Province of Damascus in the Sixteenth Century." In *Christians and Jews in the Ottoman Empire*, eds. B. Braude & B. Lewis. Vol. 2. N. Y. & London, 1982.

———. "Sidon in Mamluk and Early Ottoman Times." *al-Abḥāth* 29 (1981).

———. "Ṣafad et sa région d'après des documents de waqf et des titres de propriété 780/964H. (1378/1556)." *REMMM* 55-6 (1990).

al-Bāqī, Aḥmad 'Abd. *Sāmarrā': 'Āṣima al-dawla al-'arabīya fī 'ahd al-'Abbāsīya (Samarra: Capital of the Arab State in the 'Abbasid Period)*. Baghdād, 1989.

Barbir, K. K. *Ottoman Rule in Damascus, 1708-1758*. Princeton, 1980.

Batatu, H. *The Old Social Classes and the Revolutionary Movements of Iraq*. Princeton, 1978.

Beckwith, Ch. I. "The Plan of the City of Peace: Central Asian Iranian Factors in Early 'Abbāsid Design." *Acta Orientalia Academiae Scientiarum Hungaricae* 38/1-2 (1984).

Behrens-Abouseif, D. "A Circassian Mamluk Suburb North of Cairo." *Art and Archaeology Research Paper* 14 (1978).

———. "Four Domes of the Late Mamluk Period." *Annales Islamologiques* 17 (1981).

———. "The North-Eastern Extension of Cairo under the Mamluks." *Annales Islamologiques* 17 (1981).

———. "An Unlisted Monument of the Fifteenth Century: The Dome of Zāwiya al-Damirdāš." *Annales Islamologiques* 18 (1982).

———. *Azbakiyya and its Environs: From Azbak to Ismā'īl, 1476-1879*. Cairo, 1985.

———. "Change in Function and Form of Mamluk Religious Institutions." *Annales Islamologiques* 21 (1985).

———. *The Minarets of Cairo*. Cairo, 1985.

———. "Locations of Non-Muslim Quarters in Medieval Cairo." *Annales Islamologiques* 22 (1986).

———. "The Citadel of Cairo: Stage for Mamluk Ceremonial." *Annales Islamologiques* 24 (1988).

———. "The Takiyyat Ibrahim al-Kulshani in Cairo." *Muqarnas* 5 (1988).

———. *Islamic Architecture in Cairo: An Introduction*. Leiden, 1989.

Ben-Arieh, Y. "Urban Development in the Holy Land, 1800-1914." In *The Expanding City*, ed. J. Patten. London, 1983.

———. *Jerusalem in the 19th Century: The Old City*. Jerusalem & N. Y., 1984.

Berchem, M. van. "Matériaux pour un corpus inscriptionum arabicarum, 2ᵉ partie: Syrie du Sud, Jérusalem." *MIFAO* 43 (1922-3); 44 (1925-7); 45 (1920).

Berkey, J. *The Transmission of Knowledge in Medieval Cairo*. Princeton, 1992.

Berque, J. "Les capitales de l'Islam méditerranéen vues par Ibn Khaldoun et les deux Maqqarî." *Annales Islamologiques* 8 (1969).

Berque, J. & Mustafa al-Shakaa. "La Gamāliya depuis un siècle: Essai d'histoire sociale d'un quartier du Caire." *REI* 42 (1974).

Bianquis, Th. *Damas et la Syrie sous la domination fatimide (359-468/969-1070)*. 2 vols. Damas, 1986-9.

Blachère, R. "L'agglomération du Caire vue par quatre voyageurs arabes du moyen âge." *Annales Islamologiques* 8 (1969).

Blake, G. H. & R. I. Lawless, eds. *The Changing Middle Eastern City*. London, 1981.

Blanc, B., S. Denoix, J.-Cl. Garcin & R. Gordiani. "A propos de la carte du Caire de Matheo Pagano." *Annales Islamologiques* 17 (1981).

Bodman, J. H. L. *Political Factions in Aleppo 1760-1826*. Chapel Hill & North Carol, 1963.

The British School of Archaeology in Jerusalem. *al-Abniya al-atharīya fī al-Quds al-islāmīya (The Monuments in Islamic Jerusalem)*. Translated by Isḥāq Mūsā al-Ḥusaynī. al-Quds, 1977.

Brown, K. et al. eds. *État, ville et mouvements sociaux au Maghreb et au Moyen-Orient*. Paris, 1989.

Brunschvig, R. "Urbanisme médiéval et droit musulman." *REI* 15 (1947).

Burgoyne, M. H. "Some Mameluke Doorways in the Old City of Jerusalem." *Levant* 3 (1971).

———. "Ṭāriq Bāb al-Ḥadīd: A Mamlūk Street in the Old City of Jerusalem." *Levant* 5 (1973).

———. *Mamluk Jerusalem: An Architectural Study*. N. p., [1986].

Burke, E., III. "Towards a History of Urban Collective Action in the Middle East: Continuities and Change 1750-1980." In *État, ville et mouvements sociaux au Maghreb et au Moyen-Orient*, eds. K. Brown et al. Paris, 1989.

Cahen, Cl. *La Syrie du nord à l'époque des croisades et la principauté franque d'Antioche*. Paris, 1940.

———. "Zur Geschichte der städtischen Gesellschaft im islamischen Orient des Mittelalters." *Saeculum* 9/1 (1958).

———. "Movements populaires et autonomisme urbain dans l'Asie musulmane du moyen âge." *Arabica* 5/3 (1958); 6/1 (1959); 6/3 (1959).

———. "Y a-t-il eu des corporations professionnelles dans le monde musulman classique?" In *The Islamic City,* eds. A. Hourani & S. M. Stern. London, 1970.

———. "Tribes, Cities and Social Organization." In *Cambridge History of Iran*. Vol. 4. London, 1975.

Casanova, P. "Essai de reconstitution topographique de la ville d'al-Fousṭâṭ ou Miṣr." *MIFAO* 35 (1919).

Chabbi, J. "La fonction du ribat à Bagdad du Ve siècle au début du VIIe siècle." *REI* 42 (1974).

Chéhab, M. H. *Tyr à l'époque des croisades I: Histoire militaire et politique*. Paris, 1975.

———. "Tyr à l'époque des croisades II: Histoire sociale, économique et religieuse." *Bulletin du Musée de Beyrouth* 31 (1979)-32 (1979).

Chehabe Ed-Dine, S. *Géographie humaine de Beyrouth: Avec une étude sommaire sur les deux villes de Damas et de Baghdad*. Beirut, 1960.

Chevallier, D. "Signes de Beyrouth en 1834." *BEO* 25 (1972).

———. *Villes et travail en Syrie du XIXe au XXe siècle*. Paris, 1982.

Clerget, M. *Le Caire*. 2 vols. Le Caire, 1934.

Cohen, A. *Palestine in the 18th Century: Patterns of Government and Administration*. Jerusalem, 1973.

———. *Jewish Life under Islam: Jerusalem in the Sixteenth Century*. Cambridge, Mass., 1984.

———. *Economic Life in Ottoman Jerusalem*. Cambridge, 1989.

Cohen, A. & B. Lewis. *Population and Revenue in the Towns of Palestine in the Sixteenth Century*. Princeton, 1978.

Cohen, H. J. "The Economic Background and the Secular Occupations of Muslim Jurisprudents and Traditionists in the Classical Period of Islam (until the Middle of the Eleventh Century)." *JESHO* 13 (1970).

Colloque international sur l'histoire du Caire. [Cairo], [1972]. Also Arabic version was published as *Abḥāth al-nadwa al-duwalīya li-ta'rīkh al-Qāhira*. 3 vols. al-Qāhira, 1970-1.

Cornand, J. "L'artisanat du textile à Alep survie ou dynamisme?" *BEO* 36 (1986).

Coste, P. *Architecture arabe ou monuments du Caire*. Paris, 1837-9.

Coulson, N. J. "Doctrine and Practice in Islamic Law: One Aspect of the Problem." *BSOAS* 18 (1956).

Crecelius, D. "The Organization of Waqf Documents in Cairo." *IJMES* 2 (1971).

———. "The Waqfiyah of Muḥammad Bey Abū al-Dhahab." *Journal of the American Research Center in Egypt* 15 (1978); 16 (1979).

———. "The Waqf of Muhammad Bey Abu al-Dhahab in Historical Perspective." *IJMES* 23 (1991).

Creswell, K. A. C. *Early Muslim Architecture*. 2 vols. Oxford, 1932-40.

———. *The Muslim Architecture of Egypt*. 2 vols. Oxford, 1952-9.

———. *A Bibliography of the Architecture, Arts and Crafts of Islam: to 1st Jan. 1960*. Cairo, 1961.

———. *A Bibliography of the Architecture, Arts and Crafts of Islam: Supplement to Jan. 1972*. Cairo, 1973.

———. *A Bibliography of the Architecture, Arts and Crafts of Islam*. 2nd Supplement. N. Y. & Cairo, 1985.

al-Dabbāgh, Muṣṭafā Murād. *Bilādnā Filasṭīn (Our Homeland Palestine)*. 11 vols. Kafr Qar', 1991.

Dahmān, Muḥammad Aḥmad. *Mukhaṭaṭ al-Ṣāliḥīya (Historical Map of al-Ṣāliḥīya)*. Dimashq, 1947.

———. *Dimashq fī 'ahd al-mamālīk (Damascus in the Mamluk Period)*. Dimashq, 1964. New edition was published as *Wulāt Dimashq fī 'ahd al-mamālīk*. Dimashq, 1981.

Ḍāmin, Muḥammad. *Imāra Ḥalab fī ẓill al-ḥukm al-Saljūqī (The Emirate of Aleppo under the Seljuks)*. Dimashq, 1990.

David, J.-Cl. "Alep, dégradation et tentatives actuelles de réadaptation des structures urbaines traditionelles." *BEO* 28 (1975).

———. "L'urbanisation en Syrie." *Maghreb-Mashrek* 81 (1978).

———. "Les quartiers anciens dans la croissance moderne de la ville d'Alep." In *L'espace social de la ville arabe*, ed. D. Chevallier. Paris, 1979.

———. *Le waqf d'Ipšīr Pāšā à Alep (1063/1653)*. Damas, 1982.

———. "L'espace des chrétiens à Alep: Ségrégation et mixité, stratégies communautaires (1750-1950)." *REMMM* 55-56 (1990).

Dettmann, K. *Damaskus: Eine orientalische Stadt zwischen Tradition und Moderne*. Nürnberg, 1967.

al-Dewuchi (al-Dīwuhjī), Sa'īd. "Madāris al-Mawṣil fī al-'ahd al-atābekī (The Madrasas of Mosul)." *Sumer* 13 (1957).

———. *al-Mawṣil fī al-'ahd al-atābekī (Mosul in the Time of the Atabegs)*. Baghdād, 1958.

———. *Jawāmi' al-Mawṣil fī mukhtalif al-'uṣūr al-atābekī (The Friday Mosques of Mosul)*. Baghdād, 1963.

———. *al-A'lām al-ṣunnā' al-mawāṣila (Biographies of the Artisans of Mosul)*. al-Mawṣil, 1970.

———. *Baḥth fī tirāth al-Mawṣil (A Study of the Historical Sites of Mosul)*. [al-Mawṣil], 1982.

———. *Ta'rīkh al-Mawṣil (History of Mosul)*. Vol. 1. Baghdād, 1982.

Dhannūb, Yūsuf et al., eds. Vol. 1: *al-'Amā'ir al-sakanīya fī madīna al-Mawṣil,* Vol. 2: *al-'Amā'ir al-khidmīya fī madīna al-Mawṣil,* Vol. 3: *al-'Amā'ir al-dīnīya fī madīna al-Mawṣil* (The Buildings of Mosul). al-Mawṣil, 1982.

Djaït, Hichem. *al-Kūfa: Naissance de la ville islamique.* Paris, 1986.

Donner, F. M. "Tribal Settlement in Basra during the First Century A. H." In *Land Tenure and Social Transformation in the Middle East,* ed. Tarif Khalidi. Beirut, 1984.

Dopp, P. H. "Le Caire: vu par les voyageurs occidentaux du moyen âge." *Bulletin de la Société Royale de Géographie d'Égypte* 23 (1950).

Drory, J. "Jerusalem during the Mamluk Period (1250-1517)." *Jerusalem Cathedra* 1 (1981).

Ecochard, M. & Cl. Le Coeur. *Les bains de Damas.* 2 vols. Damas, 1942-3.

Eickelman, D. F. "Is There an Islamic City?: The Making of a Quarter in a Moroccan Town." *IJMES* 5 (1974).

El'ad, A. "The Coastal Cities of Palestine during the Early Middle Ages." *Jerusalem Cathedra* 2 (1982).

Elisséeff, N. "Les monuments de Nūr al-Dīn: Inventaire, notes archéologiques et bibliographiques." *BEO* 13 (1949-51).

———. "Corporations de Damas sous Nūr al-Dīn: Matériaux pour une topographie économique de Damas au XIIe siècle." *Arabica* 3 (1956).

———. *Nūr al-Dīn.* 3 vols. Damas, 1967.

———. "Damas à la lumière des théories de Jean Sauvaget." In *The Islamic City,* eds. A. Hourani & S. M. Stern. Oxford, 1970.

Escovitz, J. H. *The Office of Qâḍî al-Quḍât in Cairo under the Baḥrî Mamlûks.* Berlin, 1984.

Evrard, J. B. *Zur Geschichte Aleppos und Nordsyriens im letzten halben Jahrhundert der Mamlukenherrschaft (872-921A. H.) nach arabischen und italienischen Quellen.* München, 1974.

Fahad, Badrī Muḥammad. *al-'Āmma bi-Baghdād fī al-qarn al-khāmis al-hijrī (The Common People of Baghdad in the 5th Century of the Hijra).* Baghdād, 1967.

Fathy, Hassan. "The Qā'a of the Cairene Arab House: Its Development and Some New Usages for its Design Concepts." In *Colloque international sur l'histoire du Caire.* [Cairo], [1972].

Fawaz, L. "The City and the Mountain: Beirut's Political Radius in the Nineteenth Century as revealed in the Crisis of 1860." *IJMES* 16 (1984).

———. *Merchants and Migrants in Nineteenth-Century Beirut.* Cambridge, 1983.

Fernandes, L. "Three Ṣūfī Foundations in a 15th Century Waqfiyya." *Annales Islamologiques* 17 (1981).

———. "Some Aspects of the Zāwiya in Egypt at the Eve of the Ottoman Conquest." *Annales Islamologiques* 19 (1983).

———. "Two Variations of the Same Theme: The Zāwiya of Ḥasan al-Rūmī, the Takiyya of Ibrāhīm al-Ǧulšānī." *Annales Islamologiques* 21 (1985).

———. "The Foundation of Baybars al-Jashankir: Its Waqf, History, and Architecture." *Muqarnas* 4 (1987).

———. "Mamluk Politics and Education: The Evidence from Two Fourteenth Century Waqfiyya." *Annales Islamologiques* 23 (1987).

———. *The Evolution of a Sufi Institution in Mamluk Egypt: The Khanqah*. Berlin, 1988.

Garcin, J.-Cl. *Un centre musulman de la haute-Égypte médiévale: Qūṣ*. Cairo, 1974.

———. "Habitat médiéval et histoire urbaine à Fusṭāṭ au Caire." In *Palais et maisons du Caire*, eds. J.-Cl. Garcin et al. Paris, 1982.

———. "Toponymie et topographie urbaines médiévales à Fusṭāṭ et au Caire." *JESHO* 27 (1984).

———. "Le Caire et l'évolution urbaine dans des pays musulmans à l'époque médiévale." *Annales Islamologiques* 25 (1991).

Gardet, L. *La cité musulmane*. Paris, 1954.

Gaube, H. & E. Wirth. *Aleppo: historische und geographische Beiträge zur baulichen Gestaltung zur sozialen Organisation und zur wirtschaftliche Dynamik einer vorderasiatischen Fernhandelsmetropol*. Wiesbaden, 1984.

Gerber, H. "The Population of Syria and Palestine in the Nineteenth Century." *Asian and African Studies* 13 (1979).

———. *Ottoman Rule in Jerusalem 1890-1914*. Berlin, 1985.

Germen, A., ed. *Islamic Architecture and Urbanism*. Damman, 1983.

Ghassān Munīr Sannū. *Madīna Ṣaydā 1818-1860 (Sidon 1818-1860)*. Bayrūt, 1988.

Ghawānama, Yūsuf Darwīsh. *Ta'rīkh niyāba Bayt al-Muqaddas fī al-'aṣr al-mamlūkī (History of Jerusalem District in the Mamluk Period)*. 'Ammān, 1982.

Gibb, H. A. R. & H. Bowen. *Islamic Society and the West*. 2 vols. London, 1950-7.

Gil, M. "Dhimmī Donations and Foundations for Jerusalem (638-1099)." *JESHO* 27 (1984).

Gilbert, J. E. *The Ulama of Medieval Damascus and the International World of Islamic Scholarship*. Ph. D. dissertation, University of California. 1977.

———. "Institutionalization of Muslim Scholarship and Professionalization of the 'Ulamā' in Medieval Damascus." *SI* 52 (1980).

Goitein, S. D. "The Sanctity of Jerusalem and Palestine in Early Islam." In *Studies in Islamic History and Institutions*. Leiden, 1966.

———. *A Mediterranean Society*. 5 vols. Berkeley, 1967-88.

———. *Studies in Islamic History and Institutions*. Leiden, 1968.

———. "Cairo: An Islamic City in the Light of the Geniza Documents." In *Middle Eastern Cities*, ed. I. M. Lapidus. Berkeley & L. A., 1969.

———. "A Mansion in Fustat: A Twelfth-Century Description of a Domestic Compound in the Ancient Capital of Egypt." In *The Medieval City*, eds. H. A. Miskimin et al. New Haven & London, 1977.

———. "Urban Housing in Fatimid and Ayyubid Times as illustrated by the Cairo Geniza Documents." *SI* 47 (1978).

———. "Jerusalem in the Arab Period (638-1099)." *Jerusalem Cathedra* 2 (1982).

Goto, Akira. "Isuramu bokkoki no Arabu shakai no kozo (The Social Structure of Arab Society in the Early Islamic Period)." *Isuramu Sekai* 7 (1970); 11 (1977).

———. "Jiyu toshi Mekka (The Free City of Mecca)." In *Nairikuajia Nishiajia no shakai to bunka*, ed. Masao Mori. Tokyo, 1983.

———. "Jiyu toshi Mekka no hitobito (The People of the Free City of Mecca)." In *Isuramusekai no hitobito*. Vol. 5: *Toshimin*. Tokyo, 1984.

———. "7 seiki no Mekka to Medina (Mecca and Medina in the 7th Century)." *Shicho*, new series, 26 (1989).

———. "Isuramu no toshisei (On Urbanism in Islam)." *Sobun* 289 (1988).

———. *Mekka: Isuramu no toshishakai (Mecca and Islamic Urban Society)*. Tokyo, 1991.

Grandin, Th. "La savonnerie traditionnelle à Alep." *BEO* 36 (1986).

Greenshields, T. H. "'Quarters' and Ethnicity." In *The Changing Middle Eastern City*, eds. G. H. Blake & R. I. Lawless. London, 1980.

Grunebaum, G. von. "Die islamische Stadt." *Saeculum* 6 (1955).

———. "The Structure of the Muslim Town." *Memoir* (The American Anthropological Association) 81: *Islam: Essays in the Nature and Growth of a Cultural Tradition* (1955). Reprinted under the same title in London, 1961.

Guest, A. R. "The Foundation of Fustat and the Khittahs of that Town." *JRAS* 39 (1907).

Guest, A. R. & E. T. Richmond. "Miṣr in the Fifteenth Century." *JRAS* 35 (1903).

al-Ḥajīh, 'Azīz Jāsim. *Baghdādīyāt: Taṣwīr lil-ḥayāt al-ijtimā'īya wal-'ādāt al-baghdādīya khilāla mi'a 'ām (The Appearance of Baghdad: Society and Customs in Baghdad This Century)*. [Baghdād], 1981.

al-Ḥajjī, Ḥayāt Nāṣir. *Aḥwāl al-'āmma fī ḥukm al-mamālīk 678-784 A. H. /1279-1382 A. D. (Condition of the People under Mamluk Rule)*. al-Kuwayt, 1984.

Hakim, B. S. *Arabic-Islamic Cities: Building and Planning Principles*. London, 1986. Translated into Japanese as *Isuramu toshi: Arabu no machizukuri no genri* by Tsugitaka Sato et al. Tokyo, 1990.

Ḥallāq, Ḥassān. *al-Ta'rīkh al-ijtimā'ī wal-iqtiṣādī wal-siyāsī fī Bayrūt wal-wilāyāt al-'uthmānīya fī al-qarn al-tāsi' 'ashara: Sijillāt al-maḥkama al-shar'īya fī Bayrūt (A Social, Economic and Political History of Beirut)*. Bayrūt, 1987.

———. *Bayrūt al-maḥrūsa fī 'ahd al-'uthmānī (Ottoman Beirut)*. Bayrūt, 1987.

———. *Awqāf al-muslimīn fī Bayrūt fī al-'ahd al-'uthmānī: Musajjalāt al-maḥkama al-shar'īya fī Bayrūt (Waqf Foundations in Beirut)*. Bayrūt, 1988.

Ḥamūdī, Bāsim 'Abd al-Ḥamīd, ed. *'Ādāt wa taqālīd al-ḥayāt al-sha'bīya al-'Irāqīya (Customs of the People of Iraq)*. Baghdād, 1986.

Hanna, N. "Bayt al-Isṭambullī: An Introduction to the Cairene Middle Class House of the Ottoman Period." *Annales Islamologiques* 16 (1980).

———. *An Urban History of Būlāq in the Mamluk and Ottoman Periods*. Cairo, 1983.

———. *Construction Work in Ottoman Cairo (1517-1798)*. Cairo, 1984.

———. *Habiter au Caire: La maison moyenne et ses habitants aux XVIIe et XVIIIe siècles*. Le Caire, 1991.

Hasebe, Fumihiko. "14 seikimatsu-15 seikishoto Kairo no shokuryo bodo (Food Riots in Cairo around the Turn of the 15th Century)." *Shigaku Zasshi* 97/10 (1988).

———. "Isuramu toshi no shokuryo bodo: Mamurukucho Kairo no baai (Food Disturbances in a City of the Islamic World)." *Rekishigaku Kenkyu* 612 (1990).

Hasson, I. "Muslim Literature in Praise of Jerusalem: Faḍā'il Bayt al-Maqdis." *Jerusalem Cathedra* 1 (1981).

Hautecoeur, L. & G. Wiet. *Les mosquées du Caire*. 2 vols. Paris, 1932.

Havemann, A. *Ri'āsa und Qaḍā': Institution als Ausdruck wechselnder Kräftverhältnisse in syrischen Städte vom 10. bis zum 12. Jahrhundert*. Freiburg im Breisgau, 1975.

———. "The Vizier and the Ra'īs in Saljuq Syria: The Struggle for Urban Self-Representation." *IJMES* 21 (1989).

Hayashi, Takeshi. "Toshika to ningenruikei (Urbanization and Human Types: An Ideal Image of the Cairene Citizen)." *Shiso* 582 (1972).

Herzfeld, E. "Damascus: Studies in Architecture." *Ars Islamica* 9 (1942); 10 (1943); 11-12 (1946); 13-14 (1948).

———. *Geschichte der Stadt Samarra*. Berlin, 1948.

———. "Matériaux pour un corpus inscriptionum arabicarum, 2e partie: Syrie du Nord, Inscriptions et monuments d'Alep." *MIFAO* 76 (1955); 77 (1956); 78 (1954).

Herzfeld, E. & F. Sarre. *Archäologische Reise im Euphrat und Tigris Gebiet*. 4 vols. Berlin, 1911-20.

Hoffmann, G. *Kommune oder Staatsbürokratie?: Zur politischen Rolle der Bevölkerung syrischer Städte von 10. bis 12. Jahrhundert*. Berlin, 1975.

Hopkins, W. *Jerusalem: A Study in Urban Geography*. Michigan, 1970.

Hourani, A. "Ottoman Reform and the Politics of Notables." In *Beginnings of Modernization in the Middle East: The Nineteenth Century*, eds. W. R. Polk & R. L. Chambers. Chicago, 1968.

Hreitani, M. & J.-Cl. David. "Souks traditionnels et centre moderne: Espaces et pratiques à Alep (1930-1980)." *BEO* 36 (1984).

Humphreys, R. S. "The Expressive Intent of the Mamluk Architecture." *SI* 35 (1972).

———. *From Saladin to the Mongols: The Ayyubids of Damascus, 1193-1260*. N. Y., 1977.

———. "Politics and Architectural Patronage in Ayyubid Damascus." In *The Islamic World: From Classical to Modern Times*, eds. C. E. Bosworth et al. Princeton, 1989.

———. "Urban Topography and Urban Society: Damascus under the Ayyubids and Mamluks." In *Islamic History: A Framework for Inquiry*. Princeton, 1991.

Hütteroth, W.-D. *Palästina und Transjordanien im 16. Jahrhundert: Wirtschaftsstruktur ländlicher Siedlungen nach osmanischen Steuerregistern*. Wiesbaden, 1978.

Hütteroth, W.-D. & K. Abdulfattah. *Historical Geography of Palestine, Transjordan and Southern Syria in the Late 16th Century*. Erlangen, 1977.

Ilbert, R. "Note sur l'Égypte au XIXe siècle: Typologie architecturale et morphologie urbaine." *Annales Islamologiques* 17 (1981).

'Iṣām, Muḥammad Shabārū. *Ta'rīkh Bayrūt: Mundh aqdam al-'uṣūr ḥattā al-qarn al-'ishrīn (History of Beirut)*. Bayrūt, 1987.

Itagaki, Yuzo. "Musurimu dohodan o megutte (On Muslim Brethren)." In *Isuramuka ni kansuru kyodo kenkyu hokoku*. Vol. 4. ILCAA, Tokyo University of Foreign Studies. Tokyo, 1971.

———. "Arabu no seijibunka to kokumin keisei: Aidentiti kuraishisu o meguru shiron (Arab Political Culture and Nation Building)." In *Nenpo Seijigaku*, 1978.

———. *Ishi no sakebi ni mimi o sumasu: Chuto wahei no tansaku (Listening to the Voice of the Stones)*. Tokyo, 1992.

al-Jāmi'a al-Urdunīya (The University of Jordan). *Buyūt 'Ammān al-ūlā (Dwellings in Amman)*. 'Ammān, 1987.

———. *Irāq al-Amīr al-Bardūn: al-Malāmiḥ al-mi'mārīya lil-qarya al-urdunīya ('Irāq al-Amīr: A Study of the Structure of a Jordanian Village)*. 'Ammān, 1988.

———. *Sūf: Dirāsa mi'mārīya fī al-bay'a al-maḥallīya (Sūf: A Study of the Structure of a Town)*. 'Ammān, 1989.

al-Janābī, Kāẓim. *Takhṭīṭ madīna al-Kūfa (An Outline of the Planning of the City of Kufa)*. Baghdād, 1967.

al-Janābī (al-Genabi), Hāshim Khuḍayr. *Der Suq (Bazar) von Baghdad: Eine wirtschafts- und social-geographische Untersuchung*. Erlangen, 1976.

———. *Tarkīb al-dākhilī li-madīna al-Mawṣil al-qadīma: Dirāsa fī jighrāfīya al-mudun (Inner Structure of the Old City of Mosul)*. al-Mawṣil, 1982.

———. *Madīna Duhāk: Dirāsa fī jighrāfīya al-mudun (Urban Geography of the City of Duhāk)*. al-Mawṣil, 1985.

———. *Madīna Irbīl: Dirāsa fī al-ḥadar (Urban Geography of the City of Irbil)*. [Irbīl], 1987.

Jawād, Muṣṭafā & Aḥmad Sūsa. *Dalīl khāriṭa Baghdād al-mufaṣṣal fī khiṭaṭ Baghdād qadīman wa ḥadīthan (Topographical Guide to Baghdad)*. Baghdād, 1958.

Johansen, B. "The All-Embracing Town and its Mosques." *Revue de l'Occident musulman et la Méditerranée* 32/2 (1981).

Johnson, M. "Political Bosses and their Gangs: Zu'ama and Qabadayat in the Sunni Muslim Quarters of Beirut." In *Patrons and Clients in Mediterranean Societies*, eds. E. Gellner & J. Waterbury. London, 1977.

———. *Class & Client in Beirut: The Sunni Muslim Community and the Lebanese State 1840-1985*. London, 1986.

Johnson, S. W. *The Monuments of Islamic Cairo*. N. p., 1979.

Jones, F. "Memoirs on Baghdad." In *Selection from the Records of the Bombey Government*. Vol. 43. Bombey, 1857.

al-Jumaylī, Rāsim, ed. *al-Baghdādīyūn: Kitāb yuṣawwiru al-ḥayāt al-baghdādīya ayyām zamān mundh binā'hā wa ḥattā sana 1936 A. D. (The People of Baghdad: Sketches of the Life of the People of Baghdad in Past Times from its Founding to 1936)*. Vol. 1. Baghdād, 1982.

Kato, Hiroshi. "Urban and Rural Societies in mid-19th Century Egypt: as Reflected in Some Unpublished Documents relating to Taxation System." In *Urbanism in Islam: The Proceedings of the International Conference on Urbanism in Islam*. Vol. 3. Tokyo, 1989.

Kayyāl, Munīr. *al-Ḥammāmāt al-dimashqīya (The Public Baths of Damascus)*. Dimashq, 1966. Reprinted in 1986.

———. *Ḥikāyāt dimashqīya fī al-adab al-sha'bī (Tales of the People of Damascus)*. Dimashq, 1987.

Kemp, P. "Mosuli Sketches of Ottoman History." *Middle Eastern Studies* 17 (1981).

———. "History and Historiography in Jalili Mosul." *Middle Eastern Studies* 19 (1983).

———. "Power and Knowledge in Jalili Mosul." *Middle Eastern Studies* 19 (1983).

Keusséoglou, A. *Le vieux Damas qui s'en va: 1930-images et 'cris' de la rue*. Damas, 1988.

Khoury, Ph. S. *Urban Notables and Arab Nationalism: The Politics of Damascus 1860-1920*. Cambridge, 1983.

———. "Syrian Urban Politics in Transition: The Quarters of Damascus during the French Mandate." *IJMES* 16 (1984).

———. *Syria and the French Mandate: The Politics of Arab Nationalim, 1920-1945*. Princeton, 1987.

———. "The Urban Notables Paradigm Revisited." *REMMM* 55-56 (1990).

al-Khūrī, Munīr 'Īsā As'ad. *Ta'rīkh Ḥimṣ (History of Homs)*. Ḥimṣ & Ṭarābulus, 1983-4.

Kikuchi, Tadayoshi. "Mamurukucho jidai Kairo no muhutashibu: Shusshin kaiso o chushin ni (Muḥtasib in Cairo during the Mamluk Dynasty: An Analysis of their Personal Histories)." *The Toyo Gakuho* 64/1-2 (1983).

———. "Wakufu ni kansuru saikin no kenkyu ni tsuite no oboegaki (Some Remarks upon Recent Studies on Waqf)." *Oriento* 31/1 (1988).

Kremer, A. von. *Mittelsyrien und Damascus*. Wien, 1853.

———. "Topographie von Damascus." In *Denkschriften d. K. Akad. d. Wissenschaften*. Wien, 1854.

al-Kubaysī, Ḥamdān 'Abd al-Majīd. *Aswāq Baghdād ḥattā bidāya al-'aṣr al-buwayhī (The Markets of Baghdad until the Beginning of the Buwayhi Age)*. Baghdād, 1979.

Kubiak, W. B. *al-Fustat: Its Foundation and Early Urban Development*. Cairo, 1987.

Kuroki, Hidemitsu. "Areppo toshi shakai no kozo: 18 seiki kohan kara 19 seiki hajime o chushin ni (The Social Structure of the City of Aleppo from the Latter Half of the18th Century to the First Half of the 19th Century)." *Hikaku Toshishi Kenkyu* 6/2 (1987).

———. "Toshi soran ni miru shakai kankei: Areppo 1819-20 nen" (Social Relations in an Urban Disturbance: Aleppo 1819-1820)." *Nihon Chuto Gakkai Nenpo* 3/1 (1988).

———. "Toshi soran ni miru shakai kankei: Areppo 1850 nen (Social Relations in an Urban Disturbance: Aleppo, 1850)." *Toyo Bunka* 69 (1989).

Labib, S. Y. *Handelsgeschichte Ägyptens im Spätmittelalter 1171-1517*. Wiesbaden, 1965.

Lane, E. W. *An Account of the Manners and Customs of the Modern Egyptians*. London, 1836.

———. *Cairo: Fifty Years Ago*. London, 1896.

Lane-Poole, S. *Cairo: Sketches of its History, Monuments, and Social Life*. London, 1892.

———. *The Story of Cairo*. Cairo, 1902.

Lapidus, I. M. *Muslim Cities in the Later Middle Ages*. Cambridge, Mass., 1967. Reprinted as student edition in 1984.

———. "Muslim Cities and Islamic Societies." In *Middle Eastern Cities*, ed. I. M. Lapidus. Berkeley & L. A., 1969.

———. "Ayyubid Religious Policy and the Development of Schools of Law in Cairo." In *Colloque international sur l'histoire du Caire*. [Cairo], [1972].

———. "The Evolution of Muslim Urban Society." *Comparative Studies in Society and History* 15 (1973).

———. "Hierarchies and Networks: A Comparison of Chinese and Islamic Societies." In *Conflict and Control in Late Imperial China*, ed. F. J. Wakemann. Berkeley, 1975.

———. "The Separation of State and Religion in the Development of Early Islamic Society." *IJMES* 6 (1975).

———. "Islam and Modernity." In *Patterns of Modernity, Beyond the West*, ed. S. N. Eisenstadt. London, 1987.

———. *A History of Islamic Societies*. Cambridge, 1988.

———. "Muslim Cities as Plural Societies: The Politics of Intermediary Bodies." In *Urbanism in Islam: The Proceedings of the International Conference on Urbanism in Islam*. Vol. 1. Tokyo, 1989.

Lassner, J. "Massignon and Baghdad: The Complexities of Growth in an Imperial City." *JESHO* 9 (1966).

———. *The Topography of Baghdad in the Early Middle Ages: Text and Studies*. Detroit, 1970. Translated into Arabic as *Khiṭaṭ Baghdād fī al-'uhūd al-'abbāsīya al-ūlā*, by Ṣāliḥ Aḥmad al-'Alī. Baghdād, 1983.

Le Strange, G. *Baghdad during the Abbasid Caliphate*. London, 1900.

Lecerf, J. & R. Tresse. "Les 'arāḍa de Damas." *BEO* 7-8 (1937-8).

Leiser, G. "The Madrasa and the Islamization of the Middle East: The Case of Egypt." *Journal of the American Research Center in Egypt* 22 (1985).

Lev, Y. "Fāṭimid Policy towards Damascus (358/968-386/996): Military, Political and Social Aspects." *Jerusalem Studies in Arabic and Islam* 3 (1981-2).

———. "The Fāṭimids and the Aḥdāth of Damascus 386/996-411/1021." *Die Welt des Orients* 13 (1982).

Lewis, B. "The Islamic Guilds." *Economic History Review* 8/1 (1937).

Lézine, A. "Les salles nobles des palais mamelouks." *Annales Islamologiques* 10 (1972).

———. "Persistence de traditions pré-islamiques dans l'architecture domestique de l'Égypte musulmane." *Annales Islamologiques* 11 (1972).

Lézine, A. & 'Abdul-Tawwab. "Introduction à l'étude des maisons anciennes de Rosette." *Annales Islamologiques* 10 (1972).

Liauzu, Cl. "Sociétés urbaines et mouvements sociaux." *Maghreb-Machreq* 111 (1986).

Little, D. P. "Ḥaram Documents related to the Jews of Late Fourteenth Century Jerusalem." *Journal of Semitic Studies* 30/2 (1985).

Lutfi, H. *al-Quds al-Mamlûkiyya: A History of Mamlûk Jerusalem based on the Ḥaram Documents*. Berlin, 1985.

al-Ma'āḍīdī, 'Abd al-Qādir Sulaymān. *Wāsiṭ fī al-'aṣr al-umawī (Wāsiṭ in the Umayyad Era)*. Baghdād, 1976.

———. *Wāsiṭ fī al-'aṣr al-'abbāsī (Wāsiṭ in the 'Abbasid Era)*. Baghdād, 1983.

MacKenzie, N. D. *Ayyubid Cairo: A Topographical Study*. Cairo, 1992.

Maejima, Shinji. "Isuramu to toshi (Islam and the City)." In *Isuramuka ni kansuru kyodo kenkyu hokoku*. Vol. 4. ILCAA, Tokyo University of Foreign Studies, 1971.

Makdisi, G. "Autograph Diary of an Eleventh-Century Historian of Baghdād." *BSOAS* 18 (1956); 19 (1957).

———. "The Topography of Eleventh Century Baghdad: Materials and Notes." *Arabica* 6 (1959).

———. "Muslim Institutions of Learning in Eleventh-Century Baghdad." *BSOAS* 24 (1961).

———. *The Rise of Colleges: Institutions of Learning in Islam and the West*. Edinburgh, 1981.

Makovsky, A. "Sixteenth-Century Agricultural Production in the Liwā of Jerusalem: Insights from the Tapu Defters and an Attempt at Quantification." *Archivum Ottomanicum* 9 (1984).

Ma'oz, M. "Syrian Urban Politics in the Tanzimat between 1840 and 1861." *BSOAS* 19 (1966).

Marcus, A. "Men, Women and Property: Dealers in Real Estate in Eighteenth-Century Aleppo." *JESHO* 26 (1983).

———. "Privacy in Eighteenth-Century Aleppo: The Limits of Cultural Ideals." *IJMES* 18 (1986).

———. *The Middle East on the Eve of Modernity: Aleppo in the Eighteenth Century*. New York, 1989.

———. "Poverty and Poor Relief in Eighteenth Century Aleppo." *REMMM* 55-56 (1990).

Margoliouth, D. *Cairo, Jerusalem and Damascus*. London, 1907.

Marthelot, P. "Le Caire, nouvelle métropole." *Annales Islamologiques* 8 (1969).

Maṣlaḥa al-Misāḥa (The Egyptian Department of Survey). *Kharīṭa al-Qāhira tubayyina al-āthār al-islāmīya (Map of Islamic Historical Monuments in Cairo)*. al-Qāhira, 1948-51.

El-Masry, Ahmed M. *Die Bauten von Ḫādim Sulaimān Pascha (1468-1548) nach seinen Urkunden im Ministerium für Fromme Stiftungen im Kairo*. Berlin, 1991.

Massignon, L. "Mission en Mésopotamie (1907-08)." *MIFAO* 31 (1912).

———. "Les corps de métiers et la cité islamique." *Rev. Internat. de Sociologie*. 1920. Reprinted in *Opera Minora*. Vol. 1. Beirut, 1963.

———. "Enquête sur les corporations d'artisans et de commerçants au Maroc (1923-1924)." *RMM* 58 (1924).

———. "Explication du plan de Kufa (Irak)." *Mélanges Maspéro* 3 (1935). Reprinted in *Opera Minora*. Vol. 3. Beirut, 1963.

———. "Cadis et naqibs baghdadiens." *Wiener Zeitschrift für die Kunde des Morgenlandes* 51 (1948-52). Reprinted in *Opera Minora*. Vol. 1. Beirut, 1963.

———. "La 'futuwwa', ou 'pacte d'honneur artisanal' entre les travailleurs musulmans au moyen âge." *La Nouvelle Clio* 4 (1952). Reprinted in *Opera Minora*. Vol. 1. Beirut, 1963.

———. "La structure du travail à Damas en 1927." *Cahiers Internat. de Sociologie* 15 (1953). Reprinted in *Opera Minora*. Vol. 1. Beirut, 1963.

———. "Explication du plan de Basra (Irak)." In *Westöstliche Abhandlungen R. Tschudi*. Wiesbaden, 1954. Reprinted in *Opera Minora*. Vol. 1. Beirut, 1963.

———. "La cité des morts au Caire (Qarāfa-Darb al-Aḥmar)." *BIFAO* 57 (1958). Reprinted in *Opera Minora*. Vol. 3. Beirut, 1963.

Masters, B. *The Origins of Western Economic Dominance in the Middle East: Mercantilism and the Islamic Economy in Aleppo, 1600-1750*. N. Y., 1988.

———. "The 1850 Events in Aleppo: An Aftershock of Syria's Incorporation into the Capitalist World System." *IJMES* 22 (1990).

Maury, B., J.-Cl. Garcin, A. Raymond, J. Revault & M. Zakariya, eds. *Palais et maisons du Caire*. 2 vols. Paris, 1982-3.

al-Mawswī, Muṣṭafā 'Abbās. *al-'Awāmil al-ta'rīkhīya li-nash'a wa taṭawwur al-mudun al-'arabīya al-islāmīya (Historical Factors in the Formation and Development of the Arab-Islamic City)*. Baghdād, 1982.

Mazloum, S. "L'ancienne canalisation d'eau d'Alep." *Documents d'Études Orientales* 5 [1936].

Meinecke, M. "Der Survey des Damaszener Altstadtviertels aṣ-Ṣāliḥīya." *Damaszener Mitteilungen* 1 (1983).

Meinecke-Berg, V. "Eine Stadtansicht des mamlukischen Kairo aus dem 16. Jahrhundert." *Mitteilungen der Deutschen Archäologischen Instituts, Abteilung Kairo* 32 (1976).

al-Messiri Nadim, Nawal. "The Concept of the Ḥāra: A Historical and Sociological Study of al-Sukkariyya." *Annales Islamologiques* 15 (1979).

———. "Changing Lifestyle in Cairo." In *Urbanism in Islam: The Proceedings of the International Conference on Urbanism in Islam*. Vol. 4. Tokyo, 1989.

el-Messiri, Sawsan. "The Changing Role of the Futuwwa in the Social Structure of Cairo." In *Patrons and Clients in the Mediterranean Societies*, eds. E. Gellner & J. Waterbury. London, 1977.

———. *Ibn al-Balad: A Concept of Egyptian Identity*. Leiden, 1978.

———. "Self-Images of Traditional Urban Women in Cairo." In *Women in the Muslim World*, eds. L. Beck & N. Keddie. Cambridge, Mass., 1978.

Mez, A. *Die Renaissance des Islams*. Heidelberg, 1922.

The Middle Eastern Culture Center of Japan (Chukinto Bunka Senta). *Ejiputo Isuramu toshi aru-Fusutato (An Islamic City of Egypt, al-Fustat)*. Chukinto Bunka Senta Kenkyukai Hokoku 1. Tokyo, 1980.

Miki, Wataru. "Kairo no kusuridon'yatachi (Wholesale Druggists in Cairo)." In *Isuramusekai no hitobito*. Vol. 5: *Toshimin*. Tokyo, 1984.

Miura, Toru. "Damasukusu kogai no toshi keisei: 12-16 seiki no Sarihiya (The Urbanization of the Suburbs of Damascus: The Ṣāliḥīya Quarter from the 12th Century to the 16th Century)." *The Toyo Gakuho* 68/1-2 (1987).

———. "Mamurukucho jidai no Sarihiya: Gaiku to urama shakai (The Ṣāliḥīya Quarter in the Mamlūk Period: Its Structure and the Role of the'Ulamā' Society)." *Nihon Chuto Gakkai Nenpo* 4/1 (1989).

———. "Mamurukucho makki no toshishakai: Damasukusu o chushin ni (Urban Society at the End of the Mamlūk Era)." *Shigaku Zasshi* 98/1 (1989).

———. "Gaiku to minshu hanran: 15-16 seiki no Damasukusu (The Quarter and Popular Movements)." In *Sekaishi eno toi*. Vol. 4: *Shakaiteki ketsugo*. Tokyo, 1989.

———. "The Structure of the Quarter and the Role of the Outlaws: The Ṣāliḥīya Quarter and the Zu'r in the Mamlūk Period." In *Urbanism in Islam: The Proceedings of the International Conference on Urbanism in Islam*. Vol. 3. Tokyo, 1989.

———. "Isuramu no toshisei o megutte (Some Remarks on Urbanism in Islam)." *Chichukaigaku Kenkyu* 13 (1990).

———. "Nettowakuron no kozai (The Network Theory Reconsidered)." *Madiniya* (Institute of Oriental Culture, University of Tokyo) 38 (1991).

———. "The Ṣāliḥīya Quarter in the Suburbs of Damascus: Its Formation, Structure, and Transformation in the Ayyūbid and the Mamlūk Periods." *BEO* 47 (1994).

Mostafa, Saleh Lamei. *Kloster und Mausoleum des Farağ Ibn Barqūq in Kairo*. Glückstadt, 1968.

———. *Moschee des Farağ Ibn Barqūq in Kairo*. Glückstadt, 1972.

———. *Madrasa, Ḫānqāh und Mausoleum des Barqūq in Kairo*. Glückstadt, 1982.

Mottahedeh, R. P. *Loyalty and Leadership in an Early Islamic Society*. Princeton, 1980.

al-Mudīrīya al-'Āmma lil-Āthār wal-Matāḥif (La Direction Générale des Antiquités et des Musées). *Qā'ima al-mabānī al-athrīya al-musajjala wal-mu'adda lil-tasjīl fī madīna Dimashq ḥattā bidāya 'ām 1983 (A General Survey of Historical Monuments in Damascus)*. Dimashq, 1983.

Müller-Wiener, M. *Eine Stadtgeschichte Alexandrias von 564/1169 bis in die Mitte des 9./15. Jahrhunderts: Verwaltung und innerstadtische Organisationsformen*. Berlin, 1992.

al-Mumayyiz, Amīn. *Baghdād kamā 'araftuhā (Baghdad as I Saw it)*. [Baghdād], 1985.

al-Munajjid, Ṣalāḥ al-Dīn. *Khiṭaṭ Dimashq (Topography of Damascus)*. Dimashq, 1949.

Mūsā, 'Alī & Muḥammad Ḥurba. *Muḥāfaẓa Ḥamā (Hama District)*. [Dimashq], 1985.

Muṣṭafā, Firāl. *al-Bayt al-'arabī fī al-'Irāq fī al-'aṣr al-islāmī (Arab Dwellings in Iraq during the Islamic Period)*. Baghdād, 1983.

Nahdī, al-Naqīb Ṣubḥī al-Ḥimṣī. *Ta'rīkh Ṭalābulus min khilāli wathā'iq al-shar'īya fī al-niṣf al-thānī min la-qarn al-sābi' 'ashara al-mīlādī (A History of Tripoli in the 17th Century)*. Bayrūt, 1986.

Naito, Masanori. "Damasukasu ni okeru minzoku shuhabetsu sumiwake to sono hen'yo (Change in Spatial Segregation by Race and Religion in Damascus)." *Tokyo Daigaku Kyoyo Gakubu Kyoyo Gakka Kiyo* 17 (1985).

Najāt, Qaṣṣāb Ḥasan. *Ḥadīth Dimashqī 1884-1983 (Story of Damascus)*. Vol. 1. Dimashq, 1988.

Naji, A. J. & Y. N. Ali. "The Suqs of Basrah: Commercial Organization and Activity in a Medieval Islamic City." *JESHO* 24 (1981).

Nāṣif, Aḥmad 'Abd al-Salām. *al-Shurṭa fī Miṣr al-islāmīya (The Police in Islamic Egypt)*. al-Qāhira, 1987.

Niqāba al-Muhandisīn al-Sūrīyīn (The Syrian Department of Construction). *Nadwa Dimashq al-qadīma (Old Damascus)*. Dimashq, 1982.

Northedge, A. "Creswell, Herzfeld, and Samarra." *Muqarnas* 8 (1991).

Nu'aysa, Yūsuf Jamīl. *Mujtama' madīna Dimashq: 1186-1256 A. H./ 1772-1840 A. D. (Urban Society in Damascus)*. 2 vols. Dimashq, 1986.

Ota, Keiko. "Mirudasucho no guntai hensei (The Military Organization of the Mirdasid Dynasty)." *Isuramu Sekai* 25-26 (1986).

———. "Areppo Banakusa chiku no rekishi (The History of Bānaqūsa in Aleppo)." *Isuramu Sekai* 33-34 (1990).

Panzac, D. "Alexandrie: Évolution d'une ville cosmopolite au XIXe siècle." *Annales Islamologiques* 14 (1978).

Pascual, J.-P. *Damas à la fin du XVIe siècle d'après trois actes de waqf ottomans*. Vol. 1. Damas, 1983.

———. "Meubles et objets domestiques quotidiens des intérieurs damascains du XVIIe siècle." *REMMM* 55-56 (1990).

Pellat, Ch. *Le milieu baṣrien et la formation de Ǧāḥiẓ*. Paris, 1953.

Peters, F. E. *Jerusalem and Mecca: The Typology of the Holy City in the Near East*. N. Y. & London, 1986.
Petry, C. F. *The Civilian Elite of Cairo in the Later Middle Ages*. Princeton, 1981.
Philipp, Th. "The Rise and Fall of Acre: Population and Economy between 1700 and 1850." *REMMM* 55-56 (1990).
Pickvance, Ch. "Social Movements in the City or Urban Movements." In *État, ville et mouvements sociaux au Maghreb et au Moyen-Orient,* eds. K. Brown et al. Paris, 1989.
Piterberg, G. "The Formation of an Ottoman Egyptian Elite in the 18th Century." *IJMES* 22 (1990).
Popper, W. *History of Egypt, 1382-1469: Systematic Notes to Ibn Taghrî Birdî's Chronicles of Egypt*. 2 vols. Berkeley, 1955-7.
Pouzet, L. "Maghrébins à Damas au VIIIe/ XIIIe siècle." *BEO* 28 (1975).
———. *Damas au VIIe/ XIIIe siècle: Vie et structures religieuses d'une métropole islamique*. Beyrouth, 1988.
Powders, D. S. "Revenues of Public Waqfs in Sixteenth-Century Jerusalem." *Archivum Ottomanicum* 9 (1984).
al-Qāsimī, Muḥammad Sa'īd & Jamāl al-Dīn al-Qāsimī. *Qāmūs al-ṣinā'āt al-shāmīya (Dictionary of the Artisans of Damascus)*. Paris, 1960. Reprinted in Dimashq, 1988.
Qudsī, Ilyās 'Abduh (Qoudsî, Elia). "Notice sur les corporations de Damas." In *Actes du VIe Congrès des Orientalistes à Leyde, 1883*. Vol. 2. Leiden, 1885.
Rafeq, Abdul-Karim. *The Province of Damascus 1723-1783*. Beirut, 1966.
———. "The Law-court Registers of Damascus, with Special Reference to Crafts Corporations during the First Half of the Eighteenth Century." In *Les arabes par leurs archives,* eds. J. Berque & D. Chevallier. Paris, 1976.
———. "Maẓāhir min al-tanẓīm al-ḥirfī fī Bilād al-Shām fī al-'ahd al-'uthmānī (Syrian Craft Corporations in the Ottoman Period)." *Dirāsāt Ta'rīkhīya* 4 (1981). Reprinted in *Buḥūth fī al-ta'rīkh al-iqtiṣādī wal-ijtimā'ī li-Bilād al-Shām fī al-'aṣr al-ḥadīth,* ed. Abdul-Karim Rafeq. Dimashq, 1985.
———. "Ghazza: Dirāsāt 'imrānīya wa ijtimā'īya wa iqtiṣādīya min khilāli al-wathā'iq al-shar'īya 1273-1277/ 1857-1861 (Ghaza: The Architectural and Socio-economic Study based on the Sharia-court Registers during the Years of 1857-1861)." In *Buḥūth fī al-ta'rīkh al-iqtiṣādī wal-ijtimā'ī li-Bilād al-Shām fī al-'aṣr al-ḥadīth,* ed. Abdul-Karim Rafeq. Dimashq, 1985.
———. "New Light on the 1860 Riots in Ottoman Damascus." In *Gegenwart als Geschichte,* eds. A. Havemann & B. Johansen. Leiden, 1988.
———. "The Social and Economic Structure of Bāb-al-Muṣallā (al-Mīdān), Damascus, 1825-1875." In *Arab Civilization, Challenges and Responses,* eds. G. N. Atiyeh & I. M. Oweiss. N. Y., 1988.
———. "Public Morality in 18th Century Ottoman Damascus." *REMMM* 55-56 (1990).

Rāġib, Yūsuf. "Les sanctuaires des gens de la famille dans la cité des morts au Caire." *RSO* 51 (1977).

———. "Deux monuments fatimides au pied du Muqaṭṭam." *REI* 46 (1978).

———. "Les mausolées fatimides du quartier d'al-Mašāhid." *Annales Islamologiques* 17 (1981).

Ra'ūf, 'Imād 'Abd al-Salām. *al-Mawṣil fī al-'ahd al-'uthmānī (Mosul in the Ottoman Period).* al-Najaf, 1975.

Raymond, A. "Une liste des corporations de métiers au Caire." *Arabica* 4/2 (1957).

———. "Essai de géographie des quartiers de résidence aristocratique au Caire au XVIIIᵉ siècle." *JESHO* 6 (1963).

———. "Une 'révolution' au Caire sous les Mamlouks: La crise de 1123/ 1711." *Annales Islamologiques* 6 (1965).

———. "Quartiers et mouvements populaires au Caire." In *Political and Social Change in Modern Egypt,* ed. P. M. Holt. London, 1968.

———. "Les bains publics au Caire à la fin du XVIIIᵉ siècle." *Annales Islamologiques* 8 (1969).

———. "Les grandes épidémies de peste au Caire aux XVIIᵉ et XVIIIᵉ siècles." *BEO* 25 (1972).

———. "Problèmes urbains et urbanisme au Caire aux XVIIᵉᵐᵉ et XVIIIᵉᵐᵉ siècles." In *Colloque international sur l'histoire du Caire.* [Cairo], [1972].

———. *Artisans et commerçants au Caire au XVIIIᵉ siècle.* 2 vols. Damas, 1973.

———. "Signes urbains et étude de la population des grandes villes arabes à l'époque ottomane." *BEO* 27 (1974).

———. "La population du Caire, de Maqrīzī à la Description de l'Égypte." *BEO* 28 (1975).

———. "The Sources of Urban Wealth in Eighteenth Century Cairo." In *Studies in Eighteenth Century Islamic History,* eds. Th. Naff & R. Owen. Carbondale & Edwardsville, 1977.

———. "La conquête ottomane et le développement des grandes villes arabes: Le cas du Caire, de Damas et d'Alep." *Revue de l'Occident musulman et la Méditerranée* 27 (1979).

———. "Les fontaines publiques (sabīls) du Caire à l'époque ottomane (1517-1798)." *Annales Islamologiques* 15 (1979).

———. "Les grands waqfs et l'organisation de l'espace urbain à Alep et au Caire à l'époque ottomane (XVIᵉ-XVIIᵉ siècles)." *BEO* 31 (1979).

———. "La géographie des ḥāra du Caire, au XVIIIᵉ siècle." In *Livre du centenaire de l'IFAO.* Le Caire, 1980.

———. "Les quartiers de résidence des commerçants et artisans maghrébins au Caire aux XVIIᵉ et XVIIIᵉ siècles." *Revue d'Histoire Maghrébine* 10 (1983).

———. *The Great Arab Cities in the 16th-18th Centuries: An Introduction.* N. Y. & London, 1984.

———. "The Population of Aleppo in the Sixteenth and Seventeenth Centuries according to Ottoman Census Documents." *IJMES* 16 (1984).

———. "Cairo's Area and Population in the Early Fifteenth Century." *Muqarnas* 2 (1984).

———. *Grandes villes arabes à l'époque ottomane*. Paris, 1985.

———. "Urban Networks and Popular Movements in Cairo and Aleppo (End of the 18th-Beginning of the 19th Centuries)." *Urbanism in Islam: The Proceedings of the International Conference on Urbanism in Islam*. Vol. 2. Tokyo, 1989.

———. "L'activité architecturale au Caire à l'époque ottomane (1517-1798)." *Annales Islamologiques* 25 (1991).

Raymond, A. & G. Wiet. *Marchés du Caire: Traduction annotée du texte de Maqrīzī*. Le Caire, 1979.

Reimer, M. J. "Colonial Bridgehead: Social and Spatial Change in Alexandria, 1850-1882." *IJMES* 20 (1988).

Revault, J. "Espace comparé des habitations citadines du Caire et de Tunis entre le XVIe et le XVIIIe siècle." *Annales Islamologiques* 15 (1979).

Revault, J., B. Maury & M. Zakariya. *Palais et maisons du Caire du XIVe au XVIIIe siècle*. 4 vols. Le Caire, 1975-83.

Rhode, H. "The Geography of the Sixteenth-Century Sancak of Ṣafad." *Archivum Ottomanicum* 10 (1985).

al-Riḥāwī, 'Abd al-Qādir. *Makhaṭaṭ madīna Dimashq fī al-'ahd al-mamlūkī (A Map of Mamluk Damascus)*. [Dimashq], 1971.

Rishād, al-Imām. *Madīna al-Quds fī al-'aṣr al-wasīṭ (Medieval Jerusalem)*. Tūnis, 1976.

Roded, R. "Ottoman Service as a Vehicle for the Rise of New Upstarts among the Urban Elite Families of Syria in the Last Decades of Ottoman Rule." *Asian and African Studies* 17 (1983).

———. "The Syrian Urban Notables: Elite, Estates, Class?" *Asian and African Studies* 20 (1986).

Rogers, J. M. "Sāmarrā; A Study in Medieval Town-Planning." In *The Islamic City*, eds. A. Hourani & S. M. Stern. Oxford, 1970.

Rosen, M. "The Naqīb al-Ashrāf Rebellion in Jerusalem and its Repercussions on the City's Dhimmīs." *Asian and African Studies* 18 (1984).

Ruppert, H. *Beirut: Eine westlich geprägte Stadt des Orient*. Erlangen, 1969.

Russell, A. *The Natural History of Aleppo and Parts Adjacent: Containing a Description of the City, and the Principal Natural Productions in its Neighborhood*. 2 vols. London, 1794.

Sabari, S. *Mouvements populaires à Baghdad à l'époque 'abbasside, IXe-XIe siècle*. Paris, 1981.

al-Ṣabbāgh, Laylā. *al-Mujtama' al-'arabī al-sūrī fī maṭla' al-'ahd al-'uthmānī (Syrian-Arab Society in the Early Ottoman Period)*. Dimashq, 1973.

Sabbānū, Aḥmad Ghassān. *Mamlaka Ḥamā al-ayyūbīya (Ayyubid Kingdom of Hama)*. Dimashq, 1984.

Sack, D. "Damaskus: die Stadt intra muros." *Damaszener Mitteilungen* 2 (1985).

———. *Damaskus: Entwicklung und Struktur einer orientalisch-islamischen Stadt*. Mainz, 1989.

Sadek, Mohamed-Moain. *Die mamlukische Architektur der Stadt Gaza*. Berlin, 1991.

Sakurai, Kiyohiko & Mutsuo Kawatoko. "Ejiputo aru-Fusutato iseki no hakkutsu chosa: Daiichiji (Exacavations in al-Fustat: The 1st Exacavation)." *Museum* 341 (1979).

———. "Ejiputo aru-Fusutato iseki no hakkutsu chosa: Dainiji–dainanaji (Exacavations in al-Fustat: The 2nd-7th Exacavations)." *Kokogaku Zasshi* 66/3 (1980); 67/3 (1982); 68/2 (1982); 69/4 (1984); 72/1 (1986); 72/4 (1987).

———. *Ejiputo Isuramu toshi aru-Fusutato: Hakkutsu chosa 1978-1985 (An Islamic City of Egypt, al-Fustat: Exacavation Report 1978-1985).*" Tokyo, 1992.

Salam-Liebich, H. *The Architecture of the Mamluk City of Tripoli*. Cambridge, Mass.,1983.

Salibi, K. S. "The 1860 Upheaval in Damascus as Seen by al-Sayyid Muhammad Abu'l-Su'ud al-Hasibi, Notable and Later Naqib al-Ashraf of the City." In *Beginnings of the Modernization in the Middle East: The Nineteenth Century*, eds. W. R. Polk & R. L. Chambers. Chicago, 1968.

Ṣāliḥ Aḥmad al-'Alī. *al-Tanẓīmāt al-ijtimā'īya wal-iqtiṣādīya fī al-Baṣra fī al-qarn al-awwal al-hijrī (The Social and Economic Systems of Basra in the First Century of the Hijra)*. Bayrūt, 1953. Translated into Japanese as "Hijurareki 1 seiki ni okeru Basura no shakai keizai seido" by Yoshiko Sasaki. *Isuramu Sekai* 13 (1978); 15 (1979); 17 (1980).

———. *Baghdād madīna al-salām: Inshā'hā wa tanẓīm sukkānhā fī al-'uhūd al-'abbāsīya al-ūlā, 1 (al-Jānib al-gharbī) (Baghdad, the City of Peace: Buildings and the Residential System at the Beginning of the 'Abbasid Caliphate, Part 1, West Bank)*. 2 vols. Baghdād, 1985.

———. *Khiṭaṭ al-Baṣra wa minṭaqahā: Dirāsa fī aḥwālhā al-'imrānīya wal-mālīya fī al-'uhūd al-islāmīya al-ūlā (Topography of Basra in the Early Islamic Period)*. Baghdād, 1986.

———. *Ma'ālim Baghdād al-idārīya wal-'imrānīya: Dirāsa takhṭīṭīya (Administrative Institutions and Public Facilities in Baghdad)*. Baghdād, 1988.

———, ed. *al-Madīna wal-ḥayāt al-madanīya (The City and City Life)*. 3 vols. Baghdād, 1988.

Sālim, 'Abd al-'Azīz. *Ta'rīkh madīna Ṣaydā fī al-'ahd al-islāmī (Sidon in the Islamic Period)*. Iskandarīya, 1986.

al-Sāmarrā'ī, Yūnis al-Shaykh Ibrāhīm. *Ta'rīkh madīna Sāmarrā' (History of Samarra)*. 3 vols. Baghdād, 1968-73.

Ṣamīḥ Wajīh al-Zayn. *Ta'rīkh Ṭarābulus qadīman wa ḥadīthan: Mundh aqdam al-azmina ḥattā 'aṣrnā al-ḥāḍir (A History of Tripoli)*. Bayrūt, 1969.

Sanders, P. "From Court Ceremony to Urban Language: Ceremonial in Fatimid Cairo and Fusṭāṭ." In *The Islamic World: From Classical to Modern Times*, ed. C. E. Bosworth. Princeton, 1989.

Saqqaf, Abdulaziz Y. *The Middle East City: Ancient Traditions Confront a Modern World*. N. Y., 1987.

Sato, Tsugitaka. "Isuramu shakaishi eno shiten (A View of Islamic Social History: The Case of Fayyūm Province)." In *Rekishigaku,* ed. K. Kabayama. Tokyo, 1977. Reprinted in *Chusei Isuramu kokka to Arabu shakai: Ikutasei no kenkyu*. Tokyo, 1986.

———. "Musurimu toshi no seikaku (The Characteristics of the Muslim City)." *Chuto Tsuho* 284 (1982).

———. "Bagudado no ninkyo burai shudan ('Ayyārūn in Baghdad)." *Shakaishi Kenkyu* 3 (1983).

———. *The Syrian Coastal Town of Jabala*. Studia Culturae Islamicae (ILCAA, Tokyo University of Foreign Studies) 35. Tokyo, 1988.

———. "Nusairi kyoto no hanran: Jabara 1318 nen 2 gatsu (The Revolt of al-Nuṣayrīs at Jabala, 1318)." *The Toyo Gakuho* 71/1-2 (1989).

———. "11-2 seiki Shiria chiho shakai no saibankan: Toripori to Jabara no baai (Qāḍīs in the Syrian Coastal Towns of Tripoli and Jabala during the 11th-12th Centuries)." *Oriento* 34/2 (1991).

Sauvaget, J. "L'enceinte primitive de la ville d'Alep." *Mélanges de l'IFD* 1 (1929). Reprinted in *Mémorial Jean Sauvaget*. Vol. 1. Damas, 1954.

———. "La citadelle de Damas." *Syrie* 11 (1930).

———. *Monuments ayyoubides de Damas*. Damas, 1930.

———. "Un bain damasquin du XIIIe siècle." *Syrie* 11 (1930).

———. "Inventaires des monuments musulmans de la ville d'Alep." *REI* 5 (1931).

———. *Les monuments historiques de Damas*. Beyrouth, 1932.

———. "Décrets mamelouks de Syrie." *BEO* 2 (1932); 3 (1933); 12 (1947-8).

———. "Esquisse d'une histoire de la ville de Damas." *REI* 8 (1934).

———. "Le plan de Laodicée-sur-Mer." *BEO* 4 (1934).

———. *Alep: Essai sur le développement d'une grande ville syrienne des origines au milieu du XIXe siècle*. Paris, 1941.

———. "Le plan antique de Damas." *Syrie* 26 (1949).

Sauvaire, H. "Description de Damas." *JA*, 9th ser., 3 (1894); 4 (1894); 5 (1895); 6 (1895); 7 (1896).

Sayed, H. I. "The Development of the Cairene Qā'a: Some Considerations." *Annales Islamologiques* 23 (1987).

al-Sayyid-Marsot, A. L. "The Political and Economic Functions of the 'Ulamā' in the 18th Century." *JESHO* 16 (1973).

———. "Religion or Opposition?: Urban Protest Movements in Egypt." *IJMES* 16 (1984).

Scanlon, G. T. "Housing and Sanitation: Some Aspects of Medieval Public Service." In *The Islamic City,* eds. A. Hourani & S. M. Stern. London, 1970.

———. "Fusṭāṭ: Archaeological Reconsideration." In *Colloque international sur l'histoire du Caire*. [Cairo], [1972].

———. "Fustat Expedition Preliminary Report: Back to Fostat-A 1973." *Annales Islamologiques* 17 (1981).

Scharabi, M. "Drei traditionelle Handelsanlagen in Kairo: Wakālat al-Bāzar'a, Wakālat Ḏu l-Fiqār und Wakālat al-Quṭn." *Mitteilungen der Deutschen Archäologischen Instituts, Abteilung Kairo* 34 (1978).

———. "Bemerkungen zur Bauform des Sūqs von Aleppo." *Mitteilungen der Deutschen Archäologischen Instituts, Abteilung Kairo* 36 (1980).

———. *Der Bazar: Das traditionelle Stadtzentrum im Nahen Osten und seine Handelseinrichtungen*. Tübingen, 1985.

———. *Kairo: Stadt und Architektur im Zeitalter des europäischen Kolonialismus*. Tübingen, 1989.

Schilcher, L. Sch. *Families in Politics: Damascene Factions and Estates of the 18th and 19th Centuries*. Stuttgart, 1985.

Schölch, A. "The Demographic Development of Palestine, 1850-1882." *IJMES* 17 (1985).

Serageldin, Ismail & Samer El-Sadek, eds. *The Arab City*. Riyadh, 1982.

Serjeant, R. B., ed. *The Islamic City*. Paris, 1980.

Shafīq Jāsir Aḥmad Maḥmūd. *Ta'rīkh al-Quds wal-'allāqa bayna al-muslimīn wal-masīḥīyīn fīhā ḥattā al-ḥurūb al-ṣalībīya (History of Jerusalem: Relations between Muslims and Christians until the Crusade)*. 'Ammān, 1984.

al-Shaykhlī, Ṣabbāḥ Ibrāhīm Sa'īd. *al-Aṣnāf fī al-'aṣr al-'abbāsī: nash'ahā wa taṭawwurhā (Craft-Guilds in the 'Abbasid Period)*. Baghdād, 1976.

al-Shihābī, Qutayba. *Dimashq: Ta'rīkhhā wa ṣuwar (Damascus History and Pictures)*. Dimashq, 1986.

———. *Aswāq Dimashq al-qadīma wa mushayyadāthā al-ta'rīkhīya: Baḥth maydānī bi-'adasa al-mu'allif (The Old Souks of Damascus and their Historical Monuments: A Field Research, Illustrated & Photographed by the Author)*. Dimashq, 1990.

Shimizu, Kosuke. "Toshi seikatsusha no mita sekai: Arupu Arusuran jidai no Bagudado (The World of an Urban Dweller: Baghdad in the Reign of Alp Arslān)." In*Toshi ni okeru esunishiti to bunka*. Monbusho tokutei kenkyu hokoku 13-14. Tokyo University of Foreign Studies. Tokyo, 1989-90.

Shoshan, B. "Grain Riots and the 'Moral Economy': Cairo, 1350-1517." *Journal of Interdisciplinary History* 10/3 (1980).

———. "Fāṭimid Grain Policy and the Post of the Muḥtasib." *IJMES* 13 (1981).

———. "The 'Politics of Notables' in Medieval Islam." *Asian and African Studies* 20 (1986).

Shumaysānī, Ḥasan. *Madāris Dimashq fī al-'aṣr al-ayyūbī (Madrasas in Damascus in the Ayyubid Period)*. Bayrūt, 1983.

Singer, A. "The Countryside of Ramle in the Sixteenth Century: A Study of Villages with Computer Assistance." *JESHO* 33 (1990).

Sivan, E. "Le caractère sacré de Jérusalem dans l'Islam aux XIIe-XIIIe siècles." *SI* 27 (1967).

———. "The Beginnings of the Fada'il al-Quds Literature." *Israel Oriental Studies* 1 (1971).

Sievers, P. von. "Military, Merchants and Nomads: The Social Evolution of the Syrian Cities and Countryside during the Classical Period, 780-969/164-358." *Der Islam* 56/2 (1979).

Soberheim, M. "Die arabischen Inschriften von Aleppo." *Der Islam* 15 (1926).

Sourdel, D. "Les professeurs de madrasa à Alep aux XIIe-XIIIe siècle d'après Ibn Šaddād." *BEO* 13 (1949-51).

———. "Esquisse topographique d'Alep intra-muros à l'époque ayyoubide." *Les Annales Archéologiques de Syrie* 2 (1952).

Spies, O. "Islamisches Nachbarrecht nach schafiitischer Lehre." *Zeitschrift für vergleichende Rechtswissenschaft* 42 (1927).

Staffa, S. J. *Conquest and Fusion: The Social Evolution of Cairo A. D. 642-1850.* Leiden, 1977.

Stern, S. M. "The Constitution of the Islamic City." In *The Islamic City*, eds. A. Hourani & S. M. Stern. Oxford, 1970.

Strika, V. & Jābil Khalīl. "Preliminary Report of the Survey of Islamic Monuments in Baghdād." *Mesopotamia* 8-9 (1973-4).

———. "The Islamic Architecture of Baghdād: The Results of a Joint Italian-Iraqi Survey." *Annali* 47/3, Supplemento 52 (1987).

Su'ād Māhir Muḥammad. *Masājid Miṣr wa awliyā'hā al-ṣāliḥūn (Egyptian Mosques and Pious Saints).* 5 vols. al-Qāhira, 1971-3.

al-Sulaymān, 'Abd al-Mājūd Aḥmad. *al-Mawṣil fī al-'ahdayn al-rāshidī wal-umawī (Mosul in the Time of the Orthodox Caliphs and the Umayyads).* al-Mawṣil, 1985.

al-Sulaymān, 'Īsā et al. *al-'Imārāt al-'arabīya al-islāmīya fī al-'Irāq (Arab-Islamic Architecture in Iraq).* Vol. 1. Baghdād, 1982.

Sūsa, Aḥmad. *Aṭlas Baghdād (A Collection of Maps of Baghdad).* Baghdād, 1952.

Tadmurī, 'Umar 'Abd al-Salām. *Ta'rīkh Ṭarābulus al-siyāsī wal-ḥaḍārī 'abra al-'uṣūr: 'Aṣr al-ṣirā' al-'Arabī al-Bizanṭī wal-ḥurūb al-ṣalībīya (History of Tripoli: The Times of Arab-Byzantine Conflict and the Crusade).* Vol. 1. Ṭarābulus, 1978.

Ṭalas, Muḥammad As'ad. "Dhayl (Supplementary Survey to Ibn al-Mibrad's Description of Mosques in Damascus)." In *Thimār al-maqāṣid fī dhikr al-masājid*, ed. Muḥammad As'ad Ṭalas. Bayrūt, 1943.

———. *al-Āthār al-islāmīya wal-ta'rīkhīya fī Ḥalab (Islamic Historical Monuments in Aleppo).* Dimashq, 1956.

Taniguchi, Junichi. "11 seiki no Harabu ni okeru karua to madina (The Qal'a and Madīna of Aleppo in the 11th Century)." *Toyoshi Kenkyu* 49/2 (1990).

al-Ṭarāwina, Ṭāhā Thaljī. *Mamlaka Ṣafad fī 'ahd al-mamālīk (The Province of Safad in the Mamluk Period).* Bayrūt, 1982.

Tate, J. *Une waqfiyya du XVIIIe siècle à Alep: La waqfiyya d'al Ḥāǧǧ Mūsā al-Amīrī.* Damas, 1990.

Terasaka, A. & M. Naito, eds. *Geographical Views in the Middle Eastern Cities*. Vol. 2: *Syria*. Tokyo, 1990.

Thieck, J.-P. "Décentralisation ottomane et affirmation urbaine." In *Mouvements communautaires et espaces urbains au Machreq*. Beyrouth, 1985.

Thoumin, R. "Deux quartiers de Damas." *BEO* 1 (1931).

———. "Notes sur l'aménagement et la distribution des eaux à Damas et dans sa Ghouta." *BEO* 4 (1934).

———. "Damas: Notes sur la répartition de la population par origine et par religion." *Revue de Géographe Alpine* 25 (1937).

Tibawi, A. L. *The Islamic Pious Foundations in Jerusalem: Origins, History and Usurpation by Israel*. London, 1978.

Toledano, E. "The Sanjaq of Jerusalem in the Sixteenth Century: Aspects of Topography and Population." *Archivum Ottomanicum* 9 (1984).

Tresse, R. "L'irrigation dans la Ghouta de Damas." *REI* 3 (1929).

al-'Ubaydī, Ṣalāḥ Ḥusayn. *al-Malābis al-'arabīya al-islāmīya fī al-'aṣr al-'abbāsī min al-maṣādir al-ta'rīkhīya wal-athrīya (Arab-Islamic Clothing during the 'Abbasid Period)*. Baghdād, 1980.

al-'Ulabī, Akram Ḥasan. *Dimashq bayna 'aṣr al-mamālīk wal-'uthmānīyīn 906-922 A. H./ 1500-1520 A. D. (Damascus at the Turn from the Mamluk Period to Ottoman Rule)*. Dimashq, 1982.

———. *Khiṭaṭ Dimashq: Dirāsa ta'rīkhīya shāmīya (Topographie historique de la ville de Damas)*. Dimashq, 1989.

Université de Provence, Groupe de Recherches et d'Études sur le Proche-Orient, ed. *L'habitat traditionnel dans les pays musulmans autour de la Méditerranée*. 3 vols. Le Caire, 1988-91.

'Uthmān, Muḥammad 'Abd al-Sattār. *al-Madīna al-islāmīya (The Islamic City)*. al-Kuwayt, 1988.

Vial, Ch. "Le Caire des romanciers égyptiens." *Annales Islamologiques* 8 (1969).

Vincent, H. & F. M. Abel. *Jérusalem: Recherches de topographie d'archéologie et d'histoire*. Paris, 1926.

Voll, J. "Old 'Ulama' Families and Ottoman Influence in Eighteenth Century Damascus." *American Journal of Arabic Studies* 3 (1975).

Walz, T. "Wakālat al-Ğallāba: The Market for Sudan Goods in Cairo." *Annales Islamologiques* 13 (1977).

———. "Asyūṭ in the 1260's (1844-53)." *Journal of the American Research Center in Egypt* 15 (1978).

Warren, J. & Ihsan Fethi. *Traditional Houses in Baghdad*. Horsham, 1982.

Weulersse, J. "Antioche: Essai de géographie urbaine." *BEO* 4 (1934).

Wiet, G. "Fêtes et jeux au Caire." *Annales Islamologiques* 8 (1969).

Wikan, U. *Life among the Poor in Cairo*. Translated by A.Henning. London,1980. Translated into Japanese as *Kairo no shomin seikatsu* by Y. Kosugi. Tokyo, 1986.

Williams, C. "The Cult of 'Alid Saints in the Fatimid Monuments of Cairo." *Muqarnas* 1 (1983); 3 (1985).

Winter, M. "The Ashrāf and Niqābat al-Ashrāf in Egypt in Ottoman and Modern Times." *Asian and African Studies* 19 (1985).

Wirth, E. "Damaskus-Aleppo-Beirut: Ein geographischer Vergleich dreier nahöstlicher Städt im Spiegel ihrer sozial und wirtschaftlich tonangebenden Schichten." *Die Erde* 96 (1966).

Wulzinger, K. & C. Watzinger. *Damaskus*. 2 vols. Berlin, 1921-4.

Yajima, Hikoichi. "Tozaikoshojo no aru-Fusutato (al-Fustat in the History of East-West Contacts)." In *Ejiputo Isuramu toshi aru-Fusutato,* ed. Chukinto Bunka Senta (The Middle Eastern Culture Center of Japan). Tokyo, 1980.

Yukawa, Takeshi. "Chusei isuramu girudo kenkyushi gaikan (An Historical Outline of Studies concerning the Medieval Islamic Guild)." In *'Toruko minzoku to isuramu' ni kansuru kyodo kenkyu hokoku*. ILCAA, Tokyo University of Foreign Studies. Tokyo, 1974.

———. "Chusei kami Ejiputo no urama kyodotai (The Ulama Community in Medieval Upper Egypt)." In *Oriento gakkai 25 shunen kinen Orientogaku ronshu*. Tokyo, 1979.

———. "6/12 seiki no Shiria ni okeru madorasa no hatten (The Development of the Madrasa in Syria in the 6th/12th Century)." *Shigaku* 50 (1980).

Yusuf, M. D. *Economic Survey of Syria*. Berlin, 1985.

Zakariya, M. "Le rab' de Tabbāna." *Annales Islamologiques* 16 (1980).

Zakī, 'Abd al-Raḥmān. *Marāji' ta'rīkhīya al-Qāhira: mundh inshā'hā ilā al-yawm (Bibliography related to the History of Cairo)*. al-Qāhira, 1964.

———. *al-Qāhira: ta'rīkhhā wa āthārhā 969-1825 (History and Historical Monuments of Cairo 969-1825)*. al-Qāhira, 1966.

Zakkar, S. *The Emirate of Aleppo 1004-1094*. Beirut, 1971.

Ziadeh, N. *Urban Life in Syria under the Early Mamlūks*. Beirut, 1953. Reprinted in Westport, 1970.

———. *Damascus under the Mamlūks,* Norman, 1964.

Zubaida, S., "Class and Community in Urban Politics," In *État, ville et mouvements sociaux au Maghreb et au Moyen-Orient,* eds. K. Brown et al. Paris, 1989.

TURKEY

Kayoko Hayashi

Introduction

This chapter focuses on historical studies of Ottoman cities in the region of present day Turkey. Urban studies of cities other than Istanbul hardly existed until two decades ago. Though cities were frequently mentioned in historical studies about the socio-economic formation of the Ottoman Empire, the city itself was seldom the primary target of concern. In recent years, however, the study of Anatolian cities has a central place in Ottoman studies because of a growing interest in pre-modern local society and culture. In the course of this chapter I will discuss the major trends in Ottoman historical studies relating to cities, both by Turkish and Western scholars after the late 19th century.

Turkish urban studies have of course a close relationship with those on Arab and Balkan cities under Ottoman rule. However the question though of whether or not there are common characteristics among cities under Ottoman rule must await further study, even though an outline of the characteristics of Turkish Ottoman cities is a prerequisite to such studies. In this sense, the concept of "Turkish Ottoman cities" is of pragmatic significance.

In this chapter, I will introduce the scholarship in three parts according to the date of publication: (I) urban studies from the 19th century to the 1940s, (II) urban studies mainly in socio-economic history between the 1940s and 1970s, and (III) recent studies, of the 1980s in particular. I do not intend to give an exhaustive introduction to the field, since *Turkologischer Anzeiger*, a general bibliography of Turkish studies which includes urban studies, has been published since 1975 and should be consulted. Also of use regarding works published in the Republic of Turkey is the chapter on "local histories" (*mahalli tarihler*) in E. Koray, *Bibliography of Publications on History in Turkey* (T., 1952 to the present).

I. The Formative Period of Turkish Urban Studies

1. Studies in Western Countries

The oldest existing descriptions of Ottoman cities are contained in travel accounts by Europeans who visited cities under Ottoman rule such as Istanbul or Jerusalem as diplomats, pilgrims or merchants. They left many such records, either because of their interest in the pre-Islamic Classical culture of the region or in the existing Oriental Islamic civilization. Though no general catalogue of them exists, M. V. de Saint-Martin, *Description historique et géographique de l'Asie Mineure* (1852) is an old but good guide which introduces and summarizes 381 travel accounts about Anatolia that had been written before the author visited the region. In Turkey, *A Bibliography of Studies on the Geography of Turkey* (T., 1942) was published by S. Trak. A number of 17th century travel accounts about Istanbul are contained in the bibliography of R. Mantran, *Istanbul dans la seconde moitié du XVII*e *siècle* (1962). An additional collection of quotations from such travel descriptions is K. Ritter, *Die Erdkunde* (1832-59). More recently, the very useful S. Yerasimos, *Les voyageurs dans l'Empire Ottoman* (1991) gives bibliographical information about travel accounts written between the 14th and 16th centuries and includes comprehensive descriptions of their contents, such as routes of travel and places where the traveller stayed.

The following is a list of the most representative of the large number of works written. Perhaps the pioneer of Ottoman historiography is M. d'Ohsson, *Tableau général de l'Empire Ottoman* (1787-1820). d'Ohsson, an Armenian born in Istanbul in the late 18th century who later became a Swedish citizen, acted as an interpreter and was a Swedish ambassador to Istanbul. His book, which was published in Paris, contains much valuable information, even about the social customs in the cities under Ottoman rule, and retains its value today thanks to its pertinent observations and beautiful illustrations. C. White, *Three Years in Constantinople* (1846) describes everyday life in the bazars and mosques based on the personal experience of the author and contains quotations from a Turkish travel account by Evliya Çelebi. Two significant travel accounts describing Anatolian cities are W. F. Ainsworth, *Travels and Researches in Asia Minor, Mesopotamia, Chaldea and Armenia* (1842) and H. von Moltke, *Briefe über Zustände und Begebenheiten in der Türkei aus den Jahren 1835 bis 39* (1841) by a German military man.

Of all the cities of Turkey, the most popular subject in travel accounts has been Constantinople (Istanbul), the ancient capital of the Roman and Byzantine Empires, and its topography has been actively studied from the point of view of historical geography. P. Gyllius, *De topographia Constanti-*

nopoleos et de illius antiquitatibus (1561) is a very old study in this field. Later works include J. von Hammer, *Constantinopolis und der Bosporos* (1822) and A. D. Mordtmann, "Esquisse topographique de Constantinople" (1891). E. Oberhummer, a scholar of historical geography, has provided a comprehensive introduction to studies on Constantinople to the end of the 19th century in his article "Constantinopolis" in the *Real-Encyclopädie der classischen Altertumswissenschaft* (1901). Additionally, Oberhummer, *Konstantinopel unter Sultan Suleiman dem Großen* (1902) recreates the city of Istanbul in the 16th century on the basis of contemporary travel accounts. R. Mayer, *Byzantion, Konstatinopolis, Istanbul* (1943) contains a useful bibliography of these early geographical studies on Constantinople and a listing of historical maps.

Studies of human geography in the Anatolian region include references to the cities there. Well-known works include V. Cuinet, *La Turquie d'Asie* (1892-4) and C. Texier, *Asie Mineure* (1862). They record details about the economic activity of each city and its population, agricultural production in the surrounding villages, the composition of the population, transportation, topography and historical monuments and in some cases have maps. They apply modern geographical methodology, developed in 19th century Europe, but detailed local information owes much to the existence of the yearbooks (*salname*) that the Ottoman government published periodically for every province. Useful as a catalogue of *salname* is H. Duman (ed.), *Yearbooks of the Ottoman Empire* (T., 1982).

Thus the earliest studies to touch on Turkish cities were largely studies of historical and human geography. This is a common characteristic shared by studies of both Turkish, and Arab and Iranian, cities. Compared though to studies of Arab cities, those concerning Turkish cities done in the 19th century and the early years of the 20th century are undeniably inadequate in quantity as well as quality. There are two reasons for that. The first is the absence of field research. Turkey had not fallen victim to direct European colonization, and the involved political situation in late Ottoman times virtually precluded academic field research in Anatolia by scientific missions. Only after the birth of the Republic in 1923 did field-based research into the existing arts and architecture finally begin. In comparison with the Arab lands, which came under the direct colonial rule of the Western powers, cities in modern Turkey began a large-scale urban transformation through Westernization before basic data about the traditional society could be collected. This was to be a handicap for later urban studies in the region.

The first actual field survey in Turkish region was probably that conducted by Albert Gabriel at the request of the government of the Republic of Turkey. Gabriel, a teacher at the University of Istanbul, conducted detailed surveys of historical monuments in certain Anatolian cities and introduced them through detailed drawings, photographs and epitaphs. Gabriel's most important works are *Monuments turcs d'Anatolie* (1931-4) and *Voyages archéologiques dans la Turquie orientale* (1940). The former introduces the central Anatolian cities of Kayseri, Niğde, Amasya, Tokat and Sivas and the latter the south-eastern Anatolian cities of Mardin, Diyarbakır and Bitlis together with Jean Sauvaget's study on epitaphs. Gabriel's descriptions are generally the oldest reliable records we have for the cities covered, outside the fragmentary descriptions in early travel accounts. In addition, id., "Les mosquées de Constantinople" (1926) and *Une capitale turque: Brousse* (1958) were the springboard for later archaeological and architectural studies concerning Istanbul and Bursa.

A second reason for the inadequacies of Turkish urban studies is the relative scarcity of information produced by urban dwellers in the form of local histories, geographies and travel accounts as compared with the situation in the Arab lands or the Iranian sphere. Philological studies based on such materials were, along with field studies, a pillar of the formative years of urban studies in the other regions. Studies of Turkish cities were handicapped in that area too. One exception though is J. von Hammer, *A Narrative of Travels in Europe, Asia and Africa in the Seventeenth Century by Evliyá Efendí* (1834-46), an abridged translation of the travel account of Evliya Çelebi. Full-blown urban studies on the Turkish region appear to have begun only after Ottoman archival material became accessible to scholars. Another point is that there are astonishing differences in quality and accuracy between studies about Istanbul and those concerning other cities. This situation was to continue in the following decades as well.

2. Studies by Turkish Scholars

There are few local histories in Turkish classical literature, in contrast to the Arab and Iranian situation, and efforts by local scholars to write systematic histories of their own towns date only from the end of 19th century. One factor in this is the difference in the characteristics of urban notables in the Turkish region. Local histories are found only in a few works concerning Istanbul such as *Hadîkatü'l-Cevâmi (The Flower Gardens of Mosques)* written by Hâfız Hüseyin Ayvansarayî (d. 1786) and *Mecmu'a-i Tekaya (The Collection of Sufi Convents),* by Zâkir Şükrî Efendi (latter half of the 19th century), which is a listing of the majority of *tekke* (convents) belonging to Sufi orders. The well-known book written in the late 17th century by Evliya Çelebi is one of the very few example of travel accounts written in Turkish. (Recent studies on the travel accounts of Evliya Çelebi include M. van

Bruinessen and H. Boeschoten, *Evliya Çelebi in Diyarbekir,* 1988, and R. Dankoff, *Evliya Çelebi in Bitlis,* 1990.)

Works by intellectuals who were influenced by late Ottoman Westernization acted as a catalyst for local scholars to write about their cities. Mehmed Râif, *The Mirror of Istanbul* (T., 1896-1912), Celâl Esad, *Constantinople, de Byzance à Stamboul* (1909), id., *Old Galata and its Monuments* (T., 1913), and Mehmed Ziya, *Istanbul and the Bosphorus* (T., 1920-8) are general works reflecting the time when they were written, although none could be called an academic study. The work of Mehmed Râif, in particular, was responsible for the descriptive style adopted by later local histories, mentioning the origins of buildings and monuments, providing chronological histories, and recording the biographies of famous people. İ. H. Konyalı, for example, later continued this descriptive style of local history. Numerous such works have been, and are continuing to be, published in Turkey. Many are simple guides to local religious buildings and are of mixed value, but they do represent the heightening of interest local history and culture after the establishment of the Republic.

Local histories dealing with Istanbul are the most numerous. Studies of manners and customs in Istanbul include Ali Rıza, *Memories of Istanbul* (T., 1922), Ahmet Refik (Sevengil), *The Amusements of Istanbul* (T., 1927) and Musahipzade Celâl, *The Old Life Style of Istanbul* (T., 1946). Among studies of the city's historical geography are Ali Saim (Ülgen), *Istanbul and its Buildings* (T., 1933) and İ. H. Tanışık, *Fountains of Istanbul* (T., 1943-5). Ülgen, *Constantinople during the Era of Mohammed the Conqueror* (1939) includes a map of 15th century Istanbul in which the sites of Byzantine ruins and the new structures built immediately after the conquest are identified. R. E. Koçu, *The Encyclopedia of Istanbul* (T., 1959-71) is a voluminous work and extremely useful as a compendium of the local history and culture of Istanbul. Unfortunately it remains incomplete.

Local histories dealing with the Anatolian cities include, to give only a few examples, Hüseyin Hüsameddin, *A History of Amasya* (T., 1911-35), Rıdvan Nafız and İsmail Hakkı (Uzunçarşılı), *City of Sivas* (T., 1927-8), Uzunçarşılı, *City of Kütahya* (T., 1932), B. Konyar, *Diyarbekir* (T., 1936), Z. Eroğlu, *A History of Muğla* (T., 1939), O. N. Peremeci, *A History of Edirne* (T., 1939), H. Asarkaya, *Tokat during the Ottoman Period* (T., 1941) and O. Bayatlı, *Turko-Islamic Buildings in the History of Bergama* (T., 1956).

The growth of interest in local history owes much to the culture movement led by the "House of the People (*halk evi*)" in the 1930s and 40s. *Halk evi,* the locally-based organization of the Republican People's Party, aimed at the eventual creation of a national culture and so fostered an enlightenment movement and worked to introduce local cultures. One such activity associated with the organization was the compilation of local histories. K. Su, *Urban Life in Balıkesir in the 17th and 18th Centuries* (T., 1937), İ. Gökçen, *Waqf Endowments and Charitable Institutions in the History of Manisa* (T., 1946-50) and many other such works were published by the organization, which was also instrumental in the publication of Gökçen, *The Nomads and Turkmen in Saruhan in the 16th and 17th Centuries through Sharia-Court Registers* (T., 1946) and id., *Sufi Convents and Saints' Mausolea in Saruhan in the 16th and 17th Centuries through Sharia-Court Registers* (T., 1946), the first studies to use once obscure historical material preserved locally, like the sharia-court registers.

Among the relatively recent works that belong to the category of local history are a number of studies by İ. H. Konyalı, including *A History of Erzurum* (T., 1960), *A History of Konya* (T., 1964), *A History of Karaman* (T., 1967) and *A History of Üsküdar* (T., 1976-7). Konyalı arranges political history in chronological order, and not only sheds light on the origins of historical structures through their epitaphs but also provides much valuable information such as the biographies of local people.

Such studies, however, aim primarily at collecting specific information about each city and are not concerned with wider ranging questions concerning the common characteristics of Turkish cities or their internal social structure. What we can call urban studies proper, that is, the study of urban institutions and social structure, began with the pioneering work of Osman Nuri Ergin that appeared during the chaotic period that preceded the birth of the Republic of Turkey, *The Compendium of Municipal Administration* (T., 1914-22).

Ergin, a civil servant in a municipal office in Istanbul since the age of 17, studied various kinds of historical materials, such as *ferman* (Imperial decrees), *kannunname* (Sultanic laws), and sharia-court registers. These he consolidated in *The History of Urban Systems* (T., 1922), the first of the five volumes of the above-mentioned *Compendium*. His purpose was to compare the urban institutions of the West and the East at a time of contradictions in Turkey when Western systems were being introduced and many felt the necessity of maintaining the traditional system. *The History of Urban Systems* consists of three parts, discussing the urban institutions of Western countries, those of Islamic countries, and those which existed in Turkey after Tanzimat. The second section, which deals particularly with Istanbul, is extremely valuable even today as a collection of archival material which includes historical documents of the central government and the sharia-courts. Discussed in that section are the qadi, the muhtasib, the *narh* system, guilds, the supply of food to Istanbul, night guards, cleaning, lighting, the construction and maintenance of roads, fires and the water supply. Ergin describes the situation of each before Tanzimat in detail through documents and the eye of a contemporary. Though critical methodology regarding archival materials and the citation of sources are somewhat inadequate, we must remember that Ergin was writing before Ottoman archival material began to be used in a modern way. When using the work we must take into account the fact that it was intended as a kind of administrative guide and so the focus is on the administrative aspect of urban organizations and institutions, and most of the examples cited are from Istanbul.

Ergin's attempt to discover the essential nature of Turkish cities by comparing Western and Eastern institutions is clearly demonstrated in *The Historical Development of the Municipal Administration (şehircilik) in Turkey* (T., 1936). Here he argues that Turkish cities before Tanzimat did not have self-governing organizations like those of the European cities, and the roles played by the modern municipality belonged to the individual Muslim through waqf endowments. Non-Muslims belonged to half-autonomous communities organized according to religion and sect, and the quarter community of Muslims, with its functions of mutual aid centered on the mosque and coffee shop, played an important part in regional society.

Ergin placed special stress on the importance of waqf system and in *The Imâret System in Turkish Cities* (T., 1939) refers to the construction of the *imâret* (a complex of religious and charitable institutions supported by waqf revenue) as the most typical example of the way waqf endowments contributed to urban life. In *The Waqf Endowment Deeds of Imâret of Mehmet II* (T., 1945), he takes Istanbul as a general example of how *imâret* played an important role in building the city. Unfortunately the work contains many errors. It should be pointed out too that many of Ergin's works, including *The Compendium of Municipal Administration,* were intended to be educational, not modern historical studies. When Ergin discusses Turkish or Islamic cities he does so only to compare them with their European counterparts, and he is not concerned with comparing cities within the Islamic world. Nevertheless his work was the starting point for urban studies in Turkey, since he pointed out the existence of archival material capable of shedding light on various facets of the city and indicated for the first time certain general characteristics of Turkish Ottoman cities in terms of the mechanisms of rule and administration and of systems like the guild and waqf.

II. From the 1940s to the 1970s

During the 1940s full-scale study of socio-economic history began in Turkey, using the abundant archival materials of the Ottoman period. When the concept of the "Islamic city" began to gain influence in the West in the 1950s and after, the Turkish city was rarely discussed in that framework. The study of Turkish cities, until recently considered to be part of Ottoman institutional studies or studies of Ottoman economic structure, was not considered an independent research field. In fact, in view of the dominant trend in socio-economic history to study Ottoman social structure, in particular relations between state and peasant and the rural economy, "urban studies" had no real place.

All of the works mentioned below are studies of socio-economic history in the wider sense, yet it is possible to extract from them information concerning cities. First, there are some important studies on the Turkish guild. Second, studies on how cities were built in Anatolia and the Balkans deserve mention. They are mostly concerned with the early years of the Ottoman Empire, and look at the characteristics of Turkish cities in terms of how their establishment was related to the Turkicization and Islamization of an area. Third, concrete information about the Turkish cities was given through the Ottoman documentary studies. I will now introduce from those three aspects historical studies concerning cities produced between the 1940s and 1970s.

1. Guilds

One reason for the popularity of the guild in particular as an object of study may be that Western scholars "discovered" the *esnaf* system of Istanbul described in Evliya Çelebi's travel account and in Ergin's work and understood it to have been a "guild." Scholars looked particularly at the religious aspect of the Turkish guild as depicted in initiation ceremonies and the worship of a patron saint and at its centralized organizational structure. A pioneering study on the subject was B. Lewis, "The Islamic Guilds" (1937), which sees Anatolia's *ahî* organizations and the Turkish guilds as elements in the link between the Qarmatian movement in Baghdad in the 9th and 10th centuries and the occupational organizations in the Middle East in the early 20th century.

The *ahî* organization was a brotherhood type organization widespread in Anatolia in the 13th and 14th centuries which maintained the tradition of the *futuwwa* (*fütüvvet* in Turkish) spirit. It is considered the origin of the Ottoman occupational guild mentioned in historical materials from the 16th century. F. Taeschner, in a series of studies on 13th and 14th century thought including "Futuwwa-Studien, die Futuwwabünde in der Türkei und ihre Literatur" (1932), "Das Zunftwesen in der Türkei" (1941) and "a<u>kh</u>ī," "a<u>kh</u>ī baba," "futuwwa" (*EI*², 1956-65), states that the *futuwwa* spirit as found in *fütüvvetname* (the book of *futuwwa*) played an important role in organizing Anatolian urban dwellers in the 13th century, giving birth to the *ahî* organization with its self-governing function; however in the process of centralization by the Ottoman government it became weakened and was transformed in the 16th century to an occupational guild with a rather strong administrative character.

Studies on the *ahî* organization by Turkish scholars, such as A. Gölpınarlı, "The *Futuwwa* Organizations in Turkey and the Islamic World and Historical Material concerning it" (T., 1949-50), N. Çağatay, *The Ahî Organization as a Turkish Organization* (T., 1974) and the papers presented at the symposium "Turkish Culture and the Ahî Organization" (the proceedings were published in 1986) tend to emphasize its uniqueness as part of Turkish culture and its continued existence in the form of guild organization until modern times. Certainly, there is a continuity between the *ahî* organization and the Turkish guild in terms of spiritual and ritual elements, but the actual functions and organization of the Turkish guild, which was obviously an occupational one, cannot be explained in religious terms alone.

Studies on the actual organization of the guild owe a great deal to Ergin's *Compendium*. "City: Industry and Commerce," the sixth chapter of H. A. R. Gibb and H. Bowen, *Islamic Society and the West* (1950-7) contains a considerably detailed description of the Islamic guild based on Massignon's and Lewis's theory about the origin of the guild and depends almost entirely on Ergin's *Compendium* for specific information about the pre-modern guild. Gibb and Bowen speak of the Istanbul guilds, with their remaining strongly religious tinge and their tight control by the government as being typical of guilds in the pre-modern Islamic world.

In the 1960s, R. Mantran, who studied late 17th century Istanbul and who consolidated the work that had been done on guilds in the capital, wrote in *Istanbul dans la seconde moitié du XVII*^{e} *siècle*, "Il n'entre pas dans notre propos de retracer l'histoire des Corporations dans le monde musulman, ni même dans l'Empire Ottoman avant la période qui nous intéresse. Il nous paraît plus important d'étudier en quoi consistent les corporations d'İstanbul au XVIIe siècle, et ce qu'elles représentent dans la vie économique et sociale de la capitale" (p. 349). Thus recent work on the Turkish guild is putting more emphasis on what it actually was rather than how it originated. Mantran, regarding the characteristics of the 17th century guild, wrote that in a situation of a strong government heading the state, guilds in Istanbul in the 17th century could no longer continue the religious and political activities of the medieval *ahî* organization. As a result, the former religious mentality was virtually lost and replaced by an occupational mentality.

Studies on the Turkish guild were summarized in two articles by G. Baer in 1970, "The Administrative, Economic and Social Functions of Turkish Guilds" and "Monopolies and Restrictive Practices of Turkish Guilds." Baer uses much the same materials as had previous scholars in the field to reexamine the guild in Istanbul. He criticizes scholars who confuse the guild with the *ahî* organization, which was not an occupational group so much as a popular organization in the 13th and 14th centuries. Having strictly defined the guild as an occupational group, he analyzes the administrative, economic and social functions of Turkish guilds mainly in the 17th and 18th centuries. He finds that a distinguishing characteristic of Turkish guilds was their close relationship with the Ottoman government and he concludes that guilds functioned as points of contact between the ruling organization and urban dwellers and were the means by which a ruler controlled and governed the urban population. The administrative aspects of the guild were highlighted because studies on Turkish guilds had concentrated on those in the capital, Istanbul. Baer himself suggested that there were considerable differences in terms of the self-governing capability of guilds according to industry and location, but he left such investigations to others.

Other than in these studies, Turkish cities were hardly ever discussed within the framework of studies on the "Islamic city" mainly by Western scholars. While subjects such as the quarter, administrative organization, urban outlaws and popular movements have been studied widely in urban studies of the Arabic lands as they relate to the "Islamic city," virtually no such studies were done in regard to Turkish cities until the 1980s. Apart from the different situation concerning historical materials, the reason for this neglect can be basically attributed to the particular structure of Ottoman society, or what was thought to be the structure, whereby the social framework consisted of the capital Istanbul and the regional rural society subordinated to it.

2. Studies on the Formation of Cities

Within the context of Turkish historical studies, one particular topic that excited the interest of historians was the process of the Turkicization in Anatolia and Balkans after the immigration of the Turkish people.

Ö. L. Barkan, "Waqf Endowment and Private Land as the Means of Sedentarization and Settlement in the Ottoman Empire" (T., 1942) studies the part played by *dervîş* in Sufi orders and their convents in the sedentarization of Turkish people in Anatolia and the Balkans. Barkan shows through archival materials that *dervîş*' convents, supported economically by waqf endowments, became the nucleus around which villages and cities later formed and that *dervîş* protected caravan routes and were the nucleus of regional society.

In another article, "Forced Migration (*sürgün*) as the Means of Sedentarization and Settlement in the Ottoman Empire" (T., 1949-54), Barkan points out that Ottoman government policy forced artisans and merchants, as well as nomads, to migrate from Anatolia to the Balkans and from the Balkans to Anatolia as a means of systematically reorganizing newly conquered areas. Although his studies are all concerned mainly with the formation of the governing system in the early Ottoman period, he also points out that basic principles in the formation of cities in the early Ottoman period were the activities of the Sufi order, the utilization of the waqf system and forced migration.

In *The Settlement of Nomads in the Ottoman Empire* (T., 1963) and *The Derbend Organization in the Ottoman Empire* (T., 1967), C. Orhonlu discusses how the policy of settling nomads and the role of the *derbend* organization, which worked to secure and maintain traffic routes, contributed to the Islamization of the "frontier" and the shaping of newly formed villages along caravan routes or in uncultivated lands. id., "Comments on the Occupation of Road Construction (*kaldırmıcılık*) and Roads in Ottoman Cities" (T., 1972) deals with transportation routes such as roads, marine traffic and bridges, and provides valuable information about intra- and inter-city transportation, a subject closely related to city construction. Orhonlu's articles have been reprinted in *Studies on Urban Administration (şehircilik) and Transportation in the Ottoman Empire* (T., 1984). Basic material for information about the traffic routes is F. Taeschner, *Das anatolische Wegenetz nach osmanischen Quellen* (1924-6).

Planned construction of *imâret* carried out within the framework of the waqf system played an important role in urban construction during the Ottoman period. Besides the above-mentioned *The Imâret System in Turkish Cities* by Ergin, there is a notable work by Barkan, "A Study on the Construction and Administration of *Imâret* in the Ottoman Empire from the Historical Viewpoint of the Formations and Development of Cities" (T., 1962-3), which analyzes the incomes and expenditures of a number of *imâret*. Barkan points out that tax revenues collected from the villages endowed as Sultanic waqfs were the main source of revenue for the urban *imâret* built by the Ottoman Sultans and that religious and welfare demands by cities were met by revenues from the countryside. H. İnalcık, *The Ottoman Empire: The Classical Age 1300-1600* (1973) likewise sees the construction of *imâret* and commercial institutions by the ruling class as representative of the measures taken by the Ottoman government to protect and promote the development of cities. The construction of an *imâret* seems to be now widely accepted as what characterizes Ottoman cities in Anatolia and the Balkans.

Many of the studies about city construction, such as Ergin, *The Reconstruction Work of Istanbul* (T., 1938) and E. H. Ayverdi's *Quarters, Settlement and Population in Istanbul in the Late Part of the Reign of Mehmed*

II (T., 1958) are concerned with Istanbul after the conquest. Both these works summarize the measures taken for the reconstruction of Istanbul based on forced migrations and the construction of *imâret*. İnalcık, "The Policy of Mehmed II toward the Greek Population of Istanbul and the Byzantine Buildings of the City" (1970) investigates the treatment of the Greek population and their landed property in the course of the city's reorganization. id., "Ottoman Methods of Conquest" (1954) is a valuable discussion of the principles behind the reorganization of conquered land.

D. Kuban, "Historical Development and Social and Structural Development of Anatolian Turkish City" (T., 1968) studies what kind of cities with what kind of spatial characteristics emerged in the process of urban formation. Kuban attempts to explain from the standpoint of an historian of architecture with an interest in the domestic architecture of Anatolia the characteristics of the spatial structure of Turkish cities in Anatolia. Kuban remarks that "almost nothing is known about the cities of Anatolia. In the past, changes in the spatial structure of Turkish cities and the historical and social information related to those changes have not been considered subjects for systematic study," and his article is probably the first study from this angle. He comments that the way nomads settled has had a great deal of influence on domestic architecture in Anatolian cities, and that even if a Turkish city does not have a deliberate arrangement of urban institutions or some kind of central point like the cathedral in Europe, it is in no way "disordered," but should be understood as functional urban space adapted to the natural environment. Kuban rejects the framework of the "Islamic city" and emphasizes that Anatolian Turkish cities reflect the unique historical and natural conditions of Anatolia. He has had a great influence on later studies of the architectural history of Anatolian cities.

3. Ottoman Cities in Socio-economic Studies

The mainstream of Turkish historiography has been occupied with studies of socio-economic history based on Ottoman archival materials, as represented by Ö. L. Barkan and his school. Such studies have given us valuable information about cities, and I will summarize first some of the more important documentary studies.

A pioneering study of the documents relating to Istanbul is the series of works by Ahmet Refik (Altınay) on the records of the Ottoman Imperial Council (*mühimme defteri*), *Life in Istanbul in the 10th Century A. H.* (T., 1917), *Life in Istanbul in the 11th Century A. H.* (T., 1931) and *Life in Istanbul in the 12th Century A. H.* (T., 1930). Ahmet Refik has organized Imperial decrees relating to the life of the capital in Imperial Council records, and for example introduces all the 258 such decrees of the 10th century A. H. which concern the Imperial court, waqf endowments and mosques, scholarship and education, women, non-Muslims, architecture, sanitation, currency and wages, food, commerce and industry, tariffs and the police. Studying the Imperial decrees that were handed down to deal with specific problems allows us to construct an image of the life of the time. In addition, the very fact that such problems were discussed by the supreme council of the government, attests to the distinctiveness of the administration of the capital.

Among the most useful of Ottoman archival material for the study of local societies are land survey registers (*tahrir defteri*) and collections of Sultanic laws (*kanunname*). In the 15th and 16th centuries, land surveys containing much detailed information were made for each province whenever there were new conquests or on the accession of a new Sultan. Each register was prefaced with the *kanunname* governing that province, and these show how the central government ruled the province and collected tax. *Kanunname* and land survey registers have been used mainly to study the land system or socio-economic formation under the *timar* system, but they are also an important documentary source for urban studies, since they contain information about urban population and tax collection in the towns. The most extensive coverage of the *kanunname* published is Barkan, *The Legal and Financial Foundation of Agricultural Economy in the Ottoman Empire in the 15th and 16th Centuries*, vol. 1, *Collection of Kanunnames* (T., 1943). It gives a good idea of the diversity of the area stretching from the Balkans to the Arab lands and the Ottoman government's ways of responding to the demands of such diverse regions. N. Beldiceanu and I. Beldiceanu-Steinherr, *Recherche sur la province de Qaraman au XVIᵉ siècle* (1968) is a study of the *kanunname* of the Province of Qaraman. Among the published land survey registers, R. Yinanç and M. Elibüyük, *A Land Survey Register of Malatya during the Period of Süleyman I* (T., 1983) and Barkan and E. Meriçli, *A Land Survey Register of Bursa District* (T., 1988) include references to cities.

Representative of local histories mainly employing land survey registers and *kanunnames* are T. Gökbilgin, *Edirne and Rumeli Province in the 15th and 16th Centuries* (T., 1952), N. Göyünç, *Mardin Province in the 16th Century* (T., 1969) and İ. Miroğlu, *Bayburt Province in the 16th Century* (T., 1975) and such recently published works as B. Yediyıldız, *A Social History of Ordu District, 1455-1613* (T., 1985), H. Özdeğer, *Ayıntab Province in the 16th Century* (T., 1988), M. Ç. Varlık, "16th Century Kütahya and its Historical Structures" (T., 1988), M. A. Ünal, *Harput Province in the 16th Century, 1518-1566* (T., 1989), F. Emecen, *Manisa District in the 16th Century* (T., 1989) and İ. Miroğlu, *Kemah Province and Erzincan District* (T., 1990).

These studies use land survey registers and waqf registers to record details about the central city of each region such as population and changes in population, the names of quarters, the demographic composition, occupations and economic activities, and religious institutions and the administration of waqf endowments. Nevertheless the main purpose of these studies of local history is to summarize the information available about each administrative unit of the Ottoman Empire, encompassing the urban administrative center and its surrounding villages, and not to explain the internal structure of cities to any extent. In fact, they tend to over-emphasize administration and tax collection because of the nature of the archival material, primarily records of land surveys conducted by the central government. By the same token, though, because as far as the 16th century is concerned there remain a large number of registers for a variety of regions, it should be possible to examine the total situation by putting all of the dispersed local information together to allow a spatial comparison to be made concerning a regional society comprising a city, its surrounding villages and the nomads.

In addition, the value of the land survey registers as historical material is discussed in three works by Barkan, "Historical Demography and Ottoman History" (T., 1953), "Essai sur les données statistiques des registres de recensement dans l'Empire Ottoman aux XVe et XVIe siècles" (1957), and "Research on the Ottoman Fiscal Surveys" (1970). They attest the usefulness of the land survey registers particularly for making population estimates.

Ottoman archival material related to cities, other than the land survey registers and Sultanic laws *(kanunname),* includes waqf survey registers. Barkan and E. H. Ayverdi, *A Waqf Survey Register of Istanbul Dated 1546* (T., 1970) is the most important contribution to the publication of archival materials about urban waqfs. In the 16th century, besides frequent surveys of farming villages and local cities, investigations of waqf endowments in each area were made. The results of the investigation into all waqfs of Istanbul were recorded in 1546. This register, which contains summary of each waqf endowment deed with its detailed record of the income and expenditure, not only provides information about urban religious institutions but also sheds light on economic and social life in 16th century Istanbul.

The waqfs of the Ottoman royal family were under the direct control of the Ottoman government and a large number of administrative records, registers of income and expenditure (*muhasebe defteri*), have been preserved in the National Archives. Barkan has published parts of them in "The 1489-1490 *Muhasebe* Register of the Fatih Mosque and its *Imâret*" (T., 1962-3), "The 1489-1491 *Muhasebe* Register of the Ayasofya Mosque and the Eyüp Mausoleum" (T., 1962-3), "The Annual *Muhasebe* Register of Some Soup Kitchens in Edirne and its Surroundings" (T., 1965) and "The Annual

Muhasebe Register of the Mosque of Süleyman I and its *Imâret*" (T., 1971). Since such documents show how the prescriptions of waqf endowment deeds were actually carried out, they are very relevant to urban life. They also give actual figures for wages and prices of foodstuffs and consumer items. Barkan, *The Construction of the Mosque of Süleyman and its Imâret* (T., 1972-9) presents a huge amount of historical material, including the account book of expenditures recorded at the time of the construction of the *imâret* of Süleyman I, one of the largest constructions of the Ottoman period, which provides detailed data about building material, labour, wages, etc.

Of the enormous number of individual waqf endowment deeds which exist, only a small part has been published, centering on those of the Sultans, including T. Öz (ed.), *Zwei Stiftungsurkunden des Sultans Mehmed II. Fatih* (1935), K. E. Kürkçüoğlu (ed.), *The Waqf Endowment Deed of Süleyman I* (T., 1962) and M. A. Simsar, *The Waqfiyah of 'Aḥmed Pāšā* (1940). T. Gökbilgin, *Edirne and Rumeli Province in the 15th and 16th Centuries* introduces a number of waqf documents concerned with Edirne. Several waqf endowment deeds are also introduced in each issue of *Vakıflar Dergisi,* published periodically since 1938 by the General Directorate of Waqfs (Vakıflar Genel Müdürlüğü) in Ankara, which possesses the great proportion of extant waqf documents.

Further archival material are the *narh* (official price) documents, related to the activities of merchants and guilds. Official prices were decided by the qadi on the basis of the Islamic concept of "fairness." As they were changed when necessary according to season and product availability, many references to *narh* are found in sharia-court registers. H. Sahillioğlu, "The *Narh* System in the Ottoman Empire and Prices in Istanbul at the End of 1525" (T., 1967) contains an example of one such document. The maintenance of the *narh* system was one of the tasks of Ottoman urban administration and especially in the case of Istanbul, the *narh* could be decided in the form of an Imperial decree, being considered a part of state administration with the grand vizier in charge. Market laws (*kanunname-i ihtisab*) were also sometimes promulgated when it was necessary to decide prices over the long term. Barkan, "*Kanun* Enacted for the Purpose of Controlling Prices of Goods and Foodstuffs in Some Major Cities in the Late 15th Century" (T., 1942) introduces three such laws for Istanbul, Bursa and Edirne. M. Kütükoğlu, "Prices and Wages in Istanbul through a *Narh* Register Dated 1009/1600" (T., 1978) and id., *The Ottoman Narh System and a Narh Register of 1640* (T., 1983) deal with two *narh* registers from Istanbul which cover all the goods in the market. These materials are valuable since they show not only the prices of a number of goods and changes in those prices, but also the range of a guild's activity and the abundance of goods traded in Istanbul. Mantran, *Un document sur l'ihtisâb de Stamboul à la fin du XVIIe siècle* (1957) introduces material concerning *hisba*. A valuable introduction to the extraordinary tax imposed on each quarter (*avâriz vergisi*) is M. Aktepe, "An *Avâriz* Register of 17th Century Istanbul" (T., 1957).

It is undeniable that the overwhelming majority of Ottoman archival material preserved in the National Archives is, because it is concerned with the needs of the "centre," related either to rule, particularly tax collection, or to the capital city, Istanbul. There is difficulty as a result in knowing how ordinary people actually lived, particularly in regional cities. For such studies, useful source is the sharia-court registers (*kadı sicilleri*) preserved in each regional town. During the Ottoman period, qadis were both administrators and judges at the local (district) level and the records of their activities, the sharia-court registers, contain a variety of information about urban life.

Ergin, *The Compendium of Municipal Administration* was probably the first work in Turkey to introduce sharia-court registers in relation to their relevance for Istanbul. The situation in Manisa is studied in M. Ç. Uluçay, "A Study on the Sharia-Court Registers of Manisa" (T., 1953) and in a series introducing historical material by İ. Gökçen, including *The Waqf Endowments and Charitable Institutions in the History of Manisa* (T., 1946-50). H. Ongan, *The First Sharia-Court Register of Ankara* (T., 1958) and id., *The Second Sharia-Court Register of Ankara* (T., 1974) deal with Ankara. A general catalogue of all the sharia-court registers scattered in libraries and museums in Turkey has been published by the Foundation for the Study of the Turkish World (Türk Dünyası Araştırmaları Vakfı) under the title of *Sharia-Court Registers* (T., 1988-9), which has brought to light the entire range of registers, from the oldest, of 15th century Bursa, to the numerous registers from all regions in the 18th and 19th centuries.

Sharia-court registers, since they contain records of commercial transactions, loans and trials, can be used to study various aspects of urban economic activity, such as industries, the activities of wealthy merchants and guild organization. Works which utilize them in this way include M. Ç. Uluçay, *Agriculture, Trades, and Guild Organizations in 17th Century Manisa* (T., 1942), F. Dalsar, *Bursa's Silk Textile Industry in the History of Turkish Industry and Trade* (T., 1960), and a series of studies on Bursa by İnalcık, "Bursa and the Commerce of the Levant" (1960), "Bursa I: Historical Materials concerning 15th Century Industry and Trade" (T., 1960) and "Historical Materials concerning Ottoman Administrative, Social, and Economic History" (T., 1981). R. Özdemir, *Ankara in the First Half of the 19th Century* (T., 1986) summarizes the various urban institutions, population, administration and economic activities of Ankara, based mainly on sharia-court registers.

Sharia-court registers even include inheritance lists (*tereke defteri*), which record occupations and properties of the dead. Inheritance lists are introduced in Barkan, "Inheritance Lists Preserved at the Inheritance Office of Military Personnel in Edirne" (T., 1968), Y. Nagata, *Materials on the Bosnian Notables* (1979) and H. Özdeğer, *Inheritance Lists of Bursa from 1463 to 1640* (T., 1988) among others. Inheritance lists provide information about the accumulation of wealth and details about the property of urban residents such as military personnel, the ulama, merchants and artisans. They reveal that monetary loans were very common among all urban classes.

One of the most significant works in Ottoman urban studies to this day, a study of the society and economy of a particular city based on research into archival materials is R. Mantran, *Istanbul dans la seconde moitié du XVII*[e] *siècle* (1962). Using the travel account of Evliya Çelebi, Ottoman and Venetian documentary sources, and European travel accounts, it studies Istanbul in the second half of the 17th century from three aspects, urban structure, economic life and the foreigners there. Rather than being a political history, it seeks to draw a picture of Istanbul in terms of the life of its residents and provides not only detailed information about its administrative structure and the machinery for production and distribution, but also clues to the city's complicated internal structure. However, as the author himself admits, Istanbul as the capital of Empire is too particular a case to be dealt with as an ordinary city. It was administered as part of central government, and in terms of economic activity and the presence of foreigners and members of religious minorities it was not typical of Ottoman cities in general. Many of the issues important to the city which affected Ottoman national policy, such as the influence of population increase on the supply of foodstuffs and the presence of foreign merchants, go beyond the framework of urban studies. Thus while the work is an excellent, though static, summary of Istanbul, it is not easy to apply its findings to Ottoman cities in general.

Another important study based on Ottoman archival materials is N. Todorov, *The Balkan City: 1400-1900* (in Bulgarian, 1972), translated into English in 1983. It deals with the socio-economic and demographic development of the cities in the Balkans and describes the emergence of an urban bourgeoisie in 18th and 19th century Bulgaria. A great amount of statistical information is derived from an analysis of Ottoman documents such as the inheritance lists of urban residents.

A summary of the characteristics of the urban economy as culled from studies in Ottoman period socio-economic history up to the 1970s has been made by H. Inalcık in "Capital Formation in the Ottoman Empire" (1969) and "The Ottoman Economic Mind and Aspects of the Ottoman Economy" (1970). İnalcık examines the Ottoman economic system, emphasizing that it derives from the traditional view of state and society in Western Asia. He points out a number of elements as being characteristic of Ottoman cities and their economic activity on the basis of his study of Bursa. (1) Urban prosperity and decline were related to the policies for the protection and promotion of interregional trade by the state. (2) Wealthy merchants (*tüccâr*) and exchange brokers (*sarrâf*) with a privileged status among urban dwellers accumulated a large amount of capital but not to the degree of the military class. (3) Relationships based on monetary loans permeated every social class and investment in high interest loans and the caravan trade was common. (4) Some medium- and small-scale merchants and artisans belonging to guilds were able to accumulate capital, but in general the accumulation of capital was strictly controlled and this prevented independent development.

İnalcık emphasizes the influence of the Ottoman state in social life and urban economic activity in particular. Most urban facilities were constructed by the governing class within the framework of the waqf system and the cities and interregional trade routes were carefully protected by the central government. All economic processes, such as marketing and price controls, were conducted as a part of state administration. The example of Bursa shows that there was some accumulation of wealth, but in the long run, the government tended to hinder the freedom of activity of urban dwellers. However, as we will see in the next section, concrete studies of Anatolian cities made in recent years has forced this subordinate image of Turkish Ottoman cities to be revised in some respects.

III. Recent Trends

While in past years the study of cities was undertaken within the broad field of Turkish history, it is noticeable that an independent field of study that can be termed urban studies has emerged in the last two decades or so. The main concerns of this emergent area may be summarized as:

1. Studies about the development of Anatolian cities and their networks.
2. Studies about the internal structure of cities.
3. Studies about the spatial structure of cities.
4. Studies about the transformation of cities in the 19th century.

A common characteristic of these studies is that they deal with regional cities in Anatolia rather than with Istanbul. Research into Ottoman archival material is still under many restraints and topics of study have therefore been limited both temporally and spatially. As yet no studies have appeared which use the concept of a "Turkish city" or an "Ottoman city" rigorously. Nevertheless, considering the abundant historical source material that remains untouched and the growing concentration of interest on urban studies, research into Turkish Ottoman cities is expected to influence greatly the direction of urban studies about the Middle East.

1. The Development of Anatolian Cities and Their Networks

The first new type of study is in the field of socio-economic history and concerns the development of Anatolian regional cities and the formations of their networks in relation to the social changes of the 16th and 17th centuries.

The first scholar to consider this question in terms of world history was F. Braudel in *La Méditerranée et le monde méditerranéen à l'époque de Philippe II* (2nd ed. 1966), which dealt with the Mediterranean world in the tumultuous 16th century. It clearly indicates the integral role of the Ottoman Empire in the Mediterranean world and points out that the economic situation of and the demographic changes in the Ottoman Empire greatly influenced the whole Mediterranean world. The empirical studies of Barkan underlie his work. In studies such as "Historical Demography and Ottoman History," "Essai sur les données statistiques des registres de recensement dans l'Empire Ottoman aux XVe et XVIe siècles" and "Price Fluctuations in the Latter Half of the 16th Century in Turkey" (T., 1970), Barkan gives concrete evidence for demographic changes and price fluctuations in the Ottoman Empire in the 16th century.

As a result of Braudel's and Barkan's work, a more detailed study about the population of Anatolia became an important theme in Ottoman period socio-economic history. M. A. Cook, *Population Pressure in Rural Anatolia* (1972), which deals with demographic changes in three provinces of Anatolia (Aydın, Hamit and Tokat) from the 15th to the late 16th century, reveals one segment of long-term change in the excess of population growth over the development of agricultural productivity and the accompanying social changes in this period.

The following picture emerges of Ottoman history from the work in socio-economic history by some of the leading Turkish scholars in the field like Barkan, İnalcık and M. Akdağ with also some influence by Braudel. In the 16th century the population of Anatolia doubled, due to improved agricultural productivity and a healthy interregional trade. Late that century resulting social pressures and price rises caused Ottoman society to experience confusion and disorder, and a long period of political and economic decline set in from the 17th century onward. This situation at length invited the incursion of Western capital. In a sense recent studies in socio-economic history such as those by S. Faroqhi have emerged with the purpose of re-examining this view of Ottoman history. The study of the socio-economic history of cities also had its beginning in this context. For the influence of

Braudel and his school on the study of Ottoman history, see İnalcık, "Impact of the *Annales* School on Ottoman Studies and New Findings" (1978).

An important subject in recent years is population dynamics. R. Jennings, "Urban Population in Anatolia in the Sixteenth Century" (1976) focuses on population changes in the 16th century of five cities in Central Anatolia, Kayseri, Karaman, Amasya, Trabzon and Erzurum. Jennings gives details of demographic change in each city together with the ratios of Muslims and non-Muslims in the population and the population of each quarter and how it changed. He points out that while these cities fell under Ottoman rule relatively late they all took part in the population growth of the 16th century, though each had developed in different ways. In light of this, he recommends further careful study. H. W. Lowry, *Islamization and Turkicization of Trabzon, 1461-1583* (T., 1981) makes a close examination of the population of Trabzon and how the quarters of Trabzon were formed after the Ottoman conquest. L. Erder and S. Faroqhi, "Population Rise and Fall in Anatolia 1550-1620" (1979) deals with the period of the "*Celâlî* Rebellions" in Anatolia from the late 16th century to the beginning of the 17th century and studies the differences in population decrease between the two provinces of Karahisar and Kocaeli in this period, principally through a consideration of the relationship between cities and their agricultural hinterlands.

One useful means of elucidating social change is to make population estimates from the Ottoman land survey registers. However, since the land survey registers themselves were not compiled as a census of the population, they should be used with caution. Basic studies in this area, such as Erder, "The Measurement of Pre-Industrial Population Changes" (1975), N. Göyünç, "On the Term *hane*" (T., 1979) and Faroqhi, "Taxation and Urban Activities in Sixteenth-Century Anatolia" (1979-80), are also very important from the point of view of urban studies.

Studies on Anatolian population such as the above-mentioned are now enabling scholars to examine the formation of inter-city networks based on the spatial and size distribution of cities. Erder and Faroqhi, "The Development of the Anatolian Urban Network during the Sixteenth Century" (1980) describes how urban networks were formed in Anatolia during the 16th century in terms of the Central Place Theory, a method for detecting hierarchical integration among cities. At the beginning of the 16th century Anatolian cities were very small in scale but fifty years later small to medium sized cities were growing up on the trade routes and so an urban network was formed. Urban growth itself encourages further growth, and the cities of 16th century Anatolia are typical of that process.

What were the causes of urban development in 16th century Anatolia? In a series of studies, Faroqhi examines this subject from the economic aspect of the development of regional trade and the political aspect of the influence of the Ottoman state, using a number of Ottoman archival materials. Faroqhi believes that the development of regional trade in Anatolia was aided by the establishment of regional markets into which surrounding villages were integrated and by the development of manufactures distinctive to each city. In "Sixteenth Century Periodic Markets in Various Anatolian Sancaks" (1979), she studies the distribution of periodic markets in West Anatolia from this point of view and demonstrates how regional markets were formed in each district. Since the periodic markets were places of tax collection and conversion of agricultural products into money by both *timar* holders and peasants, the formation of hierarchical urban networks centring on the periodical market is indicative of the penetration of Ottoman rule. But it is important that the economic network was not necessarily in accordance with the administrative one. id., "A Map of Anatolian Friday Mosques" (1984) studies the distribution of Friday mosques to indicate density of urban settlement and relationship of construction of religious foundations by the ruling class to urban development.

In *Town and Townsmen of Ottoman Anatolia* (1984), she deals broadly with trade and manufacture, which supported the development of the cities, and examines the lives of urban dwellers in the 16th century Anatolia and the degree of crisis of the last decade of the 16th century in regards to regional urban society. She discusses urban autonomous development from three angles, namely, urban markets and trade routes, manufacturing (the weaving industry, the leather industry and the metal craft industry) and the agricultural hinterland, and investigates the Ottoman influence over local societies and its limits. It is certainly clear that the powerful centralized system greatly influenced the development of Anatolian cities. In the first place, many Anatolian cities were made centres of Ottoman administration. Within this administrative hierarchy, cities became bases to rule the villages, principally in regard to tax collection, and the presence of bureaucrats, military regiments, qadis and *timar* holders from the central government made for a distinction between the city and the village. Secondly, the principal consumers of Anatolian manufactures were the military. Economic demand by the state therefore affected the prosperity or decline of many industries. Thirdly, waqf endowments by the ruling class provided the hardware for urban trade and the manufacturing industry, satisfying urban functions. Further, stable government under Ottoman rule guaranteed regional and interregional trade. Thus, the political and administrative factors had great influence upon urban development. However, according to Faroqhi, the process of urban development of Anatolia can not be explained only by these factors. For example, many Anatolian cities developed regardless of the interregional trade that state protection had influenced to a large extent; political situation in the 16th century did not change so much, none the less cities developed rather rapidly. Moreover, the fact that in the 17th century the Anatolian cities enjoyed a certain order and prosperity after the political chaos of former decades suggests that, even under the centralized government, there actually existed local societies with quite extensive political autonomy as well as economic and social independence.

In *Men of Modest Substance* (1987), Faroqhi examines various aspects of Anatolian urban development by looking inside urban society. She uses records of real estate dealings in sharia-court registers of Ankara and Kayseri to reconstruct the dwellings that belonged to the urban dwellers and from that to examine the degree of wealth, and changes in it, of each group that made up the city. This study confirms the continuing stability and prosperity of Anatolian cities in the 17th century following recovery from the period of confusion in the late 16th century.

The relations between urban networks and the state are discussed in Faroqhi, "Towns, Agriculture and the State in Sixteenth-Century Ottoman Anatolia" (1990). After comparing Syrian cities during the Mamluk period and Anatolian cities during the Ottoman period, Faroqhi concludes that the relationship between the state and the urban economy was completely different in the two regions. Whereas I. M. Lapidus argues that "political conditions" were the main factor determining the rise and fall of cities in Mamluk Syria, Faroqhi says that the relationship of the Ottoman state with the city was indirect, maintained through the administrative system. Lapidus argues that a fluid and unorganized state of urban society characterizes Mamluk Syrian cities, but Ottoman urban society seems to be much more structured. Faroqhi points out that it is completely meaningless to abstract from the particular case of Syrian urban society the norm of an "Islamic society" assumed to be amorphous and unchangeable.

Faroqhi's studies basically concern the urban development of Anatolia, which was both the principal factor for, and the main result of, socio-economic changes in Ottoman society in the 16th and 17th centuries. She describes the development of urban networks as reflecting the dynamism of Ottoman society, and is critical to the concept of the "Islamic city" or "Islamic society" as a static model. In comparison to İnalcık, Faroqhi lays more stress on the energy within local society and considers interregional trade and political factors as secondary in importance.

Other studies in socio-economic history look more narrowly at the economic structure of one city and have concentrated most particularly on Bursa and Izmir. Bursa, in Anatolia, is where relatively old sharia-court registers have been preserved, and portions concerning international trade and the silk textile industry have been introduced in the studies of İnalcık and Dalsar. They describe Bursa as experiencing prosperity in the 16th century and an economic crisis at its end. M. Çızakça, "A Short History of the Bursa Silk Industry" (1980) and "Price History and the Bursa Silk Industry" (1980) deal with economic activity and the international situation from the late 16th to the 17th century, centring on price fluctuations. On the other hand, H. Gerber, *Economy and Society in an Ottoman City: Bursa* (1988) treats 17th century Bursa from more varied angles, including population, the degree of wealth of merchants and artisans, guilds, the structure of labor force, economic relations with the agricultural hinterland, interregional trade, financial loans and credit relations. Gerber concludes by doubting the established view that the Ottoman Empire fell into the period of decline in the 17th century, stating that despite cyclical economic change, Bursa did not witness any structural change and its entire structure functioned well throughout the 17th century and it is therefore impossible to consider this period as one of decline in terms of structure. This conclusion has much in common with the studies on Ankara and Kayseri by Faroqhi.

Essential when considering the economic structure of the Ottoman state are studies about changes in the cities and their networks before the economic advances of Europe from the 18th century onward. However, as Faroqhi remarks in the introduction to *Towns and Townsmen* in 1984, hardly any studies have been done on Ottoman cities between 1650 and 1850. This gap is now beginning to be filled, with a spate of recent studies on Izmir, a city situated on the Aegean Sea which developed rapidly after the 17th century as a trading port for Europe due to the presence of speculative foreign merchants busily exporting cheap grain to Europe. D. Goffman, *Izmir and the Levantine World, 1550-1650* (1990) deals with the rapid development of Izmir as a city and as an international commercial port in the first half of the 17th century. S. Anderson, *An English Consul in Turkey* (1989) describes the society of Izmir in the middle of the 17th century through the eyes of an English consul, Paul Rycaut. E. Frangakis-Syrett, "The Raya Communities of Smyrna in the 18th Century" (1985), "Trade between Ottoman Empire and Western Europe" (1988) and "The Greek Mercantile Community of Izmir in the First Half of the Nineteenth Century" (1991), are studies about the prosperity of Izmir in the 18th and 19th centuries and the role of the non-Muslim merchants whose influence increased at that time. Since the prosperity of 18th century Izmir was directly related with the productivity of its agricultural hinterland, and with the cultivation of commercial crops in particular, this prosperity seemed to be regarded as a natural consequence of the development of economic networks of Anatolia from the 16th century onward. But phenomena like the predominance of non-Muslim merchants was not seen in previous centuries.

In 18th century Izmir there may be detected the embryonic change in "stability" that Faroqhi and Gerber have shown as existing in 17th century Anatolian cities. However because of the scarcity of studies on other cities during this period, it remains difficult to say whether this situation was shared by other Anatolian cities or not. Studies which attempt to understand changes in urban society and their networks in the long years of Ottoman period from the 16th to the 19th centuries are awaited.

2. The Internal Structure of Cities

A second trend in recent studies is an interest in urban social groups and organizations, with sharia-court registers the main documentary source. I will discuss these studies according to theme.

Urban Administration

N. Beldiceanu, *Recherche sur la ville ottomane au XVe siècle* (1973) studies the local administrative system as a unit of the Ottoman political and military organization. Beldiceanu discusses the military, tax collection, and the machinery of administration in a 15th century urban setting in terms of institutional history using *kanunname*s, and other archival material. Another example of the administrative organization of an individual city is found in R. Özdemir, *Ankara in the First Half of the 19th Century* (T., 1986).

Of the various local administrative organizations, it was the qadi and his representative the *naib,* who had direct relations with the urban dwellers through being in charge of administration and trials at (district) level. As a result of recent progress in studies of the sharia-court registers, more detailed information about the sharia-court itself is becoming available. Jennings, "Kadi, Court and Legal Procedure in 17th C. Ottoman Kayseri" (1978) and "Limitations of the Judicial Powers of the Kadi in 17th C. Ottoman Kayseri" (1979) discuss in detail the functions of the qadi and the judicial system in 17th century Kayseri. Gerber, "Sharia, Kanun and Custom in the Ottoman Law" (1981) studies how the law was actually handled in the sharia-court of 17th Century Bursa and demonstrates that in actual judgments, customary law was given priority. Gerber does not agree that the qadi grew corrupt in 17th century Bursa as was suggested by U. Heyd in *Studies in Old Ottoman Criminal Law* (1973).

Apart from the administrative aspects, what was the actual decision making system in cities? The top of the urban social hierarchy was occupied by ulama such as qadis, and by bureaucrats, tax farmers and others connected with the central government, but they were moved from post to post and had only a limited connection with local society. On the other hand, urban notables in regional cities were called *eşrâf* and *âyan*. Although few studies have been done on their contribution to the urban society of Anatolia from the 15th to the 17th century, two articles by Ö. Ergenç on *eşrâf* and *âyan*, "Some Notes on the Administration Units of Ottoman Cities" (T., 1981) and "*Eşrâf* and *Âyan* in the Ottoman Classical Period" (T., 1982) demonstrate that regional cities in Anatolia might have had autonomy to some extent. Urban notables, identified as wealthy merchants, guild elders, native ulamas, Sufi sheikhs and others, played an intermediary role between rulers and the urban population as town officials (*şehir kethüdası*) or native agents of tax farmers and various officials appointed by the central government. Ergenç attributes semi-autonomous functions to them, since they had a voice in the appointment of officials to local office by the central government and in determining *narh*, and direct petitions made to the Sultan by them as representatives of urban dwellers were generally approved by the central government.

In and after the 18th century, local *âyan* emerged to control local society backed by their extensive land holdings and tax farming. Their economic basis was agricultural activity, but they lived in cities, having obtained certain government posts, and were influential in local urban society through their offices and because they made many waqf endowments. İnalcık, "Centralization and Decentralization in Ottoman Administration" (1977) discusses the role of *âyan* in local administration as a result of changes in the centralized system of government. Studies on the social and economic basis of the *âyan* as central figures in local society in the 18th and 19th centuries include Y. Özkaya, *The Âyan System in the Ottoman Empire* (T., 1977) and Y. Nagata, "*Âyan* in History: The Prosperity of Turkish Local Society in the Early 19th Century" (J., 1986).

Guilds and Merchants

If Baer's studies of the guild as administrative, with a close relationship with the state, were the springboard for recent research into the guild, the works on the guild by scholars such as by İnalcık, Ergenç and Gerber deal on the whole with the autonomous nature of the guild and its regional differences. Because the guild was the most important organization in Ottoman cities, the question arises that it may have been directly related to the afore-mentioned urban autonomy.

İnalcık, *The Ottoman Empire: The Classical Age* (1973), based particularly on the author's study of Bursa, gives detailed summaries of arguments concerning the Turkish guild. Since the guilds of Bursa were far more autonomous than those of Istanbul, as Gerber showed, the Turkish guild is a more autonomous organization for İnalcık than for Baer. On the other hand, İnalcık's conclusion that the guild respected the higher authorities of the state and that it had an important role in tax collection is in accord with Baer. An important observation by İnalcık is that the embryo tendency towards class differentiation among guild members was obstructed by government intervention for the sake of maintaining the established order. Ergenç "A Study on the Economic History of Ankara from 1600 to 1615" (T., 1975) on the other hand portrays the guilds of Ankara as being on the whole under stronger control by the state. Gerber, "Guilds in Seventeenth-Century Anatolian Bursa" (1976) is the most specific recent study of guilds in an Anatolian city. Gerber understands the guilds of Bursa to have been flexible in structure, quite different from those of Istanbul. In Bursa members did not need to have strong qualifications to join guilds and no strict restrictions were placed on the number of shops allowed for each industry or business. As a result, anyone could become a guild member as long as he had the necessary technical skill and paid tax. All the same guilds made regulations by themselves to standardize quality and to monopolize business, and these regulations were ratified by the sharia-court. Gerber considers that the guilds of Bursa, that city of the embryonic "class differentiation" noted by İnalcık, were able to develop such autonomy because they were conscious of protecting their privileges as a whole and of the equality of their members. The state allowed guild monopolies and restrictions as long as taxes were collected. Bursa is known as the case where guilds were involved in everything, up to deciding prices and determining quality.

Regional differences, and temporal ones as well, probably grew out of differences in such factors as city size, industrial structure and the city's relations with the state. In discussing the Turkish guild, therefore, we are now at the stage of making studies of individual cities. Recommended is Baer, "Ottoman Guilds: A Reassessment" (1980), which comments on recent studies about Ottoman period guilds together with the work of A. Raymond on Cairo and of A. K. Rafeq on Damascus.

The activities of wealthy merchants outside the scope of the guilds have been discussed in relation to interregional trade in İnalcık, "Bursa and the Commerce of the Levant" and "Capital Formation in the Ottoman Empire." No outstanding studies on the subject have appeared recently, perhaps because the main thrust of research has turned now to regional markets, as represented by Faroqhi's studies. Foreign merchants have been studied in Mantran, "Minoritaires, métiers-marchands étrangers à Istanbul aux XVIe et XVIIe siècles" (1980) and the afore-mentioned Frangakis-Syrett's works on Izmir.

Quarters

Like other cities in the Middle East, Turkish cities are divided into quarters called *mahalle*. It is clear that each *mahalle* was named after a mosque, market or the dominant characteristic of its inhabitants, but the role the quarters played in the social life of urban dwellers has not yet been fully studied. The quarter as an administrative unit is described in local histories based on the 16th century land survey registers and we know from these that each person was identified in terms of his quarter and the local imam was considered to be the quarter's representative, at the base of the governing pyramid. Similar to the situation with guild studies, to look at the social function of the quarter we need to know more about the actualities of life there for its inhabitants through sources such as sharia-court registers. A first step in this direction is Ergenç, "Functions and Characteristics of Quarters in Ottoman Cities" (T., 1984). Ergenç describes the quarter as a single undivided unit whose members were all known to each other, as well as a unit for tax collection and administration. Under Ottoman rule, quarters were not as closed as those in Arab cities, since the strength of the central government precluded the need to have systems of defence. Each quarter was concerned with mutual aid, waqf funds (*avâriz* waqf) being set up to provide against provisional taxes.

When the quarter is discussed as a fragment of the urban "mosaic," the composition of its inhabitants (for example, Muslims and non-Muslims) often becomes an issue. The detailed reports available for Turkish urban quarters tell us that some segregation was apparent but it was not extreme and many quarters had a mixed population. Faroqhi, *Men of Modest Substance* deals with the quarters in relation to houses and notes the frequent trade in real estate between Muslims and non-Muslims, the predominance of mixed habitation, and the lack of difference in style between dwellings of Muslims and non-Muslims in 17th century Kayseri and Ankara. Faroqhi concludes that the sense of unity through sharing a common urban culture exceeds, in the urban setting, the sense of division through quarter or religious group.

Waqf Endowments

The study of waqf endowments, especially of Anatolian and Syrian cities, has recently become one of the most active fields of Ottoman urban studies. I will restrict my remarks here to publications concerning the waqf endowments in the Turkish region, though it goes without saying that they share a close relation with those concerning the waqfs in the Arab region.

The contribution that the waqf endowment has made to cities is most apparent in urban buildings. K. Hayashi-Yamamoto, "Istanbul in the Latter Half of the 15th Century: The Reconstruction Policy of Mehmet II" (J., 1982) and Y. Nagata, "The Formation of Regional Society and the Waqf System in Pre-Modern Turkey" (J., 1985) study waqf endowments in Istanbul and Manisa. The construction of religious institutions like mosques and waqf properties like bazars and caravansaries was of course directly related to urban formation, and a topic for future research will be how they were related to the distinctive spatial structure of Ottoman cities.

An important point to consider is that the larger part of urban commercial facilities had been provided within the framework of the waqf system as waqf property. Because merchants and artisans rented such properties, the waqf system was directly related to urban economic activity. In the first chapter of *Towns and Townsmen,* Faroqhi uses 16th and 17th century waqf survey registers to discuss the role of the waqf system in urban development through the leasing system.

In the eighth chapter of *Economy and Society in an Ottoman City: Bursa,* Gerber examines the role of the waqf system in Bursa's social and economic activities. He criticizes the view of Gibb and Bowen in *Islamic Society and the West* (1950-7) that the waqf system was a factor in urban collapse and demonstrates that waqf administrators (*mütevelli*), the qadi and the ulama (as waqf beneficiaries) coordinated well to control it. 17th century Bursa, he says, did not witness the destruction of waqf property, and the system continued to function smoothly. Gerber shows that, as has been seen already in the case of the guilds and the quarters, the various systems constituting Ottoman society were reasonably flexible in structure and the confusion that characterized the 19th century did not extend as far back in time as people might imagine.

A characteristic of the Ottoman period is that as far as small scale endowments were concerned the cash waqf was ubiquitous. Cash was invested at a ten to twenty percent interest rate, and so provided a portion of the city's demand for cash. This question is discussed in E. Mandaville, "Usurious Piety: The Cash Waqf Controversy in the Ottoman Empire" (1979). Studies of financial relations, including the cash waqf, are Jennings, "Loan and Credit in Early 17th Century Judicial Records" (1973) dealing with Kayseri, and the seventh chapter of Gerber's *Economy and Society in an Ottoman City: Bursa.* Gerber gives figures to show that about sixteen percent of all the financial funding of cities came from waqf endowments.

Any socio-historical study of the waqf system from the social historical point necessitates an examination of waqf founders, who were in effect the users of the waqf system. B. Yediyıldız, "Social Classes of Waqf Founders in Turkey" (T., 1982) discusses the relationship between social class under

Ottoman rule and waqf founders through an exhaustive study of the waqf endowment deeds kept in the General Directorate of Waqfs in Ankara. Yediyıldız has also written "The Cultural Effects of the Waqf System in the 18th Century" (T., 1980) and "The Role of the Waqf System in 18th Century Turkish Society" (T., 1982). His Ph. D. dissertation, *Institution du vaqf au XVIII*^{e} *siècle en Turquie*, upon which the above articles are based, was published in 1985.

An interesting study of female waqf founders is G. Baer, "Women and Waqf" (1983). Baer demonstrates, from an analysis of the waqf survey register of Istanbul dated 1546 published by Barkan and Ayverdi that 36.8% of all waqf founders were women and that many of those waqf properties were originally inheritances of a relatively modest scale. After they died, men, often from the ulama class, were appointed as administrators of the waqf, and so sooner or later waqfs tended to shift into the possession of male beneficiaries, against the initial intention of the waqf endowment to protect the property of females from husbands and third persons. This is indicative of women's economic status.

Gerber, "The Waqf Institution in Early Ottoman Edirne" (1983) is a quantitative analysis of the waqf institution which attempts, on the basis of approximately 300 waqfs from Edirne mentioned in Gökbilgin, *Edirne and Rumeli Province in the 15th and 16th Centuries,* to evaluate the role of the waqf system as a whole. Gerber does not cite enough instances to be persuasive, but in method and objectivity his study remains relevant especially for the comparative study of the waqf system.

K. Hayashi, "The *Vakıf* Institution in 16th-Century Istanbul" (1992) is a quantitative analysis that attempts to classify the vast information in the above mentioned Istanbul waqf survey register of 1546 according to social class of waqf founders, type of waqf property and purpose of waqf endowments. Because 75% of all examples recorded in this register are rather small in size (with an annual income of less than 1000 akçe), the characteristics of "small" waqfs are mainly clarified. For example, 51% of small waqfs contained only dwellings as waqf property. As for the purpose for founding waqfs, one half of the small waqfs benefited only founders' families for a certain period of time, though it is quite probable that transfer from private to charitable utilization did take place afterward. The other half of small waqfs and more than a half of the medium-size waqfs were donated to a certain specific charity; in most cases, to support mosques of their quarter. The role of waqf system played in quarter community was quite important. 85% of large waqfs and 34% of medium size waqfs supported the religious or charitable institutions founded by waqf founders themselves. These analyses present some general criteria for the further comparative studies of waqf system.

Social Groups

As seen in the analytical study of female waqf founders, recent developments in the study of Ottoman archival materials have brought us substantial information about the social and economic status of various urban groups. Like in many other areas of Ottoman urban studies, most work at present is devoted to collecting information about individual cities. Jennings's study of Kayseri and Gerber's study of Bursa are pioneering studies in the use of sharia-court registers.

The subject of women is studied by Baer, in the article mentioned above, and in Jennings, "Women in Early 17th Century Ottoman Judicial Records" (1975) and Gerber, "Social and Economic Position of Women in an Ottoman City, Bursa, 1600-1700" (1980). Jennings indicates that women in Kayseri in the 17th century frequently went to the sharia-court. For example, forty percent of people concerned with the sale of real estate between the years 1603 and 1627 were women. There is much evidence to show that women were on an equal standing with men in terms of court decisions, transactions and contracts, and their position was protected in judgments more than in the regulations of Islamic law. Women figure prominently as sellers of real estate probably because they were disposing of an inheritance.

A second social group to be studied is non-Muslims (*zimmi*). Noteworthy studies of the history of individual communities include A. Galanté, *Histoire des Juifs d'Istanbul* (1941-2), U. Heyd, "The Jewish Communities of Istanbul in the XVIIth Century" (1953), M. A. Epstein, *The Ottoman Jewish Communities and their Role in the Fifteenth and Sixteenth Centuries* (1980) and A. Shmuelevitz, *The Jews of the Ottoman Empire in the Late Fifteenth and the Sixteenth Centuries* (1984). Many studies have been made on minorities in Ottoman society, and important results have been obtained. A notable work in this area is B. Braude and B. Lewis (eds.), *Christians and Jews in the Ottoman Empire* (1982). It contains valuable essays concerning the position of non-Muslim communities under Ottoman rule and how that position changed in the 18th and 19th centuries. The relations between these groups and urban society have been discussed by Faroqhi in *Men of Modest Substance* where she speaks of the co-existence of Muslims and non-Muslims, and in Jennings, "Zimmis (Non-Muslims) in Early 17th Century Ottoman Judicial Records" (1978), which proves that the sharia-courts in Kayseri functioned as places where even non-Muslims could solve conflicts.

Studies of slaves as an important social group in Ottoman cities include H. Sahillioğlu, "Slaves in the Social and Economic Life of Bursa in the Late 15th and Early 16th Centuries" (T., 1981) and id., "Labour and the Industrial Life of Bursa in the Late 15th Century" (T., 1980), and İ. Sak, "Slaves in

Konya" (T., 1989). These all deal with slaves in economic terms, as a labor force or property; on the other hand, since slaves in Ottoman society were often named as beneficiaries of their masters' waqfs, they can also be studied as members of the community of the family, the smallest unit of society. So far such an approach has not been taken.

3. Studies about Urban Space

Since the main thrust of studies about Turkish Ottoman cities has been concentrated on their social and economic aspects, the historical study of their visible aspects, such as their spatial structure and the functions of their various institutions, has lagged far behind. There is a wealth, though, of accumulated study concerning religious buildings (mosques, etc.) and domestic dwellings in terms of the history of architecture. Efforts to consolidate those studies with historical studies has only just begun.

Urban Space

The first study of Turkish cities in terms of the structure of urban space was probably Kuban, "Historical Development and Social and Structural Development of Anatolian Turkish City". Kuban cites as the three roots of the Turkish city the Islamic city, the Central Asian-Iranian city and the Anatolian Byzantine city and asserts that Turkey's unique urban space grew from a fusion of the three in Anatolia, centring on the nomadic tradition of the Turks. His arguments were continued by U. Tanyeli in *The Transformation Process of Urban Space in Anatolian Turkish Cities* (T., 1987). Tanyeli looks at the spatial structure of Anatolian cities from the 11th to the 15th century, the period when the Turkish city was formed. He classifies Anatolian cities into three categories to discuss urban functions and change in urban design (the East Anatolian city surrounded by city walls, the East Anatolian city without city walls and the West Anatolian city bordering Byzantine territory) and examines citadels, streets, quarters, plazas, palaces, grand mosques and waqf institutions as urban elements. He concludes that the balance between nomadic migrants and Turkish-Iranian settled migrants fluctuated according to region and time and that characteristic Anatolian Turkish cities with regional differences emerged from the conflict or harmony between them. The basic differences, he states, can be seen in the difference between the cities of Central and Eastern Anatolia where Iranian influence remained strong and the Ottoman cities of Western Anatolia. Since Tanyeli deals with a period for which historical material is scarce, his work inevitably contains many hypotheses, which means it is not always empirical, but in that it proposes issues for discussion it is ambitious and very stimulating. As the first full-scale work to deal with the formation of cities through the process of Turkicization and Islamization, it will motivate future studies.

Studies focusing on Anatolian cities before the Ottoman period include O. Turan, "Sivas in the Seljuk Period" (T., 1951) and T. Baykara, *Konya in the Rum Seljuk Period* (T., 1985). The majority of such studies are written primarily as architectural studies, such as M. Sözen, *Akkoyunlu Architecture in Anatolia* (T., 1981) and O. C. Tuncer, *Architecture of the Rum Seljuk Period and the Mongols* (T., 1986). The spatial structure of Anatolian cities during the Ottoman period has been studied by S. Aktüre in works such as "The Changing Process of Urban Space in the Ottoman Cities of Anatolia from the Early 17th Century to the Middle of the 19th Century" (T., 1975) and *Anatolian Cities in the Late 19th Century* (T., 1978). They represent the first attempt to link social and economic structure with urban space in Turkish Ottoman cities.

Worthy of note as a short discussion of Turkish cities in relation to the concept of the "Islamic city" is İnalcık, "Istanbul: An Islamic City" (1990). Whereas scholars like Kuban and Tanyeli have completely denied that Turkish cities can be understood within the framework of the "Islamic city," İnalcık asserts that Istanbul is the very embodiment of Islamic cosmology. He uses the expression "Islamic Ottoman city" to identify an urban society ruled constantly on the basis of the semi-sacred authority of the Sultan and Islamic law. The Islamic Ottoman city was divided spatially into residential quarters with autonomous functions where the protection of privacy was given priority, and a commercial zone where planned construction was carried out by the Sultan and members of the elite through waqf endowments. İnalcık believes that because of the existence of a commercial center shared by all of the urban dwellers and the rule of Islamic law through the qadi, the residential quarters of the city were never closed, but maintained an integrated harmony. The qadi, as the representative of Islamic law, was able to keep a certain distance from the government despite of centralized Ottoman rule, and frequently appeared on behalf of local Muslim communities. İnalcık's argument offers a different perspective from previous studies on Turkish urban space in that he looks at the autonomy of various Ottoman urban systems as it has been revealed of late in an Islamic context and understands that Islamic systems and concepts appearing in the form of qadi, waqf system and the protection of privacy determined the structure of Turkish urban space.

To further the discussion of this new understanding of Turkish urban space, we should aim at a broad view rather than become bogged down in a duality, stressing either Islamic elements or Turkish and nomadic elements.

Scholars of the history of architecture and urban engineering have tended to dismiss the concept of the "Islamic city" as a prejudiced argument invented by Western scholars which asserts that the religion of Islam produced such negative urban characteristics as a labyrinthine structure due to lack of structural planning, the centrality of the mosque and the bazar, and the lack of autonomy. İnalcık's study has tried to modify the concept of the "Islamic city" itself to make it applicable to Turkish cities, giving weight to the argument by new views on the religious authority of the Sultan and the planned nature of the city. The question remains whether İnalcık's thesis can be applied to cities other than Istanbul. Whether we think of Turkish cities in the Islamic context or not, future studies should make every effort to set up a new framework to analyze the information obtained from recent research on Turkish Ottoman cities. The Aga Khan Program is currently sponsoring a project to throw light on urban spatial structure by computerizing the sharia-court registers of Istanbul. New developments can be expected as a result.

Architecture and Its Functions

This section deals first with the main studies, both old and new, on urban buildings in terms of architectural history.

A. Gabriel, "Les mosquées de Constantinople" (1926) and T. Öz, *Mosques in Istanbul* (T., 1962-5) are pioneering works concerning the monumental structures of Istanbul. The best work on Ottoman architecture as a whole is G. Goodwin, *A History of Ottoman Architecture* (1971). One of the most important contributions to the field is a number of studies on early Ottoman architecture by E. H. Ayverdi, *Early Ottoman Architecture* (T., 1966), *Ottoman Architecture in the Ages of Mehmet I and Murat II* (T., 1972) and *Ottoman Architecture in the Age of Mehmet II* (T., 1973-4) and İ. A. Yüksel, *Ottoman Architecture in the Ages of Bayazit II and Selim I* (T., 1983). The series covers the main structures of Ottoman period to the early 16th century, and its value is enhanced by detailed drawings and illustrations with comments on the origins of historical monuments drawn from historical sources. A. Kuran, *The Mosque in Early Ottoman Architecture* (1968), dealing with the development of mosque architectural style, covers the period up to the early 16th century. The middle and late 16th century is the age of Sinan in the history of the Ottoman architecture. As the greatest architect of the time, Sinan and his work have been widely studied. Some representative works are R. M. Meriç, *The Life of the Architect Sinan and his Works* (T., 1965) and A. Kuran, *Sinan: The Grand Old Master of Ottoman Architecture* (1987). For more information, see E. İhsanoğlu (ed.), *A Bibliography about the Architect Sinan and his Works* (T., 1988).

Other studies about cities from an architectural or historico-geographical point of view include *The Waqf Buildings and Historical Heritage of Turkey* (T., 1972 to the present, published by Vakıflar Genel Müdürlüğü), W. Müller-Wiener, *Bildlexikon zur Topographie Istanbuls* (1977), *Mosques in the Eminönü District* (T., 1987, published by Türkiye Diyanet Vakfı), G. Öney, *Religious and Social Buildings of the Turkish Period in Ankara* (T., 1971) and Ergenç, "On Dwelling Conditions in Ankara in the Early 17th Century" (T., 1980). Useful for Eastern Anatolia is T. A. Sinclair, *Eastern Turkey: An Architectural and Archaeological Survey* (1987-90).

Most of the monuments dealt with in these studies were sponsored by the Sultans and were constructed by Ottoman court architects. The activities of court architects as represented by Sinan are studied in Ahmet Refik (Altınay), *Turkish Architects* (T., 1936) and Ş. Turan, "Court Architects in the Ottoman Organization" (T., 1963). Actual construction work is described in Barkan's *The Construction of the Mosque of Süleyman and its Imâret,* a good source for information ranging from the prices of raw materials to the numbers of workers. Water supply was another important element of urban life sponsored by waqf endowments. Istanbul's water supply was organized around the system of the Byzantine period and run by the waqf endowments of Sultans such as Mehmet II and Süleyman I. The system grew with the expansion of the city. A recent contribution to the knowledge of Istanbul's water supply in terms of architectural history and engineering is a series of works by K. Çeçen, *Water Supply Facilities in Istanbul in the Ottoman Period* (T., 1984), *The Waterways of Süleyman I* (T., 1986), *Halkalı Waterways of Istanbul* (T., 1991) and *Üsküdar Waterways of Istanbul* (T., 1991).

A particular feature of urban commercial facilities is that many were endowed as waqf properties for lease. Commercial space in Turkish cities was composed of three elements, the *bedestan* (central market), the caravansary and the shops in the bazar, divided among the various trades. The *bedestan,* a solid building rented by rich textile merchants, money changers or the Treasury (beytü'l-mal), was an institution remarkably developed in Ottoman cities, and was, with the *imâret,* at the core of Ottoman urban planned constructions. The distribution of the *bedestan* is discussed in K. Kreiser, "Bedesten-Bauten im osmanischen Reich" (1979) and the functions of the *bedestan* in İnalcık, "The Hub of the City: The Bedestan of Istanbul" (1979-80). Almost the only historical study of the spatial structure of the market in general, including the bedestan, is E. Wirth, "Zum Problem des Bazars (sūq, çarşı)" (1974-5). M. Cezar, *Typical Commercial Buildings of the Ottoman Classical Period and the Ottoman Construction System* (1983; 1985 in Turkish), has good descriptions of the positions of commercial districts and of actual commercial buildings, but it remains only an introduction.

There are a number of valuable studies of Turkish domestic architecture. This is an important field in urban history, for it is connected with the question of the sedentarization of nomadic Turks and the origin of Turkish cities. However, as most Turkish houses are built of wood, it is difficult to trace their history earlier than the 19th century and caution is needed when applying the study of the existing domestic architecture to historical studies. The study of domestic architecture is made more meaningful when combined with historiographical methodology to reconstruct dwellings based on sharia-court registers of real estate transactions. In addition to Faroqhi's studies of Kayseri and Ankara in *Men of Modest Substance,* descriptions of real estate recorded in Istanbul's sharia-court registers are contained in M. İpşirli, "Waqf Real Estate in Istanbul through Historical Documents" (T., 1989). Studies on domestic dwellings include S. H. Eldem, *Patterns of Turkish Houses* (T., 1954) and id., *Turkish Houses* (T., 1984-7) and A. Arel, *Historical Problems concerning the Ottoman Residential Tradition* (T., 1982). They attempt to integrate studies on domestic dwellings in individual towns and classify the findings into certain patterns. Arel's study is helpful in that it includes a bibliography of the studies of domestic dwellings of each city and town.

Here, I would like to introduce a number of new studies. They share a common tendency in attempting to understand historical monuments in the cultural, political and economic settings in which they had been built and used. G. Necipoğlu, *Architecture, Ceremonial, and Power* (1991) examines the structures and functions of the Topkapı Palace within an historical context. She explains the complicated background to how space was used in the palace, covering Ottoman ceremonies and protocol, the administrative and institutional structure of the empire, and Turkish and Islamic cultural traditions. This work represents the first historical study of a Turkish edifice. Essays contained in R. Lifchez (ed.), *The Dervish Lodge* (1992) shed light on the architecture and functions of Sufi convents (*tekke*) and their cultural activities. H. Crane discusses the ideological meaning expressed in imperial mosques in "The Ottoman Sultan's Mosques" (1991), an article in I. A. Bierman, R. A. Abou-El-Haj and D. Preziosi (eds.), *The Ottoman City and its Parts* (1991), which is a discussion of the relationship between Ottoman political power and urban structure using a cross-disciplinary approach. The work shows that there is a significant trend among scholars in Arabic and Turkish studies belonging to various fields such as history, architecture and sociology to cooperate in studying society and space under Ottoman rule. A similar attempt is also made in D. Panzac (ed.), *Les villes dans l'Empire Ottoman* (1991).

4. Studies on the Transformation of Cities in the 19th Century

Most of the above-mentioned studies deal with pre-modern cities. We will now consider studies concerning urban problems in 19th century Turkey. Most look at the cities in relation to the process of Westernization after the Tanzimat. Discussions centre on two points, the process of administrative reorganization and the transformation of urban layout as a result of modern urban planning.

Studies concerning the formation of a new local administrative organization include M. Çadırcı, "The Establishment of the *Muhtar* System in Turkey" (T., 1970), İ. Ortaylı, *Local Administration after the Tanzimat* (T., 1974) and İ. Tekeli and Ortaylı, *The Evolution of Turkish Municipalities* (T., 1978). Since actual reform occurred mainly in Istanbul, several studies, such as Tekeli, "Nineteenth Century Transformation of Istanbul Metropolitan Area" (1992) and S. Yerasimos, "Occidentalisation de l'espace urbain: Istanbul 1839-1871" (1991) introduce the process of administrative and spatial transformation as it happened there. Essays focusing on social and cultural change in various cities under Ottoman rule are contained in P. Dumont and F. Georgeon (eds.) *Villes ottomanes à la fin de l'empire* (1992).

Spatial reorganization resulted from the adoption of Western methods of urban planning. Z. Çelik, *The Remaking of Istanbul* (1986) discusses the redevelopment of Istanbul and the Westernization movement there in general. Çelik succeeds in illustrating in a visual way the modernization of transportation and other aspects of the urban fabric.

The Tanzimat reforms and new construction were concentrated on the Beyoğlu district of Istanbul. M. Cezar, *19th Century Beyoğlu* (T., 1991) introduces its buildings and cultural activities. Recently in Turkey there has developed a nostalgic interest in "Old Istanbul," focused on Beyoğlu in the 19th and the beginning of the 20th century. A number of studies and memoirs have been published on this topic, and though not all can be regarded as contributing to the urban study of Istanbul, some, such as A. Özdemir, *Beyoğlu* (T., 1988), G. Scognamillo, *A Levantin's Memories of Beyoğlu* (T., 1990) and R. Schiele and W. Müller-Wiener, *Life in 19th Century Istanbul* (T., 1988) contain important information and interesting discussion.

The modernization and Westernization of Ottoman society inevitably brought changes not only in terms of administrative and spatial organization, but also in the life style of the urban population. The transformation of social life is studied in A. Duben and C. Behar, *Istanbul Households* (1991) and P. Dumont and F. Georgeon, "Un bourgeois d'Istanbul au début du XXe siècle" (1985). One reform activity was census-taking along modern lines. Census results provide important information about the exact population and the proportion of the population occupied by each religious group. Population studies which throw light on 19th century social changes and urban transformation include S. Shaw, "The Population of Istanbul in the Nineteenth Century" (1979), M. Çadırcı, "A Study on the Population of the Centre of Ankara Based on the Census in 1830" (T., 1980) and K. H. Karpat, *Ottoman Population 1830-1914: Demographic and Social Characteristics* (1985).

Conclusion

This chapter has summarized the main trend of studies primarily on a chronological basis. It is clear that most studies on Turkish Ottoman cities have been made from the viewpoint of social and economic history using Ottoman archival material, and that the recent focus of research is on the social and physical structure of middle-sized cities in Anatolia. The capital Istanbul is dealt with in the studies concerning modernization process of the Ottoman Empire.

Since my aim has been to give a compact bird's-eye view of the development of urban studies, I have not included all the studies that might be available concerning a particular topic, and am aware that certain deficiencies are consequently inevitable. Even among the limited number of studies cited here, we can still discern particular trends. Why these exist may be discussed on a comparative basis. However, the concept of the "Islamic city" is grossly insufficient as such a framework, and in recent years, joint research projects have tended to study cities under Ottoman rule as "Ottoman cites." This may provide the basis for a new attempt to compare Turkish cities with those of other regions in the Middle East.

Bibliography

Ahmet Refik (Altınay). *Onuncu Asr-ı Hicrî'de İstanbul Hayatı: 961-1000 (Life in Istanbul in the 10th Century A. H.).* İstanbul, 1917. Reprinted in 1935 and 1988.

———. *Hicrî On İkinci Asırda İstanbul Hayatı: 1100-1200 (Life in Istanbul in the 12th Century A. H.).* İstanbul, 1930. Reprinted in1988.

———. *Hicrî On Birinci Asırda İstanbul Hayatı: 1000-1100 (Life in Istanbul in the 11th Century A. H.).* İstanbul, 1931. Reprinted in1988.

———. *Türk Mimarları: Hazine-i Evrak Vesikalarına göre (Turkish Architects).* İstanbul, 1936.

Ahmet Refik (Sevengil). *İstanbul Nasıl Eğleniyordu? (The Amusements of Istanbul).* İstanbul, 1927. Reprinted in 1985.

Ainsworth, W. F. *Travels and Researches in Asia Minor, Mesopotamia, Chaldea and Armenia.* 2 vols. London, 1842.

Aktepe, M. "XVII. Asra ait İstanbul Kazası Avarız Defteri (An Avâriz Register of 17th Century Istanbul)." *İstanbul Enstitüsü Dergisi* 3 (1957).

Aktüre, S. "17. Yüzyıl Başından 19. Yüzyıl Ortasına Kadarki Dönemde Anadolu Osmanlı Şehrinde Şehirsel Yapının Değişme Süreci (The Changing Process of Urban Space in the Ottoman Cities of Anatolia from the Early 17th Century to the Middle of the 19th Century)." *ODTÜ Mimarlık Fakültesi Dergisi* 1/1 (1975).

———. *19. Yüzyıl Sonunda Anadolu Kenti, Mekânsal Yapı Çözümlemesi (Anatolian Cities in the Late 19th Century: An Analysis of Residential Structure).* Ankara, 1978.

Ali Rıza. *Bir Zamanlar İstanbul (Memories of Istanbul).* Edited by N. A. Banoğlu. Tercüman 1001 Temel Eser Series. N.p., n. d. Originally published in 1922.

Anderson, S. *An English Consul in Turkey: Paul Rycaut at Smyrna, 1667-1678.* Oxford, 1989.

Arel, A. *Osmanlı Konut Geleneğinde Tarihsel Sorunları (Historical Problems concerning the Ottoman Residential Tradition).* İzmir, 1982.

Asarkaya, H. *Osmanlı Zamanında Tokat (Tokat during the Ottoman Period).* 2 vols. Tokat, 1941.

Ayverdi, E. H. *Fatih Devri Sonlarında İstanbul Mahalleleri, Şehrin İskânı ve Nüfusu (Quarters, Settlement and Population in Istanbul in the Late Part of the Reign of Mehmed II).* Ankara, 1958.

———. *Osmanlı Mi'mârîsinin İlk Devri: Ertuğrul, Osman, Orhan Gaazîleri, Hüdavendigâr ve Yıldırım Bâyezîd: 630-805/1230-1402 (Early Ottoman Architecture: 630-805/1230-1402).* İstanbul, 1966.

———. *Osmanlı Mi'mârîsinde Çelebi ve II. Sultan Murad Devri: 806-855/1403-1451 (Ottoman Architecture in the Ages of Mehmet I and Murat II).* İstanbul, 1972.

———. *Osmanlı Mi'mârîsinde Fatih Devri: 855-886/1451-1481 (Ottoman Architecture in the Age of Mehmet II).* 2 vols. İstanbul, 1973-4.

Baer, G. "The Administrative, Economic and Social Functions of Turkish Guilds." *IJMES* 1 (1970).

———. "Monopolies and Restrictive Practices of Turkish Guilds." *JESHO* 13/2 (1970).

———. "Ottoman Guilds: A Reassessment." In *Türkiye'nin Sosyal ve Ekonomik Tarihi (1071-1920),* eds. O. Okyar & H. İnalcık. Ankara, 1980.

———. "Women and Waqf: An Analysis of the Istanbul Tahrîr of 1546." *Asian and African Studies* 17 (1983). Reprinted in *Studies in Islamic Society: Contributions in Memory of Gabriel Baer,* eds. G. R. Warburg & G. G. Gilbar. Haifa, 1984.

Barkan, Ö. L. "Osmanlı İmparatorluğunda bir İskân ve Kolonizasyon Metodu olarak Vakıflar ve Temlikler(Waqf Endowment and Private Land as the Means of Sedentarization and Settlement in the Ottoman Empire)." *Vakıflar Dergisi* 2 (1942).

———. "XV. Asrın Sonunda Bazı Büyük Şehirlerde Eşya ve Yiyecek Fiyatlarının Tesbit ve Teftişi Hususlarını Tanzim eden Kanunlar (Kanun Enacted for the Purpose of Controlling Prices of Goods and Foodstuffs in Some Major Cities in the Late 15th Century)." *Tarih Vesikaları* 1/5 (1942); 2/7 (1942); 2/9 (1942).

———. *XV ve XVIıncı Asırlarda Osmanlı İmparatorluğunda Zirâî Ekonominin Hukûkî ve Mâlî Esasları (The Legal and Financial Foundation of Agricultural Economy in the Ottoman Empire in the 15th and 16th Centuries).* Vol. 1: *Kanunlar (Collection of Kanunnames).* İstanbul, 1943.

———. "Osmanlı İmparatorluğu'nda bir İskân ve Kolonizasyon Metodu olarak Sürgünler (Forced Migration as the Means of Sedentarization and Settlement in the Ottoman Empire)." *İktisat Fakültesi Mecmuası* 11 (1949-50); 13 (1951-2); 15 (1953-4).

———. "Tarihî Demografi Araştırmaları ve Osmanlı Tarihi (Historical Demography and Ottoman History)." *Türkiyat Mecmuası* 10 (1953).

———. "Essai sur les données statistiques des registres de recensement dans l'Empire Ottoman aux XVe et XVIe siècles." *JESHO* 1/1 (1957).

———. "Ayarofya Cami'i ve Eyüp Türbesinin 1489-91 Yıllarına âit Muhasebe Bilânçoları (The 1489-1491 Muhasebe Register of the Ayasofya Mosque and the Eyüp Mausoleum)." *İktisat Fakültesi Mecmuası* 23 (1962-3).

———. "Fatih Câmi ve İmareti Tesîslerinin 1489-90 Yıllarına âit Muhasebe Bilânçoları (The 1489-1490 Muhasebe Register of the Fatih Mosque and its Imâret)." *İktisat Fakültesi Mecmuası* 23 (1962-3).

———. "Şehirlerin Teşekkül ve İnkişafı Tarihi Bakımından Osmanlı İmparatorluğunda İmâret Sitelerinin Kuruluş ve İşleyiş Tarzına âit Araştırmalar (A Study on the Construction and Administration of Imâret in the Ottoman Empire from the Historical Viewpoint of the Formations and Development of Cities)." *İktisat Fakültesi Mecmuası* 23 (1962-3).

———. "Edirne ve Civarındaki Bazı İmâret Tesislerinin Yıllık Muhasebe Bilânçoları (The Annual Muhasebe Register of Some Soup Kitchens in Edirne and its Surroundings)." *Belgeler* 1/2 (1965).

———. "Edirne Askerî Kassamı'na âit Tereke Defteri: 1545-1659 (Inheritance Lists Preserved at the Inheritance Office of Military Personnel in Edirne: 1545-1659)." *Belgeler* 3/5-6 (1968).

———. "Research on the Ottoman Fiscal Suveys." In *Studies in the Economic History of the Middle East*, ed. M. A. Cook. London, 1970.

———. "XVI. Asrın İkinci Yarısında Türkiye'de Fiat Hareketleri (Price Fluctuations in the Latter Half of the 16th Century in Turkey)." *Belleten* 136 (1970).

———. "Süleymaniye Cami ve İmareti Tesislerine âit Yıllık bir Muhasebe Bilançosu 993/994 (1585/1586) (The Annual Muhasebe Register of the Mosque of Süleyman I and its Imâret of 1585/86)." *Vakıflar Dergisi* 9 (1971).

———. *Süleymaniye Cami ve İmareti İnşaatı: 1550-1557 (The Construction of the Mosque of Süleyman and its Imâret: 1550-1557).* 2 vols. Ankara, 1972-9.

Barkan, Ö. L. & E. H. Ayverdi. *İstanbul Vakıfları Tahrîr Defteri: 953 (1546) Târîhli (A Waqf Survey Register of Istanbul of Dated1546)*. İstanbul, 1970.

Barkan, Ö. L. & E. Meriçli. *Hüdavendigâr Livası Tahrir Defteri (A Land Survey Register of Bursa District)*. Vol. 1. Ankara, 1988.

Bayatlı, O. *Bergama Tarihinde Türk-İslâm Eserleri (Turko-Islamic Buildings in the History of Bergama)*. İstanbul, 1956.

Baykara, T. *Türkiye Selçukluları Devrinde Konya (Konya in the Rum Seljuk Period)*. Ankara, 1985.

Beldiceanu, N. *Recherche sur la ville ottomane au XVe siècle: Etude et actes*. Paris, 1973.

Beldiceanu, N. & I. Beldiceanu-Steinherr. *Recherche sur la province de Qaraman au XVIe siècle: Etude et actes*. Leyde, 1968.

Bierman, I. A., R. A. Abou-El-Haj & D. Preziosi, eds. *The Ottoman City and its Parts: Urban Structure and Social Order*. New Rochelle, 1991.

Braude, B. & B. Lewis, eds. *Christians and Jews in the Ottoman Empire: The Functioning of a Plural Society*. 2 vols. New York & London, 1982.

Braudel, F. *La Méditerranée et le monde méditerranéen à l'époque de Philippe II*. 2nd ed. 2 vols. Paris, 1966.

Bruinessen, M. van & H. Boeschoten. *Evliya Çelebi in Diyarbekir: The Relevant Section of the Seyahatname edited with Translation, Commentary and Introduction*. Leiden et al. 1988.

Celâl Esad (Djelâl Essad). *Constantinople, de Byzance à Stamboul*. Paris, 1909.

———. *Eski Galata ve Binaları (Old Galata and its Monuments)*. İstanbul, 1329/1913. Reprinted in 1989.

Cezar, M. *Typical Commercial Buildings of the Ottoman Classical Period and the Ottoman Construction System*. İstanbul, 1983 . Translated into Turkish as *Tipik Yapılariyle Osmanlı Şehirciliğinde Çarşı ve Klasik Dönem İmar Sistemi*. İstanbul, 1985.

———. *XIX.Yüzyıl Beyoğlusu (19th Century Beyoğlu)*. İstanbul, 1991.

Cook, M. A. *Population Pressure in Rural Anatolia: 1450-1600*. London, 1972.

Crane, H. "The Ottoman Sultan's Mosques: Icons of Imperial Legitimacy." In *The Ottoman City and its Parts: Urban Structure and Social Order*, eds. I. A. Bierman, R. A. Abou-El-Haj & D. Preziosi. New Rochelle, 1991.

Cuinet, V. *La Turquie d'Asie: Géographie administrative, statistique descriptive et raisonée de chaque province de l'Asie Mineure*. 4 vols. Paris, 1892-4.

Çadırcı, M. "Türkiye'de Muhtarlık Teşkilatının Kurulması üzerine bir İnceleme (The Establishment of the Muhtar System in Turkey)." *Belleten* 135 (1970).

———. "1830 Genel Sayımına göre Ankara Şehir Merkezi Nüfusu üzerine bir Araştırma (A Study on the Population of the Centre of Ankara Based on the Census in 1830)." *Osmanlı Araştırmaları* 1 (1980).

Çağatay, N. *Bir Türk Kurumu olan Ahilik (The Ahî Organization as a Turkish Organization)*. Konya, 1974.

Çeçen, K. *İstanbul'da Osmanlı Devrindeki Su Tesisleri (Water Supply Facilities in Istanbul in the Ottoman Period)*. İstanbul, 1984.

———. *Süleymaniye Suyolları (The Waterways of Süleyman I)*. İstanbul, 1986.

———. *İstanbul'un Vakıf Sularından Halkalı Suları (Halkalı Waterways of Istanbul)*. İstanbul, 1991.

———. *İstanbul'un Vakıf Sularından Üsküdar Suları (Üsküdar Waterways of Istanbul)*. İstanbul, 1991.

Çelik, Z. *The Remaking of Istanbul*. Seattle & London, 1986.

Çızakça, M. "Price History and the Bursa Silk Industry: A Study in Ottoman Industrial Decline 1550-1650." *Journal of Economic History* 40/3 (1980).

———. "A Short History of the Bursa Silk Industry (1500-1900)." *JESHO* 23/1-2 (1980).

Dalsar, F. *Türk Sanayi ve Ticaret Tarihinde Bursa'da İpekçilik (Bursa's Silk Textile Industry in the History of Turkish Industry and Trade)*. İstanbul, 1960.

Dankoff, R. *Evliya Çelebi in Bitlis: The Relevant Section of the Seyahatname edited with Translation, Commentary and Introduction*. Leiden, 1990.

Duben, A. & C. Behar. *Istanbul Households: Marriage, Family and Fertility 1880-1940*. Cambridge, 1991.

Duman, H. , ed. *Osmanlı Yıllıkları (Yearbooks of the Ottoman Empire)*. İstanbul, 1982.

Dumont, P. & F. Georgeon. "Un bourgeois d'Istanbul au début du XXe siècle." *Turcica* 17 (1985).

———, eds. *Villes ottomanes à la fin de l'Empire*. Paris, 1992.

Eldem, S. H. *Türk Evi Plan Tipleri (Patterns of Turkish Houses)*. İstanbul, 1954.

———. *Türk Evi (Turkish Houses)*. 3 vols. İstanbul, 1984-7.

Emecen, F. *XVI. Asırda Manisa Kazâsı (Manisa District in the 16th Century)*. Ankara, 1989.

Eminönü Camileri (Mosques in the Eminönü District). Pulished by Türkiye Diyanet Vakfı. İstanbul, 1987.

Epstein, M. A. *The Ottoman Jewish Communities and their Role in the Fifteenth and Sixteenth Centuries*. Freiburg, 1980.

Erder, L. "The Measurement of Pre-Industrial Population Changes: The Ottoman Empire from the 15th to the 17th Century." *Middle Eastern Studies* 11/3 (1975).

Erder, L. & S. Faroqhi. "Population Rise and Fall in Anatolia 1550-1620." *Middle Eastern Studies* 15/3 (1979).

———. "The Development of the Anatolian Urban Network during the Sixteenth Century." *JESHO* 23/3 (1980).

Ergenç, Ö. "1600-1615 Yılları Arasında Ankara İktisadî Tarihine ait Araştırmalar (A Study on the Economic History of Ankara from 1600 to 1615)." In *Türkiye İktisat Tarihi Semineri*, eds. O. Okyar & Ü. Nalbantoğlu. Ankara, 1975.

———. "XVII. Yüzyıl Başlarında Ankara'nın Yerleşim Durumu üzerine Bazı Bilgiler (On Dwelling Conditions in Ankara in the Early 17th Century)." *Osmanlı Araştırmaları* 1 (1980).

———. "Osmanlı Şehirlerindeki Yönetim Kurumlarının Niteliği üzerinde Bazı Düşünceler." In *VIII. Türk Tarih Kongresi, Ankara 11-15 Ekim 1976, Kongreye Sunulan Bildiriler*. Vol. 2. Ankara, 1981. Translated into English as "Some Notes on the Administration Units of the Ottoman Cities." In *Urbanism in Islam: The Proceedings of the International Conference on Urbanism in Islam, Oct. 22-28, 1989*. Vol. 1. Tokyo, 1989.

———. "Osmanlı Klâsik Dönemindeki "Eşraf ve A'yan" üzerine Bazı Bilgiler (Eşrâf and Âyan in the Ottoman Classical Period)." *Osmanlı Araştırmaları* 3 (1982).

———. "Osmanlı Şehrindeki "Mahalle"nin İşrev ve Nitelikleri üzerine (Functions and Characteristics of Quarters in Ottoman Cities)." *Osmanlı Araştırmaları* 4 (1984).

Ergin, Osman Nuri. *Mecelle-i Umur-u Belediye (The Compendium of Municipal Administration)*. 5 vols. İstanbul, 1914-22.

———. *Türkiyede Şehirciliğin Tarihî İnkişafi (The Historical Development of the Municipal Administration in Turkey)*. İstanbul, 1936.

———. *İstanbulda İmar ve İskân Hareketleri (The Reconstruction Work of Istanbul)*. İstanbul, 1938.

———. *Türk Şehirlerinde İmaret Sistemi (The Imâret System in Turkish Cities)*. İstanbul, 1939.

———, ed. *Farih İmareti Vakfiyesi (The Waqf Endowment Deeds of Imâret of Mehmet II)*. İstanbul, 1945.

Eroğlu, Z. *Muğla Tarihi (A History of Muğla)*. İzmir, 1939.

Faroqhi, S. "Sixteenth Century Periodic Markets in Various Anatolian Sancaks." *JESHO* 22/1 (1979).

———. "Taxation and Urban Activities in Sixteenth-Century Anatolia." *International Journal of Turkish Studies* 1/1 (1979-80).

———. "A Map of Anatolian Friday Mosques: 1520-1535." *Osmanlı Araştırmaları* 4 (1984).

———. *Towns and Townsmen of Ottoman Anatolia: Trade, Crafts and Food Production in an Urban Setting, 1520-1650*. Cambridge, 1984.

———. *Men of Modest Substance: House Owners and House Property in Seventeenth-Century Ankara and Kayseri*. Cambridge, 1987.

———. "Towns, Agriculture and the State in Sixteenth-Century Ottoman Anatolia." *JESHO* 33/2 (1990).

Frangakis-Syrett, E. "The Raya Communities of Smyrna in the 18th Century (1690-1820): Demography and Economic Activities." In *The Neohelenic City: Ottoman Heritage, International Symposium of History*. Athens, 1985.

———. "Trade between Ottoman Empire and Western Europe: The Case of Izmir in the Eighteenth Century." *New Perspective on Turkey* 2/1 (1988).

———. "The Greek Mercantile Community of Izmir in the First Half of the Nineteenth Century." In *Les villes dans l'Empire Ottoman: Activités et sociétés*, ed. D. Panzac. Vol. 1. Paris, 1991.

Gabriel, A. "Les mosquées de Constantinople." *Syria* 7 (1926).
———. *Monuments turcs d'Anatolie*. 2 vols. Paris, 1931-4.
———. *Voyages archéologiques dans la Turquie orientale*. 2 vols. Paris, 1940.
———. *Une capitale turque: Brousse*. 2 vols. Paris, 1958.
Galanté, A. *Histoire des Juifs d'Istanbul*. 2 vols. Istanbul, 1941-2.
Gerber, H. "Guilds in Seventeenth-Century Anatolian Bursa." *Asian and African Studies* 11 (1976). Reprinted in *Economy and Society in an Ottoman City: Bursa*. Jerusalem, 1988.
———. "Social and Economic Position of Women in an Ottoman City, Bursa: 1600-1700." *IJMES* 12 (1980).
———. "Sharia, Kanun and Custom in the Ottoman Law: The Court Records of 17th-Century Bursa." *International Journal of Turkish Studies* 2/1 (1981). Reprinted in *Economy and Society in an Ottoman City: Bursa*. Jerusalem, 1988.
———. "The Waqf Institution in Early Ottoman Edirne." *Asian and African Studies* 17 (1983). Reprinted in *Studies in Islamic Society: Contributions in Memory of Gabriel Baer*, eds. G. R. Warburg & G. G. Gilbar. Haifa, 1984.
———. *Economy and Society in an Ottoman City: Bursa, 1600-1700*. Jerusalem, 1988.
Gibb, H. A. R. & H. Bowen. *Islamic Society and the West*. 2 vols. London, 1950-7.
Goffman, D. *Izmir and the Levantine World, 1550-1650*. Seattle & London, 1990.
Goodwin, G. *A History of Ottoman Architecture*. Baltimore & London, 1971.
Gökbilgin, T. *XV-XVI. Asırlarda Edirne ve Paşa Livâsı (Edirne and Rumeli Province in the 15th and 16th Centuries)*. İstanbul, 1952.
Gökçen, İ. *16. ve 17. Asır Sicillerine göre Saruhan'da Yürük ve Türkmenler (The Nomads and Turkmen in Saruhan in the 16th and 17th Centuries through Sharia-Court Registers)*. İstanbul, 1946.
———. *Sicillere göre XVI. ve XVII. Asırlarda Saruhan Zaviye ve Yatırları (Sufi Convents and Saints' Mausolea in Saruhan in the 16th and 17th Centuries through Sharia-Court Registers)*. İstanbul, 1946.
———. *Manisa Tarihinde Vakıflar ve Hayırlar (The Waqf Endowments and Charitable Institutions in the History of Manisa)*. 2 vols. İstanbul, 1946-50.
Gölpınarlı, A. "İslâm ve Türk İllerinde Fütüvvet Teşkilâtı ve Kaynakları (The Futuwwa Organizations in Turkey and the Islamic World and Historical Material concerning it)." *İktisat Fakültesi Mecmuası* 11 (1949-50).
Göyünç, N. *XVI. Yüzyılda Mardin Sancağı (Mardin Province in the 16th Century)*. İstanbul, 1969.
———. "Hane Deyimi Hakkında (On the Term 'hane')." *Tarih Dergisi* 32 (1979).
Gyllius, P. *De topographia Constantinopoleos et de illius antiquitatibus*. Lyon, 1561.
Hâfız Hüseyin Ayvansarayî. *Hadîkatü'l-Cevâmi (The Flower Gardens of Mosques)*. 2 vols. İstanbul, 1281/1864-5.
Hammer, J. von. *Constantinopolis und der Bosporos*. 2 vols. Budapest, 1822.

———. *Narrative of Travels in Europe, Asia, and Africa in the Seventeenth Century by Evliyá Efendí*. 2 vols. London, 1834-46.

Hayashi (Yamamoto), Kayoko. "15 seiki kohan no Isutanburu: Mehumeto Nisei no fukkosaku o chushinni (Istanbul in the Latter Half of the 15th Century: The Reconstruction Policy of Mehmet II)." *Ochanomizu Shigaku* 25 (1982).

———. "The *Vakıf* Institution in 16th-Century Istanbul: An Analysis of the *Vakıf* Survey Register of 1546." *The Memoirs of the Toyo Bunko* 50 (1992).

Heyd, U. "The Jewish Communities of Istanbul in the XVIIth Century." *Oriens* 6 (1953).

———. *Studies in Old Ottoman Criminal Law*. Edited by V. L. Ménage. Oxford, 1973.

Hüseyin Hüsameddin. *Amasya Tarihi (A History of Amasya)*. 4 volumes and a supplement. İstanbul, 1327/1911-2, 1329/1913-4, 1927, 1928, 1935.

İhsanoğlu, E., ed. *Mimar Sinan ve Yapılarıyla ilgili Eserleri Bibliyografyası (A Bibliography about the Architect Sinan and his Works)*. Ankara, 1988.

İnalcık, H. "Ottoman Methods of Conquest." *SI* 2 (1954).

———. "Bursa and the Commerce of the Levant." *JESHO* 3/2 (1960).

———. "Bursa I, XV. Asır Sanayi ve Ticaret Tarihine dair Vesikalar (Bursa I: Historical Materials concerning 15th Century Industry and Trade)." *Belleten* 24 (1960).

———. "Capital Formation in the Ottoman Empire." *Journal of Economic History* 29 (1969).

———. "The Ottoman Economic Mind and Aspects of the Ottoman Economy." In *Studies in the Economic History of the Middle East*, ed. M. A. Cook. London, 1970.

———. "The Policy of Mehmed II toward the Greek Population of Istanbul and the Byzantine Buildings of the City." *Dumbarton Oaks Papers* 23-24 (1970).

———. *The Ottoman Empire, The Classical Age 1300-1600*. Translated by N. Itzkowitz & C. Imber. London, 1973.

———. "Centralization and Decentralization in Ottoman Administration." In *Studies in Eighteenth Century Islamic History*, eds. T. Naff & R. Owen. Carbondale & Edwardsville, 1977.

———. "Impact of the *Annales* School on Ottoman Studies and New Findings." *Review* 1/3-4 (1978).

———. "The Hub of the City: The Bedestan of Istanbul." *International Journal of Turkish Studies* 1/1 (1979-80).

———. "Osmanlı İdare, Sosyal ve Ekonomik Tarihiyle ilgili Belgeler: Bursa Kadı Sicillerinden Seçmeler (Historical Materials concerning Ottoman Administrative, Social, and Economic History: A Selection of Bursa Sharia-Court Registers)." *Belgeler* 10/14 (1981).

———. "Istanbul: An Islamic City." *Journal of Islamic Studies* 1 (1990).

İpşirli, M. "Arşiv Belgelerine göre İstanbul Vakıf Evleri: Müştemilât, Tamir, Kira, Satış (Waqf Real Estate in Istanbul through Historical Documents)." In *Tarih Boyunca İstanbul Semineri, 29 Mayıs - 1 Haziran 1988, Bildiriler*. İstanbul, 1989.

Jennings, R. "Loan and Credit in Early 17th Century Judicial Records: The Sharia Court of Anatolian Kayseri." *JESHO* 16/2-3 (1973).

———. "Women in Early 17th Century Ottoman Judicial Records: The Sharia Court of Anatolian Kayseri." *JESHO* 18/1 (1975).

———. "Urban Population in Anatolia in the Sixteenth Century." *IJMES* 7 (1976).

———. "Kadi, Court and Legal Procedure in 17th C. Ottoman Kayseri." *SI* 48 (1978).

———. "Zimmis (Non-Muslims) in Early 17th Century Ottoman Judicial Records: The Sharia Court of Anatolian Kayseri." *JESHO* 21/3 (1978).

———. "Limitations of the Judicial Powers of the Kadi in 17th C. Ottoman Kayseri." *SI* 50 (1979).

Karpat, K. H. *Ottoman Population 1830-1914: Demographic and Social Characteristics*. Madison, 1985.

Koçu, R. E., ed. *İstanbul Ansiklopedisi (The Encyclopedia of Istanbul)*. 10 vols. İstanbul, 1959-71.

Konyalı, İ. H. *Abideleri ve Kitabeleri ile Erzurum Tarihi (A History of Erzurum through its Historical Structures and Epitaphs)*. İstanbul, 1960.

———. *Abideleri ve Kitabeleri ile Konya Tarihi (A History of Konya through its Historical Structures and Epitaphs)*. Konya, 1964.

———. *Abideleri ve Kitabeleri ile Karaman Tarihi (A History of Karaman through its Historical Structures and Epitaphs)*. İstanbul, 1967.

———. *Abideleri ve Kitabeleri ile Üsküdar Tarihi (A History of Üsküdar through its Historical Structures and Epitaphs)*. 2 vols. İstanbul, 1976-7.

Konyar, B. *Diyarbekir (City of Diyarbakır)*. 3 vols. N. p., 1936.

Koray, E. *Türkiye Tarih Yayınlar Bibliyografyası (Bibliography of Publications on History in Turkey)*. İstanbul, 1952-.

Kreiser, K. "Bedesten-Bauten im osmanischen Reich: Ein vorläufiger Überblick auf Grund der Schriftquellen." *Istanbuler Mitteilungen* 29 (1979).

Kuban, D. "Anadolu-Türk Şehri Tarihî Gelişmesi, Sosyal ve Fizikî Özellikleri üzerinde Bazı Gelişmeler (Historical Development and Social and Structural Development of Anatolian Turkish City)." *Vakıflar Dergisi* 7 (1968).

Kuran, A. *The Mosque in Early Ottoman Architecture*. Chicago & London, 1968.

———. *Sinan: The Grand Old Master of Ottoman Architecture*. İstanbul, 1987.

Kürkçüoğlu, K. E., ed. *Süleymaniye Vakfiyesi (The Waqf Endowment Deed of Süleyman I)*. Ankara, 1962.

Kütükoğlu, M. "1009/1600 Tarihli Narh Defterine göre İstanbul'da Çeşitli Eşya ve Hizmet Fiatları (Prices and Wages in Istanbul through a Narh Register Dated 1009/1600)." *Tarih Enstitüsü Dergisi* 9 (1978).

———. *Osmanlılarda Narh Müessesesi ve 1640 Tarihli Narh Defteri (The Ottoman Narh System and a Narh Register of 1640)*. İstanbul, 1983.

Lewis, B. "The Islamic Guilds." *Economic History Review* 8/1 (1937).

Lifchez, R., ed. *The Dervish Lodge: Architecture, Art, and Sufism in Ottoman Turkey.* Berkeley, Los Angeles & Oxford, 1992.

Lowry, H. W. *Trabzon Şehrinin İslâmlaşma ve Türkleşmesi, 1461-1583 (Islamization and Turkicization of Trabzon, 1461-1583).* İstanbul, 1981.

Mandaville, J. E. "Usurious Piety: The Cash Waqf Controversy in the Ottoman Empire." *IJMES* 10 (1979).

Mantran, R. *Un document sur l'ihtisâb de Stamboul à la fin du XVIIe siècle.* Damas, 1957.

———. *Istanbul dans la seconde moitié du XVIIe siècle.* Paris, 1962.

———. "Minoritaires, métiers-marchands étrangers à Istanbul aux XVIe et XVIIe siècles." In *Actes du colloque sur les minorités.* Aix-en-Provence, 1980.

Mayer, R. *Byzantion, Konstantinopolis, Istanbul: Eine genetische Stadtgeographie.* Wien & Leipzig, 1943.

Mehmed Râif. *Mir'ât-ı İstanbul (The Mirror of Istanbul).* 2 vols. İstanbul, 1314/1896-7, 1327/1911-2.

Mehmed Ziya. *İstanbul ve Boğaziçi (Istanbul and the Bosphorus).* 2 vols. İstanbul, 1336/1920, 1928.

Meriç, R. M. *Mimar Sinan Hayatı, Eseri (The Life of the Architect Sinan and his Works).* Ankara, 1965.

Miroğlu, İ. *XVI. Yüzyılda Bayburt Sancağı (Bayburt Province in the 16th Century).* İstanbul, 1975.

———. *Kemah Sancağı ve Erzincan Kazası, 1520-1566 (Kemah Province and Erzincan District, 1520-1566).* Ankara, 1990.

Moltke, H. von. *Briefe über Zustände und Begebenheiten in der Türkei aus den Jahren 1835 bis 39.* Berlin, 1841.

Mordtmann, A. D. "Esquisse topographique de Constantinople." *Revue de l'art chrétien* 4/2 (1891).

Müller-Wiener, W. *Bildlexikon zur Topographie Istanbuls: Byzantion-Konstantinupolis-Istanbul bis zum Beginn des 17. Jahrhunderts.* Tübingen, 1977.

Musahipzade Celâl. *Eski İstanbul Yaşayışı (The Old Life Style of Istanbul).* İstanbul, 1946.

Nagata, Yuzo. *Materials on the Bosnian Notables.* Studia Culturae Islamicae (ILCAA, Tokyo University of Foreign Studies) 11. Tokyo, 1979.

———. "Zenkindai Toruko ni okeru chiikishakai no keisei to wakufu seido (The Formation of Regional Society and the Waqf System in Pre-Modern Turkey)." In *Nishi to higashi to,* ed. Keio Gijuku Daigaku Toyoshi Kenkyushitu. Tokyo, 1985.

———. "Rekishi no nakano ayan: 19 seiki shoto Toruko chiho shakai no han'ei (Âyan in History: The Prosperity of Turkish Local Society in the Early 19th Century)." *Shakaishi Kenkyu* 7 (1986).

Necipoğlu, G. *Architecture, Ceremonial and Power: The Topkapı Palace in the Fifteenth and Sixteenth Centuries.* New York, 1991.

Oberhummer, E. "Constantinopolis." In *Real-Encyclopädie der classischen Altertums-wissenshaft* (Paulys-Wissowa). Vol. 4. Stuttgart, 1901.

———. *Konstantinopel unter Sultan Suleiman dem Großen: Aufgenommen im Jahre 1559 durch Melchior Lorichs*. München, 1902.

d'Ohsson, M. *Tableau général de l'Empire Ottoman*. 3 vols. Paris, 1787-1820.

Ongan, H. *Ankara'nın 1 Numaralı Şer'iye Sicili (The First Sharia-Court Register of Ankara)*. Ankara, 1958.

———. *Ankara'nın İki Numaralı Şer'iye Sicili (The Second Sharia-Court Register of Ankara)*. Ankara, 1974.

Orhonlu, C. *Osmanlı İmparatorluğunda Aşiretleri İskân Teşebbüsü: 1691-1696 (The Settlement of Nomads in the Ottoman Empire: 1691-1696)*. İstanbul, 1963.

———. *Osmanlı İmparatorluğunda Derbend Teşkilâtı (The Derbend Organization in the Ottoman Empire)*. İstanbul, 1967.

———. "Meslekî bir Teşekkül olarak Kaldırımcılık ve Osmanlı Şehir Yolları hakkında Bazı Düşünceler (Comments on the Occupation of Road Construction and Roads in Ottoman Cities)." *Güney-Doğu Avrupa Araştırmaları Dergisi* 1 (1972).

———. *Osmanlı İmparatorluğunda Şehircilik ve Ulaşım üzerine Araştırmalar (Studies on Urban Administration and Transportation in the Ottoman Empire)*. İzmir, 1984.

Ortaylı, İ. *Tanzimattan sonra Mahalli İdareleri, 1840-1878 (Local Administration after the Tanzimat: 1840-1878)*. Ankara, 1974.

Öney, G. *Ankara'da Türk Devri Dini ve Sosyal Yapıları (Religious and Social Buildings of the Turkish Period in Ankara)*. Ankara, 1971.

Öz, T. *İstanbul Camileri (Mosques in Istanbul)*. 2 vols. Ankara, 1962-5.

———, ed. *Zwei Stiftungsurkunden des Sultans Mehmed II. Fatih*. Istanbul, 1935.

Özdeğer, H. *1463-1640 Yılları Bursa Şehri Tereke Defterleri (Inheritance Lists of Bursa from 1463 to 1640)*. İstanbul, 1988.

———. *Onaltıncı Asırda Ayıntâb Livâsı (Ayıntab Province in the 16th Century)*. Vol. 1. İstanbul, 1988.

Özdemir, A. *Beyoğlu: Kısa Geçmişi, Argosu (Beyoğlu: Short History and Slangs)*. İstanbul, 1988.

Özdemir, R. *XIX. Yüzyılın İlk Yarısında Ankara: Fizikî, Demografik, İdarî, ve Sosyo-Ekonomik Yapısı, 1785-1840 (Ankara in the First Half of the 19th Century: Physical, Domographical, Administrative and Socio-economic Structure, 1785-1840)*. Ankara, 1986.

Özkaya, Y. *Osmanlı İmparatorluğunda Âyânlık (The Âyan System in the Ottoman Empire)*. Ankara, 1977.

Panzac, D., ed. *Les villes dans l'Empire Ottoman: Activités et sociétés*. Vol.1. Paris, 1991.

Peremeci, O. N. *Edirne Tarihi (A History of Edirne)*. İstanbul, 1939.

Rıdvan Nafız & İsmail Hakkı (Uzunçarşılı). *Sivas Şehri (City of Sivas)*. İstanbul, 1346/1927-8.

Ritter, K. *Die Erdkunde*. 22 vols. Berlin, 1832-59.

Sahillioğlu, H. "Osmanlılarda Narh Müessesesi ve 1525 Yılı Sonunda İstanbul'da Fiatlar (The Narh System in the Ottoman Empire and Prices in Istanbul at the End of 1525)." *Belgelerle Türk Tarihi Dergisi* 1 (1967); 2 (1967); 3 (1967).

———. "Onbeşinci Yüzyıl Sonunda Bursa'da İş ve Sanayi Hayatı: Kölelikten Patronluğa (Labour and the Industrial Life of Bursa in the Late 15th Century: From Slaves to Patrons)." In *Mémorial Ömer Lûtfi Barkan*, ed. R. Mantran. Paris, 1980.

———. "Onbeşinci Yüzyılın Sonu ile Onaltıncı Yüzyılın Başında Bursa'da Kölelerin Sosyal ve Ekonomik Hayattaki Yeri." *ODTÜ Gelişme Dergisi* 1979-80 Özel Sayısı (1981). Translated into English as "Slaves in the Social and Economic Life of Bursa in the Late 15th and Early 16th Centuries." *Turcica* 17 (1985).

Saint-Martin, M. V. de. *Description historique et géographique de l'Asie Mineure*. 2 vols. Paris, 1852.

Sak, İ. "Konya'da Köleler: 16. Yüzyıl Sonu-17. Yüzyıl (Slaves in Konya: From the Late 16th to the 17th Century)." *Osmanlı Araştırmaları* 9 (1989).

Schiele, R. & W. Müller-Wiener. *19. Yüzyılda İstanbul Hayatı (Life in 19th Century Istanbul)*. İstanbul, 1988.

Scognamillo, G. Bir Levantenin Beyoğlu Anıları (*A Levantin's Memories of Beyoğlu*). İstanbul, 1990.

Shaw, S. "The Population of Istanbul in Nineteenth Century." *IJMES* 10 (1979).

Shmuelevitz, A. *The Jews of the Ottoman Empire in the Late Fifteenth and the Sixteenth Centuries: Administrative, Economic, Legal and Social Relations as Reflected in the Responsa*. Leiden, 1984.

Simsar, M. A. *The Waqfiyah of 'Aḥmed Pāšā*. London, 1940.

Sinclair, T. A. *Eastern Turkey: An Architectural and Archaeological Survey*. 4 vols. London, 1987-90.

Sözen, M. *Anadolu'da Akkoyunlu Mimarisi (Akkoyunlu Architecture in Anatolia)*. İstanbul, 1981.

Su, K. *XVII ve XVIIIinci Yüzyıllarda Balıkesir Şehir Hayatı (Urban Life in Balıkesir in the 17th and 18th Centuries)*. İstanbul, 1937.

Taeschner, F. *Das anatolische Wegenetz nach osmanischen Quellen*. 2 vols. Leipzig, 1924-6.

———. "Futuwwa-Studien, die Futuwwabünde in der Türkei und ihre Literatur." *Islamica* 5 (1932).

———. "Das Zunftwesen in der Türkei." *Leipziger Vierteljahrsschrift für Südosteuropa* 5 (1941).

———. "akhī," "akhī baba," "futuwwa." In *EI*², 1956-65.

Tanışık, İ. H. *İstanbul Çeşmeleri (Fountains of Istanbul)*. 2 vols. İstanbul, 1943-5.

Tanyeli, U. *Anadolu-Türk Kentinde Fiziksel Yapının Evrim Sürecisi: 11.-15. yy (The Transformation Process of Urban Space in Anatolian Turkish Cities: 11th-15th Centuries)*. İstanbul, 1987.

Tekeli, İ. "Nineteenth Century Transformation of Istanbul Metropolitan Area." In *Villes ottomanes à la fin de l'Empire*, eds. P. Dumont & F. Georgeon. Paris, 1992.

Tekeli, İ. & İ. Ortaylı. *Türkiye'de Belediyeciliğin Evrimi (The Evolution of Turkish Municipalities)*. Ankara, 1978.

Texier, C. *Asie Mineure, description géographique, historique et archéologique des provinces et des villes de la chersonnèse d'Asie*. 2 vols. Paris, 1862.

Todorov, N. *The Balkan City, 1400-1900*. Seattle & London. 1983. English translation of *Balkanskiiat Grad, XIV-XIX Vek*. Sofia, 1972.

Trak, S. *Türkiyeye ait Coğrafî Eserler Genel Bibliyografyası (A Bibliography of Studies on the Geography of Turkey)*. Ankara, 1942.

Tuncer, O. C. *Anadolu Selçuklu Mimarisi ve Moğollar (Architecture of the Rum Seljuk Period and the Mongols)*. N. p., 1986.

Turan, O. "Selçuklular Zamanında Sivas Şehri (Sivas in the Seljuk Period)." *Ankara Üniversitesi Dil ve Tarih-Coğrafya Fakültesi Dergisi* 9/4 (1951).

Turan, Ş. "Osmanlı Teşkilâtında Hassa Mimarları (Court Architects in the Ottoman Organization)." *Tarih Araştırmaları Dergisi* 1/1 (1963).

Türk Dünyası Araştırmaları Vakfı (The Foundation for the Study of Turkish World). *Şer'iye Sicilleri (Sharia-Court Registers)*. 2 vols. İstanbul, 1988-9.

Türk Kültürü ve Ahilik: XXI. Ahilik Bayramı Sempozyumu Tebliğileri, 13-15 Eylül 1985, Kırşehir (Turkish Culture and the Ahî Organization: The Proceedings of the Symposium). İstanbul, 1986.

Türkiye'de Vakıf Abideler ve Eski Eserler (The Waqf Buildings and Historical Heritage of Turkey). Published by Vakıflar Genel Müdürlüğü. Ankara, 1972-.

Uluçay, M. Ç. *XVIIinci Yüzyılda Manisa'da Ziraat, Ticaret ve Esnaf Teşkilâtı (Agriculture, Trades, and Guild Organizations in 17th Century Manisa)*. İstanbul, 1942.

———. "Manisa Şer'iye Sicillerine dair bir Araştırma (A Study on the Sharia-Court Registers of Manisa)." *Türkiyat Mecmuası* 10 (1953).

Uzunçarşılı, İ. H. *Kütahya Şehri (City of Kütahya)*. İstanbul, 1932.

Ülgen, Ali Saim. *İstanbul ve Eski Eserleri (Istanbul and its Buildings)*. İstanbul, 1933.

———. *Constantinople during the Era of Mohammed the Conqueror, 1453-1481*. Ankara, 1939.

Ünal, M. A. *XVI. Yüzyılda Harput Sancağı, 1518-1566 (Harput Province in the 16th Century, 1518-1566)*. Ankara, 1989.

Varlık, M. Ç. "16. Yüzyılda Kütahya Şehri ve Eserleri (16th Century Kütahya and its Historical Structures)." *Türklük Araştırmaları Dergisi* 3 (1988).

White, C. *Three Years in Constantinople; or, Domestic Manners of the Turks in 1844*. 3 vols. London, 1846.

Wirth, E. "Zum Problem des Bazars (sūq, çarşı)." *Der Islam* 51/2 (1974); 52/1 (1975).

Yediyıldız, B. "Vakıf Müessesesinin XVIII. Asırda Kültür üzerindeki Etkileri (The Cultural Effects of the Waqf System in the 18th Century)." In *Türkiye'nin Sosyal ve Ekonomik Tarihi (1071-1920)*, eds. O. Okyar & H. İnalcık. Ankara, 1980.

———. "Türk Vakıf Kurucularının Sosyal Tabakalaşmadaki Yeri 1700-1800 (Social Classes of Waqf Founders in Turkey: 1700-1800)." *Osmanlı Araştırmaları* 3 (1982).

———. "Vakıf Müessesesinin XVIII. Asır Türk Toplumundaki Rolü (The Role of the Waqf System in 18th Century Turkish Society)." *Vakıflar Dergisi* 14 (1982).

———. *Institution du vaqf au XVIIIe siècle en Turquie*. Ankara, 1985.

———. *Ordu Kazası Sosyal Tarihi, 1455-1613 (A Social History of Ordu District, 1455-1613)*. Ankara, 1985.

Yerasimos, S. *Les voyageurs dans l'Empire Ottoman (XIVe-XVIe siècles): Bibliographie, itinéraires et inventaire des lieux habités*. Ankara, 1991.

———. "Occidentalisation de l'espace urbain: Istanbul 1839-1871." In *Les villes dans l'Empire Ottoman: Activités et sociétés,* ed. D. Panzac. Vol. 1. Paris, 1991.

Yinanç, R. & M. Elibüyük. *Kanunî Devri Malatya Tahrir Defteri, 1560 (A Land Survey Register of Malatya during the Period of Süleyman I, 1560)*. Ankara, 1983.

Yüksel, İ. A. *Osmanlı Mimârîsinde II. Bâyezid, Yavuz Selim Devri: 886-926/1481-1520 (Ottoman Architecture in the Ages of Bayazit II and Selim I)*. İstanbul, 1983.

Zâkir Şükrî Efendi. *Die Istanbuler Derwischkonvente und ihre Scheiche (Mecmu'a-i Tekaya)*. Edited by M. S. Tayşı & K. Kreiser. Freiburg, 1980.

IRAN

Masashi Haneda

Introduction

This chapter is concerned with studies of those cities which existed in the region of what is today Iran and Afghanistan between the 11th and 19th centuries. Iran and Afghanistan, however, though the centre of the so-called Iran-Islamic culture, represent a far more limited area than that which the culture historically influenced, and certainly there was a period when the greater whole comprised a single cultural area. This means that Western Turkestan, part of the former Soviet Union, should in particular be included in any study of Iranian cities and their history; its exclusion prevents any correct understanding of the true nature of those cities. Conversely, the study of the cities of Central Asia must take into consideration the cities of Iran. Much the same could be said about East Anatolia and Iraq. Since this volume has separate chapters for Turkey, Mashriq, and Central Asia, I will refrain, strictly for the sake of convenience, from referring to studies concerning those regions, with some particular exceptions. In addition, since H. Komatsu treats all the studies of Iranian cities made by scholars of the former Soviet Union collectively in his chapter on Central Asia, I will only touch briefly upon them here. It must also be remembered that the borders of the Iranian world were subject to dramatic changes during the period under consideration, unlike those of the Arab world which remained relatively unchanged.

The first part of this chapter is a chronological outline of the history of Iranian urban studies. The second part examines recent studies dealing with the "hardware" of cities and are relating to urban space: topics included are the necessary conditions for a city to come into existence, city planning, structures, and urban historical geography. The third part looks at studies on the "software" of cities, which focus on social groups and functions inside urban societies, a category which includes studies on urban administration, the quarters, families of notables, the ulama, outlaws, the waqf, bazars, guilds and those nomads particular to the Iranian world. In the course of a close review of these topics, I will attempt to draw attention both to points which may have been so far neglected and to important areas for future study.

I. Chronological Outline

If European studies of the "Islamic city" are considered to have begun with descriptions of cities in the other world of the "Orient," then Marco Polo in the 13th century was the precursor of later urban studies. Excellent early examples of such "studies" are P. Della Valle, *I viaggi di Pietro Della Valle* (1650) and J. Chardin, *Description particulière de la ville d'Ispahan, capitale de Perse* (1711), records by travellers to Esfahan when it was thriving as the capital of Safavid Persia which are replete with facts about the geography and social organization of this typical pre-modern Iranian city.

With the acceleration of the European political and economic advance into Western Asia in the 19th century, a great many travel records appeared, written by European diplomats and merchants. Though none was as detailed as that of Chardin, with its descriptions based on a thorough observation of one city, works such as the following include noteworthy descriptions of Iranian cities in various periods: J. Morier, *A Journey through Persia, Armenia, and Asia Minor to Constantinople, in the Years 1808 and 1809* (1812), G. Drouville, *Voyage en Perse fait en 1812 et 1813* (1825), A. Jaubert, *Voyage en Arménie et en Perse, fait dans les années 1805 et 1806* (1821) and J. A. Gobineau, *Trois ans en Asie, de 1855 à 1858* (1859). C. J. Wills, *In the Land of the Lion and Sun* (1883) vividly describes the bazar and the life of ordinary people in Esfahan. J. B. Feuvrier, *Trois ans à la cour de Perse* (1899) is a valuable personal record of a doctor at the Iranian court. G. N. Curzon, *Persia and the Persian Question* (1892) describes Iranian society in general in the most detailed way and contains chapters on geography, manners and customs, habits, the court, administration, military organization, transportation, trade, and diplomatic relations. There are separate chapters on Mashhad and Tehran.

A distinctive feature about travel books since the time of Chardin is their wealth of illustrations. P. Coste and E. Flandin, *Voyage en Perse* (1845-54) contains detailed and precise pictures of buildings and landscapes drawn by the authors which serve as important sources for studies on historical geography, the history of architecture and other fields. J. Dieulafoy, *La Perse, la Chaldée et la Susianne* (1887) is useful for its large number of etchings, based on photos taken by the author.

As with the Arab world and other regions, European study about the cities of Iran began with descriptive works and produce excellent achievements in the fields of architecture and the arts, whose objects to study are visible. Before World War II, Western expeditions were active in making field surveys of the region; it should be noted however that they were not conducted on a large scale at national request like those carried out in Syria and the Maghrib by France. Iranian cities, like those of Turkey, were to be engulfed in the wave of modernization with very few detailed and organized descriptions and records.

Studies based on field work which contain many photos and illustrations, like A. Godard, "Iṣfahān" (1937), began to appear in the first half of this century. A. U. Pope, *A Survey of Persian Art* (1938-9) is without doubt the greatest contribution in this field. The six volumes cover 1) arts since the dawn of history down to the Parthian period, 2) arts of the Sasanian period, 3) architecture, 4) ceramics, calligraphy, and inscriptions (epitaphs), 5) the arts of the book, and 6) pottery, carpets, metalwork and others. Each volume is divided into two parts, one for photoplates and illustrations and the other for collections of related essays and articles. The enormous amount of information contained in those volumes is astonishing. In the third volume, which deals with the architecture of the Islamic period, there are numerous and valuable photographs. The study is of a high level and of good academic quality, being not merely an architectural history but including in its broad perspective, studies on urban planning, gardens, and the royal tents of nomadic people. This great work has had an important influence over later studies, and even today maintains its prestige as a classical study in the field. On the whole though, with the exception of Pope's work, it is undeniable that the emphasis of most of the field work conducted by Europeans at the time was on ancient Persian ruins such as Persepolis. This fact is all the more interesting in that it coincides with M. Kisaichi's observations about the history of French studies of the Maghrib.

Studies of urban historical geography based on philology——a science developed during the 19th century——reached its peak at the beginning of this century. Representative works are V. V. Bartol'd, *An Historical Geography of Iran* (R., 1903, English translation 1984) and G. Le Strange, *The Lands of the Eastern Caliphate* (1905). They are descriptions and studies of the pre-modern historical geography of the Iranian world and their major sources are geographical works by Arabic and Persian authors. They were to be used as basic tools for a long time.

Studies, then, on architectural history and historical geography were already producing results in the pre-World War II period, and that tradition has been maintained to this day without discontinuity. At the same time, similar to the situation *vis-à-vis* the Arab world, new attitudes towards Iranian urban studies came into prominence. First, elements close to urban life, such as the bazar and the quarter, were made objects of study, joining the more conspicuous structures such as citadels and mosques which had long been studied. Second, detailed studies based on historical documents were combined with field work to clarify various facets of urban topography. Such new directions will be examined in more detail in Part II, but here I would like to mention in this connection H. Gaube and E. Wirth, *Der Bazar von Isfahan* (1978) as an example of the first trend and H. Gaube, *Iranian Cities* (1979) and T. Allen, *Timurid Herat* (1983) as an example of the second.

Studies concerning the city itself in terms of social structure and social relationships began well after the development of studies in architectural history and historical geography. Research into Iranian cities started in earnest in the 1950s and 1960s, when G. von Grunebaum, Cl. Cahen and I. Lapidus were publishing their theories about the "Islamic city." The research of I. P. Petrushevskii in the 1940s was, as H. Komatsu points out at length in the chapter on Central Asia, the one exception. The most accessible of his numerous articles, a general survey of his contribution to the field, is "The Socio-Economic Condition of Iran under the Īl-khāns"(1968). Though Petrushevskii's works were of high quality, they aroused little discussion among Western scholars, perhaps because they were written in Russian during the period of the Cold War, or because they were based on the idea of "feudal society" as accepted, defined and perhaps limited by the Soviet academy of history, thus concerned with social and economic history in general.

In this sense, the statement of J. Aubin at the beginning of an article entitled "Eléments pour l'étude des agglomérations urbaines" (1970), that "L'histoire des villes de l'Iran islamique n'a pas été considérée en discipline particulière," is accurate. The article first points out the geographical characteristics of Iranian cities and analyzes the conditions which contributed to their rise and fall and then goes on to identify a number of important problems concerning the study of social history in Iranian urban society. Though short, the article was influential and it became the starting point for later studies of the history of pre-modern Iranian cities both in terms of their "hardware" and "software." Aubin's contributions to the study of the social history of Iran, exceeding the boundaries of "urban studies", were considerable, even before the publication of the above article. For example, *Deux sayyids de Bam au XVe siècle*(1956), describing the relations between saints, the political power, and the urban masses in one regional city in Iran in the 15th century within the larger context of contemporary currents of history, is both an interesting study in terms of social history and a useful historiographical tool.

Since the 1970s the leading figures in historical research into Iranian cities other than Aubin have been R. W. Bulliet, a specialist in the pre-Mongolian period and W. M. Floor, whose field is the post-Mongolian period. Bulliet, who in *The Patricians of Nishapur* (1972) uses *The Histories of Nishapur* (R. N. Frye, ed., 1965) as his source to describe society in the city of Nishapur in eastern Iran from the 10th to the 12th century, has been publishing a succession of original works, including a study of the historical geography of Nishapur and an investigation of changes in rates of conversion to Islam among urban dwellers. In *The Patricians of Nishapur,* he states, "The arguments adduced by various defenders of the concepts of a city type defined by the Islamic religion have not been convincing" (page ix). He is clearly on the side of those who deny the concept of the "Islamic city." Probably because his field is limited to the cities of the pre-Mongolian period, he does not seem to consider Nishapur as an Iranian city so much as a Middle Eastern medieval city. This brings to his work a subtle difference in tone as compared with that of Aubin and Floor, who are both concerned with the time after the Mongol period when strong Iranian characteristics appeared throughout society and culture in general. However, since Iranian cities did not suddenly emerge after the Mongol invasion, certain subjects remain to be examined, such as how far the image of the city as described by Bulliet was retained in later years, and to what extent it was transformed.

Floor's works extensively cover the Iranian urban system and social groups in general. His main concern seems to be to clarify the actual conditions in the transformation of the Iranian cities from pre-industrial societies to industrial ones. Typical of his ideas is the argument he makes in "The Political Role of the Lutis in Iran" (1981). He has also been giving attention to how Iranian cities compare with those of the Arab world and other areas. A characteristic of his work is his interest in the debate about the "Islamic city," which has been a concern more of scholars in the field of Arabic studies, and his use of comparative methods in his research. His energetic research activities have done much to broaden our knowledge about urban systems (such as the police and the muhtasib), social groups (for example, the guilds, merchants and outlaws) and how they have changed. However, as I will discuss further in Part III below, it is not correct to say that his research enlightens all aspects of Iranian urban history. There are occasions when, seeking a hasty answer to some question concerning a two or three hundred year time span, he needs to be more rigorous about how he collects and handles historical materials. In this sense his study is only a survey and there remains a need for further empirical research in particular areas.

Since the 1970s, as if somehow linked with the work being done in Arab and Turkish area studies, Iranian urban studies have been marked by the accelerated appearance of works analyzing urban societies based on actual documentary materials such as contract or waqf documents. Many studies have been made utilizing documents related to the Safavid Sufi order in Ardabil. They include G. Herrmann, "Urkundenfunde in Āẕarbāyǧān" (1971), A. Morton, "The Ardabīl Shrine in the Reign of Shāh Ṭahmāsp I" (1974-5), B. G. Fragner, "Das Ardabiler Heiligtum in den Urkunden" (1975), J. Aubin, "La propriété foncière en Azerbaydjan sous les Mongols" (1976-7), and M. Gronke, *Arabische und persische Privaturkunden des 12. und 13. Jahrhunderts aus Ardabil* (1982). These works show how an urban Sufi order obtained and increased their lands and properties, and the kinds of buildings it constructed in the city in accordance with that growth. A series of studies on waqf documents from the Ilkhanid to the Safavid period by Sh. Blair, R. D. McChesney and others (see pp. 264-5) are also worth noting as opening up a new phase of Iranian urban studies.

Before going into further detail, I would like to outline briefly how urban studies have developed in Iran itself. There was originally no tendency to speak of the cities of the Iranian region collectively as "Iranian cities." On the contrary, as each individual city was the center of a coherent world, individual histories about each city appeared as early as the 10th century. Histories of Bukhara, Esfahan, Qom and so on were written first in Arabic and later in Persian. This contrasts to the Turkish world where local history was rarely recorded in written form. The tradition continued without change to the 19th century and some local Iranian urban histories continued to be compiled. Many were encyclopaedic collections of information about a certain city and its surroundings gathered from existing historical materials with added items based on the author's own experience, such as A. A. Vazīrī, *History of Kerman* (P., 1364/1985-6) and *Geography of Kerman* (P., 1353/1974-5), A. Q. Kermānī, *History and Geography of Qom* (P., 1356/1977-8) and Mīrzā Ḥasan, *Book of Fārs* (P., 1312/1895). While useful, these works often fail to specify their sources of information. Nevertheless we can still find in them many contemporary descriptions of great historical value.

Works belonging to that tradition are still being published in considerable numbers in Iran. Examples include M. Maškūr, *History of Tabriz to the 9th Century A. H.* (P., 1352/1973-4), G. B. Safarī, *Ardabil: A Crossroads of History* (P., 1350-62/1971-84), H. Emdād, *Shiraz: Its Past and Present* (P., 1339/1960-1), M. Aqāsī, *History of Khoy* (P., 1350/1971-2), N. Nağmī, *Tehran: the Caliph's Capital* (P., 2nd edition, 1362/1983-4) and Ḥ. Narāqī, *Social History of Kashan* (P., 1345/1966-7). Recent publications rarely omit to note sources and their descriptions are generally reliable. *Tehran: the Caliph's Capital* contains many rare photographs and pictures, providing valuable information. All the same such works aim primarily at collecting information in general rather than using that information to analyze urban society.

While large numbers of such encyclopaedic works have been published, Anǧoman-e āṯār-e mellī (the National Heritage Association) has taken the lead in making the surviving original textual sources public (see p. 248 for details). The series of historical sources published under its auspices is extremely useful in that it contains a comprehensive listing of historical buildings in a town or locality with explanations as to their origins together with introductions to related historical materials (documents, copies of royal orders carved in walls, epitaphs etc.). Like the above encyclopaedic collections, this collection of historical sources should be regarded as source material for urban studies rather than the outcome of those studies.

Full-blown urban studies began to develop apace in Iran in the 1980s. As in Western research two broad characteristics are discernible. One is an attempt at the historical reconstruction of cities and buildings based on architectural investigation and archaeological excavation. Typical of such is the series of studies on architectural history and historical geography edited by M. Y. Keyānī, including *A General Survey of Urbanization and Urban Construction in Iran* (P., 1365/1986-7), *Architecture in Iran during the Islamic Age* (P., 1366/1987-8) and *Iranian Cities* (P., 1366-70/1987-91). Similar studies for individual cities also exist, for example, M. M. Maḥallātī, *Geography of the City of Bam* (P., 1367/1988-9) and Mo'assese-ye 'elmī va farhangī-ye faḍā (Institute for the Knowledge of Space and Culture) (ed.), *The Buildings and the City of Damghan* (P., 1368/1989-90). They do not show a sufficient awareness and understanding of developments in Western urban studies since the 19th century and their level is not always high. All the same, they cannot be ignored since they contain much local information. The second characteristic is that for the first time in Iran, studies such as Ḥ. Solṭānzāde, *Introduction to the History of Cities and Urbanization in Iran* (P., 1365/1986-7) and Ǧ. Šahrī, *Social History of Tehran in the 13th Century A. H.* (P., 1367-8/1988-9) have appeared which take a deep look at urban societies. The former work is not a collection of individual urban histories but an attempt to view Iranian cities both morphologically, in terms of historical geography and architectural history, and sociologically, in terms of urban administration and groups. Despite certain deficiencies and its rather superficial analyses, the work's intentions are praiseworthy. Šahrī's six volume work describes on the basis of the census of the year 1301 A. H. (1883-4 A. D.), people of every kind of profession then resident in Tehran. It is useful as a starting point for future study. The unsatisfactory nature of the two works is due somewhat to difficulties facing the Iranian academic world at present; nevertheless we must respect their achievements, recognizing that they have reached a certain level virtually without using the results of Western research at all.

Thus the study of the history of Iranian cities has bloomed since the 1970s not only in the field of the history of arts and architecture and historical geography, but also in the field of social structures and groups with remarkable progress both in quantity and quality. One such work that I would like to mention here is a newly published study containing various articles about Tehran, Ch. Adle and B. Hourcade (eds.), *Téhéran: Capitale bicentenaire* (1992).

In both the West and Japan little use has yet been made of historical materials and studies published in Iran (of local histories, in particular) and of unedited documents. On the other hand, in Iran, the most advanced results of studies made outside the country are not freely accessible. It should be the duty of those scholars concerned to establish a world-wide network for academic cooperation. Some excellent recently published studies give promise that research has reached a level to allow us to perceive, if only dimly, the form of the "Iranian city" in the historical sense. At long last conditions permit the development of the concept of comparative urban studies, in the Western Asian Islamic world at least. In the remainder of this chapter, I will introduce the present situation in various fields in the study of Iranian urban history together with what has gone before, keeping in mind comparisons with urban histories made in other areas, especially the Arab world and Turkey. I will place special emphasis on studies done within the past twenty-five years, and consider future themes for study. I would be happy if by so doing I can provide a means to study the cities of the Islamic world in a comparative way.

II. Urban Space

1. Geographical Characteristics

The dry climate of the Iranian highlands and the geographical situation where a large part of the land is mountainous and arid have greatly affected the basic nature of the cities existing there. Except for the region to the south of the Caspian Sea, cities were primarily established separately as independent administrative, economic and cultural centers for agricultural oasis regions. Each city and its surrounding agricultural area occupying the oasis should be understood as a single unit sharing a common destiny. This unit, consisting of a city and surrounding villages, can be compared to an island surrounded by a sea of desert. Taking the present day Kerman as an example, P. W. English described the relationship between the city and the villages in such a way in his book, *City and Village in Iran: Settlement and Economy in the*

Kirman Basin (1966). M. Bonine substantiated the connection in the case of Yazd in *Yazd and its Hinterland* (1975) and "City and Hinterland in Central Iran" (1979). A city together with its surrounding villages form a somewhat self-contained urban sphere. Yazd, for example, refers both to the city itself and to its urban sphere of surrounding villages. K. Shimizu made a similar observation about Nishapur between the 10th and 11th centuries in his article, "The Image of Cities in the History of Iran" (J., 1990).

In the first chapter of the first volume of *Les villes de l'Iran* (1969-73), F. Bémont generalizes the above-mentioned geographic features of Iranian cities and speculates on the conditions necessary for a city to come into being in the Iranian highlands. She concludes that (1) water is, above all, the main determinant of a city's establishment, (2) a number of cities developed at economically important points on trade routes, even where natural conditions were not optimum, and subsequently declined when routes changed, and (3) cities that were constructed out of political or military necessity did not in many cases last long. Almost the same conclusions were reached by J. Aubin in the aforementioned "Eléments pour l'étude des agglomérations urbaines" (1970). H. Gaube, in *Iranian Cities* (1979), also comments on the profound importance of water for Iranian cities. It need hardly be said that the securing of water supplies has been a very important issue for cities in Western Asia in general. This was particularly true in the case of Iran.

In comparison with cities in the Arab and Turkish regions, the determining characteristics of Iranian cities are considered to be their strong isolated and independent geographical location and, as an inevitable result of that, their regional nature and inclination toward decentralization. There is no huge central city in the Iranian region equivalent to Damascus or Cairo in the Arab lands or Istanbul in Turkey. Of course cities did exist which had undergone a sudden and momentary growth as capitals of dynasties, such as Tabriz in the 14th century, Herat in the 15th century and Esfahan in the 17th century. Nevertheless, such prosperity was short-lived, and the cities returned to their former local identity when the dynasties declined.

Reflecting this independence, studies have frequently been made, not only in Iran but in the West too, of a city as a single unit. Inevitably this hindered the development of studies which attempted to consider the nature of Iranian cities collectively from a wider perspective. Studies published down to the present bearing the title of "Iranian cities" are, in many cases, no more than collections of individual urban histories. L. Lockhart, *Persian Cities* (1960), a survey of the history and geography as well as the buildings of twenty-three cities is by no means a genuine urban study. F. Bémont, *Les villes de l'Iran* (1969-73) was written with the intention of examining how twenty-five cities in the Iranian region have changed from the early Qajar period (latter half of the 18th century) till today. Mainly adopting a human geographical view point, it records specific data about the social and economic conditions of each city through the 1960s. As a result, this work should be recognized as the first true encompassing study of Iranian cities, as the author herself remarks. Considering the year of publication, it is of extremely high quality; nevertheless, partly because it fails to utilize sufficiently historical sources such as local histories written in Persian, it mainly does not go beyond the description and analysis of present conditions, thus leaving the reader who is interested in the historical perspective dissatisfied. Since detailed and critical notes are added to each of the 225 reference works, a very useful bibliography has been formed; all the same, most of the works cited are general introductions or travel records concerned with only a very limited aspect of the cities. The difficulties surrounding such research at that time are apparent.

H. Gaube, *Iranian Cities* (1979) is excellent as a study of the historical geography of the three cities of Herat, Esfahan, and Bam. However, it lacks depth as a fundamental work for understanding the concept of the "Iranian city." In the general remarks of the opening chapter the author only mentions differences between ancient Oriental cities and the "Islamic city" in the course of a brief survey of Iranian cities prior to the Islamic Age. The only general feature of Iranian cities that he mentions is the importance of water. Other than this, he vigorously asserts that Iranian cities share the form of the "Islamic city" as defined in other regions by the author himself: city walls, a great mosque, and a bazar. M. Bonine, "The Morphogenesis of Iranian Cities" (1979) identifies the reason for the orthogonal network of streets in Iranian cities as being their expansion along irrigation channels. M. Kheirabadi, *Iranian Cities* (1991) is an interesting study concerning the element responsible for the formation and development of the spatial patterns and morphologies of traditional Iranian cities. Factors such as physical environment, trade and historical events, religion and sociopolitical structures are discussed in detail. The author stresses the close interrelation of these factors, but the characteristic feature of the work is the discussion on the physical environment.

2. Historical Geography

V. V. Bartol'd, *An Historical Geography of Iran* (R., 1903) is noteworthy as the first genuine work in the field of historical geography. This book, now in English translation (*An Historical Geography of Iran,* 1984), utilizes many different kinds of available documents and displays the famous Russian scholar's erudition concerning the pre-modern historical geography of Iran. The article on Khurasan, a region of particular interest to the author, is worth reading even today. G. Le Strange, *The Lands of the Eastern Caliphate* (1905), published around the same time as V. V. Bartol'd's book, is, as the title indicates, a historico-geographical study of the area between the Euphrates River and Central Asia based on Arabic and Persian geographies written chiefly in the period prior to the Mongol invasion. Partly because it is written in English, Western scholars have long relied on it more than on Bartol'd's work as a basic text. Both books are excellent as general surveys, but careful examination reveals the need for partial correction as the result of newly available sources and new findings by scholars, such as D. Krawulsky, *Īrān: Das Reich der Īlḫāne* (1978) and *Ḫorāsān zur Timuridenzeit nach dem Tārīḫ-e Ḥāfeẓ-e Abrū* (1982-4).

Together with historico-geographical studies based on textual sources, scholars are attempting to reconstruct the topography of individual cities through field surveys. Scholarly interest has tended to concentrate on the cities of Esfahan, Herat and Tehran.

The position of the city walls and main buildings of 15th century Esfahan has been estimated in R. Quiring-Zoche, *Isfahan im 15. und 16. Jahrhundert* (1980). S. Šafaqī, too, in *Geography of Esfahan* (P., 1353/1974-5), has tried to reestablish the position of the city walls in accordance with P. Coste's *Monuments modernes de la Perse* (1867). The broad divergence in their conclusions points to the difficulties of this line of research. Šafaqī's work is a full-scale study dealing with natural geography, historical geography, population and religious minorities, and provides a variety of useful data concerning the city, especially in the modern period. L. Honarfar, "Esfahan during the Timurid Period" (P., 2535/1976-7), discusses, as the title indicates, the political history of Timurid Esfahan and the buildings constructed during the period.

Many articles have been written about city planning in Esfahan as the capital of the Safavid dynasty. An early study is E. E. Beaudouin, "Ispahan sous les grands chahs (XVIIe siècle)" (1933). At the end of the 1930s, A. Godard revealed through his own field research and the records of European travellers how the Royal Square (Meydān-e Šāh) and its surroundings were constructed, thereby contributing greatly to the field (A. Godard, "Iṣfahān," 1937). This work was succeeded by A. U. Pope, *A Survey of Persian Art* (1938-9), and followed in the 1960s and after by a succession of reports about archaeological investigations, by-products of the restoration work on the Royal Square and its surroundings conducted by the Italian Institute for the Middle and Far East Studies (IsMEO) beginning in the 1960s: G. Zander (ed.), *Travaux de restauration de monuments historiques en Iran: Rapports et études préliminaires* (1968), E. Galdieri, "Two Building Phases of the Time of Šāh 'Abbās I in the Maydān-i Šāh of Isfahān: Preliminary Note"

(1970), E. Galdieri and R. Orazi, *Progretto di sistemazione del Maydān-i Šāh* (1969), E. Galdieri, *Eṣfahān: 'Alī Qāpū: An Architectural Survey* (1979), etc. As a result, knowledge of the subject became increasingly accurate.

In the first half of the 1970s, there was an outburst of studies on Esfahan. For example, *Iranian Studies,* the American journal of Iranology, published a special issue on Esfahan in 1974, though most of the articles in fact only touched on Esfahan rather than dealing directly with it. Two of them focused on the building of the city by Shah 'Abbas (L. Golombek, "Urban Patterns in pre-Safavid Isfahan" and D. Wilber, "Aspects of the Safavid Ensemble of Isfahan"). Both attempted to inquire into the reasons why the axis of the Royal Square does not align with that of the Royal Mosque; one solution is given in M. Haneda, "Maydān et Bāġ" (1990).

By the end of the 1970s, accurate drawings of the city buildings had become available. The city map of Safavid Esfahan, drawn by H. Gaube, is included in the recently published Tübingen Atlas series (TAVO). Accordingly, the discussion has moved to why Shah 'Abbas decided on such a city plan and where its origins lay. This debate still continues, and speculation on this subject may be found in works such as H. Gaube, *Iranian Cities* (1979), M. Haneda, "Maydān et Bāġ" (1990) and R. D. McChesney, "Four Sources on Shāh 'Abbās's Building of Iṣfahān" (1988). Gaube sees the proto-type of the city plan in transport routes which had existed since pre-Safavid times, while M. Haneda stresses the nomadic mentality and the tradition of city building of the tribal aristocracy since the Ilkhanid period, and R. D. McChesney notes the importance of 'Abbas' concern for the economy of the royal household. In addition, T. Sakamoto, "The Urban Structure of Esfahan in the 19th Century and Meydān" (J., 1980-1) points out the reduced city size of Esfahan during the Afghan and Qajar dynasties. A reproduction of a city map of Esfahan made in 1923 —before the modernization of the city by Reza Shah—was recently published (1984) by Sahab Publishing in Tehran. The map is a useful historical source, since it records a city landscape unchanged since the Safavid dynasty.

Two valuable works by T. Allen, *A Catalogue of the Toponyms and Monuments of Timurid Herat* (1981) and *Timurid Herat* (1983) are very instructive. The former is a comprehensive listing of historical structures remaining in Herat and its outskirts; their positions are shown on maps and they are catalogued according to their functions. The latter attempts to give meaning to urban space and analyses the historical background to the construction of the buildings and the builders' intention. Allen's work is ambitious, transcending the conventional framework of architectural studies that charts changes in the building style of mosques, madrasas, and mausolea. The historical geography of Herat at the beginning of the 16th century is treated in detail in M. Szuppe, *Entre Timourides, Uzbeks et Safavides* (1992). While Allen's study is limited to buildings of the Timurid period, A. W. Najimi, *Herat: The Islamic City* (1988), examines the topography of Old Herat considering even non-structural elements such as streets. His arguments are not far removed from the traditional one of the "Islamic city" which stresses such features as blind alleys, the bazar, and the location of the mosque.

H. Gaube, *Iranian Cities* (1979), too, studies Herat. The author asserts that the square city walls of Herat, very exceptional in the Islamic world, must have been influenced by Indian cosmology. This view is discussed in further detail in another work, "Innenstadt-Aussenstadt: Kontinuität und Wandel im Grundriss von Herāt (Afghanistan) zwischen dem X. und dem XV. Jahrhundert" (1977). Here Gaube claims that no major changes can be perceived inside the city walls of Herat for the last one thousand years, though parts of the city developed greatly outside the city walls at different periods. He makes the extremely interesting observation that the northern suburbs of the city outside the walls, which saw remarkable development as the royal residential area especially during the Timurid period, were the prototype of the "garden city" of Esfahan, the capital of the later Safavid dynasty. Moreover, N. N. Tumanovich, *Herat between the 16th and 18th Centuries* (R., 1989), a general study of Herat between the 16th and 18th centuries, is not limited to historical geography but is a helpful guide to the city of that time.

The first true geographical study of Tehran, which grew rapidly in the 19th century, is H. Bahrambeygui, *Tehran: An Urban Analysis* (1977). The first two chapters explain why the city grew so rapidly, and in so doing provide a good summary both of the geographical location of Tehran and its effects on the city's development and of the history of urban development up to World War II. The drawings and photographs it contains are valuable resources. Y. Ḏakā, *A Short History of the Construction of the Fortress of Tehran* (P., 1349/1970-1) deals mainly with discussing the many buildings including the royal palace, the main streets and the alleys built within the city walls. The approximately 200 drawings and photographs evoke the lost landscape of past Tehran. In addition, Sahab Publishing has issued a reproduction of an old map entitled "Tehran under the reign of Nāṣer al-Dīn Šāh (1891)" (P., 1984). Other important geographical studies concerning Tehran include P. Ahrens, *Die Entwicklung der Stadt Teheran: Eine städtebauliche Untersuchung ihrer zukünftigen Gestaltung* (1966), M. Ettehadieh, "Patterns in Urban Development; the Growth of Tehran (1852-1903)" (1983) and M. Seger, *Teheran: Eine stadtgeographische Studien* (1978).

Studies of the historical geography of cities other than the afore-mentioned three include R. W. Bulliet, "Medieval Nishapur: A Topographic and Demographic Reconstruction" (1976), M. Y. Keyānī, *The Islamic City of Gurgan* (1984), M. Ḥakīm, *Treasure of Knowledge: A Historical Geography of Iranian Cities* (P., 1366/1987-8) and M. A. Golrīz, *The Gate of Heaven: History and the Historical Geography of Qazvin*, vol. 1 (P., 1337/1958-9). At present M. Y. Keyānī is in charge of historical and geographical restorations of Iranian cities and his findings, exemplified by the previously cited *Iranian Cities* (p. 241), are expected to be published in succession. G. Schweizer, "Bibliographie zur Stadtgeographie des Vorderen Orients (1960-1976)" (1977), a comprehensive bibliography of geographical studies of cities of the Middle East including Iran, provides further detailed information.

Even more important to such study than historical material such as chronicles is the information provided by actually surviving structures and epitaphs. Several works have been published in Iran which deal comprehensively with the historical monuments of a certain city, giving comments about the history of each monument and introducing relevant to historical materials (documents, copies of royal orders carved in walls, epitaphs etc.). Two such works are available for Esfahan; L. Honarfar, *Treasure of Historical Monuments in Esfahan* (P., 1344/1965-6), and A. Mehrābādī, *Remains of Esfahan* (P., 1352/1973-4). The latter contains information about buildings, gardens, quarters and streets which do not remain today but whose former existence is documented. For Tehran, there is S. M. T. Moṣṭafavī, *Historical Heritage in Tehran* (P., 1361/1982-3).

A number of similar books concerning cities and local areas have been published by the National Heritage Association. They include Ḥ. Narāqī, *Historical Remains in the Old Cities of Kashan and Natanz* (P., 1348/1969-70), I. Afšār, *Historical Monuments in Yazd* (P., 1348-54/1969-76) and 'A. Kārang and S. Ǧ. Torābī Ṭabāṭabā'ī, *Ruins in Azerbaijan* (P., 1351-5/1972-7). Other works of the same kind from different sources are M. A. Moḫleṣī, *Historical Geography of Soltaniye* (P., 1363/1984-5) and M. Ḫosravī, *The Historical Geography of the Zave Region* (P., 1366/1987-8). Though they do not necessarily present new aspects in the field, they are extremely helpful as collections of research materials, not only for urban historical geography but also for studies on the relationship between a city and a political power as well as on social groups within an urban society. Only limited use has so far been made of these materials and it is to be hoped that scholars will draw more fully upon them in the future.

Photographs dating from the 19th century and later are also very useful for the study of historical geography. E. Höltzer, *Iran of 113 Years Ago* (P., 2535/1976-7) is a valuable book of photographs giving glimpses of Esfahan in the later half of the 19th century. The printing is very clear and the pictures are delightful to the eye. Q. Ṣāfī, *Historical Post Cards of Iran* (P., 1368/1989-90) contains very rare post cards dating from the 19th century and later. Unfortunately the quality of printing is not good, but this is offset by the fact that the photographs show many buildings which no longer exist. E. F. Schmidt, *Flights over Ancient Cities of Iran* (1940), dating from a time when aerial photography was in its infancy, is helpful for the study of the history of architecture and urban layout.

Iran is one of the most earthquake-prone regions of the world. Earthquakes have affected city landscapes and layout to a great extent. In this connection the following studies are worth noting: Ch. Melville, "Earthquakes in the History of Nishapur" (1980) and "Historical Monuments and Earthquakes in Tabriz" (1981), M. Szuppe, "Un tremblement de terre dans le Qohestān, 956/1549" (1989) and N. N. Ambraseys and Ch. Melville, *A History of Persian Earthquakes* (1982). Especially recommended is Melville's study with its collection of articles concerning earthquakes gathered from a great many historical sources both in the East and the West and its detailed records of damage sustained by urban structures as a result of earthquakes. This study is essential when considering a city's topography.

3. History of Architecture

Buildings are one of the most important constituents of urban space. Thus we shall here examine those studies in the field of architectural history which relate to urban topography. A survey of Iranian architectural history is contained in A. U. Pope, "Architecture" in *A Survey of Persian Art*, vol. 3 (1938). Though it is partly outdated, it still provides a good summary of the topic. A more compact study by the same author is *Persian Architecture* (1969).

One of the oldest mosques in Iran is the Friday Mosque of Esfahan. An investigation by the Italian Institute for the Middle and Far East Studies (IsMEO) has revealed changes to the building in the course of its existence, dating from as early as the Seljuk period (11th century). The findings have been published in the form of a report (E. Galdieri, *Iṣfahān: Masǧid-i Ǧum'a,* 1972-84). An analysis of the findings will provide information regarding the relationship between rulers and urban buildings and between power and faith during the period from the Seljuks to the Safavids. A recently published work, O. Graber, *The Great Mosque of Isfahan* (1990), outlines the evolution of the building of the Friday Mosque and its relationship with the people of the city. In the same vein, of continuing merit is Godard's article "Iṣfahān" (1937), mentioned above, dealing with the various historical monuments of

Esfahan. L. Golombek, "Anatomy of a Mosque: The Masjid-i Shāh of Iṣfahān" (1972) deals with the Royal Mosque.

In *The Architecture of Islamic Iran: The Il Khānid Period* (1955), D. Wilber discusses buildings constructed during the Ilkhanid period (13th-14th centuries) in the form of a catalogue and identifies the whereabouts of relevant historical sources. Wilber himself made extensive journeys throughout Iran from the 1930s and recorded a number of ruins which no longer exist, making his work a valuable document. L. Golombek and D. Wilber, *The Timurid Architecture of Iran and Turan* (1988) describes historical monuments in Timurid Central Asia and Iran following the same style as Wilber. The plans of the monuments and in some cases their elevations and photographs, are contained in a separate volume, making the text more comprehensible. The work takes the findings of recent studies (such as that about Herat by T. Allen mentioned above) into account and makes interesting analyses about the relationship between Timurid society and architecture. This is an excellent study which does not limit itself to the framework of the history of architecture alone, but attempts to explain the significance of urban space. B. O'Kane, *Timurid Architecture in Khurasan* (1987) discusses Timurid monuments in the region of Khurasan in a style following that of Golombek and Wilber. Thus, in the case of Khurasan, the two works must be compared before use.

M. Y. Keyānī, *Architecture in Iran during the Islamic Age* (P., 1366/1987-8) surveys the history of the architectural development of structures such as mosques, tombs, madrasas, citadels, bridges, caravansaries, reservoirs, public baths (*ḥammām*). M. Y. Keyānī and W. Kleiss, *A Catalogue of Caravansaries in Iran* (P., 1362-8/1983-90) lists, with abundant plates and illustrations, caravansaries, whose existence is now threatened, in many places in Iran. A comprehensive bibliography of the history of architecture and arts up to 1960 is K. A. C. Creswell, *A Bibliography of the Architecture, Arts and Crafts of Islam* (1961, 1973, 1985).

III. Studies Concerning Urban Society

1. Urban Administration

Since Iranian cities tended to be independent of each other, an important key to understanding the relationship between the central authority and a city is the question of how decisions were made for the city as a whole and how relations stood between the local agencies of the central government and the residents of the city. Previous studies have shown that an important role in this was played by the notables in each city. However, studies dealing directly with urban administration itself are still limited in number and it is hoped that more detailed research, which makes use of local histories, diaries and other such sources, will be pursued in the future.

Before the 15th century, urban leaders in Iranian cities were often called *ra'īs*. To my knowledge, no monograph has been written on this subject, though remarks about the term are to be found in such works as R. W. Bulliet, *The Patricians of Nishapur* (1972), A. K. S. Lambton, "kalāntar" (1974), R. Quiring-Zoche, *Isfahan im 15. und 16. Jahrhundert* (1980) and J. Aubin, "Notes sur quelques documents Aq-qoyunlu" (1956). In some special cases, a number of persons were collectively called *ra'īs*. According to Cl. Cahen in "Mouvements populaires et autonomisme urbain dans l'Asie musulmane du moyen âge" (1958-9), *ra'īs* as a profession was not to be found in the Mediterranean coastal regions outside Syria. The term was not much used after the end of the 15th century, when urban leaders came to be called *kalāntar*. According to Lambton, "kalāntar" and "The Office of Kalāntar under the Safawids and Afshārs" (1963) and to W. M. Floor, "The Office of Kalāntar in Qājār Persia" (1971), the *kalāntar* was formally appointed by a sovereign and was concerned with all kinds of urban issues, including police work, secular trials, the levy of guild taxes, decisions about the official prices of goods and the civil service. In order to carry out his duties, he worked in close relationship with the muhtasib, the heads of quarters and guilds, and urban outlaws. The status of *kalāntar* was often inherited. In a sense, the *kalāntar* was at one of the culminant positions in urban society, but much remains to be clarified concerning the post and its functions. Particularly needing is a study of its range of functions, which appears to have differed according to period. Neither has it been shown that *kalāntar* existed in every city. Another question remaining to be fully answered is that concerning the relationship between the duties of the *kalāntar* and those of the *dārūġa*. One of the most important tasks confronting scholars of Iranian urban history is to explain what the shift (although it is an open question whether this term "shift" is itself appropriate or not) from *ra'īs* to *kalāntar* meant for an urban society. The office of *kalāntar* impinged on many areas of urban life, and is situated at an important node, linking itself above to the *ḥākim* (or *beglerbeg*, the administrator appointed by the central government) and below to the heads of the units of urban life; chiefs of quarters and guilds. Since there is no urban administrative post corresponding to *kalāntar* in the Arab and Turkish worlds, it is an extremely important topic.

Another office considered to have had a police role is the *dārūġa*. This has been studied by A. K. S. Lambton in "The Evolution of the Office of Dārūgha" (1959-60). W. M. Floor, "The Police in Qājār Persia" (1973) discusses police power in cities throughout Iran under the Qajar dynasty and analyses the competence of the police, who were referred to differently from city to city according to whether they operated in the day or the night time. Before the "modern" police force was introduced in 1878, there were police organizations at various levels of urban society (quarters, bazar, *kalāntar*); the head of each police organization employed policemen in his own area of responsibility, and when a policeman retired, he had to recruit a replacement. There is hardly any evidence that police were conscious of having a duty to maintain public justice. A modern police force evolved haphazardly in some parts of Tehran, while in other areas the old establishments survived until the early Pahlavi period.

2. Notables and Ulama

In Iran, influencial positions in the political, economic and cultural domains of urban society often passed from father to son. As a result, such families of notables carried great weight in the cities. The continuity of urban notable families is worth noting as one of the characteristics of the Iranian city. R. W. Bulliet, *The Patricians of Nishapur* (1972), which describes the situation of urban notables in Nishapur from the 10th to the 12th century on the basis of *The Histories of Nishapur* (1965) published by R. N. Frye, is recommended reading for any study of urban notables in Iran during the Seljuk period. The book consists of two parts. The first describes the histories of more than ten families of notables and provides personal histories for each member of those families. The second part attempts to reconstitute urban society in Nishapur at the time by analyzing the data given in the first part. Bulliet describes the circumstances of the "politics of the notables." For example he shows that the notables of Nishapur were roughly divided according to school of Islamic law between the Hanafis and the Shafi'is and fought each other whenever the occasion arose; when however there was outside interference they would unite to defend themselves. The process, which Bulliet shows, whereby the shadow of state power gradually fell over the semi-independent "politics of the notables" is extremely interesting. However, as Cl. Cahen remarks in his review of this work (*JESHO*, 16, 1973), the example taken, that of the urban society of Nishapur, should be understood first and foremost as an individual case; to generalize further, deeper studies of other cities of the same period are necessary. Some questions which immediately come to mind include whether or not fights between the two law schools occurred in other cities as well, and whether or not there was any relation between such conflicts and the fighting between those quarters later separated into the *ne'matī* and the *ḥaydarī* (for further details, see pp. 258-9). These questions must await future study.

In "A Quantitative Approach to Medieval Muslim Biographical Dictionaries" (1970) and *Conversion to Islam in the Medieval Period: An Essay in Quantitative History* (1979) Bulliet shows numerically the ratio of Muslims among urban dwellers and in "The Age Structure of Medieval Islamic Education" (1983) he studies the religious education in Nishapur to calculate the ages of students and teachers and periods of education. K. Shimizu, "Races, Religions and Religious Sects" (J., 1986) uses Bulliet's research to discuss the sense of identity of individuals and groups together with the problems of conversion and "race." Shimizu, "The Image of Cities in the History of Iran" (J., 1990) is a general description of urban rule by notables. Bulliet, "City Histories in Medieval Iran" (1968) examines the intention behind compiling the history of a single city and points out their effectiveness as biographical dictionaries. J. Aubin, "L'aristocratie urbaine dans l'Iran seldjoukide: l'exemple de Sabzavâr" (1966) employs the biographical listings in *Tārīḫ-e Bayḥaq (History of Bayhaq)* to show how *sayyids*, descendants of the Prophet who gained great influence as urban notables in later years, were already playing an important political and social role in Sabzavar in the 11th century. Aubin's article, which appeared even before Bulliet's "City Histories," proved what Bulliet had claimed. Bulliet should therefore have cited this work as a reference.

From the 13th to the 15th century, the development of Yazd was centred around the silk and cotton textile industries, and its economic prosperity was accompanied by an unprecedented upsurge in cultural activity, marked by the appearance of many men of culture. Aubin, "Le patronage culturel en Iran sous les Ilkhans" (1975) describes cultural patronage by notables in Yazd in this period. A. Iwatake, "The Waqfs of the Niẓām Family in 14th Century Yazd," (J., 1989) is a detailed examination of the waqf activities of the notables covered by Aubin. This article clarifies the economic background of urban notables, and studies motivations behind religious endowments by relating them to how people of the time regarded life and death. K. Kubo, "Mīr 'Alī Shīr's Patronage of Science and Art" (J., 1990) is an interesting study dealing with the issues of patronage and the construction and restoration of religious institutions by Mīr 'Alī Šīr, one of the most influential personalities at the Timurid court in its last years though not a member of an urban notable family. The same theme is discussed more widely by M. E. Subtelny. In "Socioeconomic Bases of Cultural Patronage under the Later Timurids" (1988), she suggests that the extensive development of the so-called *soyūrghāl* system of landholding in the latter half of the Timurid period enabled social elites to patronize various cultural activities.

It is considered that during the period from the Mongol invasion of Iran to the establishment of the Safavid state in the early 16th century the traditional political and religious authorities lost their power, and were left groping to establish a new social framework. An interesting work on the influence of two saints of Bam over the people in Bam and surrounding villages is Aubin, *Deux sayyids de Bam au XVe siècle* (1956). A similar point of view is contained in Aubin, "Un santon quhistani de l'époque timouride" (1967).

Aubin, "Etudes safavides I: Šāh Isma'īl et les notables de l'Iraq persan" (1959), describing how urban notables joined forces with new regimes regardless of the rise and fall of the political power, was the first work to point out the continuing existence of Iranian urban notables after the Mongol era. The article sets out three conditions identifying urban notables: 1) the possession of religious authority (specifically, to be a *sayyid*), 2) the ability to carry out administrative duties (to be a secretary or a bureaucrat), 3) knowledge of Islamic law (to be an ulama). This work had a great influence on later studies of notables. Aubin's studies are not confined within the category of urban studies in a narrow sense, but are based on a grand conception encompassing the whole of pre-modern Iranian society, including cities, in its view. His penetrating insight and conclusions based on an exhaustive examination of the historical sources are admirable.

S. H. Modarresī Ṭabāṭabā'ī, *A Leaf from the History of Qazvin* (P., 1361/1982-3) is the history of the Mar'ašī, a *sayyid* family of Qazvin, which reconstructs the history of this family of notables from the 7th century A. H. (13th century A. D.) to the present with the aid of many documents, such as royal orders given to the family. M. A. Golrīz, *The Gate of Heaven: History and the Historical Geography of Qazvin,* vol. 2 (P., 1368/1989-90) is a collection of the biographies of ulama and intellectuals born in the city. R. Quiring-Zoche, *Isfahan im 15. und 16. Jahrhundert* (1980) discusses eight notable families who lived in Esfahan in the 15th and 16th centuries in terms of their origins and the personal histories of their members, with genealogies attached. This work clarifies in specific terms much about the administrative, economic, and religious roles played by urban notables in Esfahan during this period. M. Haneda, "La famille Ḫūzānī d'Isfahan (15e-17e siècles)" (1989) focuses on the Ḫūzānīs, a notable family of Esfahan which Quiring-Zoche only touched on in her study, and looks at the fortunes of this family, who were bureaucrats rather than ulama. Haneda also describes how a notable family and the central political power both tried to extend their own influence, turning each other to good account. These works elucidate something of the relationship between urban notables and the authorities. Since few such studies exist for cities other than Esfahan, it is to be hoped that more case studies will appear in the future. From T. Suzuki's monograph concerning the Ottoman Empire, *Elites and Power in the Ottoman Empire* (J., 1993) it has become apparent that the bureaucrat class in central government was clearly distinguished between the secretaries and the ulama, and each of the groups was dominant at various times in the Ottoman Empire. There are virtually no similar studies about the Iranian bureaucrat class. A large proportion of bureaucrats, however, probably had their origins in families of urban notables, and further research should make the relationship between state power and the cities clearer.

K. Kubo, "Herat in the Early Sixteenth Century" (J., 1988) vividly describes how those of influence in the cities reacted when directly threatened by military might following the replacement of one political power by another. This study concerning the relations between religious men of influence in Herat and the Safavid and Shibanid authorities is particularly interesting because it shows that it was not a matter of a simple change of political power but rather one related to the Safavid identification with the Shiites. The same argument is contained in the recently published M. Szuppe, *Entre Timourides, Uzbeks et Safavides* (1992). Szuppe uses a source she herself recently edited to discuss in a broader way the political and social history of Herat in the first half of the 16th century. Her line of argument is very close to Kubo's in the above article. Kubo, "The Cultural Movement and its Background in Timurid Herat" (J., 1989) sums up the type of structures influential men built in Herat in the late Timurid period.

N. Kondo, "Moḥammad Taqī Khān and his Family in Yazd" (J., 1993) focuses on the history of an influential local family of Yazd in the 18th-19th centuries and examines the process of its rise to power, its power base and its relationship to the central government. Kondo points out that the family grasped political power without tribal background and regards this phenomena as a feature of the politically unstable period after the fall of the Safavids. Their success depended, according to Kondo, on the fact that their ancestors occupied the post of the chief of the indigenous *tofangčī* corps during the Safavid period. After the establishment of the Qajar rule, the central government came to intervene in the politics of Yazd and the family lost their "independence."

19th century Tehran is dealt with in T. Sakamoto, "Mostowfī Family under the Urban Growth of the Late 19th Century Tehran" (J., 1983). The article includes details about the family composition of the head of the Mostowfīs, who held important government posts, their residence, the family's landed property, and their servants and places of origin, in order to describe the life of the elite of the time. An interesting point is that Sakamoto shows that shifts in Tehran society at a time when the population had started to increase rapidly and social classes had begun to change, were faithfully reflected in the family composition of the Mostowfīs. id. "The Demographic Census of Tehran in the 19th Century" (J., 1984) attempts to shed light on the composition of the population and the social structure of Tehran in the 19th century through an analysis of the census of 1868, taken at a time when the city was expanding. There is a considerable amount of data concerning Tehran in the transitional period from the pre-modern "Islamic city" to the modern city. M. Etteḥādīye and S. Sa'dvandiyān, *Statistics of Tehran, the Caliph's Capital* (P., 1368/1989-90) is a recently published edition which contains details about the three household checks and the census (the population statistics of which Sakamoto used in the above-mentioned article). A voluminous work by Ǧ. Šahrī, *Social History of Tehran in the 13th Century A. H.* (P., 1367-8/1988-9), has also appeared. There is also available a city map drawn by an Austrian before the expansion of the urban district: H. Slaby, *Plan von Teheran* (1977). Further progress in this area is expected.

An effective method of inquiry into the image of ulama in urban society prior to the Constitutional Revolution is to explore the roles played by the ulama in that revolution. Studies on the period of the Constitutional Revolution are so numerous that I will refrain from dealing with them here.

Notable families are discussed in W. R. Royce, "The Shirazi Provincial Elite: Status Maintenance and Change" (1981). Royce looks at how a family obtained power as an elite and how it maintained its elite status, and examines two provincial elite families in Shiraz active from the 18th century to the present century, the Qavām family, a secular elite, and the Emāmī Šīrāzī family, an ulama elite. The conditions he considers to delineate notables are (1) historical tradition and a reputation of respectability, (2) individual qualities such as educational background, manner of speaking, poetic gifts, manhood (*ǧavānmardī*) and piety, (3) making donations, (4) wealth, and (5) political power linked to the central government. This article, with its description of 19th century provincial notables provides a more detailed model of a notable than that of Aubin. It may be possible to use it to re-examine the image of notables in the pre-modern age.

If it is true that the existence of notables in Iran is more conspicuous than in any other region, it is necessary to ask which of Royce's conditions was the crucial one in guaranteeing the continuity of notable families there. H. Kano "An Image of Iranian Society" (J., 1975) analyzes, according to sociological methodology, elites in Iranian society, including the Qavām family, in the 19th century. M. D. Good, "Social Hierarchy in Provincial Iran: The Case of Qajar Maragheh" (1977) is a study of the lineage of an influential nomadic family that settled down to become a notable family in the city of Maragheh in Azerbaijan during the Qajar period. A sequel by the same author is "The Changing Status and Composition of an Iranian Provincial Elite" (1981).

It is apparent from the above outline that studies on the notables of different cities and different periods have come out separately; they need to be consolidated by comparative studies of notables of different cities of the same period and of notables of the same city over a long time span. In addition, further study is necessary concerning the roles played in urban society by influential persons in the city, such as the qadi and the ulama, whom a good proportion came from notable families; especially those roles that could only have been played by people of such family origin.

3. Guilds and Artisans

Studies about the guild (*aṣnāf* in Persian) began with general surveys of its internal constitution, as for example, A. K. S. Lambton, *Islamic Society in Persia* (1954) and A. Ashraf, "Historical Obstacles to the Development of a Bourgeoisie in Iran" (1969). Subsequently, appreciable progress has been made, particularly as a result of W. M. Floor's studies of the guild mainly in the Qajar period. Floor, a leading scholar of Iranian social and economic history, has given a good summary of his ideas about the Iranian guild in an article on the aṣnāf (1987) in the *Encyclopaedia Iranica*. T. Sakamoto, "A Memorandum on the Modern Islamic Guild" (J., 1979) introduces and sums up Floor's studies and compares them with Baer's study on the guild in modern Egypt. The article provides a convenient summary of the features of the Iranian guild and the questions concerning it which remain to be answered.

Among the studies done by Floor after the publication of Sakamoto's article, "Guilds and *futuvvat* in Iran" (1984) proves that *futuvvat* (*futuwwa* in Arabic) and guild are not one and the same, an argument which is apparent in his above-mentioned article on *aṣnāf*. In contrast to other areas, the guild in Iran played an important social role until very recently. The late 19th century guild is dealt with in T. Philipp, "Isfahan 1881-1891: A Close-up View of Guilds and Protection" (1984) while a significant recent study of the Safavid period guild is M. Keyvānī, *Artisans and Guild Life in the Later Safavid Period* (1982), an ambitious work that deals comprehensively with matters related to the guild in the late Safavid period such as internal structure, methods of control by the government, social function, relations between merchants and guild, and guild tax. Interesting is the author's claim that one of the reasons for Iran's delayed economic development in the modern era was the inconsistency of economic policies taken by the Safavid government, particularly by Shah 'Abbas.

M. Kh. Geidarov, *Cities and the Urban Craft Industry in Azerbaijan from the 13th to the 17th Century* (R., 1982) surveys the political as well as the economic condition of cities in Azerbaijan in the designated period, and describes with a wealth of detail the activities of artisans in those cities who worked in the textile, leather, dyeing, metal working and construction industries. Although the place and period under study is limited, the work is valuable for the information it provides about a blank area in the urban history of Iran.

4. Quarters

As with the cities of other regions of the Islamic world, Iranian city quarters have an important significance. Studies about Iranian cities by the Iranian scholars listed in pp. 240-2 frequently record the names of quarters at length (for example, M. Maškūr, S. Šafaqī). Information about the names and locations of present day quarters in Esfahan is contained in S. Schafaghi, "Bildung von Stadtvierteln in Eṣfahān" (1979).

Historical sources in Persian and European languages from the Safavid period onward show that the residents of urban quarters in Iranian cities were divided into two groups, *ḥaydarī* and *ne'matī*, which whenever the occasion arose fought against each other in the streets, often with deaths occurring. This phenomenon of bipartisan fighting within the quarter was a dominant characteristic of Iranian cities, one which cannot be found in the cities of any other area in the Islamic world. H. Mirjafari, "The Ḥaydarī-Ni'matī Conflicts in Iran" (1979) discusses the origin of the terms *ḥaydarī* and *ne'matī*, and shows that they derived from two Sufis who lived in the 14th century. Mirjafari also contends that the conflict between the two groups existed even before that time in the form of a conflict between Sunnis and Shiites and that such sectarian or doctrinal conflicts lost their religious meaning after the 16th century but continued as bipartisan sectarian fighting in many cities. Many questions remain, since Mirjafari's article is factual rather than analytical. Why, for example, did such conflicts occur commonly in Iranian cities with their strong tradition of independence? When did they begin to appear? Was there no horizontal communication between the *ḥaydarī* and the *ne'matī* ? What sort of man was the leader of each group? What were the relations between the two groups and urban outlaws such as *lūṭī*? An investigation of these questions would shed light on one characteristic of cities in the Iranian sphere.

As we have seen above, there were in Nishapur between the 11th and 12th centuries conflicts between the adherents of the two law schools, the Shafi'is and the Hanafis. According to Cl. Cahen, "Mouvements populaires et autonomisme urbain dans l'Asie musulmane du moyen âge" (1958), p. 232 and R. Quiring-Zoche, *Isfahan im 15. und 16. Jahrhundert* (1980), p. 14 the situation was similar in Esfahan in the same period. A subject for investigation is whether the conflict between the two law schools had any relation to that which occurred between the *ḥaydarī* and *ne'matī*. A similar conflict centring on the quarter in the period from the late 19th century to the early 20th century is discussed in H. Kagaya, "Religious Rivalry of Two Sects in Modern Muslim Society in Iran" (J., 1981).

Ḥ. Solṭānzāde, *Introduction to the History of Cities and Urbanization in Iran* (P., 1365/1986-7), devotes one section to city quarters, discussing their leaders, numbers, life, and the relationship between quarters and bazars. An interesting point is his observation that each quarter had a centre consisting of a mosque, public baths and shops for selling daily necessities and that in this centre there was often a reservoir (*āb anbār*) or a theatre (*ḥoseynīye*). This is worth noting because such centers did not exist in the quarters of 15th century Damascus, as T. Miura has shown (see pp. 119-20).

It is difficult to ascertain in the case of the Iranian city from when there occurred segregation of dwelling among the different religious groups in the city, a characteristic often regarded as definitive of the "Islamic city." Jews in Esfahan from an early time tended to live in the Jowbāre district, in the northeast of the city, according to Šafaqī, *Geography of Esfahan* (P., 1353/1974-5), p. 402, and it is a well-known fact that Shah 'Abbas made Armenians who had undergone a forced migration to reside together in Jolfa, a suburb of Esfahan. It is also known that there was a Jewish quarter in Shiraz during the period of Karim Khan (Solṭānzāde, op. cit., p. 241).

5. 'Ayyār and Lūṭī: Urban Outlaws

K. Shimizu has published two articles about *'ayyār* gangs during the Seljuk period, "'Ayyār in Sīstān" (J., 1984) and "Chivalric Groups in the History of Iran" (J., 1989). In the latter study, he raises seventeen points of issue for the study of *'ayyār* and suggests that it is possible to use literary works to study pre-modern *'ayyār*, given the fact that historical sources are scarce. Later, during the Qajar period, urban outlaws were often called *lūṭī*. As Shimizu points out, similarities and differences between the *'ayyār* and *lūṭī* have not yet been explained, nor have other significant questions such as when the shift from *'ayyār* to *lūṭī* occurred.

The first study to pay serious attention to the *lūṭī* and to point out their social significance was A. K. S. Lambton, *Islamic Society in Persia* (1954). It was followed by H. G. Migeod, "Die Lutis: Ein Ferment des städtischen Lebens in Persien" (1959) and R. Arasteh, "The Character, Organization and Social Role of the *lūṭīs* (*javānmardān*) in the Traditional Iranian Society of the 19th Century" (1961). The level of research was significantly raised by a number of articles by W. M. Floor, including "The Lūṭīs" (1971), "The Political Role of the lūṭīs in Qāǧār Iran" (1979) and "The Political Role of the Lutis in Iran" (1981). According to the first article, the term *lūṭī* was used to designate a social group in the 19th century and it can be classified into two categories by usage, one being a class of entertainers, such as itinerant jugglers, clowns and buffoons and the other being urban outlaws. Floor makes clear, regarding the second classification, that it is necessary to distinguish *lūṭī* from *awbāš*, meaning merely ruffian, and he says that the origins of the urban outlaw can often be traced back to the *'ayyār* in terms of their values, ethics, and manners and customs. He also shows that urban outlaws had a close relationship with a certain quarter of a city (though he does not elaborate on the nature of the relationship, nor on the question of what type of quarter they were associated with), that they did not form a so-called guild, and that often these urban outlaws were connected with the political power. In the second article, Floor gives specific details of how local leaders cooperated with the *lūṭī* using the example of Shiraz in the middle of the 19th century. In the third article, he summarizes the actions and social role of the *lūṭī* in the same period as that dealt with in the former two articles, and on that basis is able to analyze "*lūṭī* style" behavior on the occasion of the 1979 Revolution.

Floor's studies are very suggestive and provide hints about how to look at an urban society. Nevertheless, considering the fact that he deals mainly with the 19th and 20th centuries, he does not always probe deep enough into his sources, thus it remains necessary to undertake further research into individual cases. In addition, in order to understand how the *'ayyār* became the *lūṭī* we must also consider *'ayyār* and urban outlaws in the period from the Mongols to the Safavids. If it is correct to assume that an unstable society brings about the appearance of *'ayyār*, then the 14th and 15th centuries, prior to the establishment of the Safavid dynasty, were a particularly apt time. Although there seems to be no mention of *'ayyār* in that period, the historical sources should be reexamined. Their relations with popular movements such as the Sarbadār which broke out during the same period should also be taken into consideration. An attractive subject for future study, though it doubtless will take some time to complete, is a comparison between the role of the *'ayyār* of Iran and the *zu'r* of 15th and 16th century Damascus, elucidated by T. Miura.

6. Popular Movements in the Cities

Violent popular movements, though not reaching the intensity of those of the modern Constitutional Revolution, broke out at times in the cities of the Iranian sphere. The Sarbadār movement of the 14th century was perhaps the largest. This, a kind of "republican" movement centred on Sabzavar in

Khurasan, drew the attention of Petrushevskii in the 1950s and he published "The Sarbadār Movements in Khurasan" (R., 1956). A great advance was made with J. M. Smith, *The History of the Sarbadār Dynasty 1336-1381 A. D. and its Sources* (1970), with its use of numismatic studies in particular. A complementary work is A. H. Morton, "The History of the Sarbadārs in the Light of New Numismatic Evidence" (1976).

J. Aubin criticized the studies of Petrushevskii and Smith in two articles, "La fin de l'Etat Sarbadâr du Khorassan" (1974) and "Aux origines d'un mouvement populaire médiéval" (1976). He contends that the movement owed its success to the coming together of two groups of different characteristics, the popular urban movement, Sarbadār, on one hand, and mystic Sheikhism rooted mostly in rural areas on the other. But it was indeed the conflict and confrontation between the two that bought about the decline of the movement as a whole. Aubin has to some degree clarified the political history of the Sarbadār movement with these articles but basic questions remain, such as why a popular movement should have arisen in the mid-14th century in a not very large regional city such as Sabzavar and what were the purposes of the movement.

In Iran too, the study of the Sarbadār movement is popular. There are works such as A. Ḥaqīqat, *History of the Sarbadār Movement and Other Iranian Movements in the 8th Century A. H.* (P., 1360/1981-2) and Y. Āžand, *The Uprising of Shiite Sarbadār* (P., 1363/1984-5). Further study about the movement should include a comparative discussion of the other movement with the same name which occurred in Samarkand in the same period. There was another small-scale movement in Tabriz in the 16th century bearing the same name, Sarbadār. This is studied by G. Vercellin in "Un 'Sarbedār' del 981/1573 a Tabriz" (1970).

7. Bazars and Merchants

Eugen Wirth, whose research centres on the bazar in the cities of the Islamic world, discusses in articles such as "Strukturwandlungen und Entwicklungstendenzen der orientalischen Stadt" (1968), "Zum Problem der Bazars (sūq, çarşı)" (1974-5) and "Die orientalische Stadt" (1982), the question of where the morphological characteristics of cities of the Islamic world can be found. He contends that whereas blind alleys and courtyards already appear in the cities of the Ancient Orient prior to the Islamic Age, the form of the suq (bazar) as it remains to this day developed after the rise of Islam and, moreover, cannot be found in any European city. He therefore asserts that the bazar is the defining characteristic of an "Islamic city." X. de Planhol, "La cour, la place, le parvis" (1984) takes an almost identical position. Regardless of whether this view is right or wrong (Ḥ. Solṭānzāde has stated in his work, *Introduction to the History of Cities and Urbanization in Iran,* p. 251, that the bazar existed as early as the Sasanian period), the study of the bazar is without doubt essential to an understanding of the cities of the Islamic world. Such historical studies of the bazar in Iran are too few, given the relative importance of the subject. Such neglect may be due primarily to the lack of suitable historical materials.

Valuable, therefore, is H. Gaube and E. Wirth, *Der Bazar von Isfahan* (1978), which describes changes that the bazar in Esfahan had undergone and its present condition on the basis of fieldwork and documentary sources. The first part of the text discusses the transformation of the entire bazar and the second part contains a detailed record of the history of the individual structures within the bazar and in its vicinity. The first part is not simply a history of the bazar, but an interesting study of the historical development of the city of Esfahan. A number of fine maps which accompany the text are useful in that they are colour-coded according to the type of building and its date of construction, allowing the reader to understand at a glance how the bazar developed after the Safavid period. The chapter on Esfahan in Gaube's *Iranian Cities* (1979) is a summary of the descriptions given in *Der Bazar von Isfahan.*

T. Sakamoto, "The Urban Structure of Esfahan in the 19th Century and Meydān" (J., 1980-1) draws on Gaube's studies to discuss the political, economic and cultural roles of the Royal Square (Meydān-e Šāh) and the Old Square (Meydān-e Kohne) and proves that the *meydān* was at the centre of a large economic zone including peripheral villages and nomad areas. Sakamoto's article also looks at the decline of the political and economic status of Esfahan and its replacement in the 19th century by the expanding Tehran.

Discussions of the relationship between bazar and the political power include W. M. Floor, "The Marketpolice in Qājār Persia" (1971) and "Das Amt des Muhtasib im Iran: Zur Kontrolle der 'öffentlichen Moral' in der iranischen Geschichte" (1980; English translation "The Office of Muhtasib in Iran," 1985). The former discusses, from the viewpoint of institutional history, the authority of the *dārūġa-ye bāzār,* who maintained order in the bazar and kept control over commercial activities as the supervisor of markets. The latter argues that the position of muhtasib derived from the Byzantine *agranomos,* and that it was concerned with the control and supervision of markets, not with overseeing correct behaviour in terms of religion.

In connection with the bazar, les us look at some research on the role of merchants in urban society. (I will refrain here from mentioning studies on merchants themselves in the 19th century, though G. G. Gilbar, A. K. S.

Lambton and others have produced pertinent work.) W. M. Floor's "The Merchants (*tujjār*) in Qājār Iran" (1976) is a study on this subject. This work does not concern itself with urban history so much, but rather aims principally to shed light on the responses of Iranian merchants to European economic advances into Iran in the 19th century. Cited below from the article are points related to urban history: (1) Floor restricts himself to dealing only with wholesale merchants (*tuǧǧār*) though many other kinds existed, (2) the merchants did not form a guild, (3) many of the merchants were from notable families, and in many cases they married into the ulama class, (4) the ulama were engaged in trade, and (5) in the latter half of the 19th century, many merchants invested their money in land so as to become landowners. This extremely interesting article also includes an explanation of the various roles of the *malik al-tuǧǧār*.

T. Sakamoto, "Modern Islamic Cities and the Iranians" (J., 1984) is a compendium of the author's published articles, comprising an analysis firstly of the factors contributing to the economic decline of 19th century Esfahan and the contrasting development of Tehran, and secondly of inter-city networks extending across national borders between the cities of Iran and settlements of Iranians outside Iran, such as in Istanbul or Baku, whose influence affected Iran in a variety of ways. This is a persuasive work, linking urban prosperity and decline with 19th century international commercial networks.

While studies on post-19th century bazars and merchants are quite numerous, very little has appeared on the subject concerning the period before the 18th century. Pre-modern bazars and merchants have only been mentioned cursorily in the studies concerning the so-called guild. It has often been pointed out that bazar merchants influenced the direction of the Constitutional Revolution early this century. If this was so, much more needs to be known about the bazar and merchants in pre-modern times. The bazar should be studied in relation to the later period, especially in terms the growth of its economic sphere, order within the bazar (power of leaders, organization of merchants and artisans), and the relationship between the bazar and the government.

In addition, the relationship of merchants with bureaucrats and the ulama needs to be explained, as does the connection between urban notables and the merchant class, since it is virtually impossible to find a truebred merchant mentioned in historical sources of the pre-modern age. If a truebred merchant class did exist, we need to know how merchants backed by their accumulated wealth acted in and out of cities. In contrast to royal families, the military aristocracy, bureaucrats, and the ulama, there is almost no evidence of waqf contribution by genuine merchants. The issue of merchants in the pre-modern age is a theme that deserves particular attention in the future.

8. Waqf Endowment

Studies of waqf as a system supporting urban society have developed since the 1970s within the framework of Iranian urban history. They began as doctoral dissertations such as R. Holod-Tretiak's *The Monuments of Yazd, 1300-1450: Architecture, Patronage and Setting* (1972) and R. D. McChesney's study of the waqf of Mazar-i Sharif located in the suburbs of Balkh in Khurasan, *Waqf at Balkh: A Study of the Endowments at the Shrine of 'Alī Ibn Abī Ṭālib* (1973). McChesney went on to make general studies about waqf in the Eastern Islamic world in the 16th and 17th centuries, "Waqf and Public Policy: The Waqfs of Shāh 'Abbās, 1011-1023/1602-1614" (1981) and "Economic and Social Aspects of the Public Architecture of Bukhara in the 1560's and 1570's" (1987). Both works describe in detail the acts of waqf endowment by sovereigns and men of influence and examine the significance of endowment activities for donors as well as for urban society. Their prudent use of documents and records and the clarity of their argument make these perhaps the foremost achievements in the field. Fortunately an expanded version of McChesney's dissertation has recently been published under the title of *Waqf in Central Asia: Four Hundred Years in the History of a Muslim Shrine* (1991). M. E. Subtelny, "A Timurid Educational and Charitable Foundation: The Ikhlāṣiyya Complex of 'Alī Shīr Navā'ī in 15th-Century Herat and its Endowment"(1991) discusses the endowment by 'Alī Šīr Navā'ī, one of the great cultural patrons of the later Timurid period and gives a detailed description of the location, layout of buildings, activities and personnel of the Iḫlāsīya, his main charitable complex in Herat. M. E. Bonine, "Islam and Commerce: Waqf and the Bazaar of Yazd, Iran" (1987) uses the example of Yazd to examine the role and impact of waqf on the physical structure of the city and demonstrates the close interrelationship between the commercial and religious sectors of the city.

When McChesney studied the waqfs of Shah 'Abbas, he drew upon A. Sepantā, *A Short History of Waqf Endowments in Esfahan* (P., 1346/1967-8), a collection of summaries of the waqf documents existing in Esfahan today, helpful despite certain inadequacies deriving from the fact they are not the actual documents. It goes without saying that the foremost need in the study of waqf is to examine and analyze the actual waqf documents. The aforementioned work of M. E. Subtelny is the product of such an analysis. Looking back at previous studies we notice that it is only after a waqf document is made public in one form or another that scholarly investigation of it is pursued. For example, Holod-Tretiak's study would never have come into existence if I. Afšār and M. T. Dānešpažūh had not published *Ǧāmi' al-Ḫayrāt* (*The Record of Charities*, in Persian, 1341/1962-3), a revised edition of a collection of Yazd waqf deeds dating from the 14th century. In this sense, the present situation concerning the consolidation and publication of waqf documents from various periods that exist all over Iran is far from satisfactory. Such conditions should be improved in order to produce more substantiative research.

A. Iwatake, "The Waqfs of the Niẓām Family in 14th Century Yazd" (J., 1989) makes good use of the *Ǧāmi' al-Ḫayrāt* and describes actual waqf endowment deeds of two generations of the Niẓāms, an influential family in Yazd during the Mongol period. Deed of waqf made by Rašīd al-Dīn, vizier to the Ilkhanids, a contemporary of the Niẓāms studied by Iwatake, have been published by M. Menovī and I. Afšār as *The Waqf Deed of Rab'-e Rašīdī* (P., 2536/1977-8). Sh. Blair, "Ilkhanid Architecture and Society: An Analysis of the Endowment Deed of the Rab'-i Rashīdī" (1984) analyzes this deed. Iwatake, "A Waqf of a Tīmūrid Amīr" (J., 1990) is a case study of waqf endowment by a Timurid amir and his wife made primarily to secure property for their descendants.

Waqf endowments in the Iranian world began to grow remarkably in number in the 12th and 13th centuries. The question of why this should have been so has not yet been sufficiently answered. Generally it has been attributed to reasons such as securing inheritance of property, religious faith, and as alleged by McChesney, monarch's propaganda of his own piety. T. Allen, *Timurid Herat* (1983) argues that a Turkish amir endowed his property to a religious institution in order to link himself to religious leaders belonging to a class of influential men in urban society. Other views, such as Iwatake, "The Waqfs of the Niẓām Family" (J., 1989) and M. Haneda, "The Pastoral City and the Mausoleum City" (J., 1990) emphasize that waqf donors offered waqf properties as revenue sources for maintaining and managing their own large-scale mausolea. The popularity of waqf endowment might also have had something to do with a change in popular outlook as a result of social change. In any case, it is certain that many complicated factors contributed to the increase of waqf endowment, there is no single explanation for the occurance of such phenomenon. Since waqf endowment has a purely religious side to it, it is increasingly necessary to analyze the *mentalité* of waqf donors.

9. City and Nomads

After the establishment of the Seljuk dynasty in the early 11th century, and especially after the founding of the Ilkhanid dynasty in the 13th century, states whose existence depended almost totally on the military power of Turkic and Mongol nomadic tribesmen emerged in succession in the Iranian world. The rulers of such states were either themselves of nomad stock or deeply influenced by tribal elements, and tribal chiefs comprised the backbone of the state. As a result, monarchs and influential men of tribal origin acquired many local rights and interests and inevitably a ruler-ruled relationship emerged between the power-holding nomads and the cities. The study of this relationship is highly significant for understanding the characteristics of Iranian urban history and its history as a whole.

The relationship between the nomad and the city dweller is a persistent theme in the history of the Western Asia. T. Sato, "A View of Islamic Social History: The Case of Fayyūm Province" (J., 1977) deals with everyday relations between nomads and the cities in the region of Fayyūm in medieval Egypt. T. Sakamoto, "The Urban Structure of Esfahan in the 19th Century and Meydān" (J., 1980-1) deals with the same subject in terms of 19th century Iran. These studies however do not deal with the situation where nomads, backed by their direct connection with state power, had great dominance over a city. The works to be surveyed here will on the contrary concern the relationship between cities and nomads as rulers.

J. Aubin, "Comment Tamerlan prenait les villes" (1963) investigates how Timur, upon subjugating a city, imposed certain demands and punitive measures in response to its attitude towards him. The conclusions may perhaps be applied to the conquest of cities by nomads in general. It was the rule for leaders of tribal origin to migrate to the highlands in summer and to the cities, where food and other necessities could be obtained, in winter. M. Honda , "The Winter- and Summer-Quarters of the Ilkhans" (J., 1976) identifies the sites of the Ilkhan summer and winter quarters and proves that the Azerbaijan region was their "headquarters." "Soltaniye: The New Capital of the Ilkhanid Mongols" (J., 1986) by the same author examines the circumstances surrounding the construction of the new capital, Soltaniye, on the site of the Ilkhan summer quarters. Sh. Blair, "The Mongol Capital of Sulṭāniyya, 'The Imperial'" (1986) deals more or less with the same subject, but discusses Soltaniye in the Mongol and later periods and mentions features of architectural design. In addition Blair makes the important observation that the center of Soltaniye consisted of the mausoleum of Olǧeytū, the Ilkhan who ordered the construction of the city, which was placed inside a garden in accordance with Islamic custom since the time of the Koran.

M. Haneda, "The Pastoral City and the Mausoleum City" (J., 1990) points out two characteristics dating from the Ilkhanid period of the way the nomads constructed their cities: (1) the city was built where plenty of water and grass were available for gardens (*bāġ*) to surround it ("pastoral city"); (2) a royal mausoleum is found in the center of the city ("mausoleum city"). The article states that waqf endowment for religious and charitable institutions centred on the mausoleum was the key to the survival of this type of city and that by the Safavid period "mausoleum cities" were no longer built due to changes in the mausoleum cult. Haneda, "Maydān et Bāġ" (1990) emphasizes that in the building of the new capital of Esfahan by Shah 'Abbas in the late 16th century there is a strong persistence of certain features of tribal tradition in city construction that had been influential since the Ilkhanid period, such as in the arrangement of gardens (*bāġ*). J. M. Scarce, "The Royal Palaces of the Qajar Dynasty: A Survey" (1983) surveys the royal palaces of the Qajar dynasty in Tehran, as the title indicates. Like the Safavid rulers, the Qajar monarchs built a simple palace within a garden; it is however problematical whether this should be regarded simply as a tribal element continuing over from the Safavid period or not.

Works such as D. Wilber, "The Timurid Court: Life in Gardens and Tents" (1979) and P. A. Andrews, "The Tents of Timur" (1978) discuss how the nomads lived their lives in tents.

Gardens (*bāġ*) must have held a special meaning for tribal rulers and their close associates, since they represented valuable space which could satisfy nomadic instincts within the city. It is not within the scope of the present work to review studies concerning the historical development of Iranian gardens down to the Mughal period, and I will mention here only some of the basic works on the subject. J. Brookes, *Gardens of Paradise* (1987) is a full-scale introduction to the Islamic garden. The Iranian style of garden design is discussed in works such as D. Wilber, *Persian Gardens and Garden Pavilions* (1962); H. I. S. Kanwar, "Origin and Evolution of the Design of the Chaharbagh Garden" (1974) and R. Pinder-Wilson, "The Persian Garden: Bagh and Chahar Bagh" (1976). Sh. Parpagliolo, *Kābul: The Bāgh-i Bābur* (1972), W. Ball, "The Remains of a Monumental Timurid Garden outside Herat" (1981) and E. B. Moynihan, "The Lotus Garden Palace of Zahir al-Din Muhammad Babur" (1988) are among the studies available on Timurid period gardens. Works in Persian include P. Nīlūfarī, *Iranian Gardens* (P., 1363/1984-5) and A. R. Āryānpūr, *A Survey of Iranian Gardens and Historical Gardens in Shiraz* (P., 1365/1986-7). Nevertheless much still remains to be done on the Iranian style garden and there has appeared nothing yet about the types of garden that were created and developed by the tribal aristocracy in the city suburbs.

Studies on the relations between the politically powerful nomads and the cities are mostly concentrated on the "hardware," that is, how nomads changed the outward appearance of the cities. Future studies on the "software" of the city will perhaps answer questions such as through what channels the nomads developed their connections with urban society, how those groups and organizations constituting urban society were transformed when nomads began to rule the cities, and how urban society itself was influenced as a result. M. D. Good, "Social Hierarchy in Provincial Iran" (1977) deserves note in that it demonstrates how a nomadic tribe settled down in a town and became a noted family during the Qajar period.

10. Others

I will mention here a number of other areas that must be considered when dealing with urban history, though much remains to be done. One must concern population, since a prerequisite for any discussion of a city is its approximate population. Unlike the Ottoman Empire, where fairly exact population figures are available for as early as the 16th century in a partial way, there is no way of knowing the population and its composition for Iranian cities until the latter part of the 19th century.

T. Sakamoto, "The Demographic Census of Tehran in the 19th Century" (J., 1984) examines the composition of the inhabitants of Tehran on the basis of the demographic census carried out in 1868. The second chapter of F. Bémont, *Les villes de l'Iran*, vol. 1 (1969) and G. G. Gilbar, "Demographic Developments in Late Qajar Persia, 1810-1906" (1978) give elaborate analyses of issues in population since the 19th century. Only one such study exists for the pre-modern period; J. Aubin, "Chiffres de population urbaine en Iran Occidental autour de 1500" (1986), a work which fully utilizes documentary sources in European languages to estimate the population of the cities of western Iran in the early 16th century. The fact that this is only an estimate suggests that unless there is some epoch-making discovery of historical documentary material it will remain very difficult to apply historiographical methodology to discussions of population in the pre-modern period. It is quite understandable that Subtelny regrets: "Determining the population of Herat at the end of the 15th century seems an almost impossible task" ("A Medieval Persian Agricultural Manual in Context," 1993, p. 182).

Another important subject is immigration. It is well-known that in the Islamic world people changed their residence relatively freely. Lodgings such as *ḫānqāh* and caravansaries were built in cities and along traffic routes for the convenience of travellers. An intercity network was well established for both travel and migration. People used this network both when travelling by their own will or undergoing forced migration. F. Eršād, *The History of Iranian Immigration to India from the 8th to the 18th Century* (P., 1365/1986-7) is to my knowledge the only monograph focusing on this problem. J. R. Perry, "Forced Migration in Iran during the Seventeenth and Eighteenth Centuries" (1975) examines the immigration policies of Shah 'Abbas, Nader Shah, and Karim Khan. Since it deals mainly with the forced migration of nomadic tribes, it does not explore the subject matter in close connection with the city. Nevertheless it is a worthwhile reference in regard to topics such as the forced migration of Armenians and others during the Safavid period.

The march of the *'āšūrā* and the acting of a play about martyrdom, *ta'zīye,* on the 10th of Moharram typifies Iranian urban festivals. While studies have been made about the plays themselves, such as P. Chelkowski (ed.), *Ta'ziyeh: Ritual and Drama in Iran* (1979) there is nothing specific which discusses the meaning of this festival in the framework of urban society itself. J. Calmard, "Le mécénat des représentations de ta'ziye" (1974-7) is the only study that examines the question of official approval of *ta'zīye,* sanctioned by the authority of the Qajar to gain the support of the people.

Conclusion

In the above overview of past research, I believe that I have been able to assort, to some extent, questions concerning the study of Iranian cities. Of course, a number of shortcomings and deficiencies remain. Lack of time and knowledge on my part have forced me to omit many subjects, for instance, religious minorities in Iranian cities such as Jews and Armenians in particular, despite the fact that a considerable amount of work has been done in that area. In addition I have done no more than mention in passing the question of the urban activities of the Sufi order and Sufi influence over Iranian society, greater than in any other part of the Islamic world due to the fact that the Safavids derived from a Sufi order.

Most of the topics examined give some clue to the supposed characteristics of Iranian cities. The reader will perhaps be able to distinguish those characteristics more clearly as he or she peruses the other chapters of the book for comparison. Our future task must be to construct a total image of the Iranian city by synthesizing those characteristics considered typical of the Iranian city, in the process perhaps discovering common characteristics with other cities in the Islamic world, and so acquire the means to consider the effectiveness of the concept of the "Islamic city."

In doing so, it is necessary to compare and examine Iranian cities both before and after Islamization. H. Gaube, *Iranian Cities* (1979) and Ḥ. Solṭānzāde, *Introduction to the History of Cities and Urbanization in Iran* (P., 1365/1986-7) paid attention to this point, but not very satisfactorily. A particular task for the future will be to amass greater knowledge of Iranian cities prior to Islamization, and using that knowledge, together with comparisons with the cities of other Islamic regions, to highlight those urban characteristics belonging to the Islamic period.

Bibliography

Adle, Ch. & B. Hourcade, eds.*Téhéran: Capitale bicentenaire*. Paris & Tehran, 1992.

Afšār, I. *Yādgārhā-ye Yazd (Historical Monuments in Yazd)*. 3 vols. Tehran, 1348-54/1969-76.

Afšār, I. & M. T. Dānešpažūh, eds. *Ǧāmi' al-Ḫayrāt (The Record of Charities)*. Tehran, 1341/1962-3.

Afšār, I. & M. Menovī, eds. *Vaqfnāme-ye Rab'-e Rašīdī (The Waqf Deed of Rab'-e Rašīdī)*. Tehran, 2536/1977-8.

Ahrens, P. *Die Entwicklung der Stadt Teheran: Eine städtebauliche Untersuchung ihrer zukünftigen Gestaltung*. Berlin, 1966.

Allen, T. *A Catalogue of the Toponyms and Monuments of Timurid Herat*. Cambridge, Mass., 1981.

———. *Timurid Herat*. Wiesbaden, 1983.

Ambraseys, N. N. & Ch. Melville. *A History of Persian Earthquakes*. Cambridge, 1982.

Andrews, P. A. "The Tents of Timur: An Examination of Reports on the Quriltay at Samarqand, 1404." In *Art of the European Steppelands*, ed. P. Denwood. London, 1978.

Aqāsī, M. *Tārīḫ-e Ḫoy (History of Khoy)*. Tabriz, 1350/1971-2.

Arasteh, R. "The Character, Organization and Social Role of the *lūṭīs* (*javānmardān*) in the Traditional Iranian Society of the 19th Century." *JESHO* 4 (1961).

Āryānpūr, A. R. *Pažūhešī dar šenāḫt-e bāġhā-ye Īrān va bāġhā-ye tārīḫī-ye Šīrāz (A Survey of Iranian Gardens and Historical Gardens in Shiraz)*. Tehran, 1365/1986-7.

Ashraf, A. "Historical Obstacles to the Development of a Bourgeoisie in Iran." *Iranian Studies* 2 (1969).

Aubin, J. *Deux sayyids de Bam au XVᵉ siècle: Contribution à l'histoire de l'Iran timouride*. Wiesbaden, 1956.

———. "Notes sur quelques documents Aq-qoyunlu." In *Mélanges Louis Massignon*. Vol. 1. Damas, 1956.

———. "Etudes safavides I: Šāh Isma'īl et les notables de l'Iraq persan." *JESHO* 2/1 (1959).

———. "Comment Tamerlan prenait les villes." *SI* 19 (1963).

———. "L'aristocratie urbaine dans l'Iran seldjoukide: l'exemple de Sabzavâr." In *Mélanges offerts à René Crozet*. Poitiers, 1966.

———. "Un santon quhistani de l'époque timouride." *REI* 35 (1967).

———. "Eléments pour l'étude des agglomérations urbaines dans l'Iran médiéval." In *The Islamic City*, eds. S. M. Stern & A. Hourani. Oxford, 1970.

———. "La fin de l'Etat Sarbadâr du Khorassan." *JA* 262 (1974).

———. "Le patronage culturel en Iran sous les Ilkhans: Une grande famille de Yazd." *Le monde iranien et l'Islam* 3 (1975).

———. "Aux origines d'un mouvement populaire médiéval: Le cheykhisme du Bayhaq et du Nichapour." *Studia Iranica* 5/2 (1976).

———. "La propriété foncière en Azerbaydjan sous les Mongols." *Le monde iranien et l'Islam* 4 (1976-7).

———. "Chiffres de population urbaine en Iran Occidental autour de 1500." *Moyen Orient & Océan Indien* 3 (1986).

Ažand, Y. *Qeyām-e šī'ī sarbadārān (The Uprising of Shiite Sarbadār)*. Tehran, 1363/1984-5.

Bahrambeygui, H. *Tehran: An Urban Analysis*. Tehran, 1977.

Ball, W. "The Remains of a Monumental Timurid Garden outside Herat." *East and West* 31 (1981).

Bartol'd, V. V. *Istoriko-geograficheskii obzor Irana (An Historical Geography of Iran)*. S. Petersburg, 1903. Translated into English as *An Historical Geography of Iran* by S. Soucek. Princeton, 1984.

Beaudouin, E. E. "Ispahan sous les grands chahs (XVIIe siècle)." *Urbanisme* 2/10 (1933).

Bémont, F. *Les villes de l'Iran: Des cités d'autrefois à l'urbanisme contemporain*. 3 vols. Paris, 1969-73.

Blair, Sh. S. "Ilkhanid Architecture and Society: An Analysis of the Endowment Deed of the Rab'-i Rashīdī." *Iran* 22 (1984).

———. "The Mongol Capital of Sulṭāniyya, 'The Imperial'." *Iran* 24 (1986).

Bonine, M. E. *Yazd and its Hinterland: A Central Place System of Dominance in the Central Iranian Plateau*. Austin, 1975.

———. "City and Hinterland in Central Iran." In *Interdisziplinäre Iran-Forschung: Beiträge aus Kulturgeographie, Ethnologie, Soziologie und Neuerer Geschichte*, ed. G. Schweizer. Wiesbaden, 1979.

———. "The Morphogenesis of Iranian Cities." *Annals of the Association of American Geographers* 69/2 (1979).

———. "Islam and Commerce: Waqf and the Bazaar of Yazd, Iran." *Erdkunde* 41 (1987).

Brookes, J. *Gardens of Paradise*. London, 1987. Translated into Japanese as *Rakuen no dezain* by Takeo Kamiya. Tokyo, 1989.

Bulliet, R. W. "City Histories in Medieval Iran." *Iranian Studies* 1/3 (1968).

———. "A Quantitative Approach to Medieval Muslim Biographical Dictionaries." *JESHO* 13 (1970).

———. *The Patricians of Nishapur: A Study in Medieval Islamic Social History*. Cambridge, Mass., 1972.

———. *Conversion to Islam in the Medieval Period: An Essay in Quantitative History*. Cambridge, Mass. & London, 1979.

———. "Medieval Nishapur: A Topographic and Demographic Reconstruction." *Studia Iranica* 4 (1976).

———. "The Age Structure of Medieval Islamic Education." *SI* 57 (1983).

Cahen, Cl. "Mouvements populaires et autonomisme urbain dans l'Asie musulmane du moyen âge." *Arabica* 5/3 (1958); 6/1 (1959); 6/3 (1959).

Calmard, J. "Le mécénat des représentations de ta'ziye. I. Les précurseurs de Nâseroddin Châh." *Le monde iranien et l'Islam* 2 (1974).

———. "Le mécénat des représentations de ta'ziye. II. Les débuts du règne de Nâseroddin Châh." *Le monde iranien et l'Islam* 4 (1976-7).

Chardin, J. *Voyages du Chevalier Chardin*. Edited by L. Langlès. 10 vols. Paris, 1811.

Chelkowski, P., ed. *Ta'ziyeh: Ritual and Drama in Iran*. New York, 1979.

Coste, P. *Monuments modernes de la Perse*. Paris, 1867.

Coste, P. & E. Flandin. *Voyage en Perse*. 2 vols. Paris, 1845-54.

Creswell, K. A. C. *A Bibliography of the Architecture, Arts and Crafts of Islam: To 1st Jan. 1960*. Cairo, 1961.

———. *A Bibliography of the Architecture, Arts and Crafts of Islam: Supplement to Jan. 1972*. Cairo, 1973.

———. *A Bibliography of the Architecture, Arts and Crafts of Islam*. 2nd supplement. New York & Cairo, 1985.

Curzon, G. N. *Persia and the Persian Question*. 2 vols. London, 1892.

Ḍakā, Y. *Tārīḫče-ye sāḫtmānhā-ye arg-e solṭanatī-ye Tehrān va rāhnamā-ye kāḫ-e Golestān (A Short History of the Construction of the Fortress of Tehran and the Information on the Golestān Palace)*. Tehran, 1349/1970-1.

Della Valle, P. *I viaggi di Pietro Della Valle*. Edited by F. Gaeta & L. Lockhart. Il nuovo Ramusio VI. Roma, 1972.

Dieulafoy, J. *La Perse, la Chaldée et la Susianne*. Paris, 1887.

Drouville, G. *Voyage en Perse fait en 1812 et 1813*. 2 vols. Paris, 1825.

Emdād, H. *Šīrāz dar goḏašteh ve ḥāl (Shiraz: Its Past and Present)*. Šīrāz, 1339/1960-1.

English, P. W. *City and Village in Iran: Settlement and Economy in the Kirman Basin*. Madison, 1966.

Eršād, F. *Moḥāğerat-e tārīḫī-ye Īrāniyān be Hend; Qarn-e haštom tā heğdahom-e mīlādī (The History of Iranian Immigration to India from the 8th to the 18th Century)*. Tehran, 1365/1986-7.

Ettehadieh, M. "Patterns in Urban Development: the Growth of Tehran (1852-1903)." In *Qajar Iran: Political, Social and Cultural Change, 1800-1925*, eds. C. E. Bosworth & C. Hillenbrand. Edinburgh, 1983.

Etteḥādīye, M. & S. Sa'dvandiyān. *Āmār-e Dār al-Ḫelāfe-ye Tehrān (Statistics of Tehran, the Caliph's Capital)*. Tehran, 1368/1989-90.

Feuvrier, J. B. *Trois ans à la cour de Perse*. Paris, 1899.

Floor, W. M. "The Lūṭīs, a Social Phenomenon in Qajar Persia, a Reappraisal." *Die Welt des Islam* 13/1-2 (1971).

———. "The Office of Kalāntar in Qājār Persia." *JESHO* 14 (1971).

———. "The Marketpolice in Qājār Persia." *Die Welt des Islam* 13/3-4 (1971).

———. "The Police in Qājār Persia." *ZDMG* 123 (1973).

———. "The Guilds in Iran: An Overview from the Earliest Beginning till 1972." *ZDMG* 125 (1975).

———. "The Merchants (*tujjār*) in Qājār Iran." *ZDMG* 126 (1976).
———. "The Political Role of the lūṭīs in Qāǧār Iran." In *Interdisziplinäre Iran-Forschung: Beiträge aus Kulturgeographie, Ethnologie, Soziologie und Neuerer Geschichte,* ed. G. Schweizer. Wiesbaden, 1979.
———. "Das Amt des Muhtasib im Iran: Zur Kontrolle der 'öffentlichen Moral' in der iranischen Geschichte." In *Revolution in Iran und Afghanistan,* eds. K. Greussing & J. H. Grevemeyer. Frankfurt am Main, 1980.
———. "The Political Role of the Lutis in Iran." In *Modern Iran: The Dialectics of Continuity and Change,* eds. M. E. Bonine & N. Keddie. Albany, 1981.
———. "Guilds and *futuvvat* in Iran." *ZDMG* 134/1 (1984).
———. "The Office of Muhtasib in Iran." *Iranian Studies* 18/1 (1985).
———. "aṣnāf." *Encyclopaedia Iranica.* 1987.
Fragner, B. "Das Ardabiler Heiligtum in den Urkunden." *WZKM* 67 (1975).
Frye, R. N., ed. *The Histories of Nishapur.* Cambridge, Mass., 1965.
Galdieri, E. "Two Building Phases of the Time of Šāh 'Abbās I in the Maydān-i Šāh of Isfahān: Preliminary Note." *East and West,* new series, 20/1-2 (1970).
———. *Iṣfahān: Masǧid-i Ǧum'a: Restorations.* 3 vols. Roma, 1972-84.
———. *Eṣfahān: 'Alī Qāpū: An Architectural Survey.* Roma, 1979.
Galdieri, E. & R. Orazi. *Progretto di sistemazione del Maydān-i Šāh.* Roma, 1969.
Gaube, H. "Innenstadt-Aussenstadt: Kontinuität und Wandel im Grundriss von Herāt (Afghanistan) zwischen dem X. und dem XV. Jahrhundert." In *Beiträge zur Geographie orientalischer Städte und Märkte.* ed. G. Schweizer. Wiesbaden, 1977.
———. *Iranian Cities.* New York, 1979.
Gaube, H. & E. Wirth. *Der Bazar von Isfahan.* Wiesbaden, 1978.
Geidarov, M. Kh. *Goroda i gorodskoe remeslo Azerbaidzhana XIII-XVIIv. v. (Cities and the Urban Craft Industry in Azerbaijan from the 13th to the 17th Century).* Baku, 1982.
Gilbar, G. G. "Demographic Developments in Late Qajar Persia, 1810-1906." *Asian & African Studies* 12 (1978).
Gobineau, J. A. de. *Trois ans en Asie de 1855 à 1858.* 2 vols. Paris, 1859.
Godard, A. "Iṣfahān." *Aṯhār-é Īrān* 2 (1937).
Golrīz, M. A. *Mīnūdar yā bāb al-ǧannah-ye Qazvīn (The Gate of Heaven: History and the Historical Geography of Qazvin).* 2 vols. Tehran, 1337/1958-9, 1368/1989-90.
Golombek, L. "Anatomy of a Mosque: The Masjid-i Shāh of Iṣfahān." In *Iranian Civilization and Culture,* ed. C. J. Adams. Montreal, 1972.
———. "Urban Patterns in pre-Safavid Isfahan." *Iranian Studies* 7 (1974).
Golombek, L. & D. Wilber. *The Timurid Architecture of Iran and Turan.* 2 vols. Princeton, 1988.
Good, M. D. "Social Hierarchy in Provincial Iran: The Case of Qajar Maragheh." *Iranian Studies* 10 (1977).

———. "The Changing Status and Composition of an Iranian Provincial Elite." In *Continuity and Change in Modern Iran*, eds. M. Bonine & N. Keddie. Albany, 1981.

Graber, O. *The Great Mosque of Isfahan*. New York, 1990.

Gronke, M. *Arabische und persische Privaturkunden des 12. und 13. Jahrhunderts aus Ardabil (Aserbeidschan)*. Berlin, 1982.

Ḥakīm, M. *Ganǧ-e dāneš: Ǧoġrāfiyā-ye tārīḫī-ye šahrhā-ye Īrān (Treasure of Knowledge: A Historical Geography of Iranian Cities)*. Edited by M. A. Ṣowtī. Tehran, 1366/1987-8.

Haneda, Masashi. "La famille Ḫūzānī d'Isfahan, 15ᵉ-17ᵉ siècles." *Studia Iranica* 18/2 (1989).

———. "Maydān et Bāġ: Reflexion à propos de l'urbanisme du Šāh 'Abbās." In *Actes du Colloque franco-japonais sur les documents et archives provenant de l'Asie Centrale*. Kyoto, 1990.

———. "'Bokuchi toshi' to 'Bobyo toshi': Toho Isuramu sekai ni okeru yuboku seiken to toshi kensetsu (The Pastoral City and Mausoleum City: Nomadic Regime and City Building in the Iran-Islamic Land)." *Toyoshi Kenkyu* 49/1 (1990).

Ḥaqīqat, A. *Tārīḫ-e ǧonbeš-e sarbadārān va dīgar ǧonbešhā-ye īrāniyān dar qarn-e haštom-e heǧrī (History of the Sarbadār Movement and Other Iranian Movements in the 8th Century A. H.)*. Tehran, 1360/1981-2.

Herrmann, G. "Urkundenfunde in Āẕarbāyǧān." *Archäologische Mitteilungen aus Iran*, new series, 4 (1971).

Holod-Tretiak, R. *The Monuments of Yazd, 1300-1450: Architecture, Patronage and Setting*. Ph. D. dissertation, Harvard University, 1972.

Höltzer, E. *Īrān dar yek-ṣad o sīzdah sāl-e pīš (Iran of 113 Years Ago)*. Vol. 1: *Eṣfahān (Esfahan)*. Tehran, 2535/1976-7.

Honarfar, L. *Ganǧīne-ye āṯār-e tārīḫī-ye Eṣfahān (Treasure of Historical Monuments in Esfahan)*. Esfahan, 1344/1965-6.

———. "Eṣfahān dar dowre-ye ǧānešīnān-e Tīmūr" (Esfahan during the Timurid Period). *Honar o Mardom* 163 (2535/1976-7).

Honda, Minobu. "Iruhan no toeichi kaeichi (The Winter- and Summer-Quarters of the Ilkhans)." *Toyoshi Kenkyu* 34/4 (1976).

———. "Surutaniya kentoko (Soltaniye: The New Capital of the Ilkhanid Mongols)." In *Toho gakkai soritsu 40 shunen kinen tohogaku ronshu*. Tokyo, 1987.

Ḫosravī, M. *Ǧoġrafiyā-ye tārīḫī-ye velāyat-e Zāveh (The Historical Geography of the Zave Region)*. Mašhad, 1366/1987-8.

Iwatake, Akio. "Nizamuke no wakufu to 14 seiki no Yazudo (The Waqfs of the Niẓām Family in 14th Century Yazd)." *Shirin* 72/3 (1989).

———. "Timurucho amiru no wakufu no ichijirei: Yazudo ni okeru Chakumaku Shami no wakufu ni tsuite (A Waqf of a Tīmūrid Amīr in Yazd)." *Seinan Ajia Kenkyu* 32 (1990).

Jaubert, A. *Voyage en Arménie et en Perse, fait dans les années 1805 et 1806*. Paris, 1821.

Kagaya, Hiroshi. "Kindai Iran musurimu shakai no shuhateki nibunka taiko (Religious Rivalry of Two Sects in Modern Muslim Society in Iran)." In *Oguchi Iichi Kyoju koki kinen ronshu: Shukyo to shakai*. Tokyo, 1981.

Kano, Hiromasa. "Hitotsu no Iran shakaizo: Erito bunseki no shikaku kara (An Image of Iranian Society: From the Viewpoint of Analyzing the Elites)." *Ajia Keizai* 16/3 (1975).

Kanwar, H. I. S. "Origin and Evolution of the Design of the Chaharbagh Garden." *Islamic Culture* (Haydarabad) 48 (1974).

Kārang, 'A. *Āṯār-e bāstānī-ye Āḏarbāyǧān (Ruins in Azerbaijan)*. Vol. 1. Tehran, 1351/1972-3.

Kermānī, A. Q. *Tārīḫ va ǧoǧrafiyā-ye Qom (History and Geography of Qom)*. Tehran, 1356/1977-8.

Keyānī, M. Y. *The Islamic City of Gurgan*. Berlin, 1984.

———. *Naẓarī-ye eǧmalī be-šahrnešīnī va šahrsāzī dar Īrān (A General Survey of Urbanization and Urban Construction in Iran)*. Tehran, 1365/1986-7.

———. *Me'mārī-ye Īrān, dowre-ye islāmī (Architecture in Iran during the Islamic Age)*. Tehran, 1366/1987-8.

———. *Šahrhā-ye Īrān (Iranian Cities)*. 4 vols. Tehran, 1366-70/1987-91.

Keyānī, M. Y. & W. Kleiss. *Fehrest-e kārvānsarāhā-ye Īrān (A Catalogue of Caravansaries in Iran)*. 2 vols. Tehran, 1362/1983-4, 1368/1989-90.

Keyvānī, M. *Artisans and Guild Life in the Later Safavid Period: Contribution to the Social-Economic History of Persia*. Berlin, 1982.

Kheirabadi, M. *Iranian Cities: Formation and Development*. Austin, 1991.

Kondo, Nobuaki. "Yazudo no Mohanmado Tagi Han to sono ichizoku: 18-19 seiki Iran ni okeru chihou yuryokusha no jitsuzo (Moḥammad Taqī Khān and his Family in Yazd: Portraits of Iranian Local Elites during the 18th and 19th Centuries)." *Shigaku Zasshi* 102/1 (1993).

Krawulsky, D. *Īrān: Das Reich der Īlḫāne*. Wiesbaden, 1978.

———. *Ḫorāsān zur Timuridenzeit nach dem Tārīḫ-e Ḥāfeẓ-e Abrū*. 2 vols. Wiesbaden, 1982-4.

Kubo, Kazuyuki. "16 seiki shoto no Herato: Futatsu no shinko ocho no shihai (Herat in the Early Sixteenth Century: Under the Reign of Two Rising Dynasties)." *Shirin* 71/1 (1988).

———. "Timurucho makki no Herato (The Cultural Movement and its Background in Timurid Herat)." *Isuramu no Toshisei Kenkyu Hokoku, Kenkyu Hokokuhen* (Institute of Oriental Culture, Univesity of Tokyo) 35 (1989).

———. "Miru Ari Shiru no gakugei hogo ni tsuite (Mīr 'Alī Shīr's Patronage of Science and Art)." *Seinan Ajia Kenkyu* 32 (1990).

Lambton, A. K. S. *Islamic Society in Persia*. Oxford, 1954.

———. "The Evolution of the Office of Dārūgha." *Mağalla-ye mardom-šenāsī*, 3, 1338/1959-60.

———. "The Office of Kalāntar under the Safawids and Afshārs." In *Mélanges d'Orientalisme offerts à Henri Massé*. Tehran, 1963.

———. "kalāntar." In *EI²*, 1974.

Le Strange, G. *The Lands of the Eastern Caliphate*. London, 1905.

Lockhart, L. *Persian Cities*. London, 1960.

Maḥallātī, M. M. *Ğoġrāfiyā-ye šahr-e Bam (Geography of the City of Bam)*. Tehran, 1367/1988-9.

Maškūr, M. *Tārīḫ-e Tabrīz tā pāyān-e qarn-e nohom-e heğrī (History of Tabriz to the 9th Century A. H.)*. Tehran, 1352/1973-4.

McChesney, R. D. *Waqf at Balkh: A Study of the Endowments at the Shrine of 'Alī Ibn Abī Ṭālib*. Ph. D. dissertation, Princeton University, 1973.

———. "Waqf and Public Policy: The Waqfs of Shāh 'Abbās, 1011-1023/1602-1614." *Asian and African Studies* 15 (1981).

———. "Economic and Social Aspects of the Public Architecture of Bukhara in the 1560's and 1570's." *Islamic Art* 2 (1987).

———. "Four Sources on Shāh 'Abbās's Building of Iṣfahān." *Muqarnas* 5 (1988).

———. *Waqf in Central Asia: Four Hundred Years in the History of a Muslim Shrine, 1480-1889*. Princeton, 1991.

Mehrābādī, A. *Āṯār-e mellī-ye Eṣfahān (Remains of Esfahan)*. Tehran, 1352/1973-4.

Melville, Ch. "Earthquakes in the History of Nishapur." *Iran* 18 (1980).

———. "Historical Monuments and Earthquakes in Tabriz." *Iran* 19 (1981).

Migeod, H. G. "Die Lutis: Ein Ferment des städtischen Lebens in Persien." *JESHO* 2 (1959).

Mirjafari, H. "The Ḥaydarī-Ni'matī Conflicts in Iran." *Iranian Studies* 12/3-4 (1979).

Mīrzā Ḥasan Šīrāzī. *Fārs Nāme-ye Nāṣerī (Book of Fārs)*. Tehran, 1312/1895.

Mo'assese-ye 'elmī va farhangī-ye faḍā (Institute for the Knowledge of Space and Culture). *Banāhā va šahr-e Dāmġān (The Buildings and the City of Damghan)*. Tehran, 1368/1989-90.

Modarresī Ṭabāṭabā'ī, S. H. *Bargī az tārīḫ-e Qazvīn (A Leaf from the History of Qazvin)*. Qom, 1361/1982-3.

Moḫleṣī, M. A. *Ğoġrafiyā-ye tārīḫī-ye Solṭānīye (Historical Geography of Soltaniye)*. Tehran, 1363/1984-5.

Morier, J. *A Journey through Persia, Armenia, and Asia Minor to Constantinople, in the Years 1808 and 1809*. London, 1812.

Morton, A. H. "The Ardabīl Shrine in the Reign of Shāh Ṭahmāsp I." *Iran* 12 (1974); 13 (1975).

———. "The History of the Sarbadārs in the Light of New Numismatic Evidence." *Numismatic Chronicle* 17 (1976).

Moṣṭafavī, S. M. T. *Āṯār-e tārīḫī-ye Tehrān (Historical Heritage in Tehran)*. Edited by S. M. P. Moḥaddeṯ. Tehran, 1361/1982-3.

Moynihan, E. B. "The Lotus Garden Palace of Zahir al-Din Muhammad Babur." *Muqarnas* 5 (1988).

Nağmī, N. *Dār al-ḫelāfe-ye Tehrān (Tehran: the Caliph's Capital)*. 2nd edition. Tehran, 1362/1983-4.

Najimi, A. W. *Herat: The Islamic City*. London, 1988.

Narāqī, Ḥ. *Tārīḫ-e eğtemā'ī-ye Kāšān (Social History of Kashan)*. Tehran, 1345/1966-7.

———. *Āṯār-e tārīḫī-ye šahrestānhā-ye Kāšān va Naṭanz (Historical Remains in the Old Cities of Kashan and Natanz)*. Tehran, 1348/1969-70.

Nīlūfarī, P. *Bāğhā-ye Īrānī (Iranian Gardens)*. Tehran, 1363/1984-5.

O'Kane, B. *Timurid Architecture in Khurasan*. Costa Mesa, 1987.

Parpagliolo, Sh. M. T. *Kābul: The Bāgh-i Bābur: A Projects and a Research into the Possibilities of a Complete Reconstruction*. Roma, 1972.

Perry, J. R. "Forced Migration in Iran during the Seventeenth and Eighteenth Centuries." *Iranian Studies* 8/4 (1975).

Petrushevskii (Petrushevsky), I. P. *Dvizhenie serbedarov v Khorasanie (The Sarbadār Movements in Khurasan)*. Uchenie Zapiski Instituta Vostokovedeniya Akademiya Nauk SSSR 14. Moaka, 1956.

———. "The Socio-Economic Condition of Iran under the Īl-khāns." In *The Cambridge History of Iran*. Vol. 5. Cambridge, 1968.

Philipp, T. "Isfahan 1881-1891: A Close-up View of Guilds and Protection." *Iranian Studies* 17/4 (1984).

Pinder-Wilson, R. "The Persian Garden: Bagh and Chahar Bagh." In *The Islamic Garden*, eds. E. B. McDougall & R. Ettinghausen. Washington, 1976.

Planhol, X. de. "La cour, la place, le parvis; éléments pour une morphologie sociale comparée des villes islamiques et ouest européennes." In *Géographie historique des villes d'Europe occidentale*, ed. P. Claval. Vol. 1. Paris, 1984.

Pope, A. U. *A Survey of Persian Art*. 6 vols. Oxford, 1938-9.

———. *Persian Architecture*. Tehran, 1969. Translated into Japanese as *Perushia kenchiku* by Akira Ishii. Tokyo, 1981.

Quiring-Zoche, R. *Isfahan im 15. und 16. Jahrhundert*. Berlin, 1980.

Royce, W. R. "The Shirazi Provincial Elite: Status Maintenance and Change." In *Modern Iran: The Dialectics of Continuity and Changes*, eds. M. E. Bonine & N. Keddie. Albany, 1981.

Šafaqī (Schafaghi), S. *Ğoğrafiyā-ye Eṣfahān (Geography of Esfahan)*. Esfahan, 1353/1974-5.

———. "Bildung von Stadtvierteln in Eṣfahān." In *Interdisziplinäre Iran-Forschung: Beiträge aus Kulturgeographie, Ethnologie, Soziologie und Neuerer Geschichte*, ed. G. Schweizer. Wiesbaden, 1979.

Safarī, G. B. *Ardabīl dar gog̱argāh-e tārīḫ (Ardabil: A Crossroads of History)*. 3 vols. Tehran, 1350-62/1971-84.

Ṣāfī, Q. *Kārtpostālhā-ye tārīḫī-ye Īrān (Historical Post Cards of Iran)*. Tehran, 1368/1989-90.

Šahrī, Ǧ. *Tārīḫ-e eǧtemā'ī-ye Tehrān dar qarn-e sīzdahom (Social History of Tehran in the 13th Century A. H.)*. 6 vols. Tehran, 1367-8/1988-9.

Sakamoto, Tsutomu. "Kindai Isuramu girudo ni tsuite no oboegaki (A Memorandum on the Modern Islamic Guild)." *Oriento* 21/2 (1979).

———. "19 seiki Isufahan no toshikosei to Meidan (The Urban Structure of Esfahan in the 19th Century and Meydān)." *Shigaku* 50 (1980); 51/1-2(1981); 51/3 (1981).

———. "19 seiki Teheran to Mosutoufike (Mostowfī Family under the Urban Growth of the Late 19th Century Tehran)." *Oriento* 25/2 (1983).

———. "19 seiki Teheran no jinko chosa shiryo (The Demographic Census of Tehran in the 19th Century)." *Oriento* 27/1 (1984).

———. "Kindai Isuramu toshi to Iranjin (Modern Islamic Cities and the Iranians)." In *Isuramusekai no hitobito*. Vol. 5: *Toshimin*. Tokyo, 1984.

Sato, Tsugitaka. "Isuramu shakaishi eno shiten: Faiyumu no jirei kara (A View of Islamic Social History: The Case of Fayyūm Province)." In *Rekishigaku,* ed. Koichi Kabayama. Tokyo, 1977. Revised in *Chusei Isuramu kokka to Arabu shakai: Ikutasei no kenkyu*. Tokyo, 1986.

Scarce, J. M. "The Royal Palaces of the Qajar Dynasty: A Survey." In *Qajar Iran: Political, Social and Cultural Change, 1800-1925,* eds. E. Bosworth & R. Hillenbrand. Edinburgh, 1983.

Schmidt, E. F. *Flights over Ancient Cities of Iran*. Chicago, 1940.

Schweizer, G. "Bibliographie zur Stadtgeographie des Vorderen Orients (1960-1976)." In *Beiträge zur Geographie orientalischer Städte und Märkte,* ed. G. Schweizer. Wiesbaden, 1977.

Seger, M. *Teheran: Eine stadtgeographische Studien*. Wien & New York, 1978.

Sepantā, A. *Tārīḫče-ye awqāf-e Eṣfahān (A Short History of Waqf Endowments in Esfahan)*. Esfahan, 1346/1967-8.

Shimizu, Kosuke. "Minzoku to shukyo shuha (Races, Religions and Religious Sects)." In *Gaisetsu Isuramushi,* eds. Yuzo Itagaki & Tsugitaka Sato. Tokyo, 1986.

———. "Shisutan no aiyaru ('Ayyār in Sīstān)." In *Daisan sekai no shakai hendo to chiiki kenkyu*. Tokyo University of Foreign Studies. Tokyo, 1984.

———. "Iranshi ni okeru ninkyo shudan (Chivalric Groups in the History of Iran)." *Isuramu no Toshisei Kenkyu Hokoku, Kenkyu Hokokuhen* (Institute of Oriental Culture, Univesity of Tokyo) 11 (1989).

———. "Iranshi no naka no toshizo: 10-11seiki no Nishapuru (The Image of Cities in the History of Iran: The Case of Nīšāpūr in 10-11th Centuries)." *Shicho,* new series, 28 (1990).

Slaby, H. *Plan von Teheran*. Graz, 1977.

Smith, J. M. *The History of the Sarbadār Dynasty 1336-1381 A. D. and its Sources*. Den Haag & Paris, 1970.

Solṭānzāde, Ḥ. *Moqaddameyī bar tārīḫ-e šahr o šahrnešīnī dar Īrān (Introduction to the History of Cities and Urbanization in Iran)*. Tehran, 1365/1986-7.

Subtelny, M. E. "Socioeconomic Bases of Cultural Patronage under the Later Timurids." *IJMES* 20/4 (1988).

———. "A Timurid Educational and Charitable Foundation: The Ikhlāṣiyya Complex of 'Alī Shīr Navā'ī in 15th-Century Herat and its Endowment." *JAOS* 111/1 (1991).

———. "A Medieval Persian Agricultural Manual in Context: the *Irshād al-Zirā'a* in Late Timurid and Early Safavid Khorasan." *Studia Iranica* 22/2 (1993).

Suzuki, Tadashi. *Osuman teikoku no kenryoku to erito (Elites and Power in the Ottoman Empire)*. Tokyo, 1993.

Szuppe, M. "Un tremblement de terre dans le Qohestān, 956/1549." *Studia Iranica* 18/2 (1989).

———. *Entre Timourides, Uzbeks et Safavides: Questions d'histoire politique et sociale de Hérat dans la première moitié du XVᵉ siècle*. Paris, 1992.

Torābī Ṭabāṭabā'ī, S. Ǧ. *Āṯār-e bāstānī-ye Āḏarbāyǧān (Ruins in Azerbaijan)*. Vol 2, Tehran, 1355/1976-7.

Tumanovich, N. N. *Gerat v XVI-XVIII vekakh (Herat between the 16th and 18th Centuries)*. Moskva, 1989.

Vazīrī, A. A. *Ǧoġrafiyā-ye Kermān (Geography of Kerman)*. Edited by M. E. Bāstānī Pārīzī. Tehran, 1353/1974-5.

———. *Tārīḫ-e Kermān (History of Kerman)*. 3rd edition. Edited by M. E. Bāstānī Pārīzī. Tehran, 1364/1985-6.

Vercellin, G. "Un 'Sarbedār' del 981/1573 a Tabriz." *Annali dell'Istituto Orientale di Napoli* 20 (1970).

Wilber, D. *The Architecture of Islamic Iran: The Il Khānid Period*. Princeton, 1955.

———. *Persian Gardens and Garden Pavilions*. Tokyo, 1962.

———. "Aspects of the Safavid Ensemble of Isfahan." *Iranian Studies* 7 (1974).

———. "The Timurid Court: Life in Gardens and Tents." *Iran* 17 (1979).

Wills, C. J. *In the Land of the Lion and Sun*. London, 1883.

Wirth, E. "Strukturwandlungen und Entwicklungstendenzen der orientalischen Stadt." *Erdkunde* 22 (1968).

———. "Zum Problem der Bazars (sūq, çarşı)." *Der Islam* 51/2 (1974); 52/1 (1975).

———. "Die orientalische Stadt: Spezifische Besonderheiten der Städte Nordafrikas und Vorderasiens aus der Sicht der Geographie." In *Forschung in Erlangen. Vortragsreihen des Collegium Alexandrunum der Universität Erlangen-Nürnberg*, ed. G. Hesse. Erlangen, 1982.

Zander, G., ed. *Travaux de restauration de monuments historiques en Iran: Rapports et études préliminaires*. Rome, 1968.

CENTRAL ASIA

Hisao Komatsu

Introduction

In this chapter Central Asia refers to the region once called Ma wara' al-Nahr (Transoxania) or Turkistan, that is, the former Soviet Central Asia including southern Kazakhstan. However, since this region had, throughout its history, close relations with neighbouring areas, particularly Iran and Afghanistan, I shall not adhere too meticulously to regional borders when discussing Central Asian cities where, in the period following the Arab conquests, Muslims constituted the major part of the population.

Many of the studies introduced here are by scholars of the former Soviet Union. It has not been easy for scholars outside the former Soviet Union to make use of the historical sources located there or to conduct field investigations in the former Soviet Central Asia. As well, though studies on Central Asian cities have mostly been undertaken by Soviet Orientalists, cities were usually called either feudal or medieval depending on the period concerned and little concern was given to the concept of the "Islamic city." The Soviet historical circles held that the "medieval" cities of Central Asia were consistently part of feudal society from the 6th century until the October Revolution of 1917 and considered them to be typical Oriental cities whose development was completely different from cities in Western Europe and Russia. Such a concept inevitably involves a large measure of prior knowledge. The long feudal period was subdivided into an early feudal period, from the 6th to the 9th century, a high feudal period, from the 9th to the 15th century, and a late-feudal period, from the 16th century onward; urban studies after the 1950s do not however adhere strictly to such periodization.

This chapter will first review the development of urban studies after the 19th century, examining the principal research, then introduce certain recent representative work through specific themes, and conclude by attempting to chart possible courses that urban studies for this region will take in the future. In spite of the fact that Central Asia is an important element of the Eastern Islamic world, very little is known about what has been achieved in the field of urban studies. Even in the Soviet Union, there was no adequate summary of Central Asian urban studies other than a work by O. G. Bol'shakov (R., 1973). It is not my intention to try to cover all the studies that have been made or to summarize the history of those studies; I would be happy if as a result of the information in this chapter, scholars might gain a greater knowledge of trends of study in Russia and the former Soviet Union, as well as in other countries.

I. Historical Survey

Although Central Asian cities have been described in many books of travel from ancient times, scholarly works concerning them appeared only in the 19th century, written by Russian Orientalists. Russia, attempting a military and economic penetration of Central Asia, was naturally inclined to be concerned with the capitals of the three khanates—Bukhara, Khiva and Khokand—and the other main cities. The most valuable achievement in pre-revolutionary Central Asian urban studies before the annexation of the region by Russia is, without a doubt, N. Khanykov, *Description of the Khanate of Bukhara* (R., 1843). Khanykov, who stayed in Bukhara for eight months in 1841-2 as a member of a Russian mission, observed the city of Bukhara for the purpose of "systematic description." He left valuable records, which are brief and to the point, of Bukhara's city gates, its area, graveyards, fountains, *ark* (citadel), jails, mosques, madrasas (including the number of rooms and students and the value of scholarships), caravansaries (including charges), public baths, *tīm* (arcades of shops), the structure of houses, the permanent bazar, suburban weekly fairs, feasts (festivals), mausolea, population (estimated as 60,000-70,000), trade with neighbouring countries and cities (Russia, Khiva, Mashhad, Kabul, Khokand, Kashghar, Yarkand), prices of goods, the machinery of government, the ulama, the *īšān* (Sufi spiritual masters), and the academic situation. In appendices he included lists of place names and terms in their original language and maps of the cities of Bukhara and Samarkand, together with their suburbs. Though the descriptions of Samarkand and Karshi are superficial, Khanykov's record of 19th century Bukhara is meticulous and well deserves the praise accorded it by later scholars such as V. V. Bartol'd and O. A. Sukhareva. Khanykov, "Urban Administration in Central Asia" (R., 1844) comments specifically about government services related to urban administration in Bukhara and writes stimulating descriptions based on actual observations, as for example: "Any hamlet, with an *ark* and a Friday mosque, and surrounded by a moat or notched clay walls, is called a "city" in Central Asia."

A number of Russian Orientalists besides Khanykov have left valuable information about the cities of 19th century Central Asia. F. Nazarov, for example, visited Khokand in the years 1813 and 1814 and in *A Memorandum concerning the Peoples and the Regions of Central Asia* (R., 1821) wrote about cities in the Farghana region where city walls were absent. Captain N. Murav'ev, who was sent on a mission to Khiva in the years 1819 and 1820, reported for the first time on general conditions in the cities of the Khanate of Khiva in *A Travel to Turkmenia and Khiva* (R., 1822) and Captain E. K. Meiendorf, a member of the Negri mission despatched in 1820-1 to expand commerce between Russia and Bukhara, wrote a keenly observed travel record, *Voyage d'Orenbourg à Boukhara* (1826; Russian translation 1975) which includes a general survey of Bukhara, the condition of the arts and sciences there and a report about negotiations with the Ottoman Empire. S. Maejima refers to this book in his article, "Bukhara in the Beginning of the 19th Century and its Culture" (J., 1977). Such travel records do not provide such systematic descriptions as Khanykov's, yet all the same they are important historical materials for the study of Central Asian cities of the period.

Though it may be thought that conditions for the study of Central Asian cities would have improved following the annexation of Central Asia by Russia, good urban studies on the area are far fewer than are generally imagined. The best study done in this period is V. A. Zhukovskii, *The Ancient Era of the Transcaspian Region: The Ruins of Old Merv* (R., 1894), which deals with the historical geography of Merv, an ancient Central Asian city that had been an important centre for the Seljuk dynasty and the Khwarazm Shah dynasty and which survived into the 18th century despite large-scale destruction at the time of the Mongol invasion. This work became a springboard for Russian and Soviet study of the cities of medieval Central Asia, though it remained unknown to scholars outside Russia. Typical of the regard in which it was held was Bartol'd (1911): "[Zhukovskii's work,] based on surveys of the ruins of Old Merv and on Arabic historical sources, remains unrivalled among the studies so far done by European scholars on any city in Central Asia and Iran." A. I. Dobrosmyslov, *Tashkent Past and Present: An Historical Introduction* (R., 1911) is the first history of Tashkent from ancient times to the present. It is a useful source for information about Tashkent as the center of Russian colonial administration, but it is deficient as a description of Tashkent as a Muslim city. M. Gavrilov, *The Risala of the Sart Artisans: A Study of the Legends of Muslim Guilds* (R., 1912) is an annotated translation of six kinds of *risāla,* legends of various guilds which attracted scholarly attention for the light they threw on the spiritual world of urban Muslims.

The period of Russian rule was also characterized by a number of urban surveys conducted by colonial and military officers. Survey reports about the *īšāns* of Tashkent and waqf properties belonging to madrasas, such as I. I. Geier (ed.), *A Collection of Materials for the Statistics of the Sir-Darya Province* (R., 1899) and articles by N. P. Ostroumov, for example, are valuable historical materials for the time. Such reports should not be neglected when studying the cities of modern Central Asia. They drew the attention of the French authorities in the Maghrib, as is evidenced by the fact that some were translated and introduced in *Revue du monde musulman* (see for example S. R., "Le Ichâns de Tachkent," 1911 and anonym, "Enquêtes sur les Vakoufs du Turkestan," 1911). V. I. Masal'skii, *The Turkistan Region* (R., 1913) is a collection of topographies of Russian Central Asia which includes descriptions for each city based on pre-revolutionary surveys and studies, and is a useful tool for information about Central Asian cities in the early 20th century. The first study by a Japanese of the "fortress towns" of Central Asia was *Description of Central Asia,* vol. 1, chapter 3 (J., 1886) by T. Nishi, a young Japanese diplomat who visited the Asian parts of the Russian Empire in 1880.

V. V. Bartol'd was the doyen of Central Asian urban studies from the last years of the Russian Empire to the post-revolutionary period. He not only elucidated the historical geography of individual cities, using a wide variety of historical sources in Arabic and Persian (almost all the items related to Central Asian cities in the first edition of *The Encyclopedia of Islam* were written by him), but, stemming from his interest in the socio-economic history of cities, also proposed an important academic theory concerning the urban developmental process. He said that Arab geographers in the 9th and 10th centuries used the following specific terms to describe the cities of Iran as well as Central Asia: (1) *quhandiz* < *kuhne dīz* (old citadel), also called *qal'a,* meaning a castle where local rulers before the Arab conquests resided. They were so called because almost everything had gone to ruin by the time the geographers observed them. (2) *šahristān* or *madīna* (inner city, old city), the oldest quarters of a city existing since the days before the Arab conquests, and the political center of each region as well as the centre of commerce and the craft industry. (3) *rabaḍ,* came into existence in the Arab period, situated adjacent to the *madīna* or in suburbs surrounding the *madīna*. In some cases, it was used to mean the city walls surrounding the *madīna* and the suburbs. (4) *balad,* the whole city including all of the above areas. Bartol'd compared the meanings of these terms with those in survey data about Samarkand and Merv in the period before the Mongol invasion and showed that the center of urban life in Central Asia in the 10th and 11th centuries moved from the *šahristān* to the *rabaḍ* and that the *rabaḍ* became the new centre for commerce and crafts industries. He concluded that the threefold structure of *quhandiz, šahristān* and *rabaḍ* characterized Central Asian cities in the pre-Mongolian period. He also discussed questions such as urbanization and the mutual relationship between city and village as being factors in social development, but as far as later scholars were concerned, his most influential theories remained those of the threefold structure and of urban development. Bartol'd had stressed from early on the importance of using both historical sources and archaeological data, and in 1904 conducted an excavation of the Afrasiyab ruins of pre-Mongolian Samarkand in company with V. L. Vyatkin, who was studying the historical geography of Samarkand using waqf documents. Despite the limitations of archaeology at the time, Bartol'd may be said to have founded the trend of urban studies in the Soviet period to combine Oriental studies with archaeology.

A. Yu. Yakubovskii succeeded Bartol'd and developed his ideas within Soviet Oriental Studies. He adopted with modifications Bartol'd's urban development theory as a way to analyze the formative process of feudal society in Central Asia. Eventually he formulated a theory concerning the formation of the *rabaḍ* as a feudal city, inspired by the progress of archaeological studies, particularly by the excavation of the ruins of Panjikant, a city abandoned in the middle of the 8th century due to the destruction caused by the Arab conquests. He held that the *šahristān* and the *rabaḍ* were established at different times and that their social and economic structures were also different. The *šahristān* was peculiar to the pre-feudal period, where a closed "manorial economy" was practiced by the native aristocrats (*dihqān*) of Transoxania in the pre-Islamic period. In the suburban *rabaḍ*, on the other hand, the craft industry, now separated from cottage industry, had begun to grow in the 8th century. In the 9th century, artisans became free from their landlords, which led, though definite evidence is lacking, to the establishment in the 10th century of artisans' corporations. Free commerce also developed in the *rabaḍ*. The triumph of feudalism meant moving everything related to urban life to the *rabaḍ*, and this was the effective end of the *šahristān* (*A History of the Peoples of Uzbekistan*, in Russian, 1950). Yakubovskii's theory mapped out theoretically the direction the study of the historical geography of Central Asian cities would later take, and as a result many leading scholars of history and archaeology became interested in the field. As archaeological studies advanced, however, the theory was found not to be always in accordance with historical reality. For example, the *šahristān* survived even after the formation of the *rabaḍ*, and, according to M. E. Masson, who conducted the archaeological excavation of Termez, Yakubovskii's theories about the threefold structure of city and about urban development do not hold true for any of the cities of Central Asia. No significant and comprehensive effort has been made to examine Central Asian cities from the standpoint of historical theory since Yakubovskii's time. Accordingly, O. G. Bol'shakov asserted in 1973 that "since 1953, various archaeological studies of cities have been undertaken in great numbers, but nothing new has emerged in terms of theory. The level of scholarship therefore remains unchanged from the 1950s."

The pioneer for new developments in the study of the Central Asian cities after Yakubovskii was I. P. Petrushevskii. In 1948, he published an ambitious thesis entitled "Urban Aristocrats in the Ilkhanid State" (R., 1948) in which he attempted to analyze the internal structure of the "Muslim cities" of the Middle East and Central Asia on the basis of historical sources and with an awareness of what was happening in the wider field of studies of medieval Western European and Russian cities. Petrushevskii considered that previous urban studies were inclined to be more concerned with archaeology, historical geography and political and cultural history, rather than with subjects such as the stages of urban history, the social composition of urban dwellers, the characteristics of urban organizations, the existence of trade associations, commercial organizations, social relationships, and types of social struggle. He also asserted that studies to date had not taken sufficiently into account historical and geographical materials and criticized the fact that almost no studies had been done on the biographies of Sufi saints, which might prove to be "important historical materials in terms of urban social relationships and life-styles," and that also historians did not pay adequate attention to archaeological and epigraphic materials. The questions he posed were to become an important lodestone for later Orientalists.

In "Urban Aristocrats in the Ilkhanid State," Petrushevskii summarizes the characteristics of the cities of Iran and Central Asia from the 12th century to the 15th century. He distinguishes the cities as falling into three types from the economic point of view: (1) medium or small scale commercial and industrial cities depending on limited regional markets, (2) cities enjoying prosperity through the presence of the Mongol rulers (e. g. Maragheh and Soltaniye) and (3) large scale cities, such as Hamadan, Esfahan, Shiraz, Herat, Bukhara and Samarkand, far surpassing contemporary Western European cities in size, located at junctions of the caravan trunk routes and acting as centers for transit trade and export. All three types, unlike the autonomous cities of Western Europe and the city-republics of Northern Russia, such as Novgorod and Pskov, lacked on the whole urban autonomy and were socially subdivided. Autonomy existed only within a social organization, such as a trade association, a religious community, or a quarter, and power was in the hands of governors appointed by the khans and of the leading local families ("urban notables with extensive land holdings") connected with them.

After a thorough study of historical sources, including manuscripts, in Persian, Petrushevskii concluded that the Mongol invasion did not result in a fundamental transformation of the social structure of Iranian cities despite the large-scale destruction. Urban notables continued to be bureaucrats, ulama, *sayyids*, Sufi sheikhs and others who were simultaneously ruling agricultural society as feudal landlords. Turko-Mongolian nomad-military notables neither settled down in cities nor had any contact with urban notables. Antagonism arose between them on occasion but the reforms conducted under the leadership of Ghazan Khan, who was able to control the nomad-military notables, brought prosperity to the cities. During the 13th and 14th centuries, the major source of antagonism in Iranian society was not the struggle between cities and villages as Bartol'd had suggested in his study of the Isma'ili movement, but that between urban-based notables on one hand and farmers and the urban lower classes on the other, typified in the Sarbadār movement of the 14th century. In both cases, the same powerful social class in the city and the surrounding countryside controlled farmers and the general urban populace in many ways, economically, legally and ideologically. This was a reason, though not the sole one, that unlike in Western Europe and Russia neither urban autonomy nor urban law flourished in Iranian cities. Under such circumstances, the emergence of a commercial bourgeoisie was hindered and so there was no progressive evolution to threaten the feudalistic production system.

Petrushevskii is generally known for his studies on the socio-economic history of Iran during the Ilkhanid period. He contributed also to an advance and deepening of Central Asian urban studies, from the previous concentration on historical geography to an analysis of the internal structure of cities and their place in "feudal society." The first paper presented at the symposium entitled "The Late-Feudal City in Central Asia," held in Tashkent in 1989, concerned Petrushevskii's significant contribution to the urban studies of Central Asia after the Mongol period.

With the publication of Petrushevskii's study, Soviet scholars became aware of the backwardness of Central Asian urban studies, and in the autumn of 1956, the Second Conference of Central Asian Archaeologists and Ethnographers held at Stalinabad (the present Dushanbe) in Tajikistan emphasized the necessity of undertaking urban studies and set up a special session called "Central Asian Cities and Crafts." The conference included the following presentations: E. A. Davidovich, "Cities, Crafts, and Money Circulation in Central Asia during the 'Silver Crisis' from the 11th to the 13th Century," N. N. Negmatov, "History of Khujand in the Late Middle Ages," O. A. Sukhareva, "An Essay on the Urban History of the Khanate of Bukhara," and I. Dzhabbarov, "Apprentice Status in the Craft Guilds of

Central Asia in the Late 19th and the Early 20th Centuries: Based on the Materials of Khwarazm." The most highly-acclaimed of the papers were Davidovich's numismatic study and Sukhareva's research that fully utilized the results of surveys taken in post-revolutionary Central Asian cities centring on Bukhara. These two scholars were to lead later study of Central Asian history in the fields of numismatics and ethnography respectively. It is worth noting that numismatics and ethnography were added as new study methods to the historical studies based on documents and archaeology. It should also be mentioned that at this conference, A. A. Semyonov, a senior scholar who had been engaged in the study of Central Asian history since the pre-revolutionary period, presented a paper concerning cultural exchange between cities under the title "Some Remarks on the Cultural and Political Relations between Bukhara and Mughal India in the 17th Century."(These papers were published in Russian in 1959.)

Since the 1950s, some of the most vigorous efforts regarding Central Asian cities have centred on archaeologists. Following the scientific excavation of Afrasiyab, excavations of "medieval cities" were conducted in areas such as Semirech'e, the Talas Valley, the Tashkent Oasis, the Middle and Lower basin of the Sir Darya and southern Turkmenistan where few historical sources remain, and much information has been accumulated about the location, size and plans of Central Asian cities. The results of these excavations have been published, among others, in *Afrasiyab: The General Archaeological Investigation of Afrasiyab* (R., 1969-75), E. I. Ageeva and G. I. Patsevich, "A History of Village Settlements and Towns in Southern Kazakhstan" (R., 1958) and G. A. Pugachenkova, "The Development of Architecture in Southern Turkmenistan during the Slavery and Feudal Periods" (R., 1958). Other than Panjikant, though, no complete excavation of a city was made, and the reports were insufficiently adequate in terms of classifications and analyses to be used as historical sources. Historians of the medieval period who used historical sources were interested in land ownership, the taxation system, and social relations in the villages rather than in cities, and the numbers of studies on "medieval cities" did not increase.

In this climate, a significant publication was A. M. Belenitskii, I. B. Bentovich and O. G. Bol'shakov, *The Medieval City of Central Asia* (R., 1973), the work of three archaeologists. The part that concerns us most closely was written by Bol'shakov and deals with Central Asian cities from the 8th to the beginning of the 13th century, that is, from the Arab conquests to the Mongol invasion. Probably for the first time in Soviet academic circles the state of urban studies of Central Asia done before 1970 was summarized and prospects for further study were surveyed. Bol'shakov points out that as long as one depends upon a few written historical sources and upon abundant but not yet systematized archaeological materials, one will not be able to present the full picture of the history of Central Asian cities nor discover the factors which determined differences in the development of Oriental and Occidental cities. He suggests a practical framework for urban studies as a first step to answering those problems. Because this framework is not only a direct reflection of the structure of his work, but also shows clearly the interests of Soviet scholarship, I will outline its main items.

The first category includes the number of cities, as classified by individual area and Central Asia as a whole, changes in the number of cities, and the effects of the Arab conquests; factors behind the rise and decline of new and old cities; the size and elements of composition (the threefold structure of city), the tempo of development and the most flourishing period, the role of political factors, and the correlation between the development of small towns and major cities; and urban population and the correlation between urban residents and village farmers. Bol'shakov identifies on a map the locations of half of the between 250 and 270 Central Asian cities listed by medieval geographers like al-Istakhrī and al-Muqaddasī, based both on historical sources and city ruins. He infers that during the pre-Mongolian period urbanization was relatively advanced, with between twenty-five and thirty percent of the population of Central Asia living in towns and cities.

The second category includes clarifying the original city plan and how it later changed; changes in architectural style; the placement of social and religious buildings, and of artisan and commercial quarters, and the degree of stability of such placement; and the correlation between residential and commercial-artisan quarters, the degree of segregation, and public facilities. The process of the development of major cities like Merv, Bukhara and Samarkand is shown in plans.

The third category deals with the types of major crafts and the numbers of people connected with various forms of economic activity; the relative importance of urban demand in terms of total demand for the crafts industry; economic relations between cities and surrounding villages, between cities and nomads and among cities, and the role of long distance transit trade; the organization of the craft industry and commerce, and financial conditions; and correlation between the crafts industry, commerce and urban and rural rents, all of which went to form urban wealth.

The fourth category includes the legal status of cities, the degree of internal autonomy, mutual relationships between cities and state administration, and taxation of urban dwellers; the city as the centre of administration, culture, and religion; and mutual relations between cities and villages.

The fifth category deals with class divisions within the urban population, the composition of the urban ruling class, the correlation among free, employed, and slave labor; and the unity of the urban population, the class struggle and its ideology, and the world view of the urban population and class consciousness.

Bol'shakov's concerns and interests are wide-ranging, extending from the horizontal expansion of cities to their internal structure and the ideologies of their inhabitants. Exceptional in a Soviet scholar, he states that it is possible to discuss a Central Asian city after the 9th century as a "Muslim city," that is, "a city living in accordance with the norms of Islamic law." Unlike his predecessors, Bol'shakov was able to discuss Central Asian cities from a wide intellectual perspective, thanks to his ability to utilize both historical sources in Arabic and Persian and archaeological materials. Another factor contributing to his broad perspective was his familiarity with Western studies about "Islamic (Muslim) cities," such as works by E. Ashtor, Cl. Cahen, A. H. Hourani, S. M. Stern and I. Lapidus. He even criticized the course of Soviet research in the area, citing Cahen that "studies on Muslim cities are being made from a geographer's point of view rather than from a historian's, and from an urban engineer's point of view rather than a social historian's." Bol'shakov, having been stimulated by Western studies on "Islamic cities," may have been aiming at constructing a systematic study of Central Asian cities, then still largely ignored in Western studies. Of particular interest in his work, although limitations of space do not permit me to go into detail here, are discussions about the lease and rent of land in cities and the maintenance of land allotment over the centuries.

Bol'shakov concludes that after a period of decline caused by the Arab conquests, Central Asia saw a rapid increase in the number of cities in the 9th century as the region was integrated within the economic and cultural worlds of Iran and the Mediterranean. As a result, cities became drastically changed in feature. Cities until then had been small in scale and were centred on the residence of the *dihqān*; crafts and commerce existed only to satisfy the needs of the *dihqān*. In the 10th century large cities like Merv and Samarkand had populations on the scale of 50,000 and were centres for crafts and commerce. These cities developed around the surviving core of old cities (*šahristān*) which had existed in the 7th and 8th centuries.

Though the tempo of urban growth slowed in the Central Asian heartland in the 10th and 11th centuries, cities in the north-east frontier area began to grow due to large-scale settlement by Turkic nomads. By the end of the 11th century, most cities had reached their maximum in terms both of size and population. Since such rapid growth had been conditioned by the existence of a centralized state, the cities inevitably lost all traces of the internal autonomy they previously enjoyed and became no more than individual cells within a centralized state. Like other Oriental cities, those in Central Asia possessed neither special legal status nor autonomous rights, since all of the main administrative positions were occupied by state bureaucrats.

Between the 9th and the 12th centuries, Central Asian cities dominated the surrounding agricultural areas politically and were also the administrative and economic centres for the nearby region. As a result, many large land-owners lived in the cities and engaged in commercial activities. The development of crafts and commerce not only concentrated immense wealth on the urban ruling class, but also created many new classes of artisans and wage labourers who were divided into small independent groups (*korporatsiya*) by quarter and occupation. These corporations did not however have much influence over urban politics. Nevertheless, cities of this period did possess urban militias, organized to some extent out of groups like the *'ayyār* which were independent of the political power.

Although the conquest of Central Asia by the Seljuks and the Karakhanids did not transform the economic structure of society, it brought the cities face to face with a group of people different to the type they had been used to dealing with, populous nomadic military groups which had never before been involved with the cities. These conditions made it impossible for a city to enjoy political autonomy. While the urban ruling class realized that the security of their own properties depended upon the might of the khan, the urban population in general sought a means of defending and protecting themselves within closed organizations; these organizations worked to fragment people into cautious and mutually hostile groups. The Mongol invasion prevented the further development of Central Asian cities.

Though Bol'shakov's discussion is rather hypothetical, it is valuable in that it attempts to draw the whole picture of Central Asian cities in the pre-Mongolian period and at the same time, by using the rich resources of archaeological research, to suggest the future direction of urban studies. Though E. A. Davidovich, in a detailed review of Bol'shakov's work entitled "Controversial Problem in *The Medieval City of Central Asia*"(R., 1978, 1979), suggests him to reconsider the historical geography of individual cities, the method of calculation of urban populations and the issue of currency circulation, she is correct in saying that Bol'shakov's study compensates for the backwardness of Central Asian urban studies and makes a great contribution to late medieval urban studies as well.

Although Bol'shakov did not put out a revised edition, he did publish a new work entitled *The Medieval City of the Near East from the 7th to the mid-13th Century* (R., 1984), perhaps the first comprehensive work by a Soviet scholar analyzing the sizes of Syrian and Egyptian cities, population movements, price fluctuations, circulation of goods, and the socio-economic system. Though the subject area is different, his concerns are clearly derived from his previous work on the cities of Central Asia. As before, his objective is to examine the factors determining the different historical development of the East and the West, and for his purpose he regards it as effective to consider the medieval West and the Near East as one integrated area. Since both of them were linked economically as well as culturally, and also had a common historical background in the Roman Empire, considering them together should highlight the factors which made their later development different. He also states that the base for comparative studies with Western medieval studies is to be found in Islamic urban studies, so productive in the last twenty years, while Oriental studies in general incline to centre on philology. Such is the perspective of Bol'shakov's work in urban studies. Of all the Western studies of "Islamic cities" made from the early 20th century, Bol'shakov was most appreciative of the work of Cl. Cahen, perhaps because Cahen points out the Byzantine tradition within the social structure of Syrian cities.

In the same way, Bol'shakov attempts to interpret world history, with cities as the framework for comparison. In his definition a city is a "gathering place where production surplus is concentrated and whose main function is its redistribution." As a result of reinterpreting Arabic source materials and Western studies on the "Islamic city" and socio-economic history in terms of the Marxist view of history, Bol'shakov concludes that during the five centuries following the Arab conquests, there was no substantial change in the number of Near Eastern cities and in urban population. Any change was temporary and limited in extent. Such constancy of population does not mean there was no development in the craft industry and in agricultural technology; such development though did not bring about a fundamental transformation in the production system and the socio-economic structure. The reason Near Eastern cities were far larger than European cities of the same period is attributable first of all to their high agricultural productivity and the state's concentration of an immense production surplus in the cities. The craft industry played little part in the economic balance of society. Merchants and artisans were engaged in the redistribution of the surplus in agricultural products, and were thus in a far happier situation than were the exploited farmers. Urban ideals were expressed in Islamic law and struggles against the state authorities concerned the strict enforcement of the sharia rather than enacting new laws. Extremely high agricultural productivity and the constant internal demand remained virtually unchanged and did nothing to stimulate commercial ambition to promote increased production by the craft industry or by technological innovation. Foreign trade was not particularly significant in the Near East, and profits from transit commerce were sought to offset excesses in imports. Long-term economic stagnation in the Near East derived from neglecting to use surpluses productively, and from their consumption and hoarding by the ruling class.

Though there are doubtless many criticisms and objections that could be raised against Bol'shakov's argument, it is worthy of notice as a point of contact between the Soviet Union, the West and the Middle East in the field of historical studies about the "Islamic city." Bol'shakov himself may have preferred to develop his urban theory from a case study of the Arab region where historical sources and studies abound unlike Central Asia where historical sources are limited.

Looking back at the history of Soviet scholarship regarding Central Asian urban studies, it is noticeable that full-scale studies on cities after the Mongol invasion began after 1970. For a while just after the October Revolution, some treatises dealing with the traditional urban craft industries were published with the aim of promoting the economy of Central Asia and there are instances, like the pioneering work of Bartol'd and that of Petrushevskii and Yakubovskii, where suggestions concerning the necessity of studying urban social and economic history from the 13th century onward were made. Yet on the whole historians specializing in the Middle Ages were more interested in agricultural villages, particularly in analyzing feudal land ownership relationships, and as a result, urban studies remained long neglected despite the relative abundance of written sources compared with the pre-Mongol period. With the progress, however, of systematic excavations of "medieval" (or "late medieval") cities of the 13th to the 18th centuries, such as Otrar, Khujand and Bukhara, and the pioneering use made of fieldwork by ethnographers like O. A. Sukhareva and E. M. Peshchereva to describe in detail social life in "medieval" cities, historians working with historical sources responded by tackling that previously uncultivated field. Good examples of such work published after 1970 are the studies of R. G. Mukminova and O. D. Chekhovich. Chekhovich's interest, for example, was in the analysis of social and economic changes in Central Asia during the 18th and the 19th centuries, with an emphasis on the urban development of Central Asia after the 18th century, particularly the rapid development of cities such as Tashkent due to an active commercial relationship between the Russians and the Kazakh nomads. An example of her work is a series of articles in which she demonstrates that Tashkent in the latter half of the 18th century was a "free city," not subordinate to any external political power.

Academic interest in the cities of the "late medieval" period was also linked with the question of the ethnogenesis of Central Asian peoples. It is generally believed that the Turkic peoples of Central Asia began consolidating from the 15th century onwards, and the heightening academic interest in the role played by cities in this, and in the urban cultural remains which provide evidence for the formative process of traditional material cultures, should also be considered as motivation for more studies of the cities of that time. Soviet archaeology supported this approach. For example, K. A. Akishev, an archaeologist from Kazakhstan, remarks in a paper entitled "Urban Study Perspectives on Kazakhstan in the Late Medieval Period" (R., 1983) that archaeology dealing with the "late medieval period" is essential for the study of traditional Kazakh, Turkmen and Kirghiz cultures because of the scarcity of historical sources, and it is also able to supplement the limited ethnographical materials. Because ethnographical materials, he says, are effective for studying societies from the 19th century at earliest, field archaeology alone is able to furnish reliable information about material and spiritual culture in the period between the 15th and 18th centuries.

The 1980s saw further developments in urban studies of the "late medieval period." B. A. Tulenbaev (ed.), *The Medieval Urban Culture of Kazakhstan and Central Asia* (R., 1983) is a collection of papers submitted to a Union-wide conference held in Alma-Ata in May, 1981, under the title of "The Medieval Archaeology of Kazakhstan and Central Asia (13th-18th centuries)." It reflects the present high level of specialized work in the area and covers a wide range of topics including archaeological methodology, currency circulation, the craft industry, architecture and cultural exchange. Archaeological research always involves the problem of how to generalize an enormous quantity of data. A joint conference held in Namangan in 1989 under the auspices of the Institute of Archaeology of the Uzbek Academy of Sciences, entitled "City and Urbanization Process of Central Asia: Antiquity and the Middle Ages," discussed in the main, theories and methodologies for synthesizing information about historical urbanization processes, with the significance of modern urban problems in mind. Comparisons were reportedly drawn between the cities of Central Asia and those in the Middle East, the Far East, Europe and North Africa. Such attempts at synthesis are steps in the right direction. We await the publication of the submitted papers (see the report by Yu. F. Buryakov and M. I. Filanovich, in Russian, 1990).

Scholars of history have, in the meantime, published a succession of detailed monographs dealing with Balkh, Herat and other cities during the 16th to the 18th centuries, based on historical sources. E. A. Davidovich, *The History of Currency Circulation in Medieval Central Asia: Copper Coinage in Ma wara' al-Nahr during the 15th and the First Quarter of the 16th Centuries* (R., 1983) is a study by a specialist in numismatics which indicates the potentialities and importance of economic history. A regional symposium, "The Late-Feudal City in Central Asia," held under the auspices of the Institute of History of the Uzbek Academy of Sciences in 1989, indicates a strong interest in manuscripts and epitaphs as source material, in commercial relations between cities and in urban social life. It is also worth noting that academic institutions in Central Asia have been promoting urban studies, and study is being carried out on previously ignored themes, such as the ulama and the Sufi orders, and relations and comparisons between cities in Central Asia and those in Azerbaijan and the Middle Volga basin. Most of the papers read at the above symposium have been published as collected papers, R. G. Mukminova (ed.), *The Late Feudal City of Central Asia* (R., 1990), and full-scale monographs on these new themes are awaited (see also the report by N. N. Khabibullaev, in Russian, 1989).

The above outlines the development in the Soviet Union of studies on Central Asian cities. We can distinguish certain common characteristics in that development. First, a multi-faceted approach employing various methodologies, such as historical studies based on historical sources, and archaeological, ethnographical, and epigraphical studies, has been evident. Archaeology is given particular weight, basically because of the lack of historical sources for Central Asian cities, especially compared the situation for Middle Eastern cities, and, in particular, the fact that many of the cities, which existed in border regions between nomadic lands and the settled agricultural area, disappeared leaving very little documentation. Second, since Central Asian cities were defined as "Oriental feudal cities," their characteristics were often discussed by comparison with the medieval cities of the Occident. Although Chekhovich's "free city" theory may have been a reaction against the obsessive thinking of the Soviet academic circles, which insisted that autonomy was never experienced in the Orient, her way of looking at the question and her style of thinking do not seem free of the duality of the Orient versus the Occident (including Russia). Third, since Central Asian cities were considered to be "medieval cities" rather than "Islamic cities," Soviet scholars have tended to ignore or overlook the Islamic elements. Thus their urban theory is of interest to us, since it attempts to describe the "Islamic city," imagined by Western Orientalists, without using the term "Islam." All the same, much remains to be done in order to define the characteristics of Central Asian cities.

II. Recent Trends

1. General

Here I will deal with studies, including chronological histories and works on historical geography, which discuss in a comprehensive way the history of specific cities.

There are few urban histories of cities in the former Soviet Central Asia which have been written as regional histories by a local person about a city's distinguished persons or notable families, its origins and the history of its historical buildings and place names. Chronological histories of Samarkand (R., 1969), Bukhara (R., 1976) and the Khwarazm region (R., 1976) edited by I. M. Muminov, of Andijan (R., 1980) by M. A. Akhunova et al., and of Tashkent (R., 1988) by Kh. Z. Ziyaev and Yu. F. Buryakov are compilations of the political, socio-economic and cultural history of the city arranged chronologically. They are useful introductions, but hardly successful as descriptions of a city's individuality, and suggest that the descriptive style of the official Republic histories was also applied to the city histories. In general, they are deficient in city plans and are weighted to the period after the October Revolution. It is strange that the Muslim intellectuals of Central Asia have not written histories of their own cities when we consider how strong was their sense of belonging to one's native city up until the beginning of this century.

Noteworthy examples among histories of specific periods include B. A. Akhmedov, *A History of Balkh* (R., 1982) and A. Mukhtarov, *Balkh in the Late Middle Ages: Materials concerning its Historical Geography from the 16th to the 18th Century* (R., 1980). Akhmedov attempts to analyze the political and social history of the Khanate of Balkh using the abundant historical sources which include detailed accounts of the cities of north Afghanistan and Balkh itself together with descriptions of the state system. Mukhtarov's work is an historico-geographical study which makes full use of both unpublished manuscript sources located in Afghanistan and the findings of field research conducted by the author himself. Mukhtarov discusses the main components of the city of Balkh (city walls, quarters, public buildings, mausolea, gardens, the irrigation system), a city which enjoyed prosperity despite being pinned between the Uzbeks in Central Asia and various political forces in Iran, India and Afghanistan. N. N. Tumanovich, *Herat between the 16th and 18th Centuries* (R., 1989), which utilizes rich historical sources in Persian, is a comprehensive study with a special focus on Herat after the collapse of the Timurid dynasty. It discusses the historical geography and geographical environment of Herat and its surroundings, its political history, characterized by an ever-changing succession of rulers, from the Timurids to the Shibanids, the Safavids, Nadir Shah (the Afsharids), and the Durranis dynasty, and the economic and cultural activities of the Barnābādīs, a landlord family living in the Herat region whose influence lasted for four centuries. The above works are document-based studies which draw on unpublished written sources, and they contribute significantly to post-16th century Central Asian urban studies, a field virtually barren until their appearance.

Historians outside the Soviet Union have also made great contributions in the field. R. N. Frye, *Bukhara, the Medieval Achievement* (1965), based on sources such as Narshakhi's *History of Bukhara,* is the standard work describing the political and cultural life of Bukhara during the Samanid period. The prosperity of the Islamic-Iranian civilization and the Turkicization of Central Asia are the main interests of this study. T. Allen, *Timurid Herat* (1983) is a history of the main city of the Eastern Islamic world in the 15th century. It is brief and to the point, written on the basis of a careful study of historical sources and field research. A valuable appendix contains an exhaustive list of place names and buildings in Herat.

Few comprehensive studies exist of post-Timurid cities in Ma wara' al-Nahr with the exception of essays such as R. G. Mukminova, "A History of Tashkent in the Late Middle Ages" (R., 1981) and O. A. Sukhareva, "The Defence Walls of Samarkand" (R., 1979). Mukminova, *Tashkent Four Hundred Years Ago* (in Uzbek, 1984) is a small but reliable introduction based on manuscript and archival sources dealing with the social, economic, cultural and political history of Tashkent from the late 15th to the early 16th century. Sukhareva, *A History of Cities in the Khanate of Bukhara: An Historical and Ethnographical Introduction* (R., 1958), though no more than the introduction it claims to be, includes comments with some plans regarding the historical geography and the inhabitants of the cities of Bukhara, Karshi and Shahr-i Sabz. Sukhareva's later studies concerning the urban society of Bukhara are detailed and useful in every sense. A. Mukhtarov, *Historical Documents concerning the History of Uratube: A Collection of Edicts from the 17th to the 19th Century* (R., 1963) is a well-prepared introduction to the Persian (Tajiki) documents obtained by the Institute of History of the Tajik Academy of Sciences from a descendant of an *īšān* residing in Uratube in 1954. Among them are a Bukhara amir's *yarlīq* (khān's edict) authorizing Friday prayers at a mosque in the quarter of Uratube and a document appointing a *mudarris.* This is not a history of Uratube, but it makes us optimistic that similar documents may be found to exist in other Central Asian cities. We look forward to their eventual discovery and publication.

Academic results from recent archaeological studies should not be overlooked as good descriptions of urban history. The dynamism of the development and decline of the cities located in particular in the northern part of Central Asia, the border region between the sedentary and nomadic patterns of existence is being clarified solely by archaeologists. T. N. Senigova, *Medieval Taras* (R., 1972) traces the development of Taras from the 6th to the 12th century on the basis of archaeological finds and shows how the city was influenced in turn by Sogdian culture, Turkicization and the penetration of Islam. K. A. Akishev, K. M. Baipakov and L. B. Erzakovich, *Otrar in the*

Late Middle Ages: From the 16th to the 18th Century (R., 1981) is one study to come out of the intensive excavations being conducted at the ruins of the city of Otrar in southern Kazakhstan. It covers urban structures such as quarters, residences and city walls, economic activities such as the craft industry, commerce and agriculture, together with the city's population, social structure and ethnic composition. The population during the 16th and the 17th centuries is estimated to fall between 4,500 and 6,300, which equals that of the city of Turkistan in 1867. The study provides new information about the tendency of the nomadic Kazakhs to settle down and their ethnogenesis. Further academic fruits are confidently expected. Also in progress are excavations of a number of medieval cities in the southwestern part of Central Asia, the present Turkmenistan and works such as E. Atagarryev, *Medieval Dihistan: A History and Culture of a City in Southwest Turkmenistan* (R., 1986) have been published. Atagarryev has shed light on the topography and culture of the city of Dihistan from the 9th to the 14th century. During the height of its prosperity in the Seljuk period between the 11th and 12th centuries, the city's population is estimated to have been around 36,000.

Archaeology has also contributed greatly to the urban history of the heartland of Central Asia. Yu. F. Buryakov (ed.), *An Historical Geography of Ancient and Medieval Samarkand* (R., 1981) is an interim report of recent archaeological studies in Afrasiyab and gives information about the quarters of ceramic artisans in the 10th and 11th centuries and the process whereby the centre of urban life shifted. However it will be a long time before the entire picture of the urban development of Samarkand becomes visible. id., *An Historical Geography of Ancient Cities of the Tashkent Oasis: An Historical and Archaeological Introduction to Chachi and Ilak* (R., 1975) deals with medieval Tashkent about which written sources are scarce. Buryakov traces the rise and decline of cities which existed before the 12th century in the region of Tashkent and identifies cities mentioned in Arabic written sources between the 9th and 10th centuries with actual city ruins. M. I. Filanovich, *Tashkent, the Formation and the Development of the City and its Urban Culture* (R., 1983) too identifies ancient and medieval urban centres that moved within the micro oasis of Tashkent, occupied by the present city, in an attempt to show how Tashkent developed before the Mongol invasion. Buryakov (ed.), *The Ancient and Medieval City of Eastern Ma wara' al-Nahr* (R., 1990), written by a number of leading archaeologists in Uzbekistan, is the latest work to study the urbanization process in the Tashkent oasis before the 13th century.

The medieval cities of the eastern Farghana region, the present Kirgizistan, are discussed in V. D. Goryacheva, *The Urban Centers of Medieval Kirgizia and its Architectural Ensembles* (R., 1983), an outline of the historical geography of Uzgen from the 10th to the 15th century, and the *mazār* complex in Safid-Bulan. A. R. Mukhamedzhanov et al., *The Ruins of Paikend City: A Study of a Medieval City in Central Asia* (R., 1988) stems from excavations of the ancient city of Paikend, sixty kilometres southwest of Bukhara on the lower Zarafshan River. Paikend came into being as a Sogdian city between the late 5th and early 6th century, and was often mentioned in Arabic histories and geographies as "a town of merchants" or "a town of bronze." The recent five year study has revealed the existence of a citadel, a *šahristān* and various kinds of defense facilities, and copper coins including the T'ang Chinese *Kai-yuan tong bao* and others dating from the Umayyad, the 'Abbassid, the Samanid and the Karakhanid dynasties as well as Ghaznavid gold coins have been found. A picture of a flourishing commercial city on the trade route between Merv and Bukhara dating from the 9th to the 11th century is now being unfolded. It is no exaggeration to say that knowledge of the history of pre-Mongolian Central Asian cities depends almost entirely on the future development of archaeological studies.

Studies concerning post 19th century urban history are not numerous and of those that exist the outstanding ones concentrate on the history of Tashkent, which developed rapidly under the stimulus of trade with Russia, the Kazakh Steppe, the Khanate of Khokand and Eastern Turkistan. H. Ziyaev, *The Incorporation of Tashkent by Russia* (in Uzbek, 1967) uses local Persian histories of Tashkent in manuscript to summarize the development of diplomatic and commercial relations between Tashkent and Russia after the 1830s and to describe in detail how Tashkent was captured by the Russian army. It is interesting that Ziyaev, while following the official line of Soviet academic circles that the annexation of Central Asia, including Tashkent, by Russia "contributed to Central Asian progress, from an objective point of view," pointed out that Russia tried to demonstrate that its annexation of Tashkent in 1865 was according to the will of the local people. Ziyaev, who since Perestroika has been one of the leaders in the movement to overturn the Soviet version of history, now clearly states that the Russian "annexation" of Central Asia was nothing but a "conquest," and criticizes his own former attitude. Ziyaev, "Tashkent from the 18th Century to the First Half of the 19th Century" (R., 1983) is a short article introducing the economy, society and culture of Tashkent based on Russian sources. Central Asian society in the 19th century underwent a great change as relations with Russia developed further and further. We await future studies that will examine the dynamism of that change in terms of the framework of the city.

F. Azadaev, *Tashkent in the Latter Half of the 19th Century: An Introduction to its Socio-Economic and Political History* (R., 1959) is the only work dealing with modern urban history. It begins with Tashkent under the rule of the Khokand khans in the first half of the 19th century and goes on to examine the administrative organization of Imperial Russia, the socio-economic development of Tashkent and the popular movement in the latter half of the 19th century. It does much to shed light on the actuality of an urban society under colonial rule. Sukhareva, an ethnographer, has also written a series of works on contemporary Bukhara, but they are aimed primarily at describing an urban society statically, and are not concerned with aspects of transformation in the modern era.

Finally, I will add a few words about maps. We do not possess a large number of maps for Central Asia, either general maps showing the locations of historical cities or individual city plans. In general, Soviet scholars did not pay much attention to maps. The exception was O. G. Bol'shakov, who in the aforementioned *The Medieval City of Central Asia* includes a map locating "medieval cities" by area and plans showing how individual cities such as Merv, Bukhara and Samarkand expanded. General maps of Central Asia from the 9th to the 13th century and from the 19th to the 20th century and the plans of above-mentioned cities, all made by Bol'shakov, appear also as appendices in the 9th volume of *The Collected Works of Academician V. V. Bartol'd* (R., 1977). These are our most useful references at present. A variety of maps must have been produced during the period of the Russian rule, but most have remained long inaccessible.

2. Architecture

A classic introduction to the architecture of Central Asian cities, though now out of date, is A. Yu. Yakubovskii, *Samarkand during Timur and the Timurid Period* (R., 1933). Studies in this field witnessed a remarkable growth after World War II; of these the contribution by G. A. Pugachenkova is outstanding. In more than four hundred books and articles she studied the architecture and history of the arts of an area covering the former Soviet Central Asia, Afghanistan and Iran and there is no important building that she did not mention. In an article jointly written with M. E. Masson, "Shahr-i Sabz during the Age of Timur and Ulugh Beg" (R., 1953) she attempts to reconstruct, on the basis of the existing ruins and written sources, the main architectural features of Shahr-i Sabz, which enjoyed prosperity under the patronage of the Timurid dynasty. Even today it remains a valuable study of Shahr-i Sabz's past magnificence. It has been translated into English by J. M. Rogers as "Shahr-i Sabz from Timur to Ulugh Beg" (1978-80). Among recent works by Pugachenkova is *The Legacy of Arts in the Soviet Union: A Handbook for Central Asia* (R., 1983), a comprehensive survey, with illustrations, of representative monuments and buildings in Central Asia during the Islamic period.

Among recent studies is A. Anarbaev, *Urban Improvement in Medieval Central Asia from the 5th to the Early 13th Century* (R., 1981), a unique work which uses archaeological data to survey the environmental facilities of medieval cities in Sogdiana such as Panjikant, Samarkand and Nasaf (Nakhshab). It also deals with questions related to streets, bazars and shopping districts, the water supply, green zones, habitation improvement and sanitation in two stages, from the 5th to the 8th century and from the 9th to the 13th century. He gives evidence that streets were paved with round stones or pottery fragments as early as the late 7th to the early 8th century, that especially after the 9th century, gardens with their own water supply were made in the *rabaḍ* districts, thus extending the green zone, and that densely populated cities had their own drainage facilities and sewage pools which despite certain inadequacies contributed greatly to maintaining environmental health. On the whole, urban improvement made great strides in the 9th century, but after that there was no major change until the period of the Mongol invasion.

N. B. Nemtseva and Yu. Z. Shvab, *The Complex of the Shah-i Zinda* (R., 1979) studies the architectural history of the largest cemetery in Central Asia, on the southern outskirts of Afrasiyab, the predecessor of Samarkand. Constructed between the 11th and 19th centuries, the Shah-i Zinda is a magnificent complex of more than forty mausolea (including ruins) embodying the essence of Central Asian architectural techniques and decorative arts. A visit to the site was considered a pious act equivalent to a pilgrimage to Mecca. According to tradition, Qutham bin 'Abbas, the "living king" Shah-i Zinda who was a cousin of the Prophet Muhammad and also one of his companions, reached Samarkand in the late 7th century as an Arab warrior and was murdered at prayer by an infidel. His *mazār,* built in the 11th century, is the foundation of the later complex of mausolea. The study draws on a large number of pictorial representations to reveal the structure of the complex, and excites curiosity concerning the religious and social meaning of this rare array. All the cities of Central Asia, and their suburbs, possessed mausolea (*mazār*) linked with Sufism. If a city is considered to be a place of association, such buildings should naturally be studied from various aspects, not only their external appearance. Nemtseva, "The Origins and Architectural Development of the Shah-i Zinda" (R., 1975), with an English translation (1977), deals with the architectural history of the Shah-i Zinda.

Russian rule changed the features of Central Asian cities. New towns were constructed adjacent to the old Muslim cities for the Russian newcomers and these were characterized by ordered streets lined with modern Russian- or Western-style buildings which contrasted to the traditional Muslim quarters. The influence of modern architecture reached in some degree even the two protectorates of Bukhara and Khiva. V. A. Nil'sen, *The Origin of Modern*

Urban Construction in Uzbekistan: From the 19th to the Early 20th Century (R., 1988) is a new type of study which focuses on representative examples of urban planning and modern architecture in such major cities as Tashkent, Samarkand, Khokand and New Marghilan.

An excellent reference for recent trends in the study of architecture and the arts of the Central Asian cities in the former Soviet Union are two collections of articles, L. I. Rempel' (ed.), *Artistic Culture in Central Asia from the 9th to the 13th Century* (R., 1983) and Pugachenkova (ed.) *Civic Engineering and Architecture* (R., 1989). The latter in particular contains the latest results of archaeological studies and a number of ground-breaking and ambitious articles, including an analysis of the structural development of Central Asian cities, a comparative study of gardens in Central Asia and India, and a discussion about harmony between tradition and modernity in Central Asian urban architecture. S. D. Rakhmatullaeva, "Central Asian Public Baths, Hammams, in 15th-17th Century Miniatures" (R., 1990) is a new attempt to reconstruct the architecture, plans, decoration and facilities of public baths, on the basis of miniatures. A number of recently published collections of photographs, including Pugachenkova (ed.), *An Open-Air Museum: The Essence of the Architecture of Uzbekistan* (R., 1981), *Samarkand: A Museum in the Open* (1986) and I. Borodina (ed.), *Central Asia: Its Architectural Heritage from the 9th to the 19th Century* (R., 1987), provide glimpses of the wealthy heritage of Central Asian architecture.

T. Allen, *A Catalogue of the Toponyms and Monuments of Timurid Herat* (1981) and L. Golombek and D. Wilber, *The Timurid Architecture of Iran and Turan* (1988) are works by scholars outside the Soviet Union, also mentioned in the chapter on Iran, which are worth noting. The latter is a voluminous work which examines the characteristics of Timurid architecture and outlines in catalogue style 257 buildings and monuments in Iran and Central Asia. The second volume is devoted to illustrations. This excellent work gives an accurate view of Central Asian Islamic architecture in its golden age. A. W. Najimi, *Herat: The Islamic City* (1988) studies the urbanization of modern Herat, with the preservation of the ancient capital a concern. The Afghani author does not confine himself just to the preservation of the landscape and functions of Herat as they remain today but seeks to produce a plan to revive the Islamic city adapted to Islamic social traditions and its natural environment, thereby taking a different path to that of Western style urbanization and urban development. The detailed description of urban life in Herat owes much to the author's talent. Unfortunately, just after he finished his field research, Afghanistan was invaded in 1979 by the Soviet Army and Herat was damaged extensively in the course of the civil war. It will take many years for Herat to revive.

3. City and Nomads

Central Asian history is dominated by the relationship between the city and the nomads. Most closely concerned with the study of this question are archaeologists who took note of the previously-mentioned urban ruins on the southern fringes of Kazakhstan. K. M. Baipakov, *The Medieval Urban Culture of South Kazakhstan and Semirech'e from the 6th to the Early 13th Century* (R., 1986) recreates solely on the basis of archaeological material, the process of urban development in the border area between the Steppes, where the nomads lived, and the agricultural land in river valleys and at the foot of mountains in the south. Baipakov concludes that the development of urban culture in this region can be classified into two stages. During the first stage, between the 6th and 9th centuries, a series of cities were established in southern Kazakhstan and southwestern Semirech'e. The cities of southern Kazakhstan depended on suburban agriculture and international commerce, while those in southwestern Semirech'e were more likely commercial bases. While Sogdian influence is discernible, Turkic cultural elements are already clear. During the second stage, from the 10th to the end of the 13th century, urban culture progressed most rapidly, and about seventy new cities and towns emerged along the commercial routes in the northeastern part of Semirech'e. The population of Isfijab (Sayram) is estimated to have been about 40,000, that of Otrar about 16,000, and that of Belasagun about 10,000. This period also saw large numbers of Turkic nomads taking up a sedentary life, and the material culture of cities changed. The penetration of Islam into the region between the 11th and 12th centuries likewise contributed to the further development and homogenization of urban culture. The Mongol invasion brought disastrous effects on the development of urban culture, and at the end of the 13th century it devastated the cities in the east of Semirech'e where the urban tradition was weakest. Then in the early 15th century, the cities southwest of Semirech'e, whose economy had depended on the caravan trade, declined and only some cities in southern Kazakhstan, whose economy was dependent primarily on agricultural production, survived. Despite some looseness of argument, Baipakov gives a clear outline of urban development in the region.

An earlier study than Baipakov's, K. A. Pishchulina, "Cities in the Sir Darya Basin and their Significance in the History of the Kazakh Khanates from the 15th to the 17th Century" (R., 1969) deals with the cities which "survived" in southern Kazakhstan. Pishchulina uses primarily historical sources to carefully examine the economic and political situation of the cities of "Turkistan" and their economic and military significance to the Kazakh Khanates. Interesting is her assertion that the Kazakh khans tended to strengthen their independence from the central khans through possession of the wealthy oasis cities, and that the conquests of "Turkistan cities" might have been one factor in the split of the nomadic Kazakhs into three tribal federations (*zhuz* or horde). We await the publication of the newly discovered historical sources such as waqf documents and khans' edicts (*yarlīq*) that she utilized.

The cities of Turkistan had military significance not only for the Kazakhs, but also for the nomadic Uzbeks under the leadership of Shaibani Khan, who conquered Ma wara' al-Nahr in the early 16th century. T. Horikawa, "Shaibani Khan and the Town of Arquq" (J., 1979) analyzes in detail the relationship between the fort town of Arquq and the nomadic forces, and on the basis of historical sources, the above-mentioned work of Pishchulina and B. A. Akhmedov, *The Nomadic Uzbek State* (R., 1965), proves the military importance of urban centres. This article provides a new viewpoint about Central Asian cities, whose commercial nature alone has tended to have been emphasized.

When we turn our gaze to Ma wara' al-Nahr itself, a number of issues come to mind, not least the mutual relationship between urban societies and the Turko-Mongolian nomads who established their political power there over settled agricultural regions after the Mongol invasion; in other words, the sedentarization and assimilation into urban society of the nomads and the associated transformation of the cities. Concering this point, E. Mano, *A History of Central Asia* (J., 1977) is a lucid presentation which emphasises the formation of the Timurid dynasty and it has been followed by a number of notable successors, particularly in Japan. K. Kato, "Amir Timur and Shahr-i Kish" (J., 1988) studies the close relationship between Timur and Kish (later Shahr-i Sabz) and notes in the construction of magnificent Timurid mausolea there how the Timur's "government" transformed itself to the Timurid "dynasty." Mano, "Babur and Herat" (J., 1980) utilizes the descriptions in the *Babur-nama* to describe how the way of life of amirs in the later Timurid dynasty was perfectly adjusted to urban culture. K. Kubo, "The Cultural Movement and its Background in Timurid Herat" (J., 1989) attempts to discover ties among the amirs, native people of influence, ulama and artists through an analysis of their cultural activities, drawing upon T. Allen, *A Catalogue of the Toponyms and Monuments of Timurid Herat* (1981). Kubo, "Herat in the Early Sixteenth Century" (J., 1988) analyzes through the attitudes of the urban notables of Herat the mutual relationship between the "Turkic nomadic forces" and sedentary society at a time after the collapse of the Timurid dynasty when two rising dynasties, the Uzbeki Shibanids and the Safavids of Iran governed the city alternately. R. D. McChesney, "The Amirs of Muslim Central Asia in the XVIIth Century" (1983) is a richly suggestive study of the amir class in the 17th century from the viewpoint of social history which discusses the mutual relationship between the amirs and the ulama. Changes in and maturity of urban society in Ma wara' al-Nahr after the Timurid period is a subject connected with the ethnogenesis of the Uzbeks, Tajiks and others, and is an important area for further study.

4. Administration: The City and Political Power

Bol'shakov has made a general summary of urban administration in the pre-Mongolian period (R., 1973). He says that the "Muslim cities" of Central Asia did not have any legal status as a city. Even Muslim geographers had no criteria for recognizing a concentration of dwellings as a city other than whether or not it was the centre for large-scale administration, in other words, whether it had a Friday mosque or not. Urban autonomy may have been established to some extent in unwritten customary law, but as far as known historical sources are concerned, city-wide autonomy did not exist in the period between the 10th and 12th centuries. Urban administration was totally in the hands of government bureaucrats like the *ra'īs*, documented for the first time in the late 10th century, the qadi and the muhtasib, and this is similar to medieval Syrian cities, about which E. Ashtor and others have studied in detail. We should however not be too hasty about defining all those holding the position of *ra'īs*, qadi, etc. as government bureaucrats, for they were often selected from local notables and therefore were able to exercise their influence on urban society. Had though they lost all autonomy? Bol'shakov was inclined to take a somewhat one-sided view of the relationship between political power and urban society.

A. A. Semyonov, *An Introduction to the Central Administrative Organization in the Late Period of the Khanate of Bukhara* (R., 1954) remains a highly rated study of urban administration after the Timurid period. Based on historical documents and contemporary observations, it reveals that the various government offices in charge of the urban administration, judicial administration, police and military affairs of Bukhara were simultaneously the top posts of the khanate government organization. Semyonov also points out that the city of Bukhara was divided into two large districts (*sahm*) which in turn were further subdivided into six smaller districts, making a total of twelve districts (*jarīb*), and that the chief of each of these districts (*dah baši*) was subject to police officials called *šabgard*. Later, Sukhareva discovered twelve districts (*maḥalla*) marked on an old map of Bukhara dating from the middle of the 19th century made by a Bukharan—perhaps Aḥmad Dānish (1827-97), a progressive ulama of Bukhara—and examined the tradition of the internal classification of the city and the terms related to the districts (See Sukhareva, "An Introduction to the History of Central Asian Cities," in Russian, 1976).

O. D. Chekhovich has presented us with a new view of urban administration in Central Asia, and of autonomy in particular. As we have seen above, she has shown, in a series of articles, that Tashkent was in effect a "free city," not subordinate to any external political power. id., "A Story of Tashkent" (R., 1970) is a scrupulous introduction to an unpublished historical narrative in Persian which describes the original "republican form of government." The narrative was written in the blank spaces of what is considered the autograph manuscript of Muḥammad Ṣāliḥ Tāshkandī's *A New History of Tashkent*. Chekhovich has added a critical text and a Russian translation to a facsimile of the text. In a later work, "Urban Autonomy in 18th Century Tashkent" (R., 1976), she uses Persian sources from Bukhara and Khokand and contemporary Russian sources as well as the above mentioned narrative to make a deeper historical inquiry to prove that Tashkent in this period enjoyed prosperity as an "independent republic," under the rule of the *khwājas*, influential merchants or landowners, supported by artisan guilds, and backed by the development of commerce and the craft industry. She further remarks that the city of Tashkent and its suburbs were divided into four districts and that each district was self-governed. Little is known however about the internal affairs of the *maḥalla* of Tashkent. Chekhovich recommends the immediate commencement of a detailed study of Tashkent, similar to those about Bukhara and Samarkand done by Sukhareva. In "Urban Autonomy in Central Asia during the Feudal Age" (R., 1979), she gives as further examples of the "free city," Paikend and Iskijukat in the 10th century, Bukhara in the 12th century, Samarkand in the 14th century, and Badakhshan, Balkh, Andijan and other cities in the 18th century. Thus she urges the reexamination of the established theory that cities in Central Asia and Iran during the feudal age had neither autonomy nor urban statutes. In spite of its brevity, the article gives a new perspective on urban studies of Central Asia in the former Soviet Union. Though at present there is no evidence that self-governing cities in Central Asia produced special urban statutes, her suggestion that urban statutes were probably not necessary given the existence of sharia established by the urban population themselves is rare in the history of Soviet Oriental studies.

5. Crafts: Production and Organization

The craft industry was the major productive activity in cities and, being related also to the guild, is an essential theme when discussing cities. Partly because historical sources are scarce, historians have not addressed the issue until recently. The initiative was in fact taken by ethnographers and some archaeologists.

E. M. Peshchereva, "Pottery Manufacture in Central Asia" (R., 1959) studies the manufacture of pottery in cities and minutely describes production technology, the forms and uses of the pottery, changes in those forms, and the organizations of pottery workers in cities such as Samarkand, Shahr-i Sabz and Tashkent and those in northern Tajikistan. Though there is danger in automatically applying the reports of ethnographers to pre-19th century "medieval cities," yet detailed factual information is useful. For example, Peshchereva shows that pottery produced in the cottage industry of modern Tajikstan is distributed within a 15-20 km radius, and G. A. Brykina, who excavated the ruins of Karabulak in southwest Farghana, comparing such local pottery manufacture and that of Karabulak, concluded that the pottery produced in Karabulak, which was almost of the same standard and quality as that produced in Samarkand and Bukhara, was made for the international market (G. A. Brykina, *Karabulak,* in Russian, 1974). Brykina identifies the ruins as Asbanikat, an important city in the Farghana region mentioned by al-Muqaddasī. N. Tursunov, "An Essay on the History of Artisanal Guilds in Central Asia" (R., 1972) uses ethnographical materials collected from former weavers of Khujand to report on the internal organization and functions of guilds (*kasaba*) from the late 19th to the beginning of the 20th century and various aspects about their transformation.

O. A. Sukhareva, *The Late-Feudal City of Bukhara at the Turn of the 20th Century: Artisanal Industry*(R., 1962) is one of a series of three works about Bukhara which sets out to describe the totality of the craft industry of a particular city, Bukhara. The study is based on materials collected from the elders of Bukhara in the 1940s and 50s and is a rich source of data on such subjects as the various crafts, including metal processing, textiles, construction, leather tanning, tailoring, food dispensing, pottery manufacture, woodwork, soap making, tent making, their technologies, products, organizations for production, and the social relationships they engendered. The study is unparalleled in its breadth. It also provides useful maps showing that certain types of industry inclined to concentrate in specific areas, and lists terms related to the industry. The Khanate of Bukhara, which was a protectorate under the Imperial Russian rule, maintained to a large extent the traditional structure and features of a Central Asian city up to 1920, the year of "People's Soviet Revolution." Sukhareva's work is suggestive for the craft industry of "medieval cities" as well. She has conducted similar research for Samarkand, but the results have been published only as articles under specific titles, for example "The Textile Industry in Samarkand" (R., 1981). H. Kano, "Bukhara, an Islamic Industrial City" (J., 1976) makes good use of Sukhareva's work.

Perhaps stimulated by studies on the craft industry by ethnographers, R. G. Mukminova has studied the subject through historical sources. id., *An Introduction to the History of Crafts in Samarkand and Bukhara in the 16th Century* (R., 1976) is the best study in the field. She begins by making detailed comments concerning the historical sources and by examining the various crafts, including textiles, dyeing, paper manufacture, metalwork, armory making and tailoring. She then studies particular issues, such as the social and economic conditions of artisans, their workshops and markets for their products, tax collection and social contradictions. Mukminova utilized three kinds of source material, (1) the comparatively rich amount of historical documents from the Shibanid period, including more than 700 qadi documents from 16th-century Samarkand, *yarlīq* collections (unpublished), the Jūybārī Sheikhs' documents, waqf documents and others, (2) *risāla,* later records of regulations and ceremonies for artisans of various industries, and (3) chronicles and literary works including *Babur-nama* and *Shaybani-nama*. Contemporary documents may still await discovery. Subsequently Mukminova presented the fruits of her study of documentary sources in "An Unexamined Document concerning the Socio-Economic History of a Central Asian City" (R., 1984). She considers that the Shibanid dynasty appears largely to have relied on taxes collected from urban artisans, merchants and those engaged in agriculture and stock farming and she points out that tax registers for the urban population probably existed. Additionally, we have fragmentary glimpses of artisans who took part in urban riots opposing the governing authority. In that she has introduced into the urban studies of Central Asia the perspective of social history, Mukminova's contribution to the field has been great, and we await future results.

Field work by ethnographers has confirmed the existence of artisan guilds. Guilds were regarded as a vestiges of feudalism and an institution characteristic of the "middle ages." Bol'shakov and Mukminova, whose studies are based on historical sources, take a rather more cautious attitude about the guild due to the small number of historical sources. Nevertheless, Mukminova speculates that in the 16th century, guilds of the Western European type played an important role in Central Asian cities. Historical sources of the 16th century, incidentally, call guilds *jamā'at.* Still to be investigated is how guilds formed and developed.

Risāla, discussed by Mukminova and previously M. Gavrilov (see p. 283), existed for almost every industry, including agriculture and stock farming. Many of those that have been handed down from generation to generation were produced or written down after the 18th century (most of them in the Persian-Tajik language), but they are thought to have originated long before that time and have been widespread throughout Central Asia as a genre of popular literature. Though the collection and study of *risāla* were promoted by Orientalists and ethnographers in the 1920s, they have never drawn much scholarly attention. Sukhareva, "The Risala as Historical Materials" (R., 1984) understands that *risāla,* reflecting the influence of patron saints and of the narrative tradition, were formed out of a mixture of pre-Islamic traditions and customs and Islamic norms, and suggests that they could be employed as historical materials to study the social and spiritual history of artisans. Though Sukhareva died before completing any work along those lines, we must not ignore the importance of these kinds of historical material in allowing us to take a new and vigorous look at the history of Central Asia.

6. Urban Dwellers

Sukhareva, *Bukhara in the 19th and the Early 20th Centuries: A Late Feudal City and its Population* (R., 1966) studies urban population as a whole as well as specific social groups and was written as a case study of the historical ethnography of Bukhara, which had "survived" as a "medieval city" to the early 20th century, in response to questions about the internal structure of Central Asian cities and its historical development that had been raised by Petrushevskii and others. This work includes exhaustive descriptions of the topography of Bukhara and its integral elements (springs, bazars, caravansaries, public baths, mosques, madrasas, the *mazār,* graveyards, quarters, the traditional four urban districts) and of its population and family composition, the ethnic composition and the process of formation of its urban population, and the social composition of the population and occupations (artisans, merchants, governing and military classes, clergymen, intellectuals, and people engaged in essential services such as water-carriers). It is a veritable ethnography of Bukhara. Sukhareva estimates that the native population of Bukhara at the time exceeded 60,000 or even 65,000, giving a total population of between 75,000 and 80,000, with the difference made up with foreign students in madrasas (5,000), soldiers (5,000), travellers in caravansaries (3,000) and those who lived in the citadel (500). Though the study is somewhat weak from the point of view of dealing with urban unity and integrity, and descriptions are based on individual cases, there exists no other study which gives such a realistic image of a Central Asian city. The work is also extremely useful as a study of how the Bukharans came into being from the basic Tajik stock which had assimilated Turkic and Mongolian newcomers over a long period both culturally and linguistically. It is invaluable too as a consolidation of historical studies about Bukhara.

Sukhareva, *The Quarter Community of the Late Feudal City of Bukhara:*

In Relation to the History of Quarters (R., 1976) is the brilliant final work of Sukhareva's series on Bukhara. It describes in detail the mode of life of quarter (*guḏar*) community, and it records for all the 220 quarters of the city where they were located and what their names were, the number of houses, languages and occupations of inhabitants, waqf documents which referred to the names of quarters (historical sources for the quarters concerned) and other features. Sukhareva then uses the available historical sources to examine the history of the Bukhara quarters in five periods: (1) 8th-12th century, (2) 13th-early 16th century, (3) late 16th-17th century, (4) 18th-the first half of the 19th century, (5) latter half of the 19th century-early 20th century. She shows how the quarters grew and subdivided and points out the strong durability of their names. For example, forty-nine names of the seventy-six known in the third period were still being used up till the modern times. In conclusion she compares Bukhara with other "medieval cities" in China, Europe and Russia to generalize, though unfortunately not very successfully, about the question of the division of cities in feudal times into quarter societies. She seems not to be interested in what device or idea integrated Bukhara, separated as it was into so many quarter societies. If it is true that Bukhara was one of the most urbanized and advanced cities of Central Asia, more consideration should be given to this question. All the same, there is no other study as concrete as this about the urban cells that are the quarters, and it deserves high praise for how it has consolidated factual material concerning quarter societies before the Octorber Revolution. Detailed introductions to this work include H. Komatsu, "The Mahallas of Bukhara" (J., 1978) and A. Khalid, "The Residential Quarter in Bukhara before the Revolution" (1991). The latter attests to the importance of Russian-language works for Islamic studies, especially for reintegrating modern Central Asian history into the mainstream of Islamic studies.

A powerful argument for Sukhareva's emphasis on the urbanization of Bukhara is the fact that the city's inhabitants lived there all the year round. In "Customary Combination of Urban and Rural Occupations in Central Asia from the Late 19th Century to the Beginning of the 20th Century" (R., 1979) she shows that in pre-revolutionary Central Asia urban dwellers used to move to villages outside the city in spring to farm their own or rented land. Similarly artisans moved to their summer houses, taking with them the tools needed for their own work and engaged in farming as well as craft. In Samarkand, seventy to eighty percent of the city's population stayed away until late autumn, and only those too poor to afford a summer house in the suburbs remained in the city during summer. In 19th century Tashkent quite a number of orchards and farms were inside the city, to the extent that some travellers thought that the main occupation of the urban population was agriculture. In a society where the urban population was in general closely associated with agriculture the case of Bukhara where agriculture was not a routine of life was unique. The custom disappeared in the course of agricultural collectivization after the Revolution, but its existence is a fact that cannot be ignored when reconstructing the actual conditions of traditional urban life.

Sukhareva referred to this question again in another essay, "The Defence Walls of Samarkand" (R., 1979). In the course of an attempt to restore the defensive walls that used to surround the city and its suburbs, she conjectures that "medieval" urban dwellers thought of a city (*šahr*) as including both the city in a narrow sense and its suburban villages, and therefore city and village were not differentiated in pre-modern Central Asia. This coincides with the suggestion of B. Kh. Karmysheva, an ethnographer, who writes in *An Introduction to the Ethnic History of the Southern Regions of Tajikistan and Uzbekistan* (R., 1976) that in the southern part of the Khanate of Bukhara between the late 19th and the early 20th century, "boundaries of cities were not clear. Many urban dwellers engaged in agriculture as well as in crafts and commerce, and moved in summer to live in houses and gardens in suburban villages. A good number of those who lived in suburban villages were engaged in some kind of craft such as textiles in addition to agriculture. Suburban villages therefore were considered, in effect, one of the elements of the city, just as the urban quarters were, though they were called *qïshlaq* (village) and not *guḏar* (urban quarters)." Sukhareva, in "The Tradition of Competition between Districts in the Cities of Uzbekistan" (R., 1958) reports on the custom of "competition" among urban dwellers who were divided among a number of districts. The custom survived until the early years of the present century in many Central Asian cities, and similar customs in Iranian cities have been reported. It may be a remnant of an old custom dating back to the pre-Islamic period.

M. Abramov, *The Quarters of Samarkand* (R., 1989) uses methodology similar to Sukhareva's to describe briefly the *guḏar* of Samarkand before the Revolution. Samarkand, whose population exceeded 55,000 in the late 19th century, was divided into four administrative districts (*qiṭ'a*), Qalandarkhani, Khayrabadi, Suzangari and Khwaja Ahrari, and subdivided into a total of ninety-six quarters. Abramov has identified ninety quarters out of ninety-six on the basis of interviews conducted in the 1960s and 1970s, and records the history of each quarter and the origins and occupations of its inhabitants, as well as the names of the main buildings in the quarter and well-known persons born there. Although the work does not present a particularly new perspective on the theory of urban society, it is a useful source for the historical geography of Samarkand and its plans of all the administrative districts are of interest.

Studies concerning pre-19th century urban society include M. Haider, "Urban Classes in the Uzbek Khanates XVI-XVII Centuries" (presented in 1976, and published in 1982). This work analyzes the composition and social classes of Central Asian cities in the 16th and 17th centuries through manuscripts and historical records existing in Tashkent and by utilizing the travel records of the 16th century Jenkinson and others. Haider focuses on artisans and merchants in particular and makes good and critical use of Soviet studies, giving us new perspectives for the study of contemporary urban society. Haider has noted the vitalization of craft production in the 16th century; an important topic for future study is an examination of the international and local factors of this phenomenon.

A further discussion of Haider's theme is to be found in Mukminova, *Social Differentiation among the Urban Population of Uzbekistan in the 15th and 16th Centuries* (R., 1985), an analysis of the social and economic situation of various urban social classes from the late 15th to the early 17th century employing the colourful documents mentioned above. The social classes examined include artisans (classified into master, craftman, apprentice and others), urban poor and "stragglers," the "landlord class" made up of khans, Uzbeki amirs, and influential Sufi or sheikh families like the Jūybārī family, merchants, slaves and so on. The core of the study is an analysis of the vigorous economic activities in 16th century Samarkand of Ustad Tangri Berdi, who made a considerable fortune as a leading master artisans and mediator between masters and their artisans and wholesale stores, and between rulers and the guilds. Mukminova also studies the economic activities of the "landlord class" who owned not only huge amounts of land in agricultural villages but also a number of workshops, stores, residences, bazar sites and commercial facilities in the cities. The description is rather desultory, but the work is very helpful in that it is the first attempt to portray the actuality of the urban population of Central Asia through written sources, and it also gives us a number of relevant terms, including some left unexplained.

The existence in Bukhara and Samarkand of the old place name of "tower of the*'ayyār*" suggests that the*'ayyār* played an important role in the cities of Ma wara' al-Nahr. Despite this no complete study on the subject existed in the Soviet Union, perhaps because of the paucity of written sources. One exception is Bol'shakov, who in *The Medieval City of Cental Asia* attempted to discuss it by means of Tartusi's *A Story of Abu Muslim,* in which a good number of *'ayyār* of 11th and 12th century Merv make an appearance. A Tajik writer, Ṣadr al-Dīn 'Aynī (1878-1954), refers in his *Memoirs* (in Tajik, 1959; in Russian, 1974), which describes life in Bukhara before the Revolution, to a group called the *ālufte* who made much of chivalry and smart amusements. This may represent an offshoot of the *'ayyār*. Some articles, such as R. Hoshim, "The Tradition of Chivalry Spirit and the Ālufte of 'Aynī" (in Tajik, 1978), deal with the subject, but on the whole, the study of gangsters in the cities of Central Asia remains a topic for further study. According to 'Ayni, when an *ālufte* in Bukhara was defeated in a quarrel, he pledged, "Before God, we have sworn to surrender our *šahr* (town) to you," and it is said that the pledge was never broken.

What has been neglected in most Soviet urban studies of Central Asia is the study of the social group called "clergymen," the ulama and sheikhs of Sufi orders. In contrast to the pre-revolutionary Orientalists, Soviet scholars were long reluctant, with a few exceptions, to undertake studies of Islamic clergymen, whom they branded as reactionaries. There does exist a collection of articles, E. A. Davidovich and others (ed.), *Clergymen and Politics in the Near and Middle East in the Period of Feudalism* (R., 1985), indicative of new trends in Soviet Oriental Studies. Although the articles are not necessarily written from the standpoint of cities in particular, they contain document-based and many-sided approaches to the political and economic activities of "clergymen" in Central Asia after the Timurid period. A. N. Boldyrev, for example, points out the necessity of correctly evaluating a 15th century saint called Khwāja Aḥrār and the Naqshbandi order. The field has opened up promisingly with Perestroika and we should expect advances in the near future. Studies in the field have appeared in Japan utilizing hagiologies and chronicles. One such is M. Kawamoto, "Khwāja Aḥrār and Abū Sa'īd: Saint and Governor in the Timurid Period" (J., 1986), an analysis of the tremendous influence Khwāja Aḥrār had over the rulers and the background to that influence. Especially interesting is the fact that in 1454 Khwāja Aḥrār led the people of Samarkand in preventing the ruler from escaping when he was surrounded by the enemy and organized the system of defences. H. Komatsu, "The Īshāns of Tashkent" (J., 1985) uses Russian materials to examine the *īšāns* and their participation in the popular movement in the late 19th century. Studies on Sufi saints and Sufi orders in Central Asia are indispensable for the reconstruction of the history of the region as well as its cities.

7. Waqf Endowment

The study of waqf endowment in Central Asia is one of the major fields of Soviet Oriental Studies with its rich resources of waqf documents, and many critical texts and studies have been published, including P. P. Ivanov, *The Economy of the Juybari Sheikhs: A History of Feudal Landownership in Central Asia during the 16-17th Centuries* (R., 1954), O. D. Chekhovich, *Bukhara Documents in the 14th Century* (R., 1965), id., *Samarkand Documents in the 15th and 16th Centuries* (R., 1974) and R. G. Mukminova, *A History of Agrarian Relations in 16th-Century Uzbekistan: Based on the 'Waqf-name' Sources* (R., 1966). Chekhovich's work has been extensively introduced in Kato (J., 1970) and Mano (J., 1983). The main interest in studying waqf endowment has been in analyzing land ownership in villages during the feudal period; in terms of the waqf itself, what has been stressed are the exploitation of peasants by the ruling class and the preservation of their own property, endowment by secular rulers to influential "clergymen," and the economic basis of "clergymen." Although waqf documents have been used to study urban historical geography, the role of the waqf in urban society has hardly been examined, even where the waqf institutions were in cities or waqf properties were dedicated to urban institutions.

Scholars outside the Soviet Union trying to study Central Asian cities have long been hampered by the difficulty of utilizing primary historical sources and undertaking field research, but R. D. McChesney was able to overcome long standing restrictions by working under the auspices of the Institute of Oriental Studies in Tashkent. His research there has produced "Economic and Social Aspects of the Public Architecture of Bukhara in the 1560's and 1570's" (1987), which examines two gigantic construction projects undertaken in Bukhara in the late 16th century and their social and economic meaning. Also studied are the motives behind the construction of public buildings and the endowment of waqf properties by the three main endowers in the project, 'Abdulla Khan of the Shibanids, Khwāja Sa'd al-Dīn of the Jūybārī family, powerful throughout Central Asia as the sheikh of the Naqshbandi order, and Qul Bābā Kukaltāsh, an Uzbeki amir. Of great interest is his suggestion that such buildings allowed suburban villagers opportunities to witness the majesty and beauty of Bukhara and to give them a taste of culture and that immense waqf endowment contributed to ameliorating any sense of inequality in wealth and to justifying the position of the government. It is significant that the same types of urban development projects through waqf endowment have been identified in the contemporary Ottoman Empire and in Safavid Iran. M. E. Subtelny, "A Timurid Educational and Charitable Foundation (1991)," analyzing 'Alī Shīr's *Vaqfiyya* preserved in Saltykov-Shchedrin State Public Library in Leningrad, throws new light on the social and cultural life of late Timurid Herat. We await further publication and analysis of waqf documents existing in the former Soviet Union. Studies concerning public buildings in 16th century Bukhara based on such documents and manuscript sources have been made by G. A. Dzhuraeva, a scholar from Tashkent, in " New Sources on the Gates of Shahristan in Bukhara: Based on Waqf Documents" (R., 1983) and "New Sources on the History of Bukhara in the 16th Century" (R., 1988). Such studies by local scholars are expected to increase in the future.

M. Rogers, "Waqfiyyas and Waqf-Registers" (1976-7) examines in broad terms the waqf documents introduced by Chekhovich, and discusses their value as an historical source through comparisons with Ottoman and Iranian examples. M. Kawamoto, "A *Waqfiyya* of Khwāja Aḥrār" (J., 1989) gives us a glimpse of 15th century Samarkand through a careful analysis of a waqf document of 1470 that had been introduced by Chekhovich and points out the effectiveness of waqf studies in Islamic urban studies. Studies of the waqf system, which supported the urban economy and culture and integrated cities and villages, are significant in that they explain not only urban society in pre-modern Central Asia but also its transformation as a result of Russian colonization and the Soviet Revolution.

Not to be omitted is a remarkable work by McChesney, *Waqf in Central Asia: Four Hundred Years in the History of a Muslim Shrine, 1480-1889* (1991). In this latest of his works, McChesney employs original documents, manuscripts and a large number of Russian language studies to examine the mutual relationship between waqf endowment and urban development, together with various aspects of waqf administration as well as the political, social and economic history of the Balkh region. This comprehensive study explains the origin and development of the famous shrine city of Mazar-i Sharif, the recipient of a great number of waqf endowments thanks to its possession of the legendary tomb of the fourth Caliph 'Ali, and which enjoyed autonomous status from the second half of the 18th to the first half of the 19th century. McChesney's study is an essential work not only for Central Asian urban studies but for waqf studies in general. He writes: "Waqf is an Islamic institution made accessible to the historian by its documentary record. But to appreciate fully the way it is woven into the fabric of human society and to assess its place in the achievements of Muslim communities, the documentary record is only a beginning. The temporal and spatial dimensions of waqf, the geographical and historical realities must also be examined. Waqf deeds form both a legal contract and a statement of hope of the way the founder would like things to be. It is only through other records that touch in one way or another on the waqf in question—narrative histories, biographies, and royal court and Shar'i court decisions—that the degree to which the intent was fulfilled may be seen."

8. Others

An issue neglected in Central Asian urban studies in the former Soviet Union is urban culture itself and its evaluation. Compared with the achievements of socio-economic history and historical geography, results from the cultural fields have been poor. This is not unrelated to the indifference of scholars towards Islamic culture itself. In this field the lead has been taken by predominantly scholars outside the Soviet Union. For example, M. E. Subtelny, "Art and Politics in Early 16th Century Central Asia" (1983) and "Socioeconomic Bases of Cultural Patronage under the Later Timurids" (1988) examine the bases and background of cultural prosperity and cultural patronage under the Timurids together with the question of the continuity of Timurid cultural traditions under the succeeding Shibanids. Kubo, "Mīr 'Alī Shīr's Patronage of Science and Art" (J., 1990) employs the above-mentioned studies of Subtelny and Allen to discuss the nature of cultural patronage by Navā'ī, a high official and a man of letters in the late 15th century, through a clear examination of what actually happened. The literature of the Timurid period was considered the classical literature of Central Asia until the 19th century. A. Qayumov, *The Literary Circle of Khokand from the 18th to the 19th Century* (in Uzbek, 1961) studies the literary activities of those associated with the Khokand Court who attempted to revive the classics in the first half of the 19th century. Though this is not a study of the city itself, it is an excellent description of the Tajik-Uzbek bilingual tradition of literature in Khokand. H. Komatsu, "Bukhara and Kazan" (J., 1983) examines the significance of the movement from the end of the 18th century to the first half of the 19th century by Tatar students living in the Middle Volga to study in Bukhara, and concludes that Bukhara in this period contributed to the revival of Islamic culture in Tatar society under Russian rule. I eagerly await further studies in the cultural and social history of the Central Asian cities in the near future.

CONCLUSION

This chapter has attempted to summarize the history of scholarship concerning the "Islamic cities" of Central Asia as it has progressed primarily in Russia and the former Soviet Union. I have mentioned only a small proportion of the studies that exist and have omitted completely those of Eastern Turkistan. Although the history of urban studies for Eastern Turkistan is quite different to that described in this chapter, both Eastern and Western Turkistan comprised a common historical sphere up to the modern era. Hence, this deficiency should remedied at all costs in the near future. I should mention here that in the last decade, Japanese specialists in the area such as Y. Sanada, Y. Shin'men and S. Hori have been steadily attaining fine results (For bibliography of their works see E. Mano, "Turkistan" in Japanese, 1984; The Center for East Asian Cultural Studies, ed., *Bibliography of Central Asian Studies in Japan,* 1988-89; and Y. Shin'men, "Research in Japan on Islamic Central Asian History: 1984-91," 1993).

Despite the many omissions, I believe that to some degree I have been able to isolate trends of study in Russia and the former Soviet Union. The methods and areas of interest of Soviet scholars are substantially different to what is to be found in studies on "Islamic cities" of other areas. It is very obvious that Soviet scholars have paid little attention to Islam. I should also point out that among the scholars concerned with the cities of Central Asia, very few are native to the area, and on the whole Soviet scholars were indifferent to the trends and results of studies of the "Islamic cities" in the Arab region, Iran and Anatolia. Nevertheless, their academic results, based on the practical use of abundant written sources and backed by wide-ranging field work, are of value. The future progress of Central Asian urban studies will depend, as demonstrated by the work of McChesney, on the degree to which cooperative efforts can be maintained with local scholars and the research institutes. Such conditions appear to be evolving slowly but steadily.

Since Perestroika, Central Asia has began to take a new look at its own history and to reevaluate its national cultures, including Islam. The Koran has been translated into the local languages and published, and people are being encouraged to learn the Arabic script that had been used in the region until the 1920s. For many years the traditional residential quarter community, *maḥalla,* suffered criticism from Soviet atheist propaganda because it was considered a closed society maintaining Islamic "old-fashioned, medieval customs." Today it is considered an intimate community which does not alienate people. Abramov's recent work (*The Quarters of Samarkand*) has been high evaluated in a book review as contributing to the drive to restore the old place names lost in the course of "the unjust and opportunistic name changes" of the Soviet period. With each national language now legislated as the state's official language, there is increasing interest in the traditional terms describing urban space and functions like *šahristān*, *mazār*, and *čarsu*. The progress of the movement to reconstruct the cultural heritage will positively affect the study of Central Asian cities.

It is also true however that Central Asian cities have been damaged by the series of violent ethno-political conflicts which broke out in the last years of the Soviet Union. For example, the town of Osh, whose beauty was praised by Babur in the 16th century, has become a brutal battleground between the Uzbeks and Kirghizis, old neighbours. Bukhara and Samarkand, which were incorporated into Uzbekistan under the "National Delimitation" of Central Asia in 1924, have yet to solve the ethnic issues of the Tajiki population. However difficult and complicated the factors behind the ethnic conflicts may be, it is not impossible to perceive part of those factors as arising from changes to the urban social structure in modern times. Unfortunately we do not yet have enough studies to show us how Central

Asian cities originally were and which can throw light on the transformation process in modern times down to the present. It is safe to say however that since the Arab invasions, the cities of Central Asia have been the dynamic force of Central Asian history. We await the opening before us of new perspectives in urban studies.

Bibliography

Abramov, M. *Guzary Samarkanda (The Quarters of Samarkand)*. Tashkent, 1989.

Afrasiab: Afrasiabskaya kompleksnaya arkheologicheskaya ekspeditsii (Afrasiyab: The General Archaeological Investigation of Afrasiyab). 4 vols. Tashkent, 1969-75.

Ageeva, E. I. & G. I. Patsevich. "Iz istorii osedlykh poselenii i gorodov yuzhnogo Kazakhstana (A History of Village Settlements and Towns in Southern Kazakhstan)." *Trudy instituta istorii, arkheologii i etnografii AN Kaz SSR*. (Alma-Ata) 5 (1958).

Aini, S. *Sobranie sochinenii (The Collected Works)*. Vol. 4 & 5: *Bukhara: Vospominaniya (Bukhara: Memoirs)*. Translated by S. Borodin. Moskva, 1974.

Akhmedov, B. A. *Gosudarstvo kochevykh uzbekov (The Nomadic Uzbek State)*. Moskva, 1965.

———. *Istoriya Balkha: XVI-pervaya polovina XVIII v. (A History of Balkh: From the 16th to the First Half of the 18th Century)*. Tashkent, 1982.

Akhunova, M. A. et al., eds. *Istoriya Andizhana (A History of Andijan)*. Tashkent, 1980.

Akishev, K. A. "Perspektivy izucheniya pozdnesrednevekovykh gorodov Kazakhstana (Urban Study Perspectives on Kazakhstan in the Late Medieval Period)." In *Srednevekovaya gorodskaya kul'tura Kazakhstana i Srednei Azii, Materialy vsesoyuznogo soveshchaniya 13-15 maya 1981 g. g. Alma-Ata*, ed. B. A. Tulenbaev. Alma-Ata, 1983.

Akishev, K. A., K. M. Baipakov & L. B. Erzakovich. *Pozdnesrednevekovyi Otrar, XVI-XVIII vv. (Otrar in the Late Middle Ages: From the 16th to the 18th Century)*. Alma-Ata, 1981.

Allen, T. *A Catalogue of the Toponyms and Monuments of Timurid Herat*. Cambridge, Mass., 1981.

———. *Timurid Herat*. Wiesbaden, 1983.

Anarbaev, A. *Blagoustroistvo srednevekovogo goroda Srednei Azii, V-nachalo XIII v. (Urban Improvement in Medieval Central Asia from the 5th to the Early 13th Century)*. Tashkent, 1981.

Anonymous. "Enquêtes sur les vakoufs du Turkestan." *RMM* 13/2 (1911).

Atagarryev, E. *Srednevekovy Dekhistan: Istoriya i kul'tura goroda Yugo-Zapadnogo Turkmenistana (Medieval Dihistan: A History and Culture of a City in Southwest Turkmenistan)*. Leningrad, 1986.

'Aynī, Ṣadr al-Dīn. *Yāddāšthā (Memoirs)*. 4 vols. Istalinabad, 1959. Reprinted in one volume. Tehran, 1362/1983-4.

Azadaev, F. *Tashkent vo vtoroi polovine XIX veka: Ocherki sotsial'no-ekonomicheskoi i politicheskoi istorii (Tashkent in the Latter Half of the 19th Century: An Introduction to its Socio-Economic and Political History)*. Tashkent, 1959.

Baipakov, K. M. *Srednevekovaya gorodskaya kul'tura yuzhnogo Kazakhstana i Semirech'ya VI-nachalo XIII v. (The Medieval Urban Culture of South Kazakhstan and Semirech'e from the 6th to the Early 13th Century)*. Alma-Ata, 1986

Barthold, V. V. *Four Studies on the History of Central Asia*. 3 vols. Translated by V. Minorsky & T. Minorsky. Leiden, 1956-62.

Barthold, W. *Turkestan down to the Mongol Invasion*. 3rd edition. London, 1968. Originally published in1928.

Bartol'd, V. V. *Akademik V. V. Bartol'd sochineniya (The Collected Works of Academician V. V. Bartol'd)*.

Volume 1: *Turkestan v epokhu mongol'skogo nashestviya (Turkistan down to the Mongol Invasion)*. Moskva, 1963.

Volume 2/1: *Obshchie raboty po istorii Srednei Azii (General Works of Central Asian History)*. Moskva, 1963.

Volume 2/2: *Raboty po otdel'nym problemam istorii Srednei Azii (Problems in Central Asian History)*. Moskva, 1964.

Volume 3:*Raboty po istoricheskoi geografii (Works of Historical Geography)*. Moskva, 1965.

Volume 4: *Raboty po arkheologii, numizmatike, epigrafike i etnografii (Works of Archaeology, Numismatics, Epigraphy and Ethnography)*. Moskva, 1966.

Volume 5: *Raboty po istorii i filologii tyurkskikh i mongol'skikh narodov (Historical and Philological Studies of the Turkic and Mongolian Peoples)*. Moskva, 1968.

Volume 7: *Raboty po istoricheskoi geografii i istorii Irana (The Historical Geography and History of Iran)*. Moskva, 1971.

Volume 8: *Raboty po istochinikovedeniyu (Works of Historiography)*. Moskva, 1973.

Volume 9: *Raboty po istorii vostokovedeniya (The History of Oriental Studies)*. Moskva, 1977.

Belenitskii, A. M., I. B. Bentovich & O. G. Bol'shakov. *Srednevekovyi gorod Srednei Azii (The Medieval City of Central Asia)*. Leningrad, 1973.

Bol'shakov, O. G. *Srednevekovyi gorod Blizhnego Vostoka, VII-seredina XIIIv.: Sotsial'no-ekonomicheskie otnosheniya (The Medieval City of the Near East from the 7th to the mid-13th Century: Social and Economic Relations)*. Moskva, 1984.

Borodina, I., ed. *Srednyaya Aziya: Arkhitekturnye pamyatniki IX-XIX vekov (Central Asia: Its Architectural Heritage from the 9th to the 19th Century)*. Moskva, 1987.

Brykina, G. A. *Karabulak*. Moskva, 1974.

Buryakov, Yu. F. *Istoricheskaya topografiya drevnikh gorodov Tashkentskogo oazisa: Istoriko-arkheologicheskii ocherk Chacha i Ilaka (An Historical Geography of Ancient Cities of the Tashkent Oasis: An Historical and Archaeological Introduction to Chachi and Ilak)*. Tashkent, 1975.

———, ed. *K istoricheskoi topografii drevnego i srednevekovogo Samarkanda (An Historical Geography of Ancient and Medieval Samarkand)*. Tashkent, 1981.

———, ed. *Drevnii i srednevekovyi gorod vostochnogo Maverannakhra (The Ancient and Medieval City of Eastern Ma wara' al-Nahr)*. Tashkent, 1990.

Buryakov, Yu. F. & M. I. Filanovich. "Mezhregional'naya konferentsiya 'Gorod i protsess urbanizatsii Srednei Azii: Drevnost' i srednevekov'e' (The Interregional Conference 'City and Urbanization Process of Central Asia: Antiquity and the Middle Ages')." *Obshchestvennye nauki v Uzbekistane* 1 (1990).

The Center for East Asian Cultural Studies, ed. *Bibliography of Central Asian Studies in Japan: 1879 - March 1987*. 2 vols. Tokyo, 1988-9.

Chekhovich, O. D. *Bukharskie dokumenty XIV v. (Bukhara Documents in the 14th Century)*. Tashkent, 1965.

———. "Skazanie o Tashkenta (A Story of Tashkent)." In *Pis'mennye pamyatniki Vostoka: Istoriko-filologicheskie issledovaniya, Ezhegodnik 1968*. Moskva, 1970.

———. *Samarkandskie dokumenty XV-XVI vv. (Samarkand Documents in the 15th and 16th Centuries)*. Moskva, 1974.

———. "Gorodskoe samoupravlenie v Tashkente XVIII v. (Urban Autonomy in 18th Century Tashkent)." In *Istoriya i kul'tura narodov Srednei Azii: Drevnost' i srednie veka*. Moskva, 1976.

———. "Gorodskoe samoupravlenie v Srednei Azii feodal'nogo perioda (Urban Autonomy in Central Asia during the Feudal Age)." In *Tovarno-denezhnye otnosheniya na Blizhnem i Srednem Vostoke v epokhu srednevekov'ya*. Moskva, 1979.

Davidovich, E. A. "Gorod, remeslo i denezhnoe obrashchenie v Srednei Azii perioda tak nazyvaemogo 'serebryannogo krizisa', XI-XIII vv. (Cities, Crafts, and Money Circulation in Central Asia during the 'Silver Crisis' from the 11th to the 13th Century)." In *Materialy vtorogo soveshchaniya arkheologov i etnografov Srednei Azii 29 oktyabrya-4 noyablya 1956 goda Stalinabad*. Moskva & Leningrad, 1959.

———. "Diskussionnye voprosy v knige A. M. Belenitskogo, I. B. Bentovicha, O. G. Bol'shakova 'Srednevekovyi gorod Srednei Azii' (Controversial Problems in the Book by A. M. Belenitskii, I. B. Bentovich & O. G. Bol'shakov, The Medieval City of Central Asia)." In *Drevnost' i srednevekov'e narodov Srednei Azii*. Moskva, 1978.

———. "Diskussionnye voprosy v knige A. M. Belenitskogo, I. B. Bentovicha, O. G. Bol'shakova 'Srednevekovyi gorod Srednei Azii' (Controversial Problems in the Book by A. M. Belenitskii, I. B. Bentovich & O. G. Bol'shakov, The Medieval City of Central Asia)." In *Kul'tura i iskusstvo narodov Srednei Azii v drevnost' i srednevekov'e*. Moskva, 1979.

———. *Istoriya denezhnogo obrashcheniya srednevekovoi Srednei Azii: Mednye monety XV-pervoi chetverti XVI v. v Maverannakhre (The History of Currency Circulation in Medieval Central Asia: Copper Coinage in Ma wara' al-Nahr during the 15th and the First Quarter of the 16th Centuries)*. Moskva, 1983.

Davidovich, E. A. et al., eds. *Dukhovenstvo i politicheskaya zhizn' na Blizhnem i Srednem Vostoke v period feodalizma (Clergymen and Politics in the Near and Middle East in the Period of Feudalism)*. Moskva, 1985.

Dobrosmyslov, A. I. *Tashkent v proshlom i nastoyashchem: Istoricheskii ocherk (Tashkent Past and Present: An Historical Introduction)*. Tashkent, 1911.

Dzhabbarov, I. "Ob uchenichestve v remeslennykh tsekhakh Srednei Azii v kontse XIX i nachale XX v.: Po materialam Khorezma (Apprentice Status in the Craft Guilds of Central Asia in the Late 19th and the Early 20th Centuries: Based on the Materials of Khwarazm)." In *Materialy vtorogo soveshchaniya arkheologov i etnografov Srednei Azii 29 oktyabrya-4 noyablya 1956 goda Stalinabad*. Moskva & Leningrad, 1959.

Dzhuraeva, G. A. "Novye dannye o vorotakh shakhristana Bukhary: Po materialam vakfnykh gramot (New Sources on the Gates of Shahristan in Bukhara: Based on Waqf Documents)." *Obshchestvennye nauki v Uzbekistane* 11 (1983).

———. "Novye dannye po istorii Bukhary XVI veka (New Sources on the History of Bukhara in the 16th Century)." *Obshchestvennye nauki v Uzbekistane* 12 (1988).

Filanovich, M. I. *Tashkent, zarozhdenie i razvitie goroda i gorodskoi kul'tury (Tashkent, the Formation and the Development of the City and its Urban Culture)*. Tashkent, 1983.

Frye, R. N. *Bukhara, the Medieval Achievement*. Oklahoma-Norman, 1965.

Gavrilov, M. *Risolya sartovskikh remeslennikov: Issledovanie predanii musul'manskikh tsekhov (The Risala of the Sart Artisans: A Study of the Legends of Muslim Guilds)*. Tashkent, 1912.

Geier, I. I., ed. *Sbornik materialov dlya statistiki Syr-Dar'inskavo oblasti (A Collection of Materials for the Statistics of the Sir-Darya Province)*. Izdanie Syr-Dar'inskago oblastnogo statisticheskago komiteta 7. Tashkent, 1899.

Golombek, L. & D. Wilber. *The Timurid Architecture of Iran and Turan*. 2 vols. Princeton, 1988.

Goryacheva, V. D. *Srednevekovye gorodskie tsentry i arkhitekturnye ansambli Kirgizii (Burana, Uzgen, Safid-Bulan), Nauchno-populyarnyi ocherk (The Urban Centers of Medieval Kirgizia and its Architectural Ensembles: Burana, Uzgen, Safid-Bulan, A Scientific-general Introduction)*. Frunze, 1983.

Haider, M. "Urban Classes in the Uzbek Khanates XVI-XVII Centuries." In *Central Asia: The Proceedings of 30th International Congress of Human Sciences in Asia & North Africa,* ed. Graciela de la Lama. Mexico City, 1982.

Horikawa, Toru. "Shaibani Han to Arukuku jo (Shaibani Khan and the Town of Arquq)." *Shirin* 62/6 (1979).

Hoshim, R. "Oini Javonmardi va Oluftahoi Ayni (The Tradition of Chivalry Spirit and the Ālufte of 'Ayni)." In *Chashnnomai Ayni.* Vol. 5. Dushanbe, 1978.

Ivanov, P. P. *Khozyaistvo Dzhuibarskikh sheikhov: K istorii feodal'nogo zemlevladeniya v Srednei Azii v XVI-XVII vv. (The Economy of the Juybari Sheikhs: A History of Feudal Landownership in Central Asia during the 16-17th Centuries).* Moskva & Leningrad, 1954.

Kano, Hiromasa. "Isuramu no seisansha toshi Buhara (Bukhara, an Islamic Industrial City)." In *Hatten tojokoku no toshika,* ed. Takeshi Hayashi. Tokyo, 1976.

Karmysheva, B. Kh. *Ocherki etnicheskoi istorii yuzhnykh raionov Tadzhikistana i Uzbekistana: Po etnograficheskim dannym (An Introduction to the Ethnic History of the Southern Regions of Tajikistan and Uzbekistan: Based on Ethnographical Materials).* Moskva, 1976.

Kato, Kazuhide. "O. D. Chehovichi hencho '14 seiki Buhara no wakufu monjo' (Book Review: Chekhovich, O. D., Bukharskie dokumenty XIV veka)." *TheToyo Gakuho* 52/4 (1970).

———. "Amiru Timuru to Shafuru-i-Kishu (Amir Timur and Shahr-i Kish)." *Seinan Ajia Kenkyu* 29 (1988).

Kawamoto, Masatomo. "Hoja Afuraru to Abu Saido: Timuru cho ni okeru seija to shihaisha (Khwāja Aḥrār and Abū Sa'īd: Saint and Governor in the Timurid Period)." *Seinan Ajia Kenkyu* 25 (1986).

———. "Hoja Afuraru no wakufu monjo (A *Waqfiyya* of Khwāja Aḥrār: A Study of Waqf)." *Jinbun Gakuho* 63 (1989).

Khabibullaev, N. N. "Regional'nyi simpozium 'Pozdnefeodal'nyi gorod v Srednei Azii' (The Regional Conference 'The Late Feudal City in Central Asia')." *Obshchestvennye nauki v Uzbekistane* 8 (1989).

Khalid, A. "The Residential Quarter in Bukhara before the Revolution (The Work of O. A. Sukhareva)." *Middle East Studies Association Bulletin* 25 (1991).

Khanykov, N. *Opisanie Bukharskago khanstva (Description of the Khanate of Bukhara).* Sanktpeterburg, 1843. Translated into English as *Bokhara: Its Amir and its People,* by De Bode. London, 1845.

———. "Gorodskoe upravlenie v Srednei Azii (Urban Administration in Central Asia)." *Zhurnal Ministerstva vnutrennikh del* (Sanktpeterburg) 8/5 (1844).

Komatsu, Hisao. "Buhara no maharra ni kansuru noto: O. A. Suharewa no firudo waku kara (The Mahallas of Bukhara: From the Ethnographical Material Collected by O. A. Sukhareva)." *Ajia Afurika Gengo Bunka Kenkyu* 16 (1978).

———. "Buhara to Kazan (Bukhara and Kazan)." In *Nairikuajia Nishiajia no shakai to bunka,* ed. Masao Mori. Tokyo, 1983.

———. "Tashukento no ishan ni tsuite (The Īshāns of Tashkent)." *Isuramu Sekai* 23-24 (1985).

Kubo, Kazuyuki. "16 seiki shoto no Herato: Futatsu no shinko ocho no shihai (Herat in the Early Sixteenth Century: Under the Reign of Two Rising Dynasties)." *Shirin* 71/1 (1988).

———. "Timurucho jidai no Herato ni okeru bunka katsudo to sono haikei (The Cultural Movement and its Background in Timurid Herat)." *Isuramu no Toshisei Kenkyu Hokoku, Kenkyu Hokokuhen* (Institute of Oriental Culture, University of Tokyo) 35 (1989).

———. "Miru Ari Shiru no gakugei hogo ni tsuite (Mīr 'Alī Shīr's Patronage of Science and Art)." *Seinan Ajia Kenkyu* 32 (1990).

Maejima, Shinji. "19 seiki shoto no Buhara to sono bunka (Bukhara in the Beginning of the 19th Century and its Culture)." *Toyo Gakujutsu Kenkyu* 16/1 (1977).

Mano, Eiji. *Chuo Ajia no rekishi (A History of Central Asia).* Tokyo, 1977.

———. "Baburu to Herato (Babur and Herat)." *Oriento* 23/2 (1980).

———. "Nakushubandi kyodan ni kansuru saikin no kenkyu ni tsuite (Recent Studies on the Naqshbandīya)." *Isuramu Sekai* 21 (1983).

———. "Torukisutan (Turkistan)." In *Ajia rekishi kenkyu nyumon.* Vol. 4: *Nairikuajia Nishiajia.* Kyoto, 1984.

Masal'skii, V. I. *Turkestanskii krai (The Turkistan Region), Rossiya Polnoe Geograficheskoe Opisanie Nashego Otechestva.* S.-Peterburg, 1913.

Masson, M. E. & G. A. Pugachenkova. "Shakhrisyabz pri Timure i Ulugbeke (Shahr-i Sabz during the Age of Timur and Ulug Beg)." *Trudy SAGU* 61, *Gumanitarnye nauki 6: Arkheologiya Srednei Azii* (1953).

———. "Shakhrisyabz pri Timure i Ulug Beke (Shahr-i Sabz from Timur to Ulugh Beg)." Translated into English by J. M. Rogers. *Iran* 16 (1978); 18 (1980).

McChesney, R. D. "The Amirs of Muslim Central Asia in the XVIIth Century." *JESHO* 26/1 (1983).

———. "Economic and Social Aspects of the Public Architecture of Bukhara in the 1560's and 1570's." *Islamic Art* 2 (1987).

———. *Waqf in Central Asia: Four Hundred Years in the History of a Muslim Shrine, 1480-1889.* Princeton, 1991.

Meiendorf, E. K. *Puteshestvie iz Orenburga v Bukharu (A Journey from Orenburg to Bukhara).* Translated by E. K. Betger. Moskva, 1975. Originally published in French as *Voyage d'Orenbourg à Boukhara* by E. K. Meyendorff in 1826.

Mukhamedzhanov, A. R. et al. *Gorodishche Paikend: K probleme izucheniya srednevekovogo goroda Srednei Azii (The Ruins of the Paikend City: A Study of a Medieval City in Central Asia).* Tashkent, 1988.

Mukhtarov, A. *Materialy po istorii Ura-Tyube: Sbornik aktov XVII-XIX vv. (Historical Documents concerning the History of Uratube: A Collection of Edicts from the 17th to the 19th Century).* Moskva, 1963.

———. *Pozdnesrednevekovyi Balkh: Materialy k istoricheskoi topografii goroda v XVI-XVIII vv. (Balkh in the Late Middle Ages: Materials concerning its Historical Geography from the 16th to the 18th Century).* Dushanbe, 1980. Translated into English as *Balkh in the Late Middle Ages* by R. D. McChesney, N. Jamal and M. Lustig. Bloomington, 1993.

Mukminova, R. G. *K istorii agrarnykh otnoshenii v Uzbekistane XVI v., po materialam 'vakf-name' (A History of Agrarian Relations in 16th-Century Uzbekistan, Based on the 'Waqf-name' Sources).* Tashkent, 1966.

———. *Ocherki po istorii remesla v Samarkande i Bukhare v XVI veke (An Introduction to the History of Crafts in Samarkand and Bukhara in the 16th Century).* Tashkent, 1976.

———. "Iz istorii pozdnesrednevekovogo Tashkenta (A History of Tashkent in the Late Middle Ages)." *Obshchestvennye nauki v Uzbekistane* 11 (1981).

———. *Tort Äsr Aldingi Tashkent (Tashkent Four Hundred Years Ago).* Tashkent, 1984.

———. "Neissledovannyi dokument po sotsial'no-ekonomicheskoi istorii sredneaziatskogo goroda (An Unexamined Document concerning the Socio-Economic History of a Central Asian City)." In *Istochnikovedenie i tekstologiya srednevekovogo Blizhnego i Srednego Vostoka.* Moskva, 1984.

———. *Sotsial'naya differentsiatsiya naseleniya gorodov Uzbekistana konets XV-XVI v. (Social Differentiation among the Urban Population of Uzbekistan in the 15th and 16th Centuries).* Tashkent, 1985.

———, ed. *Pozdne-feodal'nyi gorod Srednei Azii (The Late Feudal City of Central Asia).* Tashkent, 1990.

Muminov, I. M., ed. *Istoriya Samarkanda (The History of Samarkand).* Vol. 1: *S drevneishikh vremen do Vel'koi Oktyabr'skoi sotsialisticheskoi revolyutsii (From the Earliest Times to the Great October Socialist Revolution).* Tashkent, 1969.

———, ed. *Istoriya Bukhary s drevneishikh vremen do nashikh dnei (The History of Bukhara from the Earliest Times to the Present).* Tashkent, 1976.

———, ed. *Istoriya Khorezma s drevneishikh vremen do nashikh dnei (The History of Khwarazm from the Earliest Times to the Present).* Tashkent, 1976.

Murav'ev, N. *Puteshestvie v Turkmeniyu i Khivu v 1819 i 1820 godakh kapitana Nikolaya Murav'eva, poslannogo v sii strany dlya peregovorov (A Travel to Turkmenia and Khiva in the Years of 1819 and 1820 by Captain Murav'ev, Sent to these Countries for Negotiation).* 2 vols. Moskva, 1822. Translated into French as *Voyage en Turcomanie et à Khiva, fait en 1819 et 1820 par M. N. Mouraviev* by M. G. Lecointe de Laveau. Paris, 1823.

Najimi, A. W. *Herat: The Islamic City, a Study in Urban Conservation.* London, 1988.

Nazarov, F. *Zapiski o nekotorykh narodakh i zemlyakh srednei chasti Azii (A Memorandum concerning the Peoples and the Regions of Central Asia).* S. Peterburg, 1821.

Negmatov, N. N. "Iz istorii pozdnesrednevekovogo Khodzhenta (History of Khujand in the Late Middle Ages)." In *Materialy vtorogo soveshchaniya arkheologov i etnografov Srednei Azii 29 oktyabrya-4 noyablya 1956 goda Stalinabad.* Moskva & Leningrad, 1959.

Nemtseva, N. B. "Istoki kompozitsii etapy formirobaniya ansamblya Shakhi-Zinda (The Origins and Architectural Development of the Shah-i Zinda)." *Sovetskaya arkheologiya* 3 (1975).

———. "Istoki kompozitsii i etapy formirovaniya ansamblya Shah-i Zinda (The Origins and Architectural Development of the Shah-i Zinda)." Translated, with additions, by J. M. Rogers & Adil Yasin. *Iran* 15 (1977).

Nemtseva, N. B. & Yu. Z. Shvab. *Ansambl' Shakhi-Zinda: Istoriko-arkhitekturnyi ocherk (The Complex of the Shah-i Zinda: An Historical-Architectural Introduction).* Tashkent, 1979.

Nil'sen, V. A. *U istokov sovremennogo gradostroitel'stva Uzbekistana: XIX - nachalo XX vekov (The Origin of Modern Urban Construction in Uzbekistan: From the 19th to the Early 20th Century).* Tashkent, 1988.

Nishi, Tokujiro. *Chuajia kiji (Description of Central Asia).* Tokyo, 1886. Reprinted in 1987.

Ostroumov, N. P. "Madrasy v Turkestanskom krae (Madrasas in the Turkistan Region)." *Zhurnal ministerstva narodnago prosveshcheniya* 7/1 (1907).

Peshchereva, E. M. "Goncharnoe proizvodstvo Srednei Azii (Pottery Manufacture in Central Asia)." *Trudy Instituta Etnografii AN SSSR* 42 (1959).

Petrushevskii, I. P. "Gorodskaya znat' v gosudarstve Khulaguidov (Urban Aristocrats in the Ilkhanid State)." *Sovetskoe vostokovedenie* 5 (1948).

Pishchulina, K. A. "Prisyrdar'inskie goroda i ikh znachenie v istorii kazakhskikh khanstv v XV-XVII vekakh (Cities in the Sir-Darya Basin and their Significance in the History of Kazakh Khanates from the 15th to the 17th Century)." In *Kazakhstan v XV-XVIII vekakh: Vaprosy sotsial'no politicheskoi istorii,* ed. B. S. Suleimenov. Alma-Ata, 1969.

Pugachenkova, G. A. "Puti razvitiya arkhitektury yuzhnogo Turkmenistana pory rabovladeniya i feodalizma (The Development of Architecture in Southern Turkmenistan during the Slavery and Feudal Periods)." *Trudy yuzhno-turkmenistanskoi arkheologicheskoi kompleksnoi ekspeditsii* 6 (1958).

———. *Pamyatniki iskusstva Sovetskogo Soyuza, Srednyaya Aziya, Spravochnik-putevoditel' (The Legacy of Arts in the Soviet Union: A Handbook for Central Asia).* Moskva, 1983.

———, ed. *Muzei pod otkrytym nebom: Arkhitekturnye sokrovishcha Uzbekistana (An Open-Air Museum: The Essence of the Architecture of Uzbekistan).* Tashkent, 1981.

———, ed. *Gradostroitel'stvo i arkhitektura, Kul'tura Srednego vostoka - Razvitie, svyazi i vzaimodeistviya / s drevneishikh vremen do nashikh dnei (Civic Engineering and Architecture, Middle Eastern Culture - Development, Relation and Interactions: From the Earliest Times to the Present).* Tashkent, 1989.

Qayumov, A. *Qoqan Ädäbiy Muhiti, XVIII-XIX äsrlär (The Literary Circle of Khokand, from the 18th to the 19th Century).* Tashkent, 1961.

Rakhmatullaeva, S. D. "Sredneaziatskie bani-khammom v miniatyurakh XV-XVII vv. (Central Asian Public Baths, Hammams, in 15th-17th Century Miniatures)." *Izvestiya Akademii Nauk Tadzhikskoi SSR, Seriya: Vostokovedenie, istoriya, filologiya* 1 (1990).

Rempel', L. I., ed. *Khudozhestvennaya kul'tura Srednei Azii IX-XIII veka (Artistic Culture in Central Asia from the 9th to the 13th Century).* Tashkent, 1983.

Rogers, M. "Waqfiyyas and Waqf-Registers: New Primary Sources for Islamic Architecture." *Kunst des Orients* 11/1-2 (1976-7).

S. R. "Le Ichâns de Tachkent." *RMM* 13/1 (1911).

Samarkand: A Museum in the Open. Tashkent, 1986.

Semyonov, A. A. *Ocherk ustroistva tsentral'novo administrativnogo upravleniya Bukharskogo khanstva pozdneishego vremeni (An Introduction to the Central Administrative Organization in the Last Period of the Khanate of Bukhara).* Stalinabad, 1954.

———. "K voprosu o kul'turno-politicheskikh svyazyakh Bukhary i 'velikomogol'skoi' Indii v XVII v. (Some Remarks on the Cultural and Political Relations between Bukhara and Mughal India in the 17th Century)." In *Materialy vtorogo soveshchaniya arkheologov i etnografov Srednei Azii 29 oktyabrya 1956 goda Stalinabad.* Moskva & Leningrad, 1959.

Senigova, T. N. *Srednevekovyi Taraz (Medieval Taras).* Alma-Ata, 1972.

Shin'men, Yasushi. "Research in Japan on Islamic Central Asian History: 1984-91." *Asian Research Trends* (Tokyo) 3 (1993).

Subtelny, M. E. "Art and Politics in Early 16th Century Central Asia." *CAJ* 27/1-2 (1983).

———. "Socioeconomic Bases of Cultural Patronage under the Later Timurids." *IJMES* 20/4 (1988).

———. "A Timurid Educational and Charitable Foundation: The Ikhlāṣiyya Complex of 'Alī Shīr Navā'ī in 15th-Century Herat and its Endowment." *Journal of the American Oriental Society* 111/1 (1991).

Sukhareva, O. A. *K istorii gorodov Bukharskogo khanstva: Istoriko-etnograficheskie ocherki (A History of Cities in the Khanate of Bukhara: An Historical and Ethnographical Introduction).* Tashkent, 1958.

———. "Traditsionnoe sopernichestvo mezhdu chastyami gorodov v Uzbekistane, konets XIX-nachalo XX v. (The Tradition of Competition between Districts in the Cities of Uzbekistan)." *Kratkie soobshcheniya Instituta Etnografii AN SSSR* 30 (1958).

———. "K istorii gorodov Bukharskogo khanstva (An Essay on the Urban History of the Khanate of Bukhara)." In *Materialy vtorogo soveshchaniya arkheologov i etnografov Srednei Azii 29 oktyavrya -4 noyablya 1956 goda Stalinabad*. Moskva-Leningrad, 1959.

———. *Pozdnefeodal'nyi gorod Bukhara kontsa XIX-nachala XX veka: Remeslennaya promyshlennost' (The Late Feudal City of Bukhara at the Turn of the 20th Century: Artisanal Industry)*. Tashkent, 1962.

———. *Bukhara XIX - nachala XX v.: Pozdnefeodal'nogo gorod i ego naselenie (Bukhara in the 19th and the Early 20th Centuries: A Late Feudal City and its Population)*. Moskva, 1966.

———. *Kvartal'naya obshchina pozdnefeodal'nogo goroda Bukhary: V svyazi s istoriei kvartalov (The Quarter Community of the Late Feudal City of Bukhara: In Relation to the History of Quarters)*. Moskva, 1976.

———. "Ocherki po istorii sredneaziatskikh gorodov (An Introduction to the History of Central Asian Cities)." In *Istoriya i kul'tura narodov Srednei Azii: Drevnost' i srednie veka*. Moskva. 1976.

———. "Oboronitel'nye steny Samarkanda (The Defence Walls of Samarkand)." In *Kul'tura i iskusstvo narodov Srednei Azii v drevnosti i srednevekov'e*. Moskva, 1979.

———. "Traditsiya sochetaniya gorodskikh i sel'skikh zanyatii v Srednei Azii kontsa XIX-nachala XX v. (Customary Combination of Urban and Rural Occupations in Central Asia from the Late 19th Century to the Beginning of the 20th Century)." In *Tovarno-denezhnye otnosheniya na Blizhnem i Srednem Vostoke v epokhu srednevekov'ya*. Moskva, 1979.

———. "O tkatskikh remeslakh v Samarkande (The Textile Industry in Samarkand)." In *Istoriya i etnografiya narodov Srednei Azii (Sbornik statei)*. Dushanbe, 1981.

———. "Risala kak istoricheskii istochinik (The Risala as Historical Materials)." In *Istochnikovedenie i tekstologiya srednevekovogo Blizhnego i Srednego Vostoka*. Moskva, 1984.

Tulenbaev, B. A., ed. *Srednevekovaya gorodskaya kul'tura Kazakhstana i Srednei Azii: Materialy vsesoyuznogo soveshchaniya 13-15 maya 1981 g. g. Alma-Ata (The Medieval Urban Culture of Kazakhstan and Central Asia: Collected Papers Submitted to the All-Union Conference Held in Alma-Ata from May 13-15, 1981)*. Alma-Ata, 1983.

Tumanovich, N. N. *Gerat v XVI-XVIII vekakh (Herat between the 16th and 18th Centuries)*. Moskva, 1989.

Tursunov, N. "Is istorii remeslennykh tsekhov Srednei Azii: Na materialakh tkatskikh promyslov Khodzhenta kontsa XIX - nachala XX v. (An Essay on the History of Artisanal Guilds in Central Asia: Based on Materials of Khujand at the Turn of the 20th Century)." *Sovetskaya etnografiya* 1 (1972).

Yakubovskii, A. Yu. *Samarkand pri Timure i Timuridakh (Samarkand during Timur and the Timurid Period)*. Leningrad, 1933.

———. "Dofeodal'nyi gorod v Mavarannakhre v VII-VIII v. (The Pre-Feudal City in Ma wara' al-Nahr in the 7th and 8th Centuries)." In *Istoriya narodov Uzbekistana*. Vol.1. Tashkent, 1950.

———. "Slozhenie feodal'nogo goroda v Mavarannakhre v IX-X v. (The Structure of the Feudal City in Ma wara' al-Nahr in the 9th and 10th Centuries)." In *Istoriya narodov Uzbekistana*. Vol.1. Tashkent, 1950.

Zhukovskii, V. A. *Drevnosti Zakaspiiskogo kraya: Razvaliny starogo Merva (The Ancient Era of the Transcaspian Region: The Ruins of Old Merv)*. Sankt-Peterburg, 1894.

Ziyaev, H. *Tashkentning Rossiyagä Qoshib Alinishi (The Incorporation of Tashkent by Russia)*. Tashkent, 1967.

Ziyaev, Kh. "Tashkent v XVIII-pervoi polovine XIX veka: po dannym russkikh istochnikov (Tashkent from the 18th Century to the First Half of the 19th Century: Based on Russian Sources)." *Obshchestvennye nauki v Uzbekistane* 4 (1983).

Ziyaev, Kh. Z. & Yu. F. Buryakov, eds. *Istoriya Tashkenta s drevneishikh vremen do pobedy Febral'skoi burzhuazno-demokraticheskoi revolyutsii (The History of Tashkent from the Earliest Times to the Victory of the February Bourgeois-Democratic Revolution)*. Tashkent, 1988.

CONCLUSION
Reinterpreting Urban Studies: Towards a New Perspective

Toru Miura

1. The City as a Frame of Reference

In this final chapter we will examine certain themes likely to exercise the interest of scholars of urban studies in the future and discuss prospects for the field as a whole. At the same time we will take the opportunity to reflect on the history of scholarship concerning the study of Middle Eastern and Central Asian cities as it has been described in the preceding chapters. In particular, we attempt to suggest the sort of common framework required for the study of cities in the region, given the inadequacy of that of the "Islamic city." We would suggest that the reader peruse this chapter in conjunction with the related topics in the five main chapters, and to this end we include page numbers in parentheses.

When we look back on the process of the formation of the model of the "Islamic city," including the "Islamic city" of Orientalists, it is evident that the assumption that a city consists of a particular space, society, economy and culture has proved a stumbling block. In particular, definitions of the city based on contrasts between dualities, like the city versus the village, or urban dwellers versus farmers and nomads, are, as I. M. Lapidus has showed, out of keeping with the reality of Middle Eastern and Central Asian cities, characterized as they are by a continuum between the two. Though the majority of scholars would agree with this objection, such a model has continued to be used, related no doubt to the fondness of Western scholars for comparative analyses such as Islam versus Greece and Rome or Islam versus Europe. As a result, cities in the Middle East and Central Asia have been pressed into a static model within which the existence of both temporal and physical diversity and change has been lost. On the other hand, a number of scholars, beginning with S. D. Goitein, G. Baer and K. Shimizu, have raised basic questions concerning the view of Lapidus and A. Goto that there is no fundamental difference between city and rural village, either in terms of physical form, social structure, production or culture (see pages 144, 153, 333). Furthermore, the view of the identicality of the city and the rural village has become interwoven with the view that the city and society are identical, since Lapidus and Goto consider the city to be a microcosm of Islamic society and have tried to abstract from that the structure of society as a whole. The result has been the neglect of specific individual characteristics in rural and nomadic society even if they existed. Consequently, rather than continuing to ask whether or not cities and rural villages are the same, might it not be preferable to aim at setting up a framework with the city as the starting point, so that we can look at rural villages and nomadic society continuously, encompassing both their similarities and their differences? This is not a problem peculiar just to Middle Eastern and Central Asian cities; similar questions have been proposed concerning European and Chinese cities too. For example, it has been pointed out that Italian cities constituted territorial states which included their immediate surroundings (*contad*), and that socially they were multistratified and included outsiders. Rather than a dichotomy between the city and the rural village there is evidence rather of mutual connections between them. In recent years considerable success has been achieved by applying the economic and geographical methodology called the "Zentralörtliche System (Central Place Theory)" to the study of cities in Western Europe and China. This methodology examines the subject in terms of a hierarchy of central places, a continuum from the periodical market to the large urban centre.[1]

The phenomenon of the city exists throughout the world. From ancient times cities existed to the same degree as farming communities; compared to the latter, however, which are greatly influenced by their environment, the former share certain common features, whether it be in terms of physical forms or of society and culture. The urban characteristics possessed by cities have a commonality over and above regional differences. Is it perhaps because of this that we are attracted to the city itself and the theme of the city and attempt to use it as a comparative framework? Y. Sanada, a scholar of Central Asian history, sees the decisive differences between the city and the village as centring not only on wealth but also on non-material movables like information, learning and the arts.[2] It is true of course that the characteristics of the city which have been pointed out since ancient times, like the political system, commerce, industry and culture, can all, like movable property, be transferred and transplanted and this makes it possible to consider that cities share common features which give them a universality. Y. Itagaki, who spent three years in the research project "Urbanism in Islam," emphasizes the universality of "urbanity" this goes in hand with his advocacy of the concept of "urbanism" as a tool of discovery from a comparative standpoint.[3] It is difficult to deny the attraction of the universality of the city however much we stress the points of commonality between city and village.

As noted in the Introduction, a concept like the "Islamic city" which encourages a convenient generalization for the purposes of comparison, should be abandoned both as a framework for understanding Middle Eastern and Central Asian cities and as a framework for comparison. Having abandoned the concept, though, we have to ask what the future direction of urban studies should be. In this connection, D. Eickelman has proposed two responses to Weber's "ideal type" of a city. The first rejects the Weberian ideal of the commune city as a framework for comparison and redefines the city as a specific form of association. The second moves away from the city as a unit for discussion and compares social systems in the broadest sense in terms of concepts such as hierarchy and authority which underlie forms of association.[4] Even so, an attractive feature of the city as a frame of reference has been that because it has an individual substance, whether it be physical form, facilities or the people who live there, it has particular and concrete aspects, but at the same time it remains continually open in the direction of universality. The attraction of universality draws diverse people to the city, with the resultant collision between the values of particularity and universality. An overriding order is thus necessary to resolve that potential conflict. In these terms, the theory of the commune city which is constructed on the single standard of citizenship is obviously limited. We must therefore construct a framework to study the city as a place which condenses themes of human history, such as particularity and universality.

A second problem is that of place and time. Already from the latter half of the 1960s, when the framework of the "Islamic city" was being criticized, joint research was being undertaken on the theme of the "Middle Eastern city." These studies addressed the necessity of looking at the cities of the Middle East, with a tradition of urbanization dating from 3000 B. C., over a long time-span, and concerned themselves with subjects like the pre-Islamic Mesopotamian cities and modern industrialization and urbanization. These were themes necessarily missing from the framework of the "Islamic city" as it had been set up. While the complex nature of the Middle Eastern city, in existence from ancient times, and continuities with rural villages were discussed,[5] there was still a clear tendency to concentrate on the Arab world and treat the Iranian and Turkish regions as footnotes. In recent years the designation "Ottoman city" has been proposed (see p. 221), and M. Haneda points out that since the Iranian region and Central Asia have much in common, geographically and culturally,[6] it should be possible to add a more dynamic element to the discussion of the development of cities in the Iranian and

Turkish regions by adding the Central Asian cities to the general perspective. E. Wirth, in a number of works including "Villes islamiques" and "Zur Konzeption der islamischen Stadt," has, by utilizing a wide range of Western references, proposed a method of studying whether or not the morphological characteristics that are considered peculiar to the "Islamic city" are in fact unique to the Islamic region or based on Islamic factors by comparing cities in the ancient Orient, ancient Greece and Rome, the Islamic region, and medieval and modern Western Europe.[7] As mentioned above, the blanket use of the concept of the commune is being criticized even in European urban studies and scholars are instituting various regional models, such as Northwestern Europe, Southern Europe and the Mediterranean area. We must broaden our horizon, both geographically and temporally, and consider complex associations. By instituting a more complex framework we will do away with the dichotomies of the past which set up Europe against Islam, and by comparing cities in different regions we may receive new insight on the religious and cultural role of Islam in urban forms and functions. It needs hardly be said that when we mention in this volume "dismantling the concept of the 'Islamic city'" we are criticizing concepts of the "Islamic city" and "Islamic society" based on dichotomy and essentialism, and that denying a direct connection between Islam and the city does not mean denying the validity of an "Islamic world" or an "Islamic" framework.

On further consideration, we are convinced that the bottleneck within which Middle Eastern and Central Asian urban studies have become stuck has its origins in the definition of the city which arises from a model of dichotomy contrasting city and rural village. Such a definition presupposes the existence of the city and attempts to extract from that presupposition the distinctive features of the city. There is a great danger that such a methodology will slide into an *a priori* and exclusive definition of the city. By starting from the issue of the city, rather than based on an *a priori* premise that the city exists, it becomes possible to consider a framework that is able to encompass rural villages and nomadic societies also and allows comparisons with cities and societies in other regions. Our review of urban studies concerning the Middle East and Central Asia leads me to propose that we study cities "as a frame of reference," through a framework which uses the city as the starting point for an insight into geography, the economy, society, history and culture, rather than regarding it as the *a priori* premise and having as its final purpose the definition of the city. To this end it is necessary to create a frame of reference that will allow the mutual overlap of pluralities. To this end we will spend the remainder of this chapter examining trends in urban studies as they are described in the preceding chapters on each region in terms of five themes: the city as space, the city as a point of intersection, the city as an association, the city as history and the city as culture. In the interests of understanding the city as a frame of reference, we deliberately use the expression "the city as space" rather than "urban space."

2. The City as Space

The clearest and most positive definition of the city as spatial expanse, that is, physical form, appears in the urban studies of Central Asia. N. Khanykov testifies that "any hamlet surrounded by walls and a moat and containing a citadel and a Friday mosque is called a city" (p. 282). V. V. Bartol'd, from an analysis of terminology used by Arab geographers, suggests a threefold structure of (1) *quhandiz* or *qal'a* (citadel), (2) *šahristān* or *madīna* (inner city, old city), and (3) *rabaḍ* (suburbs), plus (4) *balad* (the city as a whole incorporating all of the three above elements) (p. 284). K. Shimizu shows, using 10th-11th century Nishapur as an example, that the territory called Nishapur at that time consisted of three distinct spaces: Nishapur as a city, with the threefold structure mentioned above, Nishapur as a municipal region, made up of towns and villages within a day's travel of the city, and Nishapur as a district, the area within 100 to 200 kilometres of the city, connected by radial highways. He asserts the continuation of space from the city to the district, including rural villages, and their close and mutual social and economic relations[8] and this should be regarded as a general characteristic of cities in Central Asia and the Iranian sphere. He also says that city inhabitants had three levels of consciousness about themselves corresponding with the above differentiation. While Lapidus took the oasis cities of Central Asia and the Iranian sphere into consideration, he extracted the importance of continuities between the city and the rural village and their groupings as a region including both urban and rural elements in terms of the morphological characteristics of Islamic society. Research into Ottoman social and economic history using land survey registers and sharia-court registers reveals economic connections between regional cities and surrounding villages in Anatolia (pp. 204-5), but were these a network extending in all directions or local independent groupings like the "small islands surrounded by the sea of the desert" which characterize cities in the Iranian sphere? (p. 242) Such research is rare in the Arab lands, whether the Maghrib or Mashriq, where the centripetal tendency and cosmopolitanism of large cities like Cairo, Damascus, Baghdad, Fez and Tunis tend to be emphasized. Is this merely a difference in point of view, or does it reflect differences in geographical conditions between Turkey and the Iranian sphere on one hand and the Arab lands on the other?

If we follow the narrowest definition of urban space, the best summary of the issues regarding the morphological characteristics of the *madīna* has been presented by the geographer E. Wirth. He made extensive surveys of Esfahan and Aleppo and a wide study of the structure of pre-Islamic and Islamic period cities and came to the conclusion that if the morphological characteristics of the city in the Islamic period are considered to be (1) the courtyard-type house, (2) the blind alleys, (3) the quarter, and (4) the suq (the permanent market), then of these four spaces only the suq did not exist either in the ancient Orient or in Europe, and so must be the distinctive feature of the Islamic period city (p. 40). Similarly, the geographer H. Gaube saw the city walls, the great mosque (*jāmi'*) and the bazar as the three distinctive features of the "Islamic city" in Iran and thought they should be considered common to the region as a whole rather than to Iran alone (p. 244). The question whether they can be considered characteristic of the "city" in the "Islamic" sphere needs to be examined in terms of the following three points. First, we should make comparisons over a long time span, asking in particular whether a comparison with the physical forms of the pre-Islamic city reveal an Islamic influence on urban morphology. Both Wirth and N. Elisséeff have written that the courtyard-style house, blind alleys and the quarter have precedents in ancient Mesopotamia and Roman Syria, and Ḥ. Solṭānzāde contends that the bazar also has a tradition reaching back to the ancient period (pp. 40, 111-2, 261-2). As a result, the conclusion is reached that other than the *jāmi'* mosque there is no other unique feature representative of the city in the Islamic period. We await further elucidation on this point from the results of the numerous archaeological excavations and investigations being undertaken in Central Asia and Iraq.

Another important subject is comparative studies with the modern city. For example, is the fact that there are no courtyard houses or blind alleys in modern Istanbul or the main cities of Anatolia related to Turkish modernizing plans in the 19th century and later? Regional comparisons are also necessary, to study the influence of geographical elements like temperature, aridity, rainfall, wind and snow on urban morphology. For example, an examination of cities with differing geographical conditions might show if the development of courtyard houses and blind alleys in the city was an outcome of provisions in Islamic law to protect female privacy or a response to the arid climate. Rather than suddenly turning our attention to the cities of South East Asia or tropical Africa for such comparisons we should look first at countries in the Arab, Turkish and Iranian regions which maintain a common Islamic tradition. We look forward to the formation of an international project to undertake such a study. Of note here are the morphological studies of urban forms in Anatolia, where there is a mixture of Byzantine, Islamic, Central Asian-Iranian and Turkish traditions (p. 215). Comparisons with cities like Istanbul and Aleppo, with their large non-Muslim populations, might also be an effective way of studying Islamic elements. We must also ask whether these morphological characteristics assigned to the "Islamic city" are distinctive to the city or not. Lapidus has already asserted that the city and the rural village are homogeneous, since after the 10th century *jāmi'* mosques had spread to the countryside, and he has been in correspondence on this point with O. Graber, who does not agree.[9] The same argument could be made about the suq. Nevertheless there is little meaning in arguing whether or not facilities such as *jāmi'* mosques or suqs existed in the villages. Discussion should progress rather in the lines of defining terms, including scale and function.

Another question to be considered is not only whether particular facilities (elements) occupying urban space exist or not, but why they occupy a certain location and what ideas (planning) underlie their placement. For example, architectural history makes a clear division between public space, characterized by the *jāmi'* mosque and the great suq, and private space, characterized by the courtyard-type house and the blind alley; this division has been described as a distinctive feature of cities in the Islamic region and used to suggest the existence of urban planning. Islamic legal texts have been employed to show that in residential areas Islamic law offered guidelines concerning the placement of doors and windows and access to streets.[10] As a result, the formerly-held opinion that cities of the Islamic region are chaotic and unplanned has been criticized and undergone a radical revision. Still needing to be clarified is the philosophy upon which urban planning was based, and what or who promoted and supervised that plan. One suggestion has been Islamic law and the law court of the qadi, its executive organ, but such arguments are still conceptual, limited to the legal texts. How effective the provisions of the legal texts were in practice has not yet been examined using sharia-court registers. H. İnalcık, with Istanbul as his example, has shown that the sultans effected positive urban planning through waqf (p. 216) but it does not seem possible to put the method of linking the waqf to town planning as a whole to general use, since Istanbul displays certain unique conditions in that it was treated as conquered territory and made the land of the sultan. Rather it might be effective to consider urban planning from a study of the planning of individual facilities, using historical sources and waqf documents. M. Haneda offers an example of this, looking at the unique city planning of the nomadic rulers of Esfahan through the relative placement of the *jāmi'* mosque and the *maydān* (pp. 246, 266-7). As studies which reveal more of the philosophy behind the planning of individual facilities accumulate, we may gain an understanding of the planning of the city as a whole and of the consciousness of the urban dweller about space. In this sense, the attempts of D. Behrens-Abouseif and N. Hanna to study planning based on historical documents like waqf documents as well as architectural field survey should bridge the gap between architectural history and historical research that has existed till recently (p. 149).

3. The City as a Point of Intersection

The city is the point of intersection of people, goods and information. Here we would like to consider the location and functions of the city in both region and society in terms of the flow of people and goods. Though the basis for such discussion is demography and social and economic history, it must be admitted that reliable research and historical documents are scarce for urban populations in the premodern Middle East and Central Asia. Ottoman period land survey registers remain for the Balkans, Anatolia and Syria, where the *timar* system was in place, and they include the household census for each quarter in the cities, scholars like Ö. L. Barkan and A. Raymond have carried out studies of the populations of regional urban centres and their fluctuations, and made comparisons with rural villages (pp. 129, 134, 151, 198, 203-4). Because there are no such records for other times and places, estimates have been made using hints contained in descriptive sources like chronicles and topographies (regarding for example the number of quarters, mosques and public baths, the area of residential quarters, the number of soldiers in the army, and the death count from plague) and from reports in the travel records of Europeans (pp. 59, 125). For example, estimates of the population of Baghdad in the 10th century range from 300,000 to 1,500,000.[11] Needless to say even such hints are not available for medium to small cities and rural villages. Therefore, though the ratio of urban population to the total is generally thought to be high, there is little that can be done other than to collect data of differing quality from various types of historical document and make estimates from them. O. G. Bol'shakov, after a laborious study of archaeological remains of cities and domestic dwellings, estimated a ratio of between 25% and 30% for pre-Mongol Central Asian cities (p. 289). A project for the future will be to construct a model of population distribution and movement for Ottoman period Anatolia and Syria, for which we have data that can be used for statistical analysis, and use it in conjunction with pre-Ottoman narrative sources to consider fluctuations over the long term and from region to region. Another important theme is movement and migration between cities and between the city and its surroundings. In this sense, even reports that in pre-20th century Central Asian cities 70% to 80% of the population left the city in summer to engage in farming and other activities are of great value (pp. 310-1).

The same problems occur in studying the movement of goods, that is, trade and commerce. Much socio-economic research exists for the Ottoman period, which is fortunate to have a wealth of documentary sources such as land survey registers, sharia-court registers and waqf documents. Practical research is continuing regarding international and interregional trade as well as regional trade. Whereas S. Faroqhi places importance on regional trade and local energy, H. İnalcık stresses international and interregional trade and the state policies which protected and encouraged it (pp. 201-2, 205-6). For the Iranian and Arab spheres, poor in documentary sources, most attention has been given to international and interregional trade. Scholars such as N. Pacha, E. Ashtor, S. Labib, A. Darrag, and H. Yajima have studied routes, commodities, prices and the relationship between merchants and the state.[12] Faroqhi, however, has criticised the sole attention scholars of Arab history have given to international and interregional trade, saying that this has given rise to a model like Lapidus's which make light of economic conditions and implies that urban and economic growth will naturally occur if there is political stability. She welcomes the appearance of studies like that of A. Abdel Nour which stress the importance of regional trade (p. 206). In this connection it should be noted that Muḥammad Mazzīn recently published a detailed study on urban-rural relations around Fez using unpublished materials (p. 61). In terms of Central Asia, scholars from V. V. Bartol'd to I. P. Petrushevskii, O. D. Chekhovich and K. M. Baipakov have, using historical sources and actual surveys, linked a city's prosperity or decline to its commerce and industry. Is this view simply a result of the influence of Soviet socio-economic historiography, or are there internal factors whereby commerce and industry determine urban prosperity or decline in Central Asia? If the latter is true, what is such commerce and industry based on? The question of the relationship between commerce and industry and urban prosperity is an important one that needs further consideration, not so much in terms of alternatives like international and interregional trade versus regional trade, or state guidance versus internal factors, as of the nature and function of economic networks. A bridge to this will be resolving the unfortunate rift between Lapidus's socio-political model and Faroqhi's socio-economic model. In this sense, the work of B. Masters which begins to discuss the nature of "Islamic economy" using sharia-court registers is worthy of note (p. 131).

When thinking of the city as a point of intersection of people and goods, the role of the waqf system is extremely important. In that religious and charitable institutions (waqf institutions) like mosques and madrasas were built and provided with economic foundations (waqf properties) to finance their upkeep, the waqf system differs from charitable systems in other parts of the world. First, waqf founders (*wāqif*) were in the main rulers, the military, merchants and ulama. In many cases soldiers and merchants from outside a particular city made donations in order to establish ties with that city and its inhabitants, and this enabled wealth accumulated outside the city to flow into it. Second, waqf institutions, because they provided for the Islamic community as a whole, not just the townspeople, were instrumental in the acceptance of ulama and Muslims who came to live in the city. Third, as has been shown by the studies of Faroqhi, H. Lutfi and al-Moutabassir, commercial facilities and residences that became waqf properties were, regardless of region, leased out and so became a base for commercial and industrial activities in the cities (pp. 45, 134, 212). In addition, A. K. Rafeq has indicated that agricultural land also was managed by lease agreements, with the result that land was accumulated by urban power holders (pp. 121-2). Waqf properties, which escaped confiscation by those in power through a ban on transferring proprietary rights, stimulated urban economy in that they could be used constantly and safely in the form of lease. During the Ottoman period, cash waqf were set up and they even supplied financial capital (p. 212). It is readily apparent, therefore, that the study of the waqf system is one key to understanding the movement of people and goods in the city.

4. The City as an Association

Many scholars have pointed out that the cities of the Middle East and Central Asia were not only inhabited by the ruling military class, the ulama, merchants and artisans, with their wide-ranging networks encompassing the city and the state, but were also entered freely by various people, including farmers and nomads. Even newcomers could gain various kinds of work as day labourers or acting as officials for waqf institutions or influential people. Urban dwellers were variegated by many factors including occupation, class, origin, and religion, and they acted and moved through a variety of networks. Consequently it is difficult to define the city as an association through occupation, status, or the social groups a person belonged to. A second method therefore is to define it by asking what brings order to those diverse, pluralistic and fluid individuals and groups.

M. Kishimoto, a scholar of Chinese history, reading through this volume, has commented, "we think we should understand Islamic urban society to be neither a strict autocratic order nor a strict autonomous order. There is a tendency to give attention to flexible and informal functions to maintain that order. Can though a 'general order' be formed out of such an individual and private order? If it is true that Islamic urban society maintained social order even at times when factional disputes raged, it seems to indicate the existence of order at a more fundamental level, as 'rules of dispute'."[13] This we think points to a way to understand how research on urban order should be approached.

When considering the political order of Middle Eastern and Central Asian cities, the first point that can be made is that in most cases rulers were considered by the townspeople to be foreigners, in origin or race, even when they were Muslims.[14] A foreign authority appointed military provincial governors in territories under its rule and entrusted the government of whole provinces, including cities, villages and nomads, to them. The machinery of rule of the cities overlapped with that of the state and the province and virtually no individual machinery existed for the city alone. Posts such as muhtasib, *shurṭa* (police chief), qadi and *amīn / kethüda* (guild head) were created to deal with day to day administrative matters, such as tax collection, maintenance of peace and order, and judicial concerns, but the nature of the underlying machinery and how administration actually worked are not sufficiently clear. It is rare to find problems arising between the external power and the townspeople from demands to instigate or reform some part of the machinery of urban rule. This is surprising when compared with European urban history or with that of China and Japan. Perhaps the external power and the townspeople came into conflict over the way the system worked, rather than over the system itself.

Concerning urban autonomy, E.Ashtor and Cl. Cahen and others draw attention to how the cities of Syria, as represented by the *ra'īs* and the qadi and backed by militias and the *aḥdāth,* established their autonomy from the external power particularly in the period of the Crusades. Here "autonomy" refers externally to independence from a foreign power and internally to the administration and participation in the city's defence by representatives of the people themselves. Self-government in this sense was also accomplished in 11th-14th century Tripoli in Ifriqiya, in the joint rule of merchants and ulama and then of the *ra'īs* (p. 37). In Central Asia too examples have been reported of the position of *ra'īs* and of the "free city" where the foreign power had been expelled by the *khwāja* class of influential merchants and landowners with religious authority who were supported by artisan guilds (p. 306). In Iran there existed the tradition of rule by influential families centring on the urban *a'yān* (notables), who held the positions of *ra'īs* and *kalāntar,* etc. (pp. 252-7). It has recently been shown that even during the Ottoman period, with its centralized and bureaucratic government machinery, the *eşrâf* and the *âyan* played a "semiautonomous" role, acting for the benefit of townspeople as local officials (pp. 208-9).

The problem here is what supported such urban independence and autonomy. In most cases more importance was placed on the informal social relations and actions of social groups that underlie it than on the formal system. In Iran, notable families who possessed scholarship, religious authority, bureaucratic position and wealth fulfilled an important role. The same tendency is discernible in Central Asia and Turkey. It has been shown that in the Maghrib, and in Central Asia and Iran, Sufis and saints performed a significant role in the economic and social integration of the cities and regions through religious orders, *zāwiyas* and guilds (pp. 53-5, 253, 313). Also in the Iranian and Arab spheres, particularly in Mashriq, the social and political role of urban outlaws with chivalrous spirit, called variously *'ayyārūn, lūṭī, shuṭṭār, aḥdāth* and *zu'r,* should be noted (pp. 89, 102-3, 112-5, 119-20, 259-60, 312-3). Studies which do not consider the nature of the external authority, like those which do not discuss the internal system of the city, remain one-sided as discussions of the nature of the urban order. Lapidus's proposal, that "the Mamluks governed not by administration but by holding all of the vital social threads in their hands,"[15] offers "networks" among various groups as a new way to explain Mamluk power and the nature of urban society. Lapidus treats the state as one network and emphasizes the "unstructured" nature of society as a whole (pp. 116-7). Such stress on horizontal relationships has given rise, as Kishimoto has pointed out, to the question what it is that supports urban and social order as a whole, which is implicit in the criticism of Faroqhi and İnalcık, historians of the Ottoman period who place great importance on the institutional aspect of the state, about any general application of Lapidus's "unstructuredness" (pp. 206, 216). A. Raymond stresses on the role of social networks which gave a coherence to the urban society in opposition to the Orientalist idea of inorganic society (p.152). G. Baer also questions Lapidus's position, pointing out the separateness of cities and rural villages in premodern Egypt and their political and economic unity under the modern state (p. 153). K. Brown and N. Cigar also throw doubt on the idea of the unstructured network, showing through an analysis of dwellings, family relationships and religious networks in studies of Salé and Fez that a citizen consciousness and ties based on a common culture and religion are the foundation of autonomy (pp. 36-7).

Concerning this point, Lapidus appears to consider that Islam is a receptacle which guarantees the plurality of the networks and at the same time gives unity to the state and society as a whole. However, if this concept of "pre-established harmony" by "an invisible hand" is adopted, there is a danger that temporal changes and regional differences will be overlooked. A second problem is that Lapidus has not investigated to any great extent either the individual social groupings he calls "networks," nor their internal structure and binding ties. Rather he follows a communal model when speaking of the law schools and quarters that he suggests are the basic networks of Islamic urban society. In recent years scholars have given their attention to the pluralistic strata and functions, as well as the antagonisms, of the ulama as a group, and have become interested in the political and social role of the Sufi.

Such studies question the approach that would clearly differentiate the Sufi and the ulama in their role as jurists (pp. 49-51, 119, 148). Lapidus understands law schools to have organized the ulama in a broad sense and says that the ulama acted on behalf of urban dwellers in relation to the rulers and maintained daily contacts with the quarters and their residents. Recent studies point out though that within the ulama network there were hierarchies and confrontations. There are growing doubts too about the nature of the quarter, and it is thought that the ethnic and religious segregation apparent in premodern times is the exception rather than the rule (pp. 144, 149, 211). Miura sees a twofold distinction in the quarter: the quarter as a small community which encompasses daily life, and the quarter as an administrative and political unit. He criticizes the communal theory and hypotheses that in regard to the second aspect, unity was achieved through the role of the quarter gangs, who both ruled and protected the quarter (pp. 119-20). Eickelman, as a result of his own field work, shows that the solidity of the quarter is formed on an ideological and cultural identity based on the idea of *qrāba*, "closeness" (p. 39), and so largely refines the image of the quarter as a "neighbourhood community." Guilds have been studied, using documentary sources, in post 16th century Anatolia, Syria, Egypt and Central Asia, and much light has been thrown on their roles in terms of tax collection and business regulation, as well as on certain aspects of their internal structure, such as initiation ceremonies and the apprenticeship system (pp. 124, 153, 209-10, 308). Here too the picture of a horizontal, free network is in the process of being revised.

Such criticism will, it is hoped, lead to an examination of the internal structure of individual networks and their quality, that is, the nature of their ties. This in turn will lead to further inquiry concerning the mutual connections among networks and similarities and differences in their functions, so that more the fundamental questions of order and values may be approached. It is important too that a model for a more persuasive explanation regarding temporal and regional differences should be found. Through such efforts we may perhaps be enabled to reconsider the distinctive features of the city as an association, focusing again on a city-based theory built on the base of the previous expansion from a city-based theory to a social-based one.[16] On this point, the aforementioned work of Brown and Cigar may perhaps be said to assert that the city as an association is formed both consciously and politically. The recent heightening of interest in saints' cults, pilgrimages to tombs (*ziyāra*) and festivals reflects a new direction in the concept of association, hitherto dominated by organizations and institutions.[17]

Research has so far not raised many questions on the political and social systems common to the cities of the Middle East and Central Asia. Perhaps this is because historians, who have criticized and reacted against the abstract and ideological concept of the "Islamic city," have been concerning themselves principally with questions about the specific nature of the networks, and to the extent individual areas have been highlighted, they have tended not to be too interested in discussion that goes beyond a particular period or place. All the same, the more urban and social diversity, pluralism and fluidity is revealed, the more it becomes necessary to ask what it is that gives order to the parts. Having lost the lodestone of the "Islamic city," we seem, both methodology and practice, to be in a position of antinomy. Investigations into the social roles of the qadi and the muhtasib and into the sense of morality held by urban dwellers which use sharia-court registers and *ḥisba* manuals as sources are continuing (pp. 47-9, 124, 131-2, 208) and attention is being given to the actual role played by the Islamic legal concepts of *'adl* (justice) and *ẓulm* (injustice).[18] An resulting important task for future study is whether order should be considered the node between ideas and actuality.

5. The City as History

If cities in the Middle East and Central Asia are considered to be points of intersection between people, goods and information, it may be possible to understand historical change in the region as a whole through changes in urban economies and social and political orders (pp. 117, 284-5, 290-2). We hope that the future will see the establishment of a model that takes an extensive view of mutual relationships, aware of morphology, economics, politics and society, and culture. Large numbers of questions that go beyond the borders of architectural, cultural, political or socio-economic history need to be raised. Since this Conclusion has been written with that purpose in mind and each separate chapter is seasoned with a discussion of historical change, we will not go further into the specific question here.

6. The City as Culture

The research project, "Urbanism in Islam," attempted to define "urbanism" at different levels. Broadly speaking, the urban characteristics of the city come first, followed by the urban characteristics of society and the urban characteristics of culture. If "urbanism" is defined as that which is to be found only in a city, then we can talk about urban space (facilities), the urban economy (merchandise), urban order (safety), and urban culture (the arts and sciences). What we would like to regard here as culture includes the more abstract elements of behaviour and values. Such a definition enables us to discuss as related matters the mentality and values which underlie the use of space, the economy and urban order and to extend our argument beyond the limitation of the physical fact of the city. Nevertheless, there are very few studies about urban-based behaviour and values which take their distinctive form from the city. Pioneering studies in this field include the work of Cahen and others on the *futuwwa* spirit of outlaw groups, culled from historical sources (p. 113), the fieldwork of S. el-Messiri, which brought to light the existence of the *ibn al-balad* (son of the city) consciousness (p. 154), and the study of W. Miki concerning the sense of fairness (*'adāla*) held in common by those ulama and merchants who stood at the point of intersection between people, goods and information (p. 155). Deficiencies in approach to such questions arise perhaps from the lack of urban studies by specialists in thought and literature, in the more narrow sense of culture.[19] However as is clear from what has gone before, studies about urban space and about politics and economics cannot continue to avoid the question of mentality and values; indeed it has become mandatory to treat them. We do not mean that we should use abstract concepts like "diversity," or "choice," or "universality" which have been part of the word "urbanism" from the first, but we look forward to the appearance of empirical and persuasive hypotheses concerning the internal criteria of social groups and individual and group behaviour. Therefore studies which employ waqf documents to elucidate motivations for waqf endowment and a philanthropic sense (p. 265) and those which throw light on the actuality of arts patronage by power holders and the intentions behind such activity (pp. 253, 316) are very welcome.

We very much fear that we are guilty of the folly of bringing coals to Newcastle in raising the above questions. We are also very much aware that we could never have attempted to write this Conclusion without the separate discussions that appear in this volume for each of the five regions or without the stimulating comments from a great many people at conferences and seminars. In the preceding chapters, we have already mentioned new trends in urban research by local scholars, which are neither overly theoretical nor overly descriptive and which make full use of the historical sources. We should be happy if this work provides scholars with a springboard for studies, both empirical and rich in conception, which serve us meeting-places to discuss urban studies on the same ground beyond any demarcation of location or discipline.

Notes

1. Koichiro Shimizu, *Urban Society in Medieval Italy* (in Japanese) (Tokyo, 1990); id., *Medieval Italian Cities and Merchants* (in Japanese) (Tokyo, 1989). On the Zentralörtliche System of R. Christaller and others and its applications to historical

studies, see R. Kiesling, "Stadt-Land-Beziehung im Spätmittelalter," *Zeitschrift für bayerische Landgeschichte* 40 (1977); translated into Japanese by H. Takita in *Towns and Countryside in Medieval Western Europe,* ed. Y. Morimoto (Fukuoka, 1987). For China, see G. W. Skinner, "Marketing and Social Structure in Rural China," *Journal of Asian Studies* 24/1(1964); 24/2(1965); 24/3 (1965) and id., "Regional Urbanization in Nineteenth Century China" in *The City in Late Imperial China* (Stanford, 1977). Y. Morimoto, a scholar of the European history, makes comparisons with the study of the history of European cities and says that by drawing attention to "cosmology, networks and outlaws" the "Urbanism in Islam" project gives a new outlook on urban studies. See Morimoto, "New Directions in the Study of Urban History" (in Japanese), *Rekishigaku Kenkyu* 607 (1990).

2. Y. Sanada, "Comments on Shimizu's Thesis" (in Japanese), *Shicho,* new series, 28 (1990).
3. Y. Itagaki, "Urbanism in Islam, Opening Message," *Madiniya* (Institute of Oriental Culture, University of Tokyo), English edition, 1 (1988); "A Proposal for the Reconsideration of Urbanism" (in Japanese), *Isuramu no Toshisei Kenkyu Hokoku, Kenkyukai Hokokuhen* (Institute of Oriental Culture, University of Tokyo) 11 (1989), pp. 53-5; and papers presented at the Third Plenary Session (Tokyo, 2 December 1990) and the Closing Seminar (Tokyo, 23 March 1990) of the "Urbanism in Islam" project.
4. D.F. Eickelman, "Is There an Islamic City?" *IJMES* 5 (1974), p. 275; "The Comparative Study of 'Islamic Cities'" (paper prepared at the 2nd International Conference on Urbanism in Islam, Tokyo, 27-29 November 1990), pp. 6-7.
5. See I. M. Lapidus, ed., *Middle Eastern Cities* (Berkeley, 1969), in particular, "the Conclusion" by R. C. Adams; G. H. Blake and R. I. Lawless, eds., *The Changing Middle Eastern City* (London, 1980), in particular, introduction of this volume.
6. M. Haneda, "The Pastoral City and the Mausoleum City: Nomadic Regimes and City Building in the Iran-Islamic Land" (in Japanese), *Toyoshi Kenkyu* 49/1 (1990).
7. E. Wirth, "Villes islamiques, villes arabes, villes orientales? Une problématique face au changement," in *La ville arabe dans l'Islam,* eds. A. Bouhdiba and D. Chevallier (Tunis and Paris, 1982); "Zur Konzeption der islamischen Stadt: Privatheit im islamischen Orient versus Öffentlichkeit in Antike und Okzident," *Die Welt des Islams* 31 (1991).
8. Kosuke Shimizu, "The Image of the Cities in the History of Iran: The Case of Nīšāpūr in10-11th Centuries"(in Japanese), *Shicho,* new series, 28 (1990).
9. Lapidus, ed., *Middle Eastern Cities* (Berkeley & L. A., 1969), pp. 78-9.
10. A. Raymond, *The Great Arab Cities in the 16th-18th Centuries.* (New York & London, 1984); B. S. Hakim, *Arabic-Islamic Cities: Building and Planning Principles* (London,1986); and 'A. S. 'Uthmān, *The Islamic City* (in Arabic) (al-Kuwayt, 1988).
11. J. Lassner, *The Topography of Baghdad in the Early Middle Ages* (Detroit, 1970), pp. 155-60, 282-3 (note 3).

12. A. Darrag, *L'Égypte sous le règne de Barsbay 825-841/1422-1438* (Damas, 1961). H. Yajima, *The Formation of the Islamic World and International Trade: Focusing on International Trading Networks* (in Japanese) (Tokyo, 1991); *A Sea-Created Civilization: The History of the Indian Ocean Sphere* (in Japanese) (Tokyo, 1993). For Pacha, Ashtor and Labib, see p. 61 and p. 158.
13. Comments made at the seminar titled "Reflections about and Prospects for the History of Islamic Urban Studies," Matsuyama, 21 December 1990; see *Madiniya* 38 (1991).
14. See M. Kisaichi, "The Character of the Islamic City and the Stages of its Urban History: A Rough Sketch based on the History of Fez" (in Japanese), *Isuramu no Toshisei Kenkyu Hokoku, Kenkyu Hokokuhen* 43 (1989).
15. Lapidus, *Muslim Cities in the Later Middle Ages* (Cambridge, Mass., 1967), p. 187.
16. For the significance and limitations of Lapidus's network theory, see Miura, "The Network Theory Reconsidered" (in Japanese), *Madiniya* 38 (1991).
17. For example, B. Shoshan's recently published work, *Popular Culture in Medieval Cairo* (Cambridge, 1993) has a well of detailed information on this topic, but his understanding of popular culture is vague and insufficiently persuasive.
18. Hypothetical questions are raised in H. Kato, "Freedom and Order in Islamic Society" (in Japanese), *Sobun* 293 (1988) and T. Miura, "The Quarter and Popular Movements" (in Japanese), in *Sekaishi eno toi*, vol. 4: *Shakaiteki ketsugo* (Tokyo, 1989).
19. For example, Hussein Bayyud, *Die Stadt in der arabischen poesie, bis 1258 n. Chr.* (Berlin, 1988) is noteworthy in that it analyzes descriptions of cities appearing in Arabic poetry and the formation of an urban consciousness; less satisfactory are its underlying Orientalist assumptions that Islam is an urban religion.

Index of Authors Names

(including research institutions)

INDEX OF CITY NAMES

Index of Terms

āb anbār 259. *See also* reservoir
'adāla 343
'adl 342
agha 123
aḥdāth 35, 88-9, 111-5, 129, 339-40. *See also* outlaws
ahî 192-4
ahl al-balad 130
ālufte 312-3. *See also* outlaws
amīn 13, 15, 20, 47-8, 50, 64, 339
amir 36, 104, 120, 265, 297, 304-5, 312, 314
'āmma 102
amṣār. *See miṣr*
'arīf 119
ark 282-3. *See also* citadel
Armenians 259, 269
artisans 20-2, 28, 38, 47, 65, 91, 104, 125, 128, 144, 149-51, 158, 195, 201-2, 207, 212, 257, 263, 283, 285, 289, 291-2, 298, 306, 308-10, 312, 338-9
'aṣabīya 41, 117
ashrāf. *See sharīf*
'āshūrā', *'āšūrā* 18, 269. *See also* festival
aṣnāf 257. *See also* guild
'aṭṭār 155
avâriz 200, 211
awbāš 260
a'yān, *âyan* 50, 153, 209, 339. *See also* notables
'ayyār 35, 89, 95, 102-3, 113, 259-60, 291, 312, 340. *See also* outlaws
bādiya 29
bāġ 266-7. *See also* garden
balad 284, 333
baladī 63, 65
baltagi 154. *See also* outlaws
banat al-balad 155
baraka 47
bayt al-māl, *beytü'l-mal* 15, 218
bazar 65, 86, 104, 212, 217-8, 235-6, 238, 244, 247, 252, 259, 261-3, 282, 301, 309, 312, 334. *See also* market
bedestan 218
beggars 116
beglerbeg 251
belghajia 21
bey 15, 47, 150, 153
bildīyīn 37
blind alley 17, 28, 35, 40, 42, 108, 247, 261, 334-5
café (coffee shop) 55, 129, 191
caravansary 86, 105, 108, 140, 212, 218, 250, 268, 282, 309. *See also funduq*, *khān*, *qaysarīya*, *wakāla*
čarsu 317. *See also* market
Christians 26, 45, 47, 51, 110, 119, 122, 128, 130-1, 133, 137, 145-6, 214
citadel 28, 59, 85, 94, 104, 107, 109, 111, 126, 139, 146, 215, 238, 250, 284, 299, 309, 333. *See also ark*, *qal'a*, *quhandiz*, *ribāṭ*
city wall 27-8, 41, 53, 65, 87, 98-100, 104, 107-8, 111, 126, 129, 139, 145, 215, 244-5, 247, 283-4, 296-8, 311, 333-4
courtyard 35, 40, 42, 118, 124, 141-2, 152, 156, 261, 334-5

For Product Safety Concerns and Information please contact our EU
representative GPSR@taylorandfrancis.com
Taylor & Francis Verlag GmbH, Kaufingerstraße 24, 80331 München, Germany

www.ingramcontent.com/pod-product-compliance
Lightning Source LLC
Chambersburg PA
CBHW060135280326
41932CB00012B/1531

* 9 7 8 0 4 1 5 7 6 0 1 0 2 *